Excerpted from *Fodor's Florida 2013*

FODOR'S SOUTH FLORIDA 2013

Writers: Lynne Helm, Paul Rubio, Dorthea Hunter Sönne, Chelle Koster Walton

Editor: Douglas Stallings

Production Editors: Jennifer DePrima, Carrie Parker
Maps & Illustrations: David Lindroth; Mark Stroud, *cartographers;* Rebecca Baer, *map editor;* William Wu, *information graphics*
Design: Fabrizio La Rocca, *creative director*; Tina Malaney, Chie Ushio, Jessica Ramirez, *designers*; Melanie Marin, *associate director of photography;* Jennifer Romains, *photo research*
Cover Photos: Front cover: (Miami Beach) Raquel Gisbert Gil/age fotostock. Back cover (left to right): Chuck Wagner/Shutterstock; Tap10/Shutterstock; ShaneKato/iStockphoto. Spine: Michael Phillips/iStockphoto
Production Manager: Angela McLean

ISBN 978-0-307-92943-3

ISSN 1526-2219

SPECIAL SALES

This book is available at special discounts for bulk purchases for sales promotions or premiums. Special editions, including personalized covers, excerpts of existing books, and corporate imprints, can be created in large quantities for special needs. For more information, write to Special Markets/Premium Sales, 1745 Broadway, MD 3-1, New York, NY 10019, or e-mail specialmarkets@randomhouse.com.

AN IMPORTANT TIP & AN INVITATION

Although all prices, opening times, and other details in this book are based on information supplied to us at press time, changes occur all the time in the travel world, and Fodor's cannot accept responsibility for facts that become outdated or for inadvertent errors or omissions. So **always confirm information when it matters,** especially if you're making a detour to visit a specific place. Your experiences—positive and negative—matter to us. If we have missed or misstated something, **please write to us.** Share your opinion instantly through our online feedback center at fodors.com/contact-us.

PRINTED IN COLOMBIA

10 9 8 7 6 5 4 3 2 1

CONTENTS

Fodor's Features

MAPS

ABOUT THIS GUIDE

Fodor's Ratings

Everything in this guide is worth doing—we don't cover what isn't—but exceptional sights, hotels, and restaurants are recognized with additional accolades. Fodor's Choice★ indicates our top recommendations; ★ highlights places we deem highly recommended; and **Best Bets** call attention to notable hotels and restaurants in various categories. Care to nominate a new place? Visit Fodors.com/contact-us.

Trip Costs

We list prices wherever possible to help you budget well. Hotel and restaurant price categories from **$** to **$$$$** are noted alongside each recommendation. For hotels, we include the lowest cost of a standard double room in high season. For restaurants, we cite the average price of a main course at dinner or, if dinner isn't served, at lunch. For attractions, we always list adult admission fees; discounts are usually available for children, students, and senior citizens.

Hotels

Our local writers vet every hotel to recommend the best overnights in each price category, from budget to expensive. Unless otherwise specified, you can expect private bath, phone, and TV in your room. For expanded hotel reviews, facilities, and deals visit Fodors.com.

TripAdvisor

Our expert hotel picks are reinforced by high ratings on TripAdvisor. Look for representative quotes in this guide, and the latest TripAdvisor ratings and feedback at Fodors.com.

Restaurants

Unless we state otherwise, restaurants are open for lunch and dinner daily. We mention dress code only when there's a specific requirement and reservations only when they're essential or not accepted. To make restaurant reservations, visit Fodors.com.

Ratings

- ★ Fodor's Choice
- ★ Highly recommended
- Family-friendly

Listings

- Address
- Branch address
- Telephone
- Fax
- Website
- E-mail
- Admission fee
- Open/closed times
- Subway
- Directions or Map coordinates

Hotels & Restaurants

- Hotel
- Number of rooms
- Meal plans
- Restaurant
- Reservations
- Dress code
- No credit cards
- Price

Other

- See also
- Take note
- Golf facilities

Credit Cards

The hotels and restaurants in this guide typically accept credit cards. If not, we'll say so.

1

Experience South Florida

WHAT'S WHERE

The following numbers refer to chapters.

2 Miami and Miami Beach. Greater Miami is hot—and we're not just talking about the weather. Art deco buildings and balmy beaches set the scene. Vacations here are as much about lifestyle as locale, so prepare for power shopping, club hopping, and decadent dining.

3 The Everglades. Covering more than 1.5 million acres, the fabled "River of Grass" is the state's greatest natural treasure. Biscayne National Park (95% of which is underwater) runs a close second. It's the largest marine park in the United States.

4 The Florida Keys. This slender necklace of landfalls, strung together by a 113-mi highway, marks the southern edge of the continental United States. It's nirvana for anglers, divers, literature lovers, and Jimmy Buffett wannabes.

5 Fort Lauderdale with Broward County. The town *Where the Boys Are* has grown up. The beaches that first attracted college kids are now complemented by luxe lodgings and upscale entertainment options.

6 Palm Beach with the Treasure Coast. This area scores points for diversity. Palm Beach and environs are famous for their golden sand and glitzy residents, whereas the Treasure Coast has unspoiled natural delights.

GEORGIA
ATLANTIC OCEAN
Gulf of Mexico
Chattahoochee
Quincy
TALLAHASSEE
Perry
Eastpoint
Apalachicola
Osceola National Forest
St. Mary's R.
Amelia Island
Jacksonville
Lake City
Santa Fe R.
St. Johns R.
St. Augustine
Gainesville
Suwannee
Ocala National Forest
Ocala
Daytona Beach
Cedar Keys
Titusville
Kennedy Space Center
Cape Canaveral
Orlando
Cocoa Beach
Walt Disney World
Kissimmee
Merritt Island
Melbourne
Tarpon Springs
Clearwater
Tampa
Tampa Bay
Winter Haven
Florida's Turnpike
Sebastian Inlet Recreation Area
St. Petersburg
Vero Beach
Fort Pierce
Bradenton
Sarasota
Hutchinson Island
Kissimmee R.
Peace R.
Venice
Lake Okeechobee
Singer Island
West Palm Beach
Palm Beach
Caloosahatchee R.
Fort Myers
Cape Coral
Captiva Island
Sanibel Island
Big Cypress National Preserve
Boca Raton
Naples
Fort Lauderdale
Miami Beach
Everglades City
Miami
Biscayne Bay
Everglades National Park
Florida City
Homestead
Cape Sable
Key Largo
Florida Bay
FLORIDA KEYS
Key West
0 50 miles
0 75 kilometers
10
19
65
319
98
95
75
301
41
40
4
1
27
50
528
70
80
9336

WHEN TO GO

South Florida is a year-round vacation venue, but it divides the calendar into regional tourism seasons. Holidays and school breaks are major factors. However, the clincher is weather, with the milder months being designated as peak periods.

High season starts with the run-up to Christmas and continues through Easter. Snowbirds migrate down then to escape frosty weather back home, and festival-goers flock in because major events are held this time of year to avoid summer's searing heat and high humidity. Winter is also *the* time to visit the Everglades, as temperatures, mosquito activity, and water levels are all lower (making wildlife easier to spot).

Climate

Florida is rightly called the Sunshine State, but it could also be dubbed the "Humid State." From June through September, 90% humidity levels aren't uncommon. Nor are accompanying afternoon thunderstorms; in fact, more than half of the state's rain falls during these months, although these afternoon showers usually pass as quickly as they arrive. Florida's two-sided coastline also makes it a target for tropical storms. Hurricane season officially begins June 1 and ends November 30.

MIAMI EVENTS

HOMERUN HOMETOWN

The eagerly awaited first pitch was thrown at the new **Marlins Park** to start the 2012 baseball season. Catch baseball games and bask in the team's sparkling digs, which made a huge splash with a L.E.E.D.-certified retractable roof, air-conditioning, and glass walls showcasing panoramic views of the Miami skyline. 🌐 *miami.marlins.mlb.com.*

LITTLE HAVANA

Each winter during **Carnaval Miami**, salsa tunes blare and the smell of spicy chorizo fills the air on Calle Ocho, the commercial thoroughfare and heart of Miami's Little Havana. The roaring street festival, which culminates in the world's longest conga line, is the last of 10 events comprising the Latin-spiked Carnaval. Ambience- and amenity-wise, it is as close as you'll get to Cuba without actually going there. 🌐 *www.carnavalmiami.com.*

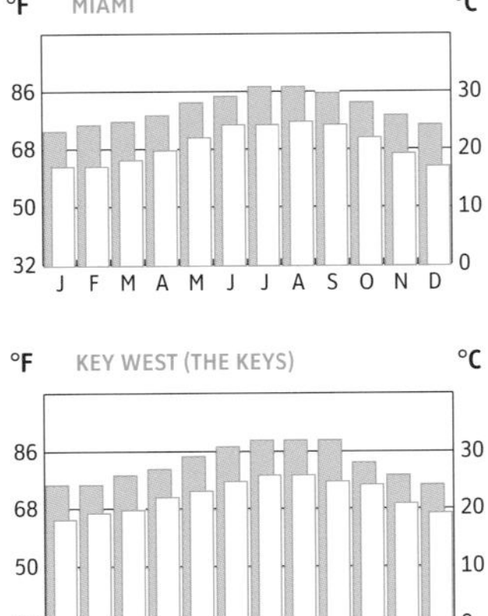

WORD OF MOUTH

"On this particular day, the beach was strewn with starfish. They were everywhere. And they were still alive. I took a quick picture and then proceeded to run up and down the beach trying to save every one of them. I hope that I succeeded."
—photo by funinthetub, Fodors.com member

QUINTESSENTIAL SOUTH FLORIDA

Food, Glorious Food

Geography and gastronomy go hand in hand in Florida. Seafood is a staple almost everywhere, yet the way it is prepared changes considerably as you maneuver around the state. In South Florida, menus highlight "Floribbean" cuisine, which marries Floridian, Caribbean, and Latin flavors (think mahimahi with mango salsa), while inland, expect catfish, gator tails, and frogs' legs, all of which are best enjoyed at a Cracker-style fish camp with a side order of hush puppies. A trip to the Miami area is not complete without a taste of Cuban food. The cuisine is heavy, with pork dishes like lechon asado (roast suckling pig) but also arroz con frijoles (the staple side dish of rice and black beans) and arroz con pollo (chicken in sticky yellow rice). Key West is a mecca for lovers of Key lime pie and conch fritters. Stone-crab claws can be savored from October through May.

The Arts

Floridians celebrate the arts year-round. Miami Beach's annual Art Basel festival draws 40,000 art lovers to town in the first week of December. Meanwhile, every April the Palm Beach International Film Festival hosts documentaries, shorts, and feature films. It's easy to catch a bit of bluegrass, country, classical, jazz, blues, or Americana with such festivals as the week-long SunFest in West Palm Beach, or hear some of the nation's best jazz performers at the annual Hollywood Jazz Fest. Miami's ArtCenter South Florida is dedicated to incubating Florida's cultural life with programs for emerging artists of all ages. The oral tradition remains vibrant with the South Florida Storytelling Project, where live readings, storytelling slams, and festivals are free and open to the public through Florida Atlantic University in Boca Raton.

Florida is synonymous with sunshine: every year, more than 80 million visitors revel in it. However, the people who live here—a diverse group that includes Mouseketeers, millionaires, and rocket scientists—know that the state's appeal rests on more than those reliable rays.

Water, Water Everywhere

Spanish explorer Ponce de León didn't find the Fountain of Youth when he swung through Florida in 1513. But if he'd lingered longer, he could have located 7,700 lakes, 1,700 rivers and creeks, and more than 700 springs. Over the centuries these have attracted American Indians, immigrants, opportunists, and countless outdoor adventurers. Boaters come for inland waterways and a 1,200-mile coast, and anglers are lured by more than 700 species of fish. (Florida claims 4,780 past and present world-record catches, so concocting elaborate "fish tales" may not be necessary.) Snorkelers and divers eager to see what lies beneath can get face time with the marine life that thrives on the world's third-largest coral reef or bone up on maritime history in underwater archaeological preserves (🌐 *www.museumsinthesea.com*). Back on dry land, all those beaches are pretty impressive, too.

Superlative Sports

South Florida is teeming with teams—and residents take the games they play *very* seriously. Baseball fans work themselves into a fever pitch: after all, the state has a pair of Major League franchises (the Miami Marlins christened a new stadium in 2012) and hosts another 13 in spring when the Grapefruit League goes to bat (three alone are in the Palm Beach area). Those who prefer pigskin might cheer for the Miami Dolphins. The state is also home to top-rated college teams, like the Hurricanes. Basketball lovers feel the "Heat" in Miami, especially now that Dwyane Wade, Chris Bosh, and three-time MVP LeBron James are on the roster, and hockey fans stick around to watch the Florida Panthers. The Professional Golfers Association (PGA) is headquartered here as well, and two big annual tennis tournaments serve up fun in Miami and Delray Beach each winter.

SOUTH FLORIDA TOP ATTRACTIONS

The Florida Keys

(A) Little wonder these 800-plus islands are a prime destination for divers and snorkelers: they boast the world's third-largest reef and aquarium-clear waters that are brimming with sea life. Under the turquoise-blue waters lies a colorful world populated by 60-plus species of coral and more than 500 species of fish, which means you can spot purple sea fans, blue tangs, yellowtail snappers, stoplight parrotfish, and more. Locals debate the premiere place for viewing them, but **John Pennekamp Coral Reef State Park** is high on everyone's list. Underwater excursions organized by park concessionaires let you put your best flipper forward. (*See ⇨ Chapter 4.*)

South Beach

(B) You can't miss the distinctive forms, vibrant colors, and extravagant flourishes of SoBe's architectural gems. The world's largest concentration of Art Deco edifices is right here; and the **Art Deco District**, with more than 800 buildings, has earned a spot on the National Register of Historic Places (*see ⇨ "A Stroll Down Deco Lane"*). The 'hood also has enough "beautiful people" to qualify for the Register of Hippest Places. The glitterati, along with assorted vacationing hedonists, are drawn by trendy shops and a surfeit of celeb-studded clubs. Stellar eateries are the icing—make that the ganache—on South Beach's proverbial cake. (*See ⇨ Chapter 2.*)

The Everglades

(C) No trip to southern Florida is complete without seeing the Everglades. At its heart is a river—50 miles wide but only 6 inches deep—flowing from Lake Okeechobee into Florida Bay. For an up-close look, speed demons can board an airboat that careens through the marshy waters. Purists, alternately, may placidly canoe or kayak within the boundaries of

Everglades National Park. Just remember to keep your hands in the boat. The critters that call this unique ecosystem home (alligators, Florida panthers, and cottonmouth snakes, for starters) can add real bite to your visit! (*See* ⇨ *Chapter 3.*)

Palm Beach

(D) If money could talk, you'd hardly be able to hear above the din in Palm Beach. The upper crust started residing there, during the winter months at least, back in the early 1900s. And today it remains a ritzy, glitzy enclave for both old money and the nouveau riche (a coterie led by "The Donald" himself). Simply put, Palm Beach is the sort of place where shopping is a full-time pursuit and people don't just wear Polo—they play it. Oooh and ahhh to your heart's content; then, for more conspicuous consumption, continue south on the aptly named Gold Coast to Boca Raton. (*See* ⇨ *Chapter 6.*)

Fort Lauderdale

(E) Mariners should set their compass for Fort Lauderdale (aka the Venice of America), where vessels from around the world moor along some two dozen finger isles between the beach and the mainland. Sailors can cruise Broward County's 300 miles of inland waterways by water taxi and tour boat, or bob around the Atlantic in a chartered yacht. If you're in a buying mood, come during October for the annual Fort Lauderdale International Boat Show. Billed as the world's largest, it has more than a billion dollars' worth of boats in every conceivable size, shape, and price range. (*See* ⇨ *Chapter 5.*)

IF YOU LIKE

Animals

The state has more than 1,200 different kinds of critters.

■ **Alligators.** "Gator spotting" in roadside waterways is itself a favorite pastime, but get a good close-up—and even hold a baby one—at **Everglades Gator Park** near Miami (see ⇨ *Chapter 3*). Farther north, canoeing around the **Arthur R. Marshall Loxahatchee National Wildlife Refuge** or the **Jonathan Dickinson State Park** will almost definitely yield a sighting (e ⇨ *Chapter 6*).

■ **Birds.** The state draws hundreds of species, from bald eagles and burrowing owls to bubblegum-pink flamingos, and the 2,000-mile **Great Florida Birding Trail** (🌐 *www.floridabirdingtrail.com*) with locations all over the Southeast helps you find them. For a squawkishly good time, feed parrots and budgies at **Lion Country Safari** (see ⇨ *Chapter 6*).

■ **Manatees.** Florida's official marine mammals are nicknamed sea cows and resemble walruses, and you can scan canals for a telltale glassy "footprint" patch indicating one is swimming below; however, for a surefire viewing, visit the gentle giants who live at the **Miami Seaquarium** (⇨ *Chapter 2*).

■ **Sea Turtles.** Ready for a late-night rendezvous with loggerheads that lumber ashore to lay eggs? Walks are organized throughout South Florida in June and July, but the **Treasure Coast** has a trove of spots (⇨ *Chapter 6*). Elsewhere try the **Museum of Discovery and Science** in Fort Lauderdale (⇨ *Chapter 5*) and **Gumbo Limbo Nature Center** in Boca Raton (⇨ *Chapter 6*).

Beaches

Each of us defines the "perfect" beach differently. But whether you want to swim, surf, lounge, or leer, Florida has one to suit your preference. Best of all, in this skinny state—bounded by the Atlantic *and* Gulf of Mexico—the coast is never more than 60 miles away.

■ **South Beach, Miami.** Over the past 20 years, no American beach has generated as much buzz as the one that hugs Ocean Drive, and it's easy to see why. Fringed with palms, backed by Art Deco architecture, and pulsating with urban energy, South Beach is the place to stretch out or strut (see ⇨ *Chapter 2*).

■ **Crandon Park Beach, Key Biscayne.** You'll see why this beach is continually ranked among the nation's top ten. After two miles of lagoon-style beach, there's an amusement center and gardens to explore (see ⇨ *Chapter 2*).

■ **Delray Municipal Beach, Delray Beach.** This super-popular stretch of sand dotted with trademark royal blue umbrellas intersects trendy Atlantic Avenue in the alluring Village by the Sea; delicious nosh and cute boutiques are a short stroll from the waves (⇨ *Chapter 6*).

■ **Matheson Hammock Park Beach, Miami.** Pack a picnic and bring the family to the safe, warm waters of this palm-tree fringed beach. Loll in the balmy breezes as you take in the amazing views or hit up the nature trails, full-service marina, and restaurant built into a historic coral rock building (see ⇨ *Chapter 2*).

■ **Dry Tortugas National Park, the Florida Keys.** Forget lazily reading a book on these shores. Come here if you're looking for a beach where you can dive in—literally. Set among coral reefs, this cluster of seven islands (accessible only by boat or seaplane) offers outstanding snorkeling and diving (see ⇨ *Chapter 4*).

Golf

With more than 1,200 courses (and counting), Florida has more greens than any other state in the Union. Palm Beach County alone is home to more than 140 courses. The trend began in 1897, when Florida's first golf course opened in Palm Beach at The Breakers, whose guests included the Rockefellers, Vanderbilts, and Astors. In Southeast Florida there are enough golf courses to allow you to play a new course every week for two years. Even if you're new to the game, you can tee up with a PGA pro for a lesson and soak in the beauty of Florida's tropical flora from one of the country's most exquisitely designed courses. Floridians play golf twelve months out of the year, although the courses are less crowded (and cheaper) between May and October.

- **Boca Raton Resort & Club.** This scenic course has some of the most exotic terrain, water features, and floral landscapes outside of Hawaii *(⇨ Chapter 6)*.
- **The Breakers, Palm Beach.** The 70-par Ocean Course offers spectacular views of the Atlantic and challenging shots on 140 acres *(⇨ Chapter 6)*.
- **Doral Golf Resort & Spa.** Home of the "Blue Monster": Doral's famous 18th hole has been ranked the best in South Florida. The par-4 hole leaves little room for error with bunkers aplenty and a green that slopes toward water *(⇨ Chapter 2)*.
- **The Club at Emerald Hills.** Test your skills on the course that has been the host site for the U.S. Amateur and U.S. Open Qualifiers since 2003 *(⇨ Chapter 5)*.
- **PGA National Resort & Spa.** Its five championship courses were all done by master designers, plus the pro tour's Honda Classic is held here *(⇨ Chapter 6)*.

Scenic Views

Florida is more than its sunsets, from aerial panoramic views to architectural wonders to nature's many surprises. Here are some views we find delightful.

- **Everglades National Park, from the tower on Shark Valley loop.** This 50-foot observation tower, about 35 miles from downtown Miami, yields a splendid panorama of the wide River of Grass as it sweeps southward toward the Gulf of Mexico. To get to the tower, you can hike or take the tram *(⇨ Chapter 3)*.
- **Ocean Drive in the Art Deco district, Miami Beach.** Feast your eyes on brilliantly restored vintage Art Deco hotels at every turn. The palm-lined beachfront that the hotels are set along hops 24 hours a day. And when you're finished looking at the colorful hotels, you can catch the sea of colorful swimsuits parading by on nearby South Beach. *(⇨ "A Stroll Down Deco Lane" in Chapter 2)*.
- **The Mansions of Palm Beach, from South Ocean Boulevard.** Some old, some new. Some ginormous—and the very definition of over-the-top—others a bit more subdued. But all are incredible, particularly the historic Mediterranean-inspired ones built by Addison Mizner and his Gilded Age-peers *(⇨ Chapter 6)*.
- **Sunset scene at Mallory Square, Key West.** Don't be surprised if someone claps for the sunset in Key West. It's that amazing, and those watching can't help but applaud. Along the waterfront the sunset draws street performers, vendors, and thousands of onlookers to the dock at Mallory Square. Fun attractions, like the Key West Aquarium, are nearby *(⇨ Chapter 4)*.

GREAT ITINERARIES

2 to 3 Days: Gold Coast and Treasure Coast

The opulent mansions of Palm Beach's Ocean Boulevard give you a glimpse of how the richer half lives. For exclusive boutique shopping, art gallery browsing, and glittery sightseeing, sybarites should wander down "The Avenue" (that's Worth Avenue to non–Palm Beachers). The sporty set will find dozens of places to tee up (hardly surprising given that the PGA is based here), along with tennis courts, polo clubs, and even a croquet center. Those who'd like to see more of the Gold Coast can continue traveling south through Boca Raton to Fort Lauderdale (justifiably known as the "Yachting Capital of the World"). But to balance the highbrow with the low-key, turn northward for a tour of the Treasure Coast. You can also look for the sea turtles that lay their own little treasures in the sands from May through October.

2 to 3 Days: Miami Area

Greater Miami lays claim to the country's most celebrated strand—South Beach—and lingering on it tops most tourist itineraries. (The Ocean Drive section, lined with edgy clubs, boutiques, and eateries, is where the see-and-be-seen crowd gathers.) Once you've checked out the candy-colored Art Deco architecture, park yourself to ogle the parade of stylish people, or join them by browsing Lincoln Road Mall, and admire its latest addition, the gleaming Frank Gehry–designed New World Symphony. Later, merengue over to Calle Ocho, the epicenter of Miami's Cuban community. Elsewhere in the area, Coconut Grove, Coral Gables, and the Miami Design District (an 18-block area crammed with showrooms and galleries) also warrant a visit. Miami is a convenient base for eco-excursions, too. You can take a day trip to the Everglades or get a spectacular view of the reefs from a glass-bottom boat in Biscayne National Park.

TIPS

Now that one-way airfares are commonplace, vacationers visiting multiple destinations can fly in to and out of different airports. Rent a car in between, picking it up at your point of arrival and leaving it at your point of departure. If you do these itineraries as an entire vacation, your best bet is to fly in to and out of Miami and rent a car from there.

2 to 3 Days: Florida Keys

Some dream of "sailing away to Key Largo," others of "wasting away again in Margaritaville." In any case, almost everybody equates the Florida Keys with relaxation. And they live up to their reputation, thanks to offbeat attractions and that fabled come-as-you-are, do-as-you-please vibe. Key West, alternately known as the Conch Republic, is a good place to get initiated. The Old Town has a funky, laid-back feel. So take a leisurely walk; pay your regards to "Papa" (Hemingway, that is); then rent a moped to tour the rest of the island. Clear waters and abundant marine life make underwater activities another must. After scoping out the parrotfish, you can always head back into town and join local "Parrotheads" in a Jimmy Buffett sing-along. When retracing your route to the mainland, plan a last pit stop at Bahia Honda State Park (it has ranger-led activities plus the Keys' best beach) or John Pennekamp Coral Reef State Park, which offers unparalleled snorkeling and scuba-diving opportunities for beginners and veterans alike.

GONE FISHIN'

by Gary McKechnie

My favorite uncle has a passion for fishing. It was one I didn't really understand—I'm more of a motorcycle guy, not a fishing pole–toting one. But one day he piqued my curiosity by telling me that fishing has many of the same enticements as motorcycling. Come again? He beautifully described the peaceful process of it all—how the serenity and solitude of the sport wash away concerns about work and tune him into the wonder of nature, just like being on a bike (minus the helmet and curvy highways).

I took the bait, and early one morning a few weeks later, my Uncle Bud and I headed out in a boat to a secluded cove on the St. Johns River near DeLand. We'd brought our rods, line, bait, and tackle—plus hot chocolate and a few things to eat. We didn't need much else. We dropped in our lines and sat silently, watching the fog hover over the water. There was a peaceful stillness as we waited (and waited) for the fish to bite. There were turtles sunning themselves on logs and herons perched in the trees. We waited for hours for just a little nibble. I can't even recall now if we caught anything, but it didn't matter. My uncle was right: it was a relaxing way to spend a Florida morning.

REEL TIME

Florida is recognized as the "Fishing Capital of the World" as well as the "Bass Capital of the World." It's also home to some of the nation's most popular crappie tournaments.

When he wasn't writing, Ernest Hemingway loved to fish in the Florida Keys. He's shown here in Key West in 1928.

Florida and fishing have a bond that goes back to thousands of years before Christ, when Paleo-Indians living along Florida's rivers and coasts were harvesting the waters just as readily as they were harvesting the land. Jump ahead to the 20th century and along came amateur anglers like Babe Ruth, Clark Gable, and Gary Cooper vacationing at central Florida fishing camps in pursuit of bream, bluegill, and largemouth bass, while Ernest Hemingway was scouring the waters off Key West in hopes of snagging marlin, tarpon, and snapper. Florida was, and is, an angler's paradise.

A variety of fish and plentiful waterways—7,800 lakes and 1,700 rivers and creeks, not to mention the gulf and the ocean—are just two reasons why Florida is the nation's favorite fishing spot. And let's not forget the frost-free attributes: unlike their northern counterparts, Florida anglers have yet to drill through several feet of ice just to go fishing in the wintertime. Plus, a well-established infrastructure for fishing—numerous bait and tackle shops, boat rentals, sporting goods stores, public piers, and charters—makes it easy for experts and first-time fishermen to get started. For Floridians and the visitors hooked on the sport here, fishing in the Sunshine State is a sport of sheer ease and simplicity.

An afternoon on the waters of Charlotte County in southwest Florida.

CASTING WIDE

The same way Florida is home to rocket scientists and beach bums, it's home to a diverse variety of fishing methods. What kind will work for you depends on where you want to go and what you want to catch.

From the Panhandle south to the Everglades, fishing is as easy as finding a quiet spot on the bank or heading out on freshwater lakes, tranquil ponds, spring-fed rivers, and placid inlets and lagoons.

Perhaps the biggest catches are found offshore—in the Atlantic Ocean, Florida Straits, or the Gulf of Mexico. For saltwater fishing, you can join a charter, be it a private one for small groups or a large party one; head out along the long jetties or public piers that jut into the ocean; or toss your line from the shore into the surf (known as surf casting). Some attempt a tricky yet effective form of fishing called net casting: tossing a circular net weighted around its perimeter; the flattened net hits the surface and drives fish into the center of the circle.

Surf casting on Juno Beach, about 20 mi north of Palm Beach.

FRESHWATER FISHING VS. SALTWATER FISHING

FRESH WATER

With nearly 8,000 lakes to choose from, it's hard to pick the leading contenders, but a handful rise to the top: Lake George, Lake Tarpon, Lake Weohyakapka, Lake Istokpoga, Lake Okeechobee, Crescent Lake, Lake Kissimmee, Lake George, and Lake Talquin. Florida's most popular freshwater game fish is the largemouth bass. Freshwater fishermen are also checking rivers and streams for other popular catches, such as spotted bass, white bass, Suwannee bass, striped bass, black crappie, bluegill, redear sunfish, and channel catfish.

SALT WATER

The seas are filled with some of the most challenging (and tasty) gamefish in America. From piers, jetties, private boats, and charter excursions, fishermen search for bonefish, tarpon, snook, redfish, grouper, permit, spotted sea trout, sailfish, cobia, bluefish, snapper, sea bass, dolphinfish (the short, squat fish, not Flipper), and sheepshead.

Tarpon

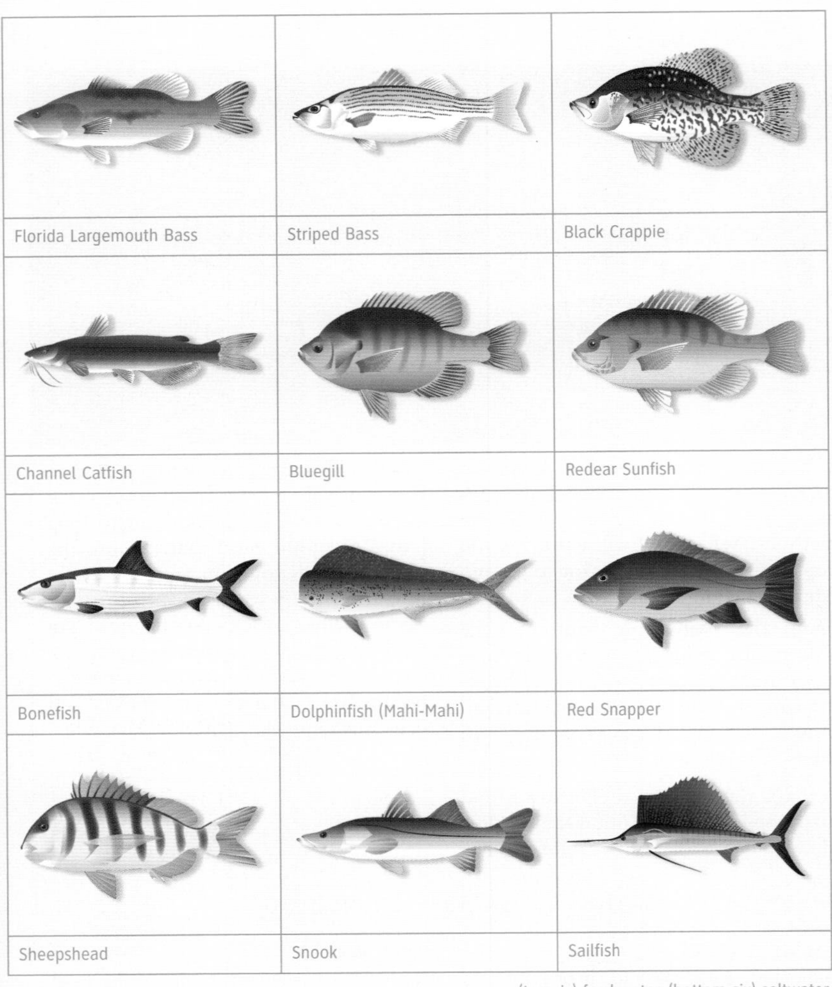

(top six) freshwater, (bottom six) saltwater

HERE'S THE CATCH

The type of fish you're after will depend on whether you fish in Florida's lake, streams, and rivers, or head out to sea. The Panhandle has an abundance of red snapper, while Lake Okeechobee is the place for bass fishing—although the largemouth bass is found throughout the state (they're easiest to catch in early spring, when they're in shallower waters). If you're looking for a good charter, Destin has a very large charter-boat fishing fleet. In the Florida Keys, you can fish by walking out in the very shallow water for hundreds of yards with the water only up to your knees; the fish you might reel in this way include bonefish, tarpon, and permit.

CHARTING THE WATERS

TYPE OF TRIP	COST	PROS	CONS
LARGE PARTY BOAT	Approx. $40/person for 4 hrs.	The captain's fishing license covers all passengers; you keep whatever you catch.	Not much privacy, assistance, or solitude: boats can hold as many as 35 passengers.
PRIVATE CHARTER	Roughly $1,200 for up to six people for 9 hrs.	More personal attention and more time on the water.	Higher cost ($200 per person instead of $40); tradition says you split the catch with the captain.
GUIDED TRIP FOR INLAND WATERS	Around $300–$400 for one or two people for 6 hrs.	Helpful if your time is limited and you want to make sure you go where the fish are biting.	Can be expensive and may not be as exciting as deep-sea fishing.
GOING SOLO	Cost for gear (rod, line, bait, and tackle) and license ($30–$100 depending on where you fish and if you need gear).	Privacy, flexibility, your time and destination are up to you; you can get fishing tips from your fellow anglers.	If you require a boat, you need to pay for and operate it yourself, plus pay for gear and a fishing license and find a fishing spot!

With a little hunting (by calling marinas, visiting bait and tackle stores, asking at town visitor centers), you can find a fishing guide who will lead you to some of the best spots on Florida's lakes and rivers. The guide provides the boat and gear, and his or her license should cover all passengers. A guide is not generally necessary for freshwater fishing, but if you're new to the sport, it might be a worthwhile investment.

On the other hand, if you're looking for fishing guides who can get you into the deep water for tarpon, redfish, snook, snapper, and dolphinfish, your best bet is to hang out at the marinas along the Florida coast and decide whether price or privacy is more important. If it's price, choose one of the larger party boats. If you'd prefer some privacy and the privilege of creating an exclusive passenger list, then sign up for a private charter. The average charter runs about nine hours, but some companies offer overnight and extended trips, too. Gear is provided in both charter-boat methods, and charters also offer the service of cleaning your catch. All guided trips encourage tipping the crew.

Most people new to the sport choose to do saltwater fishing via a charter party boat. The main reasons are expert guidance, convenience, and cost. Plus, fishing with others can be fun. Charter trips depart from marinas throughout Florida.

CREATING A FLOAT PLAN

If you're fishing in a boat on your own, let someone know where you're headed by providing a float plan, which should include where you're leaving from, a description of the boat you're on, how many are in the boat with you, what survival gear and radio equipment you have onboard, your cell phone number, and when you expect to return. If you don't return as expected, your friend can call the Coast Guard to search for you. Also be sure to have enough life jackets for everyone on board.

RULES AND REGULATIONS

To fish anywhere in (or off the coast of) Florida, you need a license, and there are separate licenses for freshwater fishing and saltwater fishing.

For non-residents, either type of fishing license cost $47 for the annual license, $30 for the 7-day one, or $17 for a 3-day license. Permits/tags are needed for catching snook ($2), crawfish/lobster ($2), and tarpon ($51.50). License and permit costs help generate funds for the Florida Fish and Wildlife Conservation Commission, which reinvests the fees into ensuring healthy habitats to sustain fish and wildlife populations, to improve access to fishing spots, and to help ensure public safety.

You can purchase your license and permits at county tax collectors' offices as well as wherever you buy your bait and tackle, such as Florida marinas, specialty stores, and sporting goods shops. You can also buy it online at www.myfwc.com/license and have it mailed to you; a surcharge is added to online orders.

If you're on a charter, you don't need to get a license. The captain's fishing license covers all passengers. Also, some piers have their own saltwater fishing licenses that cover you when you're fishing off them for recreational purposes—if you're pier fishing, ask the personnel at the tackle shop if the pier is covered.

RESOURCES

For the latest regulations on gear, daily limits, minimum sizes and seasons for certain fish, and other fishing requirements, consult the extraordinary **Florida Fish and Wildlife Conservation Commission** (888/347–4356 www.myfwc.com).

WEB RESOURCES

Download the excellent, and free, Florida Fishing PDF at www.visitflorida.com/guides. Other good sites:

www.floridafishinglakes.net
www.visitflorida.com/fishing
www.floridasportsman.com

2

Miami and Miami Beach

WORD OF MOUTH

"South beach is perfect . . . plenty of shopping, beautiful beach . . . great restaurants, lots of fun."

—flep

WELCOME TO MIAMI AND MIAMI BEACH

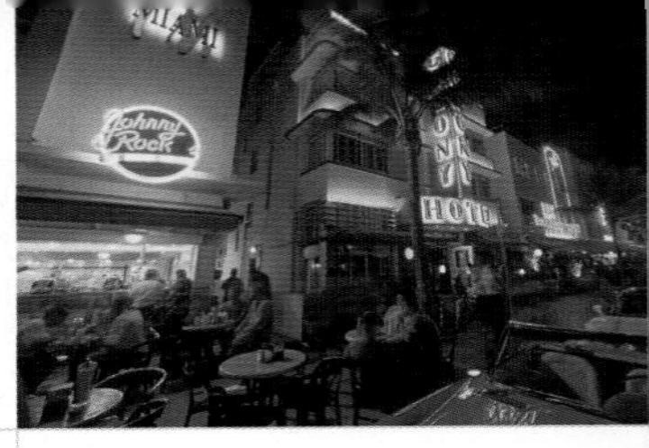

TOP REASONS TO GO

★ **The Beach:** Miami Beach has been rated as one of the 10 best in the world. White sand, warm water, and bronzed bodies everywhere provide just the right mix of relaxation and people-watching.

★ **Dining Delights:** Miami's eclectic residents have transformed the city into a museum of epicurean wonders, ranging from Cuban and Argentine fare to fusion haute cuisine.

★ **Wee-Hour Parties:** A 24-hour liquor license means clubs stay open until 5 am, and after-parties go until noon the following day.

★ **Picture-Perfect People:** Miami is a watering hole for the vain and beautiful of South America, Europe, and the Northeast. Watch them—or join them—as they strut their stuff and flaunt their tans on the white beds of renowned art deco hotels.

★ **Art Deco District:** Iconic pastels and neon lights accessorize the architecture that first put South Beach on the map in the 1930s.

1 Downtown Miami. Weave through the glass-and-steel labyrinth of new condo construction to catch a Miami Heat game at the American-Airlines Arena or a show at the Adrienne Arsht Center for the Performing Arts.

2 Coconut Grove. Catch dinner and a movie, listen to live music, or cruise the bohemian shops and locals' bars in this hip neighborhood.

3 Coral Gables. Dine and shop on family-friendly Miracle Mile, and take a driving tour of the Mediterranean-style mansions in the surrounding neighborhoods.

4 Key Biscayne. Pristine parks and tranquillity make this upscale enclave an antithesis to the South Beach party.

5 Wynwood/Midtown/Design District. These three trendy, creative neighborhoods north of downtown have shops and galleries, see-and-be-seen bars, and slick restaurants.

6 Miami Beach. People-watch from cafés and party 'til dawn at the hottest clubs in South Beach. Mid-Beach is home to the latest hotel trends and a booming restaurant scene. North Beach is more sedate and moneyed.

LITTLE HAITI
95
N.W. 79th St.
JFK Causeway
9
441
N. Miami Ave.
N.E. 2nd Ave.
Biscayne Blvd.
↑NORTH BEACH
N.W. 62nd St.
N.W. 54th St.
944
1
DESIGN DISTRICT
MID-BEACH
6
Robert Frost Expwy.
N.W. 36th St.
MIDTOWN
Julia Tuttle Causeway
195
27
5
N.W. 17th Ave.
WYNWOOD
N.W. 20th St.
SOUTH BEACH
Art Center
Venetian Causeway
395
A1A
DOWNTOWN MIAMI
Watson Island
American Airlines Arena
95
MacArthur Causeway
Art Deco District
W. Flagler St.
1
N.W. 27th Ave.
S.W. 12th Ave.
41
S.W. 8th St.
41
LITTLE HAVANA
S.W. 3rd.
S.W. 22nd St.
Fisher Island
S. Dixie Hwy.
Marine Stadium
Rickenbacker Causeway
COCONUT GROVE
2
Virginia Key
Grove Isle
Coco Walk
Biscayne Bay
ATLANTIC OCEAN
4 KEY BISCAYNE
Cape Florida Lighthouse

GETTING ORIENTED

Long considered the gateway to Latin America, Miami is as close to Cuba and the Caribbean as you can get within the United States. The 36-square-mile city is at the southern tip of the Florida peninsula, bordered on the east by Biscayne Bay. Over the bay lies a series of barrier islands, the largest being a thin 18-square-mile strip called Miami Beach. To the east of Miami Beach is the Atlantic Ocean. To the south are the Florida Keys.

CUBAN FOOD

If the tropical vibe has you hankering for Cuban food, you've come to the right place. Miami is the top spot in the country to enjoy authentic Cuban cooking.

The flavors and preparations of Cuban cuisine are influenced by the island nation's natural bounty (yucca, sugarcane, guava), as well as its rich immigrant history, from near (Caribbean countries) and far (Spanish and African traditions). Chefs in Miami tend to stick with the classic versions of beloved dishes, though you'll find some variation from restaurant to restaurant, as recipes have often been passed down through generations of home cooks. Try the popular **Versailles** (✉ *3555 S.W. 8th St.* ☎ *305/444–0240*) in Little Havana, appealing to families seeking a home-cooked, Cuban-style meal. For a fun and modern interpretation of Cuban eats, head to South Miami's **OYE Cuban Grill** (✉ *11327 S. Dixie Hwy.* ☎ *786/249–4001* 🌐 *www.oyecubangrill.com*), where the motto is "Inspired in Cuba, Made in America." The South Beach late-night institution **David's Café** (✉ *1058 Collins Ave.* ☎ *305/534–8736* ✉ *1654 Meridian Ave.* ☎ *305/672–8707*) is the beach's favorite hole-in-the-wall.

THE CUBAN SANDWICH

A great *cubano* (Cuban sandwich) requires pillowy Cuban bread layered with ham, garlic-citrus-marinated slow-roasted pork, Swiss cheese, and pickles (plus salami, in Tampa; lettuce and tomatoes in Key West), with butter and/or mustard. The sandwich is grilled in a sandwich press until the cheese melts and all the elements are fused together. Try one at **Enriqueta's Sandwich Shop** (✉ *2830 N.E. 2nd Ave.* ☎ *305/573–4681* ⏲ *Weekdays 6 am–4 pm, Sat. 6 am–2 pm*) in the Design District, or **Exquisito Restaurant** (✉ *1510 S.W. 8th St.* ☎ *305/643–0227* ⏲ *Daily 7 am–midnight*) in Little Havana.

2

KEY CUBAN DISHES

ARROZ CON POLLO

This chicken-and-rice dish is Cuban comfort food. Found throughout Latin America, the Cuban version is typically seasoned with garlic, paprika, and onions, then colored golden or reddish with saffron or achiote (a seed paste), and enlivened with a sizable splash of beer near the end of cooking. Green peas and sliced, roasted red peppers are a standard topping.

BISTEC DE PALOMILLA

This thinly sliced sirloin steak is marinated in lime juice and garlic, and fried with onions. The steak is often served with chimichurri sauce, an olive oil, garlic, and cilantro sauce that is sometimes served with bread as a dip (slather bread with butter and dab on the chimichurri). Also try *ropa vieja*, a slow-cooked, shredded flank steak in a garlic-tomato sauce.

DESSERTS

Treat yourself to a slice of *tres leches* cake. The "three milks" come from the sweetened condensed milk, evaporated milk, and heavy cream that are poured over the cake until it's an utterly irresistible gooey mess. Also, don't miss the *pastelitos*, Cuban fruit-filled turnovers. Traditional flavors include plain guava, guava with cream cheese, and cream cheese with coconut. Yum!

DRINKS

Sip *guarapo* (gwa-RA-poh), a fresh sugarcane juice that isn't really as sweet as you might think, or grab a straw and enjoy a frothy *batido* (bah-TEE-doe), a Cuban-style milk shake made with tropical fruits like mango, *piña* (pineapple), or *mamey* (mah-MAY, a tropical fruit with a melon-cherry taste). For a real twist, try the *batido de trigo*—a wheat shake that will remind you of sugar-glazed breakfast cereal.

FRITAS

If you're in the mood for an inexpensive, casual Cuban meal, have a *frita*—a hamburger with distinctive Cuban flair. It's made with ground beef that's mixed with ground or finely chopped chorizo, spiced with pepper, paprika, and salt, topped with sautéed onions and shoestring potato fries, and then served on a bun slathered with a special tomato-based ketchuplike sauce.

LECHON ASADO

Fresh ham or an entire suckling pig marinated in *mojo criollo* (parsley, garlic, sour orange, and olive oil) is roasted until fork tender and served with white rice, black beans, and *tostones* (fried plantains) or yucca (pronounced YU-kah), a starchy tuber with a mild nut taste that's often sliced into fat sticks and deep-fried like fries.

Updated by Paul Rubio

Three-quarters of a century after the art deco movement, Miami remains one of the world's trendiest and flashiest hot spots. Luckily for visitors, South Beach is no longer the only place to stand and pose in Miami. North of downtown Miami's megamakeover, the growing Wynwood and Design districts—along with nearby Midtown—are home to Miami's hipster and fashionista scenes, and South Beach continues to extend both north and west, with the addition of new venues north of 20th Street and along the bay on West Avenue. Following the reopening of the mammoth Fontainebleau and its enclave of nightclubs and restaurants along Mid-Beach, other globally renowned resorts have moved into the neighborhood, like the Soho Beach House and Canyon Ranch.

Visit Miami today and it's hard to believe that 100 years ago it was a mosquito-infested swampland, with an Indian trading post on the Miami River. Then hotel builder Henry Flagler brought his railroad to the outpost known as Fort Dallas. Other visionaries—Carl Fisher, Julia Tuttle, William Brickell, and John Sewell, among others—set out to tame the unruly wilderness. Hotels were erected, bridges were built, the port was dredged, and electricity arrived. The narrow strip of mangrove coast was transformed into Miami Beach—and the tourists started to come. They haven't stopped since!

Greater Miami is many destinations in one. At its best it offers an unparalleled multicultural experience: melodic Latin and Caribbean tongues, international cuisines and cultural events, and an unmistakable joie de vivre—all against a beautiful beach backdrop. In Little Havana the air is tantalizing with the perfume of strong Cuban coffee. In Coconut Grove,

Caribbean steel drums ring out during the Miami/Bahamas Goombay Festival. Anytime in colorful Miami Beach, restless crowds wait for entry to the hottest new clubs.

Many visitors don't know that Miami and Miami Beach are really separate cities. Miami, on the mainland, is South Florida's commercial hub. Miami Beach, on 17 islands in Biscayne Bay, is sometimes considered America's Riviera, luring refugees from winter with its warm sunshine; sandy beaches; graceful, shady palms; and tireless nightlife. The natives know well that there's more to Greater Miami than the bustle of South Beach and its Art Deco District. In addition to well-known places such as Ocean Drive and Lincoln Road, the less reported spots—like the burgeoning Design District in Miami, the historic buildings of Coral Gables, and the secluded beaches of Key Biscayne—are great insider destinations.

PLANNING

WHEN TO GO

Miami and Miami Beach are year-round destinations. Most visitors come November through April, when the weather is close to perfect; hotels, restaurants, and attractions are busiest; and each weekend holds a festival or event. The "Season" kicks off in December with Art Basel Miami Beach, and hotel rates don't come down until after the college kids have left from spring break in late March.

It's hot and steamy from May through September, but nighttime temperatures are usually pleasant. Also, summer is a good time for the budget traveler. Many hotels lower their rates considerably, and many restaurants offer discounts—especially during **Miami Spice** in August, when slews of top restaurants offer special tasting menus at a steep discount. (Sometimes Spice runs for two months. Check ⊕ *www.iLoveMiamiSpice.com* for details.)

GETTING HERE AND AROUND

Greater Miami resembles Los Angeles in its urban sprawl and traffic. You'll need a car to visit many attractions and points of interest. If possible, avoid driving during the rush hours of 7–9 am and 5–7 pm—the hour just after and right before the peak times also can be slow going. During rainy weather, be especially cautious of flooding in South Beach and Key Biscayne.

AIR TRAVEL

Miami is serviced by Miami International Airport (MIA), 8 miles northwest of downtown, and Fort Lauderdale–Hollywood International Airport (FLL), 26 miles northeast. Many discount carriers, like Spirit Airlines, Southwest Airlines, and AirTran, fly into FLL, making it a smart bargain if you are renting a car. Otherwise, look for flights to MIA on American Airlines, Delta, and Continental. MIA recently underwent an extensive face-lift, improving facilities, common spaces, and the overall aesthetic of the airport.

CAR TRAVEL

Interstate 95 is the major expressway connecting South Florida with points north; State Road 836 is the major east–west expressway and connects to Florida's Turnpike, State Road 826, and Interstate 95. Seven causeways link Miami and Miami Beach, with Interstate 195 and Interstate 395 offering the most convenient routes; the Rickenbacker Causeway extends to Key Biscayne from Interstate 95 and U.S. 1. The high-speed lanes on the left-hand side of I–95 require a prepaid toll gadget called a "Sunpass," available in most drug and grocery stores.

Remember U.S. 1 (aka Biscayne Boulevard)—you'll hear it often in directions. It starts in Key West, hugs South Florida's coastline, and heads north straight through to Maine.

PUBLIC TRANSPORTATION

Some sights are accessible via the public transportation system, run by the **Metro-Dade Transit Agency**, which maintains 740 Metrobuses on 90 routes; the 23-mile Metrorail elevated rapid-transit system; and the Metromover, an elevated light-rail system. Those planning to use public transportation should get an EASY Card or EASY Ticket available at any Metrorail station and most supermarkets. Fares are discounted, and transfer fees are nominal. The bus stops for the **Metrobus** are marked with blue-and-green signs with a bus logo and route information. The fare is $2 (exact change only if paying cash). Cash-paying customers must pay for another ride if transferring. Some express routes carry a surcharge of 35¢. Elevated **Metrorail** trains run from downtown Miami north to Hialeah and south along U.S. 1 to Dadeland. The system operates daily 5 am–midnight. The fare is $2; 50¢ transfers to Metrobus are available only for EASY Card and EASY Ticket holders. **Metromover** resembles an airport shuttle and runs on two loops around downtown Miami, linking major hotels, office buildings, and shopping areas. The system spans 4 miles, including the 1-mile Omni Loop and the 1-mile Brickell Loop. There is no fee to ride; transfers to Metrorail are $2.

Tri-Rail, South Florida's commuter-train system, stops at 18 stations north of MIA along a 71-mile route. There is a Metrorail transfer station two stops north of MIA. Prices range from $2.50 to $6.90 for a one-way ticket.

Contacts **Metro-Dade Transit Agency** ☎ *305/891–3131* 🌐 *www.miamidade.gov/transit.* **Tri-Rail** ☎ *800/874–7245* 🌐 *www.tri-rail.com.*

TAXI TRAVEL

Except in South Beach, it's difficult to hail a cab on the street; in most cases you'll need to call a cab company or have a hotel doorman hail one for you. Fares run $4.90 for the first mile and $2.40 every mile thereafter; flat-rate fares are also available from the airport to a variety of zones, including Miami Beach for $32. Expect a $2 surcharge on rides leaving from Miami International Airport. For those heading from MIA to downtown, the 15-minute, 7-mile trip costs around $22. Many cabs now accept credit cards; inquire before you get in the car.

Taxi Companies **Central Cabs** ☎ *305/532–5555.* **Metro Taxi** ☎ *305/888–8888.* **Society Cab Company** ☎ *305/757–5523.* **Super Yellow Cab Company** ☎ *305/888–7777.* **Tropical Taxi** ☎ *305/945–1025.*

TRAIN TRAVEL

Amtrak provides service from 500 destinations to the Greater Miami area. The trains make several stops along the way; north–south service stops in the major Florida cities of Jacksonville, Orlando, Tampa, West Palm Beach, and Fort Lauderdale. Note that these stops are often in less than ideal locations for immediate city access. For extended trips, or if you want to visit other areas in Florida, you can come via Auto Train (where you bring your car along) from Lorton, Virginia, just outside Washington, D.C., to Sanford, Florida, just outside Orlando. From there it's less than a four-hour drive to Miami. Fares vary, but expect to pay between around $275 and $350 for a basic sleeper seat and car passage each way. ■ **TIP→ You must be traveling with an automobile to purchase a ticket on the Auto Train.**

VISITOR INFORMATION

For additional information about Miami and Miami Beach, contact the city's visitor bureaus. You can also pick up a free Miami Beach INcard at the Miami Beach Visitors Center 10 am–4 pm seven days a week, entitling you to discounts and offers at restaurants, shops, galleries, and more.

Contacts **Coconut Grove Chamber of Commerce** ✉ *2820 McFarlane Rd., Coconut Grove* ☎ *305/444–7270* 🌐 *www.coconutgrovechamber.com.* **Coral Gables Chamber of Commerce** ✉ *224 Catalonia Ave., Coral Gables* ☎ *305/446–1657* 🌐 *www.coralgableschamber.org.* **Greater Miami Convention & Visitors Bureau** ✉ *701 Brickell Ave., Suite 2700* ☎ *305/539–3000, 800/933–8448 in U.S.* 🌐 *www.miamiandbeaches.com.* **Key Biscayne Chamber of Commerce and Visitors Center** ✉ *88 W. McIntyre St., Suite 100, Key Biscayne* ☎ *305/361–5207* 🌐 *www.keybiscaynechamber.org.* **Miami Beach Visitors Center** ✉ *1901 Convention Center Dr., Hall C, Miami Beach* ☎ *786/276-2763, 305/673-7400 Miami Beach Tourist Hotline* 🌐 *www.miamibeachguest.com.*

EXPLORING MIAMI AND MIAMI BEACH

If you had arrived here 50 years ago with a guidebook in hand, chances are you'd be thumbing through listings looking for alligator wrestlers and you-pick strawberry fields or citrus groves. Things have changed. While Disney sidetracked families in Orlando, Miami was developing a unique culture and attitude that's equal parts beach town/big business, Latino/Caribbean meets European/American—all of which fuels a great art and food scene, as well as exuberant nightlife and myriad festivals.

To find your way around Greater Miami, learn how the numbering system works (or better yet, use a GPS). Miami is laid out on a grid with four quadrants—northeast, northwest, southeast, and southwest—that meet at Miami Avenue and Flagler Street. Miami Avenue separates east from west, and Flagler Street separates north from south. Avenues and courts run north–south; streets, terraces, and ways run east–west. Roads run diagonally, northwest–southeast. But other districts—Miami Beach, Coral Gables, and Hialeah—may or may not follow this system, and along the curve of Biscayne Bay the symmetrical grid shifts diagonally. It's best to buy a detailed map, stick to the major roads, and ask directions early and often. However, make sure you're in a safe neighborhood or public place when you seek guidance; cabdrivers and cops are good resources.

DOWNTOWN MIAMI

Downtown Miami dazzles from a distance. The skyline is fluid, thanks to the sheer number of sparkling glass high-rises between Biscayne Boulevard and the Miami River. Business is the key to downtown Miami's daytime bustle. However, the influx of massive, modern, and affordable condos has lured a young and trendy demographic to the areas in and around downtown, giving Miami much more of a "city" feel come nightfall. In fact, downtown has become a nighttime hot spot in recent years, inciting a cultural revolution that has fostered burgeoning areas north in Wynwood, Midtown, and the Design District, and south along Brickell Avenue. The pedestrian streets here tend to be very restaurant-centric, complemented by lounges and nightclubs.

The free, 23-mile, elevated commuter system known as the Metromover runs inner and outer loops through downtown and to nearby neighborhoods south and north. Many attractions are conveniently located within a few blocks of a station.

Note that if you have a vehicle, you can combine a visit to this neighborhood with one to Little Havana, which is just southwest of downtown. ⇨ *See the illustrated feature "Caribbean Infusion" for a map of Little Havana as well as one of Little Haiti in north Miami.*

TOP ATTRACTIONS

Adrienne Arsht Center. Culture vultures and other artsy types are drawn to this stunning performing arts center, home of the Florida Grand Opera, Miami City Ballet, New World Symphony, Concert Association of Florida, and other local and touring groups, which have included Broadway hits like *Wicked* and *Jersey Boys*. Think of it as a sliver of savoir faire to temper Miami's often-over-the-top vibe. Designed by architect César Pelli, the massive development contains a 2,400-seat opera house, a 2,200-seat concert hall, a black-box theater, and an outdoor Plaza for the Arts. Restaurateur Barton G. presents his pretheater dining extravaganza at the Arsht Center's restaurant, **Prelude by Barton G.,** with a $39 prix-fixe menu (*305/357–7900* 🌐 *www.preludebybartong.com*). ✉ *1300 Biscayne Blvd., at N.E. 13th St., Downtown* ☎ *305/949–6722* 🌐 *www.arshtcenter.org*.

Freedom Tower. In the 1960s this ornate Spanish-baroque structure was the Cuban Refugee Center, processing more than 500,000 Cubans who entered the United States after fleeing Fidel Castro's regime. Built in 1925 for the *Miami Daily News*, it was inspired by the Giralda, an 800-year-old bell tower in Seville, Spain. Preservationists were pleased to see the tower's exterior restored in 1988. Today it is owned by Miami Dade College (MDC), functioning as a cultural and educational center, principally for premiere exhibitions of MDC's Art Gallery System. ✉ *600 Biscayne Blvd., at N.E. 6th St., Downtown* ☎ *305/237–7700* 🌐 *www.mdc.edu/ags/freedom_tower* 🕓 *Tues.–Fri. noon–5*.

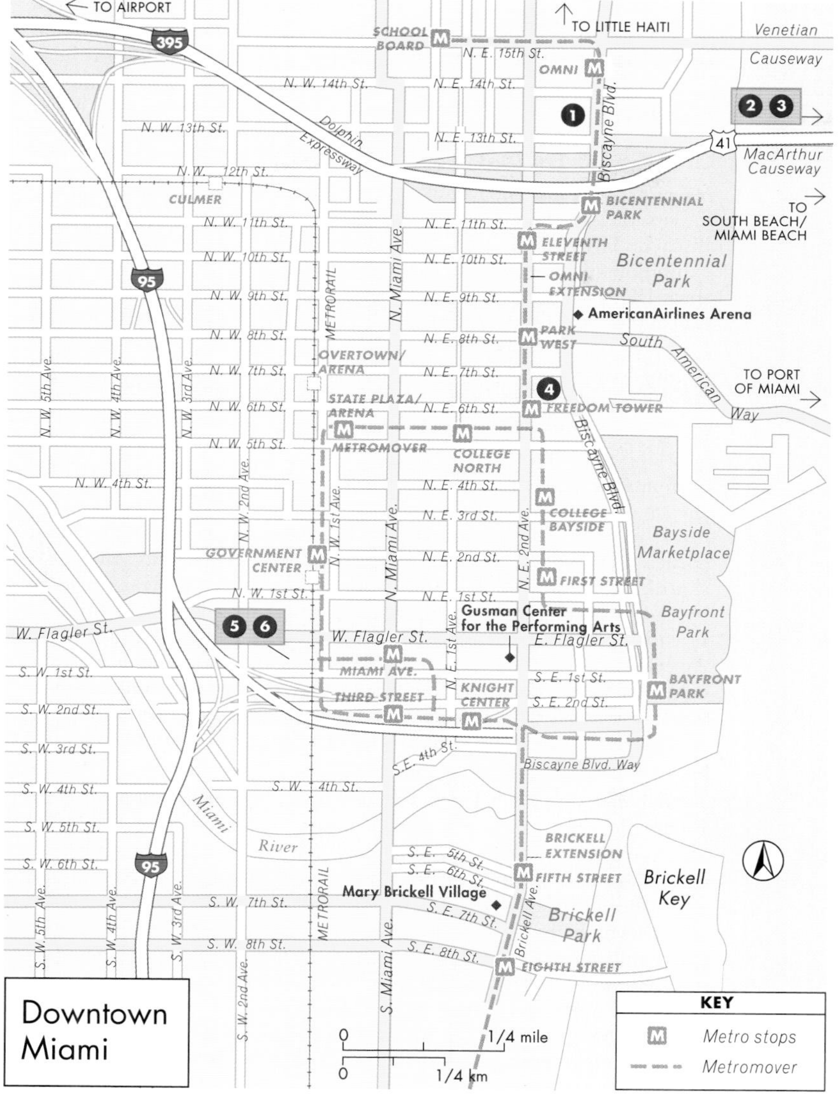
Downtown Miami
TO AIRPORT
395
TO LITTLE HAITI
Venetian Causeway
SCHOOL BOARD
N. E. 15th St.
OMNI
N. W. 14th St.
N. E. 14th St.
Biscayne Blvd.
N. W. 13th St.
Dolphin Expressway
N. E. 13th St.
41
MacArthur Causeway
N. W. 12th St.
CULMER
BICENTENNIAL PARK
TO SOUTH BEACH/ MIAMI BEACH
N. W. 11th St.
N. E. 11th St.
ELEVENTH STREET
N. W. 10th St.
N. E. 10th St.
Bicentennial Park
95
OMNI EXTENSION
N. W. 9th St.
N. E. 9th St.
METRORAIL
N. Miami Ave.
AmericanAirlines Arena
N. W. 8th St.
N. E. 8th St.
PARK WEST
South American Way
N. W. 5th Ave.
N. W. 4th Ave.
N. W. 3rd Ave.
OVERTOWN/ ARENA
N. W. 7th St.
N. E. 7th St.
TO PORT OF MIAMI
N. W. 6th St.
STATE PLAZA/ ARENA
N. E. 6th St.
FREEDOM TOWER
N. W. 5th St.
METROMOVER
COLLEGE NORTH
N. W. 4th St.
N. E. 4th St.
N. W. 2nd Ave.
N. W. 1st Ave.
N. E. 3rd St.
COLLEGE BAYSIDE
N. E. 2nd Ave.
Bayside Marketplace
GOVERNMENT CENTER
N. E. 2nd St.
FIRST STREET
N. W. 1st St.
N. E. 1st St.
Gusman Center for the Performing Arts
Bayfront Park
W. Flagler St.
E. Flagler St.
N. E. 1st Ave.
S. W. 1st St.
MIAMI AVE.
S. E. 1st St.
BAYFRONT PARK
S. W. 2nd St.
THIRD STREET
KNIGHT CENTER
S. E. 2nd St.
S. W. 3rd St.
S. E. 4th St.
Biscayne Blvd. Way
S. W. 4th St.
S. W. 4th St.
Miami River
S. W. 5th St.
BRICKELL EXTENSION
S. W. 6th St.
S. E. 5th St.
S. E. 6th St.
FIFTH STREET
Brickell Key
Mary Brickell Village
S. W. 7th St.
S. E. 7th St.
Brickell Ave.
Brickell Park
S. W. 5th Ave.
S. W. 4th Ave.
S. W. 3rd Ave.
S. W. 8th St.
S. E. 8th St.
EIGHTH STREET
S. W. 2nd Ave.
S. Miami Ave.
0
1/4 mile
0
1/4 km
KEY
Metro stops
Metromover

HistoryMiami. Discover a trove of colorful stories about the region's history at HistoryMiami, formerly known as the Historical Museum of Southern Florida. Exhibits celebrate the city's multicultural heritage, including an old Miami streetcar and unique items chronicling the migration of Cubans to Miami. ✉ *101 W. Flagler St., between N.W. 1st and 2nd Aves., Downtown* ☎ *305/375–1492* 🌐 *www.historymiami.org* 🎫 *$8* 🕒 *Tues.–Fri. 10–5, weekends noon–5.*

Miami Art Museum. The Miami Art Museum (MAM) is slated to move into its long-awaited, 120,000-square-foot home in Museum Park along Biscayne Bay in mid-2013. Until then, MAM presents major touring exhibitions of work by international artists, with an emphasis on art since 1945. It's currently amassing new pieces for a permanent collection in the expanded facility, including works by such contemporary artists as Morris Louis, Fred Wilson, and George Sanchez-Calderón. Every second Saturday, entrance is free for families. ✉ *101 W. Flagler St., between N.W. 1st and 2nd Aves., Downtown* ☎ *305/375–3000* 🌐 *www.miamiartmuseum.org* 🎫 *$8* 🕒 *Tues.–Fri. 10–5, weekends noon–5.*

WORTH NOTING

Bayfront Park. This pedestrian-friendly waterfront park sits on a 32-acre site smack in the heart of downtown Miami on Biscayne Bay—with a lovely bay walk and a number of monuments. In the park's southwest corner is the white *Challenger* Memorial, commemorating the space shuttle that exploded in 1986. A little north is Plaza Bolivar, a tribute by Cuban immigrants to their adopted country, and the JFK Torch of Friendship, a plaza with plaques representing all South and Central American countries except Cuba. To the north, the park ends with the colossal Bayside Marketplace entertainment, dining, and retail complex, which is particularly popular with cruise passengers as well as visitors from South America. ✉ *301 N. Biscayne Blvd., Downtown* 🌐 *www.bayfrontparkmiami.com.*

Jungle Island. Originally located deep in south Miami and known as Parrot Jungle, South Florida's original tourist attraction opened in 1936 and moved closer to Miami Beach in 2003. Located on Watson Island, a small stretch of land off of I–395 between Downtown Miami and South Beach, Jungle Island is far more than a park where cockatoos ride tricycles; this interactive zoological park is home to just about every unusual and endangered species you would want to see, including a rare albino alligator, a liger (lion and tiger mix), and myriad exotic birds. The most intriguing offerings are the VIP animal tours, including the Lemur Experience ($45 for 45 minutes), in which the highly social primates make themselves at home on your lap or shoulders. Jungle Island offers complimentary shuttle service to most Downtown Miami and South Beach hotels. ✉ *1111 Parrot Jungle Trail, off MacArthur Causeway (I–395), Downtown* ☎ *305/400–7000* 🌐 *www.jungleisland.com* 🎫 *$32.95, plus $8 parking* 🕒 *Weekdays 10–5, weekends 10–6.*

Miami Children's Museum. This Arquitectonica-designed museum, both imaginative and geometric in appearance, is directly across the MacArthur Causeway from Jungle Island. Twelve galleries house hundreds of interactive, bilingual exhibits. Children can scan plastic groceries in the supermarket, scramble through a giant sand castle, climb a rock wall, learn about the Everglades, and combine rhythms in the world-music studio. ✉ *980 MacArthur Causeway, off I–395, Downtown* ☎ *305/373–5437* 🌐 *www.miamichildrensmuseum.org* 🎟 *$16, parking $1/hr* ⏲ *Daily 10–6.*

COCONUT GROVE

Eclectic and intriguing, Miami's Coconut Grove can be considered a loose tropical equivalent of New York's Greenwich Village. A haven for writers and artists, the neighborhood has never quite outgrown its image as a small village. During the day it's business as usual in Coconut Grove, much as in any other Miami neighborhood. But in the evening, especially on weekends, it seems as if someone flips a switch and the streets come alive. Locals and tourists jam into small boutiques, sidewalk cafés, and stores lodged in two massive retail-entertainment complexes. For blocks in every direction, students, families, and prosperous retirees flow in and out of a mix of galleries, restaurants, bars, bookstores, comedy clubs, and theaters. With this weekly influx of traffic, parking can pose a problem. There's a well-lighted city garage at 3315 Rice Street (behind the Mayfair and CocoWalk), or look for police to direct you to parking lots where you'll pay $10 and up for an evening's slot. If you're staying in the Grove, leave the car behind, and your night will get off to an easier start.

Nighttime is the right time to see Coconut Grove, but in the day you can take a casual drive around the neighborhood to see its diverse architecture. Posh estates mingle with rustic cottages, modest frame homes, and stark modern dwellings, often on the same block. If you're into horticulture, you'll be impressed by the Garden of Eden–like foliage that seems to grow everywhere without care. In truth, residents are determined to keep up the Grove's village-in-a-jungle look, so they lavish attention on exotic plantings even as they battle to protect any remaining native vegetation.

EXPLORING

Barnacle Historic State Park. A pristine bay-front manse sandwiched between cramped luxury developments, Barnacle is Miami's oldest house still standing on its original foundation. To get here, you'll hike along an old buggy trail through a tropical hardwood hammock and landscaped lawn leading to Biscayne Bay. Built in 1891 by Florida's first snowbird—New Yorker Commodore Ralph Munroe—the large home, built of timber that Munroe salvaged from wrecked ships, has many original furnishings, a broad sloping roof, and deeply recessed verandas that channel sea breezes into the house. If your timing is right, you may catch one of the monthly Moonlight Concerts, and the old-fashioned picnic on July 4 is popular. ✉ *3485 Main Hwy.* ☎ *305/442–6866* 🌐 *www.floridastateparks.org/thebarnacle* 🎟 *$2 park entry, tours $3, concerts $7* ⏲ *Fri.–Mon. 9–5; tours at 10, 11:30, 1, and 2:30; groups Wed. and Thurs.; concerts Sept.–May on evenings near the full moon 6–9, call or check the website for date.*

Greater Miami
N.W. 79th St.
JFK Causeway
9
441
N.W. 62nd St.
N. Miami Ave.
N.E. 2nd Ave.
Biscayne Blvd.
MIAMI BEACH
Hialeah Dr.
944
N.W. 54th St.
1
N.W. 72nd Ave.
27
Robert Frost Expwy.
N.W. 39th St.
Julia Tuttle Causeway
195
N.W. 36th St.
WYNWOOD ARTS DISTRICT
Dairy Rd.
Miami River
Miami International Airport
N.W. 17th Ave.
N.W. 20th St.
SOUTH BEACH
Venetian Causeway
395
836
East-West Expressway
A1A
Alton Rd.
Art Deco District
Parrot Jungle Island
N.W. 7th St.
95
S.W. 12th Ave.
N.W. 27th Ave.
MacArthur Causeway
959
W. Flagler St.
Collins Ave.
Ocean Dr.
968
41
MIAMI
OCEAN
S.W. 8th St.
S.W. 8th St.
Tamiami Trail
Granada Blvd.
Le Jeune Rd.
Ponce de León Blvd.
S.W. 37th Ave. (Douglas Rd.)
S.W. 13th St.
S.W. 3rd. Ave.
826
Brickell Ave.
Fisher Island
Coral Way
S.W. 22nd St.
Coral Way
972
COCONUT GROVE
Marine Stadium
Rickenbacker Causeway
Sevilla Ave.
Virginia Key
S.W. 57th Ave.
953
S. Dixie Hwy.
Bird Rd.
976
CocoWalk
Grove Isle
Grand Ave.

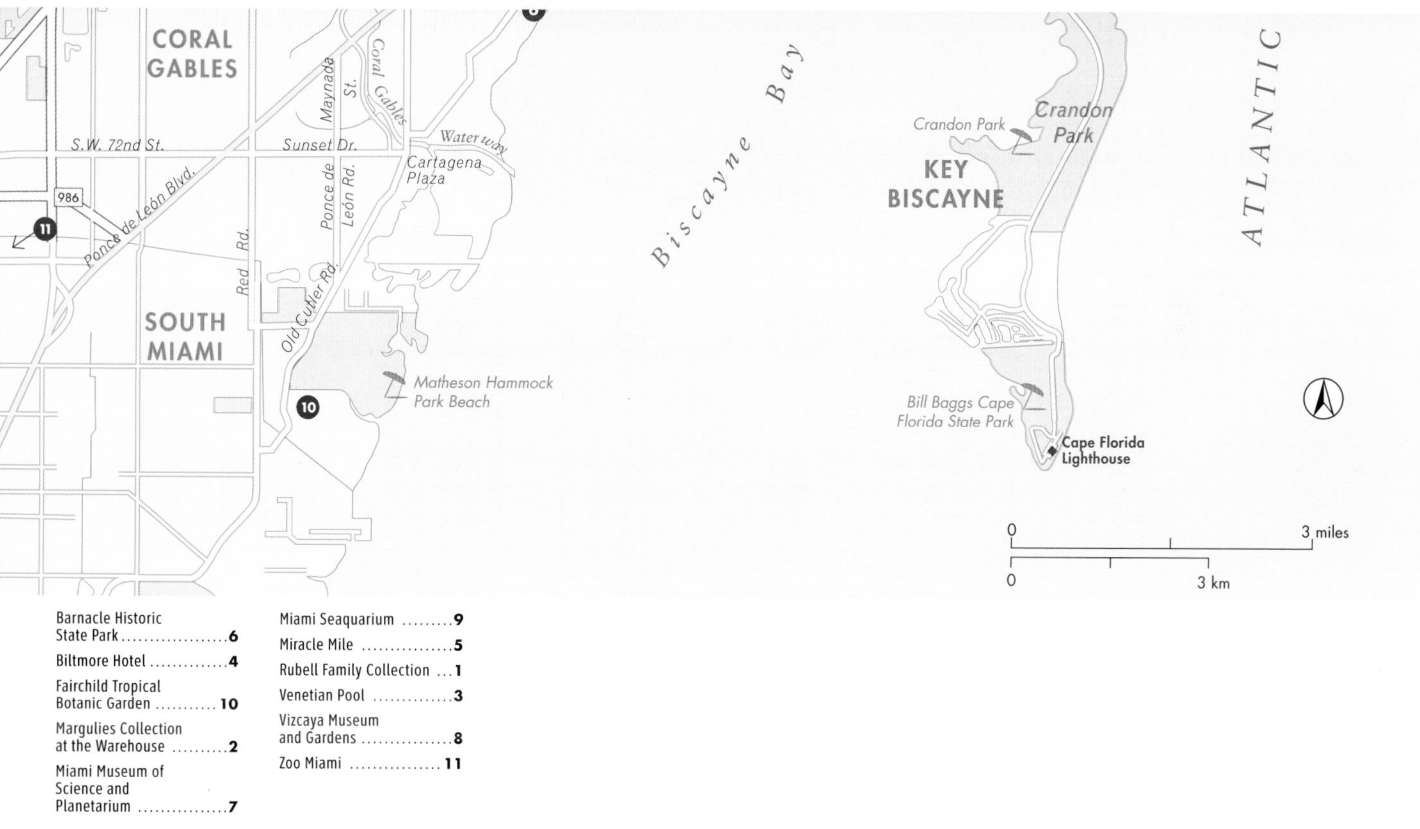

Barnacle Historic State Park ... 6
Biltmore Hotel ... 4
Fairchild Tropical Botanic Garden ... 10
Margulies Collection at the Warehouse ... 2
Miami Museum of Science and Planetarium ... 7
Miami Seaquarium ... 9
Miracle Mile ... 5
Rubell Family Collection ... 1
Venetian Pool ... 3
Vizcaya Museum and Gardens ... 8
Zoo Miami ... 11

Miami Museum of Science and Planetarium. This small fun museum is chock-full of hands-on sound, gravity, and electricity displays for children and adults alike. For animal lovers, its wildlife center houses native Florida snakes, turtles, tortoises, and birds of prey. Check the museum's schedule for traveling exhibits that appear throughout the year. If you're here the first Friday of the month—called Fabulous First Fridays—stick around for the free star show at 7:30 pm and then gaze at the planets through two powerful Meade telescopes at the Weintraub Observatory. Also enjoy a laser-light rock-and-roll show nightly at 9, 10, 11, or midnight to the tunes of the Doors, the Beatles, or Pink Floyd, to name a few. *3280 S. Miami Ave. 305/646–4200 www.miamisci.org Museum exhibits, planetarium shows, and wildlife center $14.95; laser show $8 Museum daily 10–6.*

Fodor's Choice ★ **Vizcaya Museum and Gardens.** Of the 10,000 people living in Miami between 1912 and 1916, about 1,000 of them were gainfully employed by Chicago industrialist James Deering to build this European-inspired residence. Once comprising 180 acres, this National Historic Landmark now occupies a 30-acre tract that includes a rockland hammock (native forest) and more than 10 acres of formal gardens with fountains overlooking Biscayne Bay. The house, open to the public, contains 70 rooms, 34 of which are filled with paintings, sculpture, antique furniture, and other fine and decorative arts. The collection spans 2,000 years and represents the Renaissance, baroque, rococo, and neoclassical periods. The 90-minute self-guided Discover Vizcaya Audio Tour is available in multiple languages for an additional $5. Guided tours are also available in English, Wednesday through Monday at 11:30, 12:30, 1:30, and 2:30. Moonlight tours, offered on evenings that are nearest the full moon, provide a magical look at the gardens; call for reservations. *3251 S. Miami Ave. 305/250–9133 www.vizcayamuseum.org $15 Wed.–Mon. 9:30–4:30.*

CORAL GABLES

You can easily spot Coral Gables from the window of a Miami-bound jetliner—just look for the massive orange tower of the Biltmore Hotel rising from a lush green carpet of trees concealing the city's gracious homes. The canopy is as much a part of this planned city as its distinctive architecture, all attributed to the vision of George E. Merrick nearly 100 years ago.

The story of this city began in 1911, when Merrick inherited 1,600 acres of citrus and avocado groves from his father. Through judicious investment he nearly doubled the tract to 3,000 acres by 1921. Merrick dreamed of building an American Venice here, complete with canals and homes. Working from this vision, he began designing a city based on centuries-old prototypes from Mediterranean countries. Unfortunately for Merrick, the devastating no-name hurricane of 1926, followed by the Great Depression, prevented him from fulfilling many of his plans. He died at 54, an employee of the post office. Today Coral Gables has a population of about 45,000. In its bustling downtown more than 150 multinational companies maintain headquarters or regional offices, and the University of Miami campus in the southern part of the Gables brings a youthful vibrancy to the area. A southern branch of the city extends down the shore of Biscayne Bay through neighborhoods threaded with canals.

EXPLORING

TOP ATTRACTIONS

Biltmore Hotel. Bouncing back stunningly from its dark days as an army hospital, this hotel has become the jewel of Coral Gables—a dazzling architectural gem with a colorful past. First opened in 1926, it was a hot spot for the rich and glamorous of the Jazz Age until it was converted to an Army A Force regional hospital in 1942. Until 1968, the Veterans Administration continued to operate the hospital after World War II. The Biltmore then lay vacant for nearly 20 years before it underwent extensive renovations and reopened as a luxury hotel in 1987. Its 16-story tower, like the Freedom Tower in downtown Miami, is a replica of Seville's Giralda Tower. The magnificent pool is reportedly the largest hotel pool in the continental United States. Because it functions as a full-service hotel, your ticket in—if you aren't staying here—is to patronize one of the hotel's several restaurants or bars. Sunday champagne brunch is a local legend; try to get a table in the courtyard. ✉ *1200 Anastasia Ave., near De Soto Blvd.* ☎ *305/445–1926* 🌐 *www.biltmorehotel.com.*

Fodor's Choice ★ **Fairchild Tropical Botanic Garden.** With 83 acres of lakes, sunken gardens, a 560-foot vine pergola, orchids, bellflowers, coral trees, bougainvillea, rare palms, and flowering trees, Fairchild is the largest tropical botanical garden in the continental United States. The tram tour highlights the best of South Florida's flora; then you can set off exploring on your own. A 2-acre rain-forest exhibit showcases tropical plants from around the world complete with a waterfall and stream. The conservatory, Windows to the Tropics, is home to rare tropical plants, including the Titan Arum (*Amorphophallus titanum*), a fast-growing variety that attracted thousands of visitors when it bloomed in 1998. (It was only the sixth documented bloom in this country in the 20th century.) The Keys Coastal Habitat, created in a marsh and mangrove area in 1995 with assistance from the Tropical Audubon Society, provides food and shelter to resident and migratory birds. Check out the Montgomery Botanical Center, a research facility devoted to palms and cycads. Spicing up Fairchild's calendar are plant sales, afternoon teas, and genuinely special events year-round, such as the International Mango Festival the second weekend in July. The excellent bookstore–gift shop carries books on gardening and horticulture, and the Garden Café serves sandwiches and, seasonally, smoothies made from the garden's own crop of tropical fruits. ✉ *10901 Old Cutler Rd.* ☎ *305/667–1651* 🌐 *www.fairchildgarden.org* 🎫 *$25* 🕒 *Daily 9:30–4:30.*

★ **Venetian Pool.** Sculpted from a rock quarry in 1923 and fed by artesian wells, this 820,000-gallon municipal pool had a major face-lift in 2010. It remains quite popular because of its themed architecture—a fantasy version of a waterfront Italian village—created by Denman Fink. The pool has earned a place on the National Register of Historic Places and showcases a nice collection of vintage photos depicting 1920s beauty pageants and swank soirees held long ago. Paul Whiteman played here, Johnny Weissmuller and Esther Williams swam here, and you should, too (but no kids under 3). A snack bar, lockers, and showers make this must-see user-friendly as well. ✉ *2701 De Soto Blvd., at Toledo St.* ☎ *305/460–5306* 🌐 *www.gablesrecreation.com* 🎫 *$11; free parking across De Soto Blvd.* ⏲ *Usually open Tues.–Sun. 11–4:30, but best to call ahead.*

WORTH NOTING

Miracle Mile. Even with competition from some impressive malls, this half-mile stretch of colorful retail stores continues to thrive because of its intriguing mixture of unique boutiques, bridal shops, art galleries, charming restaurants, and upscale nightlife venues. It attracts Latin America's power players as well as the kinds of women you might see on *The Real Housewives of Miami.* ✉ *Coral Way, between S.W. 37th and S.W. 42nd Aves.* 🌐 *www.shopcoralgables.com.*

OFF THE BEATEN PATH

Zoo Miami. Don't miss a visit to this top-notch zoo, 14 miles southwest of Coral Gables, in the Miami suburbs. The only subtropical zoo in the continental United States, it has 320-plus acres that are home to more than 2,000 animals, including 40 endangered species, which roam on islands surrounded by moats. Amazon & Beyond encompasses 27 acres of simulated tropical rain forests showcasing 600 animals indigenous to the region, such as giant river otters, harpy eagles, anacondas, and jaguars. You can feed veggies to the giraffes at Samburu Station. The Wings of Asia aviary has about 300 exotic birds representing 70 species flying free within the junglelike enclosure. There's also a petting zoo with a meerkat exhibit and interactive opportunities, such as those at Wacky Barn and Dr. Wilde's World and the Ecology Theater, where kids can touch Florida animals like alligators and opossums. An educational and entertaining wildlife show is given three times daily. ✉ *12400 S.W. 152nd St., Richmond Heights, Miami* ☎ *305/251–0400* 🌐 *www.miamimetrozoo.com* 🎫 *$15.95, $11.95 children ages 3 to 12; 45-min tram tour $4.95* ⏲ *Daily 9:30–5:30, last admission at 4.*

KEY BISCAYNE

Once upon a time, the two barrier islands that make up the village of Key Biscayne (Key Biscayne itself and Virginia Key) were an outpost for fishermen and sailors, pirates and salvagers, soldiers and settlers. The 95-foot Cape Florida Lighthouse stood tall during Seminole Indian battles and hurricanes. Coconut plantations covered two-thirds of Key Biscayne, and there were plans as far back as the 1800s to develop the picturesque island as a resort for the wealthy. Fortunately, the state and county governments set much of the land aside for parks, and both keys are now home to top-ranked beaches and golf, tennis, softball, and picnicking facilities. The long and winding bike paths that run through the islands are favorites for in-line skaters and cyclists. Incorporated in 1991, the village of Key Biscayne is a hospitable community of about 12,500; Virginia Key remains undeveloped at the moment, making these two playground islands especially family-friendly.

Miami Beach is dotted with lifeguard towers.

EXPLORING

Miami Seaquarium. This classic family attraction stages shows with sea lions, dolphins, and Lolita the killer whale. The Crocodile Flats exhibit has 26 Nile crocodiles. Discovery Bay, an endangered mangrove habitat, is home to sea turtles, alligators, herons, egrets, and ibis. You can also visit a shark pool, a tropical reef aquarium, and West Indian and Florida manatees. A popular interactive attraction is the Stingray Touch Tank, where you can touch and feed cow-nose rays and southern stingrays. Another big draw are the Dolphin Interaction programs, including the quite intensive Dolphin Odyssey ($199) experience and the lighter shallow-water Dolphin Encounter ($139). Make reservations for either experience. ✉ *4400 Rickenbacker Causeway, Virginia Key, Miami* ☎ *305/361–5705* 🌐 *www.miamiseaquarium.com* 🎫 *$39.95, parking $8* ⏲ *Daily 9:30–6, last admission at 4:30.*

WYNWOOD/MIDTOWN/DESIGN DISTRICT

These three trendy, creative neighborhoods are 3 to 4 miles north of downtown and have developed an impressive mix of one-of-a-kind shops and galleries, see-and-be-seen bars, and slick restaurants. **Midtown** (🌐 *midtownmiami.com*) lies between Northeast 29th and 36th streets, from North Miami Avenue to Northeast 2nd Avenue.

Just southwest, the funky and edgy **Wynwood Art District** (🌐 *www.wynwoodmiami.com)* is peppered with galleries, art studios, and private collections accessible to the public. Though the neighborhood hasn't completely shed its dodgy past, artist-painted graffiti walls and reinvented urban, industrial buildings have transformed the area from grimy and gritty to fresh and trendy. The Wynwood Walls on Northwest 2nd Avenue between Northeast 25th and 26th streets are a cutting-edge enclave of modern urban murals. Visit during Wynwood's monthly gallery walk on the second Saturday evening of each month, when studios and galleries are all open at the same time.

To reach the Design District (*www.miamidesigndistrict.net*), head north up Miami Avenue just beyond Interstate 195. From about Northeast 38th to Northeast 42nd streets, east to North Federal Highway, you'll find 18 blocks of clothiers, antiques shops, design stores, and bars and eateries.

> **SAIL AWAY**
>
> If you can sail in Miami, do. Blue skies, calm seas, and a view of the city skyline make for a pleasurable outing—especially at twilight, when the fabled "moon over Miami" casts a soft glow on the water. Key Biscayne's calm waves and strong breezes are perfect for sailing and windsurfing, and although Dinner Key and the Coconut Grove waterfront remain the center of sailing in Greater Miami, sailboat moorings and rentals sit along other parts of the bay and up the Miami River.

Margulies Collection at the Warehouse. Make sure a visit includes a stop at the Margulies Collection at the Warehouse. Martin Margulies's collection of vintage and contemporary photography, videos, and installation art in a 45,000-square-foot space makes for eye-popping viewing. Admission proceeds go to a local homeless shelter for women and children. *591 N.W. 27th St., between N.W. 5th and 6th Aves., Wynwood, Miami 305/576–1051 www.margulieswarehouse.com $10 Nov.–Apr., Wed.–Sat. 11–4*

Rubell Family Collection. Fans of edgy art will appreciate the Rubell Family Collection. Mera and Don Rubell have accumulated work by artists from the 1970s to the present, including Jeff Koons, Cindy Sherman, Damien Hirst, and Keith Haring. *95 N.W. 29th St., between N. Miami and N.W. 1st Aves., Wynwood, Miami 305/573–6090 www.rfc.museum $10 Dec.–July, Tues.–Sat. 10–6*

SOUTH BEACH

The hub of Miami Beach is South Beach (better known as SoBe), with its energetic Ocean Drive, Collins Avenue, and Washington Avenue. Here life unfolds 24 hours a day. Beautiful people pose in hotel lounges and sidewalk cafés, bronzed cyclists zoom past palm trees, and visitors flock to see the action. On Lincoln Road, café crowds spill onto the sidewalks, weekend markets draw all kinds of visitors and their dogs, and thanks to a few late-night lounges, the scene is just as alive at night. To the north, a Mid-Beach renaissance is unfolding on Collins Avenue, with swanky new hotels and restaurants popping up between 40th and 60th streets.

Quieter areas still farther north on Collins Avenue are Surfside (from 88th to 96th streets), fashionable Bal Harbour (beginning at 96th Street), and Sunny Isles (between 157th and 197th streets).

TOP ATTRACTIONS

> **WORD OF MOUTH**
>
> "Stay in South Beach and take a drive out to Key Biscayne—you'll love it!! Nice place to ride bikes."
>
> —JerseySue

★ **Española Way.** There's a bohemian feel to this street lined with Mediterranean-revival buildings constructed in 1925. Al Capone's gambling syndicate ran its operations upstairs at what is now the Clay Hotel, a youth hostel. At a nightclub here in the 1930s, future bandleader Desi Arnaz strapped on a conga drum and started beating out a rumba rhythm. Visit this quaint avenue on a weekend afternoon, when merchants and craftspeople set up shop to sell everything from handcrafted bongo drums to fresh flowers. Between Washington and Drexel avenues the road has been narrowed to a single lane and Miami Beach's trademark pink sidewalks have been widened to accommodate sidewalk café's and shops selling imaginative clothing, jewelry, and art. ✉ *Española Way, between 14th and 15th Sts. from Washington to Jefferson Aves., South Beach.*

Holocaust Memorial. A bronze sculpture depicts refugees clinging to a giant bronze arm that reaches out of the ground and 42 feet into the air. Enter the surrounding courtyard to see a memorial wall and hear the music that seems to give voice to the 6 million Jews who died at the hands of the Nazis. It's easy to understand why Kenneth Treister's dramatic memorial is in Miami Beach: the city's community of Holocaust survivors was once the second-largest in the country. ✉ *1933–1945 Meridian Ave., at Dade Blvd., South Beach* ☎ *305/538–1663* 🌐 *www.holocaustmmb.org* 🎫 *Free* ⏲ *Daily 9–sunset.*

Fodor's Choice ★ **Lincoln Road Mall.** This open-air pedestrian mall flaunts some of Miami's best people-watching. The eclectic interiors of myriad fabulous restaurants, colorful boutiques, art galleries, lounges, and cafés are often upstaged by the bustling outdoor scene. It's here among the prolific alfresco dining enclaves that you can pass the hours easily beholding the beautiful people. Indeed, outdoor restaurant and café seating takes center stage along this wide pedestrian road adorned with towering date palms, linear pools, and colorful broken-tile mosaics. Some of the shops on Lincoln Road are owner-operated boutiques carrying a smart variety of clothing, furnishings, jewelry, and decorative elements. You'll also find typical upscale chain stores—French Connection, Banana Republic, and so on. Lincoln Road is fun, lively, and friendly for people–old, young, gay, and straight—and their dogs.

Two landmarks worth checking out at the eastern end of Lincoln Road are the massive 1940s keystone building at 420 Lincoln Road, which has a 1945 Leo Birchanky mural in the lobby, and the 1921 Mission-style Miami Beach Community Church, at Drexel Avenue. The Lincoln Theatre (No. 541–545), at Pennsylvania Avenue, is a classical four-story art deco gem with friezes. At Euclid Avenue there's a monument to Morris Lapidus, the brains behind Lincoln Road Mall, who in his 90s watched the renaissance of his whimsical South Beach creation. At Lenox Avenue, a black-and-white art deco movie house with a Mediterranean barrel-tile roof is now the Colony Theater (1040 Lincoln Rd.),

Continued on page 53

CARIBBEAN INFUSION

by Michelle Delio

Miami has sun, sand, and sea, but unlike some of Florida's other prime beach destinations, it also has a wave of cultural traditions that spice up the city.

It's with good reason that people in Miami fondly say that the city is an easy way for Americans to visit another country without ever leaving the United States. According to the U.S. Census Bureau, approximately half of Miami's population is foreign born and more than 70% speak a language other than English at home (in comparison, only 35.7% of New York City residents were born in another country). The city's Latin/Caribbean immigrants and exiles make up the largest segments of the population.

Locals merrily merge cultural traditions, speaking "Spanglish" (a mix of Spanish and English), sipping Cuban coffee with Sicilian pastries, eating Nuevo Latino fusion food, and dancing to the beat of other countries' music. That said, people here are just as interested in keeping to their own distinct ways—think of the city as a colorful mosaic composed of separate elements rather than a melting pot.

Miami's diverse population creates a city that feels alive in a way that few other American cities do. And no visit to the city would be complete without a stop at one of the two neighborhoods famed for their celebrations of cultural traditions—Little Haiti and Little Havana—places that have a wonderful foreign feel even amid cosmopolitan Miami.

⚠ **Safety can be an issue in Little Haiti. Exercise special caution and do not visit at night.**

Playing dominoes is a favorite pastime at Maximo Gomez Park in Little Havana (left).

LA PETITE HAÏTI—LITTLE HAITI

Little Haiti is a study in contrasts. At first glance you see the small buildings painted in bright oranges, pinks, reds, yellows, and turquoises, with signs, some handwritten, touting immigration services, lunch specials with *tassot* (fried cubed goat), and voodoo supplies.

But as you adjust to this dazzle of color, you become aware of the curious juxtapositions of poverty and wealth in this evolving neighborhood. Streets dip with potholes in front of trendy art galleries, and dilapidated houses struggle to survive near newly renovated soccer fields and arts centers.

Miami's Little Haiti is the largest Haitian community outside of Haiti itself, and while people of different ethnic backgrounds have begun to move to the neighborhood, people here tend to expect to primarily see other Haitians on these streets. Obvious outsiders may be greeted with a few frozen stares on the streets, but owners of shops and restaurants tend to be welcoming. Creole is commonly spoken, although some people—especially younger folks—also speak English.

WHEN TO GO

The neighborhood is best visited during the daytime, combined with a visit to the nearby Miami Design District, an 18-block section of art galleries, interior design showrooms, and restaurants between N.E. 41st Street and N.E. 36th Street, Miami Avenue, and Biscayne Boulevard.

CREOLE EXPRESSIONS

Creole, one of Haiti's two languages (the other is French), is infused with French, African, Arabic, Spanish, and Portuguese words.

Komon ou ye? How are you? *(also spelled Kouman)
N'ap boule! Great!
Kisa ou ta vla? What would you like?
Mesi. Thanks.
Souple. Please.

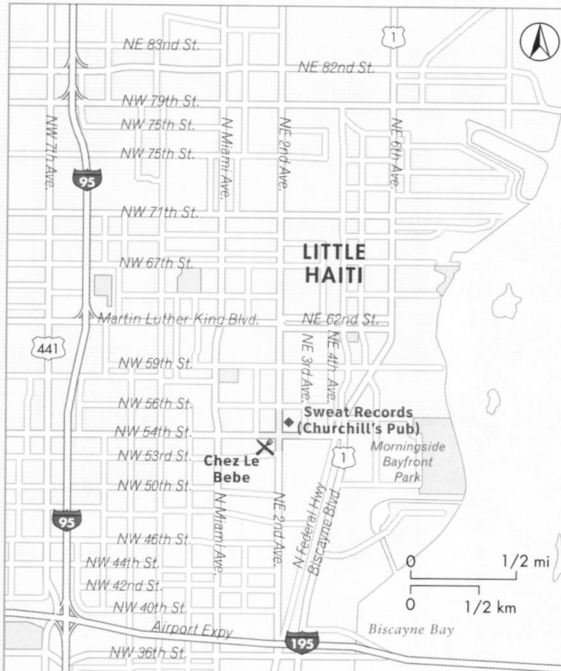

GETTING ORIENTED

Little Haiti, once a small farming community outside of Miami proper, is slowly becoming one of the city's most vibrant neighborhoods. Its northern and southern boundaries are 85th Street and 36th Street, respectively, with Interstate–95 to the west and Biscayne Boulevard to the east. The best section to visit is along North Miami Avenue from 54th to 59th streets. Driving is the best way to get here; parking is easy to find on North Miami Avenue. Public transit (☎ *305/891–3131*) is limited.

SHOPPING

The cluster of botanicas at N.E. 54th Street and N.E. 2nd Avenue offer items intended to sway the fates, from candles to plastic and plaster statues of Catholic saints that, in the voodoo tradition, represent African deities. While exploring, don't miss **Sweat Records** (✉ *5505 N.E. 2nd Ave.* ☎ *786/693–9309* 🌐 *www.sweatrecordsmiami.com*). Sweat sells a wide range of music—rock, pop, punk, electronic, hip-hop, and Latino. Check out the vegan-friendly organic coffee bar at the store, which is open from noon to 10 PM every day but Sunday.

MANGÉ KRÉYOL (HAITIAN FOOD)

Traditional Caribbean cuisines tend to combine European and African culinary techniques. Haitian can be a bit spicier—though never mouth-scorching hot—than many other island cuisines. Rice and beans are the staple food, enlivened with a little of whatever people might have: fish, goat, chicken, pork, usually stewed or deep-fried, along with peppers, plantains, and tomatoes.

Chez Le Bebe (✉ *114 N.E. 54th St.* ☎ *305/751–7639* 🌐 *www.chezlebebe.com*) offers Haitian home cooking—if you want to try stewed goat, this is the place to do it. Chicken, fish, oxtail, and fried pork are also on the menu; each plate comes with rice, beans, plantains, and salad for less than $12.

Tap Tap restaurant (✉ *819 Fifth St.* ☎ *305/672–2898*) is outside of Little Haiti, but this Miami institution will immerse you in the island's culture with an extensive collection of Haitian folk art displayed everywhere in the restaurant. On the menu is pumpkin soup, *spageti kreyol* (pasta, shrimp, and a Creole tomato sauce), goat stewed in Creole sauce (a mildly spicy tomato-based sauce), conch, and "grilled goat dinner." You can eat well here for $15 or less.

LITTLE HAVANA

First settled en masse by Cubans in the early 1960s, after Cuba's Communist revolution, Little Havana is a predominantly working-class area and the core of Miami's Hispanic community. Spanish is the main language, but don't be surprised if the cadence is less Cuban than Salvadoran or Nicaraguan: the neighborhood is now home to people from all Latin American countries.

If you come to Little Havana expecting the Latino version of New Orleans's French Quarter, you're apt to be disappointed—it's not yet that picturesque. But if great, inexpensive food (not just Cuban; there's Vietnamese, Mexican, and Argentinean here as well), distinctive, affordable art, cigars, and coffee interest you, you'll enjoy your time in Little Havana. It's not a prefab tourist destination, so don't expect Disneyland with a little Latino flair—this is real life in Miami.

WHEN TO GO

The absolute best time to visit Calle Ocho is the last Friday evening of every month, between 6:30 and 11 PM on 8th Street from 14th to 17th avenues. Known as **Viernes Culturales** (🌐 *www.viernes-culturales.org*), it's a big block party that everyone is welcome to attend. Art galleries, restaurants, and stores stay open late, and music, mojitos, and avant-garde street performances bring a young, hip crowd to the neighborhood where they mingle with locals.

If you come in mid-March, your visit may coincide with the annual **Calle Ocho festival** (🌐 *www.carnavalmiami.com*), which draws more than a million visitors in search of Latin music, food, and shopping.

GETTING ORIENTED

Little Havana's semi-official boundaries are 27th Avenue to 4th Avenue on the west, Miami River to the north, and S.W. 11th Street to the south. Much of the neighborhood is residential, but its heart and tourist hub is Calle Ocho (8th Street), between 14th and 18th avenues.

The best way to get here is by car. Park on the side streets off **Calle Ocho** (some spots have meters; most don't). Other options include the free **Metromover** (☎ *305/891–3131*) and a cab ride. From Miami Beach the 15-minute ride should cost just under $30 each way.

THE SIGHTS

Stroll down Calle Oche from 12th to 17th avenues and look around you: cafés are selling guava pastries and rose petal flan, a botanica brims with candles and herbs to heal whatever ails you. Small galleries showcasing modern art jostle up next to mom-and-pop food shops and high-end Cuban clothes and crafts. At Domino Park (officially Maximo Gomez Park), guayabera-clad seniors bask in the sun and play dominoes, while at corner bodegas and coffee shops (particularly Versailles) regulars share neighborhood gossip and political opinions. A few steps away is the "Paseo de las Estrellas" (Walk of Stars), honoring the likes of Julio Iglesias and Gloria Estefan.

At SW 13th Street, the Cuban Memorial Boulevard fills 2 blocks with monuments to Cuba's freedom fighters. At family-owned El Credito Cigar Factory, watch workers assemble cigars fit for presidents and celebs.

SPANISH EXPRESSIONS

Algo más? Anything else?

Muchas gracias! Thank you very much!

No hay de qué. / De nada. You're welcome.

No entiendo. I don't understand.

Oye! All-purpose word used to get attention or express interest, admiration, and appreciation.

Calle Ocho Carnaval

Rolling cigars by hand in a Little Havana factory.

THE SOUNDS

Salsa and merengue pour out of storefronts and restaurants, while other businesses cater to the snap and shuffles of flamenco performances and Sevillaña *tablaos* (dances performed on a wood-plank stage, using castanets). If you want to join in the merriment along Calle Ocho, dance with locals on the patio of **El Pub Restaurant** (near 15th Avenue), or snack on tapas at **Casa Panza Restaurant** (near 16th), where the background music is the restaurant owner's enthusiastic singing. Any time of day, you can hear the constant backbeat of people speaking Spanish and the occasional crowing of a stray, time-confused rooster. To take these sounds home with you, wander over to **Lily's Records** (✉ *1419 S.W. 8th St, near 14th* ☎ *305/856–0536*), for its huge selection of Latin music.

THE SCENTS

Bottled, the essence of Little Havana would be tobacco, café cubano, and a whiff of tropical fruit. To indulge your senses in two of these things, head to **Los Pinareños Fruteria** on Calle Ocho just west of 13th Avenue. Here you can sip a sweet, hot *cortadito* (coffee with milk), a *cafecito* (no milk), or a cool *coco frio* (coconut water). For more subsistence, dig into a Cuban-style tamale. There are stools out front of the shop, or take your drink to go and wander over to S.W. 13th Avenue, which has monuments to Cuban heroes, and sit under the ceiba trees. For cigars, head to Calle Ocho near 11th Avenue and visit **El Titan de Bronze**. At this family-owned business employees deftly hand-roll millions of stogies a year.

TOURS

If a quick multicultural experience is your goal, set aside an hour or two to do your own self-guided walking tour of the neighborhood. For real ethnic immersion, allow more time; eating is a must, as well as a peek at the area's residential streets lined with distinctive homes.

Especially illuminating are **History Miami, Little Havana City Tours** (✉ *101 W. Flagler St.* ☎ *305/375–1621* 🌐 *www.historymiami.org/tours*). Those led by Dr. Paul George, a history professor at Miami Dade College and historian for History Miami, covers architecture and community history. These take place only a few times a year.

Private three-hour tours are available for groups of up to 20 people for $400 ($20 per person above 20 people).

A PDF on the Web site has up-to-date information on tour dates and times.

For customized offerings, try **Miami Cultural Tours** (✉ *305/416-6868* 🌐 *www.miamiculturaltours.com*), interactive tours that introduce people to Little Havana and Little Haiti. Group and private tours are available, with prices ranging from $39 to $79 a person.

where live theater and experimental films are presented. ✉ *Lincoln Rd., between Washington Ave. and Alton Rd., South Beach* 🌐 *www.lincolnroad.org.*

DID YOU KNOW?

The Miami Circle, an archaeological site and a National Historic Landmark, halted a multimillion-dollar development when work on the site led to the discovery of a circular stone formation and other ancient artifacts. Archaeologists believe they belonged to the Tequesta Indians.

QUICK BITES

Lincoln Road is a great place to cool down with an icy treat while touring South Beach. If you visit on a Sunday, stop at one of the many juice vendors, who will whip up made-to-order smoothies from mangoes, oranges, and other fresh local fruits.

Frieze Ice Cream Factory. Delight in mouthwatering homemade ice cream and sorbets—including Indian mango, key lime pie, cashew toffee crunch, and chocolate decadence. ✉ ***1626 Michigan Ave., just south of Lincoln Rd., South Beach*** ☎ ***305/538–0207*** 🌐 ***www.thefrieze.com.***

Gelateria Parmalat. Authentic Italian gelato (or the Spanish-inspired delicious *dulce de leche* gelato) is scooped up at this sleek glass-and-stainless-steel sweet spot. ✉ ***670 Lincoln Rd., between Euclid and Pennsylvania Aves., South Beach*** ☎ ***786/276–9475.***

WORTH NOTING

Art Deco District Welcome Center. Run by the Miami Design Preservation League, the center provides information about the buildings in the district. An improved gift shop sells 1930s–50s art deco memorabilia, posters, and books on Miami's history. Several tours—covering Lincoln Road, Española Way, North Beach, and the entire Art Deco District, among others—start here. You can choose from a self-guided iPod audio tour or join one of the regular morning walking tours at 10:30 am, every day except Thursday, when the tour takes place at 6:30 pm. Arrive at the center 15 minutes beforehand. All of the options provide detailed histories of the art deco hotels as well as an introduction to the art deco, Mediterranean revival, and Miami Modern (MiMo) styles found within the Miami Beach Architectural Historic District. Don't miss the special boat tours during Art Deco Weekend, in early January. *(⇨ For a map of the Art Deco District and info on some of the sites there, see the "A Stroll Down Deco Lane" in-focus feature.)* ✉ *1001 Ocean Dr., at Ocean Dr., South Beach* ☎ *305/672–2014* 🌐 *www.mdpl.org* 🎫 *Tours $20* ⏲ *Daily 9:30–7.*

Bass Museum of Art. Special exhibitions join a diverse collection of European art at this museum whose original building is constructed of keystone and has unique Maya-inspired carvings. An expansion designed by Japanese architect Arata Isozaki houses another wing and an outdoor sculpture garden. Works on permanent display include *The Holy Family,* a painting by Peter Paul Rubens; *The Tournament,* one of several 16th-century Flemish tapestries; and works by Albrecht Dürer and

Miami Beach and South Beach

Art Deco District Welcome Center 2

Bass Museum of Art 8

Española Way 5

Holocaust Memorial 7

Lincoln Road Mall 6

Miami Children's Museum 9

Jungle Island .. 10

Sanford L. Ziff Jewish Museum of Florida 1

Wolfsonian–Florida International University 3

World Erotic Art Museum 4

Henri de Toulouse-Lautrec. Docent tours are by appointment but free with entry. ✉ *2100 Collins Ave., South Beach* ☎ *305/673–7530* 🌐 *www.bassmuseum.org* 🎫 *$8* 🕐 *Wed.–Sun. noon–5.*

Jewish Museum of Florida. Listed on the National Register of Historic Places, this former synagogue, built in 1936, contains art deco chandeliers, 80 impressive stained-glass windows, and a permanent exhibit, MOSAIC: Jewish Life in Florida, which depicts more than 235 years of the Florida Jewish experience. The museum, which includes a store filled with books, jewelry, and other souvenirs, also hosts traveling exhibits and special events. ✉ *301 Washington Ave., at 3rd St., South Beach* ☎ *305/672–5044* 🌐 *www.jewishmuseum.com* 🎫 *$6, free on Sat.* 🕐 *Tues.–Sun. 10–5. Museum store closed Sat.*

Wolfsonian–Florida International University. An elegantly renovated 1926 storage facility is now a research center and museum showcasing a 120,000-item collection of modern design and "propaganda arts" amassed by Miami native Mitchell ("Micky") Wolfson Jr., a world traveler and connoisseur. Broad themes of the 19th and 20th centuries—nationalism, political persuasion, industrialization—are addressed in permanent and traveling shows. Included in the museum's eclectic holdings, which represent art deco, art moderne, art nouveau, Arts and Crafts, and other aesthetic movements, are 8,000 matchbooks collected by Egypt's King Farouk. ✉ *1001 Washington Ave., South Beach* ☎ *305/531–1001* 🌐 *www.wolfsonian.org* 🎫 *$7, free after 6 pm Fri.* 🕐 *Mon., Tues., Thur., and weekends noon–6, Fri. noon–9. Closed Wed.*

World Erotic Art Museum (WEAM). The sexy collection of more than 4,000 erotic items, all owned by millionaire Naomi Wilzig, unfolds with unique art of varying quality—fertility statues from around the globe and historic Chinese *shunga* books (erotic art offered as gifts to new brides on the wedding night) share the space with some kitschy knickknacks. If this is your thing, an original phallic prop from Stanley Kubrick's *A Clockwork Orange* and an over-the-top Kama Sutra bed is worth the price of admission, but the real standout is "Miss Naomi," who is usually on hand to answer questions and provide behind-the-scenes anecdotes. Kids 17 and under are not admitted. ✉ *1205 Washington Ave., at 12th St., South Beach* ☎ *305/532–9336* 🌐 *www.weam.com* 🎫 *$15* 🕐 *Mon.–Thurs. 11–10, Fri.–Sun. 11–midnight.*

BEACHES

CORAL GABLES

Matheson Hammock Park Beach. Kids love the gentle waves and warm water of this beach in Coral Gables suburbia, near Fairchild Tropical Botanic Garden. But the beach is only part of the draw—the park includes a boardwalk trail, a playground, and a golf course. The manmade lagoon, or "atoll pool," is perfect for inexperienced swimmers, and it's one of the best places in mainland Miami for a picnic. But the water can be a bit murky, and with the emphasis on families, it's not

DID YOU KNOW?

From sidewalk cafés, diners enjoy the bohemian ambience of Miami Beach's Española Way.

the best place for singles. **Amenities:** parking (fee); toilets. **Best for:** swimming. ✉ *9610 Old Cutler Rd.* ☎ *305/665–5475.*

KEY BISCAYNE

Fodor's Choice ★ **Bill Baggs Cape Florida State Park.** Thanks to inviting beaches, sunsets, and a tranquil lighthouse, this park at Key Biscayne's southern tip is worth the drive. In fact, the 1-mile stretch of pure beachfront has been named several times in Dr. Beach's revered America's Top 10 Beaches list. It has 18 picnic pavilions available as daily rentals, two cafés that serve light lunches (Lighthouse Café, overlooking the Atlantic Ocean, and the Boater's Grill, on Biscayne Bay), and plenty of space to enjoy the umbrella and chair rentals. A stroll or ride along walking and bicycle paths provides wonderful views of Miami's dramatic skyline. From the southern end of the park you can see a handful of houses rising over the bay on wooden stilts, the remnants of Stiltsville, built in the 1940s and now protected by the Stiltsville Trust. The nonprofit group was established in 2003 to preserve the structures, because they showcase the park's rich history. Bill Baggs has bicycle rentals, a playground, fishing piers, and guided tours of the **Cape Florida Lighthouse,** South Florida's oldest structure. The lighthouse was erected in 1845 to replace an earlier one damaged in an 1836 Seminole attack, in which the keeper's helper was killed. Free tours are offered at the restored cottage and lighthouse at 10 am and 1 pm Thursday to Monday. Be there a half hour beforehand. **Amenities:** food and drink, lifeguards, parking, showers, toilets. **Best for:** solitude, sunsets, walking. ✉ *1200 S. Crandon Blvd., Key Biscayne* ☎ *305/361–5811* 🌐 *www.floridastateparks.org/capeflorida* 🎫 *$8 per vehicle; $2 per person on bicycle, bus, motorcycle, or foot* ⏲ *Daily 8–dusk.*

THE OCEAN DRIVE HUSTLE

As you stroll by the sidewalk restaurants lining Ocean Drive, don't be surprised if you are solicited by a pretty hostess, who will literally shove a menu in your face to entice you to her café—which is exactly like every other eatery on the strip. Be warned that reputable restaurants refrain from these aggressive tactics. If you are indeed enticed by the fishbowl drinks, use the chance to bargain. A request for free drinks with dinner may very well be accommodated!

Crandon Park Beach. This relaxing oasis in northern Key Biscayne is dotted with palm trees, which provide a respite from the steamy sun until it's time to take a dip in the blue waters. Families really enjoy the beaches here—the sand is soft, there are no rip tides, there's a great view of the Atlantic, and parking is both inexpensive and plentiful. However, on weekends be prepared for a long hike from your car to the beach. There are bathrooms, outdoor showers, plenty of picnic tables, concession stands, and golf and tennis facilities. The family-friendly park offers abundant options for kids who find it challenging to simply sit and build sand castles. **Crandon Gardens** at Crandon Park was once the site of a zoo. There are swans, waterfowl, and dozens of huge iguanas running loose. Nearby you'll find a restored carousel (it's open weekends and major holidays 10–5, until 6 in summer, and you get three rides for $1), an old-fashioned outdoor roller rink, a dolphin-shape spray fountain, and a playground. **Amenities:** food and drink; lifeguards; parking (fee); showers; toilets. **Best for:** swimming; walking. ✉ *6747 Crandon Blvd., Key Biscayne* ☎ *305/361–5421* 🌐 *www.biscaynenaturecenter.org* 🎫 *$5 per vehicle* ⏲ *Daily 8–sunset.*

WORD OF MOUTH

"The best people-watching spots are News Cafe on Ocean Drive and Van Dyke Cafe or Segafredo on Lincoln Road. Go in the evening when it's cooler and the beautiful people are out."

—SoBchBud1

Marjory Stoneman Douglas Biscayne Nature Center. At the north end of the beach is the free Marjory Stoneman Douglas Biscayne Nature Center, where you can explore sea-grass beds on a tour with a naturalist; see red, black, and white mangroves; and hike along the beach and hammock in the Bear Cut Preserve. The park also sponsors hikes and tours. ✉ *Key Biscayne* ☎ *305/361–6767* 🌐 *www.biscaynenaturecenter.org* ⏲ *Daily 10–4*

SOUTH BEACH

Fodor's Choice ★

South Beach. A 10-block stretch of white sandy beach hugging the turquoise waters along Ocean Drive—from 5th to 15th streets—is one of the most popular in America, known for drawing unabashedly modelesque sunbathers and posers. With the influx of new luxe hotels and hot spots from 16th to 25th streets, the South Beach stand-and-pose scene is now bigger than ever. The beaches crowd quickly on the weekends with a blend of European tourists, young hipsters, and sun-drenched locals offering Latin flavor. Separating the sand from the traffic of Ocean Drive is palm-fringed **Lummus Park**, with its volleyball nets and chickee huts (huts made of palmetto thatch over a cypress frame) for shade. The beach at **12th Street** is popular with gays, in a section often marked with rainbow flags. Locals hang out on 3rd Street Beach, in an area called **SoFi** (South of Fifth), where they watch fit Brazilians play foot volley, a variation of volleyball that uses everything but the hands. Because much of South Beach leans toward skimpy sunning—women are often in G-strings and casually topless—many families prefer the tamer sections of Mid- and North Beach. Metered parking spots next to the ocean are a rare find. Instead, opt for a public garage a few blocks away and enjoy the people-watching as you walk to find your perfect spot on the sand. **Amenities:** food and drink; lifeguards; parking (fee); showers; toilets. **Best for:** partiers; sunrise; swimming; walking. ✉ *Ocean Dr., from 5th to 15th Sts., then Collins Ave. to 25th St., South Beach, Miami Beach* ☎ *305/673–7714.*

2

NORTH BEACH AND AVENTURA

Haulover Beach Park. This popular clothing-optional beach is embraced by naturists of all ages, shapes, and sizes; there are even sections primarily frequented by families, singles, and gays. However, Haulover has more claims to fame than its casual attitude toward swimwear—it's also the best beach in the area for bodyboarding and surfing, as it gets what passes for impressive swells in these parts. Plus the sand here is fine-grain white, unusual for the Atlantic coast. Once you park in the North Lot, you'll walk through a short tunnel covered with trees and natural habitat until you emerge on the unpretentious beach, where nudity is rarely met by gawkers. There are volleyball nets, and plenty of beach chair and umbrella rentals to protect your birthday suit from too much exposure—to the sun, that is. The sections of beach requiring swimwear are popular, too, given the park's ample parking and relaxed atmosphere. Lifeguards stand watch. More active types might want to check out the kite rentals, or charter-fishing excursions. **Amenities:** food and drink; lifeguards; parking (fee); showers; toilets. **Best for:** nudists; surfing; swimming; walking. ✉ *10800 Collins Ave., north of Bal Harbour, North Beach and Aventura, North Miami Beach* ☎ *305/944–3040* 🌐 *www.hauloverbeach.org* 🎟 *$6 per vehicle if parking in lot* ⏲ *Daily sunrise–sunset.*

★ **Oleta River State Park.** Tucked away in North Miami Beach, this urban park is a ready-made family getaway. Nature lovers will find it easy to embrace the 1,128 acres of subtropical beauty along Biscayne Bay. Swim in the calm bay waters and bicycle, canoe, kayak, and bask among egrets, manatees, bald eagles, and fiddler crabs. Dozens of picnic tables, along with 10 covered pavilions, dot the stunning natural habitat, which was restored with red mangroves to revitalize the ecosystem and draw endangered birds, like the roseate spoonbill. There's a playground for tots, a mangrove island accessible only by boat, 15 miles of mountain-bike trails, a half-mile exercise track, concessions, and outdoor showers. **Amenities:** food and drink; parking (fee); showers; toilets; water sports. **Best for:** solitude; sunrise; sunset; walking. ✉ *3400 N.E. 163rd St., North Beach and Aventura, North Miami Beach* ☎ *305/919–1846* 🌐 *www.floridastateparks.org/oletariver* 🎟 *$6 per vehicle; $2 per person on foot or bike* ⏲ *Daily 8–sunset.*

WHERE TO EAT

Miami's restaurant scene has exploded in the last few years, with dozens of great new restaurants springing up left and right. The melting pot of residents and visitors has brought an array of sophisticated, tasty cuisine. Little Havana is still king for Cuban fare, and Miami Beach is swept up in a trend of fusion cuisine, which combines Asian, French, American, and Latin cooking with sumptuous—and pricey—results. Locals spend the most time in downtown Miami, Wynwood, Midtown, and the Design District, where the city's ongoing foodie and cocktail revolution is most pronounced. Since Miami dining is a part of the trendy nightlife scene, most dinners don't start until 8 or 9 pm, and may go well into the night. To avoid a long wait among the late-night partyers at hot spots, come before 7 or make reservations. Attire is usually casual-chic, but patrons like to dress to impress. Don't be surprised to see large tables of women in skimpy dresses—this is common in Miami. Prices tend to stay high in hot spots like Lincoln Road, but if you venture off the beaten path you can find delicious food for reasonable prices. When you get your bill, check whether a gratuity is already included; most restaurants add between 15% and 20% (ostensibly for the convenience of, and protection from, the many Latin American and European tourists who are used to this practice in their homelands), but supplement it depending on your opinion of the service.

Use the coordinate (⊕ C2) at the end of each review to locate a property on the Where to Eat in the Miami Area map.

DOWNTOWN MIAMI

$$$$ ECLECTIC Fodor's Choice ★

✕ **Azul.** A restaurant known for producing celebrity chefs and delivering dining fantasies of Food Network proportions, Azul is a Miami foodie insitution. With its award-winning team, Azul offers a haute-cuisine experience on par with a two- or three-Michelin-star restaurant. Chefs fuse disparate ingredients, merging as decadent, gastronomic art. Headliners include almond gazpacho with foie gras "snow," Moroccan argan oil, orange essence, and golden-raisin pudding, and the "silver and gold egg" with American caviar, 63-degree quail egg, caramelized onions, and potato espuma (a foaming technique). Dine here and you'll undoubtedly experience bold new taste sensations while enjoying one of the finest wine lists in the city and an incomparable skyline view. *$ Average main: $48 ✉ Mandarin Oriental, Miami, 500 Brickell Key Dr., Downtown ☎ 305/913–8358 ⊕ www.mandarinoriental.com/miami ⚠ Reservations essential ⊗ Closed Sun. No lunch ⊕ D5.*

$$$ MODERN AMERICAN

✕ **City Hall Restaurant.** This snazzy, double-decker eatery channels a bright-lights-big-city vibe, yet delivers a modern twist on old-fashioned Southern home cooking. Chef Tom Azar—of Emeril's fame—helms the kitchen, showcasing decadent delights such as the seafood and andouille gumbo and meat loaf with chorizo-maple mac-and-cheese. Given its proximity to the Adrienne Arsht Center for the Performing Arts and the AmericanAirlines Arena, City Hall is a top pick for pretheater and pregame dining. It's also wildly popular with locals. *$ Average main: $24 ✉ 2004 Biscayne Blvd., Downtown ☎ 305/764–3130 ⊕ www.cityhalltherestaurant.com ⊕ D4.*

$$$$ FRENCH Fodor's Choice ★

✕ **db Bistro Moderne Miami.** One of America's most celebrated French chefs, Daniel Boulud brings his renowned cooking to the Miami scene. The menu of Boulud's latest outpost pays homage to the different cuisines and specialties of his homeland and surrounding regions, beginning with a fabulous raw bar alongside regional tasting plates such as the "Assiette Provencale" with mackerel escabeche, black olive tapenade, goat cheese with pear, and Swiss chard *barbajuan*. Moving on to the second course, chose from a dozen hot and cold small plates, like the signature "Daniel Boulud's Smoked Salmon," escargots persillade with wild burgundy snails simmered in parsley, garlic, salted butter

BEST BETS FOR MIAMI DINING

Fodor's writers and editors have selected their favorite restaurants by price, cuisine, and experience in the Best Bets lists below. In the first column, Fodor's Choice designations represent the "best of the best" in every price category. Find specific details about a restaurant in the full reviews, listed alphabetically by neighborhood.

Fodor's Choice ★

1500°, Mid-Beach, p. 74

Azul, Downtown Miami, p. 60

BLT Steak, South Beach, p. 67

Cantina Beach, Key Biscayne, p. 65

db Bistro Moderne Miami, Downtown Miami, p. 60

The Forge, Mid-Beach, p. 74

Gotham Steak, Mid-Beach, p. 74

Hakkasan, Mid-Beach, p. 74

Il Mulino New York, North Beach and Aventura, p. 75

Joe's Stone Crab Restaurant, South Beach, p. 70

La Gloutonnerie, p. 71

Lantao, South Beach, p. 71

Meat Market, South Beach, p. 72

Michael's Genuine Food & Drink, Design District, p. 66

Michy's, Design District, p. 66

NAOE, Downtown Miami, p. 62

Ortanique on the Mile, Coral Gables, p. 64

Perricone's Marketplace and Café, Downtown Miami, p. 62

Pied à Terre, South Beach, p. 72

Rusty Pelican, Key Biscayne, p. 65

Yardbird Southern Table & Bar, South Beach, p. 73

Yes Pasta! Trattoria Italiana, North Beach and Aventura, p. 76

By Price

$

Palacio de los Jugos, Coral Gables, p. 64

$$

Hy-Vong Vietnamese Cuisine, Little Havana, p. 63

Versailles, Little Havana, p. 63

$$$

Michael's Genuine Food & Drink, Downtown Miami, p. 66

$$$$

Cioppino, Key Biscayne, p. 65

The Forge, Mid-Beach, p. 74

By Cuisine

AMERICAN

Big Pink, South Beach, p. 67

Michael's Genuine Food & Drink, Downtown Miami, p. 66

ASIAN

Hakkasan, Mid-Beach, p. 74

SushiSamba Dromo, South Beach, p. 73

CUBAN

Havana Harry's, Coral Gables, p. 64

Versailles, Little Havana, p. 63

ITALIAN

Ceconni's, Mid-Beach, p. 73

Cioppino, Key Biscayne, p. 65

SEAFOOD

Joe's Stone Crab Restaurant, South Beach, p. 70

STEAKHOUSE

Bourbon Steak, North Miami and Aventura, p. 75

The Forge, Mid-Beach, p. 74

Red, the Steakhouse, South Beach, p. 73

By Experience

CHILD-FRIENDLY

Versailles, Little Havana, p. 63

Yes Pasta! Trattoria Italiana, North Beach and Aventura, p. 76

HOT SPOTS

Meat Market, South Beach, p. 72

Michael's Genuine Food & Drink, Downtown Miami, p. 66

with yellow tomatoes and wild mushrooms, and the tomato *tarte tatin*. For the main course, the authentic coq au vin and the *moules piquante* are guaranteed crowd pleasers, channeling images and/or memories of France through the tastes and smells of the restaurant's flagship dishes. *$ Average main: $42 ✉ JW Marriott Marquis Miami, 255 Biscayne Blvd. Way, Downtown ☎ 305/421–8800 🌐 www.danielnyc.com ✥ D4.*

$$$ STEAKHOUSE **✕ Edge, Steak & Bar.** It's farm-to-table surf-and-turf at this elegantly understated restaurant in the Four Seasons, where hefty portions of the finest cuts and freshest seafoods headline the menu. The innovative tartares are a surefire way to start the night right—try the corvina with baby cucumber, green apple, and celery leaf in a yellow-pepper sauce, or ahi tuna with pickled shallots, watermelon, and mint. For the main event, Edge offers a variety of small, medium, and large cuts from the infrared grill, the most popular being the black Angus filet mignon. For a more casual experience, enjoy your meal and the restaurant's artisan cocktails under the skies in the alfresco section. *$ Average main: $30 ✉ Four Seasons Miami, 1435 Brickell Ave, Downtown ☎ 305/358–3535 🌐 www.edgerestaurantmiami.com ✥ D5.*

$$$$ JAPANESE Fodor's Choice ★ **✕ NAOE.** Once in a rare while you discover a restaurant so authentic, so special, yet still undiscovered by the masses. By virtue of its petite size (less than two-dozen max) and strict seating times (twice per night at 6:30 and 9:30), the Japanese gem NAOE will forever remain intimate and original. The menu changes daily, based on the day's best and freshest seafood. Beginning with a Bento Box and continuing on to rounds of Nigirizushi, every visit ushers in a new exploration of the senses. Chef Kevin Cory prepares the gastronomic adventure a few feet from his patrons, using only the best ingredients and showcasing family treasures, like the renowned products of his centuries' old family shoyu (soy sauce) brewery and sake brewery. From start to finish, you'll be transported to Japan through the stellar service, the tastes of bizarre sea creatures, the blanching of live scallops, and the smoothness of spectacular sakes. *$ Average main: $46 ✉ 661 Brickell Key Dr., Downtown ☎ 305/947–6263 🌐 www.naoemiami.com ✍ Reservations essential ✥ D5.*

$$ ITALIAN Fodor's Choice ★ **✕ Perricone's Marketplace and Café.** Brickell Avenue south of the Miami River is burgeoning with Italian restaurants, and this lunch place for local bigwigs is the biggest and most popular among them. It's housed partially outdoors and partially indoors in an 1880s Vermont barn. Recipes were handed down from generation to generation, and the cooking is simple and good. Buy your wine from the on-premises deli, and enjoy it (for a small corking fee) with homemade minestrone; a generous antipasto; linguine with a sauté of jumbo shrimp, scallops, and calamari; or gnocchi with four cheeses. The homemade tiramisu and cannoli are top-notch. *$ Average main: $22 ✉ Mary Brickell Village, 15 S.E. 10th St., Downtown ☎ 305/374–9449 🌐 www.perricones.com ✥ D5.*

$$ ITALIAN **✕ Tutto Pasta.** Locals love Tutto Pasta, where for around $18 per entrée they feast on delicious homemade Italian pasta with a Brazilian twist. Start with fresh-baked goat-cheese focaccia with truffle oil. Then try the famous lobster ravioli garnished with plantain chips, or the tilapia

sautéed with shrimp, calamari, scallops, and tomato sauce. Hop over to reconceptualized Tutto Pizza Beer House next door to enjoy innovative Brazilian-inspired thin pizzas like the Portuguesa, topped with ham, mozzarella, black olives, eggs, and onions. Finish with Tutto chocolate cake or creamy Brazilian pave (not unlike an English trifle but made with cachaça). *Average main: $18 ✉ 1751 S.W. 3rd Ave., at S.W. 18th Rd., Downtown ☎ 305/857–0709 ⊕ www.tuttopasta.com ⊙ Closed Sun. ✣ D5.*

LITTLE HAVANA

$$ VIETNAMESE ★ **Hy-Vong Vietnamese Cuisine.** Spring springs forth in spring rolls of ground pork, cellophane noodles, and black mushrooms wrapped in homemade rice paper. People are willing to wait on the sidewalk for hours—come before 7 pm to avoid a wait—to sample the fish panfried with mango or with *nuoc man* (a garlic-lime fish sauce), not to mention the thinly sliced pork barbecued with sesame seeds, almonds, and peanuts. Beer-savvy proprietors Kathy Manning and Tung Nguyen serve a half-dozen top brews (Double Grimbergen, Peroni, and Spaten, among them) to further inoculate the experience from the ordinary—well, as ordinary as a Vietnamese restaurant on Calle Ocho can be. *Average main: $16 ✉ 3458 S.W. 8th St. ☎ 305/446–3674 ⊕ www.hyvong.com ⊙ Closed Mon. ✣ C5.*

$$ CUBAN **Versailles.** *¡Bienvenido a Miami!* To the area's Cuban population, Miami without Versailles is like rice without black beans. The storied eatery, where old émigrés opine daily about all things Cuban, is a stop on every political candidate's campaign trail, and it should be a stop for you as well. Order a heaping platter of *lechon asado* (roasted pork loin), *ropa vieja* (shredded beef), or *picadillo* (spicy ground beef), all served with rice, beans, and fried plantains. Battle the oncoming food coma with a cup of the city's strongest *cafecito,* which comes in the tiniest of cups but packs a lot of punch. Versailles operates a bakery next door as well—take some *pastelitos* home. *Average main: $13 ✉ 3555 S.W. 8th St., between S.W. 35th and S.W. 36th Aves. ☎ 305/444–0240 ✣ C5.*

COCONUT GROVE

$$$ PERUVIAN ★ **Jaguar Ceviche Spoon Bar & Grill.** A fabulous fusion of Peruvian and Mexican flavors, Jaguar is a gastronomic tour of Latin America in a single restaurant. As the name implies, there is a heavy emphasis on ceviches. The best option for experiencing this delicacy is the sampler, which includes six distinct Peruvian and Mexican ceviches served in oversized spoons. Meals come with blue corn tortilla and pita chips served with authentic Mexican salsa. Dishes, such the Mexican Tortilla Lasagna (chicken, poblano peppers, corn, tomato sauce, and cream, topped with melted cheese), are colorful, flavorful, and innovative. *Average main: $25 ✉ 3067 Grand Ave. ☎ 305/444–0216 ⊕ www.jaguarspot.com ✣ C5.*

$$$ AMERICAN **Peacock Garden Café.** Reinstating the artsy and exciting vibe of Coconut Grove circa once-upon-a-time, this lovely spot offers an indoor-outdoor, tea-time setting for light bites. By day, it's one of Miami's

most serene lunch spots. The lushly landscaped courtyard is lined with alfresco seating, drawing some of Miami's most fabulous ladies who lunch. Come evening, the café buzzes with a multigenerational crowd, enjoying the South Florida zephyrs and the delicious flatbreads, salads, homemade soups, and entrées. *Average main: $22 ✉ 2889 McFarlane Rd., Coconut Grove ☎ 305/774–3332 🌐 www.peacockspot.com ✥ C5.*

CORAL GABLES

$ CUBAN ★ **El Palacio de los Jugos.** To the west of Coral Gables proper, this joint is one of the easiest and truest ways to see Miami's local Latin life in action. It's also one of the best fruit-shake shacks you'll ever come across (ask for a tropical juice of mamey, melón, or guanabana). Besides the rows and rows of fresh tropical fruits and vegetables, and the shakes you can make with any of them, this boisterous indoor-outdoor market has numerous food counters where you can get just about any Cuban food—tamales, rice and beans, a *pan con lechón* (roast pork on Cuban bread), fried pork rinds, or a coconut split before you and served with a straw. Order your food at a counter and eat it along with local families at rows of outdoor picnic-style tables next to the parking lot. It's disorganized, chaotic, and not for those cutting calories, but it's delicious and undeniably the real thing. *Average main: $8 ✉ 5721 W. Flagler St., West Miami, Miami ☎ 305/264–4557 ▭ No credit cards ✥ B4.*

$$ CUBAN **Havana Harry's.** When Cuban families want an affordable home-cooked meal but don't want to cook it themselves or go supercheap at the Cuban fast-food joint, Pollo Tropical, they come to this big, unassuming restaurant. In fact, you're likely to see whole families here representing multiple generations. The fare is traditional Cuban: the long thin steaks known as *bistec palomilla* (a panfried steak), roast chicken with citrus marinade, and fried pork chunks; contemporary flourishes—mango sauce and guava-painted pork roast—are kept to a minimum. Most dishes come with white rice, black beans, and a choice of ripe or green plantains. The sweet ripe ones offer a good contrast to the savory dishes. Start with the $5.25 *mariquitas* (plantain chips) with mojo. Finish with the acclaimed flan. *Average main: $12 ✉ 4612 Le Jeune Rd. ☎ 305/661–2622 🌐 www.havanaharrys.net ✥ C5.*

$$$ CARIBBEAN Fodor's Choice ★ **Ortanique on the Mile.** Cascading *ortaniques*, a Jamaican hybrid orange, are hand-painted on columns in this warm, welcoming yellow dining room. Food is vibrant in taste and color, as delicious as it is beautiful. Though there is no denying that the strong, full flavors are imbued with island breezes, chef-partner Cindy Hutson's personal "cuisine of the sun" goes beyond Caribbean refinements. The menu centers on fish, since Hutson has a special way with it, and the Caribbean bouillabaisse is not to be missed. On Sunday there's live jazz. The mojitos here are amazing. *Average main: $30 ✉ 278 Miracle Mile ☎ 305/446–7710 🌐 www.cindyhutsoncuisine.com ⊙ No lunch weekends ✥ C5.*

$$$$ FRENCH **Pascal's on Ponce.** This French gem amid the Coral Gables restaurant district is always full, thanks to chef-proprietor Pascal Oudin's assured and consistent cuisine. Oudin forgoes the glitz and fussiness often associated with French cuisine, and instead opts for a simple, small, refined dining room that won't overwhelm patrons. The equally sensible menu

includes a creamy lobster bisque starter. The main course is a tough choice between oven-roasted duck with poached pears and diver sea scallops with beef short rib. Ask your expert waiter to pair dishes with a selection from Pascal's impressive wine list, and, for dessert, order the bittersweet-chocolate soufflé with chocolate ganache. [$] *Average main: $34* ✉ *2611 Ponce de León Blvd.* ☎ *305/444–2024* 🌐 *www.pascalmiami.com* ⏲ *Closed Sun. No lunch Sat.* ✢ *C5.*

KEY BISCAYNE

$$$ MEXICAN Fodor's Choice ★

✕ **Cantina Beach.** Leave it to The Ritz-Carlton Key Biscayne, Miami to bring a small, sumptuous piece of coastal Mexico to Florida's fabulous beaches. The pool- and ocean-side Cantina Beach showcases authentic and divine Mexican cuisine, including fresh guacamole made tableside. The restaurant also boasts the region's only *tequilier*, mixing and matching 108 high-end tequilas. It's no surprise then that Cantina Beach has phenomenal margaritas. And the best part is that you can enjoy them with your feet in the sand, gazing at the ocean. [$] *Average main: $21* ✉ *Ritz-Carlton Key Biscayne, Miami, 455 Grand Bay Dr., Key Biscayne* ☎ *305/365–4622* 🌐 *www.ritzcarlton.com/keyiscayne* ✢ *E6.*

$$$$ ITALIAN

✕ **Cioppino.** Few visitors think to venture out to the far end of Key Biscayne for dinner, but making the journey to the soothing grounds of this quiet Ritz-Carlton property on the beach is well worth it. Choose your view: the ornate dining room near the exhibition kitchen or the alfresco area with views of landscaped gardens or breeze-brushed beaches. Choosing your dishes may be more difficult, given the many rich, luscious Italian options, including imported cheeses, olive oils, risottos and fresh fish flown in daily. Items range from the creamy *burrata* mozzarella and authentic pasta dishes to tantalizing risotto with organic spinach and roasted quail, all expertly matched with fine, vintage, rare, and boutique wines. An after-dinner drink and live music at the old-Havana-style RUMBAR inside the hotel is another treat. [$] *Average main: $35* ✉ *Ritz-Carlton Key Biscayne, Miami, 455 Grand Bay Dr., Key Biscayne* ☎ *305/365–4156* 🌐 *www.ritzcarlton.com/keybiscayne* ✢ *E6.*

$$$$ MODERN AMERICAN Fodor's Choice ★

✕ **Rusty Pelican.** Whether you're visiting Miami for the first or 15th time, a meal at the Rusty Pelican could easily stand out as your most memorable experience. The legendary Key Biscayne restaurant's $7 million reinvention is nothing short of spectacular. Vistas of the bay and Miami skyline are sensational—whether you admire them

FULL-MOON DINNERS

The Full Moon Dinner Series at Cioppino is fun, romantic, geeky, and one of Miami's most memorable experiences. Held from October to May on the exact night of the full moon, the dinner is a four-course Italian gastronomic extravaganza under the magical path of the rising full moon. Tabletop telescopes serve as centerpieces. The restaurant's Constellation Concierge visits each table to point out key stars and constellations, and then invites guests to look at the moon through the mega-telescope. Meanwhile the highly attentive staff serve the divine creations of Chef de Cuisine Ezio Gamba.

through the floor-to-ceiling windows or from the expansive outdoor seating area, lined with alluring fire pits. The menu is split between tropically inspired small plates, ideal for sharing, and heartier entrées from land and sea. Standouts include sea bass ceviche; baked crab cakes; crispy fried, whole local red snapper; and the bouillabaisse served tableside—a beautiful shallow bowl of fresh lobster, sea scallops, crab, roasted tomatoes, and toasted-corn relish swimming in a creamy lobster bisque. *Average main: $38 ✉ 3201 Rickenbacker Causeway, Key Biscayne ☎ 305/361–3818 ⊕ www.therustypelican.com ✣ E5.*

WYNWOOD/MIDTOWN/DESIGN DISTRICT

$$ ITALIAN

Joey's. Veneto-native chef Ivo Mazzon pays homage to fresh ingredients prepared simply in his small, modern Italian café, which carries a full line of flatbread pizzas, including the legendary *dolce e piccante* with figs, Gorgonzola, honey, and hot pepper—it's sweet and spicy goodness through and through. Joey's also serves the full gamut of Italian favorites. One of the first nongallery tenants and the first restaurant in the Wynwood Art District, it's become a favorite in this thriving neighborhood. The wine list is small but the result of much discernment. *Average main: $18 ✉ 2506 N.W. 2nd Ave., Wynwood ☎ 305/438–0488 ⊕ www.joeyswynwood.com ⊗ Closed Sun. ✣ D4.*

$$$ AMERICAN Fodor's Choice ★

Michael's Genuine Food & Drink. Michael's is often cited as Miami's top restaurant, and it's not hard to see why. This indoor-outdoor bistro in Miami's Design District relies on fresh ingredients and a hip but unpretentious vibe to lure diners. Beautifully arranged combinations like crispy beef cheek with whipped celeriac, and sweet-and-spicy pork belly with kimchi explode with unlikely but satisfying flavor. Owner and chef Michael Schwartz aims for sophisticated American cuisine with an emphasis on local and organic ingredients. He gets it right. Portions are divided into small, medium, and large plates, and the smaller plates are more inventive, so you can order several and explore. Reserve two weeks in advance for weekend tables; also, consider brunch. *Average main: $26 ✉ 130 N.E. 40th St. ☎ 305/573–5550 ⊕ www.michaelsgenuine.com ⚠ Reservations essential ⊗ No lunch Sat. ✣ D3.*

$$$ ECLECTIC Fodor's Choice ★

Michy's. Even before multiple stints on any and every great food show on TV, Miami's homegrown star and James Beard winner Michelle Bernstein was making national headlines with her self-named restaurant, Michy's. Bernstein's regulars often pack the small eatery, which serves exquisite Latin- and Mediterranean-influenced dishes at over-the-causeway (non–tourist-trap) prices. The food is bold, eclectic, and beyond tasty— everything you'd expect from a culinary wizard. Can't-miss entrées include seared turbot with sweet shrimp, potato gnocchi, artichoke *barigoule* (braised artichokes in a seasoned broth), and short ribs "falling off the bone." Both appetizers and mains (aptly termed Plates of Resistance on the menu) come in half and full portions, which makes dining here an even more amazing deal. *Average main: $26 ✉ 6927 Biscayne Blvd., Upper East Side ☎ 305/759–2001 ⊕ www.michysmiami.com ⊗ Closed Mon. No lunch ✣ E3.*

$$ ECLECTIC ★ ✕ **Wynwood Kitchen & Bar.** At the center of Miami's artsy gallery-driven neighborhood, Wynwood Kitchen & Bar offers an experience completely different from anything else in the state. While you enjoy Latin-inspired small plates, you can marvel at the powerful, hand-painted murals characterizing the interiors and exteriors, which also spill out onto the captivating Wynwood Walls. Designed for sharing, tapas-style dishes include wood-grilled octopus skewers, lemon-pepper calamari, roasted beets, bacon-wrapped dates, and ropa vieja empanadas. It's best to allot a good chunk of time to thoroughly enjoy the creative food, the artist-inspired cocktails, and the coolio crowd, and to venerate the sensational works of art all around you. *Average main: $22 ✉ 2550 N.W. 2nd Ave., Wynwood Art District ☎ 305/7228959 www.wynwoodkitchenandbar.com ✣ D4.*

SOUTH BEACH

$$$$ ITALIAN ✕ **Bianca.** In a hotel where style reigns supreme, the latest high-profile restaurant at the Delano Hotel provides both glamour and solid cuisine. The main attraction of dining here is to see and be seen, but you may leave talking about the food just as much as the outfits, hairdos, and celebrity appearances. This Italian restaurant doles out some pretty amazing fare, including fresh baby-artichoke salad and lobster tagliolini—perfection in every bite. The dessert menu may seem a bit back-to-basics, with tiramisu and cheesecake among the favorites, but these sweet classics are done right. For something a bit more casual at the Delano, try sushi from the Philippe Starck countertop sushi bar at the front of the hotel. *Average main: $45 ✉ Delano Hotel, 1685 Collins Ave., South Beach ☎ 305/674–5752 www.delano-hotel.com Reservations essential ✣ H2.*

$$ AMERICAN ✕ **Big Pink.** The decor in this innovative, superpopular diner may remind you of a roller-skating rink—everything is pink Lucite, stainless steel, and campy (think sports lockers as decorative touches)—and the menu is 3 feet tall, complete with a table of contents. Food is solidly all-American, with dozens of tasty sandwiches, pizzas, turkey or beef burgers, and side dishes, each and every one composed with gourmet flair. Big Pink also makes a great spot for brunch. *Average main: $14 ✉ 157 Collins Ave., South Beach ☎ 305/532–4700 www.mylesrestaurantgroup.com ✣ H5.*

$$$$ STEAKHOUSE Fodor's Choice ★ ✕ **BLT Steak.** This Ocean Drive favorite, renowned for seriously divine Gruyère cheese popovers and succulent steak and fish dishes, illuminates the vibrant, open lobby of the snazzy Betsy Hotel. It has the distinction among all of Miami's steak houses of serving breakfast daily and consistently impressing even the most finicky eaters. You can count on the highest-quality cuts of USDA prime, certified Black Angus, and American Wagyu beef, in addition to blackboard specials and raw-bar selections. Though the name may say steak, the fresh fish is arguably the highlight of the entire menu—the sautéed Dover sole with soy-caper brown butter is legendary. *Average main: $32 ✉ The Betsy Hotel, 1440 Ocean Dr., South Beach ☎ 305/673–0044 www.bltrestaurants.com ✣ H2.*

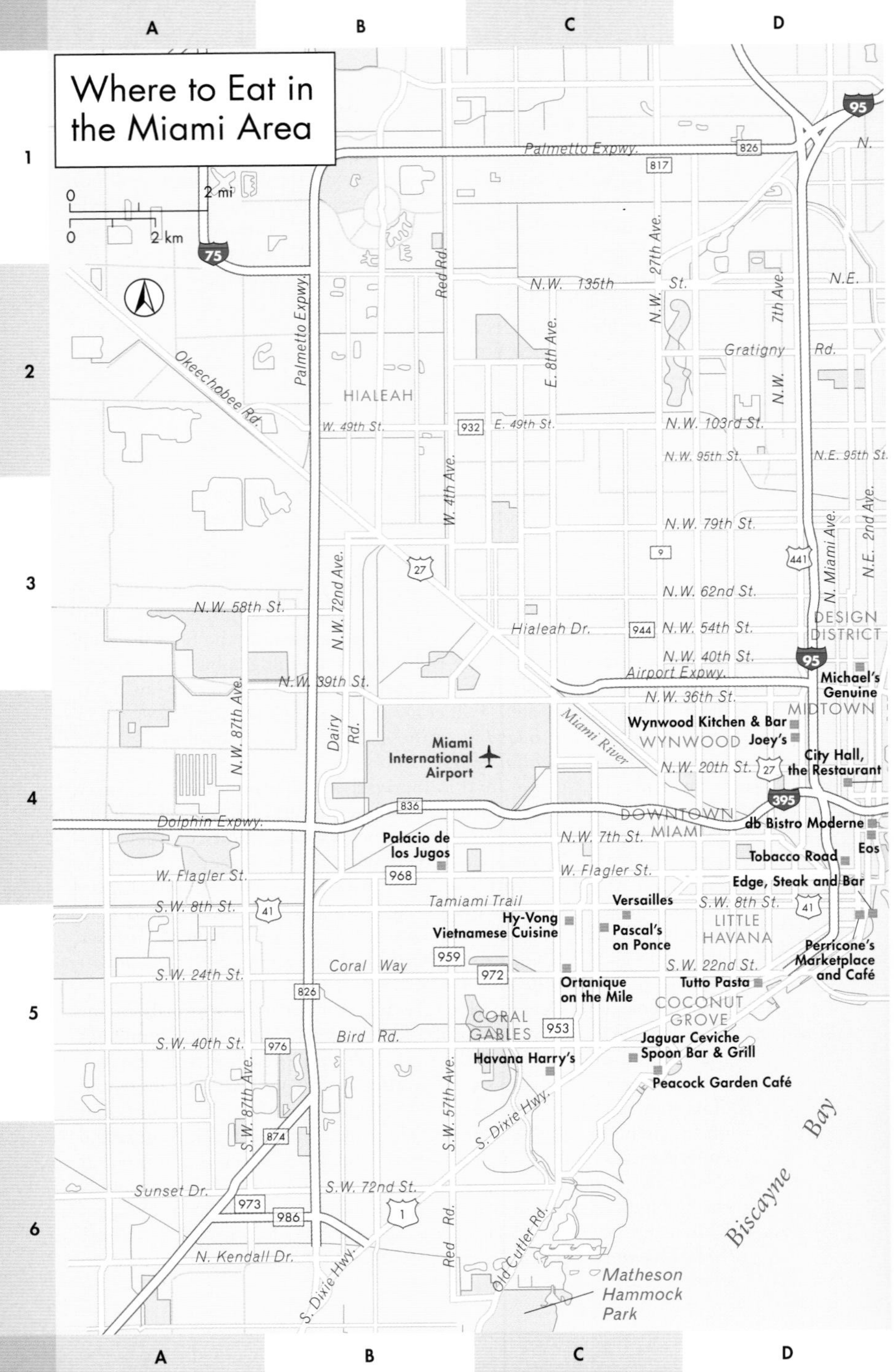
Where to Eat in the Miami Area
A
B
C
D
1
2
3
4
5
6
0
2 mi
0
2 km
Palmetto Expwy.
N.W. 135th St.
Gratigny Rd.
HIALEAH
W. 49th St.
E. 49th St.
N.W. 103rd St.
N.W. 95th St.
N.E. 95th St.
N.W. 79th St.
N.W. 62nd St.
N.W. 58th St.
Hialeah Dr.
N.W. 54th St.
N.W. 40th St.
DESIGN DISTRICT
Airport Expwy.
N.W. 39th St.
N.W. 36th St.
Michael's Genuine
MIDTOWN
Wynwood Kitchen & Bar
WYNWOOD
Joey's
Miami River
City Hall, the Restaurant
N.W. 20th St.
Miami International Airport
Dolphin Expwy.
DOWNTOWN MIAMI
db Bistro Moderne
N.W. 7th St.
Palacio de los Jugos
Eos
Tobacco Road
W. Flagler St.
Edge, Steak and Bar
S.W. 8th St.
Tamiami Trail
Versailles
Hy-Vong Vietnamese Cuisine
Pascal's on Ponce
LITTLE HAVANA
Perricone's Marketplace and Café
S.W. 24th St.
Coral Way
S.W. 22nd St.
Ortanique on the Mile
Tutto Pasta
COCONUT GROVE
CORAL GABLES
S.W. 40th St.
Bird Rd.
Jaguar Ceviche Spoon Bar & Grill
Havana Harry's
Peacock Garden Café
S. Dixie Hwy.
Biscayne Bay
Sunset Dr.
S.W. 72nd St.
N. Kendall Dr.
Old Cutler Rd.
Matheson Hammock Park
Okeechobee Rd.
Palmetto Expwy.
Red Rd.
E. 8th Ave.
N.W. 27th Ave.
N.W. 7th Ave.
W. 4th Ave.
N.W. 72nd Ave.
N.W. 87th Ave.
Dairy Rd.
N. Miami Ave.
N.E. 2nd Ave.
S.W. 57th Ave.
S.W. 87th Ave.
75
95
826
817
932
27
9
944
441
395
836
968
41
959
972
953
976
874
973
986
1

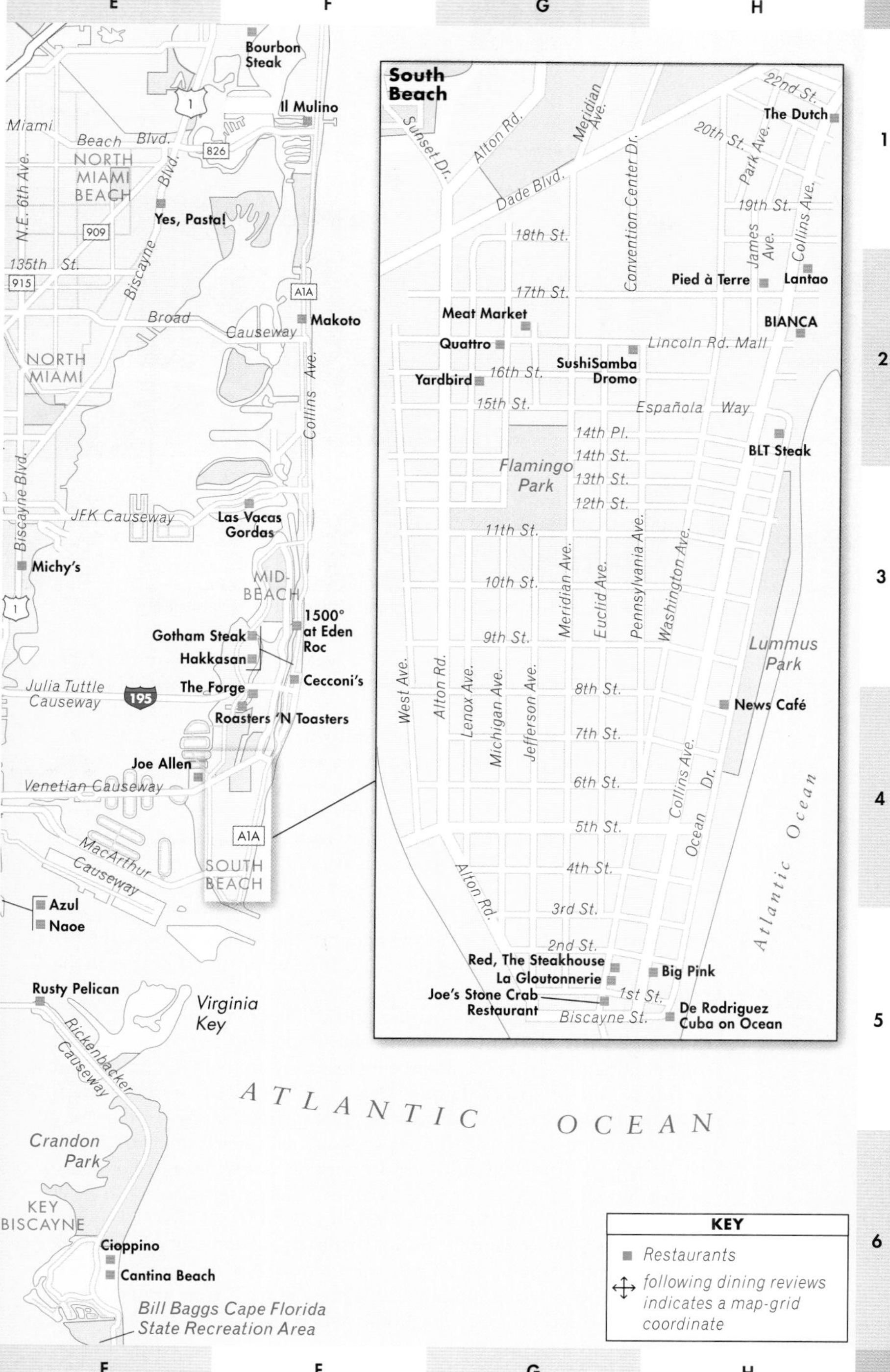

E
F
G
H
1
2
3
4
5
6
Bourbon Steak
Il Mulino
Yes, Pasta!
Makoto
Las Vacas Gordas
Michy's
1500° at Eden Roc
Gotham Steak
Hakkasan
Cecconi's
The Forge
Roasters 'N Toasters
Joe Allen
Azul
Naoe
Rusty Pelican
Cioppino
Cantina Beach
Miami Beach Blvd.
NORTH MIAMI BEACH
N.E. 6th Ave.
Biscayne Blvd.
135th St.
Broad Causeway
Collins Ave.
NORTH MIAMI
Biscayne Blvd.
JFK Causeway
MID-BEACH
Julia Tuttle Causeway
Venetian Causeway
MacArthur Causeway
SOUTH BEACH
Virginia Key
Rickenbacker Causeway
Crandon Park
KEY BISCAYNE
Bill Baggs Cape Florida State Recreation Area
ATLANTIC OCEAN
South Beach
The Dutch
Pied à Terre
Lantao
Meat Market
BIANCA
Quattro
SushiSamba Dromo
Yardbird
BLT Steak
News Café
Red, The Steakhouse
La Gloutonnerie
Big Pink
Joe's Stone Crab Restaurant
De Rodriguez Cuba on Ocean
Sunset Dr.
Alton Rd.
Meridian Ave.
Dade Blvd.
Convention Center Dr.
22nd St.
20th St.
Park Ave.
19th St.
James Ave.
Collins Ave.
18th St.
17th St.
Lincoln Rd. Mall
16th St.
15th St.
Española Way
14th Pl.
14th St.
13th St.
12th St.
11th St.
10th St.
9th St.
8th St.
7th St.
6th St.
5th St.
4th St.
3rd St.
2nd St.
1st St.
Biscayne St.
Flamingo Park
Lummus Park
West Ave.
Lenox Ave.
Michigan Ave.
Jefferson Ave.
Euclid Ave.
Pennsylvania Ave.
Washington Ave.
Ocean Dr.
Atlantic Ocean
KEY
Restaurants
following dining reviews indicates a map-grid coordinate

Pink as cotton candy and bubble gum, the Big Pink diner fits right in with its art deco surroundings.

$$$$ CUBAN ★ **De Rodriguez Cuba on Ocean.** If you're seeking a classy joint in which to experience a superlative Miami incarnation of old-world Havana, look no further than this fabulous waterfront eatery run by noteworthy chef Douglas Rodriguez, which captures the essence of circa-1950s Cuba—from the decor to the music to the incredible mojitos. Although you'll find some Cuban classics on this menu, Chef Rodriguez also showcases his gastronomic prowess with sensational ceviches and creative tapas, including braised short ribs with a smoked-tomato sauce, and foie gras–and–fig empanadas with arugula salad and Serrano ham. *Average main: $36 ✉ Hilton Bentley Hotel, 101 Ocean Dr., South Beach ☎ 305/672–6624 ⊕ www.drodriguezcuba.com ✣ H5.*

$$$$ MODERN AMERICAN **The Dutch Miami.** Loft meets cozy kitchen at the Miami outpost of Chef Andrew Carmellini's farm-to-table NYC foodie hot spot. Located in the swank W South Beach Hotel, the Dutch takes on a personality all its own, adorned with cute tchotchkes and ornamental objects set along white bookshelves. There's a bit of everything on the "roots-inspired American menu," from local line-caught fish to homemade pastas and the full gamut of steaks. Dinner begins with a twist on a Southern classic—a corn-bread loaf with a hint of jalapeño. Two dishes that may blow your mind are the Maine sea scallops with heirloom cauliflower and citrus, and the yellowtail crudo with watermelon and jalapeño. It's worth coming here for this dish alone. *Average main: $36 ✉ W South Beach, 2201 Collins Ave., South Beach ☎ 305/938–3111 ✣ H1.*

$$$$ SEAFOOD Fodor's Choice ★ **Joe's Stone Crab Restaurant.** In South Beach's decidedly new-money scene, the stately Joe's Stone Crab is an old-school testament to good food and good service. South Beach's most storied restaurant started as a turn-of-the-century eating house when Joseph Weiss discovered

2

CHEAP EATS ON SOUTH BEACH

Miami Beach is notorious for overpriced eateries, but locals know better. **Pizza Rustica** (✉ *8th St. and Washington Ave., 14th St. and Washington Ave., and at 667 Lincoln Rd.*) serves up humongous slices overflowing with mozzarella, steak, olives, and barbecue chicken until 4 am. **LaSandwicherie** (✉ *14th St. between Collins and Washington Aves.*) is a South Beach classic that has been here since 1988, serving gourmet French sandwiches, a delicious prosciutto salad, and healthful smoothies from a walk-up bar. **Lime Fresh Mexican Grill** (✉ *1439 Alton Rd., at 14th St.*) serves fresh and tangy fish tacos and homemade guacamole.

succulent stone crabs off the Florida coast. Almost a century later, the restaurant stretches a city block and serves 2,000 dinners a day to local politicians and moneyed patriarchs. Stone crabs, served with legendary mustard sauce, crispy hash browns, and creamed spinach, remain the staple. Though stone-crab season runs from October 15 to May 15, Joe's remains open year-round (albeit with a limited schedule) serving other phenomenal seafood dishes. Finish your meal with tart key lime pie, baked fresh daily. ■**TIP→ Joe's famously refuses reservations, and weekend waits can be three hours long—yes, you read that correctly—so come early or order from Joe's Take Away next door.** $ *Average main: $42* ✉ *11 Washington Ave., South Beach* ☎ *305/673–0365, 305/673–4611 for takeout* 🌐 *www.joesstonecrab.com* *Reservations not accepted* ⏲ *No lunch Sun. and Mon. and mid-May–mid-Oct.* ✣ *G5*

$$$ MODERN FRENCH Fodor's Choice ★

✕ **La Gloutonnerie.** Far removed from South Beach's mass-market deco drive strip, this intimate "vintage kitchen" brings the best of French old-school cuisine to the beach's more refined SoFi (South of Fifth) neighborhood. The chef presents everything you'd desire from a renowned French kitchen from *escargots Bourgogne* to *chateubriand* while adding new-world flavors and fusions to the mix with dishes such as the shrimp carpaccio Santa Margherita (cured in peach and citrus juice) and an assortment of fresh pasta entrées. Within the restaurant, a retro mini-market offers cheese, cold cuts, and imported French products. Add stylish black and white decor, stellar service, and a hip crowd, and you have the perfect recipe for keeping history in style. $ *Average main: $28* ✉ *81 Washington Ave., South Beach* ☎ *305/503–3811* 🌐 *www.lagloutonnerie.com* ✣ *G5.*

$$$ MODERN ASIAN Fodor's Choice ★

✕ **Lantao.** Inside the Kimpton Group's trendy Surfcomber Hotel, Lantao brings the best of Asian street food to America's sexiest city. Forget food trucks—this is a one-stop shop for touring the food stalls of an entire continent. Transport yourself to Southeast Asia with the Singapore chili prawns and crispy kale, or head to the Land of the Morning Calm, Korea, for barbecue pork ribs. The cocktails are equally impressive and colorful. It's not every day you're able to knock back a Hibiki Highball (Hibiki Japanese Whiskey with Fever-Tree soda) and gawk at Miami's profusion of pretty people. $ *Average main: $28*

✉ *Surfcomber Hotel, 1717 Collins Ave., South Beach* ☎ *305/604–1800* 🌐 *www.lantaorestaurant.com* ✥ *H2.*

$$$$ STEAKHOUSE Fodor's Choice ★ ✕ **Meat Market.** On Lincoln Road, where most of the restaurants emphasize people-watching over good food, this is one spot where you can find the best of both. Indeed, this is a meat market in every sense of the phrase, with great cuts of meat and plenty of sexy people passing by in skimpy clothes and enjoying fruity libations at the bar. Hardcore carnivores go wild over the the 14-ounce center-cut prime New York steak as well as the "mixed-grill special," a creative trio of meats and seafood that changes nightly. The tuna tartare is exceptional here, lightly tossed in ginger and soy with mashed avocados and mango mole. Also consider the wood-grilled blackened local snapper cooked to perfection and topped with a light sun-dried-tomato pesto and dollops of black-garlic sauce. The broccolini side makes a nice complement to any meal. [$] *Average main: $34* ✉ *915 Lincoln Rd., South Beach* ☎ *305/532–0088* 🌐 *www.meatmarketmiami.com* ⏲ *No lunch* ✥ *G2.*

$$ AMERICAN ✕ **News Café.** No trip to Miami is complete without a stop at this Ocean Drive landmark, though the food is nothing special. The 24-hour café attracts a crowd with snacks, light meals, drinks, periodicals, and the people-parade on the sidewalk out front. Most prefer sitting outside, where they can feel the salt breeze and gawk at the human scenery. Seagrape trees shade a patio where you can watch from a quiet distance. Offering a little of this and a little of that—bagels, pâtés, chocolate fondue, sandwiches, and a terrific wine list—this joint has something for everyone. Although service can be indifferent to the point of laissez-faire and the food is mediocre at best, News Café is just one of those places visitors love. [$] *Average main: $15* ✉ *800 Ocean Dr., South Beach* ☎ *305/538–6397* 🌐 *www.newscafe.com* ✍ *Reservations not accepted* ✥ *H4.*

$$$$ BISTRO Fodor's Choice ★ ✕ **Pied à Terre.** This cozy, 30-seat French bistro resides in the heart of South Beach, but it's everything the beach is not. Quiet, classic, and elegant, this small gem within the historic Cadet Hotel forgoes glitz and gimmicks for taste and sophistication. The resto recalls the ambience of a bona fide, intimate Parisian eatery—the kind you'd randomly discover on a side street in the City of Light's 5th or 6th arrondisment—and doles out succulent French cuisine with a Peruvian twist (think sea bass Provençal with quinoa salad). [$] *Average main: $38* ✉ *Cadet Hotel, 1701 James Ave., South Beach* ☎ *305/672–6688* 🌐 *piedaterrerestaurant.com* ✍ *Reservations essential* ⏲ *Closed Sun.–Mon. No lunch* ✥ *H2.*

$$$$ ITALIAN ✕ **Quattro Gastronomia Italiana.** Helmed by twin chefs Nicola and Fabrizio Carro, this sleek northern Italian restaurant has been a favorite with Miami's "in" crowd since it opened in 2006. The beautiful interior is adorned with Murano glass chandeliers and strking floor-to-ceiling wine towers. However, it's the alfresco dining area on busy Lincoln Road where most of the action happens. Be sure to try the *parmigiana di melanzane in forma* (baked organic eggplant), one of the homemade ravioli, or the Mediterranean sea bass while enjoying a selection from the astounding wine collection. [$] *Average main: $38* ✉ *1014 Lincoln Rd., South Beach* ☎ *305/531–4833* 🌐 *www.quattromiami.com* ✥ *G2.*

$$$$ STEAKHOUSE **Red, the Steakhouse.** Just when it seemed that South Beach had become all too saturated with steak houses, Red arrived and raised the bar on SoBe's steak-house experience. The carnivore glamour den seduces with its red and black dominatrix color scheme and overloads the senses with the divine smells and tastes of the extensive menu. Red boasts an equal number of seafood and traditional carnivorous offerings, each delicately prepared, meticulously presented, and gleefully consumed. Start with the tuna tartare, the mussels *diavolo*, or crisp chili calamari and then continue with fresh lobster or the many variations of Angus Beef Prime. And don't forget about the dozen or so sides, often the most exciting part of any steak-house experience. *Average main: $50 ✉ 119 Washington Ave., South Beach ☎ 305/534–3688 www.redthesteakhouse.com Reservations essential ✣ G5.*

$$$ JAPANESE **SushiSamba Dromo.** This sibling to the New York City SushiSamba makes an eclectic pairing of Japanese, Peruvian, and Brazilian cuisines. The results are fabulous if a bit mystifying: miso-marinated sea bass, hamachi *taquitos* (basically a yellowtail tartare), *mocqueca mista* (Brazilian seafood stew), and caramel–passion fruit sponge cake. Loaded with customers in the heart of pedestrian Lincoln Road, colorful SushiSamba has a vibe that hurts the ears but warms the trendy heart. *Average main: $32 ✉ 600 Lincoln Rd., South Beach ☎ 305/673–5337 www.sushisamba.com ✣ G2.*

$$ SOUTHERN Fodor's Choice ★ **Yardbird Southern Table & Bar.** *Top Chef* contestant Jeff McInnis brings a helluva lot of Southern lovin' from the Lowcountry to South Beach at this lively and funky spot. Miami's see-and-be-seen crowd puts calorie-counting aside for decadent nights filled with comfort foods and innovative drinks. The family-style menu is divided between "small shares" and "big shares," but let's not kid ourselves—all the portions are huge (and surprisingly affordable). You'll rave about the pimento cheese jar, fried-green-tomato BLT, grilled-mango salad, 27-hour-fried chicken, and shrimp and grits. Oh, and then there are the sides, like the house-cut waffle fries with a buttermilk dipping sauce and bacon salt, and the super-creamy macaroni-and-cheese. Don't plan on hitting the beach in a bikini the next day. *Average main: $18 ✉ 1600 Lenox Ave., South Beach ☎ 305/538–5220 www.runchickenrun.com ✣ G2.*

MID-BEACH

$$$ ITALIAN **Cecconi's.** After the New York restaurant scene invaded Miami Beach, it was only a matter of time until L.A. made its way down southeast, too. With the unveiling of the Soho Beach House in Miami came the company's iconic Italian restaurant, Cecconi's. The wait for a table at this outpost is just as long as at its West Hollywood counterpart, and the dining experience just as fabulous. Eating here is a real scene of who's who and who's eating what. Without a doubt, the truffle pizza, which servers shave huge hunks of black or white truffle onto table-side, is the restaurant's most talked about dish. The fish carpaccios are light and succulent while the classically hearty pastas and risottos provide authentic Italian fare. *Average main: $28 ✉ Soho Beach House, 4385 Collins Ave., Mid-Beach ☎ 786/507–7900 www.cecconismiamibeach.com Reservations essential ✣ F4.*

$$$$ BRAZILIAN Fodor's Choice ★ ✕ **1500°.** Thanks to the superb vision and prowess of Executive Chef Paula DaSilva, 1500° launches the farm-to-table revolution into an entirely new dimension. The menu changes seasonally, many items daily, but a few staples remain over the passing months, including the mouthwatering, tender steaks broiled to perfection (at 1500°, natch), and the delicate Florida wahoo ceviche. All side dishes (you have a whopping 17 to choose from) are beyond robust in flavor and ingenuity—the Vidalia onion–and–potato gratin is an entire, mammoth sweet onion stuffed and baked with potatoes, cheese, cream, and grilled onions. The restaurant's interiors scream modern luxury, flaunting showroom elegance spiced with trendy design elements. *Average main: $32 ✉ Eden Roc Renaissance Hotel, 4525 Collins Ave., Mid-Beach ☎ 305/674–5594 🌐 www.1500degreesmiami.com ✧ F3.*

$$$$ STEAKHOUSE Fodor's Choice ★ ✕ **The Forge.** Legendary for its opulence, this restaurant has been wowing patrons since 1968. After a renovation, The Forge reemerged in 2010 more decadent than ever. It is a steak house, but a steak house the likes of which you haven't seen before. Antiques, gilt-framed paintings, a chandelier from the Paris Opera House, and Tiffany stained-glass windows from New York's Trinity Church are the fitting background for some of Miami's best cuts. The tried-and-true menu also includes prime rib, bone-in fillet, lobster *thermidor*, chocolate soufflé, and sinful side dishes like creamed spinach and roasted-garlic mashed potatoes. The focaccia bread is to die for. For its walk-in humidor alone, the over-the-top Forge is worth visiting. The automated wine machine spans the perimeter of the restaurant and allows you to pick your own pour and sample several wines throughout your meal. *Average main: $38 ✉ 432 Arthur Godfrey Rd., Mid-Beach ☎ 305/538–8533 🌐 www.theforge.com ✍ Reservations essential ⏲ No lunch ✧ F4.*

$$$$ STEAKHOUSE Fodor's Choice ★ ✕ **Gotham Steak.** The Miami outpost of this NYC institution—set inside the fabulous Fontainebleau resort—is often cited as the best steak house in South Florida's oversaturated meat market. It's not hard to see why. The apps, meats, seafood, and sides are all stellar. The Gotham Raw bar presents top-of-the-line stone crabs, succulent sashimis, excellent ceviches, and a fantastic chilled Maine lobster salad with fresh hearts of palm, mango puree, avocado, and pineapple-vanilla dressing. Classic cuts from the grill, namely the Kansas City Strip and Niman Ranch Strip, wow even hard-core carnivores—these can be prepared simply or with one of six sauces, such as cognac-peppercorn. Naturally, Gotham offers the full gamut of decadent sides, including the must-try creamed corn with Manchego cheese and jalapeño. *Average main: $54 ✉ Fontainebleau Hotel, 4441 Collins Ave, Mid-Beach ☎ 305/674–4780 🌐 www.fontainebleau.com ✧ F3.*

$$$$ CANTONESE Fodor's Choice ★ ✕ **Hakkasan.** This stateside sibling of the Michelin-star London restaurant brings the haute-Chinese-food movement to South Florida, adding Pan-Asian flair to even quite simple and authentic Cantonese recipes, and producing an entire menu that can be classified as blow-your-mind delicious. Seafood and vegetarian dishes outnumber meat options, with the scallop-and-shrimp dim sum, Szechuan-style braised eggplant, and charcoal-grilled silver cod with champagne and Chinese honey reaching new heights of excellence. Superb eats notwithstanding, another reason

to experience Hakkasan is that it's arguably the sexiest, best-looking restaurant on Miami Beach. Intricately carved, lacquered-black-wood Chinois panels divide seating sections, creating a deceptively cozy dining experience for such a large restaurant. Dress to impress. *Average main: $40 ✉ Fontainebleau Hotel, 4441 Collins Ave., 4th floor, Mid-Beach ☎ 305/538–2000 ⊕ www.hakkasan.com ⚠ Reservations essential ⊙ No lunch weekdays ✣ F3.*

$$$$ ARGENTINE **Las Vacas Gordas.** Since the early '90s this Argentinean steak house has welcomed the who's who of Latin high society, fulfilling their wildest carnivore cravings. Recently expanded and reinvented as a glamorous enclave where the Pampas meets contemporary Miami, Vacas's grill sizzles day and nights to the hordes of patrons who patiently wait to feast on mounds of fresh meat from the Argentinean lowlands. The reasonably priced house Malbecs complement the high-end selections showcased in the floor-to-ceiling, glass-enclosed wine cellar. Those less enthused about massive meat slabs can opt for the *Berecava* (eggplant with tomato sauce and cheese), homemade pastas, grilled peppers, fish and shrimp, or fill up on homemade rolls with spicy chimmichurri. *Average main: $35 ✉ 933 Normandy Dr., Mid-Beach ☎ 305/867–1717 ⊕ www.lasvacasgordas.com ⊙ No lunch weekdays ✣ F3.*

$ DELI **Roasters 'N Toasters.** This small Jewish delicatessen chain took over from Arnie and Richie's, a longtime family establishment, in 2008. Long gone are the baskets of plastic silverware. The prices are slightly higher, but the faithful still come for the onion rolls, smoked whitefish salad, as well as the new "Corky's Famous Zaftig Sandwich," a deliciously juicy skirt steak served on twin challah rolls with a side of apple sauce. Service can be brusque, but it sure is quick. *Average main: $10 ✉ 525 Arthur Godfrey Rd., Mid-Beach ☎ 305/531–7691 ⊕ www.roastersntoasters.com ✣ F4.*

NORTH BEACH AND AVENTURA

$$$$ STEAKHOUSE ★ **Bourbon Steak.** Michael Mina's sole restaurant in the southeastern United States is one of his best. The restaurant design is seductive, the clientele sophisticated, the wine list outstanding, the service phenomenal, and the food exceptional. Dinner begins with a skillet of fresh potato focaccia and chive butter. Mina then presents a bonus starter—his trio of famous fries (fried in duck fat) with three robust sauces. Appetizers are mainly seafood. The raw bar impresses, and classic appetizers like the ahi tuna tartare are delightful and super fresh. Entrées like the Maine lobster potpie and any of the dozen varieties of wood-grilled steaks (from natural, organic, hormone-free beef) are cooked to perfection. *Average main: $35 ✉ Turnberry Isle Miami, 19999 W. Country Club Dr., Aventura, Miami ☎ 786/279–6600 ⊕ www.michaelmina.net ⚠ Reservations essential ✣ F1.*

$$$$ ITALIAN Fodor's Choice ★ **Il Mulino New York.** For more than two decades, Il Mulino New York has ranked among the top Italian restaurants in Gotham, so it's no surprise that the Miami outpost is similarly venerable. Even before the antipasti arrive, you may find yourself in a phenomenal carb coma from the fresh breads and the bruschetta. Everything that touches your palate is prepared to perfection, from simply prepared fried calamari

and gnocchi pomodoro to the more complex scampi oregenata and ever-changing risottos. The restaurant is seductive, quiet, and intimate, and a favorite hangout of A-list celebs seeking a refined spot where crowds won't gawk over their presence. $ *Average main: $52* ✉ *Acqualina Resort, 17875 Collins Ave., Sunny Isles* ☎ *305/466–9191* 🌐 *www.acqualinaresort.com* *Reservations essential* ✣ *F1.*

$$$$ JAPANESE ✕ **Makoto.** Stephen Starr's Japanese headliner is one of the most popular restaurants in the swanky and prestigious Bal Harbor Shops. The ambience, service, and food all impress; and given its location in haute-couture central, the patrons definitely dress to impress. There are two menus, one devoted solely to sushi, sashimi, and maki; the other to Japanese hot dishes like tempuras, meats, and vegetables grilled over Japanese charcoal (robata), rice and noodle dishes, and steaks and fish inspired by the Land of the Rising Sun. $ *Average main: $34* ✉ *9700 Collins Ave., North Beach and Aventura, Bal Harbour* ☎ *305/864–8600* 🌐 *www.makoto-restaurant.com* ✣ *F2.*

$ ITALIAN Fodor's Choice ★ ✕ **Yes Pasta! Trattoria Italiana.** This tiny restaurant may be out of the way, but it's well worth the drive. It's in a tacky strip mall, next to T.G.I. Friday's, but this hole-in-the-wall, authentic, family-run trattoria is a slice of Italian foodie heaven. The Italian owners wanted to create a restaurant to satisfy both expats and Italian-Americans, and they've completely succeeded. Although there are pizzas, chicken, and fish on the menu, it's the extraordinarily fresh pastas that take center stage. The concept is simple: just mix and match your pasta with your sauce. The bona fide fresh fettuccine, gnocchi, and linguine are something you'd taste in rural Italy, as are sauces like tomato, garlic, and basil "*sugo della* Nonna," and the *quattro formaggi.* This is also a great place to bring the kids, who especially love the mix-and-match concept. $ *Average main: $14* ✉ *14871 N. Biscayne Blvd., North Beach and Aventura, North Miami Beach* ☎ *305/944–1006* 🌐 *www.yes-pasta.com* ✣ *E1.*

WHERE TO STAY

Room rates in Miami tend to swing wildly. In high season, which is January through May, expect to pay at least $150 per night, even at low-budget hotels. In summer, however, prices can be as much as 50% lower than the dizzying winter rates. You can also find great values between Easter and Memorial Day, which is actually a delightful time in Miami. Business travelers tend to stay in downtown Miami, and most vacationers stay on Miami Beach, as close as possible to the water. South Beach is no longer the only "in" place to stay. Mid-Beach and downtown have taken the hotel scene by storm in the past few years, home to some of the region's most avant-garde and luxurious properties to date. If money is no object, stay in one of the glamorous hotels lining Collins Avenue between 15th and 23rd streets. Otherwise, stay on the quiet beaches farther north, or in one of the small boutique hotels on Ocean Drive, Collins, or Washington avenues between 10th and 15th streets. Two important considerations that affect price are balcony and view. If you're willing to have a room without an ocean view, you can sometimes get a much lower price than the standard rate.

2

BEST BETS FOR MIAMI LODGING

Fodor's offers a selective listing of high-quality lodging experiences in every price range, from the city's best budget beds to its most sophisticated luxury hotels. Here, we've compiled our top recommendations by price and experience. The very best properties are designated in the listings with the Fodor's Choice logo. Find specific details about a hotel in the full reviews, listed alphabetically by neighborhood.

Fodor's Choice ★

Acqualina Resort & Spa on the Beach, p. 89
Cadet Hotel, p. 83
Epic Hotel, p. 80
JW Marriott Marquis Miami, p. 80
Ritz-Carlton Key Biscayne, Miami, p. 82
The Setai, p. 86
The Surfcomber, p. 87
St. Regis Bal Harbour Resort, p. 92
W South Beach, p. 87

By Price

$

Circa 39 Hotel, p. 88
Townhouse Hotel, p. 87
Villa Paradiso, p. 87

$$$

Biltmore Hotel, p. 81
Fontainebleau, p. 88
Ritz-Carlton Key Biscayne, Miami, p. 82

$$$$

Acqualina Resort, p. 89
Four Seasons Hotel Miami, p. 80
Mandarin Oriental Miami, p. 81
The Setai, p. 86
W South Beach, p. 87

By Experience

BEST POOL

Biltmore Hotel, p. 81
National Hotel, p. 85
Ritz-Carlton South Beach, p. 86
The Standard, p. 82
Viceroy Miami, p. 81

BEST HOTEL BAR

National Hotel, p. 85
Viceroy Miami (rooftop bar), p. 81
W South Beach, p. 87

BEST SERVICE

Acqualina Resort, p. 89
Four Seasons Hotel Miami, p. 80
Ritz-Carlton Key Biscayne, Miami, p. 82

BEST VIEWS

Epic Hotel, p. 80
St. Regis Bal Harbour Resort, p. 92
W South Beach, p. 87

HIPSTER HOTELS

Catalina Hotel & Beach Club, p. 83
Thompson Ocean Drive, p. 87
Shore Club, p. 87
Soho Beach House, p. 89

BEST LOCATION

National Hotel, p. 85
The Surfcomber, p. 87

BEST-KEPT SECRET

Acqualina Resort, p. 89
Soho Beach House, p. 89

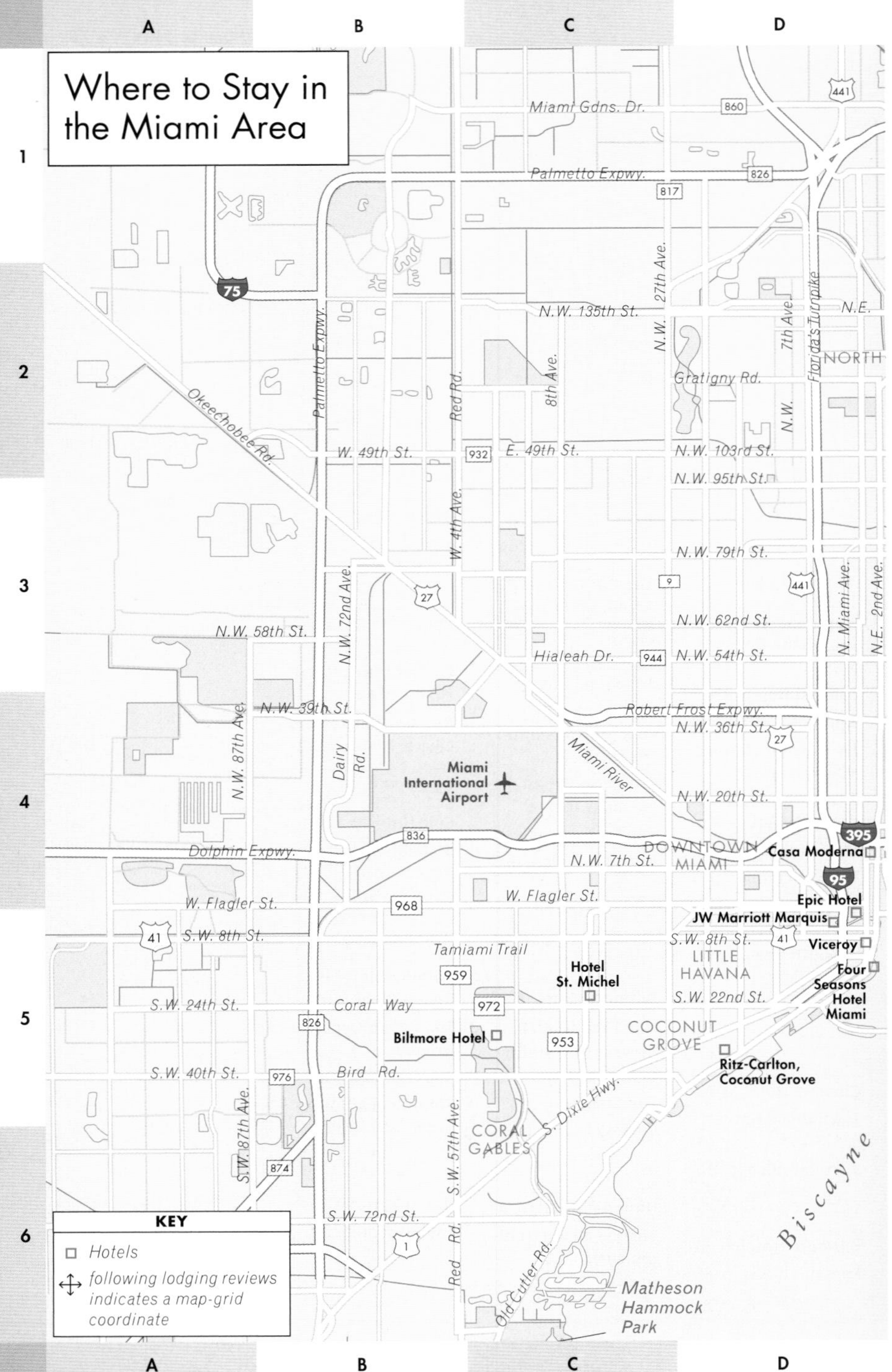

A
B
C
D
Where to Stay in the Miami Area
1
2
3
4
5
6
Miami Gdns. Dr.
Palmetto Expwy.
860
441
826
817
75
N.W. 135th St.
27th Ave.
N.W.
7th Ave.
Florida's Turnpike
N.E.
NORTH
Palmetto Expwy.
Okeechobee Rd.
Red Rd.
8th Ave.
Gratigny Rd.
N.W.
W. 49th St.
932
E. 49th St.
N.W. 103rd St.
N.W. 95th St.
W. 4th Ave.
N.W. 79th St.
N.W. 72nd Ave.
27
9
441
N. Miami Ave.
N.E. 2nd Ave.
N.W. 62nd St.
N.W. 58th St.
Hialeah Dr.
944
N.W. 54th St.
N.W. 87th Ave.
N.W. 39th St.
Robert Frost Expwy.
N.W. 36th St.
27
Dairy Rd.
Miami River
Miami International Airport
N.W. 20th St.
836
395
Dolphin Expwy.
DOWNTOWN MIAMI
N.W. 7th St.
Casa Moderna
95
W. Flagler St.
968
W. Flagler St.
Epic Hotel
JW Marriott Marquis
41
S.W. 8th St.
S.W. 8th St.
41
Viceroy
Tamiami Trail
Hotel St. Michel
LITTLE HAVANA
Four Seasons Hotel Miami
959
S.W. 24th St.
Coral Way
972
S.W. 22nd St.
826
Biltmore Hotel
953
COCONUT GROVE
S.W. 40th St.
976
Bird Rd.
Ritz-Carlton, Coconut Grove
S. Dixie Hwy.
S.W. 87th Ave.
S.W. 57th Ave.
CORAL GABLES
874
Biscayne
S.W. 72nd St.
KEY
Hotels
following lodging reviews indicates a map-grid coordinate
1
Red Rd.
Old Cutler Rd.
Matheson Hammock Park
A
B
C
D

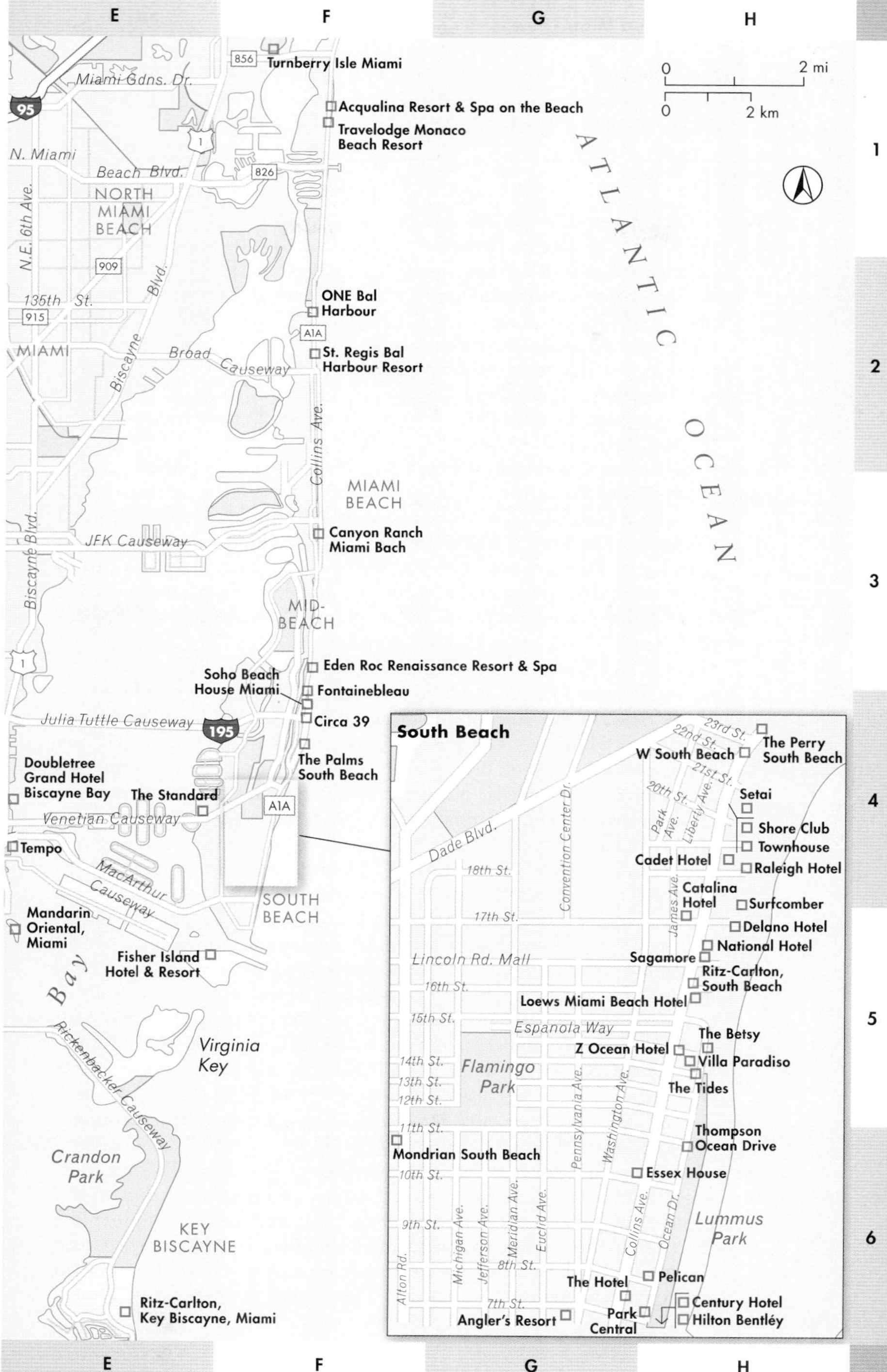
E
F
G
H
1
2
3
4
5
6
Turnberry Isle Miami
Acqualina Resort & Spa on the Beach
Travelodge Monaco Beach Resort
ONE Bal Harbour
St. Regis Bal Harbour Resort
Canyon Ranch Miami Bach
Eden Roc Renaissance Resort & Spa
Soho Beach House Miami
Fontainebleau
Circa 39
The Palms South Beach
Doubletree Grand Hotel Biscayne Bay
The Standard
Tempo
Mandarin Oriental, Miami
Fisher Island Hotel & Resort
Ritz-Carlton, Key Biscayne, Miami
ATLANTIC OCEAN
NORTH MIAMI BEACH
MIAMI
MIAMI BEACH
MID-BEACH
SOUTH BEACH
KEY BISCAYNE
Virginia Key
Crandon Park
Bay
Miami Gdns. Dr.
N. Miami Beach Blvd.
N.E. 6th Ave.
135th St.
Biscayne Blvd.
Broad Causeway
Collins Ave.
JFK Causeway
Julia Tuttle Causeway
Venetian Causeway
MacArthur Causeway
Rickenbacker Causeway
South Beach
W South Beach
The Perry South Beach
Setai
Shore Club
Townhouse
Cadet Hotel
Raleigh Hotel
Catalina Hotel
Surfcomber
Delano Hotel
National Hotel
Sagamore
Ritz-Carlton, South Beach
Loews Miami Beach Hotel
The Betsy
Z Ocean Hotel
Villa Paradiso
The Tides
Thompson Ocean Drive
Mondrian South Beach
Essex House
Pelican
The Hotel
Century Hotel
Park Central
Hilton Bentléy
Angler's Resort
Dade Blvd.
Convention Center Dr.
Lincoln Rd. Mall
Espanola Way
Flamingo Park
Lummus Park
Alton Rd.
Michigan Ave.
Jefferson Ave.
Meridian Ave.
Euclid Ave.
Pennsylvania Ave.
Washington Ave.
Collins Ave.
Ocean Dr.
James Ave.
Park Ave.
Liberty Ave.
23rd St.
22nd St.
21st St.
20th St.
18th St.
17th St.
16th St.
15th St.
14th St.
13th St.
12th St.
11th St.
10th St.
9th St.
8th St.
7th St.
0
2 mi
2 km

For expanded reviews, facilities, and current deals, visit Fodors.com. Use the coordinate (⊕ C2) at the end of each review to locate a property on the Where to Stay in the Miami Area map.

DOWNTOWN MIAMI

$$$ HOTEL **Casa Moderna.** In the Marquis high-rise residential building in downtown, Casa Moderna (formerly Tempo Miami) offers a splendid boutique experience of contemporary luxury, with LCD TV screens built into bathroom mirrors and floor-to-ceiling windows peering over downtown. **Pros:** spacious rooms; quiet respite; amazing bathrooms. **Cons:** some open-floor-plan bathrooms lack privacy; windy pool area; amenities shared with condo residents. **TripAdvisor:** "great rooms," "affordable luxury," "modern and refreshing." *Rooms from: $319 ✉ 1100 Biscayne Blvd. ☎ 786/369–0300 🌐 www.casamodernamiami.com 56 rooms No meals ⊕ D4.*

$ HOTEL **Doubletree Grand Hotel Biscayne Bay.** Near the Port of Miami at the north end of downtown, this waterfront hotel offers relatively basic, spacious rooms and convenient access to and from the cruise ships and downtown, making it a good crash pad for budget-conscious cruise passengers. **Pros:** marina; proximity to port. **Cons:** still need a cab to get around; dark lobby and neighboring arcade of shops; worn rooms. **TripAdvisor:** "quiet place with all amenities," "stylish rooms with beautiful views," "just great." *Rooms from: $171 ✉ 1717 N. Bayshore Dr. ☎ 305/372–0313, 800/222–8733 🌐 www.doubletree.com 152 rooms, 56 suites No meals ⊕ E4.*

$$$ HOTEL Fodor's Choice ★ **Epic Hotel.** In the heart of downtown, Kimpton's pet-friendly, freebie-heavy Epic Hotel has 411 guest rooms, each with a spacious balcony (many of them overlook Biscayne Bay) and fabulous modern amenities—Frette linens, iPod docks, slick bath products—that match the modern grandeur of the trendy common areas, which include a fabulous rooftop pool. **TripAdvisor:** "beautiful," "beyond all expectations," "epic by name and nature." *Rooms from: $389 ✉ 270 Biscayne Blvd. ☎ 305/424–5226 🌐 www.epichotel.com 411 rooms No meals ⊕ D4.*

$$$$ HOTEL ★ **Four Seasons Hotel Miami.** Stepping from downtown's busy, business-centric Brickell Avenue into this plush sanctuary, you enter a world of serenity—a soothing water wall greets you, the understated rooms impress you, and the seventh-floor, 2-acre-pool terrace relaxes you. **Pros:** rooms renovated in 2011; sensational service; amazing gym and pool deck. **Cons:** no balconies; caters mostly to business travelers. **TripAdvisor:** "wonderful service and people," "first rate food and service," "best concierge we have ever used." *Rooms from: $459 ✉ 1435 Brickell Ave. ☎ 305/358–3535, 800/819–5053 🌐 www.fourseasons.com/miami 182 rooms, 39 suites No meals ⊕ D5.*

$$ Fodor's Choice ★ **JW Marriott Marquis Miami.** The marriage of Marriott's JW and Marquis brands has created a truly tech-savvy, contemporary, and stylish business-minded hotel—you may never have seen a Marriott quite like this one. **Pros:** excellent gym; amazing technology; pristine rooms. **Cons:** swimming pool receives limited sunshine; lots of conventioneers on weekdays. **TripAdvisor:** "top notch," "spectacular in every way," "utter

elegance." *Rooms from: $289* ✉ *255 Biscayne Blvd Way* ☎ *305/421-8600* 🌐 *www.marriott.com* *257 rooms, 56 suites* *No meals* ✣ *D5.*

$$$$ HOTEL **Mandarin Oriental, Miami.** Clandestinely situated at the tip of prestigious Brickell Key in Biscayne Bay, the Mandarin Oriental feels as exclusive as it does glamorous, with luxurious rooms, exalted restaurants, and the city's top spa, all of which marry the brand's signature Asian style with Miami's bold tropical elegance. **Pros:** man-made beach; intimate vibe; ultraluxurious. **Cons:** small infinity pool; few beach cabanas. **TripAdvisor:** "serenity and class," "simply perfect," "exceptional service." *Rooms from: $519* ✉ *500 Brickell Key Dr.* ☎ *305/913–8288, 866/888–6780* 🌐 *www.mandarinoriental.com* *326 rooms, 31 suites* *No meals* ✣ *E5.*

2

$$$ HOTEL ★ **Viceroy Miami.** This hotel cultivates a brash, supersophisticated South Beach attitude, likely stemming from its flawless guest rooms decked out with dramatic Kelly Wearstler, Asian-inspired interiors and larger-than-life common areas designed by Philippe Starck—note the 15th-floor pool deck and massive spa adorned with awesome, whimsical furnishings and ornaments of Alice in Wonderland proportions. **Pros:** amazing design elements; exceptional pool deck and spa; sleek rooms. **Cons:** poor views from rooms; tiny lobby; some amenities shared with ICON Miami residents. **TripAdvisor:** "rock star getaway," "beautiful," "romantic and unique." *Rooms from: $319* ✉ *485 Brickell Ave.* ☎ *305/503–4400, 866/781–9923* 🌐 *www.viceroymiami.com* *150 rooms, 18 suites* *No meals* ✣ *D5.*

COCONUT GROVE

Coconut Grove is blessed with a number of excellent luxury properties. All are within walking distance of its principal entertainment center, CocoWalk, as well as its marinas. Although this area certainly can't replace the draw of Miami Beach or the business convenience of downtown, about 20 minutes away, it's an exciting bohemian-chic neighborhood with a gorgeous waterfront.

$$$ HOTEL **Ritz-Carlton, Coconut Grove.** Overlooking Biscayne Bay, this business-centric Ritz-Carlton hotel in the heart of Coconut Grove received a face-lift in 2012 that gave its rooms—all with marble baths and private balconies—a refreshed, livelier look. **Pros:** elevated pool deck; high-quality spa; service excellence. **Cons:** near residential area; more business- than leisure-oriented. **TripAdvisor:** "very nice hotel and staff," "wonderful stay," "excellent service." *Rooms from: $329* ✉ *3300 S.W. 27th Ave.* ☎ *305/644–4680, 800/241–3333* 🌐 *www.ritzcarlton.com* *88 rooms, 27 suites* *No meals* ✣ *D5.*

CORAL GABLES

Beautiful Coral Gables is set around its beacon, the national landmark Biltmore Hotel. It also has a couple of big business hotels and one smaller boutique property. The University of Miami is nearby.

$$$ HOTEL **Biltmore Hotel.** Built in 1926, this landmark hotel has had several incarnations over the years—including a stint as a hospital during

World War II—but through it all, this grande dame has remained an opulent reminder of yesteryear, with its palatial lobby and grounds, enormous pool (largest in the lower 48), and distinctive 315-foot tower, which rises above the canopy of trees shading Coral Gables. **Pros:** historic property; gorgeous pool; great tennis and golf. **Cons:** in the suburbs; a car is necessary to get around. **TripAdvisor:** "a classy South Florida retreat," "truly excellent in everything," "magical." *Rooms from: $343 ✉ 1200 Anastasia Ave. ☎ 305/445–1926, 800/727–1926 www.biltmorehotel.com 241 rooms, 39 suites No meals ✥ C5.*

$ B&B/INN **Hotel St. Michel.** The charming, European bed-and-breakfast–inspired Hotel St. **Pros:** personal service; free Continental breakfast; European sensibility. **Cons:** small rooms; could use a renovation; far from the Miami action. **TripAdvisor:** "old country charm," "a European boutique hotel," "step back in time." *Rooms from: $159 ✉ 162 Alcazar Ave. ☎ 305/444–1666, 800/848–4683 www.hotelstmichel.com 29 rooms Breakfast ✥ C5.*

KEY BISCAYNE

There is probably no other place in Miami where slowness is lifted to a fine art. On Key Biscayne there are no pressures, there's no nightlife outside of the Ritz-Carlton's great live Latin music weekends, and the dining choices are essentially limited to the hotel (which has four dining options, including the languorous, Havana-style RUMBAR).

$$$ RESORT Fodor's Choice ★ **Ritz-Carlton Key Biscayne, Miami.** In this ultra-laid-back Key Biscayne setting, it's natural to appreciate the Ritz brand of pampering with luxurious rooms, attentive service, and ample recreational activities for the whole family. **Pros:** on the beach; quiet; luxurious family retreat. **Cons:** far from Miami's nightlife and restaurants. **TripAdvisor:** "great beach," "friendly staff," "amazing stay." *Rooms from: $340 ✉ 455 Grand Bay Dr., Key Biscayne ☎ 305/365–4500, 800/241–3333 www.ritzcarlton.com/keybiscayne 365 rooms, 37 suites No meals ✥ E6.*

FISHER AND BELLE ISLANDS

$$$$ RESORT **Fisher Island Hotel & Resort.** An exclusive private island, just south of Miami Beach but accessible only by ferry, Fisher Island houses an upscale residential community that includes a small inventory of overnight accommodations divided among a few dozen exquisite beachside condos and a handful of opulent cottages and villas, which surround the island's original 1930s Vanderbilt mansion. **Pros:** great private beaches; never crowded; varied on-island dining choices. **Cons:** ferry ride to get on and off island; limited cell service. **TripAdvisor:** "a beautiful hideaway," "private luxury in very relaxed ambience," "amazing resort." *Rooms from: $853 ✉ 1 Fisher Island Dr., Fisher Island ☎ 305/535–6000, 800/537–3708 www.fisherislandclub.com 50 condo units, 7 villas, 3 cottages No meals ✥ E5.*

$$ RESORT **The Standard.** An extension of André Balazs's trendy and hip yet budget-conscious hotel chain, the shabby-chic Standard is a mile from South Beach on an island just over the Venetian Causeway and boasts one of South Florida's most renowned spas and hottest pool scenes. **Pros:** free

bike and kayak rentals; swank pool scene; great spa; inexpensive. **Cons:** slight trek to South Beach; small rooms with no views. **TripAdvisor:** "amazing spa," "perfect relaxing getaway," "great service." *Rooms from: $269 ✉ 40 Island Ave., Belle Isle ☎ 305/673–1717 ⊕ www.standardhotel.com 104 rooms, 1 suite No meals ✥ E4.*

SOUTH BEACH

$$ HOTEL **Angler's Boutique Resort.** This enclave of upscale studios, bi-level duplexes, and villas captures the feel of a sophisticated private Mediterranean villa community, making it easy to forget that the hotel is on busy Washington Avenue, two blocks from the beach. **Pros:** gardened private retreat; excellent service. **Cons:** on busy Washington Avenue; beach is a 10-minute walk. **TripAdvisor:** "best of the best," "great location," "top notch." *Rooms from: $299 ✉ 660 Washington Ave. ☎ 305/534–9600 ⊕ www.theanglersresort.com 24 rooms, 20 suites No meals ✥ G6.*

$$$ HOTEL ★ **The Betsy Hotel.** An art deco treasure elegantly refurbished and totally retro-chic, The Betsy sits directly on world-famous Ocean Drive and delivers the full-throttle South Beach experience with style and pizzazz. **Pros:** unbeatable location; super-fashionable; rooftop lounge; great beach club. **Cons:** rooms are small and often don't have views; service hit or miss (often miss); no pool scene. **TripAdvisor:** "the perfect stay in every way," "great food and great people." *Rooms from: $399 ✉ 1440 Ocean Dr., South Beach ☎ 305/771–0767 ⊕ www.thebetsyhotel.com 41 rooms, 20 suites No meals ✥ H5.*

$$$ HOTEL Fodor's Choice ★ **Cadet Hotel.** A former home to World War II Air Force cadets, this gem has been reimagined as one of the sweetest, quietest hotels in South Beach, offering the antithesis of the sometimes maddening jet-set scene with 35 distinctive rooms exuding understated luxury, beautiful antiques from all around the world, and friendly, stellar service. **Pros:** excellent service; lovely garden and spa pool; originality. **Cons:** tiny swimming pool; limited appeal for the party crowd. **TripAdvisor:** "relaxed," "comfortable place to stay," "friendly staff." *Rooms from: $187 ✉ 1701 James Ave. ☎ 305/672–6688, 800/432–2338 ⊕ www.cadethotel.com 32 rooms, 3 suites Breakfast ✥ H4.*

$$ HOTEL **Catalina Hotel & Beach Club.** The Catalina is the budget party spot in the heart of South Beach's hottest block and attracts plenty of twenty-somethings with its free nightly drink hour, airport shuttles, bike rentals, two fun pools, and beach chairs, all for around $200 a night. **Pros:** free drinks; free bikes; free airport shuttle; good people-watching. **Cons:** service not a high priority; loud; rooms not well maintained. **TripAdvisor:** "relaxing," "excellent choice for party people," "epically amazing." *Rooms from: $209*

WORD OF MOUTH

"I just returned from a trip to the Keys and spent the last night of the trip at the Cadet Hotel (in Miami). Just around the corner from the Delano, it is a little jewel. The rooms are small but immaculate, and the furnishings are very tasteful."

—bon_voyage

✉ 1732 Collins Ave. ☎ 305/674–1160 🌐 www.catalinahotel.com ⇨ 200 rooms 🍴 No meals ✥ H5.

$$ HOTEL **Crowne Plaza Z Ocean Hotel South Beach.** The lauded firm of Arquitectonica designed the rooms and suites at this glossy and bold hideaway, including 27 rooftop suites with terraces, each complete with Jacuzzi, plush chaise longues, and a view of the South Beach skyline. **Pros:** incredible balconies; huge rooms; space-maximizing closets. **Cons:** gym is tiny and basic; not much privacy on rooftop suite decks. **TripAdvisor:** "pretty good lush looking hotel," "friendly service," "provided the perfect stay." *Rooms from: $287* ✉ *1437 Collins Ave.* ☎ *305/672–4554* 🌐 *www.zoceanhotelsouthbeach.com* ⇨ *79 suites* 🍴 *No meals* ✥ *H5.*

$$$ HOTEL **Delano Hotel.** The decor of this grand hotel is inspired by Lewis Carroll's *Alice in Wonderland*, and as you make your way from the sparse, busy, spacious lobby past cascading white curtains and through rooms dotted with strange, whimsical furniture pieces, you will feel like you are indeed falling down a rabbit hole. **Pros:** electrifying design; lounging among the beautiful and famous. **Cons:** crowded; scene-y; small rooms; expensive. **TripAdvisor:** "went the extra mile," "classy and upscale," "amazing location on the beach." *Rooms from: $361* ✉ *1685 Collins Ave.* ☎ *305/672–2000, 800/555–5001* 🌐 *www.delano-hotel.com* ⇨ *184 rooms, 24 suites* 🍴 *No meals* ✥ *H5.*

$$ HOTEL **Essex House.** This restored art deco gem is a favorite with Europeans desiring good location and a somewhat no-frills practical base—expect average-size rooms with midcentury-style red furniture and marble tubs. **Pros:** a social, heated pool; great art deco patio. **Cons:** small pool; not on the beach. **TripAdvisor:** "perfect accommodation," "great location," "beyond my expectations." *Rooms from: $275* ✉ *1001 Collins Ave.* ☎ *305/534–2700* 🌐 *www.essexhotel.com* ⇨ *61 rooms, 15 suites* 🍴 *No meals* ✥ *G6.*

$$$ HOTEL ★ **Hilton Bentley Miami/South Beach.** One of the area's only kid-friendly boutique hotels, this contemporary, design-driven, and artsy Hilton in the emerging and trendy SoFi (South of 5th) district offers families just the right mix of South Beach flavor and wholesome fun while still providing couples a romantic base without any party madness. **Pros:** quiet location; style and grace; family-friendly. **Cons:** small pool; small lobby. **TripAdvisor:** "relaxing," "great location and attitude," "spacious rooms." *Rooms from: $360* ✉ *101 Ocean Dr, South Beach* ☎ *305/938–4600* 🌐 *www.hilton.com* ⇨ *104 rooms, 5 suites* 🍴 *No meals* ✥ *H6.*

$$ HOTEL **The Hotel of South Beach.** Fashion designer Todd Oldham preserved the art deco roots of The Hotel, which inhabits the historic Tiffany building on Collins Avenue, and has expanded the property with 20 new deluxe oceanfront rooms and suites along fabulous Ocean Drive. **Pros:** great service; coolest roof-deck bar in town; good for couples. **Cons:** pool is tiny; rooms in original building lack good views. **TripAdvisor:** "great staff," "great location," "friendly." *Rooms from: $280* ✉ *801 Collins Ave.* ☎ *305/531–2222* 🌐 *www.thehotelofsouthbeach.com* ⇨ *68 rooms, 5 suites* 🍴 *No meals* ✥ *G6.*

$$$ HOTEL **King & Groves Tides South Beach.** Formerly the crown jewel of the Viceroy Hotel Group, the Tides is an exclusive Ocean Drive art deco hotel of

just 45 ocean-facing suites adorned with soft pinks and corals, gilded accents, and marine-inspired decor. **Pros:** superior service; great beach location; ocean views from all suites plus the terrace restaurant. **Cons:** tiny elevators; ubiquitous taxidermy. **TripAdvisor:** "wonderful staff," "doesn't disappoint," "great experience." *Rooms from: $339 ✉ 1220 Ocean Dr. ☎ 305/604–5070 🌐 www.kingandgrove.com/tides-south-beach 45 suites No meals ✥ H5.*

WORD OF MOUTH

"If you can get a hotel room at a good price then you should come to Miami during Art Basel week (first weekend in Dec.). It's a very, very cosmopolitan atmosphere. It will be busy but if you like being in a city then you'll enjoy the energy with all sorts of interesting people, art lovers, artists, celebrities, and art everywhere. It's the best week to feel alive in Miami."

—SoBchBud1

$$$ HOTEL **Loews Miami Beach Hotel.** Loews Miami Beach, a two-tower 800-room megahotel with top-tier amenities, a massive spa, a great pool, and direct beachfront access, is good for families, businesspeople, groups, and pet-lovers. **Pros:** top-notch amenities including a beautiful oceanfront pool and immense spa; pets welcome. **Cons:** intimacy is lost due to its large size. **TripAdvisor:** "right on the beach," "fun for all," "amazing." *Rooms from: $399 ✉ 1601 Collins Ave. ☎ 305/604–1601, 800/235–6397 🌐 www.loewshotels.com/miamibeach 733 rooms, 57 suites No meals ✥ H5.*

$$ HOTEL **Mondrian South Beach.** Just when it seemed that South Beach's spotlight was fading, the Mondrian South Beach infused new life into the beach's lesser-known western perimeter and catalyzed the revival of young SoBe glam—head to toe, the hotel is a living and functioning work of art, an ingenious vision of provocateur Marcel Wanders. **Pros:** trendy; perfect sunsets; party vibe. **Cons:** busy lobby; doses of South Beach attitude; no direct beach access. **TripAdvisor:** "top notch service," "great pool area," "luxurious accommodation paired with excellent service." *Rooms from: $270 ✉ 1100 West Ave., South Beach ☎ 305/514–1500 🌐 www.mondrian-miami.com 233 rooms, 102 suites No meals ✥ F6.*

$$$ HOTEL **National Hotel.** Unlike its neighbors, the National Hotel has maintained its distinct art deco heritage while also keeping up with SoBe's glossy newcomers with its beautifully renovated cabana wing. **Pros:** stunning pool; perfect location. **Cons:** tower rooms are really dated; neighboring hotels can be noisy on the weekends. **TripAdvisor:** "friendly staff," "good atmosphere," "great pool." *Rooms from: $305 ✉ 1677 Collins Ave. ☎ 305/532–2311, 800/327–8370 🌐 www.nationalhotel.com 143 rooms, 9 suites No meals ✥ H5.*

$ HOTEL **Park Central.** This seven-story, oft-photographed 1937 archetypal art deco building on Ocean Drive offers a wide range of somewhat dated, Old Florida–style rooms decorated with black-and-white photos of old beach scenes. **Pros:** spacious rooftop sundeck; comfy beds; perfect location for first trip to Miami. **Cons:** furnishings are so not South Beach; small bathrooms; most rooms have limited views. **TripAdvisor:** "excellent location," "art deco paradise," "great staff." *Rooms* *from: $160 ✉ 640 Ocean Dr. ☎ 305/538–1611, 800/727–5236 ⊕ www.theparkcentral.com ⇆ 113 rooms, 12 suites 🍴 No meals ✣ H6.*

$$ HOTEL **Pelican Miami Beach.** Each awesome room of this Ocean Drive boutique hotel is completely different, fashioned from a mix of antique and garage-sale furnishings selected by the designer of Diesel's clothing-display windows. **Pros:** unique, over-the-top design; central Ocean Drive location. **Cons:** rooms are so tiny that the quirky charm wears off quickly; not smoke-free. **TripAdvisor:** "relaxing and eclectic," "wonderful and unique," "must stay." *$ Rooms from: $225 ✉ 826 Ocean Dr. ☎ 305/673–3373 ⊕ www.pelicanhotel.com ⇆ 28 rooms, 4 suites 🍴 No meals ✣ H6.*

$$ RESORT **The Perry, South Beach.** In late 2011, after parting ways with New York's Gansevoort brand, the Gansevoort Miami Beach was rebranded and revamped, its iconic rooftop pool, pool bar, guest-room balconies, and colossal lobby upgraded to celebrate the divorce. **Pros:** spacious rooms (averaging 700 square feet); big, fun setting with huge pool deck and rooftop. **Cons:** room views aren't amazing; sliding-glass doors are old. **TripAdvisor:** "beautiful property," "amazing pool," "hip vibe." *$ Rooms from: $286 ✉ 2377 Collins Ave. ☎ 305/604–1000 ⊕ www.perrysouthbeachhotel.com ⇆ 334 rooms 🍴 No meals ✣ H4.*

$$$ HOTEL ★ **Raleigh Hotel.** This classy art deco gem balances the perfect amount of style, comfort, and South Beach sultriness, highlighted by the beach's sexiest pool, which was created for champion swimmer Esther Williams. **Pros:** amazing swimming pool; elegance. **Cons:** lobby is a bit dark; not as social as other South Beach hotels. **TripAdvisor:** "relaxing," "awesome all around," "comfortable character." *$ Rooms from: $400 ✉ 1775 Collins Ave., South Beach ☎ 305/534–6300 ⊕ www.raleighhotel.com ⇆ 95 rooms, 10 suites 🍴 No meals ✣ H4.*

$$$$ HOTEL **Ritz-Carlton, South Beach.** A sumptuous affair, the Ritz-Carlton is the only truly luxurious property on the beach that feels like it's on the beach, because its long pool deck leads you right out to the water. **Pros:** luxury rooms; great service; pool with VIP cabanas; great location. **Cons:** too big to be intimate. **TripAdvisor:** "every time it gets better," "superb service," "comfortable rooms." *$ Rooms from: $629 ✉ 1 Lincoln Rd. ☎ 786/276–4000, 800/241–3333 ⊕ www.ritzcarlton.com/southbeach ⇆ 375 rooms 🍴 No meals ✣ H5.*

$$$ HOTEL **Sagamore Hotel.** This supersleek, all-white, all-suite hotel in the middle of the action looks and feels more like an edgy art gallery, filled with brilliant contemporary works, the perfect complement to the posh, gargantuan, 500-square-foot crash pads. **Pros:** sensational pool; great location; good rate specials. **Cons:** can be quiet on weekdays; patchy Wi-Fi. **TripAdvisor:** "friendly chic," "excellent service," "fantastic art." *$ Rooms from: $345 ✉ 1671 Collins Ave. ☎ 305/535–8088 ⊕ www.sagamorehotel.com ⇆ 93 suites 🍴 No meals ✣ H5.*

$$$$ RESORT Fodor's Choice ★ **The Setai.** This opulent hotel feels like an Asian museum, serene and beautiful, with heavy granite furniture lifted by orange accents, warm candlelight, and the soft bubble of seemingly endless ponds complemented by three oceanfront infinity pools (heated to 75, 85, and 95 degrees) that further spill onto the beach's downy sands. **Pros:** quiet and classy; beautiful grounds. **Cons:** somewhat cold aura; TVs are far

from the beds. $ *Rooms from: $775* ✉ *101 20th St.* ☎ *305/520–6000* 🌐 *www.setai.com* *110 rooms* *No meals* ✥ *H4.*

$$$ HOTEL **Shore Club.** In terms of lounging, people-watching, partying, and poolside glitz, the Shore Club ranks among the ultimate South Beach adult playgrounds, despite rather basic guest rooms. **Pros:** good restaurants and bars; nightlife in your backyard. **Cons:** spartan rooms; late-night music. **TripAdvisor:** "home away from home," "awesome rooms," "always fun." $ *Rooms from: $330* ✉ *1901 Collins Ave.* ☎ *305/695–3100, 877/640–9500* 🌐 *www.shoreclub.com* *309 rooms, 79 suites* *No meals* ✥ *H4.*

2

$$ Fodor's Choice ★ **The Surfcomber.** In 2012 the legendary Surfcomber joined the hip Kimpton Hotel group, spawning a fantastic nip-and-tuck that has rejuvenated the rooms and common spaces to reflect vintage luxe and oceanside freshness, and offering a price point that packs the place with a young, vibrant, and sophisticated yet unpretentious crowd. **Pros:** stylish but not pretentious; pet-friendly; on the beach. **Cons:** small bathrooms; front desk often busy. **TripAdvisor:** "amazing staff," "great property," "perfect location." $ *Rooms from: $259* ✉ *1717 Collins Ave., South Beach* ☎ *305/532–7715* 🌐 *www.surfcomber.com* *182 rooms, 6 suites* *No meals* ✥ *H4.*

$$$ HOTEL **Thompson Ocean Drive.** Thompson Hotels has purchased the sleek Hotel Victor, created by the Parisian designer Jacques Garcia, and was as of this writing planning to transform the property piece by piece through late 2013. **Pros:** views from pool deck; high hip factor; good service. **Cons:** small rooms; in process of renovation. **TripAdvisor:** "best on the beach," "excellent location," "great service." $ *Rooms from: $379* ✉ *1144 Ocean Dr.* ☎ *305/779–8700* 🌐 *www.thompsonhotels.com* *91 rooms* *No meals* ✥ *H6.*

$ HOTEL ★ **Townhouse Hotel.** Though sandwiched between the Setai and the Shore Club—two of the coolest hotels on the planet—the Townhouse doesn't try to act all dolled up: it's comfortable being the shabby-chic, lighthearted, relaxed fun hotel on South Beach (and rates include a Parisian-style breakfast). **Pros:** a great budget buy for the style-hungry; direct beach access; hot rooftop lounge. **Cons:** no pool; small rooms not designed for long stays. **TripAdvisor:** "very friendly," "lovely experience," "best place for leisure." $ *Rooms from: $156* ✉ *150 20th St., east of Collins Ave.* ☎ *305/534–3800, 877/534–3800* 🌐 *www.townhousehotel.com* *69 rooms, 2 suites* *Breakfast* ✥ *H4.*

$ B&B/INN **Villa Paradiso.** One of South Beach's best deals, Paradiso has huge rooms with kitchens and a charming tropical courtyard with benches for hanging out at all hours. **Pros:** great hangout spot in courtyard; good value; great location. **Cons:** no pool; no restaurant. **TripAdvisor:** "tons of space," "terrific find," "super sized room." $ *Rooms from: $149* ✉ *1415 Collins Ave.* ☎ *305/532–0616* 🌐 *www.villaparadisohotel.com* *17 studios* *No meals* ✥ *H5.*

$$$$ HOTEL Fodor's Choice ★ **W South Beach.** Fun, fresh, and funky, this W is also the flagship for the brand's evolution toward young sophistication, which means less club music in the lobby, more lighting, and more attention to the $40 million art collection lining the lobby's expansive walls. **Pros:** pool scene; masterful design; ocean-view balconies in each room. **Cons:** not

a classic art deco building; hit-or-miss service. **TripAdvisor:** "hip," "super chic," "amazing suites." *Rooms from: $431 2201 Collins Ave. 305/938–3000 www.whotels.com/southbeach 334 rooms No meals H4.*

MID-BEACH

Where does South Beach end and Mid-Beach begin? With the massive amount of money being spent on former 1950s pleasure palaces like the Fontainebleau and Eden Roc, it could be that Mid-Beach will soon just be considered part of South Beach. North of 24th Street, Collins Avenue curves its way to 44th Street, where it takes a sharp left turn after running into the Soho House Miami and then the Fontainebleau resort. The area between these two points—24th Street and 96th Street—is Mid-Beach. This stretch is undergoing a renaissance, as formerly run-down hotels are renovated and new hotels and condos are built.

$$$$ RESORT **Canyon Ranch Miami Beach.** Physical and mental well-being top the agenda at this 150-suite beachfront hotel, defined by its 70,000-square-foot wellness spa, including a rock-climbing wall, 54 treatment rooms, and 30 exercise classes daily. **Pros:** directly on the beach; spacious suites (mininum 720 square feet); spa treatments exclusive to hotel guests. **Cons:** far from nightlife; not a very gregarious clientele.**TripAdvisor:** "this is the life," "amazing hotel experience," "beyond expectations." *Rooms from: $420 6801 Collins Ave. 305/514–7000 www.canyonranch.com 150 suites No meals F3.*

$ HOTEL ★ **Circa 39 Hotel.** This stylish yet affordable boutique hotel pays attention to every detail and gets them all right. **Pros:** affordable; chic; intimate; beach chairs provided; art deco fireplace. **Cons:** not on the beach side of Collins Avenue. **TripAdvisor:** "a great getaway," "met all our needs," "loved the courtyard." *Rooms from: $169 3900 Collins Ave. 305/538–4900, 877/824–7223 www.circa39.com 96 rooms No meals F4.*

$$$$ RESORT **Eden Roc Renaissance Resort & Spa.** This grand 1950s hotel designed by Morris Lapidus retains its old glamour even as $200 million in renovations and expansions has added sparkle to the rooms and grounds, renewing the allure and swagger of a stay at the Eden Roc. **Pros:** modern rooms; great pools; revival of Golden Age glamour. **Cons:** expensive parking; taxi needed to reach South Beach. **TripAdvisor:** "great location," "beautiful," "absolutely perfect." *Rooms from: $459 4525 Collins Ave. 305/531–0000, 800/327–8337 www.edenrocmiami.com 535 rooms, 96 suites No meals F3.*

$$$ RESORT **Fontainebleau.** Vegas meets art deco at this colossal classic deemed Miami's biggest hotel after its $1 billion reinvention, which spawned more than 1,500 rooms (split among 658 suites in two new all-suite towers and 846 rooms in the two original buildings), 11 renowned restaurants and lounges, LIV nightclub, several sumptuous pools with cabana islands, a state-of-the-art fitness center, and a 40,000-square-foot spa. **Pros:** excellent restaurants; historic design mixed with all-new facilities; fabulous pools. **Cons:** away from the South Beach pedestrian scene; too big to be intimate; bizarre mix of guests doesn't always

mesh. **TripAdvisor:** "beautiful," "great Miami experience," "memorable stay." *Rooms from: $369* ✉ *4441 Collins Ave.* ☎ *305/538–2000, 800/548–8886* 🌐 *www.fontainebleau.com* *846 rooms, 658 suites* *No meals* ✥ *F4.*

$$$ HOTEL **The Palms Hotel & Spa.** Stay here if you're seeking an elegant, relaxed property away from the noise but still near South Beach. **Pros:** tropical garden; relaxed and quiet. **Cons:** standard rooms do not have balconies (but suites do). **TripAdvisor:** "quality and organization," "luxury," "perfect relaxation spot." *Rooms from: $359* ✉ *3025 Collins Ave.* ☎ *305/534–0505, 800/550–0505* 🌐 *www.thepalmshotel.com* *220 rooms, 22 suites* *No meals* ✥ *F4.*

$$$ HOTEL **Soho Beach House.** The Soho Beach House is a throwback to swanky vibes of bygone decades, bedazzled in faded color palates, maritime ambience, and circa-1930s avant-garde furnishings, luring A-listers and wannabes to indulge in the amenity-clad, retro-chic rooms. **Pros:** trendy; two pools; fabulous restaurant; full spa. **Cons:** patchy Wi-Fi; members have priority for rooms; lots of pretentious patrons. **TripAdvisor:** "made me feel young again," "a great Miami experience for adults," "chic and authentic." *Rooms from: $375* ✉ *4385 Collins Ave., Mid-Beach, Miami Beach* ☎ *786/507–7900* 🌐 *www.sohobeachhouse.com* *55 rooms* *No meals* ✥ *F4.*

NORTH MIAMI BEACH AND AVENTURA

Nearing the 100th Street mark on Collins Avenue, Mid-Beach gives way to North Beach. In particular, at 96th Street, the town of Bal Harbour takes over Collins Avenue from Miami Beach. The town runs a mere 10 blocks to the north before the bridge to Sunny Isles. Bal Harbour is famous for its outdoor high-end shops. If you take your shopping seriously, you'll probably want to stay in this area. At 106th Street, the town of Sunny Isles is an appealing, calm, predominantly upscale choice for families looking for a beautiful beach. There is no nightlife to speak of in Sunny Isles, and yet the half-dozen megaluxurious skyscraper hotels that have sprung up here in the past decade have created a niche-resort town from the demolished ashes of much older, affordable hotels. Farther west are the high-rises of Aventura.

$$$$ RESORT Fodor's Choice ★ **Acqualina Resort & Spa on the Beach.** Acqualina raises the bar on Miami beachfront luxury, delivering a fantasy of Mediterranean opulence, with oceanfront lawns and pools that evoke Vizcaya. **Pros:** excellent beach; in-room check-in; luxury amenities; huge spa. **Cons:** no nightlife near hotel; hotel's towering height shades the beach by early afternoon. **TripAdvisor:** "ultimate luxury," "excellent property," "beautiful beach and fabulous service." *Rooms from: $625* ✉ *17875 Collins Ave., Sunny Isles, Miami Beach* ☎ *305/918–8000* 🌐 *www.acqualinaresort.com* *54 rooms, 43 suites* *No meals* ✥ *F1.*

$$$$ RESORT **ONE Bal Harbour.** In one of South Florida's poshest neighborhoods, ONE Bal Harbour exudes contemporary beachfront luxury design, with decadent mahogany-floor rooms, large terraces offering panoramic views of the water and city, over-the-top bathrooms with 10-foot floor-to-ceiling windows, and LCD TVs built into the bathroom mirrors.

Acqualina Resort & Spa on the Beach

Circa 39 Hotel

Biltmore Hotel

Delano Hotel

Fodor's Choice ★

Ritz-Carlton, Key Biscayne

Four Seasons Hotel Miami

The Tides South Beach

Mandarin Oriental

Pros: proximity to Bal Harbour Shops; beachfront; great contemporary-art collection. **Cons:** narrow beach is a bit disappointing; far from nightlife. **TripAdvisor:** "a quiet luxury escape," "a truly luxurious experience," "nice rooms." *Rooms from: $525* ✉ *10295 Collins Ave., North Beach and Aventura, Bal Harbour* ☎ *305/455–5400* 🌐 *www.oneluxuryhotels.com* *124 rooms, 63 suites* *No meals* ✣ *F2.*

$$$$ RESORT Fodor's Choice ★ **St. Regis Bal Harbour Resort.** With the 2012 opening of this $1 billion–plus resort, Miami's North Beach is enjoying a revival of glamour and haute living, with A-list big spenders rushing to stay in this 27-story, 243-room, triple-glass-tower masterpiece. **Pros:** beachfront; beyond glamorous; large rooms. **Cons:** limited lounge space around main pool; limited privacy on balconies. **TripAdvisor:** "clean rooms with great views," "serenity and genie-like service," "absolutely gorgeous." *Rooms from: $659* ✉ *9703 Collins Ave., North Beach and Aventura, Bal Harbour* ☎ *305/993–3300* 🌐 *www.stregisbalharbour.com* *190 rooms, 53 suites* *No meals* ✣ *F2.*

$ HOTEL **Travelodge Monaco Beach Resort.** The last of a dying breed, the dated Travelodge Monaco is a no-frills step up from a youth hostel and caters to those looking for nothing more than a super basic crash pad to return to come nightfall. **Pros:** steps to great beach; bottom-dollar cost; free shuttle to South Beach and Aventura. **Cons:** older rooms; not service-oriented; no Wi-Fi in room, and public Wi-Fi in hotel has a fee. **TripAdvisor:** "inexpensive getaway," "cheap and cheerful," "great location." *Rooms from: $144* ✉ *17501 Collins Ave., Sunny Isles, Miami Beach* ☎ *305/932–2100, 800/227–9006* 🌐 *www.monacomiamibeachresort.com* *110 rooms* *No meals* ✣ *F1.*

$$$$ RESORT **Turnberry Isle Miami.** Golfers and families favor this service-oriented, 300-acre tropical resort with jumbo-size rooms and world-class amenities, including a majestic lagoon pool (winding waterslide and lazy river included), an acclaimed three-story spa and fitness center, and celeb chef Michael Mina's Bourbon Steak restaurant. **Pros:** great golf, pools, and restaurants; free shuttle to Aventura Mall; situated between Miami and Fort Lauderdale. **Cons:** far from the beach; no nightlife. **TripAdvisor:** "beautiful accommodations and great staff," "huge room," "exceptional service." *Rooms from: $499* ✉ *19999 W. Country Club Dr., North Beach and Aventura, Aventura* ☎ *305/932–6200, 855/201–8027* 🌐 *www.turnberryislemiami.com* *408 rooms, 34 suites* *No meals* ✣ *F1.*

NIGHTLIFE

One of Greater Miami's most popular pursuits is bar-hopping. Bars range from intimate enclaves to showy see-and-be-seen lounges to loud, raucous frat parties. There's a New York–style flair to some of the newer lounges, which are increasingly catering to the Manhattan party crowd who escape to South Beach for long weekends. No doubt, Miami's pulse pounds with nonstop nightlife that reflects the area's potent cultural mix. On sultry, humid nights with the huge full moon rising out of the ocean and fragrant night-blooming jasmine intoxicating the senses, who can resist Cuban salsa with some disco and hip-hop thrown in for good measure? When this place throws a party, hips shake, fingers snap,

From salsa and merengue to disco and hip-hop, Miami's dance clubs cater to diverse styles of music.

bodies touch. It's no wonder many clubs are still rocking at 5 am. If you're looking for a relatively nonfrenetic evening, your best bet is one of the chic hotel bars on Collins Avenue.

The *Miami Herald* (*www.miamiherald.com*) is a good source for information on what to do in town. The Weekend section of the newspaper, included in the Friday edition, has an annotated guide to everything from plays and galleries to concerts and nightclubs. The "Ticket" column of this section details the week's entertainment highlights. Or, you can pick up the *Miami New Times* (*www.miaminewtimes.com*), the city's largest free alternative newspaper, published each Thursday. It lists nightclubs, concerts, and special events; reviews plays and movies; and provides in-depth coverage of the local music scene. *Night & Day* is another rundown of the week's cultural highlights. *MIAMI* (*www.modernluxury.com/miami*) and *Ocean Drive* (*www.oceandrive.com*), Miami's model-strewn, upscale fashion and lifestyle magazines, squeeze club, bar, restaurant, and events listings in with fashion spreads, reviews, and personality profiles. Paparazzi photos of local party people and celebrities give you a taste of Greater Miami nightlife before you even dress up to paint the town.

The Spanish-language *El Nuevo Herald* (*www.elnuevoherald.com*), published by the *Miami Herald*, has extensive information on Spanish-language arts and entertainment, including dining reviews, concert previews, and nightclub highlights.

THE VELVET ROPES

How to get past the velvet ropes at the hottest South Beach nightspots? First, if you're staying at a hotel, use the concierge. Decide which clubs you want to check out (consult *Ocean Drive* magazine celebrity pages if you want to be among the glitterati), and the concierge will email, fax, or call in your names to the clubs so you'll be on the guest list when you arrive. This means much easier access and usually no cover charge (which can be upward of $20) if you arrive before midnight. Guest list or no guest list, follow these pointers: Make sure there are more women than men in your group. Dress up—casual chic is the dress code. For men this means no sneakers, no shorts, no sleeveless vests, and no shirts unbuttoned past the top button. For women, provocative and seductive is fine; overly revealing is not. Black is always right. At the door: don't name-drop—no one takes it seriously. Don't be pushy while trying to get the doorman's attention. Wait until you make eye contact, then be cool and easygoing. If you decide to tip him (which most bouncers don't expect), be discreet and pleasant, not big-bucks obnoxious—a $10 or $20 bill quietly passed will be appreciated, however. With the right dress and the right attitude, you'll be on the dance floor rubbing shoulders with South Beach's finest clubbers in no time.

DOWNTOWN MIAMI

BARS AND LOUNGES

Gordon Biersch. This popular brewhouse chain in Downtown's Financial District has glass-enclosed copper pots cranking out tasty ales and lagers, an inspired menu, live music on Thursday and Friday, and a steady happy-hour crowd. ✉ *1201 Brickell Ave., Downtown* ☎ *786/425–1130* 🌐 *www.gordonbiersch.com.*

Fodor's Choice ★ **Tobacco Road.** Opened in 1912, this classic holds Miami's oldest liquor license: No. 0001. Upstairs, in a space that was occupied by a speakeasy during Prohibition, local and national blues bands perform nightly. There is excellent bar food, a dinner menu, and a selection of single-malt scotches, bourbons, and cigars. This is the hangout of grizzled journalists, bohemians en route to or from nowhere, and club kids seeking a way station before the real parties begin. Live blues, R&B, and jazz bands are on tap, along with food and drink, seven days a week. If you like your food and drink the way you like your blues—gritty, honest, and unassuming—then this vintage joint will quickly earn your respect. ✉ *626 S. Miami Ave., Downtown* ☎ *305/374–1198* 🌐 *www.tobacco-road.com.*

DANCE CLUBS

Fodor's Choice ★ **Space Miami.** Want 24-hour partying? Here's the place. Space revolutionized the Miami party scene over a decade ago and still gets accolades as one of the country's best dance clubs. Created from four downtown warehouses, it has two levels (one blasts house music; the other reverberates with hip-hop), an outdoor patio, a New York–style industrial look, and a 24-hour liquor license. It's open on weekends only, and you'll need to look good to be allowed past the velvet ropes. Note that the crowd can sometimes be sketchy. ✉ *34 N.E. 11th St., Downtown* ☎ *305/375–0001* 🌐 *www.clubspace.com.*

COCONUT GROVE

BARS AND LOUNGES

Monty's Raw Bar. The outdoor bar here has Caribbean flair, thanks especially to live calypso and island music. It's very kid-friendly on weekends, when Mom and Dad can kick back and enjoy a beer and the raw bar while the youngsters dance to live music. Evenings bring a DJ and reggae music. ✉ *2550 S. Bayshore Dr., at Aviation Ave.* ☎ *305/856–3992.*

Improv Comedy Club. This long-standing comedy club hosts nationally touring comics nightly. Comedy-club regulars will recognize Margaret Cho and George Wallace, and everyone knows Damon Wayans and Chris Rock, both of whom have taken the stage here. Comedy Jam is held Tuesday. ✉ *Streets of Mayfair, 3390 Mary St., Suite 182, at Grand Ave.* ☎ *305/441–8200* 🌐 *www.miamiimprov.com.*

WYNWOOD/MIDTOWN/DESIGN DISTRICT

BARS AND LOUNGES

Cafeina Wynwood Lounge. This awesome Wynwood watering hole takes center stage during the highly social Gallery Night and Artwalk through the Wynwood Art District, the second Saturday of every month, which showcases the cool and hip art galleries between Northwest 20th and Northwest 36 streets west of North Miami Avenue. For those in the know, the evening either begins or ends at Cafeina, a seductive, design-driven lounge with a gorgeous patio and plenty of art on display. Other weekends, this is still a great place to hang out and get a true feel for Miami's cultural revolution. Open only Thursday–Saturday. ✉ *297 N.W. 23rd St., Wynwood* ☎ *305/438–0792* 🌐 *www.cafeinamiami.com.*

Fodor's Choice ★ **Ricochet Bar & Lounge.** In Miami's booming Midtown district (east of Wynwood and south of the Design District), this upscale, culture-centric bar and lounge presents rotating evenings of live music, DJ-led dance-offs, and chill nights filled with amazing handcrafted cocktails and light bites. Owners Alan Roth and Tommy Pooch wanted to create a quintessential meeting place for art and music lovers—and they definitely succeeded. Paying homage to the artsy neighborhood, the Ricochet Art Series takes shape as limited-edition, disposable coasters displaying custom works from local artists. ✉ *3250 N.E. 1st Ave., Suite 122B, Midtown* ☎ *786/353–0846* 🌐 *www.ricochetlounge.com.*

SOUTH BEACH

BARS AND LOUNGES

Buck 15. In late 2011, this hidden second-floor lounge on Lincoln Lane, just off of Lincoln Road, moved two blocks down to its new home and quickly reestablished itself in the South Beach scene. The tiny club never charges a cover and manages to play amazing music—a rock-heavy mix of songs you loved but haven't heard in ages—and maintain a low-key, unpretentious, hipster attitude. It's a bit of a kitschy frat party for grown-ups. The drinks are reasonably priced, and the well-worn couches are great to dance on. Note that Thursday's long-running

"Simple Life" gay nights have ended. ✉ *437 Lincoln La., Miami Beach* ☎ *305/538–5488* 🌐 *www.buck-15.com.*

Mac's Club Deuce Bar. Although it's a complete dive bar, this pool hall attracts a colorful crowd of clubbers, locals, celebs—and just about anyone else. Locals consider it a top spot for an inexpensive drink and cheap thrills. ✉ *222 14th St., at Collins Ave.* ☎ *305/531–6200.*

Lost Weekend. Slumming celebs and locals often patronize this pool hall–dive bar on quaint Española Way. The hard-core locals are serious about their pastime, so it can be challenging to get a table on weekends. However, everyone can enjoy the full bar, which has 150 kinds of beer and draws an eclectic crowd, from yuppies to drag queens to celebs on the down-low. ✉ *218 Española Way, at Collins Ave.* ☎ *305/672–1707.*

CULTURAL FRIDAYS

On the last Friday of every month Little Havana takes its culture to the streets for *Viernes Culturales* (Cultural Friday 🌐 *www.viernesculturales.org*), held between 7 and 11 pm on 8th Street from 14th to 17th avenues. Art galleries and stores stay open late, and music, mojitos, and avant-garde street performances bring a young, hip crowd to the neighborhood, where they mingle with locals. The annual Calle Ocho festival, held in March, draws more than a million visitors in search of Latin music, food, and shopping.

MOVA. Formerly known as Halo Lounge, this gay bar and lounge off of Lincoln Road is where most GLBT South Beach nights begin (and some end), with ample eye candy to whet the palate for a scintillating night of drinking and partying. The minimalist lounge gives off an undeniably sexy vibe, augmented by the handsome bartenders muddling fresh fruits for the ever-changing avant-garde drink menu. The place gets packed on Friday and Saturday; other nights are hit-or-miss. ✉ *1625 Michigan Ave., South Beach* ☎ *305/534–8181* 🌐 *www.movalounge.com.*

Fodor's Choice ★ **Mynt Lounge.** This is the quintessential celeb-studded, super-VIP, South Beach party where you may or may not be let in, depending on what you wear or whom you know. It's the kind of place where LiLo acts out, Brit-Brit chills out, and Paris Hilton zones out, namely because of the club's "no paparazzi" policy. Admittedly, owner Romain Zago says that "Mynt is for the famous and fabulous." Every summer the lounge undergoes renovations to stay at the top of its game, revealing a slightly different look. ✉ *1921 Collins Ave., Miami Beach* ☎ *305/532–0727* 🌐 *www.myntlounge.com.*

The National. Though it's a low-key affair, don't miss a drink at the National Hotel's nifty wooden bar, one of many elements original to the 1939 building, which give it such a sense of its era that you'd expect to see Ginger Rogers and Fred Astaire hoofing it along the polished lobby floor. The adjoining Martini Room has a great collection of cigar and old airline stickers and vintage Bacardi ads on the walls. ✉ *National Hotel, 1677 Collins Ave., Miami Beach* ☎ *305/532–2311* 🌐 *www.nationalhotel.com.*

Fodor's Choice ★ **Rose Bar and FDR at the Delano.** Renovated in late 2011, the airy lobby lounge at South Beach's trendiest hotel manages to look dramatic but not cold, with long, snow-white, gauzy curtains and huge white pillars separating conversation nooks (this is where Ricky Martin shot the video for "La Vida Loca"). A pool table brings the austerity down to earth. There's also an expansive poolside bar, dotted with intimate poolside beds (bottle service required) and private cabanas to reserve for the evening—for a not-so-nominal fee, of course. What's more is that the famous Florida Room was reinvented and reopened in spring 2012 as FDR, an über-exclusive subterranean lounge, developed by Las Vegas's Light Group. ✉ *1685 Collins Ave., Miami* ☎ *305/672–2000* 🌐 *www.delano-hotel.com.*

★ **SkyBar at the Shore Club.** An entire enclave dedicated to alcohol-induced fun for grown-ups, the SkyBar is actually a collection of adjoining lounges at the Shore Club, including a chic outdoor lounge, the indoor Red Room, and the areas in between, which teem with party-hungry visitors. Splendor-in-the-garden is the theme in the outdoor lounge, accessorized with daybeds and glowing Moroccan lanterns. Groove to dance music in the Red Room, enjoy an aperitif at Nobu, or have a cocktail at the Italian restaurant Terrazza. ✉ *Shore Club Hotel, 1901 Collins Ave., Miami Beach* ☎ *305/695–3100* 🌐 *www.shoreclub.com.*

DANCE CLUBS

Cameo. One of Miami's ultimate dance clubs, Cameo is constantly reinventing itself, but the result always seems to be the same—long lines filled with everyone claiming to be on the guest list, trust-fund babies pulling up in Daddy's wheels, hoochie mamas wearing far too little clothing, and some unsuspecting tourists trying to see what all the fuss is about. The combination makes for some insane partying, especially if the night is headlined by an all-star DJ. You'll find both plentiful dance space and plush VIP lounges. If you can brave the velvet rope and the nonsense described above, Saturday-night parties are the best. ✉ *1445 Washington Ave.* ☎ *305/531–5535* 🌐 *www.cameomiami.com.*

Nikki Beach Club. Smack-dab on the beach, the full-service Nikki Beach Club was once a favorite of SoBe's pretty people and celebrities. Nowadays it's filled with more suburbanites than the "in" crowd. Tepees and hammocks on the sand, dance floors both under the stars and inside, and beach parties make this a true South Beach experience, especially on "Sexy Saturdays." Sunday brunch at the club's restaurant is pretty spectacular. Note that the upstairs Pearl South Beach Restaurant & Champagne Lounge reopened in 2012 and offers excellent eats and a great lounge atmosphere Wednesday–Sunday until 2 am. ✉ *1 Ocean Dr.* ☎ *305/538–1111* 🌐 *www.nikkibeach.com/miami.*

Score. This popular bar is the see-and-be-seen central of Miami's gay community, with plenty of global hotties coming from near and far to show off their designer threads and six-pack abs. DJs spin every night of the week, but Planeta Macho Latin Tuesday is exceptionally popular, as are the upstairs parties on Thursday and the weekend dance-offs. Dress to impress (and then be ready to go shirtless). ✉ *727 Lincoln Rd.* ☎ *305/535–1111* 🌐 *www.scorebar.net.*

★ **Twist.** Twist is a gay institution in South Beach, having been the late-night go-to place for decades, filling to capacity around 2:30 am after the beach's fly-by-night bars and more established lounges begin to die down. There's never a cover here—not even on holidays or during gay pride events. The dark club has several rooms spread over two levels and patios, pumping out different tunes and attracting completely disparate groups. It's not uncommon to have young college boys partying to Top 40 in one room and strippers showing off their stuff to the straight girls in another area, while an all-out hip-hop throwdown is taking place upstairs. ✉ *1057 Washington Ave.* ☎ *305/538–9478* 🌐 *www.twistsobe.com.*

LIVE MUSIC

Jazid. If you're looking for an unpretentious alternative to the velvet-rope nightclubs, this unassuming, live-music hot spot is a standout on the strip. Eight-piece bands play danceable Latin rhythms, as well as reggae, hip-hop, and fusion sounds. Get ready for a late night though, as bands are just getting started at midnight. They play every night of the week. Call ahead to reserve a table. ✉ *1342 Washington Ave.* ☎ *305/673–9372* 🌐 *www.jazid.net.*

MID-BEACH

DANCE CLUBS

Fodor's Choice ★ **LIV Nightclub.** Since its 2009 opening, the Fontainebleau's LIV Nightclub has garnered plenty of attention. It's not hard to see why—if you can get in, that is. LIV is notorious for lengthy lines, so don't arrive fashionably late. Past the velvet ropes, the dance palladium impresses with its lavish decor, well-dressed international crowd, sensational light-and-sound system, and seductive bi-level club experience. ✉ *Fontainebleau Miami Beach, 4441 Collins Ave., Mid-Beach* ☎ *305/674–4680* 🌐 *www.livnightclub.com.*

SHOPPING

Miami teems with sophisticated shopping malls and the bustling avenues of commercial neighborhoods. But this is also a city of tiny boutiques tucked away on side streets—such as South Miami's Red, Bird, and Sunset roads intersection—and outdoor markets touting unusual and delicious wares. Stroll through Spanish-speaking neighborhoods where shops sell clothing, cigars, and other goods from all over Latin America. At an open-air flea-market stall, score an antique glass shaped like a palm tree and fill it with some fresh Jamaican ginger beer from the table next door. Or stop by your hotel gift shop and snap up an alligator magnet for your refrigerator, an ashtray made of seashells, or a bag of gumballs shaped like Florida oranges. Who can resist?

People fly to Miami from all over the world just to shop, and the malls are high on their list of spending spots. Stop off at one or two of these climate-controlled temples to consumerism, many of which double as mega-entertainment centers, and you'll understand what makes Miami such a vibrant shopping destination.

If you're over the climate-controlled slickness of shopping malls and can't face one more food-court "meal," you've got choices in Miami. Head out into the sunshine and shop the city streets, where you'll find big-name retailers and local boutiques alike. Take a break at a sidewalk café to power up on some Cuban coffee or fresh-squeezed OJ and enjoy the tropical breezes.

Beyond the shopping malls and the big-name retailers, Greater Miami has all manner of merchandise to tempt even the casual browser. For consumers on a mission to find certain items—art deco antiques or cigars, for instance—the city streets burst with a rewarding collection of specialty shops.

Pass the mangoes! Greater Miami's farmers' markets and flea markets take advantage of the region's balmy weather and tropical delights to lure shoppers to open-air stalls filled with produce and collectibles.

LITTLE HAVANA

SPECIALTY SHOPS

CIGARS

Sosa Family Cigars. There is a wide selection of premium and house cigars in a humidified shop, once known as Macabi. There's a selection of wines for purchase. Humidors and other accessories are also available. ✉ *3475 S.W. 8th St., Little Havana* ☎ *305/446–2606.*

ONLY IN MIAMI

La Casa de las Guayaberas. Like the name says, this shop sells custom-made guayaberas, the natty four-pocket dress shirts favored by Latin men. Hundreds are also available off the rack. ✉ *5840 S.W. 8th St., Little Havana* ☎ *305/266–9683.*

COCONUT GROVE

MALLS

CocoWalk. This popular three-story indoor-outdoor mall has three floors of nearly 40 shops that stay open almost as late as its popular restaurants. Typically 1990s chain stores like Victoria's Secret and Gap blend with a few specialty shops like Edward Beiner; the space mixes the bustle of a mall with the breathability of an open-air market. Touristy kiosks with cigars, beads, incense, herbs, and other small items are scattered around the ground level, and commercial restaurants and nightlife (Cheesecake Factory, Fat Tuesday, and Paragon Grove 13—a multiscreen, state-of-the-art movie theater with a wine bar and lounge) line the upstairs perimeter. Hanging out and people-watching is something of a pastime here. ✉ *3015 Grand Ave.* ☎ *305/444–0777* 🌐 *www.cocowalk.net.*

SPECIALTY STORES

ANTIQUES

Worth Galleries. Find an enormous selection of fine European antiques (especially lighting and chandeliers) as well as large and eclectic items—railroad crossing signs, statues, English roadsters. There's also vintage furniture, modern art, oil paintings, and silverware, all in a cluttered setting that makes shopping an adventure. ✉ *2520 S.W. 28th La.* ☎ *305/285–1330* 🌐 *www.worthgalleries.com.*

OUTDOOR MARKETS

★ **Coconut Grove Organic Farmers' Market.** This pricey, outdoor organic market is a Saturday ritual for locals. It specializes in a mouthwatering array of local produce as well as such ready-to-eat, raw vegan goodies as cashew butter, homemade salad dressings, and fruit pies. If you are looking for a downright granola crowd and experience, pack your Birkenstocks, because this is it. It's open Saturday from 10 to 7, rain or shine. ✉ *3300 Grand Ave.* ☎ *305/238–7747* 🌐 *www.glaserorganicfarms.com.*

CORAL GABLES

MALLS

Fodor's Choice ★ **Village of Merrick Park.** At this Mediterranean-style shopping-and-dining venue, Neiman Marcus and Nordstrom anchor 115 specialty shops. Designers such as Etro, Tiffany & Co., Burberry, CH Carolina Herrera, and Gucci fulfill most high-fashion needs, and Brazilian contemporary-furniture designer Artefacto provides a taste of the haute-decor shopping options. International food favorite C'est Bon and pampering specialist Elemis Day-Spa offer further indulgences. ✉ *358 San Lorenzo Ave.* ☎ *305/529–0200* 🌐 *www.villageofmerrickpark.com.*

SHOPPING DISTRICTS

Miracle Mile. The centerpiece of the downtown Coral Gables shopping district, lined with trees and busy with strolling shoppers, is home to men's and women's boutiques, jewelry and home-furnishings stores, and a host of exclusive couturiers and bridal shops. Running from Douglas Road to LeJeune Road and Aragon Avenue to Andalusia Avenue, more than 30 first-rate restaurants offer everything from French to Indian cuisine, and art galleries and the Actors' Playhouse give the area a cultural flair. ✉ *Miracle Mile (Coral Way), Douglas Rd. to LeJeune Rd., and Aragon Ave. to Andalusia Ave.* 🌐 *www.shopcoralgables.com.*

SPECIALTY SHOPS

ANTIQUES

Alhambra Antiques. The collection of high-quality furniture and decorative pieces is acquired on annual jaunts to Europe. ✉ *2850 Salzedo St.* ☎ *305/446–1688* 🌐 *www.alhambraantiques.com.*

Valerio Antiques. This shop carries fine French art deco furniture, bronze sculptures, shagreen boxes, and original art glass by Gallé and Loetz, among others. ✉ *250 Valencia Ave.* ☎ *305/448–6779* 🌐 *www.valerioartdeco.com.*

BOOKS

Fodor's Choice ★ **Books & Books, Inc.** Greater Miami's only independent English-language bookshops specialize in contemporary and classical literature as well as in books on the arts, architecture, Florida, and Cuba. At any of its half-dozen locations you can lounge at the old-fashioned in-store café or, at the Coral Gables store, browse the photography gallery. Stores host regular book signings, literary events, poetry, and other readings.

✉ *265 Aragon Ave.* ☎ *305/442–4408* 🌐 *www.booksandbooks.com* ✉ *927 Lincoln Rd., South Beach, Miami Beach* ☎ *305/532–3222* ✉ *9700 Collins Ave., Bal Harbour* ☎ *305/864–4241.*

CIGARS

Sabor Havana Cigars. Spanish wine helps patrons relax while browsing the selection of rare cigars here, where the motto is "It's more than a cigar. It's a lifestyle." ✉ *2309 Ponce de León Blvd., Coral Gables* ☎ *305/444–1764* 🌐 *www.saborhavana.com.*

CLOTHING

Koko & Palenki. Shoe shopaholics come here for the well-edited selection of trendy footwear by Alexandre Birman, Giuseppe Zanotti, Emilia Castillo, Rachel Zoe, Rebecca Minkoff, and others. Handbags and belts add to the selection. Clothing hails from designers like Catherine Malandrino, Issa, J Brand, and Citizens of Humanity. Koko & Palenki also has a store in Aventura Mall. ✉ *Village of Merrick Park, 342 San Lorenzo Ave., Suite 1090, Coral Gables, Miami* ☎ *305/444–0626* 🌐 *www.kokopalenki.com.*

Silvia Tcherassi. The Colombian designer's signature boutique in the Village of Merrick Park features ready-to-wear, feminine, and frilly dresses and separates accented with chiffon, tulle, and sequins. A neighboring atelier at 4101 Ponce de León Boulevard showcases the designer's bridal collection. ✉ *350 San Lorenzo Ave., No. 2140* ☎ *305/461–0009* 🌐 *www.silviatcherassi.com.*

JEWELRY

Jose Roca Fine Jewelry Designs. Jose Roca designs fine jewelry from precious metals and stones. If you have a particular piece that you would like to create, this is the place to have it meticulously executed. ✉ *297 Miracle Mile* ☎ *305/448–2808.*

WYNWOOD/MIDTOWN/DESIGN DISTRICT

SHOPPING NEIGHBORHOODS

★ **Miami Design District.** Miami is synonymous with good design, and this visitor-friendly shopping district is an unprecedented melding of public space and the exclusive world of design. There are more than 200 showrooms and galleries, including Kartell, Ann Sacks, Poliform, and Luminaire. Restaurants like Michael's Genuine Food & Drink and Sra. Martinez also make this trendy neighborhood a hip place to dine. Unlike most showrooms, which are typically the beat of decorators alone, the Miami Design District's showrooms are open to the public and occupy windowed, street-level spaces. The neighborhood even has its own high school (of art and design, of course) and hosts street parties and gallery walks. Although in many cases you'll need a decorator to secure your purchases, browsers are encouraged to consider for themselves the array of rather exclusive furnishings, decorative objects, antiques, and art. ✉ *N.E. 2nd Ave. and N.E. 40th St., Miami Design District* 🌐 *www.miamidesigndistrict.net.*

SPECIALTY SHOPS

ANTIQUES

Artisan Antiques Art Deco. These purveyors of china, crystal, mirrors, and armoires from the French art deco period also draw customers in with an assortment of 1930s radiator covers, which can double as funky sideboards. The shop is open weekdays. ✉ *110 N.E. 40th St., Miami Design District* ☎ *305/573–5619* 🌐 *www.artisanartdeco.com.*

ONLY IN MIAMI

ABC Costume Shop. ABC Costume Shop is a major costume source for TV, movie, and theatrical performances. Open to the public, it rents and sells outfits from Venetian kings and queens to Tarzan and Jane. Hundreds of costumes and accessories, such as wigs, masks, gloves, tights, and makeup, are available to buy off the rack, and thousands are available to rent. ✉ *575 N.W. 24th St., Miami Design District* ☎ *305/573–5657* 🌐 *www.abccostumeshop.com.*

SOUTH BEACH

SHOPPING DISTRICTS

★ **Collins Avenue.** Give your plastic a workout in South Beach shopping at the many high-profile tenants on this densely packed stretch of Collins between 5th and 10th streets, with stores like Club Monaco, M.A.C., Kenneth Cole, Barneys Co-Op, and A/X Armani Exchange. Sprinkled among the upscale vendors are hair salons, spas, cafés, and such familiar stores as the Gap, Diesel, and Urban Outfitters. Be sure to head over one street east to Ocean Drive or west to Washington Avenue for a drink or a light bite, in between shopping on Collins Avenue and Lincoln Road. ✉ *Collins Ave. between 5th and 10th Sts., South Beach, Miami Beach.*

Fodor's Choice ★ **Lincoln Road Mall.** The eight-block-long pedestrian mall is the trendiest place on Miami Beach. Home to more than 150 shops, 20-plus art galleries and nightclubs, about 50 restaurants and cafés, and the renovated Colony Theatre, Lincoln Road, between Alton Road and Washington Avenue, is like the larger, more sophisticated cousin of Ocean Drive. The see-and-be-seen theme is furthered by outdoor seating at every restaurant, where well-heeled patrons lounge and discuss the people (and pet) parade passing by. An 18-screen movie theater anchors the west end of the street, which is where most of the worthwhile shops are; the far east end is mostly discount and electronics shops. Sure, there's a Pottery Barn, a Gap, and a Williams-Sonoma, but the emphasis is on emporiums with unique personalities, like En Avance, Chroma, Base, and Jonathan Adler. ✉ *Lincoln Rd. between Alton Rd. and Washington Ave., South Beach, Miami Beach* 🌐 *www.lincolnroad.org.*

SPECIALTY SHOPS

BEAUTY

Brownes & Co. An entire store dedicated to beauty, body, and soul, Brownes & Co. is a one-stop shop for pampering and high-end vanity. Cosmetics include Molton Brown, Nars, Le Clerc, and others. It also sells herbal remedies and upscale hair and body products from Bumble and Bumble. Just try to resist something from the collection of French, Portuguese, and Italian soaps in various scents and sizes. There's also a fabulous spa and salon on-site. ✉ *1688 Jefferson Ave., South Beach, Miami Beach* ☎ *888/276–9637* 🌐 *www.brownesbeauty.com* ✉ *87 N.E. 40 St., Design District, Miami* ☎ *305/538–7544.*

WORD OF MOUTH

"South Beach is filled with cutting-edge, hip clothing shops for young women, and in addition has great nightlife and a lively street scene."

—montereybob

CLOTHING

★ **Base.** This is the quintessential South Beach fun-and-funky boutique experience. Stop here for men's eclectic clothing, shoes, jewelry, and accessories that mix Japanese design with Caribbean-inspired materials. Constantly evolving, this shop features an intriguing magazine section and groovy home accessories. The often-present house-label designer may help select your wardrobe's newest addition. ✉ *939 Lincoln Rd., South Beach, Miami Beach* ☎ *305/531–4982* 🌐 *www.baseworld.com.*

Fly Boutique. Fly Boutique is where South Beach hipsters flock for the latest arrival of used clothing. At this resale boutique '80s glam designer pieces fly out at a premium price, but vintage camisoles and Levi's corduroys are still a resale deal. Be sure to look up—the eclectic lanterns are also for sale. ✉ *650 Lincoln Rd., South Beach, Miami Beach* ☎ *305/604–8508* 🌐 *www.flyboutiquevintage.com.*

Intermix. This modern New York–based boutique has the variety of a department store. You'll find fancy dresses, stylish shoes, slinky accessories, and trendy looks by sassy and somewhat pricey designers like Chloé, Stella McCartney, Marc Jacobs, Moschino, and Diane von Furstenberg. ✉ *634 Collins Ave., South Beach, Miami Beach* ☎ *305/531–5950* 🌐 *www.intermixonline.com.*

VINTAGE CLOTHING

Consign of the Times. Consign of the Times sells vintage and consignment items by top designers at pre-owned prices, including Chanel suits, Fendi bags, and Celine and Prada treasures. ✉ *1635 Jefferson Ave., South Beach, Miami Beach* ☎ *305/535–0811* 🌐 *www.consignofthetimes.com.*

ONLY IN MIAMI

Dog Bar. Just north of Lincoln Road's main drag, this over-the-top pet boutique caters to enthusiastic animal owners with a variety of unique items for the super-pampered pet (luxurious pet sofas imported from Italy and bling-bling-studded collars). ✉ *1684 Jefferson Ave., South Beach, Miami Beach* ☎ *305/532–5654* 🌐 *www.dogbar.com* ✉ *3301 N.E. 1st Ave., Midtown 4, Wynwood, Miami* ☎ *786/837–0904.*

Genius Jones. This is a modern design store for kids and parents. It's the best—and one of few—places to buy unique children's gifts on South Beach. Pick up furniture, strollers, clothing, home accessories, and playthings, including classic wooden toys, vintage-rock T-shirts by Claude and Trunk, and toys designed by Takashi Murakami and Keith Haring. ✉ *1661 Michigan Ave., South Beach, Miami Beach* ☎ *305/571–2000* 🌐 *www.geniusjones.com.*

JEWELRY

MIA Jewels. On Alton Road, this jewelry and accessories boutique is known for its colorful, gem- and bead-laden, gold and silver earrings, necklaces, bracelets, and brooches by lines such as Cousin Claudine, Amrita, and Alexis Bittar. This is a shoo-in store for everyone: you'll find things for trend lovers (gold-studded chunky Lucite bangles), classicists (long, colorful, wraparound beaded necklaces), and ice lovers (long Swarovski crystal cabin necklaces) alike. ✉ *1439 Alton Rd., South Beach, Miami Beach* ☎ *305/532–6064* 🌐 *www.miajewels.com* ✉ *Aventura Mall, 19575 Biscayne Blvd., North Beach and Aventura, Aventura* ☎ *305/931–2000.*

OUTDOOR MARKETS

Lincoln Road Outdoor Antique and Collectible Market. Interested in picking up samples of Miami's ever-present modern and moderne furniture and accessories? About 125 vendors take over outdoor Lincoln Road Mall every other Sunday, selling multifarious goods that should satisfy postimpressionists, deco-holics, Edwardians, Bauhausers, Goths, and '50s junkies. ✉ *Lincoln Road Mall, South Beach, Miami Beach* 🌐 *www.antiquecollectiblemarket.com.*

NORTH BEACH AND AVENTURA

MALLS

Fodor's Choice ★ **Aventura Mall.** This three-story megamall offers the ultimate in South Florida retail therapy. Aventura houses many global top performers such as the most lucrative Abercrombie & Fitch in the United States, a massive Crate & Barrel, a supersize Nordstrom and Bloomingdale's, and 250 other shops like Façonnable, Coccinelle, and Braccialini, which together create the fifth-largest mall in the United States. This is the one-stop, shop-'til-you-drop retail palladium for locals, out-of-towners, and—frequently—celebrities. ✉ *19501 Biscayne Blvd., Aventura, Aventura* ☎ *305/935–1110* 🌐 *www.aventuramall.com.*

Fodor's Choice ★ **Bal Harbour Shops.** Beverly Hills meets the South Florida sun at this swank collection of 100 high-end shops, boutiques, and department stores, which include such names as Christian Dior, Gucci, Hermès, Salvatore Ferragamo, Tiffany & Co., and Valentino. Many European designers open their first North American signature store at this outdoor, pedestrian-friendly mall, and many American designers open their first boutique outside of New York here. Restaurants and cafés, in tropical garden settings, overflow with style-conscious diners. People-watching at outdoor café Carpaccio is the best in town. The ambience is oh-so-Rodeo Drive. ✉ *9700 Collins Ave., Bal Harbour, Bal Harbour* ☎ *305/866–0311* 🌐 *www.balharbourshops.com.*

SPORTS AND THE OUTDOORS

Sun, sand, and crystal-clear water mixed with an almost nonexistent winter and a cosmopolitan clientele make Miami and Miami Beach ideal for year-round sunbathing and outdoor activities. Whether the priority is showing off a toned body, jumping on a Jet Ski, or relaxing

Continued on page 110

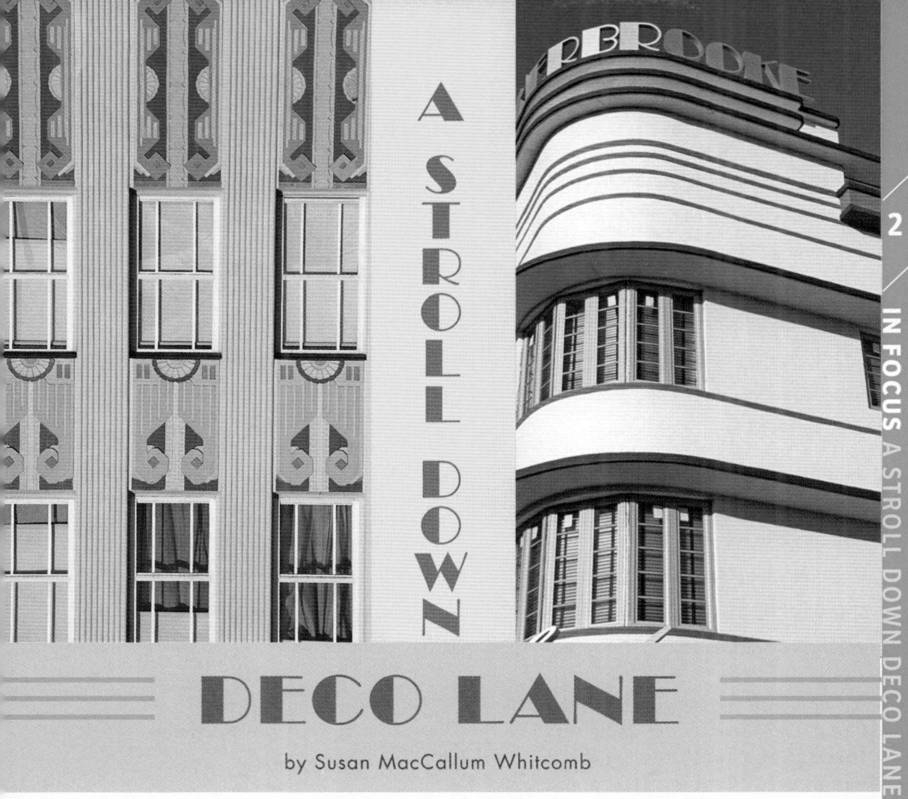

A STROLL DOWN DECO LANE

by Susan MacCallum Whitcomb

"It was an age of miracles, it was an age of art, it was an age of excess, and it was an age of satire."

—F. Scott Fitzgerald, *Echoes of the Jazz Age*

The 1920s and '30s brought us flappers and gangsters, plunging stock prices and soaring skyscrapers, and plenty of headline-worthy news from the arts scene, from talking pictures and the jazz craze to fashions where pearls piled on and sequins dazzled. These decades between the two world wars also gave us an art style reflective of the changing times: art deco.

Distinguished by geometrical shapes and the use of industrial motifs that fused the decorative arts with modern technology, art deco became the architectural style of choice for train stations and big buildings across the country (think New york's Radio City Music Hall and Empire State Building).

Using a steel-and-concrete box as the foundation, architects dipped into art deco's grab bag of accessories, initially decorating facades with spheres, cylinders, and cubes. They later borrowed increasingly from industrial design, stripping elements used in ocean liners and automobiles to their streamlined essentials.

The style was also used in jewelry, furniture, textiles, and advertising. The fact that it employed inexpensive materials, such as stucco or terrazzo, helped art deco thrive during the Great Depression.

MIAMI BEACH'S ART DECO DISTRICT

With its warm beaches and tropical surroundings, Miami Beach in the early 20th century was establishing itself as America's winter playground. During the roaring '20s luxurious hostelries resembling Venetian palaces, Spanish villages, and French châteaux sprouted up. In the 1930s, middle-class tourists started coming, and more hotels had to be built. Designers like Henry Hohauser chose art deco for its affordable yet distinctive design.

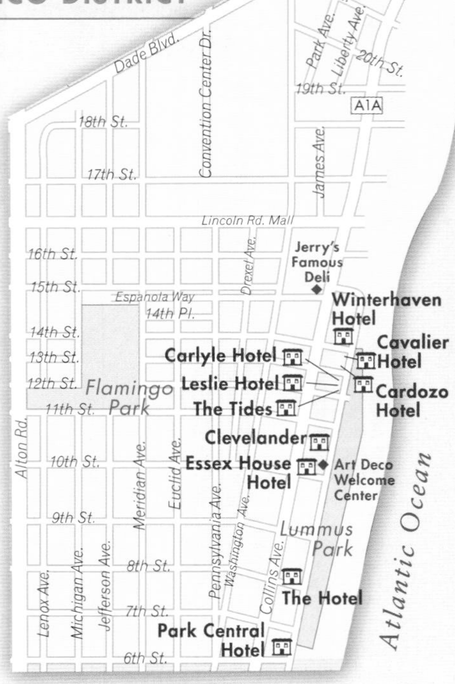

An antidote to the gloom of the Great Depression, the look was cheerful and tidy. And with the whimsical additions of portholes, colorful racing bands, and images of rolling ocean waves painted or etched on the walls, these South Beach properties created an oceanfront fantasy world for travelers.

Many of the candy-colored hotels have survived and been restored. They are among the more than 800 buildings of historical significance in South Beach's art deco district. Composing much of South Beach, the 1-square-mi district is bounded by Dade Boulevard on the north, the Atlantic Ocean on the east, 6th Street on the south, and Alton Road on the west.

Because the district as a whole was developed so rapidly and designed by like-minded architects—**Henry Hohauser, L. Murray Dixon, Albert Anis,** and their colleagues—it has amazing stylistic unity. Nevertheless, on this single street you can trace the evolution of period form from angular, vertically emphatic early deco to aerodynamically rounded Streamline Moderne. The relatively severe Cavalier and more curvaceous Cardozo are fine examples of the former and latter, respectively.

To explore the district, begin by loading up on literature in the **Art Deco Welcome Center** (✉ *1001 Ocean Dr.* ☎ *305/763–8026* 🌐 *www.mdpl.org*). If you want to view these historic properties on your own, just start walking. A four-block stroll north on Ocean Drive gets you up close to camera-ready classics: the **Clevelander** (1020), the **Tides** (1220), the **Leslie** (1244), the **Carlyle** (1250), the **Cardozo** (1300), the **Cavalier** (1320), and the **Winterhaven** (1400).

ART DECO TOURS

See the bold looks of classic Art Deco architecture along Ocean Drive.

SELF-GUIDED AUDIO TOURS

Expert insight on the architecture and the area's history is yours on the Miami Design Preservation League's (MDPL) 90-minute self-guided walks that use an iPod or cell phone and include a companion map. You can pick up the iPod version and companion map at the Art Deco Welcome Center from 9:30 AM to 5 PM daily; the cost is $15. The cell-phone option ($10) is available anytime by calling 786/312–1229 and charging the amount to your credit card; your payment allows you access to audio commentary for up to 24 hours after purchase.

WALKING TOURS

The MDPL's 90-minute "Ocean Drive and Beyond" group walking tour gives you a guided look at area icons, inside and out. (A number of interiors are on the itinerary, so it's a good chance to peek inside spots that might otherwise seem off-limits.) Morning tours depart at 10:30 AM from the Art Deco Welcome Center Gift Shop on Tuesday, Wednesday, Friday, Saturday, and Sunday. An evening tour departs at 6:30 PM on Thursdays. Reservations can't be made in advance, so arrive 15–20 minutes early to buy tickets ($20).

BIKE TOURS

Rather ride than walk? Half-day cycling tours of the city's art deco history are organized daily for groups (5 or more) by **South Beach Bike Tours** (☎ *305/673–2002* ⊕ *www.southbeach-biketours.com*). The $59 cost includes equipment, snacks, and water.

ART DECO WEEKEND

Tours, lectures, film screenings, and dozens of other '30s-themed events are on tap in mid-January, during the annual **Art Deco Weekend** (☎ *305/672–2014*, ⊕ *www.ArtDecoWeekend.com*). Festivities—many of them free—kick off with a Saturday morning parade and culminate in a street fair. More than a quarter of a million people join in the action, which centers on Ocean Drive between 5th and 15th streets.

Celebrate the 1930s during Art Deco Weekend.

ARCHITECTURAL HIGHLIGHTS

Cavalier Hotel

FRIEZE DETAIL, CAVALIER HOTEL

The decorative stucco friezes outside the Cavalier Hotel at 1320 Ocean Drive are significant for more than aesthetic reasons. Roy France used them to add symmetry (adhering to the "Rule of Three") and accentuate the hotel's verticality by drawing the eye upward. The pattern he chose also reflected a fascination with ancient civilizations engendered by the recent rediscovery of King Tut's tomb and the Chichén Itzá temples.

Park Central Hotel

LOBBY FLOOR, PARK CENTRAL HOTEL

Terrazzo—a compound of cement and stone chips that could be poured, then polished—is a hallmark of deco design. Terrazzo floors typically had a geometric pattern, like this one in the Park Central Hotel, a 1937 building by Henry Hohauser at 640 Ocean Drive.

Essex House Hotel

CORNER FACADE, ESSEX HOUSE HOTEL

Essex House Hotel, a 1938 gem that appears permanently anchored at 1001 Collins Avenue, is a stunning example of Maritime deco (also known as Nautical Moderne). Designed by Henry Hohauser to evoke an ocean liner, the hotel is rife with marine elements, from the rows of porthole-style windows and natty racing stripes to the towering smokestack-like sign. With a prow angled proudly into the street corner, it seems ready to steam out to sea.

The Hotel

NEON SPIRE, THE HOTEL

The name spelled vertically in eye-popping neon on the venue's iconic aluminum spire—Tiffany—bears evidence of the hotel's earlier incarnation. When the L. Murray Dixon–designed Tiffany Hotel was erected at 801 Collins Avenue in 1939, neon was still a novelty. Its use, coupled with the spire's rocket-like shape, combined to create a futuristic look influenced by the sci-fi themes then pervasive in popular culture.

Jerry's Famous Deli

ENTRANCE, JERRY'S FAMOUS DELI

Inspired by everything from car fenders to airplane noses, proponents of art deco's Streamline Moderne look began to soften buildings' hitherto boxy edges. But when Henry Hohauser designed Hoffman's Cafeteria in 1940 he took moderne to the max. The landmark at 1450 Collins Avenue (now Jerry's Famous Deli) has a sleek, splendidly curved facade. The restored interior echoes it through semicircular booths and rounded chair backs.

ARCHITECTURAL TERMS

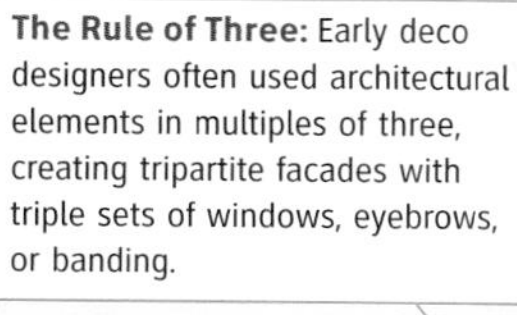

The Rule of Three: Early deco designers often used architectural elements in multiples of three, creating tripartite facades with triple sets of windows, eyebrows, or banding.

Eyebrows: Small shelf-like ledges that protruded over exterior windows were used to simultaneously provide much-needed shade and serve as a counterpoint to a building's strong vertical lines.

Tropical Motifs: In keeping with the setting, premises were plastered, painted, or etched with seaside images. Palm trees, sunbursts, waves, flamingoes, and the like were particularly common.

Banding: Enhancing the illusion that these immobile structures were rapidly speeding objects, colorful horizontal bands (also called "racing stripes") were painted on exteriors or applied with tile.

Stripped Classic: The most austere version of art deco (sometimes dubbed Depression Moderne) was used for buildings commissioned by the Public Works Administration.

(top) Hotel Marlin; (left) Sherbrooke Hotel; (right) U.S. Post Office in Miami Beach.

in a tranquil natural environment, there's a beach tailor-made to please. But tanning and water sports are only part of this sun-drenched picture. Greater Miami has championship golf courses and tennis courts, miles of bike trails along placid canals and through subtropical forests, and skater-friendly concrete paths amidst the urban jungle. For those who like their sports of the spectator variety, the city offers up a bonanza of pro teams for every season. There's even a crazy ball-flinging game called jai alai that's billed as the fastest sport on earth.

In addition to contacting venues directly, get tickets to major events from **Ticketmaster** (☎ *800/745–3000* 🌐 *www.ticketmaster.com*).

BASEBALL

Miami Marlins. Miami's baseball team, formerly known as the Florida Marlins, is settling into its new home, Marlins Park—a 37,000-seat retractable-roof baseball stadium on the grounds of Miami's famous Orange Bowl. Go see the team that came out of nowhere to beat the New York Yankees and win the 2003 World Series. Home games are April through early October. ✉ *Marlins Park, Marlin Way, N.W. 7th St. and N.W. 14th Ave., 2 miles west of downtown, Little Havana* ☎ *305/626–7378, 877/627–5467 for tickets* 🌐 *www.marlins.com* *$10–$395, parking $10.*

BASKETBALL

Miami Heat. The 2006 NBA champs play at the 19,600-seat, waterfront AmericanAirlines Arena. The state-of-the-art venue features restaurants, a wide patio overlooking Biscayne Bay, and a silver sun-shape special-effects scoreboard with rays holding wide-screen TVs. During Heat games, when the 1,100 underground parking spaces are reserved for season-ticket holders, you can park across the street at Miami's Bayside Marketplace ($20), at metered spaces along Biscayne Boulevard, or in lots on side streets, where prices range from $5 to $25, depending on the distance from the arena (a limited number of spaces for people with disabilities are available on-site for non-season-ticket holders). Better yet, take the Metromover to the Park West or Freedom Tower station. Home games are held November through April. ✉ *AmericanAirlines Arena, 601 Biscayne Blvd., Downtown* ☎ *800/462–2849 ticket hotline, 786/777–1000 arena* 🌐 *www.nba.com/heat* *$10–$500.*

BICYCLING

Perfect weather and flat terrain make Miami–Dade County a popular place for cyclists; however, biking here can also be quite dangerous. Be very vigilant when biking on Miami Beach, or better yet, steer clear and bike the beautiful paths of Key Biscayne.

Key Cycling. Rent bikes for $15 for two hours, $24 for the day, and $80 for the week. ✉ *328 Crandon Blvd., Key Biscayne* ☎ *305/361–0061* 🌐 *www.keycycling.com.*

Miami Beach residential buildings tower over the sand.

Miami Beach Bicycle Center. On Miami Beach the proximity of this shop to Ocean Drive and the ocean itself makes it worth the $24 per day, $8 per hour, or $80 for the week. ✉ *601 5th St., South Beach, Miami Beach* ☎ *305/674–0150* 🌐 *www.bikemiamibeach.com.*

BOATING AND SAILING

Boating, whether on sailboats, powerboats, luxury yachts, WaveRunners, or Windsurfers, is a passion in Greater Miami. The Intracoastal Waterway, wide and sheltered Biscayne Bay, and the Atlantic Ocean provide ample opportunities for fun aboard all types of watercraft.

The best windsurfing spots are on the north side of the Rickenbacker Causeway at Virginia Key Beach or to the south at, go figure, Windsurfer Beach. Kite surfing adds another level to the water sports craze.

MARINAS

Bayshore Landing Marina. This bustling marina is home to a lively seafood restaurant that's good for viewing the nautical eye candy. ✉ *2560 S. Bayshore Dr., Coconut Grove* ☎ *305/854–7997* 🌐 *www.bayshorelanding.com.*

Haulover Marine Center. It may be low on glamour, but this marina, with a bait-and-tackle shop and a 24-hour marine gas station, is high on service. ✉ *15000 Collins Ave., north of Bal Harbour, Miami Beach* ☎ *305/945–3934* 🌐 *www.haulovermarinecenter.net.*

Miami Beach Marina. Near the Art Deco District there is plenty to entice sailors and landlubbers alike: restaurants, charters, boat rentals, a complete marine-hardware store, a dive shop, excursion vendors, a large grocery store, a fuel dock, concierge services, and 400 slips accommodating vessels of up to 250 feet. There's also a U.S. Customs clearing station and a charter service, Florida Yacht Charters. Picnic tables along the docks make this marina especially visitor-friendly. ✉ *300 Alton Rd., South Beach, Miami Beach* ☎ *305/673–6000* 🌐 *www.miamibeachmarina.com.*

OUTFITTERS AND EXPEDITIONS

Club Nautico. You can rent 18- to 34-foot powerboats and 52- to 54-foot yachts through this national boat-rental company with two Miami locations. Half- to full-day rentals range from $399 to $3,600. ✉ *Miami Beach Marina, 300 Alton Rd., #112, Miami Beach* ☎ *305/673–2502* 🌐 *www.club-nautico.com* ✉ *Crandon Park Marina, 4000 Crandon Blvd., Key Biscayne.*

Playtime Watersports. All types of boat rentals are available from this company, but a regularly scheduled evening sunset cruise through Biscayne Bay departs nightly at 6:30 pm. ✉ *Maribella Marina, 801 Brickell Ave., Downtown* ☎ *305/216–6967* 🌐 *www.playtimewatersport.com.*

Sailboards Miami. Rent paddle boards and kayaks or learn how to windsurf. These friendly folks say they teach more windsurfers each year than anyone in the United States and promise to teach you to windsurf within two hours—for $79. ✉ *.7 miles after toll plaza on Rickenbacker Causeway, Key Biscayne* ☎ *305/361–7245* 🌐 *www.sailboardsmiami.com.*

GOLF

Greater Miami has more than 30 private and public courses. Costs at most courses are higher on weekends and in season, but you can save by playing on weekdays and after 1 or 3 pm, depending on the course—call ahead to find out when afternoon-twilight rates go into effect. For information on most courses in Miami and throughout Florida, you can visit 🌐 *www.floridagolferguide.com.*

★ **Biltmore Golf Course.** The 18-hole, par-71 championship course, known for its scenic layout, has been restored to its original Donald Ross design, circa 1925. Greens fees in season range from $145 to $165 for nonresidents. The optional cart is $27. ✉ *1210 Anastasia Ave., Coral Gables* ☎ *305/460–5364* 🌐 *www.biltmorehotel.com.*

Crandon Golf Key Biscayne. Overlooking the bay, this top-rated 18-hole, par-72 public course comes with a beautiful tropical setting. Nonresidents should expect to pay $180 for a round in season (December 15–April) and roughly half that off-season. Deeply discounted twilight rates apply after 3 pm. ✉ *6700 Crandon Blvd., Key Biscayne* ☎ *305/361–9129* 🌐 *www.crandongolfclub.com.*

★ **Shula's Hotel & Golf Club.** In northern Miami, this hotel has one of the longest championship courses in the area (7,055 yards, par 72), a lighted par-3 course, and a golf school. Greens fees are $62–$140, depending on the season and time. You'll pay in the lower range on weekdays, more on weekends, and $45 after 3 pm. Golf carts are included. The par-3 course is $12 weekdays, $15 weekends. The club hosts more than

75 tournaments a year. ✉ *7601 Miami Lakes Dr., 154th St. Exit off Rte. 826, Miami Lakes* ☎ *305/820–8106* 🌐 *www.shulasgolfclub.com.*

Fodor's Choice ★ **Doral Golf Resort and Spa.** Of its five courses and many annual tournaments this resort, just west of Miami proper, is best known for the par-72 Blue Monster course and the PGA's annual World Golf Championship. (The week of festivities planned around this tournament, which offers $8 million in prize money, brings hordes of pro-golf aficionados in late March.) Greens fees range from $65 to $325. Carts are not required. ✉ *4400 N.W. 87th Ave., 36th St. Exit off Rte. 826, Doral* ☎ *305/592–2000, 800/713–6725* 🌐 *www.doralresort.com.*

GUIDED TOURS

BOAT TOURS

Duck Tours Miami. Amphibious vehicles make daily 90-minute tours of Miami that combine land and sea views. Comedy and music are part of the mix. Tickets are $18 for children 4–12. ✉ *1661 James Ave., South Beach, Miami Beach* ☎ *305/673–2217* 🌐 *www.ducktourssouthbeach.com* 🎟 *$32.*

Island Queen, Island Lady, and Miami Lady. Double-decker, 140-passenger tour boats docked at Bayside Marketplace set sail daily for 90-minute narrated tours of the Port of Miami and Millionaires' Row. For an extra $9 the company offers transportation between Bayside Marketplace and certain hotels. ✉ *401 Biscayne Blvd., Downtown* ☎ *305/379–5119* 🌐 *www.islandqueencruises.com* 🎟 *$27.*

RA Charters. For something a little more private and luxe, sail out of the Dinner Key Marina in Coconut Grove. Full- and half-day charters include sailing lessons, with occasional extended trips to the Florida Keys. For a romantic night, have Captain Masoud pack some gourmet fare and sail sunset to moonlight while you enjoy Biscayne Bay's spectacular skyline view of Miami. ✉ *Coconut Grove* ☎ *305/666–7979, 305/989–3959* 🌐 *www.racharters.com* 🎟 *Call for prices.*

WALKING TOURS

Art Deco District Tour. Operated by the Miami Design Preservation League, this is a 90-minute guided walking tour that departs from the league's welcome center at Ocean Drive and 10th Street. It starts at 10:30 am Friday through Wednesday, and at 6:30 pm Thursday. Alternatively, you can go at your own pace with the league's self-guided iPod audio tour, which takes roughly an hour and a half. ✉ *1001 Ocean Dr., South Beach, Miami Beach* ☎ *305/763–8026* 🌐 *www.mdpl.org* 🎟 *$20 guided tour, $15 audio tour.*

Miami Urban Tours. For customized offerings, try Miami's Cultural Community Tours, offered by Urban Tours, which specializes in group and private excursions. They put together interactive tours (read: you actually step into each locale) that cover all the urban enclaves between Little Havana and Little Haiti, providing a perspective on Miami's Caribbean, African-American, and Hispanic heritage. ☎ *305/416–6868* 🌐 *www.miamiculturaltours.com.*

SCUBA DIVING AND SNORKELING

Diving and snorkeling on the offshore coral wrecks and reefs on a calm day can be very rewarding. Chances are excellent that you'll come face-to-face with a flood of tropical fish. One option is to find Fowey, Triumph, Long, and Emerald reefs in 10- to 15-foot dives that are perfect for snorkelers and beginning divers. On the edge of the continental shelf a little more than 3 miles out, these reefs are just ¼ mile away from depths greater than 100 feet. Another option is to paddle around the tangled prop roots of the mangrove trees that line the coast, peering at the fish, crabs, and other creatures hiding there. ⇨ *For the best snorkeling in Miami-Dade, head to Biscayne National Park. See the Everglades chapter for more information.*

Artificial Reefs. Perhaps the area's most unusual diving options are its artificial reefs. Since 1981, Miami-Dade County's Department of Environmental Resources Management has sunk tons of limestone boulders and a water tower, army tanks, and almost 200 boats of all descriptions to create a "wreckreational" habitat where divers can swim with yellow tang, barracudas, nurse sharks, snapper, eels, and grouper. The website offers an interactive map of wreck locations. Dive outfitters are familiar with most of these artificial reefs and can take you to the best ones. ✉ *Miami Beach* 🌐 *www.miamidade.gov/derm/artificial_reef_locator.asp*.

OUTFITTERS

Divers Paradise of Key Biscayne. This complete dive shop and diving-charter service next to the Crandon Park Marina, includes equipment rental and scuba instruction with PADI and NAUI affiliation. Dive trips are offered Tuesday through Friday at 10 and 1, weekends 8:30 and 1:30. The trip is $60. ✉ *4000 Crandon Blvd., Key Biscayne* ☎ *305/361–3483* 🌐 *www.keydivers.com*.

South Beach Dive and Surf Center. Dedicated to all things ocean, this center offers diving and snorkeling trips (at least four times weekly) as well as surfboard rentals and lessons. The Discover Scuba course trains diving newcomers on Tuesday, Thursday, and Saturday at 8 am at a PADI-affiliated dive shop. Advance classes follow at 9:45 am. Night dives take place each Wednesday at 5, and wreck and reef dives on Sundays at 7:30 am. The center also runs dives in Key Largo's Spiegel Grove, the second-largest wreck ever to be sunk for the intention of recreational diving, and in the Neptune Memorial Reef, inspired by the city of Atlantis and created in part using the ashes of cremated bodies. Boats depart from marinas in Miami Beach and Key Largo, in the Florida Keys. ✉ *850 Washington Ave., South Beach, Miami Beach* ☎ *305/531–6110* 🌐 *www.southbeachdivers.com*.

3

The Everglades

WORD OF MOUTH

"Sign up at the Ernest Coe Visitor Center or call the Flamingo Visitor Center for the free ranger-led canoe tour. . . . No experience necessary—maneuvering the long canoe through the twists and turns of the mangroves was a challenge, but very fun."

—JC98

WELCOME TO THE EVERGLADES

TOP REASONS TO GO

★ **Fun Fishing:** Cast for some of the world's fightingest game fish—600 species of fish in all—in the Everglades' backwaters.

★ **Abundant Birdlife:** Check hundreds of birds off your life list, including—if you're lucky—the rare Everglades snail kite.

★ **Cool Kayaking:** Do a half-day trip in Big Cypress National Preserve or reach for the ultimate—the 99-mile Wilderness Trail.

★ **Swamp Cuisine:** Hankering for alligator tail and frogs' legs? Or how about swamp cabbage, made from hearts of palm? Better yet, try stone-crab claws fresh from the traps.

★ **Gator-Spotting:** This is ground zero for alligator viewing in the United States, and there's a good bet you'll leave having spotted your quota.

1 Everglades National Park. Alligators, Florida panthers, black bears, manatees, dolphins, bald eagles, and roseate spoonbills call this vast habitat home.

2 Biscayne National Park. Mostly under water, this is where the string of coral reefs and islands that form the Florida Keys begins.

GETTING ORIENTED

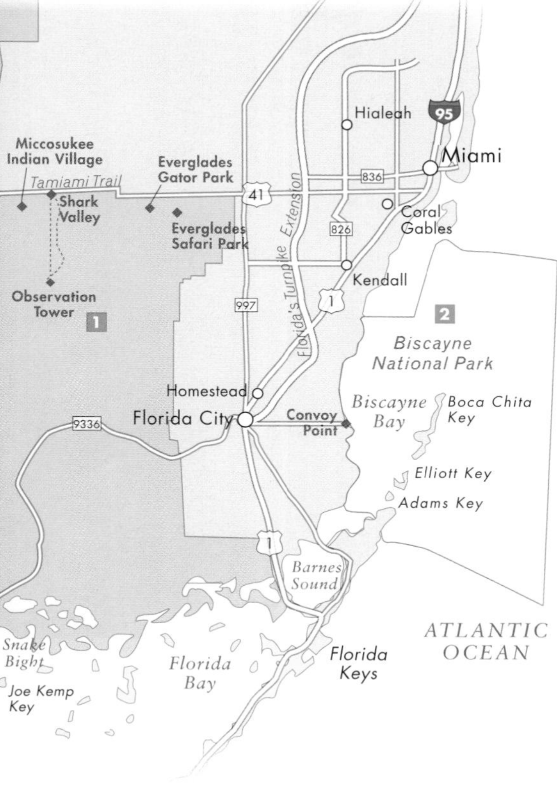

The southern third of the Florida peninsula is largely taken up by protected government land that includes Everglades National Park, Big Cypress National Preserve, and Biscayne National Park. Miami lies to the northeast, and Naples and Marco Island are northwest. Land access to Everglades National Park is primarily by two roads. The park's main road traverses the southern Everglades from the gateway towns of Homestead and Florida City to the outpost of Flamingo, on Florida Bay. In the northern Everglades, Tamiami Trail (U.S. 41) runs from the Greater Miami area on the east coast or from Naples on the west coast to the western park entrance in Everglades City at Route 29.

3 Big Cypress National Preserve. Neighbor to Everglades National Park, it's an outdoors-lover's paradise.

THE FLORIDA EVERGLADES

by Lynne Helm

Alternately described as elixir of life or swampland muck, the Florida Everglades is one of a kind—a 50-mi-wide "river of grass" that spreads across hundreds of thousands of acres. It moves at varying speeds depending on rainfall and other variables, sloping south from the Kissimmee River and Lake Okeechobee to estuaries of Biscayne Bay, Florida Bay, and the Ten Thousand Islands.

Today, apart from sheltering some 70 species on America's endangered list, the Everglades also embraces more than 7 million residents, 50 million annual tourists, 400,000 acres of sugarcane, and the world's largest concentration of golf courses.

Demands on the land threaten the Everglades' finely balanced ecosystem. Irrigation canals for agriculture and roadways disrupt natural water flow. Drainage for development leaves wildlife scurrying for new territory. Water runoff, laced with fertilizers, promotes unnatural growth of swamp vegetation. What remains is a miracle of sorts, given decades of these destructive forces.

Creation of the Everglades required unique conditions. South Florida's geology, linked with its warm, wet subtropical climate, is the perfect mix for a marshland ecosystem. Layers of porous, permeable limestone create water-bearing rock, soil, and aquifers, which in turn affects climate, weather, and hydrology.

This rock beneath the Everglades reflects Florida's geologic history—its crust was once part of the African region. Some scientists theorize that continental shifting merged North America with Africa, and then continental rifting later pulled North America away from the African continent but took part of northwest Africa with it—the part that is today's Florida. The Earth's tectonic plates continued to migrate, eventually placing Florida at its current location as a land mass jutting out into the ocean, with the Everglades at its tip.

EXPERIENCING THE ECOSYSTEMS

Eight distinct habitats exist within Everglades National Park, Big Cypress National Preserve, and Biscayne National Park.

ECOSYSTEMS	EASY WAY	MORE ACTIVE WAY
COASTAL PRAIRIE: An arid region of salt-tolerant vegetation lies between the tidal mud flats of Florida Bay and dry land. **Best place to see it: The Coastal Prairie Trail**	Take a guided boat tour of Florida Bay, leaving from Flamingo Marina.	Hike the Coastal Prairie Trail from Eco Pond to Clubhouse Beach.
CYPRESS: Capable of surviving in standing water, cypress trees often form dense clusters called "cypress domes" in natural water-filled depressions. **Best place to see it: Big Cypress National Preserve**	Drive U.S. 41 (also known as Tamiami Trail—pronounced Tammy-Amee), which cuts across Southern Florida, from Naples to Miami.	Hike (or drive) the scenic Loop Road, which begins off Tamiami Trail, running from the Loop Road Education Center to Monroe Station.
FRESH WATER MARL PRAIRIE: Bordering deeper sloughs are large prairies with marl (clay and calcium carbonate) sediments on limestone. Gators like to use their toothy snouts to dig holes in prairie mud. **Best place to see it: Pahayokee Overlook**	Drive there from the Ernest F. Coe Visitor Center.	Take a guided tour, either through the park service or from permitted, licensed guides. You also can set up camp at Long Pine Key.
FRESH WATER SLOUGH AND HARDWOOD HAMMOCK: Shark River Slough and Taylor Slough are the Everglades' two sloughs, or marshy rivers. Due to slight elevation amid sloughs, dense stands of hardwood trees appear as teardrop-shaped islands. **Best place to see it: The Observation Tower**	Take a two-hour guided tram tour from the Shark Valley Visitor Center to the tower and back.	Walk or bike (rentals available) the route to the tower via the tram road and (walkers only) Bobcat Boardwalk trail and Otter Cave Hammock Trail.
MANGROVE: Spread over South Florida's coastal channels and waterways, mangrove thrives where Everglades fresh water mixes with salt water. **Best place to see it: The Wilderness Waterway**	Picnic at the area near Long Pine Key, which is surrounded by mangrove, or take a water tour at Biscayne National Park.	Boat your way along the 99-mi Wilderness Waterway. It's six hours by motorized boat, seven days by canoe.
MARINE AND ESTUARINE: Corals, sponges, mollusks, seagrass, and algae thrive in the Florida Bay, where the fresh waters of the Everglades meet the salty seas. **Best place to see it: Florida Bay**	Take a boat tour from the Flamingo Visitor Center marina.	Canoe or kayak on White Water Bay along the Wilderness Waterway Canoe Trail.
PINELAND: A dominant plant in dry, rugged terrain, the Everglades' diverse pinelands consist of slash pine forest, saw palmettos, and more than 200 tropical plant varieties. **Best place to see it: Long Pine Key trails**	Drive to Long Pine Key, about 6 mi off the main road from Ernest F. Coe Visitor Center.	Hike or bike the 28 mi of Long Pine Key trails.

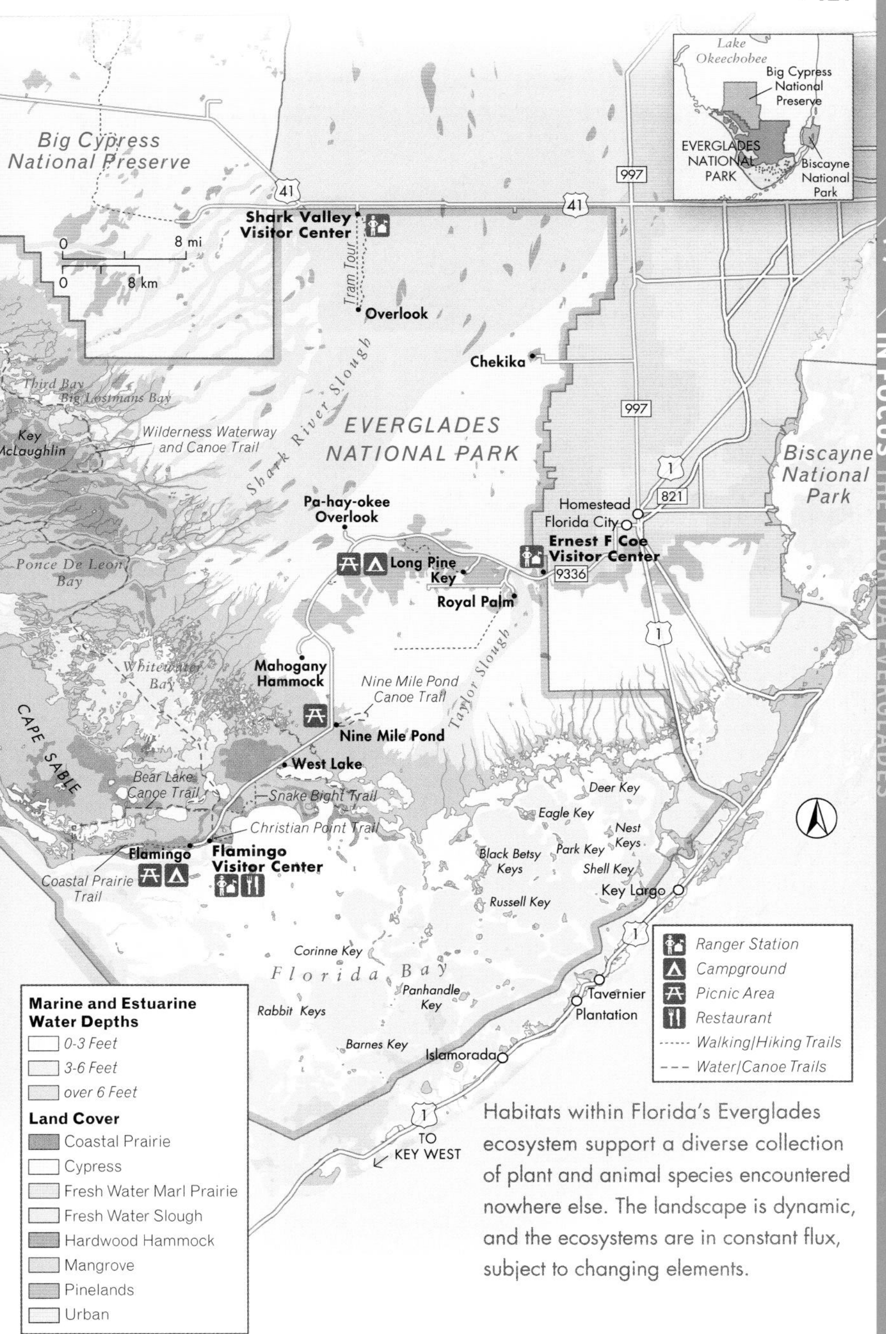

Habitats within Florida's Everglades ecosystem support a diverse collection of plant and animal species encountered nowhere else. The landscape is dynamic, and the ecosystems are in constant flux, subject to changing elements.

FLORA

❶ Cabbage Palm

It's virtually impossible to visit the Everglades and not see a cabbage palm, Florida's official state tree. The cabbage palm (or sabal palm), graces assorted ecosystems and grows well in swamps. **Best place to see them:** At Loxahatchee National Wildlife Refuge (embracing the northern part of the Everglades, along Alligator Alley), throughout Everglades National Park, and at Big Cypress National Preserve.

❷ Sawgrass

With spiny, serrated leaf blades resembling saws, sawgrass inspired the term "river of grass" for the Everglades. **Best place to see them:** Both Shark Valley and Pahayokee Overlook provide terrific vantage points for gazing over sawgrass prairie; you also can get an eyeful of sawgrass when crossing Alligator Alley, even when doing so at top speeds.

❸ Mahogany

Hardwood hammocks of the Everglades live in areas that rarely flood because of the slight elevation of the sloughs, where they're typically found.
Best place to see them: Everglades National Park's Mahogany Hammock Trail (which has a boardwalk leading to the nation's largest living mahogany tree).

❹ Mangrove

Mangrove forest ecosystems provide both food and protected nursery areas for fish, shellfish, and crustaceans.
Best place to see them: Along Biscayne National Park shoreline, at Big Cypress National Preserve, and within Everglades National Park, especially around the Caple Sable area.

❺ Gumbo Limbo

Sometimes called "tourist trees" because of peeling reddish bark (not unlike sunburns).
Best place to see them: Everglades National Park's Gumbo Limbo Trail and assorted spots throughout the expansive Everglades.

FAUNA

❶ American Alligator

In all likelihood, on your visit to the Everglades you'll see at least a gator or two. These carnivorous creatures can be found throughout the Everglades swampy wetlands.

Best place to see them: Loxahatchee National Wildlife Refuge (also sheltering the endangered Everglades snail kite) and within Everglades National Park at Shark Valley or Anhinga Trail. Sometimes (logically enough) gators hang out along Alligator Alley, basking in early morning or late-afternoon sun along four-lane I–75.

❷ American Crocodile

Crocs gravitate to fresh or brackish water, subsisting on birds, fish, snails, frogs, and small mammals.

Best place to see them: Within Everglades National Park, Big Cypress National Preserve, and protected grounds in or around Billie Swamp Safari.

❸ Eastern Coral Snake

This venomous snake burrows in underbrush, preying on lizards, frogs, and smaller snakes.

Best place to see them: Snakes typically shy away from people, but try Snake Bight or Eco Pond near Flamingo, where birds are also prevalent.

❹ Florida Panther

Struggling for survival amid loss of habitat, these shy, tan-colored cats now number around 100, up from lows of near 30.

Best place to see them: Protected grounds of Billie Swamp Safari sometimes provide sightings during tours. Signage on roadway linking Tamiami Trail and Alligator Alley warns of panther crossings, but sightings are rare.

❺ Green Tree Frog

Typically bright green with white or yellow stripes, these nocturnal creatures thrive in swamps and brackish water.

Best place to see them: Within Everglades National Park, especially in or near water.

● =Extremely Common ● =Very Common ● =Somewhat Common ● =Rare

BIRDS

❶ Anhinga

The lack of oil glands for waterproofing feathers helps this bird to dive as well as chase and spear fish with its pointed beak. The Anhinga is also often called a "water turkey" because of its long tail, or a "snake bird" because of its long neck.

Best place to see them: The Anhinga Trail, which also is known for attracting other wildlife to drink during especially dry winters.

❷ Blue-Winged Teal

Although it's predominantly brown and gray, this bird's powder-blue wing patch becomes visible in flight. Next to the mallard, the blue-winged teal is North America's second most abundant duck, and thrives particularly well in the Everglades.

Best place to see them: Near ponds and marshy areas of Everglades National Park or Big Cypress National Preserve.

❸ Great Blue Heron

This bird has a varied palate and enjoys feasting on everything from frogs, snakes, and mice to shrimp, aquatic insects, and sometimes even other birds! The all-white version, which at one time was considered a separate species, is quite common to the Everglades.

Best place to see them: Loxahatchee National Wildlife Refuge or Shark Valley in Everglades National Park.

❹ Great Egret

Once decimated by plume hunters, these monogamous, long-legged white birds with S-shaped necks feed in wetlands, nest in trees, and hang out in colonies that often include heron or other egret species.

Best place to see them: Throughout Everglades National Park, along Alligator Alley, and sometimes even on the fringes of Greater Fort Lauderdale.

❺ Greater Flamingo

Flocking together and using long legs and webbed feet to stir shallow waters and mud flats, color comes a couple of years after hatching from ingesting shrimplike crustaceans along with fish, fly larvae, and plankton.

Best place to see them: Try Snake Bight or Eco Pond, near Flamingo Marina.

❻ Osprey

Making a big comeback from chemical pollutant endangerment, ospreys (sometimes confused with bald eagles) are distinguished by black eyestripes down their faces. Gripping pads on feet with curved claws help them pluck fish from water.

Best place to see them: Look near water, where they're fishing for lunch in the shallow areas. Try the coasts, bays, and ponds of Everglades National Park. They also gravitate to trees You can usually spot them from the Gulf Coast Visitor Center, or you can observe them via boating in the Ten Thousand Islands.

❼ Roseate Spoonbill

These gregarious pink-and-white birds gravitate toward mangroves, feeding on fish, insects, amphibians, and some plants. They have long, spoon-like bills, and their feathers can have a touch of red and yellow. These birds appear in the Everglades year-round.

Best place to see them: Sandy Key, southwest of Flamingo, is a spoonbill nocturnal roosting spot, but at sunrise these colorful birds head out over Eco Pond to favored day hangouts throughout Everglades National Park.

❽ Wood Stork

Recognizable by featherless heads and prominent bills, these birds submerge in water to scoop up hapless fish. They are most common in the early spring and often easiest to spot in the morning.

Best place to see them: Amid the Ten Thousand Island areas, Nine Mile Pond, Mrazek Pond, and in the mangroves at Paurotis Pond.

● =Extremely Common ● =Very Common ● =Somewhat Common ● =Rare

THE BEST EVERGLADES ACTIVITIES

HIKING

Top experiences: At Big Cypress National Preserve, you can hike along designated trails or push through unmarked acreage. (Conditions vary seasonally, which means you could be tramping through waist-deep waters.) Trailheads for the Florida National Scenic Trail are at Loop Road off U.S. 41 and Alligator Alley at mile marker 63.

What will I see? Dwarf cypress, hardwood hammocks, prairies, birds, and other wildlife.

For a short visit: A 6.5-mi section from Loop Road to U.S. 41 crosses Robert's Lake Strand, providing a satisfying sense of being out in the middle nowhere.

With more time: A 28-mi stretch from U.S. 41 to I–75 (Alligator Alley) reveals assorted habitats, including hardwood hammocks, pinelands, prairie, and cypress.

Want a tour? Big Cypress ranger-led exploration starts from the Oasis Visitor Center, late November through mid-April.

WALKING

Top experiences: Everglades National Park magnets: wheelchair accessible walkways at Anhinga Trail, Gumbo Limbo Trail, Pahayokee Overlook, Mahogany Hammock, and West Lake Trail.

What will I see? Birds and alligators at Anhinga; tropical hardwood hammock at Gumbo Limbo; an overlook of the River of Grass from Pahayokee's tower; a subtropical tree island with massive mahogany growth along Mahogany Hammock; and a forest of mangrove trees on West Lake Trail.

For a short visit: Flamingo's Eco Pond provides for waterside wildlife viewing.

With more time: Shark Valley lets you combine the quarter-mile Bobcat Boardwalk (looping through sawgrass prairie and a bayhead) with the 1-mi-long round-trip Otter Cave, allowing you to steep in subtropical hardwood hammock.

Want a tour? Pahayokee and Flamingo feature informative ranger-led walks.

The Anhinga Trail near the Royal Palm Visitor Center at Everglades National Park

BOATING

Top experiences: Launch a boat from the Gulf Coast Visitors Center or Flamingo Marina. Bring your own watercraft or rent canoes or skiffs at either location.

What will I see? Birds from bald eagles to roseate spoonbills, plus plenty of mangrove and wildlife—and maybe even some baby alligators with yellow stripes.

For a short visit: Canoe adventurers often head for Hells Bay, a 3-mi stretch about 9 mi north of Flamingo. Or put in at the Turner River alongside the Tamiami Trail in the Big Cypress National Preserve and paddle all the way (about eight hours) to Chocoloskee Bay at Everglades City.

With more time: Head out amid the Ten Thousand Islands and lose yourself in territory once exclusively the domain of only the hardiest pioneers and American Indians. If you've got a week or more for paddling, the 99-mi Wilderness Waterway stretches from Flamingo to Everglades City.

Want a tour? Sign on for narrated boat tours at the Gulf Coast or Flamingo visitor center.

BIRD WATCHING

Top experiences: Anhinga Trail, passing over Taylor Slough.

What will I see? Anhinga and heron sightings are a nearly sure thing, especially in early morning or late afternoon. Also, alligators can be seen from the boardwalk.

For a short visit: Even if you're traveling coast to coast at higher speeds via Alligator Alley, chances are you'll spot winged wonders like egrets, osprey, and heron.

With more time: Since bird-watching at Flamingo can be a special treat early in the morning or late in the afternoon, try camping overnight even if you're not one for roughing it. Reservations are recommended. (Flamingo Lodge remains under reconstruction from 2005 hurricane damage.)

Want a tour? Ranger-led walks at Pahayokee and from Everglades National Park visitor centers provide solid birding background for novices.

(top left) Tourists cruise the Everglades by airboat; (bottom left) Green Heron; (right) Eastern Meadowlark

THE BEST EVERGLADES ACTIVITIES

BIKING

Top experiences: Shark Valley (where bicycling is allowed on the tram road) is great for taking in the quiet beauty of the Everglades. Near Ernest F. Coe Visitor Center, Long Pine Key's 14-mi nature trail also can be a way to bike happily away from folks on foot.

What will I see? At Shark Valley, wading birds, turtles, and, probably alligators. At Long Pine Key, shady pinewood with subtropical plants and exposed limestone bedrock.

For a short visit: Bike on Shark Valley tram road but turn around to fit time schedule.

With more time: Go the entire 15-mi tram road route, which has no shortcuts. Or try the 22-mi route of Old Ingraham Highway near the Royal Palm Visitor Center, featuring mangrove, sawgrass, and birds (including hawks).

Want a tour? In Big Cypress National Preserve, Bear Island Bike Rides (8 mi round-trip over four to five hours) happen on certain Saturdays.

SNORKELING

Top experiences: Biscayne National Park, where clear waters incorporate the northernmost islands of the Florida Keys.

What will I see? Dense mangrove swamp covering the park shoreline, and, in shallow waters, a living coral reef and tropical fish in assorted colors.

For a short visit: Pick a sunny day to optimize your snorkeling fun, and be sure to use sunscreen.

With more time: Advanced snorkel tours head out from the park on weekends to the bay, finger channels, and around shorelines of the barrier islands. Biscayne National Park also has canoe and kayak rentals, picnic facilities, walking trails, fishing, and camping.

Want a tour? You can swim and snorkel or stay dry and picnic aboard tour boats that depart from Biscayne National Park's visitor center.

(top left) Biking near the Shark Valley Visitor Area. (top right) Snorkeling on the surface in the Atlantic Ocean.

DID YOU KNOW?

You can tell you're looking at a crocodile if you can see its lower teeth protruding when its jaws are shut, whereas an alligator shows no teeth when his mouth is closed. Gators are much darker in color—a grayish black—compared with the lighter tan color of crocodiles. Alligators' snouts are also much broader than their long, thin crocodilian counterparts.

THE STORY OF THE EVERGLADES

Dreams of draining southern Florida took hold in the early 1800s, expanding in the early 1900s to convert large tracts from wetlands to agricultural acreage. By the 1920s, towns like Fort Lauderdale and Miami boomed, and the sugar industry—which came to be known as "Big Sugar"—established its first sugar mills. In 1947 Everglades National Park opened as a refuge for wildlife.

Meanwhile, the sugar industry grew. In its infancy, about 175,000 tons of raw sugar per year was produced from fields totaling about 50,000 acres. But once the U.S. embargo stopped sugar imports from Cuba in 1960 and laws restricting acreage were lifted, Big Sugar took off. Less than five years later, the industry produced 572,000 tons of sugar and occupied nearly a quarter of a million acres.

Fast-forward to 2008, to what was hailed as the biggest conservation deal in U.S. history since the creation of the national parks. A trailblazing restoration strategy hinged on creating a water flow-way between Lake Okeechobee and the Everglades by buying up and flooding 187,000 acres of land. The country's largest producers of cane sugar agreed to sell the necessary 187,000 acres to the state of Florida for $1.75 billion. Environmentalists cheered.

But within months, news broke of a scaled-back land acquisition plan: $1.34 billion to buy 180,000 acres. By spring 2009, the restoration plan had shrunk to $536,000 to buy 73,000 acres. With the purchase still in limbo, critics claim the state might overpay for acreage appraised at pre-recession values and proponents fear dwindling revenues may derail the plan altogether.

The Big Sugar land deal is part of a larger effort to preserve the Everglades. In 2010, two separate lawsuits charged the state, along with the United States Environmental Protection Agency, with stalling Everglades cleanup that was supposed to begin in 2006. "Glacial delay" is how one judge put it. The state must reduce phosphorus levels in water that flows to the Everglades or face fines and sanctions for violating the federal Clean Water Act. The fate of the Everglades remains in the balance.

Updated by
Lynne Helm

More than 1.5 million acres of South Florida's 4.3 million acres of subtropical, watery wilderness were given national-park status and protection in 1947 with the creation of Everglades National Park. It is one of the country's largest national parks and is recognized by the world community as a Wetland of International Importance, an International Biosphere Reserve, and a World Heritage Site. Come here if you want to spend the day biking, hiking, or boating in deep, raw wilderness with lots of wildlife.

To the east of Everglades National Park, Biscayne National Park brings forth a pristine, magical, subtropical Florida. It is the nation's largest marine park and the largest national park within the continental United States boasting living coral reefs. A small portion of the park's 172,000 acres consists of mainland coast and outlying islands, but 95% remains under water. Of particular interest are the mangroves and their tangled masses of stiltlike roots that thicken the shorelines. These "walking trees," as some locals call them, have curved prop roots, which arch down from the trunk, and aerial roots that drop from branches. The trees draw fresh water from salt water and create a coastal nursery that sustains myriad types of marine life. You can see Miami's high-rise buildings from many of Biscayne's 44 islands, but the park is virtually undeveloped and large enough for escaping everything that Miami and the Upper Keys have become. To truly escape, don scuba-diving or snorkeling gear, and lose yourself in the wonders of the coral reefs.

On the northern edge of Everglades National Park is Big Cypress National Preserve, one of South Florida's least-developed watersheds. Established by Congress in 1974 to protect the Everglades, it comprises extensive tracts of prairie, marsh, pinelands, forested swamps, and sloughs. Hunting is allowed, as is off-road-vehicle use. Come here if you like alligators. Stop at the Oasis Visitor Center to walk the boardwalk with alligators lounging underneath, and then drive Loop Road for a backwoods experience. If time permits, kayak the Turner River.

Surrounding the parks and preserve are several small communities: Everglades City, Florida City, and Homestead, home to many area outfitters.

PLANNING

WHEN TO GO

Winter is the best, and busiest, time to visit the Everglades. Temperatures and mosquito activity are more tolerable, low water levels concentrate the resident wildlife, and migratory birds swell the avian population. In late spring the weather turns hot and rainy, and tours and facilities are less crowded. Migratory birds depart, and you must look harder to see wildlife. Summer brings intense sun and afternoon rainstorms. Water levels rise and mosquitoes descend, making outdoor activity virtually unbearable, unless you swath yourself in netting. Mosquito repellent is a necessity any time of year.

GETTING HERE AND AROUND

Miami International Airport (MIA) is 34 miles from Homestead and 47 miles from the eastern access to Everglades National Park. ⇨ *For MIA airline carrier information, refer to the Miami chapter.* Shuttles run between MIA and Homestead. Southwest Florida International Airport (RSW), in Fort Myers, a little over an hour's drive from Everglades City, is the closest major airport to the Everglades' western access. On-demand taxi transportation from the airport to Everglades City is available, and costs $150 for up to three passengers ($10 each for additional passengers).

ABOUT THE RESTAURANTS

Dining in the Everglades area centers on mom-and-pop places that serve hearty home-style food, and small eateries that specialize in fresh local fare: alligator, fish, stone crab, frogs' legs, and Florida lobster from the Keys. American Indian restaurants serve local favorites as well as catfish, Indian fry bread (a flour-and-water flatbread), and pumpkin bread. A growing Hispanic population around Homestead means plenty of authentic, inexpensive Latin cuisine, with an emphasis on Cuban and Mexican dishes. Restaurants in Everglades City, especially those along the river, have fresh seafood, particularly succulent, sustainable stone crab. These places are mostly casual to the point of rustic, and are often closed in late summer or fall. For finer dining, go to Marco Island or Naples.

ABOUT THE HOTELS

Accommodations near the parks range from inexpensive to moderate and offer off-season rates in summer, when rampant mosquito populations discourage spending much time outdoors, especially at dusk. If you're spending several days exploring the east coast Everglades, stay in one of the park's campgrounds; 11 miles away in Homestead–Florida City, where there are reasonably priced motels and RV parks; or in the Florida Keys or the Greater Miami–Fort Lauderdale area. Lodgings and campgrounds are also available on the Gulf Coast in Everglades City, Marco Island, and Naples, which has the most upscale accommodations in the area. Florida City's selection is mostly of the chain variety and geared toward business travelers.

HOTEL AND RESTAURANT COSTS

Prices in the restaurant reviews are the average cost of a main course at dinner or, if dinner is not served, at lunch. Prices in the hotel reviews are the lowest cost of a standard double room in high season. Prices do not include taxes (6%, more in some counties, and 1%–5% tourist tax for hotel rooms).

ABOUT CAMPING

For an intense stay in the "real" Florida, consider one of some four-dozen backcountry campsites deep in Everglades National Park, many inland, some on the beach. You'll have to carry in your food, water, and supplies, and carry out all your trash. You'll also need a site-specific permit, available on a first-come, first-served basis from the Flamingo or Gulf Coast visitor centers. Permits cost $10, plus $2 per person per night for sites, with a 14-night limit, and are issued only up to 24 hours in advance. Front-country camping fees at park campgrounds are $16 per night.

ABOUT ACTIVITIES

⇨ *While outfitters are listed with the parks and preserve, see our What's Nearby section later in this chapter for information about each town.*

EVERGLADES NATIONAL PARK

45 miles southwest of Miami International Airport.

If you're heading across South Florida on U.S. 41 from Miami to Naples, you'll breeze right through the Everglades. Also known as Tamiami Trail, this mostly two-lane road along much of the route skirts the edge of Everglades National Park and cuts across the Big Cypress National Preserve. You'll also be near the park if you're en route from Miami to the Florida Keys on U.S. 1, which travels through Homestead and Florida City, two communities east of the main park entrance. Basically, if you're in South Florida, you can't get away from at least fringes of the Everglades. With tourist strongholds like Miami, Naples, and the Florida Keys so close by, travelers from all over the world typically make day trips to the park.

Everglades National Park has three main entry points: the park headquarters at Ernest F. Coe Visitor Center, southwest of Homestead and Florida City; the Shark Valley area, in the northern reaches and accessed by Tamiami Trail (U.S. 41); and the Gulf Coast Visitor Center, just south of Everglades City to the west and closest to Naples.

You can explore on your own or participate in free ranger-led hikes, bicycle tours, bird-watching tours, and canoe trips; the number and variety of these excursions are greatest from mid-December through Easter, and some excursions (canoe trips, for instance) typically aren't offered in the sweltering summer. Among the more popular are the

CLOSE UP

War on Snakes

In a January 2012 press conference on the Tamiami Trail, personnel from the U.S. Department of the Interior announced a nationwide ban on the import of Burmese pythons and other non-native, large constrictor snakes, including the yellow anaconda and both northern and southern African pythons. Interior Secretary Ken Salazar called the action a "milestone in the protection of the Everglades."

Pythons, sometimes freed by owners no longer wanting to care for large, growing snakes, consume native wildlife, competing with native predators. Biologists estimate thousands of Burmese pythons are now overrunning the Everglades, where they have eaten everything from marsh rabbits to alligators. Some studies suggest they could spread farther, possibly outside Florida. One python captured in the Everglades had consumed a full-grown deer.

(The U.S. Fish and Wildlife Service said it will consider listing as injurious five other non-native snake species: the reticulated python, the boa constrictor, DeSchauensee's anaconda, the green anaconda, and the Beni anaconda.)

Anhinga Amble, a 50-minute walk around the Taylor Slough (departs from the Royal Palm Visitor Center), and the Early Bird Special, a 90-minute walk centered on birdlife (departs from Flamingo Visitor Center at 7:30 am). Ask at the visitor centers for details.

PARK ESSENTIALS

Admission Fees $10 per vehicle, $5 per pedestrian, bicycle, or motorcycle. Admission, payable at gates, is good for seven consecutive days at all park entrances. Annual passes are $25.

Admission Hours The park is open daily, year-round, and both the main entrance near Florida City and Homestead, and the Gulf Coast entrance are open 24 hours. The Shark Valley entrance is open 8:30 am to 6 pm.

COE VISITOR CENTER TO FLAMINGO

About 30 miles from Miami.

The most popular access to Everglades National Park is via the park headquarters entrance just southwest of Homestead and Florida City. If you're coming to the Everglades from Miami, take Route 836 West to Route 826/874 South to the Homestead Extension of Florida's Turnpike, U.S. 1, and Krome Avenue (Route 997/old U.S. 27). To reach the Ernest F. Coe Visitor Center from Homestead, go right (west) from U.S. 1 or Krome Avenue onto Route 9336 (Florida's only four-digit route) in Florida City and follow signs to the park entrance.

EXPLORING

To explore this section of the park, follow Route 9336 from the park entrance to Flamingo; there are many opportunities to stop along the way, and an assortment of activities to pursue in the Flamingo area. The following is arranged in geographic order.

Ernest F. Coe Visitor Center. Don't just grab your park map and go; this visitor center's numerous interactive exhibits and films are well worth your time. The 15-minute film *River of Life,* updated frequently, provides a succinct park overview with emphasis on the river of grass. There is also a movie on hurricanes and a 35-minute wildlife film for children available upon request. A bank of telephones offers differing viewpoints on the Great Water Debate, detailing how last century's gung ho draining of swampland for residential and agricultural development also cut off water-supply routes for precious wetlands in the Everglades ecosystem. Here you'll also find a schedule of daily ranger-led activities, mainly walks and talks, and information on canoe rentals and boat tours at Flamingo. The Everglades Discovery Shop stocks books and jewelry including bird-oriented earrings, and you can browse through cool nature, science, and kids' stuff or pick up extra insect repellent. Coe Visitor Center, which has restrooms, is outside park gates, so you can stop in without paying park admission. ⊠ *11 miles southwest of Homestead, 40001 State Rd. 9336, Homestead* ☎ *305/242–7700* ⊙ *Daily 9–5, subject to change.*

Main road to Flamingo. Route 9336 travels 38 miles from the Ernest F. Coe Visitor Center southwest to the Florida Bay at Flamingo. It crosses a section of the park's eight distinct ecosystems: hardwood hammock, freshwater prairie, pinelands, freshwater slough, cypress, coastal prairie, mangrove, and marine-estuarine. Route highlights include a dwarf cypress forest, the transition zone between saw grass and mangrove forest, and a wealth of wading birds at Mrazek and Coot Bay ponds—where in early morning or late afternoon you can observe the hundreds of birds feeding. Boardwalks, looped trails, several short spurs, and observation platforms help you stay dry. You also may want to stop along the way to walk several short trails (each takes about 30 minutes): the popular, wheelchair-accessible **Anhinga Trail,** which cuts through saw-grass marsh and allows you to see lots of wildlife (be on the lookout for alligators and the trail's namesake water birds: anhingas); the junglelike—yet, also wheelchair-accessible—**Gumbo-Limbo Trail;** the **Pinelands Trail,** where you can see the limestone bedrock that underlies the park; the **Pahayokee Overlook Trail,** which ends at an observation tower; and the **Mahogany Hammock Trail** with its dense growth. ■ **TIP→ Before you head out on the trails, inquire about insect and weather conditions and plan accordingly, stocking up on bug repellent, sunscreen, and water as necessary. Also, even on seemingly nice days, it's probably smart to bring along rain gear.** ⊠ *Homestead.*

★ **Royal Palm Visitor Center.** A must for anyone wanting to experience the real Everglades, and ideal for when there's limited time, this small center with a bookstore and vending machines permits access to the **Anhinga Trail boardwalk,** where in winter catching sight of alligators congregating in watering holes is almost guaranteed. Or follow the neighboring **Gumbo Limbo Trail** through a hardwood hammock. Both strolls are short (½ mile) and expose you to two Everglades ecosystems. Rangers conduct daily Anhinga Ambles in season (check for dates and times by calling ahead). A Glades Glimpse program takes place afternoons daily in season. Ask also about starlight walks and bike tours. ⊠ *4 miles west* *of Ernest F. Coe Visitor Center on Rte. 9336, Everglades National Park ☎ 305/242–7700 ⏲ Daily 8–4:15.*

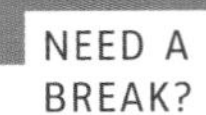

Good spots to pull over for a picnic lunch are Paurotis Pond, about 10 miles north of Florida Bay, or Nine Mile Pond, less than 30 miles from the main visitor center. Another option is along Bear Lake, 2 miles north of the Flamingo Visitor Center.

Flamingo. At the far end of the main road to Flamingo lies this community along Florida Bay, where you'll find a marina with a gift shop, visitor center, and campground, with nearby hiking and nature trails. Before hurricanes Katrina and Wilma washed them away in 2005, a lodge, cabins, and restaurants in Flamingo provided Everglades National Park's only accommodations. Rebuilding of Flamingo Lodge has long been projected, but nothing has materialized yet and won't for some time. For now, you can still pitch a tent or bring an RV to the campground, where improvements include solar-hot-water showers and electricity for RV sites. A popular houseboat-rental concession returned in December 2010. A pair of 35-foot floating homes each sleep six and are equipped with a shower, a toilet, bedding, pots, flatware, a stereo, and depth finder. Houseboats (thankfully air-conditioned) with 60-horsepower outboards rent for $350 per night, plus fuel. ✉ *Flamingo.*

Flamingo Visitor Center. Check the schedule here for ranger-led activities, such as naturalist discussions, hikes along area trails, and evening programs in the 100-seat campground amphitheater, which replaced the old gathering spot destroyed by hurricanes in 2005. Also, find natural history exhibits and pamphlets on canoe, hiking, and biking trails in the small Florida Bay Flamingo Museum on the 2nd floor of the visitor center. ✉ *1 Flamingo Lodge Hwy., Flamingo* ☎ *239/695–2945, 239/695–3101 marina* ⏲ *Exhibits always open, staffed mid-Nov.–mid-Apr., daily 8–4:30.*

SPORTS AND THE OUTDOORS

BIRDING

Some of the park's best birding is in the Flamingo area.

BOATING

The 99-mile inland **Wilderness Trail** between Flamingo and Everglades City is open to motorboats as well as canoes, although, depending on the water level, powerboats may have trouble navigating the route above Whitewater Bay. Flat-water canoeing and kayaking are best in winter, when temperatures are moderate, rainfall diminishes, and mosquitoes back off—a little, anyway. You don't need a permit for day trips, although there is a seven-day, $5 launch fee for all motorized boats brought into the park. The Flamingo area has well-marked canoe trails, but be sure to tell someone where you're going and when you expect to return. Getting lost is easy, and spending the night without proper gear can be unpleasant, if not dangerous.

Flamingo Lodge, Marina, and Everglades National Park Tours. The official Everglades National Park concessionaire runs tours and operates a marina. The one-hour, 45-minute backcountry cruise aboard the 50-passenger *Pelican* ($26.50) winds through the water under a heavy canopy of mangroves, revealing abundant wildlife—from alligators, crocodiles, and turtles to herons, hawks, and egrets. A second boat, *Sawgrass,* follows the same route in peak season (November–April). Flamingo Marina charters boats, and rents 17-foot power skiffs from 7 am for $195 per day (eight hours, if returned by 4 pm), $150 per half day, $80 for two hours. Canoes for up to three paddlers rent for $16 for two hours (minimum), $22 for four hours, $40 for eight hours. and $50 overnight. Family canoes for up to four rent for $20 for two hours (minimum), $30 for four hours, $40 for eight hours, and $50 for 24 hours. Two-person charter fishing trips can be arranged for weekends ($350 for a half day or $450 a day; each additional person pays $25). Cost includes tackle, ice, and license. The concessionaire also rents bikes, binoculars, rods, reels, and other equipment by the half and full day. Feeling sticky after a day in the 'Glades? Hot showers are $3. (Flamingo Lodge, a victim of massive hurricane damage in 2005, remains closed pending funding for a fresh start.) ✉ *1 Flamingo Lodge Hwy., on Buttonwood Canal, Flamingo* ☎ *239/695–3101* 🌐 *www.evergladesnationalparkboattoursflamingo.com.*

GOOD READS

■ *The Everglades: River of Grass.* This circa-1947 classic by pioneering conservationist Marjory Stoneman Douglas (1890–1998) is a must-read.

■ *Everglades Wildguide.* Jean Craighead George gives an informative account of the park's natural history in this official National Park Service handbook.

■ *Everglades: The Park Story.* Wildlife biologist William B. Robertson Jr. presents the park's flora, fauna, and history.

GULF COAST ENTRANCE

To reach the park's western gateway, take U.S. 41 west from Miami for 77 miles, turn left (south) onto Route 29, and travel another 3 miles through Everglades City to the Gulf Coast Ranger Station. From Naples on the Gulf Coast, take U.S. 41 east for 35 miles, and then turn right onto Route 29.

Gulf Coast Visitor Center. The best place to bone up on Everglades National Park's watery western side is at this visitor center just south of Everglades City, where rangers are on hand to address your questions. In winter, canoeists check in here for trips to the Ten Thousand Islands (for which the visitor center doubles as a gateway) and 99-mile Wilderness Waterway Trail, nature lovers view interpretive exhibits on local flora and fauna while waiting for naturalist-led boat trips, and backcountry campers purchase permits. In season (Christmas through Easter), rangers lead bike tours and canoe trips. No direct roads from here link to other sections of the park, and admission is free only to this section. ✉ *Rte. 29, 815 Oyster Bar La., Everglades City* ☎ *239/695–3311* ⏲ *Mid-Nov.–mid-Apr., daily 8–4:30; mid-Apr.–mid-Nov., daily 9–4:30.*

Much skill is required to navigate boats through the shallow, muddy waters of the Everglades.

SPORTS AND THE OUTDOORS

BOATING AND KAYAKING OUTFITTERS

Everglades National Park Boat Tours. Operating in conjunction with boat tours at Flamingo, this company runs 1½-hour trips ($26.50) through the Ten Thousand Islands National Wildlife Refuge. Adventure-seekers often see dolphins, manatees, bald eagles, and roseate spoonbills. In peak season (November–April), 49-passenger boats run on the hour and half-hour daily. Mangrove wilderness tours ($35) are also conducted on smaller boats for up to six passengers. These one-hour, 45-minute trips are the best option to see alligators. The outfitter also rents canoes and kayaks. ✉ *Gulf Coast Visitor Center, 815 Oyster Bar La., Everglades City* ☎ *239/695–2591, 866/628–7275* 🌐 *www.evergladesnationalparkboattoursgulfcoast.com/index.php.*

Fodor's Choice ★ **Everglades Rentals & Eco Adventures.** Inside the Ivey House Inn there is an established, year-round source for canoes, sea kayaks, and guided Everglades paddling tours. Canoe rentals cost $35 the first day, $27 for each day thereafter. Day-long kayak rentals are from $65. All half-day rentals are from 1 to 5 pm. Shuttles deliver you to major launching areas such as Turner River ($25.60 to $32, one-way for up to two people) and Collier-Seminole State Park ($56 to $70, one-way). Tour highlights include bird and gator sightings, mangrove forests, no-man's-land beaches, relics of hideouts for infamous and just-plain-reclusive characters, and spectacular sunsets. Longer adventures include canoe/kayak and equipment rental, all necessary camping equipment, a guide, and meals. ✉ *Ivey House, 107 Camellia St., Everglades City 877/567–0679, 239/695–3299* 🌐 *www.evergladesadventures.com.*

SHARK VALLEY

23½ miles west of Florida's Turnpike, off Tamiami Trail. Approximately 45 minutes west of Miami.

One thing you won't see at Shark Valley is sharks. The name comes from the Shark River, also called the River of Grass, which flows through the area. Several species of shark swim up this river from the coast (about 45 miles south of Shark Valley) to give birth. Young sharks (called pups), vulnerable to being eaten by adult sharks and other predators, gain strength in waters of the slough before heading out to sea to fend for themselves.

THE EVERGLADES WITH KIDS

Although kids of all ages can enjoy the park, those six and older will get the most out of the experience. Consider how much you as a parent will enjoy keeping tabs on tiny ones around so much water and so many teeth. Some younger children are frightened by sheer wilderness. NOTE: Authorities have found surprisingly high mercury content in predator pythons as well, negating their desirability for use in exotic cuisine.

EXPLORING

Though Shark Valley is the national park's north entrance, no roads here lead directly to other parts of the park. However, it's still worth stopping here to take a tram tour. Be sure to stop at the halfway point and ascend to the top of the observation tower via a ramp.

Prefer to do the trail on foot? It takes a bit of nerve to walk the paved 15-mile loop in Shark Valley, because in the winter months alligators lie on and alongside the road, basking in the sun—most, however, do move quickly out of the way.

You also can ride a bicycle (the outfitter here rents one-speed, well-used bikes daily 8:30–4 for $8 per hour) or take a two-hour guided tram tour (reservations recommended in winter). Just behind the bike-rental area a short boardwalk trail meanders through the saw grass, and another one passes through a tropical hardwood hammock. An underwater live camera in the canal behind the center (viewed from the gift shop) lets visitors sporadically see the alligators and otters.

Observation Tower. At the Shark Valley trail's end (really, the halfway point of the 15-mile loop), you can pause to navigate this tower, first built in 1984, spiraling 50 feet upward. Once on top, the River of Grass gloriously spreads out as far as your eye can see. Observe waterbirds as well as alligators, and perhaps even river otters crossing the road. The tower has a wheelchair-accessible ramp to the top. ✉ *Shark Valley Loop Rd., Miami.*

Shark Valley Visitor Center. The small center has rotating exhibits, a bookstore, and park rangers ready for your questions. ✉ *23½ miles west of Florida's Turnpike, off Tamiami Trail, 36000 S.W. 8th St., Miami* ☎ *305/221–8776* ⏲ *Late Mar.–late Dec., daily 9:15–5:15.*

SPORTS AND THE OUTDOORS

BOATING

Many Everglades-area tours operate only in season, roughly November through April.

Buffalo Tiger's Airboat Tours. A former chief of Florida's Miccosukee tribe operates this Shark Valley–area company. Though at 90 (or so) years old he no longer skippers the boat, the chief still gets out to meet and greet customers when he can. Guides narrate the trip to an old Indian camp on the north side of Tamiami Trail from the American Indian perspective. Don't worry about airboat noise, since guides shut down the engines during informative talks. The 45-minute round-trip tours go 10–5 Saturday through Thursday and cost $25 per person for two, $20 per person for more than two, up to 12 people. Reservations are not required, but cash is—no credit cards accepted. ✉ *29708 S.W. 8th St., 5 miles east of Shark Valley, 25 miles west of Florida's Turnpike, Miami* ☎ *305/559–5250* 🌐 *www.buffalotigersairboattours.com.*

WORD OF MOUTH

"We drove from Ft. Lauderdale to the Everglades and rented bikes to do the loop at Shark Valley. Lots of wildlife to see! It took us the morning. I think you get better views of the wildlife on the bikes than the tram and of course since you can stop anytime you want, better pics. It's a very easy ride since it's flat and paved."

—klam_chowder

GUIDED TOURS

★ **Shark Valley Tram Tours.** Starting at the Shark Valley visitor center, two-hour, narrated tours ($19) follow a 15-mile loop road—especially good for viewing gators—into the interior, stopping at a 50-foot observation tower. Bring your own water. Reservations are strongly recommended December through April. ✉ *Shark Valley Visitor Center, Shark Valley Loop Rd., Miami* ☎ *305/221–8455* 🌐 *www.sharkvalleytramtours.com* ⏲ *Tours Dec.–Apr., hourly 9–4; May–Nov., hourly 9–3.*

BIG CYPRESS NATIONAL PRESERVE

Through the 1950s and early 1960s the world's largest cypress-logging industry prospered in Big Cypress Swamp. As the industry died out, the government began buying parcels. Today more than 729,000 acres, or nearly half of the swamp, form this national preserve. The word big refers not to the size of the trees but to the swamp, which juts into the north edge of Everglades National Park like a jigsaw-puzzle piece. Size and strategic location make Big Cypress an important link in the region's hydrological system, where rainwater first flows through the preserve, then south into the park, and eventually into Florida Bay. Its variegated pattern of wet prairies, ponds, marshes, sloughs, and strands provides a wildlife sanctuary, and thanks to a policy of balanced land use—"use without abuse"—the watery wilderness is devoted to recreation as well as research and preservation.

The preserve allows—in limited areas—hiking, hunting, and off-road-vehicle (airboat, swamp buggy, four-wheel-drive vehicle) use by permit.

Compared with Everglades National Park, the preserve is less developed and hosts fewer visitors. That makes it ideal for naturalists, birders, and hikers who prefer to see more wildlife than humans.

Several scenic drives link from Tamiami Trail; some require four-wheel-drive vehicles, especially in wet summer months. A few lead to camping areas and roadside picnic areas.

PARK ESSENTIALS

Admission Fees There is no admission fee to visit the preserve.

Admission Hours The park is open daily, year-round. Accessible only by boat, Adams Key is for day use only.

Contacts **Big Cypress National Preserve** *239/695–1201* ⊕ *www.nps.gov/bicy.*

EXPLORING

Oasis Visitor Center. The big attraction here is the observation deck, where you can view huge gators as well as fish, birds, and other wildlife. There's also a small butterfly garden where native plants seasonally attract winged wonders. Inside the information center you'll find a small exhibit area, a bookshop, and a theater that shows a dated but informative 15-minute film on the Big Cypress Preserve swamplands. ✉ *24 miles east of Everglades City, 50 miles west of Miami, 20 miles west of Shark Valley, 52105 Tamiami Trail, Ochopee* ☎ *239/695–1201* 🎫 *Free* ⏲ *Daily 9–5.*

Ochopee Post Office. This former irrigation pipe shed, on the south side of Tamiami Trail, is North America's smallest post office. Don't blink or you'll miss it. To help keep this picturesque outpost in business during times of governmental cutbacks and layoffs, buy a postcard of the one-room shack, and mail it to someone who would appreciate such a rustic spot. ✉ *4 miles east of Rte. 29, 38000 E. Tamiami Trail, Ochopee* ☎ *239/695–2099* ⏲ *Weekdays 10–noon and 1–4:30, Sat. 10–11:30.*

SPORTS AND THE OUTDOORS

There are three types of trails—walking (including part of the extensive Florida National Scenic Trail), canoeing, and bicycling. All three trail types are easily accessed from the Tamiami Trail near the preserve visitor center, and one boardwalk trail departs from the center. Canoe and bike equipment can be rented from outfitters in Everglades City, 24 miles west, and Naples, 40 miles west.

Hikers can tackle the Florida National Scenic Trail, which begins in the preserve and is divided into segments 6.5 to 28 miles each. Two 5-mile trails, Concho Billy and Fire Prairie, can be accessed off Turner River Road, a few miles east. Turner River Road and Birdon Road form a 17-mile gravel loop drive that's excellent for birding. Bear Island has about 32 miles of scenic, flat, looped trails that are ideal for bicycling. Most trails are hard-packed lime rock, but a few miles are gravel. Cyclists share the road with off-road vehicles, most plentiful from mid-November through December.

To see the best variety of wildlife from your car, follow 26-mile Loop Road, south of U.S. 41 and west of Shark Valley, where alligators, raccoons, and soft-shell turtles crawl around beside the gravel road, often swooped upon by swallowtail kites and brown-shouldered hawks. Stop at H. P. Williams Roadside Park, west of the Oasis, and walk along the boardwalk to spy gators, turtles, and garfish in the river waters.

RANGER PROGRAMS

From the Oasis Visitor Center you can get in on one of the seasonal ranger-led or self-guided activities, such as campfire and wildlife talks, hikes, slough slogs, and canoe excursions. The 8-mile Turner River Canoe Trail begins nearby and crosses through Everglades National Park before ending in Chokoloskee Bay, near Everglades City. Rangers lead four-hour canoe trips and two-hour swamp walks in season; call for days and times. Bring shoes and long pants for the swamp walks and be prepared to wade at least knee-deep in water. Ranger program reservations are accepted up to 14 days in advance.

BISCAYNE NATIONAL PARK

Occupying 172,000 acres along the southern portion of Biscayne Bay, south of Miami and north of the Florida Keys, this national park is 95% submerged, and its altitude ranges from 4 feet above sea level to 60 feet below. Contained within from shore to sea are four distinct zones: mangrove forest along the coast, Biscayne Bay, the undeveloped upper Florida Keys, and coral reefs. Mangroves line the mainland shore much as they do elsewhere along South Florida's protected bay waters. Biscayne Bay functions as a lobster sanctuary and a nursery for fish, sponges, and crabs. Manatees and sea turtles frequent its warm, shallow waters. The park hosts legions of boaters, snorkelers, divers, and landlubbers who gaze in appreciation over the bay.

GETTING HERE

To reach Biscayne National Park from Homestead, take Krome Avenue to Route 9336 (Palm Drive) and turn east. Follow Palm Drive for about 8 miles until it becomes S.W. 344th Street, and follow signs to park headquarters in Convoy Point. The entry is 9 miles east of Homestead and 9 miles south and east of Exit 6 (Speedway Boulevard/S.W. 137th Avenue) off Florida's Turnpike.

PARK ESSENTIALS

Admission Fees There is no fee to enter Biscayne National Park, and you don't pay a fee to access the islands, but there is a $20 overnight camping fee that includes a $5 dock fee to berth vessels at some island docks. The park concessionaire charges for trips to the coral reefs and the islands.

Admission Hours The park is open daily, year-round.

Contact Information **Biscayne National Park** ✉ *Dante Fascell Visitor Center, 9700 S.W. 328th St., Homestead* ☎ *305/230–7275* 🌐 *www.nps.gov/bisc.*

DID YOU KNOW?

The Everglades shelter four types of mangroves: white, black, red, and buttonwood. The red mangrove plant (rhizophora mangle), shown here in Key Biscayne National Park, has tall, arching roots and a high tolerance for salt.

Biscayne is a great place if you want to dive, snorkel, canoe, camp, birdwatch, or learn about marine ecology. The best place to hike is Elliott Key (⇨ *see Islands, below*).

THE CORAL REEF

Biscayne's corals range from the soft, flagellant fans, plumes, and whips found chiefly in the shallower patch reefs to the hard brain corals, elkhorn, and staghorn forms that can withstand the depths and heavier wave action along the ocean's edge.

THE ISLANDS

To the east, about 8 miles off the coast, lie 44 tiny keys, stretching 18 nautical miles north–south and accessible only by boat. There's no commercial transportation between the mainland and the islands, and only a handful can be visited: Elliott, Boca Chita, Adams, and Sands keys. The rest are wildlife refuges, are too small, or have rocky shores or waters too shallow for boats. It's best to explore the keys between December and April, when the mosquito population is less aggressive. Repellent is a must.

Adams Key. A stone's throw from the western tip of Elliott Key and 9 miles southeast of Convoy Point, the island is open for day use. It was the onetime site of the Cocolobo Club, a yacht club famous for hosting presidents Harding, Hoover, Johnson, and Nixon, as well as other luminaries. It has picnic areas, restrooms, dockage, and a short trail that runs along the shore and through a hardwood hammock. Rangers live on-island. Access is by private boat, and no pets or overnight docking is allowed.

★ **Boca Chita Key.** Ten miles northeast of Convoy Point and about 12 miles south of the Cape Florida Lighthouse on Key Biscayne, this key was once owned by the late Mark C. Honeywell, former president of Honeywell Company. It is listed on the National Register of Historic Places for its 10 historic structures. A ½-mile hiking trail curves around the south side of the island. Climb the 65-foot-high ornamental lighthouse (by ranger tour only) for a panoramic view of Miami or check out the cannon from the HMS *Fowey*. There's no freshwater, access is by private boat only, and no pets are allowed. Only portable toilets are on-site, and there are no sinks or showers. A $20 fee for overnight docking between 6 pm and 6 am covers a campsite; pay at the automated kiosk near the harbor.

Elliott Key. The largest of the islands, 9 miles east of Convoy Point, has a mile-long loop trail on the bay side of the island at the north end of the campground. Boaters may dock at any of 36 slips, and a $20 fee for stays between 6 pm and 6 am covers a campsite. Take an informal, ranger-led nature walk or head out on your own to hike the 6-mile trail along so-called Spite Highway, a 225-foot-wide swath of green that developers mowed down in hopes of linking this key to the mainland. Luckily the federal government stepped in, and now it's a hiking trail through tropical hardwood hammock. Facilities include restrooms, picnic tables, fresh drinking water, cold (or, occasionally, lukewarm) water showers, grills, and a campground. Leashed pets are allowed in developed areas only, not on trails. A 30-foot-wide sandy shoreline about a mile north of the harbor on the west (bay) side of the key is the only one in the national park, and boaters like to anchor off here to swim. The beach, fun for families, is for day use only; it has picnic areas and a short trail that follows the shore and cuts through the hammock.

BISCAYNE IN ONE DAY

Most visitors come to snorkel or dive. Divers should plan to spend the morning on the water and the afternoon exploring the visitor center. The opposite is true for snorkelers, as snorkel trips (and one-tank shallow-dive trips) depart in the afternoon. If you want to hike as well, turn to the trails at Elliott Key—just be sure to apply insect repellent (and sunscreen, too, no matter what time of year).

VISITOR CENTER

★ **Dante Fascell Visitor Center.** Go outside on the wide veranda to take in views across mangroves and Biscayne Bay. Inside the museum, artistic vignettes and on-request videos including the 11-minute *Spectrum of Life* explore the park's four ecosystems, while the Touch Table gives both kids and adults a feel for bones, feathers, and coral. Facilities include the park's canoe and tour concessionaire, restrooms with showers, a ranger information area, gift shop with books, and vending machines. Various ranger programs take place daily during busy fall and winter seasons. On the second Sunday of each month from December through April, the Family Fun Fest program offers three hours of hands-on activities for kids and families. Rangers also give informal tours of Elliott and Boca Chita keys; arrange in advance. Outside are picnic tables and grills. A short trail and boardwalk lead to a jetty. This is the only area of the park accessible without a boat. ✉ *9700 S.W. 328th St., Homestead* ☎ *305/230–7275* 🌐 *www.nps.gov/bisc* 🎟 *Free* 🕘 *Daily 9–5.*

SPORTS AND THE OUTDOORS

BIRD-WATCHING

More than 170 species of birds have been identified around the park. Expect to see flocks of brown pelicans patrolling the bay—suddenly rising, then plunging beak first to capture prey in their baggy pouches. White ibis probe exposed mudflats for small fish and crustaceans. Although all the keys are excellent for birding, Jones Lagoon (south of Adams Key, between Old Rhodes Key and Totten Key) is outstanding. It's approachable only by nonmotorized craft.

DIVING AND SNORKELING

Diving is great year-around but best in summer, when calmer winds and smaller seas result in clearer waters. Ocean waters, 3 miles east of the keys, showcase the park's main attraction—the northernmost section of Florida's living tropical coral reefs. Some are the size of an office desk, others as large as a football field. You can take a glass-bottom-boat ride to see this underwater wonderland, but you really should snorkel or scuba dive to fully appreciate it.

Native plants along the Turner River Canoe Trail hem paddlers in on both sides, and alligators lurk nearby.

A diverse population of colorful fish—angelfish, gobies, grunts, parrot fish, pork fish, wrasses, and many more—flits through the reefs. Shipwrecks from the 18th century are evidence of the area's international maritime heritage, and a Maritime Heritage Trail is being developed to link six of the major shipwreck and underwater cultural sites. Thus far, three sites, including a 19th-century wooden sailing vessel, have been plotted with GPS coordinates and marked with mooring buoys. Plastic dive cards are being developed that will contain navigational and background information.

WHAT'S NEARBY

EVERGLADES CITY

35 miles southeast of Naples and 83 miles west of Miami.

Aside from a chain gas station or two, Everglades City is perfect Old Florida. No high-rises (other than an observation tower) mar the landscape at this western gateway to Everglades National Park, just off the Tamiami Trail. It was developed in the late 19th century by Barron Collier, a wealthy advertising entrepreneur, who built it as a company town to house workers for his numerous projects, including construction of the Tamiami Trail. It grew and prospered until the Depression and World War II. Today this ramshackle town draws adventure-seekers heading to the park for canoeing, fishing, and bird-watching excursions. Airboat tours, though popular, are banned within the preserve and park because of the environmental damage they cause to the mangroves.

The Everglades Seafood Festival, going strong for about 40 years and held the first full weekend of February, draws crowds of up to 75,000 for delights from the sea, music, and craft displays. At quieter times, dining choices are limited to a handful of basic eateries. The town is small, fishing-oriented, and unhurried, making it excellent for boating, bicycling, or just strolling around. Pedal along the waterfront on a 2-mile ride along the strand out to Chokoloskee Island.

Visitor Information Everglades Area Chamber of Commerce ✉ *32016 E. Tamiami Trail, at Rte. 29* ☎ *239/695–3172* 🌐 *www.evergladeschamber.com.*

EXPLORING

★ **Fakahatchee Strand Preserve State Park.** The ½-mile boardwalk through this linear swamp forest gives you an opportunity to see rare plants, bald cypress, nesting eagles, and North America's largest stand of native royal palms and largest concentration and variety of epiphytic orchids, including more than 30 varieties of threatened and endangered species blooming most extravagantly in hotter months. It's particularly famous for its ghost orchids (as featured in the novel *The Orchid Thief* by Susan Orlean), visible only on guided hikes. In your quest for ghost orchids, also keep a hopeful eye out for white-tailed deer, black bears, bobcats, and the Florida panther. For park nature on parade, take the 12-mile-long (one-way) W. J. Janes Memorial Scenic Drive, and, if you have the time, hike its spur trails. Rangers lead swamp walks and canoe trips November through April. ✉ *Boardwalk on north side of Tamiami Trail, 7 miles west of Rte. 29; W. J. Janes Scenic Dr., ¾ mile north of Tamiami Trail on Rte. 29; ranger station on W. J. Janes Scenic Dr., 137 Coastline Dr., Copeland* ☎ *239/695–4593* 🌐 *www.floridastateparks.org/fakahatcheestrand* 🎫 *Free* 🕒 *Daily 8 am–sunset.*

OFF THE BEATEN PATH

Collier-Seminole State Park. Nature trails, biking, hiking, camping, and canoeing into Everglades territory make this park a prime introduction to this often forbidding land. Of historical interest, a Seminole War blockhouse has been re-created to hold the interpretative center, and one of the "walking dredges"—a towering black machine invented to carve the Tamiami Trail out of the muck—stands silent on the grounds amid tropical hardwood forest. Campsites ($22 per night plus tax) include electricity, water, and picnic table. Restrooms have hot water, and one has a laundry. ✉ *20200 E. Tamiami Trail, Naples* ☎ *239/394–3397* 🌐 *www.floridastateparks.org/collier-seminole* 🎫 *$5 per car, $4 with lone driver* 🕒 *Daily 8–sunset.*

Museum of the Everglades. Through artifacts and photographs you can meet the American Indians, pioneers, entrepreneurs, and fishermen who played a role in the development of southwest Florida. Exhibits and a short film chronicle the tremendous feat of building the Tamiami Trail through the mosquito-ridden, gator-infested Everglades wetlands. In addition to the permanent displays, monthly exhibits rotate the work of local artists. ✉ *105 W. Broadway* ☎ *239/695–0008* 🎫 *Free* 🕒 *Tues.–Sat. 9–4.*

WHERE TO EAT

$$ SEAFOOD ✕ **Everglades Seafood Depot.** Count on affordable meals in a scenic setting at this storied 1928 Spanish-style stucco structure fronting Lake Placid. Beginning life as the original Everglades train depot, the building

later was deeded to the University of Miami for marine research, and appeared in scenes from the film *Winds across the Everglades*, before becoming a haven over the years for assorted restaurants. Well-prepared seafood including shrimp, frogs' legs, and alligator—much from local boats—dominates the menu. For big appetites, there are generously portioned entrées of steak and fish specials and combination platters that include warm, fresh-baked biscuits. All-you-can-eat specials, such as fried chicken, a taco bar, or a seafood buffet are staged on selected nights. There's also an all-you-can-eat salad bar. Save room for coconut guava cake or key lime pie. Ask for a table on the back porch or for a window seat overlooking the lake. *Average main: $20 ✉ 102 Collier Ave. ☎ 239/695–0075 ⊕ www.evergladesseafooddepot.com.*

$$ CUBAN

Havana Cafe. Cuban specialties are a tasty change from the shanty seafood houses of Everglades City. Brightly painted walls and floral tablecloths make this little eatery with 10 indoor tables and another 10 porch tables a cheerful spot. Service is order-at-the-counter for breakfast and lunch (7 am–3 pm), with dinner on Friday and Saturday nights in season. Jump-start your day with *café con leche* and a pressed-egg sandwich. For lunch, you'll find the ubiquitous Cuban sandwich, burgers, shrimp, grouper, steak, and pork plates with rice and beans and yucca. *Average main: $15 ✉ 191 Smallwood Dr., Chocoloskee ☎ 239/695–2214 ⊕ www.myhavanacafe.com ▭ No credit cards ⊙ No dinner Apr.–Oct. No dinner Sun.–Thurs. Nov.–Mar.*

$$$ SEAFOOD

Rod and Gun Club. The striking, polished pecky-cypress woodwork in this historic building dates from the 1920s, when wealthy hunters, anglers, and yachting parties from around the world arrived for the winter season. Presidents Hoover, Roosevelt, Truman, Eisenhower, and Nixon stopped by here, as have Ernest Hemingway, Burt Reynolds, and Mick Jagger. The main dining room holds overflow from the popular, expansive screened porch overlooking the river. Like life in general here, friendly servers move slowly and upkeep is minimal. Fresh seafood dominates, from stone crab claws in season (October 15–May 15) to a surf-and-turf combo of steak and grouper, a swamp-and-turf combo of frogs' legs and steak, and seafood and pasta pairings. For $14.95 you can have your own catch fried, broiled, or blackened, and served with salad, veggies, and potato. Pie offerings include key lime and chocolate–peanut butter. Be aware that separate checks are discouraged and there's a $5 plate-sharing charge. Yesteryear's main lobby is well worth a look—even if you plan to eat elsewhere. Arrive by boat or land. *Average main: $25 ✉ 200 Riverside Dr. ☎ 239/695–2101 ⊕ www.evergladesrodandgun.com ▭ No credit cards.*

WHERE TO STAY

For expanded reviews, facilities, and current deals, visit Fodors.com.

$$$ B&B/INN Fodor's Choice ★

Ivey House. A remodeled 1928 boardinghouse originally for workers building the Tamiami Trail, Ivey House today fits many budgets. **Pros:** canoe and kayak rentals and tours; pleasant; affordable. **Cons:** not on water; some small rooms. **TripAdvisor:** "best in Everglade City," "hospitable accommodation," "pleasant stay." *Rooms from: $169 ✉ 107 Camellia St. ☎ 877/567–0679, 239/695–3299 ⊕ www.iveyhouse.com 30 rooms, 18 with bath; 1 2-bedroom cottage Breakfast.*

SPORTS AND THE OUTDOORS

AIR TOURS

Wings Ten Thousand Islands Aero-Tours. These 20- to 90-minute scenic flightseeing tours of the Ten Thousand Islands National Wildlife Refuge, Big Cypress National Preserve, Everglades National Park, and Gulf of Mexico operate November through May. Aboard an Alaskan floatplane you can see saw-grass prairies, American Indian shell mounds, alligators, and wading birds. Rates start at $42 (Everglades tour) to $54 (Ten Thousand Islands Tour) per person with groups of three or four. Flights can be booked to the Florida Keys or Dry Tortugas for all- or multi-day outings. ✉ *Everglades Airpark, 650 Everglades City Airpark Rd.* ☎ *239/695–3296.*

BOATING AND CANOEING

On the Gulf Coast explore the nooks, crannies, and mangrove islands of Chokoloskee Bay and Ten Thousand Islands National Wildlife Refuge, as well as the many rivers near Everglades City. The Turner River Canoe Trail, a pleasant day trip with a guarantee of bird and alligator sightings, passes through mangrove, dwarf cypress, coastal prairie, and freshwater slough ecosystems of Everglades National Park and Big Cypress National Preserve.

OUTFITTER **Glades Haven Marina.** Get on the water to explore the Ten Thousand Islands in 16-foot Carolina skiffs and 24-foot pontoon boats. Rates start at $150 a day, with half-day and hourly options. The outfitter also rents kayaks and canoes and has a 24-hour boat ramp and dockage for vessels up to 24 feet long. ✉ *801 Copeland Ave. S* ☎ *239/695–2628* 🌐 *www.gladeshaven.com.*

FLORIDA CITY

3 miles southwest of Homestead on U.S. 1.

Florida's Turnpike ends in Florida City, the southernmost town on the peninsula, spilling thousands of vehicles onto U.S. 1 and eventually west to Everglades National Park, east to Biscayne National Park, or south to the Florida Keys. Florida City and Homestead run into each other, but the difference couldn't be more noticeable. As the last outpost before 18 miles of mangroves and water, this stretch of U.S. 1 is lined with fast-food eateries, service stations, hotels, bars, dive shops, and restaurants. Hotel rates increase significantly during NASCAR races at the nearby Homestead Miami Speedway. Like Homestead, Florida City is rooted in agriculture, with hundreds of acres of farmland west of Krome Avenue and a huge farmers' market that processes produce shipped nationwide.

VISITOR INFORMATION

Tropical Everglades Visitor Center. Run by the nonprofit Tropical Everglades Visitor Association, this pastel-pink center with teal signage offers abundant printed material plus tips from volunteer experts on south Dade County, Homestead, Florida City, and the Florida Keys. ✉ *160 U.S. 1* ☎ *305/245–9180, 800/388–9669* 🌐 *www.tropicaleverglades.com.*

WHERE TO EAT

SHUTTLES FROM MIAMI

Super Shuttle. This 24-hour service runs air-conditioned vans between MIA and the Homestead–Florida City area; pickup is outside baggage claim and costs around $55 per person depending on your destination. For the return to MIA, reserve 24 hours in advance and know your pickup zip code for a price quote. ☎ *305/871–2000* 🌐 *www.supershuttle.com.*

$$$ SEAFOOD **Captain's Restaurant and Seafood Market.** A comfortable place where the chef prepares seafood with flair, this is among the town's best bets. Locals and visitors alike gather in the cozy dining room or outdoors on the patio. Blackboards describe a varied menu of sandwiches, pasta, seafood, steak, and nightly specials, plus stone crabs in season. Inventive offerings include a lobster Reuben sandwich and pan-seared tuna topped with balsamic onions and shallots. Specials sometimes include crawfish pasta. 💲 *Average main: $20* ✉ *404 S.E. 1st Ave.* ☎ *305/247–9456.*

$ SEAFOOD ★ **Farmers' Market Restaurant.** Although this eatery is in the farmers' market on the edge of town and serves fresh vegetables, seafood figures prominently on the menu. A family of anglers runs the place, so fish and shellfish are only hours from the sea, and there's a fish fry on Friday nights. Catering to anglers and farmers, the restaurant opens at 5:30 am, serving pancakes, jumbo eggs, and fluffy omelets with home fries or grits in a pleasant dining room with checkered tablecloths. Lunch and dinner menus have fried shrimp, seafood pasta, country-fried steak, roast turkey, and fried conch, as well as burgers, salads, and sandwiches. 💲 *Average main: $13* ✉ *300 N. Krome Ave.* ☎ *305/242–0008.*

$$ SEAFOOD **Mutineer Wharf Restaurant.** Families and older couples flock to the quirky yet well-dressed setting of this roadside steak-and-seafood outpost with a fish-and-duck pond and a petting zoo for kids. It was built in 1980 to look like a ship, back when Florida City was barely on the map. Etched glass divides the bi-level dining rooms, with velvet-upholstered chairs, an aquarium, and nautical antiques. Topping the menu of about a dozen seafood entrées is the stuffed grouper, Florida lobster tails, and snapper Oscar, plus another half-dozen daily seafood specials, as well as poultry, ribs, and steaks. Burgers and seafood sandwiches are popular for lunch, as is weekday happy-hour buffet until 7 pm in the lounge with purchase of a drink. You also can dine in the restaurant's Wharf Lounge. Most Friday and Saturday nights feature live entertainment and dancing. 💲 *Average main: $16* ✉ *11 S.E. 1st Ave. (U.S. 1), at Palm Dr.* ☎ *305/245–3377* 🌐 *www.mutineerrestaurant.com.*

WHERE TO STAY

For expanded reviews, facilities, and current deals, visit Fodors.com.

$$ HOTEL **Best Western Gateway to the Keys.** For easy access to Everglades and Biscayne national parks as well as the Florida Keys, you'll be well-placed at this two-story motel two blocks off Florida's Turnpike. **Pros:** convenient to national parks, outlet shopping, and Keys; business services; pretty pool area. **Cons:** traffic noise; fills up fast during high season. **TripAdvisor:** "clean and comfortable," "attractive rooms," "great staff." 💲 *Rooms from: $135* ✉ *411 S. Krome Ave.* ☎ *305/246–5100,*

888/981–5100 www.bestwestern.com/gatewaytothekeys 114 rooms Breakfast.

$ HOTEL **Everglades International Hostel.** Stay in clean and spacious private or dorm-style rooms (generally six to a room), relax in indoor or outdoor quiet areas, and watch videos or TV on a big screen. **Pros:** affordable; Everglades tours; free services. **Cons:** communal living; no elevator; old structure. **TripAdvisor:** "very nice place," "relaxing oasis," "a place to meet interesting people." *Rooms from: $25 20 S.W. 2nd Ave. 305/248–1122, 800/372–3874 www.evergladeshostel.com 46 beds in dorm-style rooms with shared bath, 2 private rooms with shared bath, 2 suites No meals.*

$ HOTEL **Fairway Inn.** Two stories high with a waterfall pool, this motel has some of the area's lowest chain rates, and it's next to the Chamber of Commerce visitor center so you'll never be short of reading and planning material. **Pros:** affordable; convenient to restaurants, parks, and raceway. **Cons:** plain, small rooms; no-pet policy. **TripAdvisor:** "clean rooms," "great staff," "sweet home away from home." *Rooms from: $89 100 S.E. 1st Ave. 305/248–4202, 888/340–4734 160 rooms Breakfast.*

$$ HOTEL ★ **Ramada Inn.** If you're looking for an upgrade from the other chains, this pet-friendly property offers more amenities and comfort, such as 32-inch flat-screen TVs, duvet-covered beds, closed closets, and stylish furnishings. **Pros:** extra room amenities; business clientele perks; convenient location. **Cons:** chain anonymity. **TripAdvisor:** "acceptable," "pleasant place," "good location." *Rooms from: $99 124 E. Palm Dr. 305/247–8833 www.hotelfloridacity.com 124 rooms Breakfast.*

SHOPPING

★ **Robert Is Here.** This remarkable fruit stand sells vegetables, fresh-fruit milk shakes (try the key lime), 10 flavors of honey, more than 100 types of jams and jellies, fresh juices, salad dressings, and some 30 kinds of tropical fruits, including (in season) carambola, lychee, egg fruit, monstera, sapodilla, dragonfruit, genipa, sugar apple, and tamarind. The stand started in 1960, when seven-year-old Robert sat at this spot selling his father's bumper crop of cucumbers. Today Robert (still on the scene daily with his wife and kids) ships all over the United States and donates seconds to needy area families. An odd assortment of animals out back—from goats to emus—adds entertainment value for kids. Picnic tables, benches, and a waterfall with a koi pond add some serenity to the experience. The stand, on the way to Everglades National Park, opens at 8 am and stays open until at least 7. It shuts down between September and October. *19200 S.W. 344th St. 305/246–1592.*

HOMESTEAD

30 miles southwest of Miami.

In recent years Homestead has redefined itself as a destination for tropical agro- and ecotourism. At a crossroads between Miami and the Keys as well as Everglades and Biscayne national parks, the area has the added dimension of shopping centers, residential development, hotel chains, and the Homestead-Miami Speedway—when car races are scheduled, hotels hike up their rates and require minimum stays. The historic downtown has become a preservation-driven Main Street. Krome Avenue, where it cuts through the city's heart, is lined with restaurants, an arts complex, antiques shops, and low-budget, sometimes undesirable accommodations. West of north–south Krome Avenue, miles of fields grow fresh fruits and vegetables. Some are harvested commercially, and others beckon with "U-pick" signs. Stands selling farm-fresh produce and nurseries that grow and sell orchids and tropical plants abound. In addition to its agricultural legacy, the town has an eclectic flavor, attributable to its population mix: descendants of pioneer Crackers, Hispanic growers and farm workers, professionals escaping the Miami hubbub, and latter-day northern retirees.

EXPLORING

Coral Castle. Driven by unrequited love, 100-pound Latvian immigrant Ed Leedskalnin (1887–1951) built this castle in the early 1900s out of massive slabs of coral rock, a feat he likened to building the pyramids. Visitors can learn how he peopled his fantasy world with his imaginary wife and three children, studied astronomy, and created a simple home and elaborate courtyard without formal engineering education and with tools he mostly fashioned himself. Highlights of this National Register of Historic Places site include the Polaris telescope built to spot the North Star, a working sundial, a 5,000-pound heart-shape table featured in Ripley's *Believe It or Not,* a banquet table in the shape of Florida, and a playground Ed named "Grotto of the Three Bears." ✉ *28655 S. Dixie Hwy.* ☎ *305/248–6345* 🌐 *www.coralcastle.com* *$12* ⏲ *Daily 8–6.*

WHERE TO EAT

$ MEXICAN

NicaMex. Among the local Latin population, this 68-seat eatery is a low-budget favorite for Nicaraguan and Mexican flavors. It helps if you speak Spanish, but usually some staffers on hand speak English, and the menu is bilingual. Although they term it *comidas rapidas* (fast food), the cuisine is not Americanized. You can get authentic huevos rancheros or *chilaquiles* (corn tortillas cooked in red-pepper sauce) for breakfast, and specialties such as *chicharron en salsa verde* (fried pork skin in hot-green-tomato sauce) and shrimp in garlic all day. Hearty seafood and beef soups are best sellers. Choose among domestic or imported beers, and escape south of the border. [$] *Average main: $10* ✉ *32 N.W. 1st St., across from Krome Ave. bandstand* ☎ *305/247–0727.*

SPORTS AND THE OUTDOORS

AUTO RACING

Homestead-Miami Speedway. The speedway buzzes more than 280 days each year with racing, manufacturer testing, car-club events, driving schools, and ride-along programs. The facility has 65,000 grandstand seats, club seating eight stories above racing action, and two tracks—a 2.21-mile continuous road course and a 1.5-mile oval. A packed schedule includes GRAND-AM and NASCAR events. ✉ *One Speedway Blvd.* ☎ *866/409–7223* 🌐 *www.homesteadmiamispeedway.com.*

Are baby alligators more to your liking than their daddies? You can pet one at Everglades Gator Park.

WATER SPORTS

Homestead Bayfront Park. Boaters, anglers, and beachgoers give high ratings to the facilities at this recreational area adjacent to Biscayne National Park. The 174-slip marina, accommodating vessels up to 50 feet long, has a ramp, dock, bait-and-tackle shop, fuel station, ice, and dry storage. The park also has a tidal swimming area, a beach with lifeguards, a playground, ramps for people with disabilities (including a ramp that leads into the swimming area), and a picnic pavilion with grills, showers, and restrooms. ✉ *9698 S.W. 328th St.* ☎ *305/230–3033* 🎫 *$6 per passenger vehicle; $12 per vehicle with boat Mon.–Thurs., $15 Fri.–Sun.; $15 per RV or bus* ⏲ *Daily sunrise–sunset.*

TAMIAMI TRAIL

An 80-mile stretch of U.S. 41 (known as the Tamiami Trail) traverses the Everglades, Big Cypress National Preserve, and Fakahatchee Strand Preserve State Park. The road was conceived in 1915 to link Miami to Fort Myers and Tampa. When it finally became a reality in 1928, it cut through the Everglades and altered the natural flow of water as well as the lives of the Miccosukee Indians, who were trying to eke out a living fishing, hunting, farming, and frogging here. The landscape is surprisingly varied, changing from hardwood hammocks to pinelands, then abruptly to tall cypress trees dripping with Spanish moss and back to saw-grass marsh. Slow down to take in the scenery and you'll likely be rewarded with glimpses of alligators sunning themselves along the banks of roadside canals or in the shallow waters, and hundreds of waterbirds, especially in the dry winter season. The man-made landscape has

Native American villages, chickee huts, and airboats parked at roadside enterprises. Between Miami and Naples the road goes by several names, including Tamiami Trail, U.S. 41, 9th Street in Naples, and, at the Miami end, S.W. 8th Street. **■TIP→ Businesses along the trail give their addresses based on either their distance from Krome Avenue, Florida's Turnpike, or Miami on the east coast or Naples on the west coast.**

CROCS OR GATORS?

You can tell you're looking at a crocodile, not an alligator, if you can see its lower teeth protruding when its jaws are shut. Gators are much darker in color—a grayish black—compared with the lighter tan color of crocodiles. Alligator snouts—sort of U-shape—are also much broader than their long, thin A-shape crocodilian counterparts. South Florida is the world's only place where the two coexist. Alligators are primarily found in freshwater habitats, whereas crocodiles (better at expelling salt from water) are typically in coastal estuaries.

WHAT TO SEE

Gator Park. Here you can get face-to-face with and even touch an alligator—albeit a baby one—during the park's exciting Wildlife Show. You also can squirm in a "reptilium" of venomous and nonpoisonous native snakes or learn about American Indians of the Everglades through a reproduction of a Miccosukee village. The park, open rain or shine, also has 35-minute airboat tours as well as a gift shop and restaurant serving fare from burgers to gator tail. ✉ *24050 Tamiami Trail, 12 miles west of Florida's Turnpike, Miami* ☎ *305/559–2255, 800/559–2205* 🌐 *www.gatorpark.com* 🎟 *Tours, wildlife show, airboat ride $22.99* ⏲ *Daily 9–5.*

Everglades Safari Park. A perennial favorite with tour-bus operators, the park has an arena, seating up to 300, for an alligator show and wrestling demonstration. Before and after the show, get a closer look at both alligators and crocodiles on Gator Island, walk through a small wildlife museum, follow the jungle trail, or climb aboard an airboat for a 40-minute ride on the River of Grass (included in admission). There's also a restaurant, gift shop, and an observation platform looking out over the Glades. Smaller, private airboats are available for an extra charge for tours lasting 40 minutes to 2 hours. ✉ *26700 S.W. 8th St., 15 miles west of Florida's Turnpike, Miami* ☎ *305/226–6923, 305/223–3804* 🌐 *www.evergladessafaripark.com* 🎟 *$23* ⏲ *Daily 9–5, last tour departs 3:30.*

★ **Miccosukee Indian Village and Gift Shop.** Showcasing the skills and lifestyle of the Miccosukee Tribe of Florida, this cultural center offers crafts demonstrations and insight into the interactions between alligators and the American Indians. Narrated 30-minute airboat rides take you into the wilderness where these American Indians hid after the Seminole Wars and Indian Removal Act of the mid-1800s. In modern times many of the Miccosukee have relocated to this village along Tamiami Trail, but most still maintain their hammock farming and hunting camps. The village museum shows a film and displays chickee structures and artifacts. Guided tours run throughout the day, and a gift shop stocks dolls, apparel for adults and children, silver jewelry, beadwork, and other handcrafted items. The Miccosukee Everglades Music and Craft Festival falls on a July weekend, and the 10-day Miccosukee Indian Arts Festival is in late December. ✉ *U.S. 41, just west of Shark Valley entrance, 25 miles west of Florida's Turnpike at MM 70, Miami* ☎ *305/552–8365* 🌐 *www.miccosukee.com* 🎫 *Village $8, airboat rides $10* ⏲ *Daily 9–5.*

WHERE TO EAT

$ AMERICAN ✕ **Coopertown Restaurant.** Make this a pit stop for local color and cuisine fished straight from the swamp. Starting a half century ago as a sandwich stand, this small casual eatery inside an airboat concession storefront has attracted the famous and the humbly hungry. House specialties are frogs' legs and alligator tail breaded in cornmeal and deep-fried, casually served on paper ware with a lemon wedge and Tabasco. More conventional options include catfish, shrimp, burgers, hot dogs, and grilled cheese sandwiches. [$] *Average main: $12* ✉ *22700 S.W. 8th St., 11 miles west of Florida's Turnpike, Miami* ☎ *305/226–6048* 🌐 *www.coopertownairboats.com* ⏲ *No dinner.*

$$ SOUTHWESTERN ★ ✕ **Miccosukee Restaurant.** For breakfast or lunch (or dinner until 9 November–April), this roadside cafeteria a quarter mile from the Miccosukee Indian Village provides the best variety along Tamiami Trail in Everglades territory, where you won't find much choice. Atmosphere comes from the view overlooking the River of Grass, servers wearing traditional Miccosukee patchwork vests, and a mural depicting American Indian women cooking and men engaged in a powwow. Catfish and frogs' legs are breaded and deep-fried. Other favorites include Indian fry bread and pumpkin bread, but you'll also find burgers, salads, and dishes from south of the border. The Miccosukee Platter ($24.95) offers a sampling of local favorites, including gator bites. [$] *Average main: $15* ✉ *U.S. 41, 18 miles west of Miccosukee Resort & Gaming; 25 miles west of Florida's Turnpike, Miami* ☎ *305/894–2374* ⏲ *No dinner May–Oct.*

$ BARBECUE ✕ **Pit Bar-B-Q.** At the edge of Miami, this old-fashioned roadside eatery along Tamiami Trail near Krome Avenue was launched in 1965 by the late Tommy Little, who wanted anyone heading into or out of the Everglades to have access to cold drinks and rib-sticking fare. His vision remains a holdout from the Everglades' backwoods heritage and a popular, affordable option for families. Order at the counter, pick up your food, and eat at one of the picnic tables on the screened porch or outdoors. Specialties include barbecued chicken and ribs with a tangy sauce, fries, coleslaw, and a fried biscuit, plus burgers and fish sandwiches. The whopping double-decker beef or pork sandwich with slaw requires multiple napkins. Latin specialties include deep-fried pork and fried green plantains. Beer is by the bottle or pitcher. Locals flock here with kids on weekends for pony rides. [$] *Average main: $12* ✉ *16400 S.W. 8th St., 5 miles west of Florida's Turnpike, Miami* ☎ *305/226–2272* 🌐 *www.thepitbarbq.com.*

WHERE TO STAY

For expanded reviews, facilities, and current deals, visit Fodors.com.

$$$ RESORT **Miccosukee Resort & Gaming.** Like an oasis on the horizon of endless saw grass, this nine-story resort at the southeastern edge of the

Everglades can't help but attract your attention, even if you're not on the lookout for 24-hour gaming action. **Pros:** casino; most modern resort in these parts; golf. **Cons:** smoking odor in lobby; hotel guests find parking lot fills with gamblers; feels incompatible with the Everglades. **TripAdvisor:** "clean and affordable," "wonderful getaway," "great place." *Rooms from: $149* *500 S.W. 177th Ave., 6 miles west of Florida's Turnpike, Miami* *305/925–2555, 877/242–6464* *www.miccosukee.com* *256 rooms, 46 suites* *No meals.*

SPORTS AND THE OUTDOORS

BOAT TOURS

Many Everglades-area tours operate only in season, roughly November through April.

Coopertown Airboats. Running since 1945, this is the oldest airboat operator in the Everglades. The 35- to 40-minute tour ($22) takes you 9 miles to hammocks and alligator holes. Private charters of up to two hours are also available. *22700 S.W. 8th St., 11 miles west of Florida's Turnpike, Miami* *305/226–6048* *www.coopertownairboats.com.*

Everglades Alligator Farm. Southwest of Florida City near the entrance to Everglades National Park, this outfit runs a 4-mile, 30-minute airboat tour of the River of Grass with departures 25 minutes after the hour. The tour ($23) includes free hourly alligator, snake, and wildlife shows, or see the gator farm and show only ($15.50). Look for online coupons. *40351 S.W. 192nd Ave., Homestead* *305/247–2628* *www.everglades.com.*

Everglades Safari Park. A 30-minute eco-adventure airboat ride costs $23, while longer, smaller, private airboat adventures, like the eco-adventure and sunset tours, cost more. All prices include the alligator show and access to walking trails and exhibits. Discounts are available online. *26700 S.W. 8th St., 15 miles west of Florida's Turnpike, Miami* *305/226–6923, 305/223–3804* *www.evergladessafaripark.com.*

Gator Park Airboat Tours. Open daily rain or shine, Gator Park conducts 45-minute narrated airboat tours ($22.95), including a park tour and wildlife show. Discounts are available online. *24050 S.W. 8th St., 12 miles west of Florida's Turnpike, Miami* *305/559–2255, 800/559–2205* *www.gatorpark.com.*

Wooten's Everglades Airboat Tour. This classic Florida roadside attraction runs airboat tours through the Everglades for up to 18 people and swamp-buggy rides through the Big Cypress Swamp for up to 25 people. Each lasts approximately 30 minutes. (Swamp buggies are giant tractorlike vehicles with oversize rubber wheels.) More personalized airboat tours on smaller boats, seating six to eight, are also available for 45 minutes to one hour. The on-site animal sanctuary offers the typical Everglades array of alligators, snakes, and other creatures. Rates change frequently. *32330 Tamiami Trail E, 1½ miles east of Rte. 29, Ochopee* *239/695–2781, 800/282–2781* *www.wootensairboats.com* *Daily 8:30–5; last ride departs at 4:30.*

4

The Florida Keys

WORD OF MOUTH

"The Keys are definitely a get out on the water type place instead of a driving up and down U.S. 1 kind of place. Bars and restaurants open early and close early. Get out over the water. That is where the most amazing things in the keys are."

—GoTravel

WELCOME TO THE FLORIDA KEYS

TOP REASONS TO GO

★ **John Pennekamp Coral Reef State Park:** A perfect introduction to the Florida Keys, this nature reserve offers snorkeling, diving, camping, and kayaking. An underwater highlight is the massive Christ of the Deep statue.

★ **Under the Sea:** Whether you scuba dive, snorkel, or ride a glass-bottom boat, don't miss gazing at the coral reef and its colorful denizens.

★ **Sunset at Mallory Square:** Sure, it's touristy, but just once while you're here, you've got to witness the circuslike atmosphere of this nightly event.

★ **Duval Crawl:** Shop, eat, drink, repeat. Key West's Duval Street and the nearby streets make a good day's worth of window-shopping and people-watching.

★ **Get on the Water:** From angling for trophy-size fish to zipping out to the Dry Tortugas, a boat trip is in your future. It's really the whole point of the Keys.

1 The Upper Keys. As the doorstep to the islands' coral reefs and blithe spirit, the Upper Keys introduce all that is sporting and sea-oriented about the Keys. They stretch from Key Largo to the Long Key Channel (MM 106–65).

2 The Middle Keys. Centered on the town of Marathon, the Middle Keys hold most of the chain's historic and natural attractions outside of Key West. They go from Conch (pronounced *konk*) Key through Marathon to the south side of the Seven Mile Bridge, including Pigeon Key (MM 65–40).

3 The Lower Keys. Pressure drops another notch in this laid-back part of the region, where wildlife and the fishing lifestyle peak. The Lower Keys go from Little Duck Key south through Big Coppitt Key (MM 40–9).

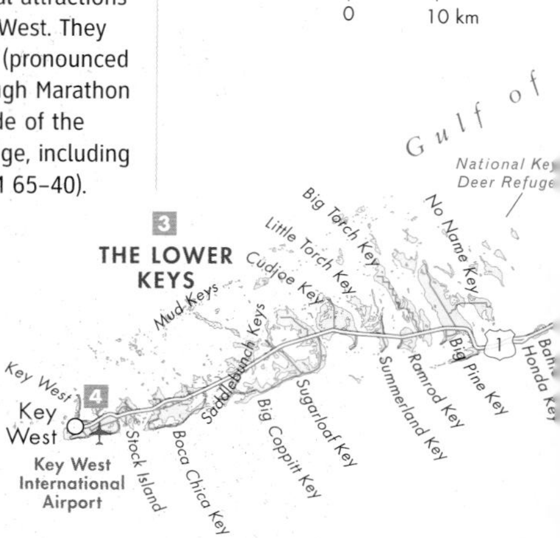

4 Key West. The ultimate in Florida Keys craziness, the party town Key West isn't the place for those seeking a quiet retreat. The Key West area encompasses MM 9–0.

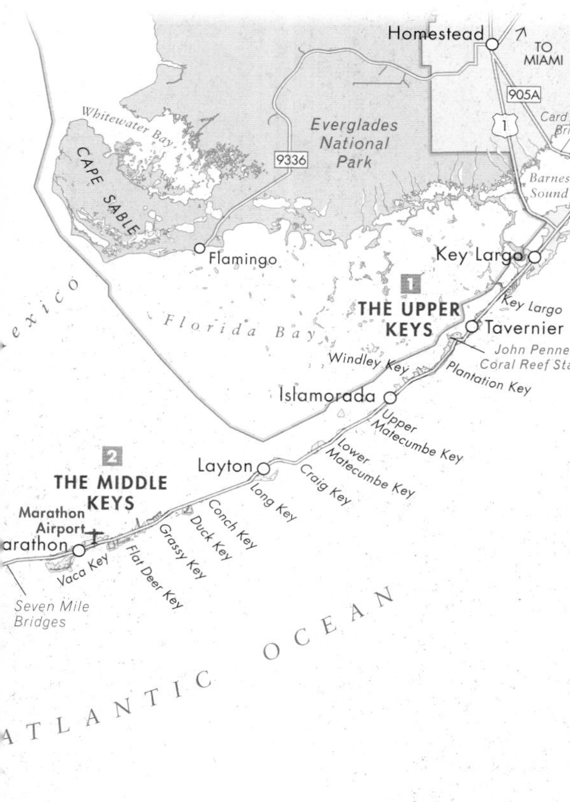

GETTING ORIENTED

The Florida Keys are the dribble of islands off the peninsula's southern tip. From Miami International Airport, Key Largo is a 56-mile drive via the Florida Turnpike and Highway 1. The rest of the keys—Islamorada, Marathon, Bahia Honda Key, and Big Pine Key—fall in succession for the 106 miles between Key Largo and Key West along the Overseas Highway. At their north end, the Florida Keys front Florida Bay, part of Everglades National Park. The Middle and Lower Keys front the Gulf of Mexico; the Atlantic Ocean borders the length of the chain on its eastern shores.

EVERYTHING'S FISHY IN THE KEYS

Fish. It's what's for dinner in the Florida Keys. The Keys' runway between the Gulf of Mexico or Florida Bay and Atlantic warm waters means fish of many fin. Restaurants take full advantage by serving it fresh, whether you caught it or a local fisherman did.

Menus at a number of colorful waterfront shacks such as **Snapper's** (✉ *139 Seaside Ave., Key Largo* ☎ *305/852–5956*) in Key Largo and **Half Shell Raw Bar** (✉ *231 Margaret St., Key West* ☎ *305/294–7496*) range from basic raw, steamed, broiled, grilled, or blackened fish to some Bahamian and New Orleans–style interpretations. Other seafood houses dress up their fish in creative haute-cuisine styles, such as **Pierre's** (✉ *MM 81.5 BS, Islamorada* ☎ *305/664–3225*) hogfish *meunière*, or yellowtail snapper with pear, ricotta pasta purses with caponata, and red pepper coulis at **Café Marquesa** (✉ *600 Fleming St., Key West* ☎ *305/292–1244* 🌐 *www.marquesa.com*). Try a Keys-style breakfast of "grits and grunts"—fried fish and grits—at the **Stuffed Pig** (✉ *3520 Overseas Hwy., Marathon* ☎ *305/743–4059*).

BUILT-IN FISH

You know it's fresh when you see a fish market as soon as you open the door to the restaurant where you're dining. It happens all the time in the Keys. You can even peruse the seafood showcases and pick the fish fillet or lobster tail you want.

Many of the Keys' best restaurants are found in marina complexes, where the commercial fishermen bring their catches straight from the sea. Those in **Stock Island** (one island north of Key West) and at **Keys Fisheries Market & Marina** (✉ *MM 49 BS, end of 35th St., Marathon* ☎ *305/743–4353 or 866/743–4353*) take some finding.

CONCH

One of the tastiest legacies of the Keys' Bahamian heritage, conch shows up on nearly every restaurant menu. It's so prevalent in local diets that natives refer to themselves as Conchs. Conch fritter is the most popular culinary manifestation, followed by cracked (pounded, breaded, and fried) conch, and conch salad, a ceviche-style refresher. Since the harvesting of queen conch is now illegal, most of the islands' conch comes from the Bahamas.

FLORIDA LOBSTER

What happened to the claws? Stop looking for them: Florida spiny lobsters don't have 'em, never did. The sweet tail meat, however, makes up for the loss. Commercial and sports divers harvest these glorious crustaceans from late July through March. Check with local dive shops on restrictions, and then get ready for a fresh feast. Restaurants serve them broiled with drawn butter or in creative dishes such as lobster Benedict, lobster sushi rolls, lobster Reuben, and lobster tacos.

GROUPER

Once central to Florida's trademark seafood dish—fried grouper sandwich—its populations have been overfished in recent years, meaning that the state has exerted more control over bag regulations and occasionally closes grouper fishing on a temporary basis during the winter season. Some restaurants have gone antigrouper to try to bring back the abundance, but most grab it when they can. Black grouper is the most highly prized of the several varieties.

STONE CRAB

In season October 15 through May 15, it gets its name from its rock-hard shell. Fishermen take only the claws, which can regenerate in a sustainable manner. Connoisseurs prefer them chilled with tangy mustard sauce. Some restaurants give you a choice of hot claws and drawn butter, but this means the meat will be cooked twice, because it's usually boiled or steamed quickly after taken from its crab trap.

YELLOWTAIL SNAPPER

The preferred species of snappers, it is more plentiful in the Keys than in any other Florida waters. As pretty as it is tasty, it's a favorite of divers and snorkelers. Mild, sweet, and delicate, its meat lends itself to any number of preparations. It is available pretty much year-round, and many restaurants will give you a choice of broiled, baked, fried, or blackened. Chefs top it with everything from key lime beurre blanc to mango chutney. **Ballyhoo's** in Key Largo (✉ *MM 97.8, in the median* ☎ *305/852–0822*) serves it 10 different ways.

Updated by Chelle Koster Walton

Being a Conch is a condition of the heart, and foreclosure on the soul. Many throughout the Florida Keys wear that label proudly, yet there's anything but a shared lifestyle here.

To the south, Key West has a Mardi Gras mood with Fantasy Festivals, Hemingway look-alike contests, and the occasional threat to secede from the Union. It's an island whose melting-pot character allows crusty natives to mingle (more or less peacefully) with eccentrics and escape artists who lovingly call this 4-mile sandbar "Paradise." Although life elsewhere in the island chain isn't quite as offbeat, it's nearly as diverse. Flowering jungles, shimmering seas, and mangrove-lined islands are also, conversely, overburdened. Key Largo, nearest the mainland, is becoming more congested as it evolves into a bedroom community and weekend hideaway for residents of Miami and Fort Lauderdale.

A river of tourist traffic gushes along Overseas Highway, the 110-mile artery linking the inhabited islands. Take pleasure, nonetheless, as you cruise along the islands. Gaze over the silvery blue-and-green Atlantic and its still-living reef, with Florida Bay, the Gulf of Mexico, and the backcountry on your right (the Keys extend southwest from the mainland). At a few points the ocean and gulf are as much as 10 miles apart; in most places, however, they are from 1 to 4 miles apart, and on the narrowest landfill islands they are separated only by the road. Try to get off the highway. Once you do, rent a boat, anchor, and then fish, swim, or marvel at the sun, sea, and sky. In the Atlantic, dive spectacular coral reefs or pursue grouper, blue marlin, dolphinfish, and other deepwater game fish. Along Florida Bay's coastline, kayak and canoe to secluded islands and bays or seek out the bonefish, snapper, snook, and tarpon that lurk in the grass flats and in the shallow, winding channels of the backcountry.

With virtually no distracting air pollution or obstructive high-rises, sunsets are a pure, unadulterated spectacle that each evening attract thousands to the waterfront.

The Keys were only sparsely populated until the early 20th century. In 1905, however, railroad magnate Henry Flagler began building the extension of his Florida railroad south from Homestead to Key West. His goal was to establish a Miami–Key West rail link to his steamships that sailed between Key West and Havana, just 90 miles across the Straits of Florida. The railroad arrived at Key West in 1912, and remained a lifeline of commerce until the Labor Day hurricane of 1935 washed out much of its roadbed. The Overseas Highway, built over the railroad's old roadbeds and bridges, was completed in 1938.

PLANNING

WHEN TO GO

High season in the Keys falls between Christmas and Easter. November to mid-December crowds are thinner, the weather is wonderful, and hotels and shops drastically reduce their prices. Summer, which is hot and humid, is becoming a second high season, especially among Floridians, families, and European travelers. If you plan to attend the wild Fantasy Fest in October, book your room at least six months in advance. Accommodations are also scarce during the last consecutive Wednesday and Thursday in July (lobster sport season) and starting the first weekend in August, when the commercial lobster season begins.

Winter is typically 10°F warmer than on the mainland; summer is usually a few degrees cooler. The Keys also get substantially less rain, around 40 inches annually, compared with an average 55–60 inches in Miami and the Everglades. Most rainfalls are quick downpours on summer afternoons, except in June through October, when tropical storms can dump rain for two or more days. Winter cold fronts occasionally stall over the Keys, dragging overnight temperatures down to the low 50s.

GETTING HERE AND AROUND

AIR TRAVEL

About 450,000 passengers use the **Key West International Airport (EYW)** each year; its most recent renovation includes a beach where travelers can catch their last blast of rays after clearing security. Because flights are few, many prefer flying into Miami International Airport (MIA) and driving the 110-mile Overseas Highway (aka U.S. 1).

Contact **Key West International Airport (EYW)** ☎ *305/296–5439* 🌐 *www.keywestinternationalairport.com.*

BOAT AND FERRY TRAVEL

Key West can be reached by high-speed catamaran ferry from Fort Myers and Marco Island through Key West Express.

Boaters can travel to and along the Keys either along the Intracoastal Waterway through Card, Barnes, and Blackwater sounds and into Florida Bay or along the deeper Atlantic Ocean route through Hawk Channel. The Keys are full of marinas that welcome transient visitors, but there aren't enough slips for all the boats heading to these waters. Make reservations far in advance and ask about channel and dockage depth—many marinas are quite shallow.

Contact **Key West Express** ✉ *100 Grinnell St., Key West* ☎ *888/539–2628* 🌐 *www.seakeywestexpress.com.*

4

BUS TRAVEL

Those unwilling to tackle the route's 42 bridges and peak-time traffic can take **Greyhound's** Keys Shuttle, which has multiple daily departures from Miami International Airport.

Contact **Greyhound** ☎ *800/231–2222* ⊕ *www.greyhound.com.*

CAR TRAVEL

By car, from Miami International Airport, follow signs to Coral Gables and Key West, which puts you on LeJeune Road, then Route 836 west. Take the Homestead Extension of Florida's Turnpike south (toll road), which ends at Florida City and connects to the Overseas Highway (U.S. 1). Tolls from the airport run approximately $3. Payment is collected via SunPass, a prepaid toll program, or with Toll-By-Plate, a system that photographs each vehicle's license plate and mails a monthly bill for tolls, plus a $2.50 administrative fee, to the vehicle's registered owner. Vacationers traveling in their own cars can obtain a mini-SunPass sticker via mail before their trips for $4.99 and receive the cost back in toll credits and discounts. The pass also is available at many major Florida retailers and turnpike service plazas. It works on all Florida toll roads and many bridges. For details on purchasing a mini-SunPass, call or visit the website. For visitors renting cars in Florida, most major rental companies have programs allowing customers to use the Toll-By-Plate system. Tolls, plus varying service fees, are automatically charged to the credit card used to rent the vehicle. For details, including pricing options at participating rental-car agencies, check the program website. Under no circumstances should motorists attempt to stop in high-speed electronic tolling lanes. Travelers can contact Florida's Turnpike Enterprise for more information about the all-electronic tolling on Florida's Turnpike.

The alternative from Florida City is Card Sound Road (Route 905A), which has a bridge toll of $1. Continue to the only stop sign and turn right on Route 905, which rejoins Overseas Highway 31 miles south of Florida City. The best Keys road map, published by the Homestead–Florida City Chamber of Commerce, can be obtained for $5.50 from the Tropical Everglades Visitor Center.

Contacts **Florida's Turnpike Enterprise** ☎ *800/749–7453* ⊕ *www.floridasturnpike.com.* **SunPass** ☎ *888/865–5352* ⊕ *www.sunpass.com.* **TOLL-BY-PLATE** ⊕ *www.sunpass.com/rentalcar.*

THE MILE MARKER SYSTEM

Getting lost in the Keys is almost impossible once you understand the unique address system. **Many addresses are simply given as a mile marker (MM) number.** The markers are small, green, rectangular signs along the side of the Overseas Highway (U.S. 1). They begin with MM 126, 1 mile south of Florida City, and end with MM 0, in Key West. **Keys residents use the abbreviation BS for the bay side of Overseas Highway and OS for the ocean side.** From Marathon to Key West, residents may refer to the bay side as the gulf side.

VISITOR INFORMATION

Contact Tropical Everglades Visitor Association ☎ *305/245–9180, 800/388–9669* ⊕ *www.tropicaleverglades.com.*

ABOUT THE RESTAURANTS

Seafood rules in the Keys, which is full of chef-owned restaurants with not-too-fancy food. Things get more exotic once you reach Key West. Restaurants serve cuisine that reflects the proximity of the Bahamas and Caribbean. Tropical fruits figure prominently—especially on the beverage side of the menu. Florida spiny lobster should be local and fresh from August to March, and stone crabs from mid-October to mid-May. And don't dare leave the islands without sampling conch, be it in a fritter or in ceviche. Keep an eye out for authentic key lime pie—yellow custard in a graham-cracker crust. If it's green, just say "no." Note: Particularly in Key West and particularly during spring break, the more affordable and casual restaurants can get loud and downright rowdy, with young visitors often more interested in drinking than eating. Live music contributes to the decibel levels. If you're more of the quiet, intimate dining type, avoid such overly exuberant scenes by eating early or choosing a restaurant where the bar is not the main focus.

ABOUT THE HOTELS

Throughout the Keys, the types of accommodations are remarkably varied, from 1950s-style motels to cozy inns to luxurious resorts. Most are on or near the ocean, so water sports are popular. Key West's lodging portfolio includes historic cottages, restored Conch houses, and large resorts. Some larger properties throughout the Keys charge a mandatory daily resort fee of $15 or more, which can cover equipment rental, fitness-center use, and other services, plus expect another 12.5% (or more) in state and county taxes. Some guesthouses and inns do not welcome children, and many do not permit smoking.

HOTEL AND RESTAURANT COSTS

Prices in the restaurant reviews are the average cost of a main course at dinner or, if dinner is not served, at lunch. Prices in the hotel reviews are the lowest cost of a standard double room in high season. Prices do not include taxes (6%, more in some counties, and 1%–5% tourist tax for hotel rooms).

THE UPPER KEYS

Diving and snorkeling rule in the Upper Keys, thanks to the tropical coral reef that runs a few miles off the seaward coast. Divers of all skill levels benefit from accessible dive sites and an established tourism infrastructure. Fishing is another huge draw, especially around Islamorada, known for its sportfishing in both deep offshore waters and in the backcountry. Offshore islands accessible only by boat are popular destinations for kayakers. In short, if you don't like the water, you might get bored here.

Other nature lovers won't feel shortchanged. Within 1½ miles of the bay coast lie the mangrove trees and sandy shores of Everglades National Park, to where naturalists lead tours of one of the world's few saltwater

GREAT ITINERARIES

3 DAYS

Spend your first morning diving or snorkeling at John Pennekamp Coral Reef State Park in **Key Largo**. If you aren't certified, sign up for a resort course and you'll be exploring the reefs by the afternoon. Dinner at a bay-side restaurant will give you your first look at a fabulous Keys sunset. On Day 2 get an early start to savor the breathtaking views on the two-hour drive to Key West. Along the way make a stop at the natural-history museum that's part of Crane Point Museum, Nature Center and Historic Site in **Marathon**. Another worthwhile detour is Bahia Honda Key State Park on **Bahia Honda Key**, where you can stretch your legs on a forest trail or snorkel on an offshore reef. Once you arrive in **Key West**, watch the sunset at one of the restaurants around Mallory Square. The next day, take a trolley tour of Old Town, stroll Duval Street, visit a museum or two, and spend some beach time at Fort Zachary Taylor State Park.

7 DAYS

Spend your first three days as you would in the above itinerary, but spend both the second and third nights in **Islamorada**. In the morning catch a boat or rent a kayak to paddle to Lignumvitae Key Botanical State Park before making the one-hour drive to **Marathon**. Visit Crane Point Museum, Nature Center and Historic Site and walk out on the Old Seven Mile Bridge or take the ferry to Pigeon Key. The next stop is just 10 miles away at Bahia Honda State Park on **Bahia Honda Key**. Take a walk on a wilderness trail, go snorkeling around the offshore reef, or wriggle your toes in the beach's soft sand. Spend the night in a waterfront cabin, letting the waves lull you to sleep. Your sixth day starts with either a half day of fabulous snorkeling or diving at Looe Key Reef or a visit to the National Key Deer Refuge on **Big Pine Key**. Then continue on to **Key West**, and get in a little sightseeing before watching the sunset.

forests. Here you'll see endangered manatees, curious dolphins, and other underwater creatures. Although the number of birds has dwindled since John James Audubon captured their beauty on canvas, the rare Everglades snail kite, bald eagles, ospreys, and a colorful array of egrets and herons delight bird-watchers. At sunset flocks take to the skies as they gather to find their night's roost, adding a swirl of activity to an otherwise quiet time of day.

The Upper Keys are full of low-key eateries where the owner is also the chef and the food is tasty and never too fussy. The one exception is Islamorada, where you'll find the more upscale restaurants. Places to eat may close for a two- to four-week vacation during the slow season between mid-September and late October.

In the Upper Keys the accommodations are as varied as they are plentiful. The majority of lodgings are in small waterfront complexes with efficiencies and one- or two-bedroom units. These places offer dockage and often arrange boating, diving, and fishing excursions. There are also larger resorts with every type of activity imaginable and smaller boutique hotels where the attraction is personalized service.

Depending on which way the wind blows and how close the property is to the highway, there may be some noise from Overseas Highway. If this is an annoyance for you, ask for a room as far from the traffic as possible. Some properties require two- or three-day minimum stays during holiday and high-season weekends. Conversely, discounts apply for midweek, weekly, and monthly stays.

GETTING HERE AND AROUND

Airporter operates scheduled van and bus pickup service from all Miami International Airport (MIA) baggage areas to wherever you want to go in Key Largo ($50) and Islamorada ($55). Groups of three or more passengers receive discounts. There are three departures daily; reservations are required 48 hours in advance. The SuperShuttle charges about $165 for two passengers for trips from Miami International Airport to the Upper Keys; reservations are required. For a trip to the airport, place your request 24 hours in advance.

Contacts Airporter ☎ *305/852–3413, 800/830–3413.* **SuperShuttle** ☎ *305/871–2000* 🌐 *www.supershuttle.com.*

KEY LARGO

The first of the Upper Keys reachable by car, 30-mile-long Key Largo is also the largest island in the chain. Key Largo—named Cayo Largo ("Long Key") by the Spanish—makes a great introduction to the region.

The history of Largo is similar to that of the rest of the Keys, with its succession of native people, pirates, wreckers, and developers. The first settlement on Key Largo was named Planter, back in the days of pineapple, and later, key lime plantations. For a time it was a convenient shipping port, but when the railroad arrived, Planter died on the vine. Today three communities—North Key Largo, Key Largo, and Tavernier—make up the whole of Key Largo.

If you've never tried diving, Key Largo is the perfect place to learn. Dozens of companies will be more than happy to show you the ropes. Nobody comes to Key Largo without visiting John Pennekamp Coral Reef State Park, one of the jewels of the state-park system. Also popular is the adjacent Key Largo National Marine Sanctuary, which encompasses about 190 square miles of coral reefs, sea-grass beds, and mangrove estuaries. Both are good for underwater exploration.

Fishing is the other big draw, and world records are broken regularly. There are plenty of charter operations to help you find the big ones and teach you how to hook the elusive (but inedible) bonefish, sometimes known as the ghost fish. On land, restaurants will cook your catch or dish up their own offerings with inimitable style.

Key Largo offers all the conveniences of a major resort town, with most businesses lined up along Overseas Highway (U.S. 1), the four-lane highway that runs down the middle of the island. Cars whiz past at all hours—something to remember when you're booking a room. Most lodgings are on the highway, so you'll want to be as far back as possible.

GETTING HERE AND AROUND

Key Largo is 56 miles south of Miami International Airport, with the mile markers going from 106 to 91. The island runs northeast–southwest, with Overseas Highway running down the center. If the highway is your only glimpse of the island, you're likely to feel barraged by its tacky commercial side. Make a point of driving Route 905 in North Key Largo and down side streets to the marinas to get a better feel for it.

VISITOR INFORMATION

Contact **Key Largo Chamber of Commerce** ✉ *MM 106 BS, 10600 Overseas Hwy.* ☎ *305/451–4747, 800/822–1088* 🌐 *www.keylargochamber.org.*

EXPLORING

Dagny Johnson Key Largo Hammock Botanical State Park. American crocodiles, mangrove cuckoos, white-crowned pigeons, Schaus swallowtail butterflies, mahogany mistletoe, wild cotton, and 100 other rare critters and plants inhabit these 2,400 acres, sandwiched between Crocodile Lake National Wildlife Refuge and Pennekamp Coral Reef State Park. The park is also a user-friendly place to explore the largest remaining stand of the vast West Indian tropical hardwood hammock and mangrove wetland that once covered most of the Keys' upland areas. Interpretive signs describe many of the tropical tree species along a wide 1-mile paved road (2-miles round-trip) that invites walking and biking. There are also more than 6 miles of nature trails accessible to bikes and wheelchairs. Pets are welcome if on a leash no longer than 6 feet. You'll also find restrooms, information kiosks, and picnic tables. ✉ *0.5 mile north of Overseas Hwy., Rte. 905 OS, North Key Largo* ☎ *305/451–1202* 🌐 *www.floridastateparks.org/keylargohammock* 🎟 *$2.50* ⏲ *Daily 8–sundown.*

Dolphin Cove. This educational program begins at the facility's lagoon with a get-acquainted session from a platform. After that, you slip into the water for some frolicking with your new dolphin pals. The cost is $135 to $185. Spend the day shadowing a dolphin trainer for $630. Admission for nonparticipants is $10 for adults. ✉ *MM 101.9 BS, 101900 Overseas Hwy.* ☎ *305/451–4020, 877/365–2683* 🌐 *www.dolphinscove.com.*

Dolphins Plus. A sister property to Dolphin Cove, Dolphin Plus offers some of the same programs. Costing $135, the Natural Swim program begins with a one-hour briefing; then you enter the water to become totally immersed in the dolphins' world. In this visual orientation, participants snorkel but are not allowed to touch the dolphins. For tactile interaction (kissing, fin tows, etc.), sign up for the Structured Swim program ($185). The same concept with different critters, the sea lion swim costs $120. ✉ *MM 99, 31 Corrine Pl.* ☎ *305/451–1993, 866/860–7946* 🌐 *www.dolphinsplus.com.*

Jacobs Aquatic Center. Take the plunge at one of three swimming pools: an 8-lane, 25-meter lap pool with a diving well; a 3- to 4-foot-deep pool accessible to people with mobility problems; and an interactive play pool with a waterslide, pirate ship, waterfall, and sloping zero entry instead of steps. ✉ *MM 99.6 OS, 320 Laguna Ave., at St.*

Croix Pl. (at Key Largo Community Park) ☎ 305/453–7946 ⊕ www.jacobsaquaticcenter.org 🎫 $8–$10 ⏲ Daily 10–6 (10–7 in summer).

BEACHES

Fodor's Choice ★ **John Pennekamp Coral Reef State Park.** This state park is on everyone's list for close access to the best diving and snorkeling sites in the Sunshine State. The underwater treasure encompasses 78 square miles of coral reefs, sea-grass beds, and mangrove swamps and lies adjacent to the Florida Keys National Marine Sanctuary, which contains 40 of the 52 species of coral in the Atlantic Reef System and nearly 600 varieties of fish, from the colorful stoplight parrot fish to the demure cocoa damselfish. The park's visitor center has a 30,000-gallon floor-to-ceiling fish tank surrounded by smaller ones, so you can get a closer look at many of the underwater creatures. When you want to head out to sea, a concessionaire rents kayaks and powerboats, as well as snorkeling and diving equipment. You can also sign up for snorkeling and diving trips ($30 and $55, respectively, equipment extra) and glass-bottom-boat rides to the reef ($24). One of the most popular excursions is the snorkeling trip to see *Christ of the Deep*, the 2-ton underwater statue of Jesus. The park also has short nature trails, two man-made beaches, picnic shelters, a snack bar, and a campground. *✉ MM 102.5 OS, 102601 Overseas Hwy. ☎ 305/451–1202 for park, 305/451–6300 for excursions ⊕ www.pennekamppark.com, www.floridastateparks.org/pennekamp 🎫 $4.50 for 1 person in vehicle, $8 for 2–8 people, $2 for pedestrians and cyclists or extra people ⏲ Daily 8–sunset.*

WHERE TO EAT

$ SEAFOOD ★ **Alabama Jack's.** Calories be damned—the conch fritters here are heaven on a plate. The crab cakes, made from local blue crabs, earn hallelujahs, too. The conch salad is as good as any you'll find in the Bahamas and a third of the price in trendy Keys restaurants. This weathered, circa-1950 restaurant floats on two roadside barges in an old fishing community. Regulars include weekend cyclists, Miamians on the lam, and boaters, who come to admire tropical birds in the nearby mangroves, the occasional crocodile in the canal, or the bands that play on weekend afternoons. ■ **TIP→ It's about a half-hour drive from Key Largo, so you may want to plan a visit for your drive in or out.** Jack's closes by 7, when the mosquitoes start biting. *$ Average main: $11 ✉ 58000 Card Sound Rd. ☎ 305/248–8741 Reservations not accepted.*

$$$ SEAFOOD ★ **The Fish House.** Restaurants not on the water have to produce the highest quality food to survive in the Keys. That's how the Fish House has succeeded since the 1980s—so much so that it built the Fish House Encore next door to accommodate fans. The pan-sautéed black grouper will make you moan with pleasure, but it's just one of many headliners in this nautical eatery. On the fin side, the choices include mahimahi, swordfish, tuna, and yellowtail snapper that can be broiled, blackened, baked, or fried. The Matecumbe Catch prepares the day's fresh fish so simply and flavorfully it should be patented—baked with tomatoes, capers, olive oil, and lemon juice. Prefer shellfish? Choose from shrimp, lobster, and (mid-October to mid-May) stone crab. For a sweet ending, try the homemade key lime pie. *$ Average main: $21 ✉ MM 102.4*

DID YOU KNOW?

The bronze *Christ of the Deep* (also called *Christ of the Abyss*) statue of Jesus Christ underwater near John Pennekamp Coral Reef State Park is modeled after one in the Mediterranean Sea near where Italian Dario Gonzatti died while scuba diving.

OS, 102341 Overseas Hwy. ☎ *305/451–4665* ⊕ *www.fishhouse.com* ✍ *Reservations not accepted* ⊙ *Closed Sept.*

$ AMERICAN ✕ **Harriette's Restaurant.** If you're looking for comfort food—like melt-in-your-mouth buttermilk biscuits—try this refreshing throwback. The kitchen makes fresh muffins daily, in flavors like mango, chocolate, and key lime. Little has changed over the years in this yellow-and-turquoise eatery. Owner Harriette Mattson often personally greets guests who come for steak and eggs with hash browns or old-fashioned hotcakes with sausage or bacon. Stick to simple dishes; the eggs Benedict are a disappointment. At lunch- and dinnertime, Harriette's shines in the burger department, but there are also hot meals such as chicken-fried steak and a fried shrimp basket. $ *Average main: $8* ✉ *MM 95.7 BS, 95710 Overseas Hwy.* ☎ *305/852–8689* ✍ *Reservations not accepted* ⊙ *No dinner Fri.–Sun.*

4

$ AMERICAN ✕ **Key Largo Conch House.** Tucked into the trees along the Overseas Highway, this Victorian-style home and its true-to-the-Keys style of cooking are worth seeking out—at least the Food Network and the Travel Channel have thought so in the past. Family-owned since 2004, it feels welcoming either indoors around the coffee bar or on the Old South veranda. Raisin pecan French toast and eight varieties of Benedicts, including conch, are reason enough to rise early and get your fresh coffee fix. Lunch and dinner menus cover all bases from conch chowder bread bowl and vegetarian wraps to lobster and conch ceviche, andouille Alfredo, and yellowtail Florentine. $ *Average main: $15* ✉ *Key Largo* ☎ *305/453–4844* ⊕ *www.keylargoconchhouse.com* ✍ *Reservations essential.*

$ SEAFOOD ✕ **Mrs. Mac's Kitchen.** Townies pack the counters and booths at this tiny eatery, where license plates are stuck on the walls and made into chandeliers. Got a hankering for meat loaf or crab cakes? You'll find them here, along with specials like grilled yellowfin tuna. Bring your appetite for the all-you-can-eat catfish special on Tuesday and all-you-can-eat spaghetti on Thursday. There's also champagne breakfast, an assortment of tasty Angus beef burgers and sandwiches, and its famous chili and key lime freeze (somewhere between a shake and a float). In season, ask about the hogfish special du jour. $ *Average main: $15* ✉ *MM 99.4 BS, 99336 Overseas Hwy.* ☎ *305/451–3722* ⊕ *www.mrsmacskitchen.com* ✍ *Reservations not accepted* ⊙ *Closed Sun.*

$$ SEAFOOD ★ ✕ **Snapper's.** "You hook 'em, we cook 'em" is the motto here. Alas, "cleanin' 'em" is not part of the bargain. If you bring in your ready-for-the-grill fish, dinner here is $12 for a single, $13 per person family style with a mix of preparations. Otherwise, they'll catch and prepare you a plank-roasted yellowtail snapper, Thai-seared tuna, fish of the day baked with 36 herbs and spices, or a little something from the raw bar. The ceviche of yellowtail, shrimp, and conch (merrily spiced) wins raves, too. The seafood burrito on the sandwich board is a keeper. All this is served up in a lively, mangrove-ringed waterfront setting with live music, an aquarium bar, Sunday brunch (including a Bloody Mary bar), killer rum drinks, and seating alongside the fishing dock. Three-course early-bird dinner specials are available 5–6 for $18.50. $ *Av-*

erage main: $15 ✉ *MM 94.5 OS, 139 Seaside Ave.* ☎ *305/852–5956* 🌐 *www.snapperskeylargo.com* ✍ *Reservations not accepted.*

$$$ AMERICAN
✕ **Sundowners.** The name doesn't lie. If it's a clear night and you can snag a reservation, this restaurant will treat you to a sherbet-hue sunset over Florida Bay. If you're here in mild weather—anytime other than the dog days of summer or the rare winter cold snap—the best seats are on the patio. The food is excellent: try the key lime seafood, a happy combo of sautéed shrimp, lobster, and lump crabmeat swimming in a tangy sauce spiked with Tabasco served over penne or rice. Wednesday and Saturday are all about prime rib, and Friday draws the crowds with an all-you-can-eat fish fry ($16). Vegetarian and gluten-free menus are available. [$] *Average main: $22* ✉ *MM 104 BS, 103900 Overseas Hwy.* ☎ *305/451–4502* 🌐 *sundownerskeylargo.com* ✍ *Reservations essential.*

WHERE TO STAY

For expanded reviews, facilities, and current deals, visit Fodors.com.

$$$ B&B/INN ★
Azul del Mar. The dock points the way to many beautiful sunsets at this adults-only boutique hotel. **Pros:** great garden; good location; sophisticated design. **Cons:** small beach; close to highway; high-priced. **TripAdvisor:** "a romantic hideaway from life," "gorgeous," "nice surprise." [$] *Rooms from: $189* ✉ *MM 104.3 BS, 104300 Overseas Hwy.* ☎ *305/451–0337, 888/253–2985* 🌐 *www.azulhotels.us* *2 studios, 3 1-bedroom suites, 1 2-bedroom suite* *No meals.*

$$ RESORT
Coconut Bay Resort & Bay Harbor Lodge. Some 200 feet of waterfront is the main attraction at this property, a combination of two lodging options. **Pros:** bay front; neatly kept gardens; walking distance to restaurants; complimentary kayak and paddleboat use. **Cons:** a bit dated; small sea-walled sand beach. **TripAdvisor:** "just paradise," "simply perfect," "a beautiful hideaway." [$] *Rooms from: $105* ✉ *MM 97.7 BS, 97702 Overseas Hwy.* ☎ *305/852–1625, 800/385–0986* 🌐 *www.coconutbaykeylargo.com* *7 rooms, 5 efficiencies, 2 suites, 1 2-bedroom villa, 6 1-bedroom cottages* *No meals.*

$$$$ B&B/INN
Dove Creek Lodge. Old-school anglers will likely be scandalized by this 2004 fishing camp's sherbet-hue paint and plantation-style furnishings. **Pros:** great for fishing enthusiasts; luxurious rooms; close to Snapper's restaurant. **Cons:** loud music next door. **TripAdvisor:** "great breakfast," "good place to unwind," "a private place." [$] *Rooms from: $229* ✉ *MM 94.5 OS, 147 Seaside Ave.* ☎ *305/852–6200, 800/401–0057* 🌐 *www.dovecreeklodge.com* *4 room, 10 suites* *Breakfast.*

$$$$ RESORT Fodor's Choice ★
Kona Kai Resort, Gallery & Botanic Gardens. Brilliantly colored bougainvilleas, coconut palms, guava trees, and a new botanical garden of rare species make this 2-acre hideaway one of the prettiest places to stay in the Keys. **Pros:** free custom tours of botanical gardens for guests; free use of sports equipment; knowledgeable staff. **Cons:** expensive; some rooms are very close together. **TripAdvisor:** "lovely property," "awesome experience," "little slice of paradise." [$] *Rooms from: $269* ✉ *MM 97.8 BS, 97802 Overseas Hwy.* ☎ *305/852–7200, 800/365–7829* 🌐 *www.konakairesort.com* *8 suites, 3 rooms* *Closed Sept.* *No meals.*

$$$ B&B/INN ★ **Largo Lodge.** When you drive under the dense canopy of foliage at the entrance to Largo Lodge you'll feel like you've escaped Overseas Highway's bustle. **Pros:** lush grounds; great sunset views; affordable rates; boat docking. **Cons:** no pool; some traffic noise outdoors. **TripAdvisor:** "tropical and quiet," "relaxation," "peaceful and beautiful." *Rooms from: $175 ✉ MM 101.7 BS, 101740 Overseas Hwy. ☎ 305/451–0424, 800/468–4378 🌐 www.largolodge.com 2 rooms, 6 cottages No meals.*

$$ RESORT ★ **Marriott's Key Largo Bay Beach Resort.** This 17-acre bay-side resort has plenty of diversions, from diving to parasailing to a day spa. **Pros:** lots of activities; free covered parking; dive shop on property; free Wi-Fi. **Cons:** rooms facing highway can be noisy; thin walls; unspectacular beach. **TripAdvisor:** "friendly staff," "lovely resort," "a little slice of heaven." *Rooms from: $139 ✉ MM 103.8 BS, 103800 Overseas Hwy. ☎ 305/453–0000, 866/849–3753 🌐 www.marriottkeylargo.com 132 rooms, 20 2-bedroom suites, 1 penthouse suite No meals.*

$ HOTEL **The Pelican.** This 1950s throwback is reminiscent of the days when parents packed the kids into the station wagon and headed to no-frills seaside motels, complete with an old-timer fishing off the dock. **Pros:** free use of kayaks and a canoe; well-maintained dock; reasonable rates. **Cons:** some small rooms; basic accommodations and amenities. **TripAdvisor:** "clean and friendly," "nice peaceful place on the water," "nothing fancy but it works." *Rooms from: $60 ✉ MM 99.3, 99340 Overseas Hwy. ☎ 305/451–3576, 877/451–3576 🌐 www.hungrypelican.com 13 rooms, 4 efficiencies, 4 suites, 2 trailers No meals.*

$ HOTEL **Seafarer Resort.** It's very basic budget lodging, but the Seafarer Resort is not without its charms. **Pros:** sandy beach; complimentary kayak use; cheap rates. **Cons:** some rooms close to road noise; some complaints about cleanliness; no toiletries of any kind provided. **TripAdvisor:** "great location," "old Florida feel," "excellent service." *Rooms from: $85 ✉ MM 97.6 BS, 97684 Overseas Hwy. ☎ 305/852–5349 🌐 www.seafarerresort.com 8 rooms, 3 studios, 3 1-bedroom cottages, 1 2-bedroom cottage, 2 apartments No meals.*

NIGHTLIFE

The semiweekly *Keynoter* (Wednesday and Saturday), weekly *Reporter* (Thursday), and Friday through Sunday editions of the *Miami Herald* are the best sources of information on entertainment and nightlife. Daiquiri bars, tiki huts, and seaside shacks pretty well summarize Key Largo's bar scene.

Breezers Tiki Bar & Grille. Mingle with locals over cocktails and sunsets at Marriott's Key Largo Bay Beach Resort. *✉ MM 103.8 BS, 103800 Overseas Hwy. ☎ 305/453–0000.*

★ **Caribbean Club.** Walls plastered with Bogart memorabilia remind customers that the classic 1948 Bogart–Bacall flick *Key Largo* has a connection with this club. It draws boaters, curious visitors, and local barfly types, all of whom happily mingle and shoot pool. Postcard-perfect sunsets and live music draw revelers on weekends. *✉ MM 104 BS, 10404 Overseas Hwy. ☎ 305/451–4466.*

4

Coconuts. Live music fills both the indoor and outdoor areas of this bar throughout most of the week. Outside around the pool it's a family scene, with food service and a bar. Inside is strictly a thirty- and fortysomething crowd, including a few seasoned townies, playing pool, watching sports TV, and enjoying the music. ✉ *MM 100 OS, Marina Del Mar Resort, 528 Caribbean Dr.* ☎ *305/453–9794.*

SHOPPING

For the most part, shopping is sporadic in Key Largo, with a couple of shopping centers and fewer galleries than you find on the other big islands. If you're looking to buy scuba or snorkeling equipment, you'll have plenty of places from which to choose.

Bluewater Potters. Bluewater Potters creates functional and decorative pieces ranging from signature vases and kitchenware to one-of-a-kind pieces where the owners' creative talent at the wheel blazes. ✉ *MM 102.9 OS, 102991 Overseas Hwy.* ☎ *305/453–1920* 🌐 *www.bluewaterpotters.com.*

SPORTS AND THE OUTDOORS

BOATING

Everglades Eco-Tours. Captain Sterling operates Everglades and Florida Bay ecology tours ($50 per person) and sunset cruises ($75 per person). ✉ *MM 104 BS, Sundowners Restaurant, 103900 Overseas Hwy.* ☎ *305/853–5161, 888/224–6044* 🌐 *www.captainsterling.com.*

M.V. *Key Largo Princess.* Two-hour glass-bottom-boat trips and sunset cruises on a luxury 75-foot motor yacht with a 280-square-foot glass viewing area (each $30) depart from the Holiday Inn docks three times a day. ✉ *MM 100 OS, 99701 Overseas Hwy.* ☎ *305/451–4655, 877/648–8129* 🌐 *www.keylargoprincess.com.*

CANOEING AND KAYAKING

Sea kayaking continues to gain popularity in the Keys. You can paddle for a few hours or the whole day, on your own or with a guide. Some outfitters even offer overnight trips. The **Florida Keys Overseas Paddling Trail,** part of a statewide system, runs from Key Largo to Key West. You can paddle the entire distance, 110 miles on the Atlantic side, which takes 9–10 days. The trail also runs the chain's length on the bay side, which is a longer route.

Coral Reef Park Co. At John Pennekamp Coral Reef State Park, this operator has a fleet of canoes and kayaks for gliding around the 2½-mile mangrove trail or along the coast. It also rents powerboats. ✉ *MM 102.5 OS, 102601 Overseas Hwy.* ☎ *305/451–6300* 🌐 *www.pennekamppark.com.*

Florida Bay Outfitters. Rent canoes or sea kayaks from this company, which sets up self-guided trips on the Florida Keys Overseas Paddling Trail, helps with trip planning, and matches equipment to your skill level. It also runs myriad guided tours around Key Largo. Take a full-moon paddle or a one- to seven-day canoe or kayak tour to the Everglades, Lignumvitae Key, or Indian Key. Trips start at $60 for three hours. ✉ *MM 104 BS, 104050 Overseas Hwy.* ☎ *305/451–3018* 🌐 *www.kayakfloridakeys.com.*

FISHING

Private charters and big head boats (so named because they charge "by the head") are great for anglers who don't have their own vessel.

Sailors Choice. Fishing excursions depart twice daily ($40 cash for half-day trips). The 65-foot boat leaves from the Holiday Inn docks. Rods, bait, and license are included. ✉ *MM 100 OS, Holiday Inn Resort & Marina, 99701 Overseas Hwy.* ☎ *305/451–1802, 305/451–0041* 🌐 *www.sailorschoicefishingboat.com.*

WORD OF MOUTH

"Went on the snorkeling trip out of John Pennekamp State Park. The total was $44 for snorkel trip, full rental including wet suit. Really enjoyed the trip, but wished I had driven down for the 9 am trip—there were fewer snorkelers and the website offered a discount coupon for the morning tour."

—starrsville

SCUBA DIVING AND SNORKELING

Much of what makes the Upper Keys a singular dive destination is variety. Places like Molasses Reef, which begins 3 feet below the surface and descends to 55 feet, have something for everyone, from novice snorkelers to experienced divers. The *Spiegel Grove,* a 510-foot vessel, lies in 130 feet of water, but its upper regions are only 60 feet below the surface. On rough days, Key Largo Undersea Park's Emerald Lagoon is a popular spot. Expect to pay about $80 for a two-tank, two-site-dive trip with tanks and weights, or $35–$40 for a two-site-snorkel outing. Get big discounts by booking multiple trips.

Amy Slate's Amoray Dive Resort. This outfit makes diving easy. Stroll down to the full-service dive shop (NAUI, PADI, TDI, and BSAC certified), then onto a 45-foot catamaran. The rate for a two-dive trip is $80. ✉ *MM 104.2 BS, 104250 Overseas Hwy.* ☎ *305/451–3595, 800/426–6729* 🌐 *www.amoray.com.*

★ **Conch Republic Divers.** Book diving instruction as well as scuba and snorkeling tours of all the wrecks and reefs of the Upper Keys. Two-location dives are $85 with tank and weights or $65 without the equipment. ✉ *MM 90.8 BS, 90800 Overseas Hwy.* ☎ *305/852–1655, 800/274–3483* 🌐 *www.conchrepublicdivers.com.*

Coral Reef Park Co. At John Pennekamp Coral Reef State Park, this company gives 3½-hour scuba ($55) and 2½-hour snorkeling ($30) tours of the park. In addition to the great location and the dependability, it's also suited for water adventurers of all levels. ✉ *MM 102.5 OS, 102601 Overseas Hwy.* ☎ *305/451–6300* 🌐 *www.pennekamppark.com.*

Ocean Divers. The PADI five-star facility offers day and night dives, a range of courses, and dive-lodging packages. The cost is $85 for a two-tank reef dive with tank and weight rental. Snorkel trips cost $35 with equipment. ✉ *MM 100 OS, 522 Caribbean Dr.* ☎ *305/451–1113, 800/451–1113* 🌐 *www.oceandivers.com .*

Quiescence Diving Services. This operator sets itself apart in two ways: it limits groups to six to ensure personal attention and offers day and night dives, as well as twilight dives when sea creatures are most active. Two-dive trips start at $69 without equipment. ✉ *MM 103.5 BS, 103680 Overseas Hwy.* ☎ *305/451–2440* 🌐 *www.quiescence.com.*

ISLAMORADA

Islamorada is between mile markers 90.5 and 70.

Early settlers named this key after their schooner, *Island Home*, but to make it sound more romantic they translated it into Spanish: *Isla Morada*. The chamber of commerce prefers to use its literal translation "Purple Island," which refers either to a purple-shelled snail that once inhabited these shores or to the brilliantly colored orchids and bougainvilleas.

Early maps show Islamorada as encompassing only Upper Matecumbe Key. But the incorporated "Village of Islands" is made up of a string of islands that the Overseas Highway crosses, including Plantation Key, Windley Key, Upper Matecumbe Key, Lower Matecumbe Key, Craig Key, and Fiesta Key. In addition, two state-park islands accessible only by boat—Indian Key and Lignumvitae Key—belong to the group.

Islamorada (locals pronounce it *eye*-la-mor-*ah*-da) is one of the world's top fishing destinations. For nearly 100 years, seasoned anglers have fished these clear, warm waters teeming with trophy-worthy fish. There are numerous options for those in search of the big ones, including chartering a boat with its own crew or heading out on a vessel rented from one of the plethora of marinas along this 20-mile stretch of the Overseas Highway. Islamorada is one of the more affluent resort areas of the Keys. Sophisticated resorts and restaurants meet the needs of those in search of luxury, but there's also plenty for those looking for something more casual and affordable. Art galleries and boutiques make Islamorada's shopping scene the best in the Upper Keys, but if you're shopping for groceries, head to Marathon or Key Largo.

ESSENTIALS

Visitor Information **Islamorada Chamber of Commerce & Visitors Center** ✉ *MM 83.2 BS, 83224 Overseas Hwy, Upper Matecumbe Key* ☎ *305/664–4503, 800/322–5397* 🌐 *www.islamoradachamber.com.*

EXPLORING

History of Diving Museum. Adding to the region's reputation for world-class diving, this museum plunges into the history of man's thirst for undersea exploration. Among its 13 galleries of interactive and other interesting displays are a submarine and helmet re-created from the film *20,000 Leagues Under the Sea*. Vintage U.S. Navy equipment, diving helmets from around the world, and early scuba gear explore 4,000 years of diving history. ✉ *MM 83 BS, 82990 Overseas Hwy., Upper Matecumbe Key* ☎ *305/664–9737* 🌐 *www.divingmuseum.org* 🎟 *$12* ⏲ *Daily 10–5.*

★ **Robbie's Marina.** Huge, prehistoric-looking denizens of the not-so-deep, silver-sided tarpon congregate around the docks at this marina on Lower Matecumbe Key. Children—and lots of adults—pay $3 for a bucket of sardines to feed them and $1 each for dock admission. Spend some time hanging out at this authentic Keys community, where you can

Islamorada's warm waters attract large fish and the anglers and charter captains who want to catch them.

grab a bite to eat, do a little shopping at the artisans' booths, or charter a boat. ✉ *MM 77.5 BS, 77522 Overseas Hwy., Lower Matecumbe Key* ☎ *305/664–9814, 877/664–8498* 🌐 *www.robbies.com* 🎫 *Dock access $1* ⏲ *Daily sunrise–sunset.*

Theater of the Sea. The second-oldest marine-mammal center in the world doesn't attempt to compete with more modern, more expensive parks. Even so, it's among the better attractions north of Key West, especially if you have kids in tow. Like the pricier parks, there are dolphin, sea lion, and stingray encounters ($55–$185, which includes general admission; reservations required) where you can get up close and personal with underwater creatures. These are popular, so reserve in advance. Ride a "bottomless" boat to see what's below the waves and take a guided tour of the marine-life exhibits. Entertaining educational shows highlight conservation issues. You can stop for lunch at the grill, shop in the boutique, or sunbathe at a lagoon-side beach. This easily could be an all-day attraction. ✉ *MM 84.5 OS, 84721 Overseas Hwy., Windley Key* ☎ *305/664–2431* 🌐 *www.theaterofthesea.com* 🎫 *$26.95* ⏲ *Daily 9:30–5 (last ticket sold at 3:30).*

Upper Matecumbe Key. This was one of the first of the Upper Keys to be permanently settled. Early homesteaders were so successful at growing pineapples in the rocky soil that at one time the island yielded the country's largest annual crop. However, foreign competition and the hurricane of 1935 killed the industry. Today life centers on fishing and tourism, and the island is filled with bait shops, marinas, and charter-fishing boats. ✉ *MM 84–79.*

OFF THE BEATEN PATH

Indian Key Historic State Park. Mystery surrounds 10-acre Indian Key, on the ocean side of the Matecumbe islands. Before it became one of the first European settlements outside of Key West, it was inhabited by American Indians for several thousand years. The islet served as a base for 19th-century shipwreck salvagers until an Indian attack wiped out the settlement in 1840. Dr. Henry Perrine, a noted botanist, was killed in the raid. Today his plants grow in the town's ruins. Most people kayak or canoe here from Indian Key Fill or Robbie's Marina (about 20 minutes away by paddle) to tour the nature trails and the town ruins or to snorkel. There are no restrooms or picnic facilities on Indian Key. ☎ *305/664–2540 park, 305/664–8070 boat tour* ⊕ *www.floridastateparks.org/indiankey* 🎫 *Free* ⏲ *Daily 8–5.*

OFF THE BEATEN PATH

Lignumvitae Key Botanical State Park. On the National Register of Historic Places, this 280-acre bay-side island is the site of a virgin hardwood forest and the 1919 home of chemical magnate William Matheson. His caretaker's cottage serves as the park's visitor center. Access is by boat—your own, a rented vessel, or a tour operated by Robbie's Marina. The tour leaves at 8:30 am Friday through Sunday and takes in both Lignumvitae and Indian keys (reservations required). Paddling here from Indian Key Fill, at MM 78.5, is a popular pastime. The only way to do the trails is by a guided ranger walk, offered at 10 am and 2 pm Friday to Sunday. Wear long sleeves and pants, and bring mosquito repellent. On the first Saturday in December is the Lignumvitae Christmas Celebration, when the historic home is decorated 1930s-style. ☎ *305/664–2540 park, 305/664–8070 boat tours* ⊕ *www.floridastateparks.org/lignumvitaekey* 🎫 *$1 for ranger tours; $35 for boat tours* ⏲ *Park Thurs.–Mon. 8–5; house tours Fri.–Sun at 10 and 2.*

Windley Key Fossil Reef Geological State Park. The fossilized-coral reef, dating back about 125,000 years, demonstrates that the Florida Keys were once beneath the ocean. Excavation of Windley Key's limestone bed by the Florida East Coast Railway exposed the petrified reef, full of beautifully fossilized brain coral and sea ferns. Visitors can see the fossils along a 300-foot quarry wall when hiking the park's three trails. There are guided (Friday, Saturday, and Sunday only) and self-guided tours along the trails, which lead to the railway's old quarrying equipment and cutting pits, where you can make rubbings of the quarry walls. The **Alison Fahrer Environmental Education Center** holds historic, biological, and geological displays about the area, including videos. The first Saturday in March is Windley Key Day, when the park sells native plants and hosts environmental exhibits. ✉ *MM 84.9 BS, Windley Key* ☎ *305/664–2540* ⊕ *www.floridastateparks.org/windleykey* 🎫 *Education center free, $2.50 for park self-tours, $1 for ranger-guided tours* ⏲ *Education center Fri.–Sun. 9–5 (tours at 10 and 2).*

BEACHES

Anne's Beach Park. On Lower Matecumbe Key is a popular village park, named for a local environmental activist. Its "beach" (really a typical Keys-style sand flat) is best enjoyed at low tide. The nicest feature here is a ½-mile, elevated, wooden boardwalk that meanders through a natural wetland hammock. Covered picnic areas along the way give you places to linger and enjoy the view. Restrooms are at the north end.

Weekends are packed with Miami day-trippers, as it's the only public beach until you reach Marathon. ✉ *MM 73.5 OS, Lower Matecumbe Key* ☎ *305/853–1685.*

WHERE TO EAT

$$$ SEAFOOD ✕ **Green Turtle Inn.** This circa-1928 landmark inn and its vintage neon sign is a slice of Florida Keys history. Period photographs decorate the wood-paneled walls. Breakfast and lunch options include surprises like coconut French toast made with Cuban bread and a yellowtail po' boy. Chef Dan Harris relies heavily on Cajun cuisine with global touches for the dinner menu; think turtle chowder (don't gasp; it's made from farm-raised freshwater turtles), osso bucco, gumbo, and five-spice blackened tuna. Naturally, there's a Turtle Sundae on the dessert menu. [$] *Average main: $24* ✉ *MM 81.2 OS, 81219 Overseas Hwy., Upper Matecumbe Key* ☎ *305/664–2006* 🌐 *www.greenturtlekeys.com* ✍ *Reservations essential* ⏲ *Closed Mon.*

4

$ SEAFOOD ★ ✕ **Island Grill.** Don't be fooled by appearances; this shack on the waterfront takes island breakfast, lunch, and dinner cuisine up a notch. The eclectic menu tempts you with such dishes as its famed "original tuna nachos," lobster rolls, and a nice selection of seafood and sandwiches. Southern-style shrimp and andouille sausage with grits join island-style specialties such as grilled ribs with guava barbecue sauce on the list of entrées. There's an air-conditioned dining room and bar as well as open seating under a vaulted porch ceiling. The outdoor bar hosts live entertainment Wednesday to Sunday. [$] *Average main: $12* ✉ *MM 85.5 OS, 85501 Overseas Hwy., Windley Key* ☎ *305/664–8400* 🌐 *www.keysislandgrill.com* ✍ *Reservations not accepted.*

$$$ JAPANESE ✕ **Kaiyó Grill & Sushi.** The decor—an inviting setting that includes colorful abstract mosaics, polished wood floors, and upholstered banquettes—almost steals the show at Kaiyó, but the food is equally interesting. The menu, a fusion of East and West, offers sushi rolls that combine local ingredients with traditional Japanese tastes. A wood grill is used to prepare such dishes as grilled catch-of-the-day and hardwood grilled rack of lamb. The rice paper–wrapped fried banana with warm chocolate ganache and vanilla ice cream exemplifies the collision of Asia and Florida on the dessert menu. [$] *Average main: $28* ✉ *MM 81.5 OS, 81701 Overseas Hwy., Upper Matecumbe Key* ☎ *305/664–5556* 🌐 *www.kaiyogrill.com* ⏲ *No lunch.*

$$$ SEAFOOD ★ ✕ **Marker 88.** A few yards from Florida Bay, this seafood restaurant has been popular since the late '60s. Large picture windows offer great sunset views, but the bay is lovely no matter what time of day you visit. Chef Sal Barrios serves such irresistible entrées as onion-crusted mahimahi, crispy yellowtail snapper, and mangrove-honey-and-chipotle–glazed rib eye. In addition, there are a half-dozen burgers and sandwiches, and you can't miss the restaurant's famous key lime baked Alaska dessert. The extensive wine list is an oenophile's delight. [$] *Average main: $28* ✉ *MM 88 BS, 88000 Overseas Hwy., Plantation Key* ☎ *305/852–9315* 🌐 *www.marker88.info* ✍ *Reservations essential.*

$$$ ECLECTIC ★ **Morada Bay Beach Café.** This bay-front restaurant wins high marks for its surprisingly stellar cuisine, tables planted in the sand, and tiki torches that bathe the evening in romance. Entrées feature alluring combinations like fresh fish of the day sautéed with Meyer lemon butter and whole fried snapper with coconut rice. Seafood takes center stage, but you can always get roasted organic chicken or prime rib. Tapas and raw bar menus cater to smaller appetites or those who can't decide with offerings like fried calamari, conch fritters, and Wagyu beef sliders. Lunch adds interesting sandwiches to the mix, plus there's breakfast Friday through Sunday. Sit in a dining room outfitted with surfboards, or outdoors on a beach, where the sunset puts on a mighty show and kids (and your feet) play in the sand. *Average main: $27 MM 81 BS, 81600 Overseas Hwy., Upper Matecumbe Key 305/664–0604 www.moradabay-restaurant.com Closed Tues. No breakfast Mon.–Thurs.*

$$$$ FRENCH Fodor's Choice ★ **Pierre's.** One of the Keys' most elegant restaurants, Pierre's marries colonial style with modern food trends. Full of interesting architectural artifacts, the place oozes style, especially the wicker chair–strewn veranda overlooking the bay. Save your best "tropical chic" duds for dinner here, so you don't stand out from your surroundings. The food, drawn from French and Floridian influences, is multilayered and beautifully presented. Among the seasonally changing appetizer choices, you might find smoked hogfish chowder and foie gras sliders with a butternut squash milk shake. A changing list of entrées might include hogfish meunière and scallops with pork belly tortellini. The downstairs bar is a perfect spot for catching sunsets, sipping martinis, and enjoying light eats. *Average main: $35 MM 81.5 BS, 81600 Overseas Hwy., Upper Matecumbe Key 305/664–3225 www.pierres-restaurant.com Reservations essential No lunch.*

$$$ ITALIAN **Uncle's Restaurant.** Former fishing guide Joe LePree adds Italian flair to standard seafood dishes. Here you can have your seafood almandine, Milanese (breaded and fried), LePree (with artichokes, mushrooms, and lemon-butter wine sauce), or any of five other different preparations. For starters, feast on mussels or littleneck clams in a marinara or garlic sauce. Specials sometimes combine game (bison, caribou, or elk) with seafood. Portions are huge, so share dishes or take home a doggie bag. Alternatively, arrive early (between 5 and 7) for the lighter menu, priced $12.95 to $17.95. Weather permitting, sit outdoors in the garden; poor acoustics make dining indoors unusually noisy. *Average main: $21 MM 81 OS, 80939 Overseas Hwy., Upper Matecumbe Key 305/664–4402 www.unclesrestaurant.com Closed Mon.*

WHERE TO STAY

For expanded reviews, facilities, and current deals, visit Fodors.com.

$$$$ B&B/INN Fodor's Choice ★ **Casa Morada.** This relic from the 1950s has been restyled into a suave, design-forward, all-suites property with outdoor showers and Jacuzzis in some of the suites. **Pros:** cool design; complimentary snacks and bottled water; complimentary use of bikes, kayaks, and snorkel gear. **Cons:** trailer park across the street; beach is small and inconsequential. **TripAdvisor:** "a perfect getaway," "pure bliss," "nice place for relaxation." *Rooms from: $299 MM 82 BS, 136 Madeira Rd., Upper*

Matecumbe Key ☎ 305/664–0044, 888/881–3030 🌐 www.casamorada.com ⇨ 16 suites 🍴 Breakfast.

$$$$ RESORT ★ **Cheeca Lodge & Spa.** In the main lodge, West Indian–style rooms boast luxurious touches like elegant balcony tubs that fill from the ceiling. **Pros:** beautifully landscaped grounds; new designer rooms; dive shop on property. **Cons:** expensive rates; $39 resort fee for activities; busy. **TripAdvisor:** "an upscale oasis," "casual elegance at its finest," "a beautiful retreat." *$ Rooms from: $299 ✉ MM 82 OS, Box 527, Upper Matecumbe Key ☎ 305/664–4651, 800/327–2888 🌐 www.cheeca.com ⇨ 60 1-bedroom suites, 64 junior suites 🍴 No meals.*

$$ HOTEL ★ **Drop Anchor Resort and Marina.** It's easy to find your cottage here, as they are painted in an array of Crayola colors. **Pros:** bright and colorful; attention to detail; laid-back charm. **Cons:** noise from the highway; beach is better for fishing than swimming. **TripAdvisor:** "pleasantly surprised," "really relaxing," "cool." *$ Rooms from: $129 ✉ MM 85 OS, 84959 Overseas Hwy., Windley Key ☎ 305/664–4863, 888/664–4863 🌐 www.dropanchorresort.com ⇨ 18 suites 🍴 No meals.*

4

$$$$ RESORT **The Islander Resort.** While the general waterfront layout here (including the retro sign) retains a 1950s feel, the decor is modern yet comfortable, with white cottage-style furnishings, elegant fabrics, and sunny yellow bedrooms. **Pros:** spacious rooms; nice kitchens; eye-popping views. **Cons:** pricey for what you get; beach has rough sand; no a/c in the screened gym. **TripAdvisor:** "great staff," "fantastic view," "ultimate relaxation." *$ Rooms from: $249 ✉ MM 82.1 OS, 82200 Overseas Hwy., Upper Matecumbe Key ☎ 305/664–2031, 800/753–6002 🌐 www.islanderfloridakeys.com ⇨ 114 rooms, 12 suites 🍴 Breakfast.*

$$$$ HOTEL Fodor's Choice ★ **The Moorings Village.** This tropical retreat is everything you imagine when you think of the Keys—from hammocks swaying between towering trees to sugar-white sand (arguably the Keys' best resort beach) lapped by aqua-green waves. **Pros:** romantic setting; good dining options with room-charging privileges; beautiful beach. **Cons:** no room service; extra fee for housekeeping; daily resort fee for activities. **TripAdvisor:** "perfect romantic getaway," "sets a very high bar," "peaceful and serene setting." *$ Rooms from: $375 ✉ MM 81.6 OS, 123 Beach Rd., Upper Matecumbe Key ☎ 305/664–4708 🌐 www.themooringsvillage.com ⇨ 6 cottages, 12 houses 🍴 No meals.*

$ HOTEL **Ragged Edge Resort.** Tucked away in a residential area at the ocean's edge, this hotel is big on value but short on style. **Pros:** oceanfront location; boat docks and ramp; cheap rates. **Cons:** dated decor; off the beaten path. **TripAdvisor:** "super friendly staff," "great quiet place," "so incredibly relaxing." *$ Rooms from: $100 ✉ MM 86.5 OS, 243 Treasure Harbor Rd., Plantation Key ☎ 305/852–5389, 800/436–2023 🌐 www.ragged-edge.com ⇨ 6 studios, 1 efficiency, 3 2-bedroom suites 🍴 No meals.*

NIGHTLIFE

Islamorada is not known for its raging nightlife, but for local fun Lorelei's is legendary. Others cater to the town's sophisticated clientele and fishing fervor.

★ **Lorelei Restaurant & Cabana Bar.** Behind a larger-than-life mermaid, this is the kind of place you fantasize about during those long cold winters up north. It's all about good drinks, tasty pub grub, and beautiful sunsets set to live bands playing island tunes and light rock nightly. ✉ *MM 82 BS, 81924 Overseas Hwy., Upper Matecumbe Key* ☎ *305/664–2692* 🌐 *www.loreleicabanabar.com.*

SHOPPING

Art galleries, upscale gift shops, and the mammoth World Wide Sportsman (if you want to look the part of a local fisherman, you must wear a shirt from here) make up the variety and superior style of Islamorada shopping.

Banyan Tree. A sharp-eyed husband-and-wife team successfully combines antiques and contemporary gifts for the home and garden with plants, pots, and trellises in a stylishly sophisticated indoor–outdoor setting. ✉ *MM 81.2 OS, 81197 Overseas Hwy., Upper Matecumbe Key* ☎ *305/664–3433* 🌐 *www.banyantreegarden.com.*

Gallery Morada. The go-to destination for one-of-a-kind gifts beautifully displays blown-glass objects, original sculptures, paintings, lithographs, and jewelry by 200 artists. ✉ *MM 81.6 OS, 81611 Old Hwy., Upper Matecumbe Key* ☎ *305/664–3650* 🌐 *www.gallerymorada.com.*

Hooked on Books. Among the best buys in town are the used best sellers at this bookstore, which also sells new titles, audiobooks, and CDs. ✉ *MM 81.9 OS, 81909 Overseas Hwy., Upper Matecumbe Key* ☎ *305/517–2602* 🌐 *www.hookedonbooksfloridakeys.com.*

Island Silver & Spice. The shop stocks tropical-style furnishings, rugs, and home accessories, as well as women's and men's resort wear and a large jewelry selection with high-end watches and marine-theme pieces. ✉ *MM 82 OS, 81981 Overseas Hwy., Upper Matecumbe Key* ☎ *305/664–2714.*

Rain Barrel Artisan Village. This is a natural and unhurried shopping showplace. Set in a tropical garden of shady trees, native shrubs, and orchids, the crafts village has shops with works by local and national artists and resident artists in studios, including John Hawver, noted for Florida landscapes and seascapes. The Main Gallery up front showcases the craftsmanship of the resident artisans, who create marine-inspired artwork while you watch. ✉ *MM 86.7 BS, 86700 Overseas Hwy., Plantation Key* ☎ *305/852–3084.*

Redbone Gallery. One of the largest sportfishing–art galleries in Florida stocks hand-stitched clothing and giftware, in addition to work by wood and bronze sculptors such as Kendall van Sant; watercolorist C.D. Clarke; and painters Daniel Caldwell, David Hall, Steven Left, and Stacie Krupa. Proceeds benefit cystic fibrosis research. ✉ *MM 81.5 OS, 200 Industrial Dr., Upper Matecumbe Key* ☎ *305/664–2002* 🌐 *www.redbone.org.*

World Wide Sportsman. This two-level retail center sells upscale fishing equipment, resort clothing, sportfishing art, and other gifts. When you're tired of shopping, relax at the Zane Grey Long Key Lounge just above World Wide Sportsman. ✉ *MM 81.5 BS, 81576 Overseas Hwy., Upper Matecumbe Key* ☎ *305/664–4615, 800/327–2880.*

SPORTS AND THE OUTDOORS

BOATING

Marinas pop up every mile or so in the Islamorada area, so finding a rental or tour is no problem. Robbie's Marina is a prime example of a salty spot where you can find it all—from fishing charters and kayaking rentals to lunch and tarpon feeding.

Bump & Jump. Fishing and deck boat rentals (from 15 to 29 feet) start at $145 per day and $745 per week. ✉ *MM 81.2 OS, 81197 Overseas Hwy., Upper Matecumbe Key* ☎ *305/664–9404, 877/453–9463* 🌐 *www.keysboatrental.com.*

Houseboat Vacations of the Florida Keys. See the islands from the comfort of your own boat (captain's cap optional). The company maintains a fleet of 42- to 55-foot boats that accommodate up to 10 people and come outfitted with everything you need besides food. (You may provision yourself at a nearby grocery store.) The three-day minimum starts at $1,112; one week costs $1,950 and up. Kayaks, canoes, and skiffs suitable for the ocean are also available. ✉ *MM 85.9 BS, 85944 Overseas Hwy., Plantation Key* ☎ *305/664–4009* 🌐 *www.floridakeys.com/houseboats.*

Robbie's Boat Rentals & Charters. This full-service company will even give you a crash course on how not to crash your boat. The rental fleet includes an 18-foot skiff with a 60-horsepower outboard for $150 for four hours and $200 for the day to a 23-foot deck boat with a 130-horsepower engine for $185 for a half day and $235 for eight hours. Robbie's also rents fishing and snorkeling gear (there's good snorkeling nearby) and sells bait, drinks and snacks, and gas. Want to hire a guide who knows the local waters and where the fish lurk? Robbie's offers offshore-fishing trips, patch-reef trips, and party-boat fishing. Backcountry flats trips are a specialty. ✉ *MM 77.5 BS, 77522 Overseas Hwy., Lower Matecumbe Key* ☎ *305/664–9814, 877/664–8498* 🌐 *www.robbies.com.*

Treasure Harbor Marine. Captains Pam and Pete Anderson provide everything you'll need for a bareboat sailing vacation at sea. They also give excellent advice on where to find the best anchorages, snorkeling spots, or lobstering sites. Vessels range from a 19-foot Cape Dory to a 41-foot Morgan Out Island. Rates start at $125 a day; $500 a week. Captained sails are $550 a day, $3,250 a week aboard the 41-footer. Marina facilities are basic—water, electric, ice machine, laundry, picnic tables, and restrooms with showers. A store sells snacks, beverages, and sundries. ✉ *MM 86.5 OS, 200 Treasure Harbor Dr., Plantation Key* ☎ *305/852–2458, 800/352–2628* 🌐 *www.treasureharbor.com.*

FISHING

Here in the self-proclaimed "Sportfishing Capital of the World," sailfish is the prime catch in the winter and dolphinfish in the summer. Buchanan Bank just south of Islamorada is a good spot to try for tarpon in the spring. Blackfin tuna and amberjack are generally plentiful in the area, too. ■ **TIP→ The Hump at Islamorada ranks highest among anglers' favorite fishing spots in Florida because of the incredible offshore marine life.**

Renting WaveRunners is a fun way to catch some surf and sun in Florida Keys. Each fits one to three people.

Captain Ted Wilson. Go into the backcountry for bonefish, tarpon, redfish, snook, and shark aboard a 17-foot boat that accommodates up to three anglers. For two people, half-day trips run $375, full-day trips $550, two-hour sunset bonefishing $225, and evening excursions $400. There's a $100 charge for an extra person. ✉ *MM 79.9 OS, 79851 Overseas Hwy., Upper Matecumbe Key* ☏ *305/942–5224, 305/664–9463* 🌐 *www.captaintedwilson.com.*

Florida Keys Fly Fish. Like other top fly-fishing and light-tackle guides, Captain Geoff Colmes helps his clients land trophy fish in the waters around the Keys ($500–$550). ✉ *105 Palm La., Upper Matecumbe Key* ☏ *305/853–0741* 🌐 *www.floridakeysflyfish.com.*

Florida Keys Outfitters. Long before fly-fishing became popular, Sandy Moret was fishing the Keys for bonefish, tarpon, and redfish. Now he attracts anglers from around the world on a quest for the big catch. Weekend fly-fishing classes, which include classroom instruction, equipment, and daily lunch, cost $695. Add $1,070 for two additional days of fishing. Guided fishing trips cost $395 for a half day, $535 for a full day. Packages combining fishing and accommodations at Islander Resort are available. ✉ *MM 81.2, Green Turtle, 81219 Overseas Hwy., Upper Matecumbe Key* ☏ *305/664–5423* 🌐 *www.floridakeysoutfitters.com.*

★ **Hubba Hubba Charters.** Captain Ken Knudsen has fished the Keys waters for more than 40 years. A licensed backcountry guide, he's ranked among Florida's top 10 by national fishing magazines. He offers four-hour sunset trips for tarpon ($425) and two-hour sunset trips for bonefish ($200), as well as half- ($375) and full-day ($550) outings. Prices are for one or two anglers, and tackle and bait are included. ✉ *MM 79.8 OS, Upper Matecumbe Key* ☎ *305/664–9281.*

Miss Islamorada. The 65-foot party boat has full-day trips for $60. Bring your lunch or buy one from the dockside deli. ✉ *Bud n' Mary's Marina, MM 79.8 OS, 79851 Overseas Hwy., Upper Matecumbe Key* ☎ *305/664–2461, 800/742–7945* 🌐 *www.budnmarys.com.*

SCUBA DIVING AND SNORKELING

San Pedro Underwater Archaeological Preserve State Park. About 1¼ nautical miles south of Indian Key is the San Pedro Underwater Archaeological Preserve State Park, which includes the remains of a Spanish treasure-fleet ship that sank in 1733. The state of Florida protects the site for divers; no spearfishing or souvenir collecting is allowed. Seven replica cannons and a plaque enhance what basically amounts to a 90-foot-long pile of ballast stones. Resting in only 18 feet of water, its ruins are visible to snorkelers as well as divers and attract a colorful array of fish. ✉ *MM 85.5 OS* ☎ *305/664–2540* 🌐 *www.floridastateparks.org/sanpedro.*

4

Florida Keys Dive Center. Dive from John Pennekamp Coral Reef State Park to Alligator Light with this outfitter. The center has two 46-foot Coast Guard–approved dive boats, offers scuba training, and is one of the few Keys dive centers to offer Nitrox and Trimix (mixed gas) diving. Two-tank dives cost $60 with no equipment; two-location snorkeling is $38. ✉ *MM 90.5 OS, 90451 Overseas Hwy., Plantation Key* ☎ *305/852–4599, 800/433–8946* 🌐 *www.floridakeysdivectr.com.*

Holiday Isle Dive Shop. This one-stop dive shop has a resort, pool, restaurant, lessons, and twice-daily dive and snorkel trips. Rates start at $50 for a two-tank dive or one-tank night dive without equipment. Snorkel trips are $30. ✉ *MM 84 OS, 84001 Overseas Hwy., Windley Key* ☎ *305/664–3483, 800/327–7070* 🌐 *www.diveholidayisle.com.*

WATER SPORTS

The Kayak Shack. Rent kayaks for trips to Indian (about 20 minutes one way) and Lignumvitae (about 45 minute one way) keys, two favorite destinations for paddlers. Kayak rental half-day rates (and you'll need plenty of time to explore those mangrove canopies) are $40 for a single kayak and $55 for a double. Pedal kayaks are available for $50 single and $65 double. The company also offers guided three-hour tours, including a snorkel trip to Indian Key ($45). It also rents stand-up paddleboards, at $50 for a half-day including lessons, and canoes. ✉ *MM 77.5 BS, Robbie's Marina, 77522 Overseas Hwy., Lower Matecumbe Key* ☎ *305/664–4878* 🌐 *www.kayakthefloridakeys.com.*

LONG KEY

Long Key isn't a tourist hot spot, making it a favorite destination for those looking to avoid the masses and enjoy some ecological history in the process.

GETTING HERE AND AROUND

Long Key runs from mile markers 70 to 65.5, with the tiny town of Layton at its heart. Many people get around by bike.

Continued on page 195

DID YOU KNOW?

The coral making up the Barrier Reef is living and provides an ecosystem for small marine creatures. Bumping against or touching the coral can kill these creatures as well as damage the reef itself.

UNDER THE SEA

SNORKELING AND DIVING IN THE FLORIDA KEYS

by Lynne Helm

Up on the shore they work all day...

While we devotin',

Full time to floatin',

Under the sea...

—"Under the Sea,"

from Disney's *Little Mermaid*

All Floridians—even those long-accustomed to balmy breezes and swaying palms—turn ecstatic at the mere thought of tripping off to the Florida Keys. Add the prospect of underwater adventure, and hot diggity, it's unparalleled bliss.

Perennially laid back, the Keys annually attract nearly 800,000 snorkeling and scuba diving aficionados, and why not? There's arguably no better destination to learn these sports that put you up close to the wonders of life under the sea.

THE BARRIER REEF

The continental United States' only living coral barrier reef stretches 5 mi offshore of the Keys and is a teeming backbone of marine life, ranging from brilliant corals to neon-colored fish from blue-striped grunts to green moray eels. This is the prime reason why the Keys are where you descend upon intricate natural coral formations and encrusted shipwrecks, some historic, others sunk by design to create artificial reefs that attract divers and provide protection for marine life. Most diving sites have mooring buoys (nautical floats away from shore, sometimes marking specific sites); these let you tie up your boat so you don't need to drop anchor, which could damage the reef. Most of these sites also are near individual keys, where dozens of dive operators can cater to your needs.

Reef areas thrive in waters as shallow as 5 feet and as deep as 50 feet. Shallow reefs attract snorkelers, while deeper reefs suit divers of varying experience levels. The Keys' shallow diving offers two benefits: longer time safely spent on the bottom exploring, and more vibrant colors because of sunlight penetration. Most divers log maximum depths of 20 to 30 feet.

(left) Shallow-water coral reef, (top) Nine Foot Stake is a popular site for underwater photography.

WHERE TO SNORKEL AND DIVE

KEY WEST

Mile Marker 0–4

Nine Foot Stake

You can soak up a mesmerizing overview of submerged watery wonders at the **Florida Keys Eco-Discovery Center**, opened in 2007 on Key West's Truman Annex waterfront. Both admission and parking are free at the 6,000 square-foot center (*⏲ 9–4 Tues.–Sat. ☎ 305/809–4750*); interactive exhibits here focus on Keys marine life and habitats. Key West's offshore reefs are best accessed via professional charters, but it's easy to snorkel from shore at **Key West Marine Park**. Marked by a lighthouse, **Sand Key Reef** attracts snorkelers and scuba divers. **Joe's Tug**, at 65-foot depths, sets up encounters with Goliath grouper. **Ten-Fathom Ledge**, with coral caves and dramatic overhangs, shelters lobster. The **Cayman Salvor**, a buoy tender sunk as an artificial reef in 1985, shelters baitfish. Patch reef **Nine Foot Stake**, submerged 10 to 25 feet, has soft corals and juvenile marine life. **Kedge Ledge** features a pair of coral-encrusted anchors from 18th-century sailing vessels. *Florida Keys main visitor line at ☎ 800/FLA-KEYS (352-5397).*

BIG PINE KEY/LOWER KEYS

Mile Marker 4–47

Many devotees feel a Florida dive adventure would not be complete without heading 5 mi from Big Pine Key to **Looe Key National Marine Sanctuary**, an underwater preserve named for the HMS Looe running aground in 1744. If you time your visit for July, you might hit the one-day free underwater music festival for snorkelers and divers. Go under here and you'll likely encounter more tropical marine species than perhaps anywhere in the hemisphere. Looe Key's reef ecosystem extends from fossilized corals to a reef flat of turtle grass and large star and brain corals, from 20 to 40 feet. A deeper reef showcases eagle rays, turtles, and sometimes the rare whale shark. About 3 mi west of Looe Key, the 210-foot island freighter **Adolphus Busch** rests on the ocean floor at 110-foot depths, sheltering a 350-pound Goliath grouper near the wheelhouse. Sunk in 1988, it acts as an artificial reef providing additional habitat for marine species. *Big Pine Key and Lower Keys Tourist information line, at MM 31, ☎ 800/872-3722.*

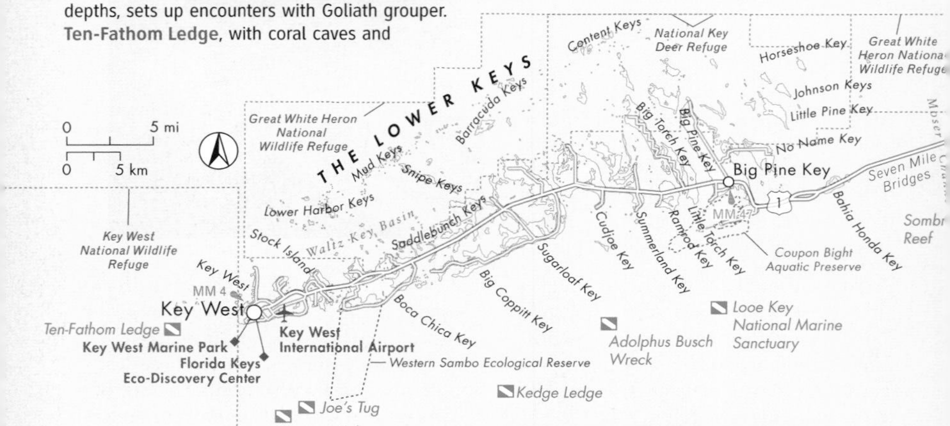

THE LOWER KEYS

National Parks
National Wildlife Refuge
Marine Ecological Reserves
Aquatic Preserve
State Parks
Dive Sites

Looe Key National Marine Sanctuary

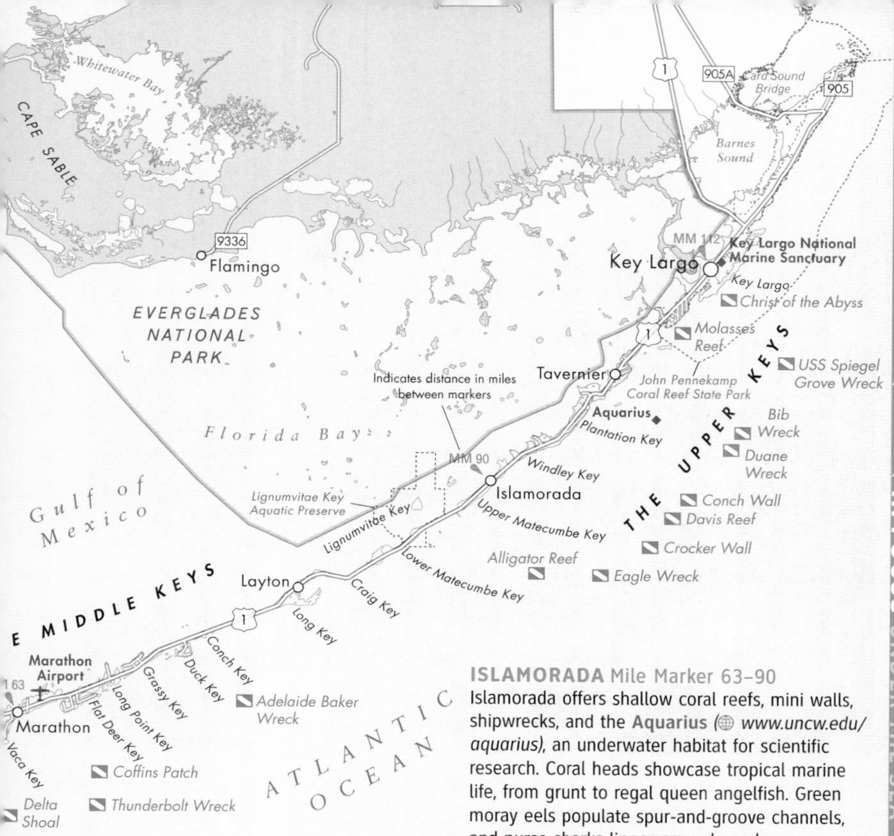

MARATHON/MIDDLE KEYS

Mile Marker 47–63

Sombrero Reef

The Middle Keys yield a marine wilderness of a spur-and-groove coral and patch reefs. The **Adelaide Baker** historic shipwreck has a pair of stacks in 25 feet of water. Popular **Sombrero Reef**, with coral canyons and archways, is marked by a 140-foot lighted tower. Six distinct patch reefs known as **Coffin's Patch** have shallow elkhorn forests. **Delta Shoals**, a network of coral canyons fanning seaward from a sandy shoal, attracts divers to its elkhorn, brain, and star coral heads. Marathon's **Thunderbolt**, a 188-foot ship sunk in 1986, sits upright at 115-foot depths, coated with sponge, coral, and hydroid, and attracting angelfish, jacks, and deep-water pelagic creatures. *Greater Marathon Chamber and visitors center at MM 53.5, ☎ 800/262–7284.*

ISLAMORADA Mile Marker 63–90

Islamorada offers shallow coral reefs, mini walls, shipwrecks, and the **Aquarius** (*www.uncw.edu/aquarius*), an underwater habitat for scientific research. Coral heads showcase tropical marine life, from grunt to regal queen angelfish. Green moray eels populate spur-and-groove channels, and nurse sharks linger around overhangs. Submerged attractions include the **Eagle**, a 287-foot ship in 110 feet of water; **Davis Reef**, with gorgonian coral; **Alligator Reef**, where the *USS Alligator* sank while fighting pirates; the sloping **Conch Wall**, with barrel sponges and gorgonian; and **Crocker Wall**, featuring spur-and-groove and block corals. *Islamorada Chamber and visitor center at MM 83.2, ☎ 800/322–5397.*

KEY LARGO Mile Marker 90–112

Key Largo marine conservation got a big leg up with creation of **John Pennekamp Coral Reef State Park** in 1960, the nation's first undersea preserve, followed by 1975's designation of the **Key Largo National Marine Sanctuary**. A popular underwater attraction is the bronze statue of **Christ of the Abyss** between coral formations. Explorers with a "lust for rust" can dive down to 60 to 90 feet and farther to see the murky cemetery for two twin 327-foot U.S. Coast Guard cutters, ***Duane*** and ***Bibb***, used during World War II; ***USS Spiegel Grove***, a 510-foot Navy transport ship sunk in 2002 to create an artificial reef; and **Molasses Reef**, showcasing coral heads. *Key Largo Chamber at MM 106, ☎ 800/822–1088.*

SCUBA DIVING

A diver explores the coral reef in the Florida Keys National Marine Sanctuary off Key Largo.

Florida offers wonderful opportunities to spend your vacation in the sun and become a certified diver at the same time. In the Keys, count on setting aside three to five days for entry-level or so-called "Open Water" certification offered by many dive shops. Basic certification (covering depths to about 60 feet) involves classroom work and pool training, followed by one or more open-water dives at the reef. After passing a knowledge test and completing the required water training (often starting in a pool), you become a certified recreational scuba diver, eligible to rent dive gear and book dive trips with most operations worldwide. Learning through video or online computer programs can enable you to complete classroom work at home, so you can more efficiently schedule time in the Keys for completing water skills and getting out to the reef for exploration.

Many would-be divers opt to take the classroom instruction and pool training at home at a local dive shop and then spend only two days in the Keys completing four dives. It's not necessarily cheaper, but it can be far more relaxing to commit to only two days of diving.

Questions you should ask: Not all dive shops are created equal, and it may be worthwhile to spend extra money for a better diving experience. Some of the larger dive shops take out large catamarans that can carry as many as 24 to 40 people. Many people prefer the intimacy of a smaller boat.

Good to know: Divers can become certified through PADI *(www.padi.com)*, NAUI *(www.naui.org)*, or SSI *(www.divessi.com)*. The requirements for all three are similar, and if you do the classroom instruction and pool training with a dive shop associated with one organization, the referral for the open water dives will be honored by most dive shops. Note that you are not allowed to fly for at least 24 hours after a dive, because residual nitrogen in the body can pose health risks upon decompression. While there are no rigid rules on diving after flying, make sure you're well-hydrated before hitting the water.

Cost: The four-day cost can range from $300 to $475, but be sure to ask if equipment, instruction manuals, and log books are extra. Some dive shops have relationships with hotels, so check for dive/stay packages. Referral dives (a collaborative effort among training agencies) run from $285 to $300 and discover scuba runs around $175 to $200.

SNUBA

Beyond snorkeling or the requirements of scuba, you also have the option of "Snuba." The word is a trademarked portmanteau or combo of snorkel and scuba. Marketed as easy-to-learn family fun, Snuba lets you breathe underwater via tubes from an air-supplied vessel above, with no prior diving or snorkel experience required.

NOT CERTIFIED?

Not sure if you want to commit the time and money to become certified? Not a problem. Most dive shops and many resorts will offer a discover scuba day-long course. In the morning, the instructor will teach you the basics of scuba diving: how to clear your mask, how to come to the surface in the unlikely event you lose your air supply, etc. In the afternoon, instructors will take you out for a dive in relatively shallow water—less than 30 feet. Be sure to ask where the dive will take place. Jumping into the water off a shallow beach may not be as fun as actually going out to the coral. If you decide that diving is something you want to pursue, the open dive may count toward your certification.

■ **TIP→** You can often book the discover dives at the last minute. It may not be worth it to go out on a windy day when the currents are stronger. Also the underwater world looks a whole lot brighter on sunny days.

(top) Scuba divers; (bottom) Diver ascending line.

SNORKELING

Snorklng lets you see the wonders of the sea from a new perspective.

The basics: Sure, you can take a deep breath, hold your nose, squint your eyes, and stick your face in the water in an attempt to view submerged habitats . . . but why not protect your eyes, retain your ability to breathe, and keep your hands free to paddle about when exploring underwater? That's what snorkeling is all about.

Equipment needed: A mask, snorkel (the tube attached to the mask), and fins. In deeper waters (any depth over your head), life jackets are advised.

Steps to success: If you've never snorkeled before, it's natural to feel a bit awkward at first, so don't sweat it. Breathing through a mask and tube, and wearing a pair of fins take getting used to. Like any activity, you build confidence and comfort through practice.

If you're new to snorkeling, begin by submerging your face in shallow water or a swimming pool and breathing calmly through the snorkel while gazing through the mask.

Next you need to learn how to clear water out of your mask and snorkel, an essential skill since splashes can send water into tube openings and masks can leak. Some snorkels have built-in drainage valves, but if a tube clogs, you can force water up and out by exhaling through your mouth. Clearing a mask is similar: lift your head from water while pulling forward on mask to drain. Some masks have built-in purge valves, but those without can be cleared underwater by pressing the top to the forehead and blowing out your nose (charming, isn't it?), allowing air to bubble into the mask, pushing water out the bottom. If it sounds hard, it really isn't. Just try it a few times and you'll soon feel like a pro.

Now your goal is to get friendly with fins—you want them to be snug but not too tight—and learn how to propel yourself with them. Fins won't help you float, but they will give you a leg up, so to speak, on smoothly moving through the water or treading water (even when upright) with less effort.

Flutter stroking is the most efficient underwater kick, and the farther your foot bends forward the more leg power you'll be able to transfer to the water and the farther you'll travel with each stroke. Flutter kicking movements involve alternately separating the legs and then drawing them back together. When your legs separate, the leg surface encounters drag from the water, slowing you down. When your legs are drawn back together, they produce a force pushing you forward. If your kick creates more forward force than it causes drag, you'll move ahead.

Submerge your fins to avoid fatigue rather than having them flailing above the water when you kick, and keep your arms at your side to reduce drag. You are in the water—stretched out, face down, and snorkeling happily away—but that doesn't mean you can't hold your breath and go deeper in the water for a closer look at some fish or whatever catches your attention. Just remember that when you do this, your snorkel will be submerged, too, so you won't be breathing (you'll be holding your breath). You can dive head-first, but going feet-first is easier and less scary for most folks, taking less momentum. Before full immersion, take several long, deep breaths to clear carbon dioxide from your lungs.

If your legs tire, flip onto your back and tread water with inverted fin motions while resting. If your mask fogs, wash condensation from lens and clear water from mask.

TIPS FOR SAFE SNORKELING

- Snorkel with a buddy and stay together.
- Plan your entry and exit points prior to getting in the water.
- Swim into the current on entering and then ride the current back to your exit point.
- Carry your flippers into the water and then put them on, as it's difficult to walk in them.
- Make sure your mask fits properly and is not too loose.
- Pop your head above the water periodically to ensure you aren't drifting too far out, or too close to rocks.
- Think of the water as someone else's home—don't take anything that doesn't belong to you, or leave any trash behind.
- Don't touch any sea creatures; they may sting.
- Wear a T-shirt over your swimsuit to help protect you from being fried by the sun.
- When in doubt, don't go without a snorkeling professional; try a guided tour.

Cayman Salvor

TOP OUTFITTERS

COMPANY	ADDRESS & PHONE	COST	DESCRIPTION
AMY SLATE'S AMORAY DIVE CENTER www.amoray.com	104250 Overseas Hwy. (MM 104.2), Key Largo 305/451–3595	Daily Scuba classes for kids ages 8 and up and adults $100-$200.	Sign up for dive/ snorkel trips, scuba instruction and kid programs.
DIVE KEY WEST www.divekeywest.com	3128 N. Roosevelt Blvd., Key West 305/296–3823	Snorkel from $49, dive from $69	Operating nearly 40 years. Has charters, instruction, and gear.
ECO SCUBA KEY WEST	5930 Peninsular Ave. (MM 5), Key West 305/851–1899	Daily Snorkel from $35, scuba from $99.	Debuted in 2009. Offers eco-tours, lobstering, snorkeling, and scuba.
FLORIDA KEYS DIVE CENTER www.floridakeys-divectr.com	90451 Old Hwy. (MM 90.5), Tavernier 305/852–4599	Daily Classes from $175.	Charters for snorkerlers and divers go to Pennekamp, Key Largo, and Islamorada.
HORIZON DIVERS www.horizondivers.com	100 Ocean Dr. #1, Key Largo 305/453–3535	Daily Snorkel from $50, scuba from $80.	Take customized dive/ snorkel trips on a 45-foot catamaran.
ISLAND VENTURES www.islandventure.com	103900 Overseas Hwy. (MM 103.9), Key Largo 305/451–4957	Two trips daily Snorkel $45, scuba from $80.	Go on snorkeling and scuba explorations to the Key Largo reef and shipwrecks.
KEYS DIVER SNORKEL TOURS www.keysdiver.com	99696 Overseas Hwy. (MM 99.6), Key Largo 305/451–1177	Three daily snorkel tours from $28. Includes gear.	Family-oriented snorkel-only tours head to coral reefs such as Pennekamp.
LOOE KEY REEF RESORT & DIVE CENTER www.diveflakeys.com	27340 Overseas Hwy. (MM 27.5), Ramrod Key 305/872–2215	Daily Snorkel from $44, scuba from $85.	Beginner and advanced scuba instruction, a photographer course, and snorkel gear rental.
RON JON SURF SHOP www.ronjons.com	503 Front St., Key West 305/293–8880	Daily Sells snorkel gear.	Several locations in Florida; its HQ is in Cocoa Beach.
SNUBA OF KEY WEST www.snubakeywest.com	600 Palm Ave., Key West 305/292–4616	Daily $99 per person, $44 for ride-alongs.	Swimmers ages 8 and up can try Snuba.
TILDENS SCUBA CENTER www.tildensscuba-center.com	4650 Overseas Hwy. (MM 49.5), Marathon 305/743–7255	Daily Snorkel from $35.99, scuba from $60.99.	Operating for 25 years. Has lessons, tours, snorkeling, scuba, snuba, gear, and a kids club.

EXPLORING

★ **Long Key State Park.** Come here for solitude, hiking, fishing, and camping. On the ocean side, the Golden Orb Trail leads to a boardwalk that cuts through the mangroves (may require some wading) and alongside a lagoon where waterfowl congregate (as do mosquitoes, so be prepared). A 1¼-mile canoe trail leads through a tidal lagoon, and a broad expanse of shallow grass flats is perfect for bonefishing. Bring a mask and snorkel to observe the marine life in the shallow water. The park is particularly popular with campers who long to stake their tent at the campground on a beach. In summer, no-see-ums (biting sand flies) also love the beach, so again—be prepared. The picnic area is on the water, too, but lacks a beach. Canoes rent for $10 per day, and kayak rentals start at $17 for a single for two hours, $21.50 for a double. Rangers lead tours every Wednesday and Thursday at 10 on birding, boating, or beachcombing. ✉ *MM 67.5 OS, 67400 Overseas Hwy.* ☎ *305/664–4815* 🌐 *www.floridastateparks.org/longkey* 🎫 *$4.50 for 1 person, $5.50 for 2 people, and 50¢ for each additional person in the group* ⏲ *Daily 8–sunset.*

4

WHERE TO STAY

For expanded reviews, facilities, and current deals, visit Fodors.com.

$$ RESORT **Lime Tree Bay Resort.** Easy on the eye and the wallet, this 2½-acre resort on Florida Bay is far from the hustle and bustle of the larger islands. **Pros:** great views; friendly staff; close to Long Key State Park. **Cons:** no restaurants nearby, shared balconies. **TripAdvisor:** "hidden oasis," "a lot of fun," "great hideaway." [$] *Rooms from: $119* ✉ *MM 68.5 BS, 68500 Overseas Hwy., Layton* ☎ *305/664–4740, 800/723–4519* 🌐 *www.limetreebayresort.com* *10 rooms, 10 studios, 14 one- and two-bedroom suites, 5 apartments, 4 efficiencies* 🍽 *No meals.*

EN ROUTE **Long Key Viaduct.** As you cross Long Key Channel, look beside you at the old viaduct. The second-longest bridge on the former rail line, this 2-mi-long structure has 222 reinforced-concrete arches. The old bridge is popular with cyclists and anglers, who fish off the sides day and night.

THE MIDDLE KEYS

Most of the activity in this part of the Florida Keys centers on the town of Marathon—the region's third-largest metropolitan area. On either end of it, smaller keys hold resorts, wildlife research and rehab facilities, a historic village, and a state park. The Middle Keys make a fitting transition from the Upper Keys to the Lower Keys not only geographically but mentally. Crossing Seven Mile Bridge prepares you for the slow pace and don't-give-a-damn attitude you'll find a little farther down the highway. Fishing is one of the main attractions—in fact, the region's commercial-fishing industry was founded here in the early 1800s. Diving is another popular pastime. There are many beaches and natural areas to enjoy in the Middle Keys, where mainland stress becomes an ever more distant memory.

If you get bridge fever—the heebie-jeebies when driving over long stretches of water—you may need a pair of blinders (or a couple of tranquilizers) before tackling the Middle Keys. Stretching from Conch Key to the far side of the Seven Mile Bridge, this zone is home to the region's two longest bridges: Long Key Viaduct and Seven Mile Bridge, both historic landmarks.

Overseas Highway takes you from one end of the region to the other in a direct line that takes in most of the sights, but you'll find some interesting resorts and restaurants off the main drag.

DUCK KEY

MM 61.

Duck Key holds one of the region's nicest marina resorts, Hawks Cay, plus a boating-oriented residential community.

EXPLORING

Dolphin Connection. Hawk's Cay Resort's Dolphin Connection offers three programs, including Dockside Dolphins, a 30-minute encounter from the dry training docks ($60); Dolphin Discovery, an in-water program that lasts about 45 minutes and lets you kiss, touch, and feed the dolphins ($165); and Trainer for a Day, a three-hour session with the animal training team ($315). ✉ *MM 61 OS, 61 Hawks Cay Blvd.* ☎ *305/743–7000* 🌐 *www.dolphinconnection.com.*

WHERE TO EAT AND STAY

For expanded hotel reviews, visit Fodors.com.

$$$ LATIN AMERICAN ★ ✕ **Alma.** A refreshing escape from the Middle Keys' same-old menus, Alma serves expertly prepared Florida and Latin-Caribbean dishes in an elegant setting. Nightly changing menus might include a trio of ceviche, ahi tuna with a wonderful garbanzo bean tomato sauce, gnocchi and exotic mushroom ragout, and pan-seared Wagyu steak. Finish your meal with the silky, smooth, passion-fruit crème brûlée, which has just the right amount of tartness to balance the delicate caramelized crust. [$] *Average main: $28* ✉ *Hawks Cay Resort, 61 Hawks Cay Blvd., Duck Cay* ☎ *305/743–7000, 888/432–2242* 🌐 *www.hawkscay.com* ⏲ *No lunch.*

$$$$ RESORT Fodor's Choice ★ **Hawks Cay Resort.** The 60-acre, Caribbean-style retreat has plenty to keep the kids occupied (and adults happy). **Pros:** huge rooms; restful spa; full-service marina and dive shop. **Cons:** no real beach; far from Marathon's attractions. **TripAdvisor:** "a great family vacation," "what a fabulous getaway," "paradise." [$] *Rooms from: $240* ✉ *MM 61 OS, 61 Hawks Cay Blvd.* ☎ *305/743–7000, 888/432–2242* 🌐 *www.hawkscay.com* *161 rooms, 16 suites, 225 2- and 3-bedroom villas* 🍽 *No meals.*

GRASSY KEY

MM 60–57.

Local lore has it that this sleepy little key was named not for its vegetation—mostly native trees and shrubs—but for an early settler by the name of Grassy. The key is inhabited primarily by a few families operating small fishing camps and roadside motels. There's no marked

DID YOU KNOW?

Dolphins in Florida are predominantly of the Atlantic bottlenose variety. These playful and smart creatures love to leap out of the water and synchronize their movements with others. By swimming next to boats, dolphins can conserve energy.

definition between it and Marathon, so it feels sort of like a suburb of its much larger neighbor to the south. Grassy Key's sights tend toward the natural, including a worthwhile dolphin attraction and a small state park.

GETTING HERE AND AROUND

Most visitors arriving by air drive to this destination either from Miami International Airport or Key West International Airport. Rental cars are readily available at both, and in the long run, are the most convenient means of transportation for getting here and touring around the Keys.

EXPLORING

Curry Hammock State Park. Looking for a slice of the Keys that's far removed from tiki bars? On the ocean and bay sides of Overseas Highway are 260 acres of upland hammock, wetlands, and mangroves. On the bay side, there's a trail through thick hardwoods to a rocky shoreline. The ocean side is more developed, with a sandy beach, a clean bathhouse, picnic tables, a playground, grills, and a 28-site campground. Locals consider the paddling trails under canopies of arching mangroves one of the best kayaking spots in the Keys. Manatees frequent the area, and it's a great spot for bird-watching. Herons, egrets, ibis, plovers, and sanderlings are commonly spotted. Raptors are often seen in the park, especially during migration periods. ✉ *MM 57 OS, 56200 Overseas Hwy., Little Crawl Key* ☎ *305/289–2690* 🌐 *www.floridastateparks.org/curryhammock* 🎟 *$4.50 for 1 person, $6 for 2, 50¢ per additional person* ⏲ *Daily 8–sunset.*

★ **Dolphin Research Center.** The 1963 movie *Flipper* popularized the notion of humans interacting with dolphins, and Milton Santini, the film's creator, also opened this center, which is home to a colony of dolphins and sea lions. The nonprofit center has educational sessions and programs that allow you to greet the dolphins from dry land or play with them in their watery habitat. You can even paint a T-shirt with a dolphin—you pick the paint, the dolphin "designs" your shirt ($55 plus admission). The center also offers five-day programs for children and adults with disabilities. ✉ *MM 59 BS, 58901 Overseas Hwy.* ☎ *305/289–1121 information, 305/289–0002 reservations* 🌐 *www.dolphins.org* 🎟 *$20* ⏲ *Daily 9–4:30.*

WHERE TO EAT AND STAY

For expanded hotel reviews, visit Fodors.com.

$$$$ AMERICAN ✕ **Hideaway Café.** The name says it all. Tucked between Grassy Key and Marathon, it's easy to miss if you're barnstorming through the middle islands. When you find it (upstairs at Rainbow Bend Resort), you'll discover a favorite of locals who appreciate a well-planned menu, lovely ocean view, and quiet evening away from the crowds—fancy with white tablecloths, but homey with worn carpeting. For starters, dig into escargots à la Edison (sautéed with vegetables, pepper, cognac, and cream). Then feast on several specialties, such as a rarely found chateaubriand for one, a whole roasted duck, or the seafood medley combining the catch of the day with scallops and shrimp in a savory sauce. $ *Average main: $30* ✉ *MM 58 OS, Rainbow Bend Resort, 57784 Overseas Hwy.* ☎ *305/289–1554* 🌐 *www.hideawaycafe.com* ⏲ *No lunch.*

$$ B&B/INN **Bonefish Resort.** Set on a skinny lot bedecked with palm trees, banana trees, and hibiscus plantings, this motel-style hideaway is the best choice among the island's back-to-basics properties. **Pros:** decent price for the location; ocean-side setting. **Cons:** decks are small; simple decor. **TripAdvisor:** "nice location," "can't say it's not unique," "cute and comfortable." *Rooms from: $119 MM 58 OS, 58070 Overseas Hwy. 305/743–7107, 800/274–9949 www.bonefishresort.com 3 rooms, 11 efficiencies No meals.*

MARATHON

Marathon runs from mile markers 53 to 47.5.

Most of what there is to see lies right off the Overseas Highway, with the exception of a couple of hidden restaurants and the town's best beach.

Marathon is a bustling town, at least compared with other communities in the Keys. As it leaves something to be desired in the charm department, Marathon will probably not be your first choice of places to stay. But there are a number of good dining options, so you'll definitely want to stop for a bite even if you're just passing through on the way to Key West.

Outside of Key West, Marathon has the most historic attractions, which merit a visit, along with its Sombrero Beach. Fishing, diving, and boating are the main events here. It throws tarpon tournaments in April and May, more fishing tournaments in June and September, a seafood festival in March, and lighted boat parades around the winter holidays.

New Englanders founded this former fishing village in the early 1800s. The community on Vaca Key subsequently served as a base for pirates, salvagers (also known as "wreckers"), spongers, and, later, Bahamian farmers who eked out a living growing cotton and other crops. More Bahamians arrived in hopes of finding work building the railroad. According to local lore, Marathon was renamed when a worker commented that it was a marathon task to position the tracks across the 6-mile-long island. During the building on the railroad, Marathon developed a reputation for lawlessness that rivaled that of the Old West. It is said that to keep the rowdy workers from descending on Key West for their off-hours endeavors, residents would send boatloads of liquor up to Marathon. Needless to say, things have quieted down considerably since then. Grassy Key segues into Marathon with little more than a slight increase in traffic and higher concentration of commercial establishments. Marathon's roots are anchored to fishing and boating, so look for marinas to find local color, fishing charters, and good restaurants. At its north end, Key Colony Beach is an old-fashioned island neighborhood worth a visit for its shops and restaurants. Nature lovers shouldn't miss the attractions on Crane Point. Other good places to leave the main road are at Sombrero Beach Road (MM 50), which leads to the beach, and 35th Street (MM 49), which takes you to a funky little marina and restaurant. Overseas Highway hightails through Hog Key and Knight Key before the big leap over Florida Bay and Hawk's Channel via the Seven Mile Bridge.

GETTING HERE AND AROUND

The SuperShuttle charges $102 per passenger for trips from Miami International Airport to the Upper Keys. To go farther into the Keys, you must book an entire 11-person van, which costs about $250 to Marathon. For a trip to or from the airport, place your request 24 hours in advance.

Miami Dade Transit provides daily bus service from MM 50 in Marathon to the Florida City Walmart Supercenter on the mainland. The bus stops at major shopping centers as well as on-demand anywhere along the route during daily round-trips on the hour from 6 am to 10 pm. The cost is $2 one-way, exact change required. The Lower Keys Shuttle bus runs from Marathon to Key West ($4 one way), with scheduled stops along the way.

ESSENTIALS

Transportation Contacts **Lower Keys Shuttle** ☎ *305/809–3910* 🌐 *www.kwtransit.com.* **Miami Dade Transit** ☎ *305/770–3131.* **SuperShuttle** ☎ *305/871–2000, 800/258–3826* 🌐 *www.supershuttle.com.*

Visitor Information **Greater Marathon Chamber of Commerce and Visitor Center** ✉ *MM 53.5 BS, 12222 Overseas Hwy.* ☎ *305/743–5417, 800/262–7284* 🌐 *www.floridakeysmarathon.com.*

EXPLORING

★ **Crane Point Museum, Nature Center, and Historic Site.** Tucked away from the highway behind a stand of trees, Crane Point—part of a 63-acre tract that contains the last-known undisturbed thatch-palm hammock—is delightfully undeveloped. This multiuse facility includes the **Museum of Natural History of the Florida Keys,** which has displays about local wildlife, a seashell exhibit, and a marine-life display that makes you feel you're at the bottom of the sea. Kids love the replica 17th-century galleon and pirate dress-up room where they can play, and the re-created **Cracker House** filled with insects, sea-turtle exhibits, and children's activities. On the 1-mile indigenous loop trail, visit the **Laura Quinn Wild Bird Center** and the remnants of a Bahamian village, site of the restored **George Adderly House.** It is the oldest surviving example of Bahamian tabby (a concretelike material created from sand and seashells) construction outside of Key West. A boardwalk crosses wetlands, rivers, and mangroves before ending at Adderly Village. From November to Easter, docent-led tours are available; bring good walking shoes and bug repellent during warm weather. ✉ *MM 50.5 BS, 5550 Overseas Hwy.* ☎ *305/743–9100* 🌐 *www.cranepoint.net* 🎫 *$12.50* ⏲ *Mon.–Sat. 9–5, Sun. noon–5; call to arrange trail tours.*

Pigeon Key. There's much to like about this 5-acre island under the Old Seven Mile Bridge. You can reach it via a ferry that departs from the behind the visitors center in an old red railroad car on Knight's Key (MM 47 OS). Once there, tour the island on your own or join a guided tour to explore the buildings that formed the early-20th-century work camp for the Overseas Railroad that linked the mainland to Key West in 1912. Later the island became a fish camp, a state park, and then government-administration headquarters. Exhibits in a small museum recall the history of the Keys, the railroad, and railroad baron Henry

M. Flagler. The ferry ride with tour lasts two hours; visitors can self-tour and catch the ferry back in a half hour. ✉ *MM 45 OS, 1 Knights Key Blvd., Pigeon Key* ☎ *305/743–5999* 🌐 *www.pigeonkey.net* 🎫 *$12* ⏲ *Daily 9:30–2:30; ferry departures at 10, 11:30, 1, 2:30.*

Seven Mile Bridge. This is one of the most photographed images in the Keys. Actually measuring slightly less than 7 mi, it connects the Middle and Lower Keys and is believed to be the world's longest segmental bridge. It has 39 expansion joints separating its various concrete sections. Each April runners gather in Marathon for the annual Seven Mile Bridge Run. The expanse running parallel to Seven Mile Bridge is what remains of the **Old Seven Mile Bridge,** an engineering and architectural marvel in its day that's now on the National Register of Historic Places. Once proclaimed the Eighth Wonder of the World, it rested on a record 546 concrete piers. No cars are allowed on the old bridge today.

4

The Turtle Hospital. More than 100 injured sea turtles check in here every year. The 90-minute guided tours take you into recovery and surgical areas at the world's only state-certified veterinary hospital for sea turtles. In the "hospital bed" tanks, you can see recovering patients and others that are permanent residents due to their injuries. Call ahead—tours are sometime cancelled due to medical emergencies. ✉ *MM 48.5 BS, 2396 Overseas Hwy.* ☎ *305/743–2552* 🌐 *www.turtlehospital.org* 🎫 *$15* ⏲ *Daily 9–5.*

BEACHES

★ **Sombrero Beach.** Here pleasant, shaded picnic areas overlook a coconut palm–lined grassy stretch and the Atlantic Ocean. Roped-off areas allow swimmers, boaters, and windsurfers to share the narrow cove. Facilities include barbecue grills, a large playground, a pier, a volleyball court, and a paved, lighted bike path off Overseas Highway. Sunday afternoons draw lots of local families toting coolers. The park is accessible for those with disabilities and allows leashed pets. Turn east at the traffic light in Marathon and follow signs to the end. **Amenities:** showers, toilets. **Best for:** families, swimming, windsurfing. ✉ *MM 50 OS, Sombrero Beach Rd.* ☎ *305/743–0033* 🎫 *Free* ⏲ *Daily 8–sunset.*

WHERE TO EAT

$ SEAFOOD **Fish Tales Market and Eatery.** This roadside eatery with its own seafood market serves signature dishes such as snapper on grilled rye with coleslaw and melted Muenster cheese and a fried fish burrito. You also can slurp luscious lobster bisque or tomato-based conch chowder. There are burgers, chicken, and dogs for those who don't do seafood. Plan to dine early; it's only open until 6:30 pm. This is a no-frills kind of place with a loyal local following, unfussy ambiance, a couple of outside picnic tables, and friendly service. [$] *Average main: $8* ✉ *MM 52.5 OS, 11711 Overseas Hwy.* ☎ *305/743–9196, 888/662–4822* 🌐 *www.floridalobster.com* *Reservations not accepted* ⏲ *Closed Sun.*

$ AMERICAN **Herbie's.** Since 1972 this has been the go-to spot for quick-and-affordable comfort food from cheeseburgers and fried oysters to shrimp scampi and filet mignon. You'll find all the local staples—conch, lobster tail, and fresh fish—to enjoy at picnic tables in the screened-in porch or inside where it's air-conditioned. Its shack-like appearance gives it an old-Keys feel. *Average main: $10 MM 50.5, 6350 Overseas Hwy. 305/743–6373 Reservations not accepted No credit cards Closed Sun. and Mon.*

$$ ITALIAN **Key Colony Inn.** The inviting aroma of an Italian kitchen pervades this family-owned favorite with a supper-club atmosphere. As you'd expect, the service is friendly and attentive. For lunch there are fish and steak entrées served with fries, salad, and bread in addition to Italian specialties. At dinner you can't miss with traditional dishes like veal Oscar and New York strip, or such specialties as seafood *Italiano*, a dish of scallops and shrimp sautéed in garlic butter and served with marinara sauce over a bed of linguine. The place is renowned for its Sunday brunch, served from November to April. *Average main: $19 MM 54 OS, 700 W. Ocean Dr., Key Colony Beach 305/743–0100 www.kcinn.com.*

$$ SEAFOOD ★ **Keys Fisheries Market & Marina.** From the parking lot, this commercial warehouse flanked by fishing boats and lobster traps barely hints at the restaurant inside. Order at the window outside, pick up your food, then dine at one of the waterfront picnic tables outfitted with rolls of paper towels. The menu is comprised of fresh seafood and a token hamburger and chicken sandwich. A huge lobster Reuben ($14.95) served on thick slices of toasted bread is the signature dish. Other delights include the shrimp burger, very rich whiskey-peppercorn snapper, and the Keys Kombo (grilled lobster, shrimp, scallops, and mahimahi for $29). There are also sushi and a bar serving beer and wine. Kids like feeding the fish while they wait for their food. *Average main: $16 MM 49 BS, 3390 Gulfview Ave., at the end of 35th St. (turn right on 35th St. off Gulfview Ave.) 305/743–4353, 866/743–4353 www.keysfisheries.com Reservations not accepted.*

$$$ SEAFOOD ★ **Lazy Days South.** Tucked into Marathon Marina a half-mile north of the Seven Mile Bridge, this restaurant offers views just as spectacular as its highly lauded food. A spin-off of an Islamorada favorite, here you'll find a wide range of daily offerings from fried or sautéed conch and a coconut-fried fish du jour sandwich to seafood pastas and beef tips over rice. Choose a table on the outdoor deck or inside underneath paddle fans and surrounded by local art. *Average main: $22 MM 47.3 OS, 725 11th St. 305/289–0839 www.keysdining.com/lazydays.*

$ AMERICAN **The Stuffed Pig.** With only nine tables and a counter inside, this breakfast-and-lunch place is always hopping. When the weather's right, grab a table out back. The kitchen whips up daily lunch specials like burgers, seafood platters, or pulled pork with hand-cut fries, but a quick glance around the room reveals that the all-day breakfast is the main draw. You can get the usual breakfast plates, but most newcomers opt for oddities like the lobster omelet, alligator tail and eggs, or "grits and grunts" (that's fish, to the rest of us). *Average main: $9 MM 49 BS, 3520 Overseas Hwy. 305/743–4059 www.thestuffedpig.com Reservations not accepted No credit cards No dinner.*

WHERE TO STAY

For expanded reviews, facilities, and current deals, visit Fodors.com.

$$$$ RESORT ★ **Tranquility Bay.** Ralph Lauren could have designed the rooms at this luxurious beach resort. **Pros:** secluded setting; gorgeous design; lovely crescent beach. **Cons:** a bit sterile; no real Keys atmosphere; cramped building layout. **TripAdvisor:** "very quiet," "beautiful grounds," "lovely grounds and facilities." *Rooms from: $399 MM 48.5 BS, 2600 Overseas Hwy. 305/289–0888, 866/643–5397 www.tranquilitybay.com 45 2-bedroom suites, 41 3-bedroom suites No meals.*

SPORTS AND THE OUTDOORS

BIKING

Tooling around on two wheels is a good way to see Marathon. There's easy cycling on a 1-mile off-road path that connects to the 2 miles of the Old Seven Mile Bridge leading to Pigeon Key.

Bike Marathon Bike Rentals. "Have bikes, will deliver" could be the motto of this company, which gets beach cruisers to your hotel door for $35 per week, including a helmet and basket. Note that there's no physical location, but services are available Monday through Saturday 9–4 and Sunday 9–2. *305/743–3204 www.bikemarathonbikerentals.com.*

Bubba's. Book a custom biking tour through the Keys along the heritage trail. A van accompanies tours to carry luggage and tired riders. Operated by former police officer Bubba Barron, Bubba's hosts an annual one-week ride down the length of the Keys every November. Riders can opt for tent camping ($645) or motel-room accommodations (prices vary). Meals are included on the annual ride and bike rentals are extra. *321/759–3433 www.bubbafestbiketours.com.*

Overseas Outfitters. Aluminum cruisers and hybrid bikes are available for rent at this outfitter for $10 to $15 per day. It's open weekdays 9–6 and Saturday 9–3. *MM 48 BS, 1700 Overseas Hwy. 305/289–1670 www.overseasoutfitters.com.*

BOATING

Sail, motor, or paddle—whatever your choice of modes, boating is what the Keys is all about. Brave the Atlantic waves and reefs or explore the backcountry islands on the calmer gulf side. If you don't have a lot of boating and chart-reading experience, it's a good idea to tap into local knowledge on a charter.

Captain Pip's. This operator rents 20- to 24-foot outboards, $195–$330 per day, as well as tackle and snorkeling gear. You also can charter a small boat with a guide, $450–$550 for a half day and $700–$800 for a full day. Multiday packages are also available. *MM 47.5 BS, 1410 Overseas Hwy. 305/743–4403, 800/707–1692 www.captainpips.com.*

Fish 'n Fun. Get out on the water on 19- to 26-foot powerboats starting at $140 for a half day, $190 for a full day. The company offers free delivery in the Middle Keys. You also can rent Jet Skis and kayaks. *MM 49.5 OS, 4590 Overseas Hwy., at Banana Bay Resort & Marina 305/743–2275, 800/471–3440 www.fishnfunrentals.com.*

FISHING

For recreational anglers, the deepwater fishing is superb in the ocean. Marathon West Hump, one good spot, has depths ranging from 500 to more than 1,000 feet. Locals fish from a half-dozen bridges, including Long Key Bridge, the Old Seven Mile Bridge, and both ends of Tom's Harbor. Barracuda, bonefish, dolphinfish, and tarpon all frequent local waters. Party boats and private charters are available.

★ ***Marathon Lady.*** Morning, afternoon, and night, fish for mahimahi, grouper, and other tasty catch aboard this 73-footer, which departs on half-day ($45) excursions from the Vaca Cut Bridge, north of Marathon. Join the crew for night fishing ($55) from 6:30 to midnight from Memorial Day to Labor Day; it's especially beautiful on a full-moon night. ✉ *MM 53 OS, at 117th St.* ☎ *305/743–5580* 🌐 *www.fishfloridakeys.com/marathonlady.*

Sea Dog Charters. Captain Jim Purcell, a deep-sea specialist for ESPN's *The American Outdoorsman,* provides one of the best values in Keys fishing. Next to the Seven Mile Grill, his company offers half- and full-day offshore, reef and wreck, and backcountry fishing trips, as well as fishing and snorkeling trips aboard 30- to 37-foot boats. The cost is $60 per person for a half day, regardless of whether your group fills the boat, and includes bait, light tackle, ice, coolers, and fishing licenses. If you prefer an all-day private charter on a 37-foot boat, he offers those, too, for $600 for up to six people. A fuel surcharge may apply. ✉ *MM 47.5 BS, 1248 Overseas Hwy.* ☎ *305/743–8255* 🌐 *www.seadogcharters.net.*

SCUBA DIVING AND SNORKELING

Local dive operations take you to Sombrero Reef and Lighthouse, the most popular down-under destination in these parts. For a shallow dive and some lobster-nabbing, Coffins Patch, off Key Colony Beach, is a good choice. A number of wrecks such as *Thunderbolt* serve as artificial reefs. Many operations out of this area will also take you to Looe Key Reef.

Hall's Diving Center & Career Institute. The institute has been training divers for more than 40 years. Along with conventional twice-a-day snorkel and two-tank dive trips ($40–$65) to the reefs at Sombrero Lighthouse and wrecks like the *Thunderbolt,* the company has more unusual offerings like photography and nitrox courses. ✉ *MM 48.5 BS, 1994 Overseas Hwy.* ☎ *305/743–5929, 800/331–4255* 🌐 *www.hallsdiving.com.*

Spirit Snorkeling. Snorkeling excursions to Sombrero Reef and Lighthouse Reef cost $30 a head. ✉ *MM 47.5 BS, 1410 Overseas Hwy., Slip No. 1* ☎ *305/289–0614* 🌐 *www.spiritsnorkeling.net.*

THE LOWER KEYS

Beginning at Bahia Honda Key, the islands of the Florida Keys become smaller, more clustered, and more numerous—a result of ancient tidal water flowing between the Florida Straits and the gulf. Here you're likely to see more birds and mangroves than other tourists, and more refuges, beaches, and campgrounds than museums, restaurants, and hotels. The islands are made up of two types of limestone, both denser than the highly permeable Key Largo limestone of the Upper Keys. As a result, freshwater forms in pools rather than percolating through the rock, creating watering holes that support alligators, snakes, deer, rabbits, raccoons, and migratory ducks. Many of these animals can be seen in the National Key Deer Refuge on Big Pine Key. Nature was generous with her beauty in the Lower Keys, which have both Looe Key Reef, arguably the Keys' most beautiful tract of coral, and Bahia Honda State Park, considered one of the best beaches in the world for its fine-sand dunes, clear warm waters, and panoramic vista of a historic bridge, hammocks, and azure sky and sea. Big Pine Key is fishing headquarters for a laid-back community that swells with retirees in the winter. South of it, the dribble of islands can flash by in a blink of an eye if you don't take the time to stop at a roadside eatery or check out tours and charters at the little marinas. In truth, the Lower Keys include Key West, but since it is as different from the rest of the Lower Keys as peanut butter is from jelly, it is covered in its own section.

GETTING HERE AND AROUND

The Lower Keys in this section include the keys between MM 37 and MM 9. The Seven Mile Bridge drops you into the lap of this homey, quiet part of the Keys.

Heed speed limits in these parts. They may seem incredibly strict given that the traffic is lightest of anywhere in the Keys, but the purpose is to protect the resident Key deer population, and officers of the law pay strict attention and will readily issue speeding tickets.

BAHIA HONDA KEY

Bahia Honda Key is between mile markers 38 and 36.

All of Bahia Honda Key is devoted to its eponymous state park, which keeps it in a pristine state. Besides the park's outdoor activities, it offers an up-close look at the original railroad bridge.

EXPLORING

Fodor's Choice ★ **Bahia Honda State Park.** Most first-time visitors to the region are dismayed by the lack of beaches—but then they discover Bahia Honda Key. The 524-acre park sprawls across both sides of the highway, giving it 2½ miles of fabulous sandy coastline. The snorkeling isn't bad, either; there's underwater life (soft coral, queen conchs, random little fish) just a few hundred feet offshore. Although swimming, kayaking, fishing, and boating are the main reasons to visit, you shouldn't miss biking along the 2½ miles of flat roads or hiking the Silver Palm Trail, with rare West Indian plants and several species found nowhere else in the nation. Along the way you'll be treated to a variety of butterflies. Seasonal ranger-led nature programs take place at or depart from the Sand and Sea Nature Center. There are rental cabins, a campground, snack bar, gift shop, 19-slip marina, nature center, and facilities for renting kayaks and arranging snorkeling tours. Get a panoramic view of the island from what's left of the railroad—the Bahia Honda Bridge. ✉ *MM 37 OS, 36850 Overseas Hwy.* ☎ *305/872–2353* 🌐 *www.floridastateparks.org/bahiahonda* 🎟 *$4.50 for 1 person, $9 for 2 people, 50¢ per additional person* ⏲ *Daily 8–sunset.*

DID YOU KNOW?

An old railroad bridge connected Bahia Honda Key with Key West until a hurricane destroyed it in 1935. Although it is no longer in operation, the bridge is used by hikers as a place from which to view the island and waters.

BEACHES

Sandspur Beach. Bahia Honda Key State Beach contains three beaches in all—on both the Atlantic Ocean and the Gulf of Mexico. Sandspur Beach, the largest, is regularly declared the best beach in Florida, and you'll be hard-pressed to argue. The sand is baby-powder soft, and the aqua water is warm, clear, and shallow. With their mild currents, the beaches are great for swimming, even with small fry. **Amenities:** food and drink, showers, toilets, water sports. **Best for:** snorkeling, swimming. ✉ *MM 37 OS, 36850 Overseas Hwy.* ☎ *305/872–2353* 🌐 *www.floridastateparks.org/bahiahonda* 🎟 *$4.50 for 1 person, $9 for 2 people, 50¢ per additional person* ⏲ *Daily 8–sunset.*

WHERE TO STAY

For expanded reviews, facilities, and current deals, visit Fodors.com.

$$$ RENTAL ★ **Bahia Honda State Park.** Elsewhere you'd pay big bucks for the wonderful water views available at these cabins on Florida Bay. **Pros:** great bay-front views; beachfront camping; affordable rates. **Cons:** books up fast; area can be buggy. **TripAdvisor:** "absolutely gorgeous beach," "breathtaking experience," "great camping experience." $ *Rooms from: $183* ✉ *MM 37 OS, 36850 Overseas Hwy.* ☎ *305/872–2353, 800/326–3521* 🌐 *www.reserveamerica.com* *80 partial hook-up campsites, 6 cabin units* 🍴 *No meals.*

SPORTS AND THE OUTDOORS

SCUBA DIVING AND SNORKELING

Bahia Honda Dive Shop. The concessionaire at Bahia Honda State Park manages a 19-slip marina; rents wet suits, snorkel equipment, and corrective masks; and operates twice-a-day offshore-reef snorkel trips ($30 plus $9 for equipment). Park visitors looking for other fun can rent kayaks ($12 per hour for a single, $18 for a double) and beach chairs. ✉ *MM 37 OS, 36850 Overseas Hwy.* ☎ *305/872–3210* 🌐 *www.bahiahondapark.com.*

BIG PINE KEY

Big Pine Key runs from mile marker 32 to 30.

Welcome to the Keys' most natural holdout, where wildlife refuges protect rare and endangered animals. Here you have left behind the commercialism of the Upper Keys for an authentic backcountry atmosphere.

How could things get more casual than Key Largo? you might wonder. Find out by exiting Overseas Highway to explore the habitat of the charmingly diminutive Key deer or cast a line from No Name Bridge. Tours explore the expansive waters of National Key Deer Refuge and Great White Heron National Wildlife Refuge, one of the first such refuges in the country. Along with Key West National Wildlife Refuge, it encompasses more than 200,000 acres of water and more than 8,000 acres of land on 49 small islands. Besides its namesake bird, the Great White Heron National Wildlife Refuge provides habitat for uncounted species of birds and three species of sea turtles. It is the only U.S. breeding site for the endangered hawksbill turtle.

ESSENTIALS

Visitor Information **Big Pine and the Lower Keys Chamber of Commerce** ✉ *MM 31 OS, 31020 Overseas Hwy.* ☎ *305/872–2411, 800/872–3722* 🌐 *www.lowerkeyschamber.com.*

EXPLORING

★ **National Key Deer Refuge.** This 84,824-acre refuge was established in 1957 to protect the dwindling population of the Key deer, one of more than 20 animals and plants classified as endangered or threatened in the Florida Keys. The Key deer, which stands about 30 inches at the shoulders and is a subspecies of the Virginia white-tailed deer, once roamed throughout the Lower and Middle Keys, but hunting, destruction of their habitat, and a growing human population caused their numbers to decline to 27 by 1957. The deer have made a comeback, increasing their numbers to approximately 750. The best place to see Key deer in the refuge is at the end of Key Deer Boulevard and on No Name Key, a sparsely populated island just east of Big Pine Key. Mornings and evenings are the best time to spot them. Deer may turn up along the road at any time of day, so drive slowly. They wander into nearby yards to nibble tender grass and bougainvillea blossom, but locals do not appreciate tourists driving into their neighborhoods after them. Feeding them is against the law and puts them in danger. The refuge also has 21 other listed endangered and threatened species of plants and animals, including five that are found nowhere else.

A quarry left over from railroad days, the **Blue Hole** is the largest body of freshwater in the Keys. From the observation platform and nearby walking trail, you might see the resident alligator, turtles, and other wildlife. There are two well-marked trails, recently revamped: the Jack Watson Nature Trail (.6 mile), named after an environmentalist and the refuge's first warden; and the Fred Mannillo Nature Trail, one of the most wheelchair-accessible places to see an unspoiled pine-rockland forest and wetlands. The visitor center has exhibits on Keys biology and ecology. The refuge also provides information on the Key West National Wildlife Refuge and the Great White Heron National Wildlife Refuge. Accessible only by water, both are popular with kayak outfitters. ✉ *MM 30.5 BS, Visitor Center–Headquarters, Big Pine Shopping Center, 28950 Watson Blvd.* ☎ *305/872–2239* 🌐 *www.fws.gov/nationalkeydeer* 🎫 *Free* 🕒 *Daily sunrise–sunset; headquarters weekdays 8–5.*

WHERE TO EAT

$ VEGETARIAN ✕ **Good Food Conspiracy.** Like good wine, this small natural-foods eatery and market surrenders its pleasures a little at a time. Step inside to the aroma of brewing coffee, and then pick up the scent of fresh strawberries or carrots blending into a smoothie, the green aroma of wheatgrass juice, followed by the earthy odor of hummus. Order raw or cooked vegetarian and vegan dishes, organic soups and salads, and organic coffees and teas. Bountiful sandwiches (available halved) include the popular tuna melt or hummus and avocado. If you can't sit down for a bite in the back courtyard, stock up on healthful snacks like dried fruits, raw nuts, and carob-covered almonds. $ *Average main: $7* ✉ *MM 30.2 OS,*

30150 Overseas Hwy. ☎ *305/872–3945* 🌐 *www.goodfoodconspiracy.com* ✍ *Reservations not accepted* ⏲ *No dinner Sun.*

$ AMERICAN ✕ **No Name Pub.** This no-frills honky-tonk has been around since 1936, delighting inveterate locals and intrepid vacationers who come for the excellent pizza, cold beer, and *interesting* companionship. The decor, such as it is, amounts to the autographed dollar bills that cover every inch of the place. The full menu printed on place mats includes a tasty conch chowder, a half-pound fried-grouper sandwich, spaghetti and meatballs, and seafood baskets. The lighting is poor, the furnishings are rough, and the music is oldies. This former brothel and bait shop is just before the No Name Key Bridge. It's a bit hard to find, but worth the trouble if you want a singular Keys experience. [$] *Average main: $15* ✉ *MM 30 BS, turn west on Wilder Rd., left on South St., right on Ave. B, right on Watson Blvd.* ☎ *305/872–9115* 🌐 *www.nonamepub.com* ✍ *Reservations not accepted.*

WHERE TO STAY

For expanded reviews, facilities, and current deals, visit Fodors.com.

$ HOTEL **Big Pine Key Fishing Lodge.** There's a congenial atmosphere at this lively family-owned lodge-campground-marina—a happy mix of tent campers (who have the fabulous waterfront real estate), RVers (who look pretty permanent), and motel dwellers (rooms start at $109) who like to mingle at the rooftop pool and challenge each other to a game of poker. **Pros:** local fishing crowd; nice pool; great price. **Cons:** RV park is too close to motel; deer will eat your food if you're camping. **TripAdvisor:** "relaxing and beautiful," "family traditions start here," "friendly old Florida vibe." [$] *Rooms from: $39* ✉ *MM 33 OS, 33000 Overseas Hwy.* ☎ *305/872–2351* *16 efficiencies, 97 campsites with full hook-ups, 61 campsites without hook-ups* *No meals.*

$$$$ B&B/INN ★ **Deer Run Bed & Breakfast.** Key deer wander the grounds of this beachfront bed-and-breakfast, set on a quiet street lined with buttonwoods and mangroves. **Pros:** quiet location; healthy breakfasts; complimentary bike, kayak, and state park passes. **Cons:** price is a bit high; hard to find. **TripAdvisor:** "beyond comparison," "wonderful food and special people," "tranquility and nature." [$] *Rooms from: $235* ✉ *MM 33 OS, 1997 Long Beach Dr.* ☎ *305/872–2015* 🌐 *www.deerrunfloridabb.com* *4 rooms* *Breakfast.*

SPORTS AND THE OUTDOORS

BIKING

A good 10 miles of paved roads run from MM 30.3 BS, along Wilder Road, across the bridge to No Name Key, and along Key Deer Boulevard into the National Key Deer Refuge. Along the way you might see some Key deer. Stay off the trails that lead into wetlands, where fat tires can do damage to the environment.

Big Pine Bicycle Center. Owner Marty Baird is an avid cyclist and enjoys sharing his knowledge of great places to ride. He's also skilled at selecting the right bike for the journey, and he knows his repairs, too. His old-fashioned single-speed, fat-tire cruisers rent for $8 per half day and $10 for a full day. Helmets, baskets, and locks are included. ✉ *MM 30.9 BS, 31 County Rd.* ☎ *305/872–0130.*

BOATING AND FISHING EXCURSIONS

Those looking to fish can cast from No Name Key Bridge or hire a charter to take them into backcountry or deep waters for fishing year-round. If you're looking for a good snorkeling spot, stay close to Looe Key Reef, which is prime scuba and snorkeling territory. One resort caters to divers with dive boats that depart from their own dock. Others can make arrangements for you.

Strike Zone Charters. Glass-bottom-boat excursions venture into the backcountry and Atlantic Ocean. The five-hour Island Excursion ($55 plus fuel surcharge) emphasizes nature and Keys history; besides close encounters with birds, sea life, and vegetation, there's a fish cookout on an island. Snorkel and fishing equipment, food, and drinks are included. This is one of the few nature outings in the Keys with wheelchair access. Deep-sea charter rates for up to six people are $650 for a half day, $850 for a full day. It also offers flats fishing in the Gulf of Mexico. Dive excursions head to the wreck of the 110-foot *Adolphus Busch* ($55), and scuba ($45) and snorkel ($35) trips to Looe Key Reef, prime scuba and snorkeling territory, aboard glass-bottom boats. ✉ *MM 29.6 BS, 29675 Overseas Hwy.* ☎ *305/872–9863, 800/654–9560* 🌐 *www.strikezonecharter.com.*

KAYAKING

There's nothing like the vast expanse of pristine waters and mangrove islands preserved by national refuges from here to Key West. The maze-like terrain can be confusing, so it's wise to hire a guide at least the first time out.

★ **Big Pine Kayak Adventures.** There's no excuse to skip a water adventure with this convenient kayak rental service, which delivers them to your lodging or anywhere between Seven Mile Bridge and Stock Island. The company, headed by *The Florida Keys Paddling Guide* author Bill Keogh, will rent you a kayak and then ferry you—called taxi-yakking—to remote islands with clear instructions on how to paddle back on your own. Rentals are by the half day or full day. Group kayak tours ($50 each for three hours) explore the mangrove forests of Great White Heron and Key Deer National Wildlife Refuges. Custom tours ($125 each and up, four hours) transport you to exquisite backcountry areas teeming with wildlife. Kayak fishing charters are also popular. ✉ *MM 30 BS, Old Wooden Bridge Fishing Camp, turn right at traffic light, continue on Wilder Rd. toward No Name Key* ☎ *305/872–7474* 🌐 *www.keyskayaktours.com.*

LITTLE TORCH KEY

Little Torch Key is between mile markers 29 and 10.

Little Torch Key and its neighbor islands, Ramrod Key and Summerland Key, are good jumping-off points for divers headed for Looe Key Reef. The islands also serve as a refuge for those who want to make forays into Key West but not stay in the thick of things.

The undeveloped backcountry at your door makes Little Torch Key an ideal location for fishing and kayaking. Nearby **Ramrod Key,** which also caters to divers bound for Looe Key, derives its name from a ship that wrecked on nearby reefs in the early 1800s.

NEED A BREAK?

Baby's Coffee. The aroma of rich roasting coffee beans arrests you at the door of "the Southernmost Coffee Roaster." Buy it by the pound or by the cup along with sandwiches and sweets. ✉ ***MM 15 OS, 3178 Overseas Hwy.*** ☎ ***305/744-9866, 800/523-2326*** 🌐 ***www.babyscoffee.com.***

WHERE TO EAT

$ AMERICAN **Geiger Key Smokehouse Bar & Grill.** There's a strong hint of the Old Keys at this oceanside marina restaurant, which came under new management in 2010 by the same folks who own Hogfish Grill on Stock Island. "On the backside of paradise," as the sign says, its tiki structures overlook quiet mangroves at an RV park marina. Locals usually outnumber tourists. For lunch, try a fish sandwich or pulled pork. The all-day menu spans an ambitious array of sandwiches, tacos, and seafood. Local fishermen stop here for breakfast before heading out in search of the big one. *$ Average main: $12 ✉ MM 10, 5 Geiger Key Rd., off Boca Chica Rd., on Geiger Key, Key West ☎ 305/296-3553, 305/294-1230 🌐 www.geigerkeymarina.com.*

$$$$ ECLECTIC ★ **Little Palm Island Restaurant.** The oceanfront setting calls to mind St. Barts and the other high-end destinations of the Caribbean. Keep that in mind as you reach for the bill, which can also make you swoon. The restaurant at the exclusive Little Palm Island Resort—its dining room and adjacent outdoor terrace lit by candles and warmed by live music—is one of the most romantic spots in the Keys. The seasonal menu is a melding of French and Caribbean flavors, with exotic little touches. Think shrimp and yellowtail ceviche or coconut lobster bisque as a starter, followed by mahimahi with creamy cilantro polenta. The Sunday brunch buffet, the full-moon dinners with live entertainment, and the Chef's Table Dinner are very popular. The dining room is open to nonguests on a reservations-only basis. *$ Average main: $65 ✉ MM 28.5 OS, 28500 Overseas Hwy. ☎ 305/872-2551 🌐 www.littlepalmisland.com ✍ Reservations essential.*

$$ ITALIAN **Zaza Pizzeria Neopolitana.** All that remains of the former Sugarloaf Lodge Restaurant is the pleasant gulf view out the picture windows; ZaZa has a new clean, open look dominated by a blue-tiled wood-fired pizza oven. Besides artisan pizzas such as béchamel with ham, you'll find hand-rolled fried risotto balls filled with ground beef, mozzarella, and peas; risotto infused with fresh lobster; pasta; bruschetta; and fried calzones. There's even pizza for breakfast (or try a frittata with ricotta and spinach or buffalo mozzarella, baby arugula, and prosciutto). Everything's fresh, most of it imported from Italy. *$ Average main: $18 ✉ MM 17 BS, 17015 Overseas Hwy. ☎ 305/745-2717.*

WHERE TO STAY

For expanded reviews, facilities, and current deals, visit Fodors.com.

$$$$ RESORT Fodor's Choice ★ **Little Palm Island Resort & Spa.** *Haute tropicale* best describes this luxury retreat, and "second mortgage" might explain how some can afford the extravagant prices. **Pros:** secluded setting; heavenly spa; easy wildlife viewing. **Cons:** expensive; might be too quiet for some. **TripAdvisor:**

"perfect experience," "beautiful little property," "romantic and relaxing." *$ Rooms from: $1590 ✉ MM 28.5 OS, 28500 Overseas Hwy. ☎ 305/872–2524, 800/343–8567 🌐 www.littlepalmisland.com 30 suites 🍽 Some meals.*

$ HOTEL **Looe Key Reef Resort & Center.** If your Keys vacation is all about diving, you'll be well served at this scuba-obsessed operation—the closest place to stay to the stellar reef (and affordable to boot). **Pros:** guests get discounts on dive and snorkel trips; fun bar. **Cons:** small rooms; unheated pool; close to road. **TripAdvisor:** "perfect for a weekend getaway," "low key," "everything you need and more." *$ Rooms from: $75 ✉ MM 27.5 OS, 27340 Overseas Hwy., Ramrod Key ☎ 305/872–2215, 877/816–3483 🌐 www.diveflakeys.com 23 rooms, 1 suite 🍽 No meals.*

$$ HOTEL **Parmer's Resort.** Almost every room at this budget-friendly option has a view of South Pine Channel, with the lovely curl of Big Pine Key in the foreground. **Pros:** bright rooms; pretty setting; good value. **Cons:** a bit out of the way; housekeeping costs extra; little shade around the pool. **TripAdvisor:** "consistently outstanding," "great staff," "peaceful slice of paradise." *$ Rooms from: $134 ✉ MM 28.7 BS, 565 Barry Ave. ☎ 305/872–2157 🌐 www.parmersresort.com 18 rooms, 12 efficiencies, 15 apartments, 1 penthouse, 1 2-bedroom cottage 🍽 Breakfast.*

BOATING AND KAYAKING

Dolphin Marina. Dolphin Marina rents 22-foot boats with 150 horsepower for up to eight people by the half day ($200) and full day ($250). *✉ 28530 Overseas Hwy. ☎ 305/872–2685 🌐 www.dolphinmarina.net.*

Sugarloaf Marina. Rent a paddle-propelled vehicle for exploring local gulf waters. Rates for one-person kayaks start at $15 for one hour to $35 for a full day. Two-person kayaks are also available. Delivery is free for rentals of three days or more. *✉ MM 17 BS, 17015 Overseas Hwy., Sugarloaf Key ☎ 305/745–3135 🌐 www.sugarloafkeymarina.com.*

SCUBA DIVING AND SNORKELING

★ **Looe Key Reef.** In 1744 the HMS *Looe,* a British warship, ran aground and sank on one of the most beautiful coral reefs in the Keys. Today the key owes its name to the ill-fated ship. The 5.3-square-nautical-mile reef, part of the **Florida Keys National Marine Sanctuary,** has strands of elkhorn coral on its eastern margin, purple sea fans, and abundant sponges and sea urchins. On its seaward side it drops almost vertically 50 to 90 feet. In its midst, **Shipwreck Trail** plots the location of nine historic wreck sites in 14 to 120 feet of water. Buoys mark the sites, and underwater signs tell the history of each site and what marine life to expect. Snorkelers and divers will find the sanctuary a quiet place to observe reef life—except in July, when the annual Underwater Music Festival pays homage to Looe Key's beauty and promotes reef awareness with six hours of music broadcast via underwater speakers. Dive shops, charters, and private boats transport about 500 divers and snorkelers to hear the spectacle, which includes classical, jazz, new age, and Caribbean music, as well as a little Jimmy Buffett. There are even underwater Elvis impersonators. *✉ MM 27.5 OS, 216 Ann St., Key West ☎ 305/292–0311.*

Looe Key Reef Resort & Dive Center. Rather than the customary morning and afternoon two-tank, two-location trips offered by most dive shops, this center, the closest dive shop to Looe Key Reef, runs a single three-tank, three-location dive ($84 for divers, $44 for snorkelers). The maximum depth is 30 feet, so snorkelers and divers go on the same boat. On Wednesday it runs a trip that visits a wreck and reefs in the area for the same price for either snorkeling or diving. The dive boat, a 45-foot catamaran, is docked at the full-service Looe Key Reef Resort. ✉ *MM 27.5 OS, Looe Key Reef Resort, 27340 Overseas Hwy., Ramrod Key* ☎ *305/872–2215, 877/816–3483* 🌐 *www.diveflakeys.com.*

EN ROUTE

The huge object that looks like a white whale floating over Cudjoe Key (MM 23–21) is not a figment of your imagination. It's Fat Albert, a radar balloon that monitors local air and water traffic.

4

KEY WEST

Situated 150 miles from Miami, 90 miles from Havana, and an immeasurable distance from sanity, this end-of-the-line community has never been like anywhere else. Even after it was connected to the rest of the country—by the railroad in 1912 and by the highway in 1938—it maintained a strong sense of detachment.

Key West reflects a diverse population: Conchs (natives, many of whom trace their ancestry to the Bahamas), freshwater Conchs (longtime residents who migrated from somewhere else years ago), Hispanics (primarily descendants of Cuban immigrants), recent refugees from the urban sprawl of mainland Florida, military personnel, and an assortment of vagabonds, drifters, and dropouts in search of refuge. The island was once a gay vacation hot spot, and it remains a decidedly gay-friendly destination. Some of the most renowned gay guesthouses, however, no longer cater to an exclusively gay clientele. Key Westers pride themselves on their tolerance of all peoples, all sexual orientations, and even all animals. Most restaurants allow pets, and it's not surprising to see stray cats, dogs, and chickens roaming freely through the dining rooms. The chicken issue is one that government officials periodically try to bring to an end, but the colorful iconic fowl continue to strut and crow, particularly in the vicinity of Old Town's Bahamian Village.

Although the rest of the Keys are known for outdoor activities, Key West has something of a city feel. Few open spaces remain, as promoters continue to churn out restaurants, galleries, shops, and museums to interpret the city's intriguing past. As a tourist destination, Key West has a lot to sell—an average temperature of 79°F, 19th-century architecture, and a laid-back lifestyle. Yet much has been lost to those eager for a buck. Duval Street looks like a miniature Las Vegas lined with garish signs for T-shirt shops and tour-company offices. Cruise ships dwarf the town's skyline and fill the streets with day-trippers gawking at the hippies with dogs in their bike baskets, gay couples walking down the street holding hands, and the oddball lot of locals, some of whom bark louder than the dogs.

KEY WEST'S COLORFUL HISTORY

The United States acquired Key West from Spain in 1821, along with the rest of Florida. The Spanish had named the island Cayo Hueso, or Bone Key, after the Native Americans' skeletons they found on its shores. In 1823 President James Monroe sent Commodore David S. Porter to chase pirates away. For three decades the primary industry in Key West was wrecking—rescuing people and salvaging cargo from ships that foundered on the nearby reefs. According to some reports, when pickings were lean, the wreckers hung out lights to lure ships aground. Their business declined after 1849, when the federal government began building lighthouses.

In 1845 the army began construction on Fort Taylor, which kept Key West on the Union side during the Civil War, even though most of Florida seceded. After the fighting ended, an influx of Cubans unhappy with Spain's rule brought the cigar industry here. Fishing, shrimping, and sponge gathering became important industries, as did pineapple canning. Through much of the 19th century and into the 20th, Key West was Florida's wealthiest city in per-capita terms. But in 1929 the local economy began to unravel. Cigar making moved to Tampa, Hawaii dominated the pineapple industry, and the sponges succumbed to blight. Then the Depression hit, and within a few years half the population was on relief.

Tourism began to revive Key West, but that came to a halt when a hurricane knocked out the railroad bridge in 1935. To help the tourism industry recover from that crushing blow, the government offered incentives for islanders to turn their charming homes—many of them built by shipwrights—into guesthouses and inns. The wise foresight has left the town with more than 100 such lodgings, a hallmark of Key West vacationing today. In the 1950s the discovery of "pink gold" in the Dry Tortugas boosted the economy of the entire region. Harvesting Key West shrimp required a fleet of up to 500 boats and flooded local restaurants with sweet luscious shrimp. The town's artistic community found inspiration in the colorful fishing boats.

GETTING HERE AND AROUND

Between mile markers 4 and 0, Key West is the one place in the Keys where you could conceivably do without a car, especially if you plan on staying around Old Town. If you've driven the 106 miles down the chain, you're probably ready to abandon your car in the hotel parking lot anyway. Trolleys, buses, bikes, scooters, and feet are more suitable alternatives. To explore the beaches, New Town, and Stock Island, you'll probably need a car.

Greyhound Lines runs a special Keys shuttle two times a day (depending on the day of the week) from Miami International Airport (departing from Concourse E, lower level) and stops throughout the Keys. Fares run about $45 for Key West (3535 S. Roosevelt, Key West International Airport). Keys Shuttle runs scheduled service six times a day in 15-passenger vans between Miami Airport and Key West with stops throughout the Keys for $70 to $90 per person. Key West Express

Sailboats big and small make their way into Key West Harbor; photo by John Franzis, Fodors.com member.

operates air-conditioned ferries between the Key West Terminal (Caroline and Grinnell streets) and Marco Island and Fort Myers Beach. The trip from Fort Myers Beach takes at least four hours each way and costs $86 one way, $146 round-trip. Ferries depart from Fort Myers Beach at 8:30 am and from Key West at 6 pm. The Marco Island ferry costs $86 one way and $146 round-trip, and departs at 8:30 am (the return trip leaves Key West at 5 pm). A photo ID is required for each passenger. Advance reservations are recommended. The SuperShuttle charges $102 per passenger for trips from Miami International Airport to the Upper Keys. To go farther into the Keys, you must book an entire 11-person van, which costs about $350 to Key West. You need to place your request for transportation back to the airport 24 hours in advance.

The City of Key West Department of Transportation has six color-coded bus routes traversing the island from 6:30 am to 11:30 pm. Stops have signs with the international bus symbol. Schedules are available on buses and at hotels, visitor centers, and shops. The fare is $2 one way. The Lower Keys Shuttle bus runs from Marathon to Key West ($4 one way), with scheduled stops along the way.

Old Town Key West is the only place in the Keys where parking is a problem. There are public parking lots that charge by the hour or day (some hotels and bed-and-breakfasts provide parking or discounts at municipal lots). If you arrive early, you can sometimes find a spot on side streets off Duval and Whitehead, where you can park for free—just be sure it's not marked for residential parking only. Your best bet is to bike or take the trolley around town if you don't want to walk. You can disembark and reboard the trolley at will.

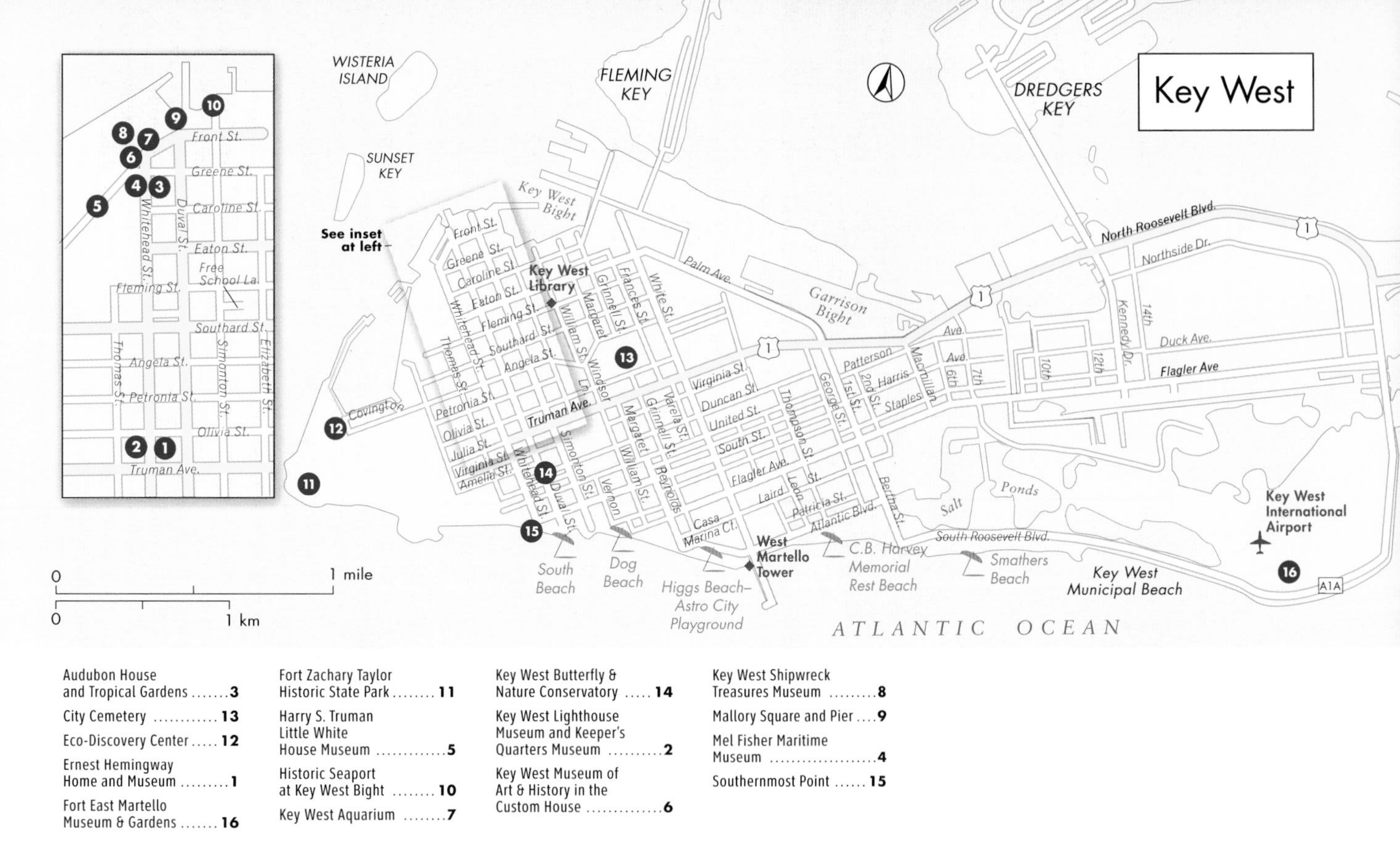
Key West
WISTERIA ISLAND
FLEMING KEY
DREDGERS KEY
SUNSET KEY
Key West Bight
See inset at left
Key West Library
Garrison Bight
North Roosevelt Blvd.
Northside Dr.
Kennedy Dr.
14th
Duck Ave.
Flagler Ave
12th
10th
7th
6th
Ave.
Patterson
Harris
Macmillan
2nd St.
1st St.
Staples
George St.
Palm Ave.
Front St.
Greene St.
Caroline St.
Eaton St.
Fleming St.
Southard St.
Angela St.
Whitehead St.
Thomas St.
Petronia St.
Olivia St.
Julia St.
Virginia St.
Amelia St.
Truman Ave.
Windsor
Ln.
William St.
Margaret
Grinnell St.
Frances St.
White St.
Covington
Virginia St.
Duncan St.
United St.
South St.
Flagler Ave.
Thompson St.
Varela St.
Reynolds
Vernon
Simonton St.
Duval St.
Laird
Leon St.
Patricia St.
Atlantic Blvd.
Bertha St.
Casa Marina Ct.
South Roosevelt Blvd.
Salt
Ponds
South Beach
Dog Beach
Higgs Beach–Astro City Playground
West Martello Tower
C.B. Harvey Memorial Rest Beach
Smathers Beach
Key West Municipal Beach
Key West International Airport
A1A
ATLANTIC OCEAN
0
1 mile
0
1 km
Front St.
Greene St.
Caroline St.
Eaton St.
Free School La.
Fleming St.
Southard St.
Angela St.
Petronia St.
Olivia St.
Truman Ave.
Thomas St.
Simonton St.
Elizabeth St.
Whitehead St.
Duval St.
Audubon House and Tropical Gardens 3
City Cemetery 13
Eco-Discovery Center..... 12
Ernest Hemingway Home and Museum 1
Fort East Martello Museum & Gardens 16
Fort Zachary Taylor Historic State Park 11
Harry S. Truman Little White House Museum 5
Historic Seaport at Key West Bight 10
Key West Aquarium 7
Key West Butterfly & Nature Conservatory 14
Key West Lighthouse Museum and Keeper's Quarters Museum 2
Key West Museum of Art & History in the Custom House 6
Key West Shipwreck Treasures Museum 8
Mallory Square and Pier 9
Mel Fisher Maritime Museum 4
Southernmost Point 15

ESSENTIALS

Transportation Contacts **City of Key West Department of Transportation** ☎ *305/809–3910* ⊕ *www.kwtransit.com.* **Greyhound Lines** ☎ *800/410–5397 Local information, 800/231–2222* ⊕ *www.greyhound.com.* **Keys Shuttle** ☎ *305/289–9997, 888/765–9997* ⊕ *www.floridakeysshuttle.com.* **Key West Express** ✉ *100 Grinnell St.* ☎ *888/539–2628* ⊕ *www.seakeywestexpress.com.* **Lower Keys Shuttle** ☎ *305/809–3910* ⊕ *www.kwtransit.com.* **SuperShuttle** ☎ *305/871–2000, 800/258–3826* ⊕ *www.supershuttle.com.*

Visitor Information **Gay & Lesbian Community Center** ✉ *513 Truman Ave.* ☎ *305/394–4603* ⊕ *www.gaykeywestfl.com.* **Greater Key West Chamber of Commerce** ✉ *510 Greene St.* ☎ *305/294–2587, 800/527–8539* ⊕ *www.keywestchamber.org.*

4

EXPLORING

OLD TOWN

The heart of Key West, this historic Old Town area runs from White Street to the waterfront. Beginning in 1822, wharves, warehouses, chandleries, ship-repair facilities, and eventually in 1891 the U.S. Custom House sprang up around the deep harbor to accommodate the navy's large ships and other sailing vessels. Wreckers, merchants, and sea captains built lavish houses near the bustling waterfront. A remarkable number of these fine Victorian and pre-Victorian structures have been restored to their original grandeur and now serve as homes, guesthouses, shops, restaurants, and museums. These, along with the dwellings of famous writers, artists, and politicians who've come to Key West over the past 175 years, are among the area's approximately 3,000 historic structures. Old Town also has the city's finest restaurants and hotels, lively street life, and popular nightspots.

TOP ATTRACTIONS

Audubon House and Tropical Gardens. If you've ever seen an engraving by ornithologist John James Audubon, you'll understand why his name is synonymous with birds. See his works in this three-story house, which was built in the 1840s for Captain John Geiger and filled with period furniture. It now commemorates Audubon's 1832 stop in Key West while he was traveling through Florida to study birds. After an introduction by a docent, you can do a self-guided tour of the house and gardens (or just the gardens). An art gallery sells lithographs of the artist's famed portraits. ✉ *205 Whitehead St.* ☎ *305/294–2116, 877/294–2470* ⊕ *www.audubonhouse.com* 🎫 *$7.50 gardens only; $12 house and gardens* ⏲ *Daily 9:30–5, last tour starts at 4:30.*

★ **Ernest Hemingway Home and Museum.** Amusing anecdotes spice up the guided tours of Ernest Hemingway's home, built in 1801 by the town's most successful wrecker. While living here between 1931 and 1942, Hemingway wrote about 70% of his life's work, including classics like *For Whom the Bell Tolls*. Few of his belongings remain aside from some books, and there's little about his actual work, but photographs help you visualize his day-to-day life. The supposed six-toed descendants of Hemingway's cats—many named for actors, artists, authors, and

See the typewriter Hemingway used at his home office in Key West. He lived here from 1931 to 1942.

even a hurricane—have free rein of the property. Tours begin every 10 minutes and take 30 minutes; then you're free to explore on your own. ✉ *907 Whitehead St.* ☎ *305/294–1136* 🌐 *www.hemingwayhome.com* 🎫 *$12.50* 🕘 *Daily 9–5.*

★ **Fort Zachary Taylor Historic State Park.** Construction of the fort began in 1845 but was halted during the Civil War. Even though Florida seceded from the Union, Yankee forces used the fort as a base to block Confederate shipping. More than 1,500 Confederate vessels were detained in Key West's harbor. The fort, finally completed in 1866, was also used in the Spanish-American War. Take a 30-minute guided walking tour of the redbrick fort, a National Historic Landmark, at noon and 2, or self-tour anytime between 8 and 5. In February a celebration called Civil War Heritage Days includes costumed reenactments and demonstrations. From mid-January to mid-April the park serves as an open-air gallery for pieces created for Sculpture Key West. One of its most popular features is its man-made beach, a rest stop for migrating birds in the spring and fall; there are also hiking and biking trails and a kayak launch. ✉ *Box 6565, end of Southard St., through Truman Annex* ☎ *305/292–6713* 🌐 *www.floridastateparks.org/forttaylor* 🎫 *$4.50 for 1 person, $7 for 2 people, 50¢ per additional person* 🕘 *Daily 8–sunset.*

NEED A BREAK?

Key West Library. Check out the pretty palm garden next to the Key West Library at 700 Fleming Street, just off Duval. This leafy, outdoor reading area, with shaded benches, is the perfect place to escape the frenzy and crowds of downtown Key West. There's free Internet access in the library, too. ✉ ***700 Fleming St.*** ☎ ***305/292–3595.***

CLOSE UP

Hemingway Was Here

In a town where Pulitzer Prize–winning writers are almost as common as coconuts, Ernest Hemingway stands out. Bars and restaurants around the island claim that he ate or drank there (except Bagatelle, where a sign in the bar reads "Hemingway never liked this place").

Hemingway came to Key West in 1928 at the urging of writer John dos Passos and rented a house with wife number two, Pauline Pfeiffer. They spent winters in the Keys and summers in Europe and Wyoming, occasionally taking African safaris. Along the way they had two sons, Patrick and Gregory. In 1931 Pauline's wealthy uncle Gus gave the couple the house at 907 Whitehead Street. Now known as the Ernest Hemingway Home & Museum, it's Key West's number-one tourist attraction. Renovations included the addition of a pool and a tropical garden.

In 1935, when the visitor bureau included the house in a tourist brochure, Hemingway promptly built the brick wall that surrounds it today. He wrote of the visitor bureau's offense in a 1935 essay for *Esquire*, saying, "The house at present occupied by your correspondent is listed as number eighteen in a compilation of the forty-eight things for a tourist to see in Key West. So there will be no difficulty in a tourist finding it or any other of the sights of the city, a map has been prepared by the local F.E.R.A. authorities to be presented to each arriving visitor. This is all very flattering to the easily bloated ego of your correspondent but very hard on production."

During his time in Key West, Hemingway penned some of his most important works, including *A Farewell to Arms, To Have and Have Not, Green Hills of Africa,* and *Death in the Afternoon.* His rigorous schedule consisted of writing almost every morning in his second-story studio above the pool, and then promptly descending the stairs at midday. By afternoon and evening he was ready for drinking, fishing, swimming, boxing, and hanging around with the boys.

One close friend was Joe Russell, a craggy fisherman and owner of the rugged bar Sloppy Joe's, originally at 428 Greene Street but now at 201 Duval Street. Russell was the only one in town who would cash Hemingway's $1,000 royalty check. Russell and Charles Thompson introduced Hemingway to deep-sea fishing, which became fodder for his writing. Another of Hemingway's loves was boxing. He set up a ring in his yard and paid local fighters to box with him, and he refereed matches at Blue Heaven, then a saloon at 729 Thomas Street.

Hemingway honed his macho image, dressed in cutoffs and old shirts, and took on the name Papa. In turn, he gave his friends new names and used them as characters in his stories. Joe Russell became Freddy, captain of the *Queen Conch* charter boat in *To Have and Have Not.*

Hemingway stayed in Key West for 11 years before leaving Pauline for wife number three. Pauline and the boys stayed on in the house, which sold in 1951 for $80,000, 10 times its original cost.

—Jim and Cynthia Tunstall

Harry S Truman Little White House Museum. Renovations to this circa-1890 landmark have restored the home and gardens to the Truman era, down to the wallpaper pattern. A free photographic review of visiting dignitaries and presidents—John F. Kennedy, Jimmy Carter, and Bill Clinton are among the chief executives who passed through here—is on display in the back of the gift shop. Engaging 45-minute tours begin every 20 minutes until 4:30. They start with an excellent 10-minute video on the history of the property and Truman's visits. On the grounds of **Truman Annex**, a 103-acre former military parade grounds and barracks, the home served as a winter White House for presidents Truman, Eisenhower, and Kennedy. **TIP→ The house tour does require climbing steps. Visitors can do a free self-guided botanical tour of the grounds with a brochure from the museum store.** ✉ *111 Front St.* ☎ *305/294–9911* 🌐 *www.trumanlittlewhitehouse.com* 🎫 *$16* ⏲ *Daily 9–5, grounds 7–6.*

Historic Seaport at Key West Bight. What was once a funky—in some places even seedy—part of town is now an 8½-acre historic restoration of 100 businesses, including waterfront restaurants, open-air bars, museums, clothing stores, bait shops, dive shops, docks, a marina, and water-sports concessions. It's all linked by the 2-mile waterfront **Harborwalk**, which runs between Front and Grinnell streets, passing big ships, schooners, sunset cruises, fishing charters, and glass-bottom boats. ✉ *100 Grinnell St.* ☎ *305/293–8309.*

NEED A BREAK?

Coffee Plantation. Get your morning (or afternoon) buzz, and hook up to the Internet in the comfort of a homelike setting in a circa-1890 Conch house. Munch on sandwiches, wraps, and pastries, and sip a hot or cold espresso beverage. ✉ ***713 Caroline St.*** ☎ ***305/295–9808*** 🌐 ***www.coffeeplantationkeywest.com.***

★ **Key West Butterfly & Nature Conservatory.** This air-conditioned refuge for butterflies, birds, and the human spirit gladdens the soul with hundreds of colorful wings—more than 45 species of butterflies alone—in a lovely glass-encased bubble. Waterfalls, artistic benches, paved pathways, birds, and lush, flowering vegetation elevate this above most butterfly attractions. The gift shop and gallery are worth a visit on their own. ✉ *1316 Duval St.* ☎ *305/296–2988, 800/839–4647* 🌐 *www.keywestbutterfly.com* 🎫 *$12* ⏲ *Daily 9–5, gallery and shop open until 5:30.*

Key West Lighthouse Museum & Keeper's Quarters Museum. For the best view in town, climb the 88 steps to the top of this 1847 lighthouse. The 92-foot structure has a Fresnel lens, which was installed in the 1860s at a cost of $1 million. The keeper lived in the adjacent 1887 clapboard house, which now exhibits vintage photographs, ship models, nautical charts, and lighthouse artifacts from all along the Key reefs. A kids' room is stocked with books and toys. ✉ *938 Whitehead St.* ☎ *305/295–6616* 🌐 *www.kwahs.com* 🎫 *$10* ⏲ *Daily 9:30–5.*

Fodor's Choice ★ **Key West Museum of Art & History in the Custom House.** When Key West was designated a U.S. port of entry in the early 1820s, a customhouse was established. Salvaged cargoes from ships wrecked on the reefs were brought here, setting the stage for Key West to become—for a time—the richest city in Florida. The imposing redbrick-and-terra-cotta Richardsonian Romanesque–style building reopened as a museum and art gallery in 1999. Smaller galleries have long-term and changing exhibits about the history of Key West, including a Hemingway room and a fine collection of folk artist Mario Sanchez's wood paintings. In 2011, to commemorate the 100th anniversary of the railroad's arrival to Key West in 1912, a new permanent Flagler exhibit opened. ✉ *281 Front St.* ☎ *305/295–6616* 🌐 *www.kwahs.com* 🎫 *$7* 🕒 *Daily 9:30–5.*

Mallory Square and Pier. For cruise-ship passengers, this is the disembarkation point for an attack on Key West. For practically every visitor, it's the requisite venue for a nightly sunset celebration that includes street performers—human statues, sword swallowers, tightrope walkers, musicians, and more—plus craft vendors, conch fritter fryers, and other regulars who defy classification. (Wanna picture with my pet iguana?) With all the activity, don't forget to watch the main show: a dazzling tropical sunset. ✉ *Mallory Sq.*

The Southernmost Point. Possibly the most photographed site in Key West (even though the actual geographic southernmost point in the continental United States lies across the bay on a naval base, where you see a satellite dish), this is a must-see. Who wouldn't want his picture taken next to the big striped buoy that marks the southernmost point in the continental United States? A plaque next to it honors Cubans who lost their lives trying to escape to America and other signs tell Key West history. ✉ *Whitehead and South Sts.*

WORTH NOTING

City Cemetery. You can learn almost as much about a town's history through its cemetery as through its historic houses. Key West's celebrated 20-acre burial place may leave you wanting more, with headstone epitaphs such as "I told you I was sick," and, for a wayward husband, "Now I know where he's sleeping at night." Among the interesting plots are a memorial to the sailors killed in the sinking of the battleship USS *Maine,* carved angels and lambs marking graves of children, and grand aboveground crypts that put to shame many of the town's dwellings for the living. There are separate plots for Catholics, Jews, and refugees from Cuba. You're free to walk around the cemetery on your own, but the best way to see it is on a 90-minute tour given by the staff and volunteers of the Historic Florida Keys Foundation. Tours leave from the main gate, and reservations are required. ✉ *Margaret and Angela Sts.* ☎ *305/292–6718* 🌐 *www.historicfloridakeys.org* 🎫 *Tours $15* 🕒 *Daily sunrise–6 pm; tours Tues. and Thurs. at 9:30 year-round, call for additional times.*

Eco-Discovery Center. While visiting Fort Zachary Taylor Historic State Park, stop in at this 6,400-square-foot interactive attraction, which encourages visitors to venture through a variety of Florida Keys habitats from pinelands, beach dunes, and mangroves to the deep sea. Walk through a model of NOAA's (National Oceanic and Atmospheric Administration) Aquarius, a unique underwater ocean laboratory 9 miles off Key Largo, to virtually discover what lurks beneath the sea. Touch-screen computer displays, a dramatic movie, a 2,450-gallon

THE CONCH REPUBLIC

Beginning in the 1970s, pot smuggling became a source of income for islanders who knew how to dodge detection in the maze of waterways in the Keys. In 1982 the U.S. Border Patrol threw a roadblock across the Overseas Highway just south of Florida City to catch drug runners and undocumented aliens. Traffic backed up for miles as Border Patrol agents searched vehicles and demanded that the occupants prove U.S. citizenship. Officials in Key West, outraged at being treated like foreigners by the federal government, staged a protest and formed their own "nation," the so-called Conch Republic. They hoisted a flag and distributed mock border passes, visas, and Conch currency. The embarrassed Border Patrol dismantled its roadblock, and now an annual festival recalls the city's victory.

aquarium, and live underwater cameras show off North America's only contiguous barrier coral reef. ✉ *35 E. Quay Rd., at end of Southard St. in Truman Annex* ☎ *305/809–4750* 🌐 *www.floridakeys.noaa.gov* *Free, donations accepted* ⏲ *Tues.–Sat. 9–4.*

Key West Aquarium. Pet a nurse shark and explore the fascinating underwater realm of the Keys without getting wet at this historic aquarium. Hundreds of tropical fish and enormous sea creatures live here. A touch tank enables you to handle starfish, sea cucumbers, horseshoe and hermit crabs, even horse and queen conchs—living totems of the Conch Republic. Built in 1934 by the Works Progress Administration as the world's first open-air aquarium, most of the building has been enclosed for all-weather viewing. Guided tours, included in the admission price, feature shark feedings. ✉ *1 Whitehead St.* ☎ *305/296–2051* 🌐 *www.keywestaquarium.com* *$15.05* ⏲ *Daily 10–8; tours at 11, 1, 2, 4:30, and 6:30.*

Key West Shipwreck Treasures Museum. Much of Key West's history, early prosperity, and interesting architecture come from ships that ran aground on its coral reef. Artifacts from the circa-1856 *Isaac Allerton*, which yielded $150,000 worth of wreckage, comprise the museum portion of this multifaceted attraction. Actors and films add a bit of Disneyesque drama. The final highlight is climbing to the top of the 65-foot lookout tower, a reproduction of the 20 or so towers used by Key West wreckers during the town's salvaging heydays. ✉ *1 Whitehead St.* ☎ *305/292–8990* 🌐 *www.shipwreckhistoreum.com* *$15.05* ⏲ *Daily 9:40–5.*

Mel Fisher Maritime Museum. In 1622 two Spanish galleons laden with riches from South America foundered in a hurricane 40 miles west of the Keys. In 1985 diver Mel Fisher recovered the treasures from the lost ships, the *Nuestra Señora de Atocha* and the *Santa Margarita*. Fisher's incredible adventure tracking these fabled hoards and battling the state of Florida for rights is as amazing as the loot you'll see, touch, and learn about in this museum. Artifacts include a 77.76-carat natural emerald crystal worth almost $250,000. Exhibits on the second floor rotate and might cover slave ships, including the excavated 17th-century *Henrietta*

Marie, or the evolution of Florida maritime history. ✉ *200 Greene St.* ☎ *305/294–2633* 🌐 *www.melfisher.org* 🎟 *$12.50* ⏲ *Weekdays 8:30–5, weekends 9:30–6.*

NEW TOWN

The Overseas Highway splits as it enters Key West, the two forks rejoining to encircle New Town, the area east of White Street to Cow Key Channel. The southern fork runs along the shore as South Roosevelt Boulevard (Route A1A), skirting Key West International Airport. Along the north shore, North Roosevelt Boulevard (U.S. 1) leads to Old Town. Part of New Town was created with dredged fill. The island would have continued growing this way had the Army Corps of Engineers not determined in the early 1970s that it was detrimental to the nearby reef.

4

★ **Fort East Martello Museum & Gardens.** This redbrick Civil War fort never saw a lick of action during the war. Today it serves as a museum, with historical exhibits about the 19th and 20th centuries. Among the latter are relics of the USS *Maine,* cigar factory and shipwrecking exhibits, and the citadel tower you can climb to the top. The museum, operated by the Key West Art and Historical Society, also has a collection of Stanley Papio's "junk art" sculptures inside and out, and a gallery of Cuban folk artist Mario Sanchez's chiseled and painted wooden carvings of historic Key West street scenes. ✉ *3501 S. Roosevelt Blvd.* ☎ *305/296–3913* 🌐 *www.kwahs.com* 🎟 *$7* ⏲ *Daily 9:30–4:30.*

BEACHES

OLD TOWN

Dog Beach. Next to Louie's Backyard, this tiny beach—the only one in Key West where dogs are allowed unleashed—has a shore that's a mix of sand and rocks. **Amenities:** none. **Best for:** dog owners. ✉ *Vernon and Waddell Sts.* 🎟 *Free* ⏲ *Daily sunrise–sunset.*

★ **Fort Zachary Taylor Beach.** The park's beach is the best and safest place to swim in Key West. There's an adjoining picnic area with barbecue grills and shade trees, a snack bar, and rental equipment, including snorkeling gear. A café serves sandwiches and other munchies. **Amenities:** food and drink, showers, toilets, water sports. **Best for:** swimming, snorkeling. ✉ *Box 6565, end of Southard St., through Truman Annex* ☎ *305/292–6713* 🌐 *www.floridastateparks.org/forttaylor* 🎟 *$4.50 for 1 motorist, $7 for 2 people, 50¢ per additional person* ⏲ *Daily 8–sunset tours noon and 2.*

Higgs Beach–Astro City Playground. This Monroe County park with its groomed pebbly sand is a popular sunbathing spot. A nearby grove of Australian pines provides shade, and the West Martello Tower provides shelter should a storm suddenly sweep in. Kayak and beach-chair rentals are available, as is a volleyball net. The beach also has a marker and cultural exhibit commemorating the gravesite of 295 enslaved Africans who died after being rescued from three South America–bound slave ships in 1860. Across the street, **Astro City Playground** is popular with young children. **Amenities:** parking, toilets, water sports. **Best for:**

WORD OF MOUTH

"The historic Key West Garrison Bight Marina is crowded with pleasure and commercial boats. We always skip the 'short cut' around the harbor and take the long walk by the boats. We never tire of seeing the variety and arrangement of boats."

—photo by John Franzis, Fodors.com member

swimming, snorkeling. ✉ *Atlantic Blvd., between White and Reynolds Sts.* 🎟 *Free* ⏲ *Daily 6 am–11 pm.*

NEW TOWN

C.B. Harvey Memorial Rest Beach. This beach and park were named after Cornelius Bradford Harvey, former Key West mayor and commissioner. Adjacent to Higgs Beach, it has half a dozen picnic areas across the street, dunes, a pier, and a wheelchair and bike path. **Amenities:** none. **Best for:** strolling. ✉ *Atlantic Blvd., east side of White St. Pier* 🎟 *Free* ⏲ *Daily 6 am–11 pm.*

Smathers Beach. This wide beach has nearly 1 mile of nice white sand, plus beautiful coconut palms, picnic areas, and volleyball courts, all of which make it popular with the spring-break crowd. Trucks along the road rent rafts, windsurfers, and other beach "toys." **Amenities:** parking, toilets, water sports. **Best for:** partying. ✉ *S. Roosevelt Blvd.* 🎟 *Free* ⏲ *Daily 7 am–11 pm.*

South Beach. On the Atlantic, this stretch of sand, also known as City Beach, is popular with travelers staying at nearby motels. It is now part of the new Southernmost Hotel on the Beach resort, but is open to the public with a fun beach bar and grill. There's little parking however, so visitors must walk or bike to the beach. **Amenities:** food and drink, parking, toilets. **Best for:** partiers, sunrise, sunset. ✉ *Duval St. at South St.* 🎟 *Free* ⏲ *Daily 7 am–11 pm.*

4

WHERE TO EAT

Bring your appetite, a sense of daring, and a lack of preconceived notions about propriety. A meal in Key West can mean overlooking the crazies along Duval Street, watching roosters and pigeons battle for a scrap of food that may have escaped your fork, relishing the finest in what used to be the dining room of some 19th-century Victorian home, or gazing out at boats jockeying for position in the marina. And that's just the diversity of the setting. Seafood dominates local menus, but the treatment afforded that fish or crustacean can range from Cuban and American to Asian and Continental.

$$ JAPANESE

✕ **Ambrosia.** Ask any savvy local where to get the best sushi on the island and you'll undoubtedly be pointed to this tiny wood-and-tatami-paneled dining room with indoor waterfall tucked away into a resort near the beach. Grab a seat at the sushi bar and watch owner and head sushi chef Masa prepare an impressive array of superfresh sashimi delicacies. Sushi lovers can't go wrong with the Ambrosia special ($40): miso soup served with a sampler of 15 kinds of sashimi, seven pieces of sushi, and sushi rolls. There's an assortment of lightly fried tempura and teriyaki dishes and a killer bento box at lunch. Enjoy it all with a glass of premium sake or a cold glass of Sapporo beer. Ⓢ *Average main: $20* ✉ *Santa Maria Resort, 1401 Simonton St.* ☎ *305/293–0304* 🌐 *keywestambrosia.com* ⏲ *No lunch weekends. Closed 2 weeks after Labor Day.*

$$$ ECLECTIC

✕ **Azur Restaurant.** Fuel up on the finest fare at this former gas station, now part of the Eden House complex. In a contemporary setting with indoor and outdoor seating, welcoming staff serves breakfast, lunch, and dinner that stand out from the hordes of Key West restaurants by virtue of originality. For instance, key lime-stuffed French toast and yellowtail snapper Benedict make breakfast a pleasant wake-up call. The fennel-roasted pork sandwich with Fontina cheese, crab cake BLT, and charred marinated octopus command notice on the lunch menu. Four varieties of homemade gnocchi are a dinner-time specialty, along with tasting plates, "almost entrées" like braised lamb ribs over Moroccan-spiced chick peas, and main courses that include seafood risotto with chorizo and grilled sea bass. *Average main: $26 ✉ 425 Grinnell St. ☎ 305/292–2987 www.azurkeywest.com Reservations essential.*

$$$ CARIBBEAN ★ ✕ **Blue Heaven.** The outdoor dining area here is often referred to as "the quintessential Keys experience," and it's hard to argue. There's much to like about this historic restaurant where Hemingway refereed boxing matches and customers cheered for cockfights. Although these events are no more, the free-roaming chickens and cats add that "what-a-hoot" factor. Nightly specials include black bean soup, Caribbean BBQ shrimp, bison strip steak with blackberry salad, and jerk chicken. Desserts and breads are baked on the premises; the banana bread and lobster Benedict with key lime hollandaise are hits during breakfast, the signature meal here. *Average main: $24 ✉ 729 Thomas St. ☎ 305/296–8666 www.blueheavenkw.com Reservations not accepted Closed after Labor Day for 6 weeks.*

$ SEAFOOD ✕ **B.O.'s Fish Wagon.** What started out as a fish house on wheels appears to have broken down on the corner of Caroline and William streets and is today the cornerstone for one of Key West's junkyard-chic dining institutions. Step up to the wood-plank counter window and order the specialty: a grouper sandwich fried or grilled and topped with key lime sauce. Other choices include fish nuts (don't be scared, they're just fried nuggets), hot dogs, cracked conch sandwich, and shrimp or soft-shell-crab sandwich. Talk sass with your host and find a picnic table or take a seat at the plank. Grab some paper towels off one of the rolls hanging around and busy yourself reading graffiti, license plates, and irreverent signs. It's a must-do Key West experience. *Average main: $10 ✉ 801 Caroline St. ☎ 305/294–9272 www.bosfishwagon.com Reservations not accepted No credit cards.*

$ VEGETARIAN ✕ **The Café.** You don't have to be a vegetarian to love this new-age café decorated with bright artwork and a corrugated tin–fronted counter. Local favorites include homemade soup, veggie sandwiches and burgers (order them with a side of sweet potato fries), grilled portobello mushroom salad, seafood, vegan specialties, stir-fry dinners, and grilled Gorgonzola pizza. There's also a nice selection of draft beer and wines by the glass, plus daily desserts (including vegan selections). *Average main: $11 ✉ 509 Southard St. ☎ 305/296–5515 Reservations not accepted.*

$$$ EUROPEAN Fodor's Choice ★ ✕ **Café Marquesa.** Chef Susan Ferry presents seven or more inspired entrées on her changing menu each night; delicious dishes can include yellowtail snapper with pear, ricotta pasta purses with caponata, and Australian rack of lamb crusted with goat cheese and a port-fig sauce. End your meal on a sweet note with key lime napoleon with tropical fruits and berries. There's also a fine selection of wines and custom

martinis such as the key limetini and the Irish martini. Adjoining the intimate Marquesa Hotel, the dining room is equally relaxed and elegant. *Average main: $29 ✉ 600 Fleming St. ☎ 305/292–1244 🌐 www.marquesa.com ✍ Reservations essential ⏲ No lunch.*

$$$ FRENCH **Café Solé.** This little corner of France hides behind a high wall in a residential neighborhood. Inside, French training intertwines with local ingredients, creating delicious takes on classics, including a must-try conch carpaccio, yellowtail snapper with mango salsa, and some of the best bouillabaisse that you'll find outside of Marseilles. Hog snapper, aka hogfish, is a house specialty here, prepared several ways by Chef John Correa, including with beurre blanc or red pepper custard sauce. From the land, there is filet mignon with a wild-mushroom demi-glaze. *Average main: $27 ✉ 1029 Southard St. ☎ 305/294–0230 🌐 www.cafesole.com ✍ Reservations essential ⏲ No lunch.*

$$ CUBAN **El Meson de Pepe.** If you want to get a taste of the island's Cuban heritage, this is the place. Perfect for after watching a Mallory Square sunset, you can dine alfresco or in the dining room on refined versions of Cuban classics. Begin with a megasized mojito while you enjoy the basket of bread and savory sauces. The expansive menu offers *tostones rellenos* (green plantains with different traditional fillings), ceviche (raw fish "cooked" in lemon juice), and more. Choose from Cuban specialties such as roasted pork in a cumin mojo sauce and *ropa vieja* (shredded beef stew). At lunch, the local Cuban population and cruise-ship passengers enjoy Cuban sandwiches and smaller versions of dinner's most popular entrées. A Latin band performs outside at the bar during sunset celebration. *Average main: $19 ✉ Mallory Sq., 410 Wall St. ☎ 305/295–2620 🌐 www.elmesondepepe.com.*

$ CUBAN **El Siboney.** Dining at this family-style restaurant is like going to Mom's for Sunday dinner—if your mother is Cuban. The dining room is noisy, and the food is traditional *cubano*. There are well-seasoned black beans, a memorable paella, traditional ropa vieja (shredded beef), and local seafood served grilled, stuffed, and breaded. Dishes come with plantains and beans and rice or salad and fries. To make a good thing even better, the prices are very reasonable. *Average main: $10 ✉ 900 Catherine St. ☎ 305/296–4184 🌐 www.elsiboneyrestaurant.com ✍ Reservations not accepted.*

$ IRISH **Finnegan's Wake Irish Pub and Eatery.** "Come for the beer. Stay for the food. Leave with the staff," is the slogan of this popular pub. The pictures of Beckett, Shaw, Yeats, and Wilde on the walls and the creaky wood floors underfoot exude Irish country warmth. Traditional fare includes bangers and mash, chicken potpie, and colcannonballs—rich mashed potatoes with scallions, cabbage, and cheese sauce. Irish bread pudding topped with whiskey sauce and custard is a true treat. Live music on weekends and daily happy hours from 4 to 7 and midnight to 2 featuring more than 30 beers on tap make it popular with the spring break and sometimes-noisy drinking crowd, but you can find quieter spots in the back room and on the porch. *Average main: $13 ✉ 320 Grinnell St. ☎ 305/293–0222 🌐 www.keywestirish.com ✍ Reservations not accepted.*

$$ SEAFOOD **Half Shell Raw Bar.** Smack-dab on the docks, this legendary institution gets its name from the oysters, clams, and peel-and-eat shrimp that are a departure point for its seafood-based diet. It's not clever recipes or fine dining (or even air-conditioning) that packs 'em in; it's fried fish, po'boy sandwiches, and seafood combos. For a break from the deep fryer, try the fresh and light conch ceviche "cooked" with lime juice. The potato salad is flavored with dill, and the "PamaRita" is a new twist in Margaritaville. *Average main: $16 Lands End Village at Historic Seaport, 231 Margaret St. 305/294–7496 www.halfshellrawbar.com Reservations not accepted.*

WORD OF MOUTH

"My favorite fine dining restaurant is Louie's Backyard, though we always go for lunch rather than dinner. The food is just as good, the view is wonderful during the day, and the prices are reasonable."

—SusanCS

$ AMERICAN **Lobo's Mixed Grill.** Famous for its selection of wrap sandwiches, Lobo's has a reputation among locals for its 8-ounce, charcoal-grilled ground chuck burger—thick and juicy and served with lettuce, tomato, and pickle on a toasted bun. Mix it up with toppings like Brie, blue cheese, or portobello mushroom. The menu of 30 wraps includes rib eye, oyster, grouper, Cuban, and chicken Caesar. The menu includes salads and quesadillas, as well as a fried-shrimp-and-oyster combo. Beer and wine are served. This courtyard food stand closes around 5, so eat early. Most of Lobo's business is takeout (it has a half-dozen outdoor picnic tables), and it offers free delivery within Old Town. *Average main: $9 5 Key Lime Sq., east of intersection of Southard and Duval Sts. 305/296–5303 www.lobosmixedgrill.com Reservations not accepted Closed Sun. Apr.–early Dec.*

$$$$ ECLECTIC ★ **Louie's Backyard.** Feast your eyes on a steal-your-breath-away view and beautifully presented dishes prepared by executive chef Doug Shook. Once you get over sticker shock on the seasonally changing menu (appetizers cost around $9–$18; entrées can hover around the $36 mark), settle in on the outside deck and enjoy dishes like grilled scallops with portobello relish, grilled king salmon with fried risotto, and mint-rubbed pork chop with salsa verde. A more affordable option upstairs is the Upper Deck, which serves tapas such as flaming ouzo shrimp, roasted olives with onion and feta, and Gruyère and duck confit pizza. If you come for lunch, the menu is less expensive but the view is just as fantastic. For night owls, the tin-roofed Afterdeck Bar serves cocktails on the water until the wee hours. *Average main: $36 700 Waddell Ave. 305/294–1061 www.louiesbackyard.com Reservations essential Closed Labor Day to mid-Sept. Upper Deck closed Sun. and Mon. No lunch at Upper Deck.*

$$ ITALIAN **Mangia Mangia.** This longtime favorite serves large portions of homemade pastas that can be matched with any of their homemade sauces. Tables are arranged in a brick garden hung with twinkling lights and in a cozy, casual dining room in an old house. Everything out of the open kitchen is outstanding, including the *bollito misto di mare* (fresh

seafood sautéed with garlic, shallots, white wine, and pasta) or the memorable spaghettini "schmappellini," homemade pasta with asparagus, tomatoes, pine nuts, and Parmesan. The wine list—with more than 350 offerings—includes old and rare vintages, and also has a good by-the-glass selection. *Average main: $16 900 Southard St. 305/294–2469 www.mangia-mangia.com Reservations not accepted No lunch.*

$$$ AMERICAN **Michaels Restaurant.** White tablecloths, subdued lighting, and romantic music give Michaels the feel of an urban eatery. Garden seating reminds you that you are in the Keys. Chef–owner Michael Wilson flies in prime rib, cowboy steaks, and rib eyes from Allen Brothers in Chicago, which has supplied top-ranked steak houses for more than a century. Also on the menu is a melt-in-your-mouth grouper stuffed with jumbo lump crab, Kobe and tenderloin meat loaf, veal saltimbocca, and a variety of made-to-order fondue dishes (try the pesto pot, spiked with hot pepper and basil). To lighten up, smaller portions of many of the favorites are available until 7:30 Sunday through Thursday. The Hemingway (mojito-style) and the Third Degree (raspberry vodka and white crème de cacao) top the cocktail menu. *Average main: $25 532 Margaret St. 305/295–1300 www.michaelskeywest.com Reservations essential No lunch.*

$$$ ECLECTIC **Nine One Five.** Twinkling lights draped along the lower- and upper-level outdoor porches of a 100-year-old Victorian mansion set an elegant—though unstuffy—stage here. If you like to sample and sip, you'll appreciate the variety of smaller plate selections and wines by the glass. Starters include a cheese platter, crispy duck confit, a tapas platter, and the signature "tuna dome" with fresh crab, lemon-miso dressing, and an ahi tuna–sashimi wrapping. There are also larger plates if you're craving something like seafood soup or steak au poivre frites. Dine outdoors and people-watch along upper Duval, or sit at a table inside while listening to light jazz. *Average main: $28 915 Duval St. 305/296–0669 www.915duval.com Reservations essential No lunch.*

$$$$ EUROPEAN ★ **Pisces.** In a circa-1892 former store and home, chef William Arnel and staff create a contemporary setting with a stylish granite bar, Andy Warhol originals, and glass oil lamps. Favorites include "lobster tango mango," flambéed in cognac and served with saffron butter sauce and sliced mangoes; Pisces Aphrodite (seafood in puff pastry); fillet *au poivre*; and black grouper braised in champagne. *Average main: $35 1007 Simonton St. 305/294–7100 www.pisceskeywest.com Reservations essential No lunch.*

$$ ITALIAN **Salute Ristorante at the Beach.** This colorful restaurant sits on Higgs Beach, giving it one of the island's best lunch views—and a bit of sand and salt spray on a windy day. Owners of the popular Blue Heaven restaurant took it over and have designed an intriguing dinner menu that includes linguine with mussels, lasagna, and white bean soup. At lunch the gazpacho refreshes with great flavor and texture, and the calamari marinara, antipasti sandwich, pasta primavera, and yellowtail sandwich do not disappoint. Plans are under way to expand the kitchen and serve breakfast. *Average main: $20 1000 Atlantic Blvd., Higgs*

Beach ☎305/292–1117 🌐saluteonthebeach.com ✍ Reservations not accepted.

$$ AMERICAN ★ ✕ **Sarabeth's.** Named for the award-winning jam-maker and pastry chef Sarabeth Levine, who runs the kitchen, it naturally is proclaimed for its all-morning, all-afternoon breakfast, best enjoyed in the picket-fenced front yard of this sweet circa-1870 cottage. Lemon ricotta pancakes, pumpkin waffles, omelets, and homemade jams make the meal. Lunch offerings range from a griddled smoked mozzarella sandwich to poached salmon "Cobb" salad. Start dinner with the signature velvety cream of tomato soup, or roasted red beets and Gorgonzola salad. The daily special augments the short entrée listing that includes meatloaf, green chile pepper macaroni with three cheeses, and grilled mahi with tomatillo sauce. In the mood for dessert? The warm orange-apricot bread pudding takes its cues from Sarabeth's most popular flavor of jam. *[$] Average main: $20 ✉530 Simonton St. ☎305/293–8181 🌐www.sarabethskeywest.com ✍ Reservations not accepted ⏲ Closed Mon. Easter through Christmas, no dinner Mon. Christmas through Easter, closed Tues.*

$$$ SEAFOOD ★ ✕ **Seven Fish.** A local hot spot, this intimate, off-the-beaten-track eatery is good for an eclectic mix of dishes like tropical shrimp salsa, wild-mushroom quesadilla, seafood marinara, and old-fashioned meat loaf with real mashed potatoes. For dessert, the sweet potato pie provides an added measure of down-home comfort. Those in the know reserve for dinner early to snag one of the 20 or so tables clustered in the bare-bones dining room. *[$] Average main: $21 ✉632 Olivia St. ☎305/296–2777 🌐www.7fish.com ✍ Reservations essential ⏲ Closed Tues. No lunch.*

$$ SEAFOOD ✕ **Turtle Kraals.** Named for the kraals, or corrals, where sea turtles were once kept until they went to the cannery, this place calls to mind the island's history. The lunch–dinner menu offers an assortment of marine cuisine that includes seafood enchiladas, mesquite-grilled fish of the day, and mango crab cakes. The slow-cook wood smoker results in wonderfully tender ribs, brisket, mesquite-grilled oysters with Parmesan and cilantro, and mesquite grilled chicken sandwich. The open restaurant overlooks the marina at the Historic Seaport. Turtle races entertain during happy hour on Monday and Friday at 6 pm. *[$] Average main: $16 ✉231 Margaret St. ☎305/294–2640 🌐www.turtlekraals.com ✍ Reservations not accepted.*

WHERE TO STAY

Historic cottages, restored century-old Conch houses, and large resorts are among the offerings in Key West, the majority charging from $100 to $300 a night. In high season, Christmas through Easter, you'll be hard-pressed to find a decent room for less than $200, and most places raise prices considerably during holidays and festivals. Many guesthouses and inns do not welcome children under 16, and most do not permit smoking indoors; rates often include an expanded continental breakfast and afternoon wine or snack.

For expanded reviews, facilities, and current deals, visit Fodors.com.

$$$$ B&B/INN ★ **Ambrosia Key West.** If you desire personal attention, a casual atmosphere, and a dollop of style, stay at these twin inns spread out on nearly 2 acres. **Pros:** spacious rooms; poolside breakfast; friendly staff. **Cons:** on-street parking can be tough to come by; a little too spread out. **TripAdvisor:** "something for everyone," "so relaxing," "quiet getaway." *Rooms from: $319 615, 618, 622 Fleming St. 305/296–9838, 800/535–9838 www.ambrosiakeywest.com 6 rooms, 3 town houses, 1 cottage, 10 suites Breakfast.*

$$ B&B/INN **Angelina Guest House.** In the heart of Old Town, this home away from home offers simple, clean, attractively priced accommodations. **Pros:** good value; nice garden; friendly staff. **Cons:** thin walls; basic rooms; shared balcony. **TripAdvisor:** "great place to relax," "liked everything about it," "awesome pool area." *Rooms from: $109 302 Angela St. 305/294–4480, 888/303–4480 www.angelinaguesthouse.com 13 rooms Breakfast.*

4

$$$$ B&B/INN **Azul Key West.** The ultramodern—nearly minimalistic—redo of this classic circa-1903 Queen Anne mansion is a break from the sensory overload of Key West's other abundant Victorian guesthouses. **Pros:** lovely building; marble-floored baths; luxurious linens. **Cons:** on a busy street. **TripAdvisor:** "beautiful," "a perfect stay," "really takes your breath away." *Rooms from: $239 907 Truman Ave. 305/296–5152, 888/253–2985 www.azulhotels.us 11 rooms, 1 suite Breakfast.*

$$$ RESORT ★ **Casa Marina Resort & Beach Club.** At any moment, you expect the landed gentry to walk across the oceanfront lawn, just as they did when this 13-acre resort was built back in the 1920s. **Pros:** nice beach; historic setting; away from the crowds. **Cons:** long walk to central Old Town; $25 resort fee. **TripAdvisor:** "nice property," "relaxing and fun," "great service." *Rooms from: $159 1500 Reynolds St. 305/296–3535, 866/203–6392 www.casamarinaresort.com 241 rooms, 70 suites No meals.*

$$$$ B&B/INN **Courtney's Place.** If you like kids, cats, and dogs, you'll feel right at home in this collection of accommodations ranging from cigar-maker cottages to shotgun houses. **Pros:** near Duval Street; fairly priced. **Cons:** small parking lot; small pool, minimum stay requirements. **TripAdvisor:** "good location," "a secret gem," "great place for the Key West experience." *Rooms from: $229 720 Whitmarsh La., off Petronia St. 305/294–3480, 800/869–4639 www.courtneysplacekeywest.com 6 rooms, 2 suites, 2 efficiencies, 8 cottages Breakfast.*

$$$ HOTEL **Crowne Plaza Key West–La Concha.** History and franchises can mix, as this 1920s-vintage hotel proves with its handsome faux-palm atrium lobby and sleep-conducive rooms. **Pros:** restaurant and Starbucks in-house; close to downtown attractions; free Wi-Fi. **Cons:** high-traffic area; confusing layout; $20/night valet-only parking. **TripAdvisor:** "amazing experience," "rooms are beautiful," "courteous staff." *Rooms from: $199 430 Duval St. 305/296–2991 www.laconchakeywest.com 160 rooms, 8 rooms with balconies, 10 suites.*

$$$ HOTEL ★ **Eden House.** From the vintage metal rockers on the street-side porch to the old neon hotel sign in the lobby, this 1920s rambling Key West mainstay hotel is high on character, low on gloss. **Pros:** free parking;

hot tub is actually hot; daily happy hour around the pool; discount at excellent Azur restaurant. **Cons:** pricey; a bit of a musty smell in some rooms; no TV in some rooms. **TripAdvisor:** "excellent staff," "the best of the best," "perfect oasis." *Rooms from: $200 ✉ 1015 Fleming St. ☎ 305/296–6868, 800/533–5397 ⊕ www.edenhouse.com 36 rooms, 8 suites No meals.*

$$$$ HOTEL Fodor's Choice ★ **The Gardens Hotel.** Built in 1875, this gloriously shaded property covers a third of a city block in Old Town, among orchids, ponytail palms, black bamboo, walks, fountains, and earthen pots imported from Cuba. **Pros:** luxurious bathrooms; secluded garden seating; free phone calls. **Cons:** hard to get reservations; expensive; $20 per night parking fee. **TripAdvisor:** "a quiet getaway," "wonderful and relaxing," "lovely gardens." *Rooms from: $385 ✉ 526 Angela St. ☎ 305/294–2661, 800/526–2664 ⊕ www.gardenshotel.com 17 rooms Breakfast.*

$$$$ RESORT **Hyatt Key West Resort and Spa.** With its own man-made beach, the Hyatt Key West is one of few resorts where you can dig your toes in the sand, then walk a short distance away to the streets of Old Town. **Pros:** a little bit away from the bustle of Old Town; plenty of activities. **Cons:** beach is small; cramped-feeling property. **TripAdvisor:** "idyllic," "luxury resort in a prime sunset location," "beautiful landscaped." *Rooms from: $290 ✉ 601 Front St. ☎ 305/809–1234 ⊕ www.keywest.hyatt.com 118 rooms No meals.*

$$$ B&B/INN **Key Lime Inn.** This 1854 Grand Bahama–style house on the National Register of Historic Places succeeds by offering amiable service, a great location, and simple rooms with natural-wood furnishings. **Pros:** free parking; some rooms have private outdoor spaces. **Cons:** standard rooms are pricey; pool faces a busy street; mulch-covered paths. **TripAdvisor:** "great location," "a quaint comfortable oasis," "quiet getaway." *Rooms from: $179 ✉ 725 Truman Ave. ☎ 305/294–5229, 800/549–4430 ⊕ www.keylimeinn.com 37 rooms Breakfast.*

$ B&B/INN ★ **Key West Bed and Breakfast/The Popular House.** There are accommodations for every budget, but the owners reason that budget travelers deserve as pleasant an experience (and lavish a tropical continental breakfast) as their well-heeled counterparts. **Pros:** lots of art; tiled outdoor shower; hot tub and sauna area is a welcome hangout. **Cons:** some rooms are small. **TripAdvisor:** "fabulous service," "charming with perfect location," "amazing hospitality." *Rooms from: $99 ✉ 415 William St. ☎ 305/296–7274, 800/438–6155 ⊕ www.keywestbandb.com 10 rooms, 6 with private bath Breakfast.*

$$$$ HOTEL **Key West Marriott Beachside Hotel.** This new hotel vies for convention business with one of the biggest ballrooms in Key West, but it also appeals to families with its spacious condo units decorated with impeccable good taste. **Pros:** private beach; poolside cabanas. **Cons:** small beach; long walk to Old Town; cookie-cutter facade. **TripAdvisor:** "nice rooms," "pure bliss," "great accommodations." *Rooms from: $228 ✉ 3841 N. Roosevelt Blvd., New Town ☎ 305/296–8100, 800/546–0885 ⊕ www.keywestmarriottbeachside.com 93 rooms, 93 1-bedroom suites, 10 2-bedroom suites, 26 3-bedroom suites No meals.*

$$$$ HOTEL Fodor's Choice ★ **Marquesa Hotel.** In a town that prides itself on its laid-back luxury, this complex of four restored 1884 houses stands out. **Pros:** elegant setting; romantic atmosphere; turndown service. **Cons:** street-facing rooms can be noisy; expensive rates. **TripAdvisor:** "romantic," "oasis of serenity," "fantastic service." *Rooms from: $330 ✉ 600 Fleming St. ☎ 305/292–1919, 800/869–4631 ⊕ www.marquesa.com ⇨ 27 rooms 🍴 No meals.*

$$$$ B&B/INN ★ **Merlin Guesthouse.** Key West guesthouses don't usually welcome families, but this laid-back jumble of rooms and suites is an exception. **Pros:** good location near Duval Street; good rates. **Cons:** neighbor noise; street parking. **TripAdvisor:** "superb location," "nice quaint guesthouse," "very relaxing." *Rooms from: $279 ✉ 811 Simonton St. ☎ 305/296–3336, 800/642–4753 ⊕ www.merlinguesthouse.com ⇨ 10 rooms, 6 suites, 4 cottages 🍴 Breakfast.*

4

$$$$ B&B/INN ★ **Mermaid & the Alligator.** An enchanting combination of flora and fauna makes this 1904 Victorian house a welcoming retreat. **Pros:** hot plunge pool; massage pavilion; island-getaway feel. **Cons:** minimum stay required (length depends on season); dark public areas; plastic lawn chairs. **TripAdvisor:** "a tropical paradise," "gracious hosts," "absolutely lovely." *Rooms from: $248 ✉ 729 Truman Ave. ☎ 305/294–1894, 800/773–1894 ⊕ www.kwmermaid.com ⇨ 9 rooms 🍴 Breakfast.*

$$$$ RESORT ★ **Ocean Key Resort & Spa.** A pool and lively open-air bar and restaurant sit on Sunset Pier, a popular place to watch the sun sink into the horizon. **Pros:** well-trained staff; lively pool scene; best spa on the island. **Cons:** $20 per night valet parking; too bustling for some; noise from plumbing and bar. **TripAdvisor:** "faultless resort," "vacation on paradise," "the most amazing place to stay." *Rooms from: $348 ✉ Zero Duval St. ☎ 305/296–7701, 800/328–9815 ⊕ www.oceankey.com ⇨ 64 rooms, 36 suites 🍴 No meals.*

$$$ HOTEL ★ **Parrot Key Resort.** This revamped destination resort feels like an old-fashioned beach community with picket fences and rocking-chair porches. **Pros:** four pools; finely appointed units; access to marina and other facilities at three sister properties in Marathon. **Cons:** outside of walking distance to Old Town; no transportation provided; hefty resort fee. **TripAdvisor:** "very pretty," "beautiful," "the nicest one on the island." *Rooms from: $199 ✉ 2801 N. Roosevelt Blvd., New Town ☎ 305/809–2200 ⊕ www.parrotkeyresort.com ⇨ 74 rooms, 74 suites, 3 3-bedroom cottages 🍴 No meals.*

$$$$ RESORT ★ **Pier House Resort and Caribbean Spa.** The location—on a quiet stretch of beach at the foot of Duval—is ideal as a buffer from and gateway to the action. **Pros:** beautiful beach; good location; nice spa. **Cons:** lots of conventions; poolside rooms are small; minimum stays during busy times. **TripAdvisor:** "a beautiful tropical getaway," "amazing stay," "perfect hotel and perfect location." *Rooms from: $339 ✉ 1 Duval St. ☎ 305/296–4600, 800/327–8340 ⊕ www.pierhouse.com ⇨ 116 rooms, 26 suites 🍴 No meals.*

$$$$ RESORT ★ **The Reach Resort.** Embracing Key West's only natural beach, this recently reinvented and reopened full-service resort has its roots in the 1980s when locals rallied against the loss of the topless beach it displaced. **Pros:** removed from Duval hubbub; great sunrise views; pullout

Sunset Key cottages are right on the water's edge, far away from the action of Old Town.

sofas in most rooms. **Cons:** $25 per day per room resort fee; expensive. **TripAdvisor:** "casual elegance," "beautiful beach," "excellent service." *Rooms from: $279 1435 Simonton St. 305/296–5000, 888/318–4316 www.reachresort.com 72 rooms, 78 suites No meals.*

$$$$ B&B/INN ★ **Simonton Court.** A small world all of its own, this lodging makes you feel deliciously sequestered from Key West's crasser side, but close enough to get there on foot. **Pros:** lots of privacy; well-appointed accommodations; friendly staff. **Cons:** minimum stays required in high season. **TripAdvisor:** "awesome place," "beautiful oasis," "wonderful relaxing getaway." *Rooms from: $260 320 Simonton St. 305/294–6386, 800/944–2687 www.simontoncourt.com 17 rooms, 6 suites, 6 cottages Breakfast.*

$$$ HOTEL **Southernmost Hotel.** This hotel's location on the quiet end of Duval means you don't have to deal with the hustle and bustle of downtown unless you want to—it's within a 20-minute walk (but around sunset, this end of town gets its share of car and foot traffic). **Pros:** pool attracts a lively crowd; access to nearby properties and beach; free parking. **Cons:** can get crowded around the pool and public areas. **TripAdvisor:** "fun in the sun," "great location," "this is the place to stay." *Rooms from: $209 1319 Duval St. 305/296–6577, 800/354–4455 www.southernmostresorts.com 125 rooms No meals.*

$$$ B&B/INN **Speakeasy Inn.** During Prohibition, Raul Vasquez made this place popular by smuggling in rum from Cuba. **Pros:** good location; reasonable rates; kitchenettes. **Cons:** no pool; on busy Duval. **TripAdvisor:** "what a lovely place," "gorgeous inn with superb hospitality," "great folks." *Rooms from: $149 1117 Duval St. 305/296–2680 www.speakeasyinn.com 4 suites Breakfast.*

$$$$ RESORT Fodor's Choice ★ **Sunset Key.** This private island retreat feels completely cut off from the world, yet you're just minutes away from the action. **Pros:** peace and quiet; roomy verandas; free 24-hour shuttle; free Wi-Fi. **Cons:** luxury doesn't come cheap. **TripAdvisor:** "a very different perspective on Key West," "exclusive quiet," "lovely views and excellent service." *Rooms from: $695* *245 Front St.* *305/292–5300, 888/477–7786* *www.westinsunsetkeycottages.com* *40 cottages* *Breakfast.*

NIGHTLIFE

Rest up: much of what happens in Key West does so after dark. Open your mind and have a stroll. Scruffy street performers strum next to dogs in sunglasses. Brawls tumble out the doors of Sloppy Joe's. Drag queens strut across stages in Joan Rivers garb. Tattooed men lick whipped cream off of women's body parts. And margaritas flow like a Jimmy Buffett tune.

BARS AND LOUNGES

Capt. Tony's Saloon. When it was the original Sloppy Joe's in the mid-1930s Hemingway was a regular. Later, a young Jimmy Buffett sang here and made this watering hole famous in his song "Last Mango in Paris." Bands play nightly while regulars play pool. *428 Greene St.* *305/294–1838.*

Durty Harry's. The megasize entertainment complex has live music in a variety of indoor-outdoor bars including Rick's Dance Club Wine & Martini Bar and the tiny Red Garter strip club. *208 Duval St.* *305/296–5513.*

Green Parrot Bar. Pause for a libation in the open air. Built in 1890, the bar is said to be Key West's oldest. The sometimes-rowdy saloon has locals outnumbering out-of-towners, especially on nights when bands play. *601 Whitehead St., at Southard St.* *305/294–6133* *www.greenparrot.com.*

Hog's Breath Saloon. Belly up to the bar for a cold mug of the signature Hog's Breath Lager at this infamous joint, a must-stop on the Key West bar crawl. Live bands play daily 1 pm–2 am (except when the game's on TV). *400 Front St.* *305/296–4222* *www.hogsbreath.com.*

Margaritaville Café. A youngish, touristy crowd mixes with aging Parrot Heads. It's owned by former Key West resident and recording star Jimmy Buffett, who has been known to perform here. The drink of choice is, of course, a margarita, made with Jimmy's own brand of Margaritaville tequila. There's live music nightly, as well as lunch and dinner. *500 Duval St.* *305/292–1435* *www.margaritaville.com.*

Pier House. The party here begins with a steel-drum band to celebrate the sunset on the beach (on select Thursdays and Fridays), then moves indoors to the Wine Galley piano bar for live jazz. *1 Duval St.* *305/296–4600, 800/327–8340* *www.pierhouse.com.*

Schooner Wharf Bar. An open-air waterfront bar and grill in the historic seaport district retains its funky Key West charm and hosts live entertainment daily. Its margarita ranks among Key West's best. *202 William St.* *305/292–3302* *www.schoonerwharf.com.*

Sloppy Joe's is one must-stop on most Key West visitors' barhop stroll, also known as the Duval Crawl.

Sloppy Joe's. There's history and good times at the successor to a famous 1937 speakeasy named for its founder, Captain Joe Russell. Decorated with Hemingway memorabilia and marine flags, the bar is popular with travelers and is full and noisy all the time. A Sloppy Joe's T-shirt is a de rigueur Key West souvenir, and the gift shop sells them like crazy. ✉ *201 Duval St.* ☎ *305/294–5717* 🌐 *www.sloppyjoes.com.*

The Top. On the seventh floor of the Crowne Plaza Key West–La Concha, this is one of the best places in town to view the sunset and enjoy live entertainment on Friday and Saturday nights. ✉ *430 Duval St.* ☎ *305/296–2991* 🌐 *www.laconchakeywest.com.*

Virgilio's. In the best traditions of a 1950s cocktail lounge, this bar serves chilled martinis to the soothing tempo of live jazz and blues nightly. ✉ *524 Duval St.* ☎ *305/296–8118* 🌐 *www.virgilioskeywest.com.*

SHOPPING

On these streets you'll find colorful local art of widely varying quality, key limes made into everything imaginable, and the raunchiest T-shirts in the civilized world. Browsing the boutiques—with frequent pub stops along the way—makes for an entertaining stroll down Duval Street.

MALLS AND SHOPPING CENTERS

Bahama Village. Where to start your shopping adventure? This cluster of spruced-up shops, restaurants, and vendors is responsible for the restoration of the colorful historic district where Bahamians settled in the 19th century. The village lies roughly between Whitehead and Fort streets and Angela and Catherine streets. Hemingway frequented the bars, restaurants, and boxing rings in this part of town. ✉ *Between Whitehead and Fort streets and Angela and Catherine streets.*

ARTS AND CRAFTS

Key West is filled with art galleries, and the variety is truly amazing. Much is locally produced by the town's large artist community, but many galleries carry international artists from as close as Haiti and as far away as France. Local artists do a great job of preserving the island's architecture and spirit.

Alan S. Maltz Gallery. The owner, declared the state's official wildlife photographer by the Wildlife Foundation of Florida, captures the state's nature and character in stunning portraits. Spend four figures for large-format images on canvas or save on small prints and closeouts. ✉ *1210 Duval St.* ☎ *305/294–0005* 🌐 *www.alanmaltz.com.*

Cuba, Cuba!. Check out this shop's stock of cigars, coffee, and paintings, sculptures, pottery, and photos by Cuban artists and artisans. ✉ *814 Duval St.* ☎ *305/295–9442, 800/621–3596* 🌐 *www.cubacubastore.com.*

Gallery on Greene. Showcasing politically incorrect art by Jeff MacNelly and three-dimensional paintings by Mario Sanchez, this is the largest gallery–exhibition space in Key West. ✉ *606 Greene St.* ☎ *305/294–1669.*

Gingerbread Square Gallery. The oldest private art gallery in Key West represents local and internationally acclaimed artists on an annually changing basis, in mediums ranging from graphics to art glass. ✉ *1207 Duval St.* ☎ *305/296–8900* 🌐 *www.gingerbreadsquaregallery.com.*

Glass Reunions. Find a collection of wild and impressive fine-art glass here. It's worth a stop just to see the imaginative and over-the-top glass chandeliers, jewelry, dishes, and platters. ✉ *825 Duval St.* ☎ *305/294–1720* 🌐 *www.glassreunions.com.*

KW Light Gallery. Historian, photographer, and painter Sharon Wells opened this gallery to showcase her own fine-art photography and painted tiles and canvases, as well as the works of other national artists. You can find historic photos here as well. ✉ *1203 Duval St.* ☎ *305/294–0566* 🌐 *www.keywestlightgallery.com.*

Lucky Street Gallery. High-end contemporary paintings are the focus here. There are also a few pieces of jewelry by internationally recognized Key West–based artists. Changing exhibits, artist receptions, and special events make this a lively venue. ✉ *1130 Duval St.* ☎ *305/294–3973* 🌐 *www.luckystreetgallery.com.*

Pelican Poop Shoppe. Caribbean art sells in a historic building (with Hemingway connections, of course). For a $2 admission or a $10 purchase, you can stroll the tropical courtyard garden. The owners buy directly from the artisans every year, so the prices are very attractive. ✉ *314 Simonton St.* ☎ *305/292–9955* 🌐 *www.pelicanpoopshoppe.com.*

Whitehead St. Pottery. Potters Charles Pearson and Tim Roeder display their porcelain stoneware and raku-fired vessels. The setting, around two koi ponds with a burbling fountain, is as sublime as the art. ✉ *322 Julia St.* ☎ *305/294–5067* 🌐 *www.whiteheadstreetpottery.com.*

Nightlife, shops, and some interesting street art can all be found on Key West's Duval Street.

BOOKS

Key West Island Bookstore. This home away from home for the large Key West writers' community carries new, used, and rare titles. It specializes in Hemingway, Tennessee Williams, and South Florida mystery writers. ⊠ *513 Fleming St.* ☎ *305/294–2904.*

CLOTHING AND FABRICS

Fairvilla Megastore. Don't leave town without a browse through the legendary shop, where you'll find an astonishing array of fantasy wear, outlandish costumes (check out the pirate section), and other "adult" toys. ⊠ *520 Front St.* ☎ *305/292–0448* 🌐 *www.fairvilla.com.*

Seam Shoppe. Take home a shopping bag full of scarlet hibiscus, fuchsia heliconias, blue parrot fish, and even pink flamingo fabric, selected from the city's widest selection of tropical-print fabrics. ⊠ *1114 Truman Ave.* ☎ *305/296–9830* 🌐 *www.tropicalfabricsonline.com.*

FOOD AND DRINK

Fausto's Food Palace. Since 1926 Fausto's has been the spot to catch up on the week's gossip and to chill out in summer—it has groceries, organic foods, marvelous wines, a sushi chef on duty 8 am–3 pm, and box lunches to go. ⊠ *522 Fleming St.* ☎ *305/296–5663* 🌐 *www.faustos.com* ⊠ *1105 White St.* ☎ *305/294–5221.*

★ **Kermit's Key West Lime Shoppe.** You'll see Kermit himself standing on the corner every time a trolley passes, pie in hand. Besides pie, his shop carries a multitude of key lime products from barbecue sauce to jellybeans. His prefrozen pies, dressed with a special long-lasting whipped cream instead of meringue, travels well. ⊠ *200 Elizabeth St., Historic Seaport* ☎ *305/296–0806, 800/376–0806* 🌐 *www.keylimeshop.com.*

Key West Winery. You'll be pleasantly surprised with the fruit wines sold here. Display crates hold bottles of wines made from blueberries, blackberries, pineapples, cherries, mangoes, watermelons, passion fruit, and, of course, key limes. Stop in for a free tasting. ✉ *103 Simonton St.* ☎ *305/292–1717, 866/880–1717* 🌐 *www.thekeywestwinery.com.*

Peppers of Key West. If you like it hot, you'll love this collection of hundreds of sauces, salsas, and sweets guaranteed to light your fire. ✉ *602 Greene St.* ☎ *305/295–9333, 800/597–2823* 🌐 *www.peppersofkeywest.com.*

GIFTS AND SOUVENIRS

Cayo Hueso y Habana. Part museum, part shopping center, this circa-1879 warehouse includes a hand-rolled cigar shop, one-of-a-kind souvenirs, a Cuban restaurant, and exhibits that tell of the island's Cuban heritage. Outside, a memorial garden pays homage to the island's Cuban ancestors. ✉ *410 Wall St., Mallory Sq.* ☎ *305/293–7260.*

★ **Montage.** For that unique (but slightly overpriced) souvenir of your trip to Key West head here, where you'll discover hundreds of handcrafted signs of popular Key West guesthouses, inns, hotels, restaurants, bars, and streets. If you can't find what you're looking for, they'll make it for you. ✉ *291 Front St.* ☎ *305/395–9101, 877/396–4278* 🌐 *www.montagekeywest.com.*

4

SPORTS AND THE OUTDOORS

Unlike the rest of the region, Key West isn't known primarily for outdoor pursuits. But everyone should devote at least half a day to relaxing on a boat tour, heading out on a fishing expedition, or pursuing some other adventure at sea. The ultimate excursion is a boat trip to Dry Tortugas National Park for snorkeling and exploring Fort Jefferson. Other excursions cater to nature lovers, scuba divers and snorkelers, anglers, and those who would just like to get out in the water and enjoy the scenery and sunset. For those who prefer their recreation land based, biking is the way to go. Hiking is limited, but walking the streets of Old Town provides plenty of exercise.

BIKING

Key West was practically made for bicycles, but don't let that lull you into a false sense of security. Narrow and one-way streets along with car traffic result in several bike accidents a year. Some hotels rent or lend bikes to guests; others will refer you to a nearby shop and reserve a bike for you. Rentals usually start at about $10 a day, but some places also rent by the half day. ■ **TIP→ Lock up! Bikes—and porch chairs!—are favorite targets for local thieves.**

A&M Rentals. Rent beach cruisers with large baskets for $15 a day. Rates for scooters start at $30 for four hours. Look for the huge American flag on the roof, or call for free airport, ferry, or cruise ship pickup. ✉ *523 Truman Ave.* ☎ *305/294–0399* 🌐 *www.amscooterskeywest.com.*

Eaton Bikes. Tandem, three-wheel, and children's bikes are available in addition to the standard beach cruisers ($18 for first day) and hybrid bikes ($25). Delivery is free for all Key West rentals. ✉ *830 Eaton St.* ☎ *305/294–8188* 🌐 *www.eatonbikes.com.*

Lloyd's Original Tropical Bike Tour. Explore the natural, noncommercial side of Key West at a leisurely pace, stopping on backstreets and in backyards of private homes to sample native fruits and view indigenous plants and trees with a 30-year Key West veteran. The behind-the-scenes tours run two hours and cost $39, including bike rental. ✉ *Truman Ave. and Simonton St.* ☎ *305/304–4700, 305/294–1882* 🌐 *www.lloydstropicalbiketour.com.*

Moped Hospital. This outfit supplies balloon-tire bikes with yellow safety baskets for adults and kids ($12 for the first day, $8 for extra days), as well as scooters ($35) and double-seater scooters ($55). ✉ *601 Truman Ave.* ☎ *305/296–3344, 866/296–1625* 🌐 *www.mopedhospital.com.*

BOAT TOURS

Dancing Dolphin Spirit Charters. Victoria Impallomeni, a 34-year wilderness guide and marine scientist, invites up to six nature lovers—especially children—aboard the *Imp II,* a 25-foot Aquasport, for four-hour ($500) and seven-hour ($700) ecotours that frequently include encounters with wild dolphins. While island-hopping, you visit underwater gardens, natural shoreline, and mangrove habitats. For her Dolphin Day for Humans tour, Impallomeni pulls you through the water, equipped with mask and snorkel, on a specially designed "dolphin water massage board" that simulates dolphin swimming motions. Sometimes dolphins follow the boat and swim among participants. All equipment is supplied. ✉ *MM 5 OS, Murray's Marina, 5710 Overseas Hwy.* ☎ *305/304–7562, 888/822–7366* 🌐 *www.captainvictoria.com.*

White Knuckle Thrill Boat Ride. For something with an adrenaline boost, book with this speedboat. It holds up to 10 people and does 360s, fishtails, and other water stunts in the gulf. Cost is $69 each, and includes pickup shuttle. ✉ *Sunset Marina, 555 College Rd.* ☎ *305/797–0459* 🌐 *www.whiteknucklethrillboatride.com.*

BUS AND TROLLEY TOURS

Conch Tour Train. The Conch Tour Train is a 90-minute narrated tour of Key West, traveling 14 miles through Old Town and around the island. Board at Mallory Square or Angela Street and Duval Street depot every half-hour (9–4:30 from Mallory Square). The cost is $29 (go online for discounted tickets). ☎ *305/294–5161, 888/916–8687* 🌐 *www.conchtourtrain.com.*

Old Town Trolley. Old Town Trolley operates trolley-style buses, departing from the Mallory Square every 30 minutes from 9 to 4:30, for 90-minute narrated tours of Key West. The smaller trolleys go places the larger Conch Tour Train won't fit. You may disembark at any of 12 stops and reboard a later trolley. The cost is $29, but you can save a little by booking online. It also offers package deals with Old Town attractions. ✉ *201 Front St.* ☎ *305/296–6688, 888/910–8687* 🌐 *www.trolleytours.com.*

City View Trolley Tours. In 2010, City View Trolley Tours began service, offering a little competition to the Conch Train and Old Town Trolley, which are owned by the same company. Its rates are more affordable at $19 per adult. Tours depart every 30 minutes from 9:30 to 4:30. Passengers can board and disembark at any of nine stops, and can reboard at will. ☎ *305/294–0644* 🌐 *www.cityviewtrolleys.com.*

Gay & Lesbian Trolley Tour. Decorated with a rainbow, the Gay and Lesbian Trolley Tour rumbles around the town beginning at 4 pm every Saturday afternoon. The 70-minute tour highlighting Key West's gay history costs $25. ✉ *513 Truman Ave.* ☎ *305/294–4603* 🌐 *www.gaykeywestfl.com.*

FISHING

Any number of local fishing guides can take you to where the big ones are biting, either in the backcountry for snapper and snook or to the deep water for the marlins and shark that brought Hemingway here in the first place.

4

Key West Bait & Tackle. Prepare to catch a big one with the live bait, frozen bait, and fishing equipment provided here. This outfitter also has the Live Bait Lounge, where you can sip ice-cold beer while telling fish tales. ✉ *241 Margaret St.* ☎ *305/292–1961* 🌐 *www.keywestbaitandtackle.com.*

Key West Pro Guides. Trips include flats and backcountry fishing ($400–$450 for a half day) and reef and offshore fishing (starting at $550 for a half day). ✉ *G-31 Miriam St.* ☎ *866/259–4205* 🌐 *www.keywestproguides.com.*

KAYAKING

Key West Eco-Tours. Key West is surrounded by marinas, so it's easy to find what you're looking for, whether it's sailing with dolphins or paddling in the mangroves. These sail-kayak-snorkel excursions take you into backcountry flats and mangrove forests. The 4½-hour trip costs $95 per person and includes lunch. Sunset sails ($295 or $65 per person) and private charters ($495) are also available. ✉ *Historic Seaport, 100 Grinnell St.* ☎ *305/294–7245* 🌐 *www.javacatcharters.com.*

Lazy Dog Kayak Guides. Take a two- or four-hour guided sea kayak–snorkel tour around the mangrove islands just east of Key West. The $35 or $60 charge, respectively, covers transportation, bottled water, a snack, and supplies, including snorkeling gear. Paddleboard tours are $40. Rentals for self-touring are also available. ✉ *5114 Overseas Hwy.* ☎ *305/295–9898* 🌐 *www.lazydog.com.*

SCUBA DIVING AND SNORKELING

The Florida Keys National Marine Sanctuary extends along Key West and beyond to the Dry Tortugas. Key West National Wildlife Refuge further protects the pristine waters. Most divers don't make it this far out in the Keys, but if you're looking for a day of diving as a break from the nonstop party in Old Town, expect to pay about $65 and upward for a two-tank dive. Serious divers can book dive trips to the Dry Tortugas.

Captain's Corner. This PADI–certified dive shop has classes in several languages and twice-daily snorkel and dive trips ($40–$65) to reefs and wrecks aboard the 60-foot dive boat *Sea Eagle*. Use of weights, belts, masks, and fins is included. ✉ *125 Ann St.* ☎ *305/296–8865* 🌐 *www.captainscorner.com.*

Snuba of Key West. Safely dive the coral reefs without getting a scuba certification. Ride out to the reef on a catamaran, then follow your guide underwater for a one-hour tour of the coral reefs. You wear a regulator with a breathing hose that is attached to a floating air tank on the surface. No prior diving or snorkeling experience is necessary, but you must know how to swim. The $99 price includes beverages. ✉ *Garrison Bight Marina, Palm Ave., between Eaton St. and N. Roosevelt Blvd.* ☎ *305/292–4616* 🌐 *www.snubakeywest.com.*

WALKING TOURS

Historic Florida Keys Foundation. In addition to publishing several good guides on Key West, the foundation conducts tours of the City Cemetery Tuesday and Thursday at 9:30. ✉ *510 Greene St., Old City Hall* ☎ *305/292–6718* 🌐 *www.historicfloridakeys.org.*

DRY TORTUGAS NATIONAL PARK

History buffs might remember long-deactivated Fort Jefferson as the prison that held Dr. Samuel Mudd for his role in the Lincoln assassination. But today's "guests" are much more captivated by this sanctuary's thousands of birds and marine life.

70 miles southwest of Key West.

GETTING HERE AND AROUND

For now, the ferryboat *Yankee Freedom II* departs from a marina in Old Town and does day trips to Garden Key. Key West Seaplane Adventures has half- and full-day trips to the Dry Tortugas, where you can explore Fort Jefferson, built in 1846, and snorkel on the beautiful protected reef. Departing from the Key West airport, the flights include soft drinks and snorkeling equipment for $265 half day, $465 full day, plus there's a $5 cash park fee. If you want to explore the park's other keys, look into renting a boat or hiring a private charter. *For more information on the two ferries and the seaplane, see the Exploring section.*

ESSENTIALS

Visitor Information **Dry Tortugas National Park** *305/242–7700* 🌐 *www.nps.gov/drto.*

EXPLORING

Dry Tortugas National Park. This park, 70 miles off the shores of Key West, consists of seven small islands. Tour the fort; then lay out your blanket on the sunny beach for a picnic before you head out to snorkel on the protected reef. Many people like to camp here ($3 per person per night, eight sites plus group site and overflow area; first come, first served), but note that there's no freshwater supply and you must carry off whatever you bring onto the island.

The typical visitor from Key West, however, makes it no farther than the waters of Garden Key. Home to 19th-century Fort Jefferson, it is the destination for seaplane and fast ferry tours out of Key West. With 2½ to 6½ hours to spend on the island, visitors have time to tour the mammoth fort-come-prison and then cool off with mask and snorkel along the fort's moat wall.

History buffs might remember long-deactivated Fort Jefferson, the largest brick building in the western hemisphere, as the prison that held Dr. Samuel Mudd, who unwittingly set John Wilkes Booth's leg after the assassination of Abraham Lincoln. Three other men were also held there for complicity in the assassination. Original construction on the fort began in 1846 and continued for 30 years, but was never completed because the invention of the rifled cannon made it obsolete. That's when it became a Civil War prison and later a wildlife refuge. In 1935 President Franklin Roosevelt declared it a national monument for its historic and natural value.

The brick fort acts as a gigantic, almost 16-acre reef. Around its moat walls, coral grows and schools of snapper, grouper, and wrasses hang out. To reach the offshore coral heads requires about 15 minutes of swimming over sea-grass beds. The reef formations blaze with the color and majesty of brain coral, swaying sea fans, and flitting tropical fish. It takes a bit of energy to swim the distance, but the water depth pretty much measures under 7 feet all the way, allowing for sandy spots to stop and rest. (Standing in sea-grass meadows and on coral is detrimental to marine life.)

Serious snorkelers and divers head out farther offshore to epic formations, including Palmata Patch, one of the few surviving concentrations of elkhorn coral in the Keys. Day-trippers congregate on the sandy beach to relax in the sun and enjoy picnics. Overnight tent campers have use of restroom facilities and achieve a total getaway from noise, lights, and civilization in general. Remember that no matter how you get here, the park's $5 admission fee must be paid in cash.

The park has set up with signage a self-guided tour that takes about 45 minutes. You should budget more time if you're into photography, because the scenic shots are hard to pass up. Ranger-guided tours are also available at certain times. Check in at the visitor center for a schedule. The small office also shows an orientation video, sells books and other educational materials, and, most importantly, provides a blast of air-conditioning on hot days.

Birders in the know bring binoculars to watch some 100,000 nesting sooty terns at their only U.S. nesting site, Bush Key, adjacent to Garden Key. Noddy terns also nest in the spring. During winter migrations, birds fill the airspace so thickly they literally fall from the sky to make their pit stops, birders say. Nearly 300 species have been spotted in the park's seven islands, including frigatebirds, boobies, cormorants, and broad-winged hawks. Bush Key is closed to foot traffic during nesting season, January through September. *305/242–7700 ⊕ www.nps.gov/drto* 🎫 *$5.*

Yankee Freedom II. The fast, sleek, 100-foot catamaran *Yankee Freedom II* travels to the Dry Tortugas in 2¼ hours. The time passes quickly on the roomy vessel equipped with three restrooms, two freshwater showers, and two bars. Stretch out on two decks: one an air-conditioned salon with cushioned seating, the other an open sundeck with sunny and shaded seating. Continental breakfast and lunch are included. On arrival, a naturalist leads a 40-minute guided tour, which is followed by lunch and a free afternoon for swimming, snorkeling (gear included), and exploring. The vessel is ADA–certified for visitors using wheelchairs. ■ **TIP→ The Dry Tortugas lie in the central time zone.** ✉ *Lands End Marina, 240 Margaret St., Key West* ☎ *305/294–7009, 800/634–0939* 🌐 *www.yankeefreedom.com* 🎫 *$169, parking $5* ⏲ *Trips daily at 8 am; check in 7:15 am.*

5

Fort Lauderdale

WITH BROWARD COUNTY

WORD OF MOUTH

"I think you'll enjoy Fort Lauderdale. The Riverwalk/Las Olas area has lots of good restaurants—you can take a water taxi there from just about anywhere on the Intracoastal waterway."

—321go

WELCOME TO FORT LAUDERDALE

TOP REASONS TO GO

★ **Blue Waves:** Sparkling Lauderdale beaches spanning Broward County's entire coast were Florida's first to capture Blue Wave Beach status from the Clean Beaches Council.

★ **Inland Waterways:** More than 300 miles of inland waterways, including downtown Fort Lauderdale's historic New River, create what's known as the Venice of America.

★ **Everglades Access:** Just minutes from luxury hotels and golf courses, the rugged Everglades tantalize with alligators, colorful birds, and other wildlife.

★ **Vegas-Style Gaming:** Since slots and blackjack tables hit Hollywood's glittering Seminole Hard Rock Hotel & Casino in 2008, smaller competitors have followed this lucrative trend on every square inch of Indian Territory.

★ **Cruise Gateway:** Port Everglades—home port for *Allure* and *Oasis of the Seas,* the world's largest cruise vessels—hosts cruise ships from major lines.

1 Fort Lauderdale. Anchored by the fast-flowing New River and its attractive Riverwalk, Fort Lauderdale embraces high-rise condos along with single-family homes, museums, parks, and attractions. Las Olas Boulevard, lined with boutiques, sidewalk cafés, and restaurants, links downtown with 20 miles of sparkling beaches.

2 North on Scenic A1A. Stretching north on Route A1A, old-school seaside charm abounds, from high-rise Galt Ocean Mile to quiet, low-rise resort communities farther north.

3 South Broward. From Hollywood's beachside Broadwalk and historic Young Circle (the latter transformed into an Arts Park) to Seminole gaming, South Broward provides grit, glitter, and diversity in attractions.

GETTING ORIENTED

Along the southeast's Gold Coast, Fort Lauderdale and Broward County anchor a delightfully chic middle ground between the posh and elite Palm Beaches and the international hubbub of Miami. From downtown Fort Lauderdale it's about a four-hour drive to either Orlando or Key West, but there's plenty to keep you in Broward. All told, Broward boasts 31 communities from Deerfield Beach to Hallandale Beach along the coast, and from Coral Springs to Southwest Ranches closer to the Everglades. Big—in fact, huge—shopping options await in Sunrise, home of Sawgrass Mills, the upscale Colonnade Outlets at Sawgrass, and IKEA Sunrise.

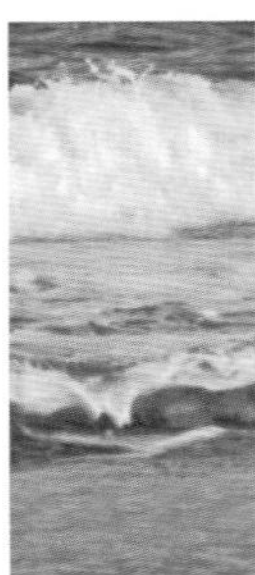

Revised and updated by Paul Rubio

Collegians of the 1960s returning to Fort Lauderdale would be hard-pressed to recognize the onetime "Sun and Suds Spring Break Capital of the Universe." Back then, Fort Lauderdale's beachfront was lined with T-shirt shops, and downtown consisted of a lone office tower and dilapidated buildings waiting to be razed.

The beach and downtown have since exploded with upscale shops, restaurants, and luxury resort hotels equipped with enough high-octane amenities to light up skies all the way to western Broward's Alligator Alley. At risk of losing small-town 45-rpm magic in iPod times—when hotel parking fees alone eclipse room rates of old—Greater Fort Lauderdale somehow seems to meld disparate eras into nouveau nirvana, seasoned with a lot of Gold Coast sand.

The city was named for Major William Lauderdale, who built a fort at the river's mouth in 1838 during the Seminole Indian wars. It wasn't until 1911 that the city was incorporated, with only 175 residents, but it grew quickly during the Florida boom of the 1920s. Today's population hovers around 165,000, and suburbs keep growing—1.75 million live in Broward County's 31 municipalities and unincorporated areas.

As elsewhere, many speculators busily flipping property here got caught when the sun-drenched real-estate bubble burst, leaving Broward's foreclosure rate to skyrocket. But the worst is far behind us. By the time the city began celebrating its centennial in 2011, it had resumed the renaissance that began before the economic crisis. The 20-mile shoreline—with wide ribbons of golden sand for beachcombing and sunbathing—remains the anchor draw for Fort Lauderdale and Broward County, but amazing beaches are now complemented by show-stopping hotels, an exploding foodie scene, and burgeoning cultural scene. In a little over 100 years, Fort Lauderdale has grown into Fort Fabulous.

PLANNING

WHEN TO GO

Peak season runs Thanksgiving through April, when concert, art, and entertainment seasons go full throttle. Expect heat and humidity and some rain in summer. Hurricane winds come most notably in August and September. Golfing tee-time waits are longer on weekends year-round. Regardless of season, remember that Fort Lauderdale sunshine can burn even in cloudy weather.

GETTING HERE AND AROUND

AIR TRAVEL

Serving more than 23 million travelers a year, **Fort Lauderdale–Hollywood International Airport** is 3 miles south of downtown Fort Lauderdale, just off U.S. 1 between Fort Lauderdale and Hollywood, and near Port Everglades and Fort Lauderdale Beach. Other options include **Miami International Airport,** about 32 miles to the southwest, and the far less chaotic **Palm Beach International Airport,** about 50 miles to the north. All three airports link to **Tri-Rail,** a commuter train operating seven days through Palm Beach, Broward, and Miami-Dade counties.

Airport Information **Fort Lauderdale–Hollywood International Airport** *(FLL).* ☎ *866/435–9355* 🌐 *www.broward.org/airport.* **Miami International Airport** *(MIA).* ☎ *305/876–7000* 🌐 *www.miami-airport.com.* **Palm Beach International Airport** *(PBI).* ☎ *561/471–7420* 🌐 *www.pbia.org.* **Tri-Rail** ☎ *800/874–7245* 🌐 *www.tri-rail.com.*

BUS TRAVEL

Broward County Transit operates bus route No. 1 between the airport and its main terminal at Broward Boulevard and Northwest 1st Avenue, near downtown Fort Lauderdale. Service from the airport is every 20 minutes and begins at 5:22 am on weekdays, 5:37 am Saturday, and 8:41 am Sunday; the last bus leaves the airport at 11:38 pm Monday–Saturday and 9:41 pm Sunday. The fare is $1.75 (cash only). ⚠ The Northwest 1st Avenue stop is in a crime-prone part of town. Exercise special caution there, day or night. Better yet, take a taxi to and from the airport. Broward County Transit (BCT) also covers the county on 303 fixed routes. The fare is $1.75 (cash only). Service starts around 5 am and continues to 11:30 pm, except on Sunday.

Bus Contact **Broward County Transit** ☎ *954/357–8400* 🌐 *www.broward.org/BCT.*

CAR TRAVEL

Renting a car to get around Broward County is highly recommended. Taxis are scarce and costly. Public transportation is rarely used.

By car, access to Broward County from north or south is via Florida's Turnpike, Interstate 95, U.S. 1, or U.S. 441. Interstate 75 (Alligator Alley, requiring a toll despite being part of the nation's interstate-highway system) connects Broward with Florida's west coast and runs parallel to State Road 84 within the county. East–west Interstate 595 runs from westernmost Broward County and links Interstate 75 with Interstate 95 and U.S. 1, providing handy access to the airport and seaport. Route A1A, designated a Florida Scenic Highway by the state's Department of Transportation, parallels the beach.

TRAIN TRAVEL

Amtrak provides daily service to Fort Lauderdale and stops at Deerfield Beach and Hollywood.

RESTAURANTS

References to "Fort Liquordale" from spring-break days of old have given way to au courant allusions for the decidedly cuisine-oriented "Fork Lauderdale." Greater Fort Lauderdale offers some of the finest, most varied dining of any U.S. city its size, spawned in part by the advent of new luxury hotels and upgrades all around. From among more than 4,000 wining-and-dining establishments in Broward, choose from basic Americana or cuisines of Asia, Europe, or Central and South America, and enjoy more than just food in an atmosphere with subtropical twists.

HOTELS

Back-to-back openings of luxury beachfront hotels have created Fort Lauderdale's upscale "hotel row"—with the Atlantic Resort & Spa, the Hilton Fort Lauderdale Beach Resort, the Ritz-Carlton, Fort Lauderdale, the W resort, and the Westin Fort Lauderdale all less than a decade old. More upscale places to hang your hat are on the horizon, whereas smaller family-run lodging spots are disappearing, though you can still find chain hotels along the Intracoastal Waterway. If you want to be *on* the beach, be sure to ask specifically when booking your room, since many hotels advertise "waterfront" accommodations that are along inland waterways or overlooking the beach from across Route A1A.

HOTEL AND RESTAURANT COSTS

Prices in the restaurant reviews are the average cost of a main course at dinner or, if dinner is not served, at lunch. Prices in the hotel reviews are the lowest cost of a standard double room in high season. Prices do not include taxes (6%, more in some counties and 1%–5% tourist tax for hotel rooms).

FORT LAUDERDALE

Like many southeast Florida neighbors, Fort Lauderdale has long been revitalizing. In a state where gaudy tourist zones often stand aloof from workaday downtowns, Fort Lauderdale exhibits consistency at both ends of the 2-mile Las Olas corridor. The sparkling look results from upgrades both downtown and on the beachfront. Matching the downtown's innovative arts district, cafés, and boutiques is an equally inventive beach area, with hotels, cafés, and shops facing an undeveloped shoreline, and new resort-style hotels replacing faded icons of yesteryear. Despite wariness of pretentious overdevelopment, city leaders have allowed a striking number of glittering high-rises. Nostalgic locals and frequent visitors fret over the diminishing vision of sailboats bobbing in waters near downtown; however, Fort Lauderdale remains the yachting capital of the world, and the water toys don't seem to be going anywhere. Sharp demographic changes are also altering the faces of

This couple tours Fort Lauderdale via a three-wheeled scooter; photo by rockindom, Fodors.com member.

Greater Fort Lauderdale communities, increasingly cosmopolitan with more minorities, including Hispanics and people of Caribbean descent, as well as gays and lesbians. In Fort Lauderdale, especially, a younger populace is growing, whereas longtime residents are heading north, to a point where one former city commissioner likens the change to that of historic New River—moving with the tide and sometimes appearing at a standstill: "The river of our population is at still point, old and new in equipoise, one pushing against the other."

GETTING HERE AND AROUND

The Fort Lauderdale metro area is laid out in a grid system, and only myriad canals and waterways interrupt the mostly straight-line path of streets and roads. Nomenclature is important here. Streets, roads, courts, and drives run east–west. Avenues, terraces, and ways run north–south. Boulevards can (and do) run any which way. For visitors, boutique-lined Las Olas Boulevard is one of the most important east–west thoroughfares from the beach to downtown, whereas Route A1A—referred to as Atlantic Boulevard, Ocean Boulevard, and Fort Lauderdale Beach along some stretches—runs along the north–south oceanfront. These names can confuse visitors, since there are separate streets called Atlantic and Ocean in Hollywood and Pompano Beach. Boulevards, composed of either pavement or water, give Fort Lauderdale its distinct "Venice of America" character.

The city's transportation system, though less congested than elsewhere in South Florida, suffers from traffic overload. I–595 connects the city and suburbs and provides a direct route to the Fort Lauderdale–Hollywood International Airport and Port Everglades, but lanes slow to a crawl during rush hours. The Intracoastal Waterway, paralleling Route A1A, is the nautical equivalent of an interstate highway. It runs north–south between downtown Fort Lauderdale and the beach and provides easy boating access to neighboring beach communities.

Catch an orange-bottomed, yellow-topped Sun Trolley, running every 15 minutes, for as little as 50¢ each way. Sun Trolley's *Convention Connection* runs round-trip from Cordova Road's Harbor Shops near Port Everglades (where you can park free) to past the Convention Center, over the 17th Street Causeway, and north along Route A1A to Beach Place. Sun Trolley's Las Olas Beaches route passes from downtown through Las Olas and then north on A1A. Wave at trolley drivers—yes, they will stop—for pickups anywhere along the route.

Taxi meters on Yellow Cab run at rates of $4.50 for the first mile and $2.40 for each additional mile; waiting time is 40¢ per minute. There's a $10-fare minimum to or from seaport or airport, and an additional $2 service charge when you are collected from the airport. All Yellow Cab vehicles accept major credit cards.

Transportation Contacts **Sun Trolley** ☎ *954/761–3543* 🌐 *www.suntrolley.com*. **Yellow Cab** ☎ *954/777–7777* 🌐 *www.taxi9547777777.com*.

TOURS

Honeycombed with some 300 miles of navigable waterways, Fort Lauderdale is home port for about 44,000 privately owned vessels, but you don't need to be a boat owner to ply the waters. For a scenic way to really see this canal-laced city, take a relaxing boat tour or simply hop on a Water Taxi, part of Fort Lauderdale's water-transportation system. See why the city is called the "Venice of America."

Carrie B. Board a 300-passenger day cruiser for a 90-minute tour on the New River and Intracoastal Waterway. Cruises depart at 11, 1, and 3 daily November through May and Thursday–Monday between June and October. The cost is $22.95. ✉ *440 N. New River Dr. E, off Las Olas Blvd.* ☎ *954/768–9920* 🌐 *www.carriebcruises.com*.

Fort Lauderdale Duck Tours. Quack, quack! The famous 45-passenger amphibious Hydra-Terra tours, which first gained popularity in Boston, have arrived in Fort Lauderdale. Ninety-minute tours include lots of of land/water family fun, cruising and driving through Venice of America neighborhoods, historic areas, and the Intracoastal Waterway. Several tours depart daily and cost $32. The schedule varies and ducks sometimes don't run in low season, so check ahead of time. ✉ *17 S. Fort Lauderdale Beach Blvd., at Beach Pl.* ☎ *954/761–4002* 🌐 *www.fortlauderdaleducktours.com*.

Jungle Queen Riverboat. The kitsch *Jungle Queen* riverboat seats more than 550 and cruises up the New River through the heart of Fort Lauderdale, as it has for more than 75 years. It's old school and totally touristy, but that's half the fun! The sightseeing cruises at 9:30 and 1:30 cost $17.50, and the 6 pm all-you-can-eat BBQ dinner cruise costs $40. ✉ *Bahia Mar Beach Resort, 801 Seabreeze Blvd.* ☎ *954/462–5596* 🌐 *www.junglequeen.com*.

Water Taxi. A great way to experience the multimillion-dollar homes, hotels, and seafood restaurants along Fort Lauderdale's waterways is via the public Water Taxi, which runs every 30 minutes beginning at 10 am and ending at midnight. An unlimited day pass serves as both a tour and a means of transportation between Fort Lauderdale's hotels and hot spots, though Water Taxi is most useful when viewed as a tour. It's possible to cruise all afternoon while taking in the waterfront sights. Captains and helpers indulge guests in fun factoids about Fort Lauderdale, white lies about the city's history, and bizarre tales about the celebrity homes along the Intracoastal. A day pass is $20. There are 12 pickup stations in Fort Lauderdale, and Water Taxi also connects Fort Lauderdale to Hollywood, where there are seven scheduled stops. ☎ *954/467–6677* 🌐 *www.watertaxi.com.*

VISITOR INFORMATION

Greater Fort Lauderdale Convention and Visitors Bureau ☎ *954/765–4466* 🌐 *www.sunny.org.*

EXPLORING

DOWNTOWN AND LAS OLAS

The jewel of downtown along New River is the small Arts and Entertainment District, with Broadway shows, ballet, and theater at the riverfront Broward Center for the Performing Arts. Clustered within a five-minute walk are the Museum of Discovery & Science, the expanding Fort Lauderdale Historical Museum, and the Museum of Art, home to stellar touring exhibits. Restaurants, sidewalk cafés, bars, and dance clubs flourish along Las Olas and its downtown extension. Tying these areas together is the Riverwalk, extending 2 miles along the New River's north and south banks. Tropical gardens with benches and interpretive displays fringe the walk on the north, boat landings on the south.

TOP ATTRACTIONS

Fort Lauderdale History Center. Surveying city history from the Seminole era to more recent times, the Fort Lauderdale Historical Society's museum has expanded into several adjacent buildings, including the historic King-Cromartie House (a typical early 20th-century Fort Lauderdale home), the 1905 New River Inn (Broward's oldest remaining hotel building), and the Hoch Heritage Center, a public research facility archiving original manuscripts, maps, and more than 250,000 photos. Daily docent-led tours run on the hour from 1 pm to 3 pm. ✉ *231 S.W. 2nd Ave.* ☎ *954/463–4431* 🌐 *www.oldfortlauderdale.org* 🎟 *$10* 🕒 *Tues.–Sun. noon–4.*

★ **Las Olas Boulevard.** What Lincoln Road is to South Beach, Las Olas Boulevard is to Fort Lauderdale. The terrestrial heart and soul of Broward County, Las Olas is the premiere street for restaurants, art galleries, shopping, and people-watching. From west to east the landscape of Las Olas transforms from modern downtown high-rises to original boutiques and ethnic eateries. Beautiful mansions and traditional Floridian homes line the Intracoastal and define Fort Lauderdale. The streets of Las Olas connect to the pedestrian friendly Riverwalk, which

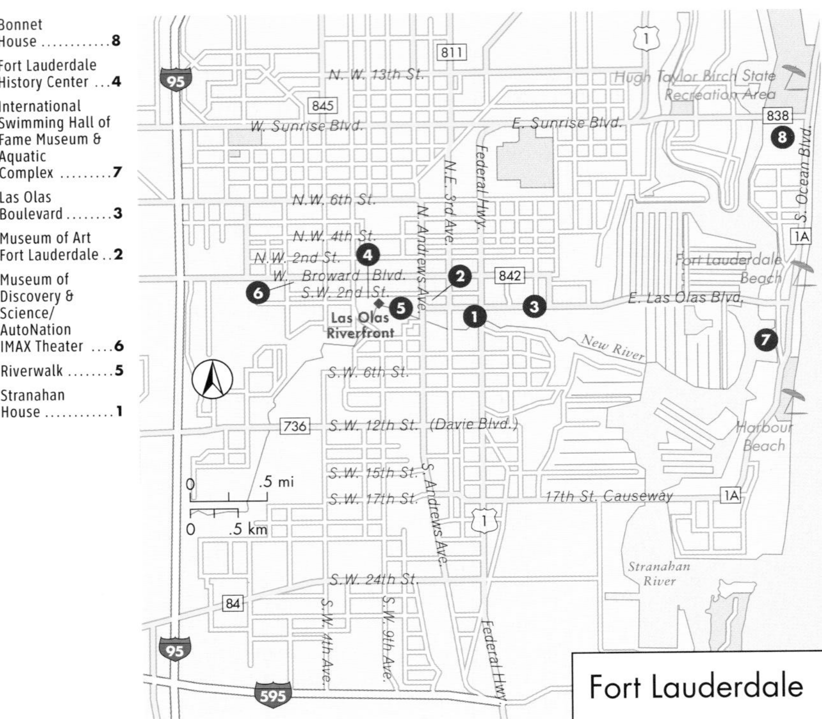

continues to the edge of the New River on Avenue of the Arts. ⊕ *www.lasolasboulevard.com*.

Museum of Art Fort Lauderdale. Currently in an Edward Larrabee Barnes–designed building that's considered an architectural masterpiece, this museum was started by activists in a nearby storefront about 50 years ago. MOAFL now coordinates with Nova Southeastern University to host world-class touring exhibits and has an impressive permanent collection of 20th-century European and American art, including works by Picasso, Calder, Dalí, Mapplethorpe, Warhol, and Stella, as well as works by celebrated Ashcan School artist William Glackens. The lobby-level bookstore and cafe combo, Books & Books/Museum Cafe often hosts book signings, author visits, and special events. ✉ *1 E. Las Olas Blvd., Downtown and Las Olas* ☎ *954/763–6464* ⊕ *www.moafl.org* 🎟 *$10* ⏲ *Tues.–Wed. and Fri.–Sat. 11–6, Thurs.11–8, Sun. noon–5.*

Fodor's Choice ★

Museum of Discovery & Science/AutoNation IMAX Theater. With more than 200 interactive exhibits, the aim here is to entertain children—*and* adults—with the wonders of science and the wonders of Florida. In 2012 the museum doubled in size, meaning twice the fun! Exhibits include the Ecodiscovery Center with an Everglades Airboat Adventure ride, resident otters, and an interactive Florida storm center. Florida Ecoscapes has a living coral reef, plus sharks, rays, and eels. Runways to

THE GHOSTS OF STRANAHAN HOUSE

These days the historic Stranahan House is as famous for its night-time ghost tours as it is for its daytime history tour. Originally built as a trading post in 1901 and later expanded into a town hall, a post office, a bank, and the personal residence of Frank Stranahan and wife, Ivy Cromartie, the historic Stranahan House was more than plagued by a number of tragic events and violent deaths, including Frank's tragic suicide. After financial turmoil, Stranahan tied himself to a concrete sewer grate and jumped into New River, leaving his widow to carry on. Sunday night at 7:30, house staff reveal the multiple tragic tales from the Stranahan crypt during the River House Ghost Tour ($25) and help visitors communicate with "the other side." Using special tools and snapping photos to search for orbs, guests are encouraged to field energy from the supposed five ghosts in the house. Given the high success rate of reaching out to the paranormal, the Stranahan House has become a favorite campground for global ghost hunters and television shows. Advance reservations are required.

Rockets offers stimulating trips to Mars and the moon while nine different cockpit simulators let you try out your pilot skills. The AutoNation IMAX theater, part of the complex, shows films, some in 3-D, on an 80-foot by 60-foot screen with 15,000 watts of digital surround sound broadcast from 42 speakers. ✉ *401 S.W. 2nd St., Downtown and Las Olas* ☎ *954/467–6637 museum, 954/463–4629 IMAX* 🌐 *www.mods.org* 🎫 *Museum $13, $18 with one IMAX show (not including full-length feature films)* ⏲ *Mon.–Sat. 10–5, Sun. noon–6.*

Riverwalk. Lovely views prevail on this paved promenade on the New River's north bank. On the first Sunday of every month a free jazz festival attracts visitors as does an organic farmers' market each Saturday from 9 to 1. From west to east, the Riverwalk begins at the residential New River Sound, passes through the Arts and Science District, then the historic center of Fort Lauderdale, and wraps around the New River until it meets with Las Olas Boulevard's shopping district.

Stranahan House. The city's oldest residence, on the National Register of Historic Places, and increasingly dwarfed by high-rise development, was once home to businessman Frank Stranahan, who arrived in 1892. With his wife, Ivy, the city's first schoolteacher, he befriended and traded with Seminole Indians, and taught them "new ways." In 1901 he built a store that would later become his home after serving as a post office, a general store, and a restaurant. Frank and Ivy's former residence is now a museum, with many period furnishings, and tours. The historic home remains Fort Lauderdale's principal link to its brief history. Note that self-guided tours are not allowed. ✉ *335 S.E. 6th Ave., at Las Olas Blvd., Downtown and Las Olas* ☎ *954/524–4736* 🌐 *www.stranahanhouse.org* 🎫 *$12* ⏲ *Tours daily at 1, 2, and 3 pm; closed Sept.*

QUICK BITES

Kilwin's of Las Olas. The sweet smell of waffle cones lures pedestrians to an old-fashioned confectionery that also sells hand-paddled fudge and

scoops of homemade ice cream. ✉ *809 E. Las Olas Blvd., Downtown and Las Olas* ☎ *954/523-8338.*

ALONG THE BEACH

★ **Bonnet House Museum & Gardens.** A 35-acre oasis in the heart of the beach area, this subtropical estate on the National Register of Historic Places stands as a tribute to the history of Old South Florida. This charming home, built in the 1920s, was the winter residence of the late Frederic and Evelyn Bartlett, artists whose personal touches and small surprises are evident throughout. If you're interested in architecture, artwork, or the natural environment, this place is worth a visit. After admiring the fabulous gardens, be on the lookout for playful monkeys swinging from trees. ✉ *900 N. Birch Rd., Along the beach* ☎ *954/563–5393* 🌐 *www.bonnethouse.org* 🎫 *$20 for house tours, $10 for grounds only* 🕒 *Tues.–Sat. 10–4, Sun. 11–4.*

International Swimming Hall of Fame Museum. This monument to underwater accomplishments has photos, medals, and other souvenirs from major swim events, and the Huizenga Theater provides an automated video experience where you can select vintageOlympics coverage or old films such as Esther Williams's *Million Dollar Mermaid*. Connected to the museum, the **Fort Lauderdale Aquatic Complex** (🌐 *www.ci.ftlaud.fl.us/flac*) has two 50-meter pools plus a dive pool open daily to the public (except mid-December to mid-January). ✉ *501 Sea Breeze Blvd., 1 block south of Las Olas at Rte. A1A, Along the beach* ☎ *954/462–6536, 954/828–4580* 🌐 *www.ishof.org* 🎫 *Museum $8, pool $5* 🕒 *Museum weekdays 9–5, weekends 9–2; pool daily 8–2, plus 6 pm–7:30 pm weekdays.*

NEED A BREAK?

Casablanca Café. For respite from the sun, duck in for a nice glass of chardonnay or a light bite. ✉ *3049 Alhambra St., Along the beach* ☎ *954/764-3500.*

Steak 954. Recover from a long day in the sun with a much-deserved, refreshing cocktail. ✉ *401 N. Fort Lauderdale Beach Blvd.* ☎ *954/414-8333.*

Starbucks addicts can get their iced-coffee fix at the beachfront outpost at the Westin Hotel, smack-dab in the center of Fort Lauderdale Beach.

WESTERN SUBURBS AND BEYOND

West of Fort Lauderdale is ever-growing suburbia, with most of Broward's golf courses, shopping, casinos, and chain restaurants. As you head farther west, the terrain takes on more characteristics of the Everglades, and you'll occasionally see alligators sunning on canal banks. Eventually, you reach the Everglades themselves after hitting the airboat outfitters on the park's periphery. Tourists flock to these airboats, but the best way of seeing the Everglades is to visit the Everglades National Park itself.

Ah-Tah-Thi-Ki Museum. A couple of miles from Billie Swamp Safari is Ah-Tah-Thi-Ki Museum, whose name means "a place to learn, a place to remember." This museum documents the traditions and culture of the

DID YOU KNOW?

Sculptor Peter Wolf Toth fashioned this totem pole for Fort Lauderdale's DC Alexander Park on Seabreeze Boulevard near the New River Sound. Toth, who has sculpted works throughout the country, often creates art that represents the lives of early Native Americans.

Sand can sometimes be forgiving if you fall, and bicyclists also appreciate the ocean views.

Seminole Tribe of Florida through artifacts, exhibits, and reenactments of rituals and ceremonies. The 60-acre site includes a living-history Seminole village, nature trails, and a wheelchair-accessible boardwalk through a cypress swamp. Guided tours are available daily at 2:30. ✉ *34725 W. Boundary Rd., Western Suburbs and Beyond, Clewiston* ☎ *863/902–1113* 🌐 *www.ahtahthiki.com* 🎫 *$9* ⏲ *9–5*

Billie Swamp Safari. At the Billie Swamp Safari, experience the majesty of the Everglades firsthand. Daily tours of wildlife-filled wetlands and hammocks yield sightings of deer, water buffalo, raccoons, wild hogs, hawks, eagles, and alligators. Animal and reptile shows entertain audiences. Ecotours are conducted aboard motorized swamp buggies, and airboat rides are available, too. The on-site Swamp Water Café serves gator nuggets, frogs' legs, catfish, and Indian fry bread with honey. ✉ *Big Cypress Seminole Indian Reservation, 30000 Gator Tail Trail, Western Suburbs and Beyond, Clewiston* ☎ *863/983–6101, 800/949–6101* 🌐 *www.swampsafari.com* 🎫 *Swamp Safari Day Package (ecotour, shows, exhibits, and airboat ride) $49.95* ⏲ *Daily 9–6*

★ **Butterfly World.** As many as 80 butterfly species from South and Central America, the Philippines, Malaysia, Taiwan, and other Asian nations are typically found within the serene 3-acre site inside Tradewinds Park in the northwest reaches of Broward County. A screened aviary called North American Butterflies is reserved for native species. The Tropical Rain Forest Aviary is a 30-foot-high construction, with observation decks, waterfalls, ponds, and tunnels filled with thousands of colorful butterflies. There are lots of birds, too; and kids love going in the lorikeet aviary, where the colorful birds land on every limb!

✉ *3600 W. Sample Rd., Western Suburbs and Beyond, Coconut Creek* ☎ *954/977–4400* 🌐 *www.butterflyworld.com* 🎫 *$24.95* ⏲ *Mon.–Sat. 9–5, Sun. 11–5.*

Everglades Holiday Park. This 30-acre park provides a decent glimpse of the Everglades and Florida's wild west circa 1950. Take an hour-long airboat tour, look at an 18th-century-style American Indian village, or catch the alligator wrestling. The airboats tend to be supersized and the experience very commercialized. ✉ *21940 Griffin Rd., Western Suburbs and Beyond* ☎ *954/434–8111* 🌐 *www.evergladesholidaypark.com* 🎫 *Free, airboat tour $22.50* ⏲ *Daily 9–5.*

★ **Sawgrass Mills.** Twenty-six million visitors a year flock to this mall, 10 miles west of downtown Fort Lauderdale, making it Florida's second-biggest tourist attraction (after the one with the mouse). The ever-growing complex has a basic alligator shape, and walking it all amounts to about a 2-mile jaunt. Count on 11,000 self-parking spaces (note your location, or you'll be working those soles), valet parking, and two information centers. More than 400 shops—many manufacturer's outlets, retail outlets, and name-brand discounters—include Chico's Outlet, Guess, Gap, and Ron Jon Surf Shop. Chain restaurants such as P.F. Chang's, the Cheesecake Factory, Grand Lux Cafe, and Rainforest Café are on-site. The Shops at Colonnade cater to well-heeled patrons with a David Yurman jewelry outlet and other shops including Valentino, Prada, Burberry, Kate Spade New York, and Barneys New York. Non-locals are entitled to a free coupon book at guest services. ✉ *12801 W. Sunrise Blvd., at Flamingo Rd., Western Suburbs and Beyond, Sunrise* ☎ *954/846–2300* 🌐 *www.sawgrassmills.com* ⏲ *Mon.–Sat. 10–9:30, Sun. 11–8.*

Sawgrass Recreation Park. A half-hour airboat ride through the Everglades allows you to view a good variety of plants and wildlife, from ospreys and alligators to turtles, snakes, and fish. Besides the ride, your entrance fee covers admission to an Everglades nature exhibit; a native Seminole village; and exhibits on alligators, other reptiles, and birds of prey. Super cool airboat nights tours are offered on Wednesdays and Saturdays at 8:30 pm to experience the nocturnal world of the 'glades. Reservations required for night tours. ✉ *1006 N. U.S. Hwy. 27, Western Suburbs and Beyond, Weston* ☎ *888/424–7262* 🌐 *www.evergladestours.com* 🎫 *$19.50; $40 night tours* ⏲ *Airboat rides daily 9–5.*

BEACHES

Fodor's Choice ★ **Fort Lauderdale Beach.** The same downy sands that once welcomed America's youth-gone-wild (aka wild spring breakers) now frame a multimile shoreline of beachside sophistication. Alone among Florida's major beachfront communities, Fort Lauderdale's principal beach remains gloriously open and uncluttered. Walkways line both sides of the beach roadway, and traffic has been trimmed to two gently curving northbound lanes. Fort Lauderdale Beach unofficially begins between the Sheraton Fort Lauderdale and the Bahia Mar Resort, starting with the quiet **South Beach Park**, where picnic tables and palm trees rule. Going north, the younger, barely legal crowd gravitates toward the section of sand at the mouth of Las Olas Boulevard. The beach is actually most crowded between Las Olas and Sunrise boulevards, directly in front of the major hotels and condominiums, namely in front of **Beach Place**, home to the Marriott time-share building and touristy places like Hooters and Fat Tuesday (and a beach-themed CVS Pharmacy). Gay men and women get their fix of vitamin D along **Sebastian Beach**, on Sebastian Street, just north of the Ritz-Carlton, Fort Lauderdale. Families with children enjoy hanging out between Seville Street and Vistamar Street, between the Westin Fort Lauderdale Beach and the Atlantic Resort and Spa. **Amenities:** food and drink; lifeguards; parking (fee). **Best for:** sunrise; swimming; walking. ✉ *A1A from Holiday Drive to Sunrise Blvd., Along the beach.*

Harbor Beach. The posh neighborhood of Harbor Beach boasts Fort Lauderdale's most opulent homes along the Intracoastal Waterway. Due east of this community, and just south of Fort Lauderdale's South Beach Park, a stunning swath of beach has adopted the name of its neighborhood—Harbor Beach. This section offers some of the few private beaches in Fort Lauderdale, most of which belong to big hotel names like the Marriott Harbor Beach and the Lago Mar. (Only hotel guests can access these beaches.) Such status permits the hotels to offer full-service amenities and eating and drinking outlets on their bespoke slices of sugarloafed heaven. **Amenities:** water sports. **Best for:** solitude; swimming; walking. ✉ *Along the beach.*

Hugh Taylor Birch State Recreation Area. North of Fort Lauderdale's bustling beachfront, past Sunrise Boulevard, the quieter sands of Fort Lauderdale beach run parallel to Hugh Taylor Birch State Recreation Area, a nicely preserved patch of primeval Florida. The 180-acre tropical park sports lush mangrove areas along the Intracoastal Waterway, and lovely nature trails. Visit the Birch House Museum, enjoy a picnic, play volleyball, or paddle a rented canoe. Since parking is limited on Route A1A, park here and take a walkway underpass to the beach (which can be accessed 9–5, daily). ✉ *3109 E. Sunrise Blvd.* ☎ *954/564–4521* 🌐 *www.floridastateparks.org* 🎟 *$6 per vehicle, $2 per pedestrian* ⏲ *Daily 8–sunset.*

WHERE TO EAT

DOWNTOWN AND LAS OLAS

$$$ ECLECTIC ✕ **Big City Tavern.** A Las Olas landmark, Big City Tavern is the boulevard's most consistent spot for good food, good spirits, and good times. The diverse menu commingles Asian entrées like pad thai, Italian options like homemade meatballs and cheese ravioli, and American dishes like the grilled skirt steak Cobb salad. The Asian calamari with peanuts, apricots, and sweet-and-sour sauce and the pistachio brown butter bundt cake with honey-roasted spiced peaches and pistachio gelato are two of the tavern's best creations. Big City is open late night for drinks, desserts, and even offers a late-night menu. [$] *Average main: $24* ✉ *609 E. Las Olas Blvd., Downtown and Las Olas* ☎ *954/727–0307* 🌐 *www.bigtimerestaurants.com.*

$ AMERICAN **Floridian.** This classic diner is plastered with photos of Monroe, Nixon, and local notables past and present in a succession of brightly painted rooms with funky chandeliers. The kitchen dishes up typical grease-pit breakfast favorites (no matter the hour), with oversize omelets that come with biscuits, toast, or English muffins, plus a choice of grits or tomato. The restaurant also has good hangover eats but don't expect anything exceptional (besides the location). It's open 24 hours—even during hurricanes, as long as the power holds out. *Average main: $16 1410 E. Las Olas Blvd., Downtown and Las Olas 954/463–4041 No credit cards.*

$ ITALIAN **Gran Forno Cafe.** The gamble of importing an entire Italian bakery direct from Brescia, Italy, definitely paid off. Most days, the sandwiches, fresh baked breads, and pastries sell out even before lunchtime. All products are made fresh daily (except Monday), beginning at 4 am, by a team of bakers who can be seen hard at work through the café's glass windows. Customers line up at the door early in the morning to get their piping-hot artisanal breads, later returning for the scrumptious panini and decadent desserts. A second branch, five blocks east on Las Olas, called Gran Forno Pronto, offers full service and a more extensive menu seven days a week. *Average main: $10 1235 E. Las Olas Blvd., Downtown and Las Olas 954/467–2244 www.granforno.com Tues.–Sun. 7:30–7; closed Mon.*

5

$$$$ STEAKHOUSE **Morton's The Steakhouse.** The South Florida steak-house craze has spawned some one-of-a-kinds, but it's also paved the way for some old-school gems to move into the Fort Lauderdale neighborhood. Case in point: Morton's The Steakhouse, which quietly took residence in a corner of downtown in 2010. The steak-house powerhouse doles out hefty portions of its internationally renowned meats and seafood, starting dinner with a freshly baked onion loaf and rich appetizers, moving on to a superb main course accompanied by a slew of indulgent side dishes. It's worth saving room for the legendary ice cream sundae. Just order your cocktails from the "skinny" drink menu, and you'll have less guilt finishing the mammoth dessert. *Average main: $50 500 E. Broward Blvd., Downtown and Las Olas 954/467–9720 www.mortons.com.*

$$ MODERN AMERICAN ★ **PL8 Kitchen.** A small-plates reinvention of Himmarshee Bar and Grill, PL8 Kitchen pushes the envelope of flavorful American cuisine. The food is utterly fantastic. Thankfully, some old favorites, like the butternut-squash purses and the wahoo over sweet-potato hash, made the new menu. In addition, the rebranded restaurant features brick-oven pizzas, skewers, and wedges, and dozens of other eclectic small plates, perfect for sharing. Next door, Side Bar is a classy lounge for simply enjoying the awesome libations on the PL8 mixology menu. *Average main: $18 210 S.W. 2nd St., Downtown and Las Olas 954/524–1818 www.pl8kitchen.com.*

$$ MODERN MEXICAN Fodor's Choice ★ **Rocco's Tacos & Tequila Bar.** The busiest spot on the Las Olas strip, Rocco's is more of a scene than just a restaurant. With pitchers of margaritas a-flowin', the middle-age crowd is boisterous and fun, recounting (and reliving) the days of spring break debauchery from their preprofessional years. In fact, Rocco's drink menu is even larger than its sizeable

food menu. Guacamole is made tableside, and Mexican dishes such as chimichangas and enchiladas have been reinvented (and made far less spicy) for the American palate. Expect a wild night and lots of fun! [$] *Average main: $20* ✉ *1313 E. Las Olas Blvd., Downtown and Las Olas* ☎ *954/524–9550* 🌐 *www.roccostacos.com.*

$$$ ITALIAN ✕ **Timpano Italian Chophouse.** Combine the likes of a high-end steak house with a typical Italian-American trattoria and you've got yourself a successful recipe for an Italian chophouse. Timpano's Italian-centric offerings include fresh pastas, flatbreads, and the full gamut of Parmesans, marsalas, and fra diavolos. Its steak-house identity plays out through a wide selection of aged beef and chops with decadent sides (including truffle mac-and-cheese). Regardless of whether you go carb or carnie for the main event, the blow-your-mind delicious salads are an essential component to the Timpano experience, namely the watercress-and-arugula salad and the chopped salad. [$] *Average main: $22* ✉ *450 Las Olas Blvd., Downtown and Las Olas* ☎ *954/462–9119* 🌐 *www.timpanochophouse.net.*

$$$ AMERICAN ✕ **YOLO.** YOLO stands for "You Only Live Once," but you will definitely want to eat here more than once. For Fort Lauderdale's bourgeoisie, this is the place to see and be seen and to show off your hottest wheels in the driveway. For others, it's an upscale restaurant with affordable prices and a great ambience. The restaurant serves the full gamut of new American favorites like tuna sashimi, fried calamari, garden burgers, and short ribs with a sophisticated spin. For example, the Szechuan calamari is flash fried, and then covered in garlic-chili sauce, chopped peanuts, and sesame seeds; the garden burger is made from bulgur wheat, cremini mushrooms, and cashews and served with thin-cut fries. [$] *Average main: $22* ✉ *333 E. Las Olas Blvd., Downtown and Las Olas* ☎ *954/523–1000* 🌐 *www.yolorestaurant.com.*

ALONG THE BEACH

$$ ECLECTIC ✕ **Casablanca Cafe.** Located along A1A in the heart of Fort Lauderdale's hotel row, Casablanca Cafe offers alfresco and indoor dining with a fabulous ocean view. The historic two-story Moroccan-style villa was built in the 1920s by local architect Francis Abreu. The menu at this piano bar and restaurant showcases a global potpourri of American, Mediterranean, and Asian flavors; however, the recommended "house favorites" focus on eclectic preparations of Florida's best fish. Prepare for long waits to eat in the outdoor section; it's wildly popular morning, noon, and night with tourists and locals alike. [$] *Average main: $18* ✉ *3049 Alhambra St., Along the beach* ☎ *954/764–3500* 🌐 *www.casablancacafeonline.com.*

$$$ MEXICAN ✕ **Dos Caminos.** An institution in the Manhattan Mexican dining scene, Dos Caminos has opened its first Florida outpost at the Sheraton Fort Lauderdale Beach Hotel. Rounds of traditional and nontraditional margaritas (like the pineapple–brown sugar margarita) begin the journey south of the border. Chips are served with a trio of authentic salsas, usually followed by fantastic guacamole, made to order. The house specialties, tacos, quesadillas, and enchiladas are a commingling of traditional Mexican and neo-Mexican gastronomy, reinvented with an American flair. [$] *Average main: $20* ✉ *Sheraton Fort Lauderdale*

Beach Resort, 1140 Seabreeze Blvd., Along the beach ☎ 954/727–7090 🌐 www.doscaminos.com.

$$$$ SUSHI Fodor's Choice ★ ✕ **SAIA Sushi.** The superlative locale for getting your sushi fix in Fort Lauderdale, SAIA offers innovative rolls and perfectly executed classics as well as a great selection of hot Thai and Japanese dishes. SAIA's master chef Subin Chenkosorn hails from the renowned Blue Sea at the Delano in Miami, bringing his amazing skill set to the Fort Lauderdale shore. The stylish restaurant doubles as a gregarious lounge come late evening, perfect for enjoying another round of saketinis, soju-based cocktails, and other specialty drinks like the divine SAIA-rita and Ruby Foo, after a fabulous dinner. $ *Average main: $35 ✉ B Ocean Fort Lauderdale, 999 N. Fort Lauderdale Beach Blvd., Along the beach ☎ 954/302–5252.*

$$$$ STEAKHOUSE ★ ✕ **Shula's on the Beach.** For anyone getting positively misty-eyed at the mere mention of Don Shula's Miami Dolphins 17–0 Perfect Season of '72, the good news is that this beachfront spot also turns out culinary winners. Despite dozens of new, trendy steak houses in Miami and Fort Lauderdale, Shula's on the Beach remains staunch competition. Carnivores rejoice over the aged premium Black Angus beef grilled over a super-hot fire for quick charring. The seafood is excellent, too, and served in generous portions. The jumbo sea scallops and jumbo lump crab cakes are indeed "jumbo" and über-delicious. For a more casual affair, check out the lively bar area adorned with sports memorabilia and large-screen TVs. $ *Average main: $38 ✉ The Westin Beach Resort & Spa, Fort Lauderdale, 321 N. Fort Lauderdale Beach Blvd., Along the beach ☎ 954/355–4000.*

5

$$$$ STEAKHOUSE ✕ **Steak 954.** It's not just the steaks that impress at Stephen Starr's superstar restaurant. The lobster and crab-coconut ceviche and the red snapper tiradito are divine; the butter-poached Maine lobster is perfection; and the raw bar showcases only the best and freshest seafood on the market. Located on the 1st floor of the swanky W Fort Lauderdale, Steak 954 offers spectacular views of the ocean for those choosing outdoor seating; or a sexy, sophisticated ambience for those choosing to dine in the main dining room, with bright tropical colors balanced with dark woods and an enormous jellyfish tank spanning the width of the restaurant. Sunday brunch is very popular, so arrive early for the best views. $ *Average main: $35 ✉ W Fort Lauderdale, 401 N. Fort Lauderdale Beach Blvd., Along the beach ☎ 954/414–8333 🌐 www.steak954.com.*

$$$$ SEAFOOD Fodor's Choice ★ ✕ **3030 Ocean.** Celebrity chef Dean James Max's fish and seafood restaurant has been the talk of the town for decades. Constantly evolving with new flavors and fusions, 3030 Ocean gives plenty of great reasons to return time and time again. The ahi tuna coconut ceviche, a kind of tuna tartare served in one-half of a shelled coconut, is so fresh, it melts in your mouth. The apricot-glazed mahi and wild gulf shrimp ravioli in butternut-squash puree are nothing short of experiential. The martini menu is also heaven-sent, advancing mixology with basil-and-passion-fruit martinis, Bellini martinis, and acai-and-sage martinis. If you treat yourself to one nice dinner in Fort Lauderdale, do it here! $ *Average*

main: $32 ✉ Marriott's Harbor Beach Resort & Spa, 3030 Holiday Dr., Along the beach ☎ 954/765–3030 ⊕ www.3030ocean.com.

INTRACOASTAL AND INLAND

$$$$ SOUTHWESTERN ✕ **Canyon Southwest Cafe.** Southwestern fusion fare helps you escape the ordinary at this small magical enclave. It's been run for the past dozen years by owner and executive chef Chris Wilber. Order, for example, bison medallions with scotch bonnets, a tequila-jalapeño smoked salmon tostada, coriander-crusted tuna, or blue-corn fried oysters. Chipotle, wasabi, mango, and red chilies accent fresh seafood and wild game. Start off with a signature prickly pear margarita or choose from a well-rounded wine list or beer selection. Save room for the divine chocolate bread pudding. $ *Average main: $35 ✉ 1818 E. Sunrise Blvd., Intracoastal and Inland ☎ 954/765–1950 ⊕ www.canyonfl.com ⊙ No lunch.*

$$$$ STEAKHOUSE ★ ✕ **The Capital Grille, Fort Lauderdale.** The Capital Grille is a rare example of a restaurant chain that has managed to uphold the superlative food quality and stellar service on which it was founded, regardless of expansion. Indeed, the Fort Lauderdale outpost of this American darlin' never fails to impress, every dish cooked to perfection and meticulously presented. The dining room feels warm and welcoming, buzzing with the constant chatter of patrons raving about the food and ordering another round of Stoli Dolis (Stoli vodka marinating in a tub of fresh-cut pineapples for two weeks and then served as a smooth martini). Though the steaks and sides are the main draw, the calamari appetizer, shrimp cocktail, sushi-grade tuna steak, and salmon should not be overlooked. They are all phenomenal. $ *Average main: $34 ✉ 2430 E. Sunrise Blvd., Intracoastal and Inland ☎ 954/446–2000 ⊕ www.thecapitalgrille.com.*

$$$$ ITALIAN ✕ **Casa D'Angelo.** Owner-chef Angelo Elia has created a gem of a Tuscan-style white-tablecloth restaurant, tucked in the Sunrise Square shopping center. Casa D'Angelo's oak oven turns out marvelous seafood and beef dishes. The pappardelle with porcini mushrooms takes pasta to pleasant heights. Another favorite is the calamari and scungilli salad with garlic and lemon. Ask about the oven-roasted fish of the day or the snapper *oreganta* at market price. $ *Average main: $38 ✉ 1201 N. Federal Hwy., Intracoastal and Inland ☎ 954/564–1234 ⊕ www.casa-d-angelo.com ⊙ No lunch.*

$$$$ ASIAN ✕ **China Grill.** China Grill takes the best of Asian cuisine and adds an American flair to create a pan-Asian eating extravaganza. This concept of global Asian fusion draws inspiration from Marco Polo and his descriptions of the Far East and its riches. While Marco Polo's travels are imprinted on the restaurant floor, the flavors of his destinations are all over the menu. Try the crackling calamari salad—a taste explosion of zest with crispy lettuce, calamari, and citrus in lime-miso dressing—or the Shanghai Lobster —a 2.5-pound female lobster, unbelievably soft and tender, drenched in ginger and curry and accompanied by crispy spinach. $ *Average main: $40 ✉ 1881 S.E. 17th St., Intracoastal and Inland ☎ 954/759–9950 ⊕ www.chinagrillmgt.com.*

$$ PIZZA ✕ **Giorgio's Brick Oven Pizza.** The delicious brick-oven pizza lures customers to this tiny restaurant, but it's really the salads and sandwiches that provide the wow factor. The blackened chicken Caesar salad and the

monstrous grilled chicken sandwiches (with grilled peppers and fresh mozzarella on freshly baked bread) are both memorable. Nevertheless, the homemade seafood salad is still Giorgio's best seller, a healthy mix of baby squid, shrimp, calamari, and scallops in a light vinaigrette. All meals are served with piping hot rolls and homemade hummus. *Average main: $20 ✉ 1499 S.E. 17th St., Intracoastal and Inland ☎ 954/767–8300.*

$$$ ECLECTIC **The Grateful Palate.** This restaurant is locally famous for catering the be-all and end-all of yacht parties in the "yachting capital of the world." The selective international menu showcases original global fusion, with starters such as watermelon-and-goat-cheese salad with rum-mint-vanilla vinaigrette and macadamia nuts, and main dishes like the tandoori-style grilled pork chop with Israeli couscous and tzatziki. For those unable to secure an invitation to a fabulous yacht party, the charming restaurant offers an initmate setting for sampling the eclectic eats. *Average main: $26 ✉ 817 S.E. 17th St., Intracoastal and Inland ☎ 954/467–1998.*

5

$$$ ITALIAN **Kitchenetta.** A modern Italian-American trattoria serving fresh Mediterranean favorites in a chic, loft-inspired setting, Kitchenetta has been pleasing Fort Lauderdale foodies for more than a decade. The outdoor seating area welcomes pet-lovers, who dine with pooch in tow. Popular items fresh out of the open kitchen include the fried calamari, fusilli escarole and cannellini beans, penne puttanesca, pollo scarpariello Siciliano, and a wide range of daily mouthwatering specials. *Average main: $24 ✉ 2850 N. Federal Hwy, Intracoastal and Inland ☎ 954/567–3333 www.kitchenetta.com.*

$$$ MODERN AMERICAN Fodor's Choice ★ **Market 17.** Using only the best ingredients from regional farmers and local fishermen, Market 17 leads the organic farm-to-table revolution in South Florida. The menu at this chic restaurant shifts seasonally, lending to an ever-changing kaleidoscope of mouthwatering creations. The Florida wahoo crudo in citrus marinade and the pan-basted Florida yelloweye snapper with leek puree are two local favorites. The desserts, too, are outstanding and include homemade ice creams in flavors like bananas Foster, chocolate cake batter, and ginger and honey. For something awesome and different with a small group, Market 17 offers "dining in the dark," where dinner is served in a blacked-out room, forcing you to rely on your senses of touch, taste, and smell to figure out what you're eating and drinking. *Average main: $30 ✉ 1850 S.E. 17th St., Suite 109, Intracoastal and Inland ☎ 954/835–5507 www.market17.net Reservations essential.*

$$ SEAFOOD Fodor's Choice ★ **Pelican Landing.** In this age of globalization and instant information, it's nearly impossible to remain the city's "best-kept secret," but somehow Pelican Landing has managed to do exactly that. Located on a second-story terrace in the Pier Sixty-Six Marina, the serene outdoor restaurant serves mouthwatering beach-shack-style eats surrounded by picturesque panoramas of boats, sea, and sunset. The fish is caught daily, served blackened or grilled, presented with sides, on a salad, or in a burrito. The ceviches and conch fritters are the best in Florida. And matched with frozen drinks and pitchers of mojitos, you'll quickly reach a state of "paradise found!" *Average main: $18 ✉ Hyatt Regency*

Pier Sixty Six, 2301 S.E. 17th St. Causeway, at end of main dock, Intracoastal and Inland ☎ *954/525–6666* 🌐 *www.pier66.hyatt.com.*

$$$$ AMERICAN Fodor's Choice ★ **PierTop at Hyatt Pier 66.** Doling out superlative views of Fort Lauderdale high in the sky, the Hyatt Pier 66's PierTop Lounge opens to the public once a week for a divine Sunday brunch. You may feel like you've entered a time warp upon exiting the elevator on the rooftop with a circa 1977 rotating floor and circa 1986 prom-dress-inspired tablecloths. However, the vistas, the food, and the service are all exceptional. Sunday brunch begins with a glass of Veuve Clicquot and continues with unlimited champagne and Bloody Marys and an all-out gourmet eating extravaganza, including a decadent sushi bar (all for $65 per head). You'll get the most eye-popping panoramic views of Fort Lauderdale as the floor slowly spins in the rooftop restaurant. This brunch is a must-do! *Average main: $65* ✉ *Hyatt Regency Pier Sixty-Six, 2301 S.E. 17th St., Intracoastal and Inland* ☎ *954/525–6666* 🌐 *www.thepiertop.com* *Reservations essential.*

$$$$ STEAKHOUSE **Ruth's Chris Steak House.** The Fort Lauderdale outpost of the steak-house juggernaut got a face-lift in late 2011, endowing the restaurant with a lighter, softer ambience. The service here is outstanding, and waitstaff are eager to guide you through the protein-rich menu. Steaks are served on a sizzling 500-degree plate to keep them piping hot and are dripping with melted butter. Appetizers include the "crabtini," a generous portion of lump crabmeat, lightly dressed in a chilled martini glass, and the sensational lobster bisque. *Average main: $38* ✉ *2525 N. Federal Hwy., Intracoastal and Inland* ☎ *954/565–2338* 🌐 *www.ruthschris.com.*

$$ SEAFOOD **Southport Raw Bar.** You can't go wrong at this unpretentious spot where the motto, on bumper stickers for miles around, proclaims, "eat fish, live longer, eat oysters, love longer, eat clams, last longer." Raw or steamed clams, raw oysters, and peel-and-eat shrimp are market priced. Sides range from Bimini bread to key lime pie, with conch fritters, beer-battered onion rings, and corn on the cob in between. Order wine by the bottle or glass, and beer by the pitcher, bottle, or can. Eat outside overlooking a canal, or inside at booths, tables, or in the front or back bars. Limited parking is free, and a grocery-store parking lot is across the street. *Average main: $18* ✉ *1536 Cordova Rd., Intracoastal and Inland* ☎ *954/525–2526* 🌐 *www.southportrawbar.com.*

$$$ VEGETARIAN ★ **Sublime.** Pamela Anderson and her celebrity pals are not the only vegetarians that love this vegan powerhouse. The vegan sushi, the portobello stack, and innovative pizzas and pastas surprisingly satisfy carnivore cravings. All dishes are organic and void of any animal by-products, showing the world how vegan eating does not compromise flavor or taste. Even items like the key lime cheesecake, and chicken scaloppini use alternative ingredients and headline an evening of health-conscious eating. *Average main: $30* ✉ *1431 N. Federal Hwy., Intracoastal and Inland* ☎ *954/539–9000* 🌐 *www.sublimerestaurant.com* *Closed Mon.*

$ MEXICAN Fodor's Choice ★ **Zona Fresca.** A local favorite on the cheap, Zona Fresca serves healthful, Mexican fast food with the best chips, salsas, burritos, and quesadillas in town. Everything is made fresh on the premises, including the authentic salsas, presented in a grand salsa bar. Zona is busy seven days a week for both lunch and dinner and offers both indoor and outdoor seating. It's likely to be your best (and cheapest) lunch in Fort Lauderdale. $ *Average main: $8* ✉ *1635 N. Federal Hwy., Intracoastal and Inland* ☎ *954/566–1777* 🌐 *www.zonafresca.com.*

WESTERN SUBURBS

$$$$ IRISH ✕ **Ireland Steakhouse.** Don't let the name fool you. Ireland Steakhouse is not particularly Irish nor is it just a steak house. In fact, this restaurant is most popular for its sustainable seafood menu. Promoting a holistic philosophy of green eating, the restaurant meticulously chooses its ingredients and the purveyors that supply them, while staying true to the international "Seafood Watch" guide. The restaurant is a warm and woodsy enclave in the back corner of the Hyatt Bonaventure. In keeping with trends of other steak houses, hearty mains (like the orange glaze wild Canadian Arctic char and the cherry balsamic yellowfin tuna) are paired with loads of decadent sides made for sharing (like lobster mac n' cheese and lobster fries). $ *Average main: $42* ✉ *Hyatt Bonaventure, 250 Racquet Club Rd., Western Suburbs and Beyond, Weston* ☎ *954/349–5656* 🌐 *www.bonaventure.hyatt.com* ⏲ *Dinner Tues.–Sat. 5:30–10:30; closed Sun. and Mon.*

5

WILTON MANORS AND OAKLAND PARK

$$ PIZZA ✕ **D'Angelo.** Having recently expanded his Casa D'Angelo restaurant empire south and north of Fort Lauderdale, locally famous restaurateur and chef Angelo Elia has now returned to his second home (Tuscany is his first) to open a casual pizza, tapas, and wine bar in the suburbs of Fort Lauderdale. D'Angelo serves affordable small plates, salads, ceviches, and pizzas and has quickly become a neighborhood favorite. Both kids and adults love the rotating selections of homemade gelati, a very necessary end to an evening at D'Angelo. $ *Average main: $14* ✉ *4215 N. Federal Hwy., Wilton Manors and Oakland Park* ☎ *954/561–7300* 🌐 *www.pizzadangelo.com.*

$$$$ AMERICAN ✕ **Hi-Life Cafe.** In a strip mall, this friendly eatery is where Cuban chef Carlos Fernandez—he's done a couple of turns on Bravo's *Top Chef*—attracts attention with inventive recipes like merlot roast duckling and chocolate Coca-Cola cake. Oft-changing menu items range from naked seafood dumplings to bronzed tuna. The neighborhood-bistro atmosphere adds a touch of romance with a bloom, typically a rose, on each table. The cafe now offers most dishes as half plates, letting you sample even more of Carlos' great cooking. $ *Average main: $38* ✉ *3000 N. Federal Hwy., Wilton Manors and Oakland Park* ☎ *954/563–1395* 🌐 *www.hilifecafe.com* ⏲ *Closed Mon.*

$ CAFÉ ✕ **Stork's Café.** Wilton Manors' legendary Stork's Café stands out as a gay-friendly, straight-friendly, and just plain friendly coffeehouse and café, ideal for chilling out or catching up on a good read. Sit indoors or outside at tables under red umbrellas and indulge in a coffee and a sweet. The white-chocolate-pistachio cheesecake is a must-try. Baked goods range from croissants, tortes, cakes, and pies to "monster cookies," including gingersnap and snickerdoodle. For lunch, try the Pilgrim (think Thanksgiving in a wrap) or the Hello Kitty (tuna salad on sourdough), or a made-from-scratch soup like vegan split pea. $ *Average* *main: $10 ✉ 2505 N.E. 15th Ave., Wilton Manors and Oakland Park, Wilton Manors ☎ 954/567–3220 ⊕ storksbakery.com.*

$$$ SEAFOOD ✕ **Sunfish Grill.** The former Pompano Beach institution migrated south in 2009 and hasn't looked back since. Quickly establishing itself in the Oakland Park area (albeit in a quiet strip mall), Sunfish Grill doles out beautifully presented contemporary American cuisine, namely well-executed, outside-the-box seafood and fish dishes. The spaghetti Bolognaise is made with ground tuna instead of beef; the Sunfish Caesar with Maytag Blue Cheese instead of Parmesan; the "not the usual" key lime pie with coconut sorbet instead of whipped cream. The results of this ingenuity are fantastic. [$] *Average main: $27 ✉ 2775 E. Oakland Park Blvd., Wilton Manors and Oakland Park ☎ 954/561–2004 ⊕ www.sunfishgrill.com.*

WHERE TO STAY

For expanded reviews, facilities, and current deals, visit Fodors.com.

DOWNTOWN AND LAS OLAS

$$$$ B&B/INN ★ **Pineapple Point.** Tucked a few blocks behind Las Olas Boulevard in the residential neighborhood of Victoria Park, Pineapple Point is a magnificent maze of posh tropical cottages and dense foliage catering to the gay community and is nationally renowned for its stellar service. **Pros:** superior service; tropical setting. **Cons:** difficult to find at first; need a vehicle for beach jaunts. **TripAdvisor:** "top-notch service and accommodations," "a never failingly happy experience," "the people made the difference." [$] *Rooms from: $289 ✉ 315 N.E. 16th Terrace, Downtown and Las Olas ☎ 954/527–0094 ⊕ www.pineapplepoint.com ⇨ 25 rooms 🍽 Breakfast.*

$$$ HOTEL **Riverside Hotel.** On Las Olas Boulevard, just steps from boutiques, restaurants, and art galleries, Fort Lauderdale's oldest hotel (circa 1936) evokes a bygone time with historical photos gracing hallways, and guest rooms outfitted with antique oak furnishings, ornamental palm trees, and a bold tropical color palate with a Tommy Bahamas throwback flair. **Pros:** historic appeal; in the thick of Las Olas action; nice views. **Cons:** questionable room decor; poor cell phone reception; dated lobby; small bathrooms. **TripAdvisor:** "elegant with great people," "charming," "great location." [$] *Rooms from: $159 ✉ 620 E. Las Olas Blvd., Downtown and Las Olas ☎ 954/467–0671, 800/325–3280 ⊕ www.riversidehotel.com ⇨ 208 rooms, 6 suites 🍽 No meals.*

ALONG THE BEACH

$$$ HOTEL **The Atlantic Resort & Spa.** The hotel that catalyzed Fort Lauderdale's luxe revolution looks better than ever after a major makeover in 2011, positioning the skyscraping, oceanfront beauty to stay at the top of her contemporary game for years to come. **Pros:** sophisticated lodging option; rooms have high-tech touches. **Cons:** no complimentary water bottles in room; expensive parking. **TripAdvisor:** "great service," "great location," "beautiful." [$] *Rooms from: $219 ✉ 601 N. Fort Lauderdale Beach Blvd., Along the beach ☎ 954/567–8020, 877/567–8020 ⊕ www.atlantichotelfl.com ⇨ 61 rooms, 58 suites, 4 penthouses 🍽 No meals.*

> **WORD OF MOUTH**
>
> "Loved Lago Mar. The rooms are spacious and clean, nice pools and nice beach. Restaurant is very good. You would need a car to get to other places in Fort Lauderdale but I think it is worth it."
>
> —lindafromNJ

$$ HOTEL **Bahia Mar Fort Lauderdale Beach Hotel.** This nicely situated Fort Lauderdale beachfront classic received a long-overdue nip/tuck in 2011 before rebranding as a DoubleTree hotel. **Pros:** crosswalk from hotel to beach; on-site yacht center. **Cons:** dated exteriors; small bathrooms; popcorn ceilings. **TripAdvisor:** "an enchanting view," "gorgeous rooms," "perfect location at the beach." *Rooms from: $111 801 Seabreeze Blvd., Along the beach 954/764–2233 www.bahiamarhotel.com 296.*

$$$ HOTEL **B Ocean Fort Lauderdale.** The first hotel launched by the new "B" hotel brand merges trendiness with affordability in a 13-story U-shaped tower overlooking the ocean. **Pros:** all rooms have ocean views; trendy but affordable; nightime fire pits. **Cons:** small pool area; lackluster exterior. **TripAdvisor:** "nice rooms," "quiet with great views," "great location with attentive staff." *Rooms from: $165 999 N. Fort Lauderdale Beach Blvd, Along the beach 954/564-1000 www.boceanfortlauderdale.com 240.*

$$$$ RESORT **Hilton Fort Lauderdale Beach Resort.** This 26-story oceanfront sparkler features 374 tastefully appointed guest rooms and a fabulous 6th-floor pool deck, colorfully and whimsically decorated. **Pros:** excellent gym; most rooms have balconies. **Cons:** charge for Wi-Fi; no outdoor bar. **TripAdvisor:** "luxurious accommodations," "amazing stay," "great ocean view." *Rooms from: $254 505 N. Fort Lauderdale Beach Blvd., Along the beach 954/760–7177 www.fortlauderdalebeachresort.hilton.com 374 rooms No meals.*

$$$ RESORT ★ **Lago Mar Resort and Club.** The sprawling, kid-friendly Lago Mar, owned by the Banks family since the early 1950s, retains its sparkle and a refreshed Old Florida feel thanks to frequent renovations. **Pros:** secluded setting; plenty of activities; on the beach. **Cons:** not easy to find; far from restaurants and beach action. **TripAdvisor:** "very relaxing," "nice beach and pool," "peaceful and charming." *Rooms from: $210 1700 S. Ocean La., Along the beach 954/523–6511, 800/524–6627 www.lagomar.com 52 rooms, 160 suites No meals.*

$$$ RESORT Fodor's Choice ★ **Marriott Harbor Beach Resort.** Bill Marriott's personal Marriott of choice for his annual four-week family vacation, the Marriott Harbor Beach Resort sits on a quarter-mile swath of private beach and bursts with the luxe beachfront personality of an upscale Caribbean resort. **Pros:** excellent gym; all rooms have balconies; great eating outlets; no resort fees. **Cons:** Wi-Fi isn't free; expensive parking; interiors are new but feel a little cookie-cutter. **TripAdvisor:** "a wonderful escape from the mundane," "nice location," "amazing property and staff." *Rooms from: $399 3030 Holiday Dr., Along the beach 954/525-4000 www.marriottharborbeach.com 681 rooms.*

$$$ RESORT **Pelican Grand Beach Resort.** Smack on Fort Lauderdale Beach, this yellow spired, Key West style property maintains its heritage of Old Florida seaside charm with rooms adorned in florals, pastels, and wicker; an old-fashioned emporium; and a small circulating lazy-river pool that allows kids to float 'round and 'round. **Pros:** free popcorn in the Postcard Lounge, directly on the beach, full-service on the beach. **Cons:** high tide can swallow most of beach area, decor appeals to older generations. **TripAdvisor:** "homey but elegant," "awesome views," "the ultimate luxury experience." *Rooms from: $224* ✉ *2000 N. Atlantic Blvd., Along the beach* ☎ *954/568–9431, 800/525–6232* 🌐 *www.pelicanbeach.com* *135 rooms (some condominiums)* *No meals.*

ULTIMATE WINE TASTING

The seductive Wine Room and sensual Wine Vault at the Ritz-Carlton, Fort Lauderdale impress with 5,000 global bottles, classic elegance, and the haute design minutia that have given the Ritz-Carlton its flawless reputation. The surprisingly affordable "Take Flight in the Wine Vault" experience entails the hotel sommelier creating a private wine tasting for guests inside the signature wine vault. Experience a journey across France, Australia, Argentina, or California through six glasses of red or white wine while enjoying informative and fascinating lessons between sips! Reservations required, $50.

$$$ B&B/INN **The Pillars Hotel.** Once a "small secret" kept by locals in the know, this elegant boutique gem, sandwiched between Fort Lauderdale Beach and the Intracoastal Waterway, rarely falls below capacity since its esteemed placement on the list of Top Small Hotels in the US by Conde Nast 2011 and a reader's choice award in the magazine's Gold List 2012. **Pros:** attentive staff; lovely decor; idyllic pool area. **Cons:** small rooms; not for families with young kids, given proximity to dock and water with no lifeguard on duty. **TripAdvisor:** "fabulous hidden gem," "faultless hospitality," "a staff second to none." *Rooms from: $219* ✉ *111 N. Birch Rd., Along the beach* ☎ *954/467–9639* 🌐 *www.pillarshotel.com* *13 rooms, 5 suites* *No meals.*

$$$$ HOTEL Fodor's Choice ★ **The Ritz-Carlton, Fort Lauderdale.** Inspired by the design of an opulent luxury liner, 24 dramatically tiered, glass-walled stories rise from the sea, forming a sumptous Ritz-Carlton hotel with guest rooms that reinvent a golden era of luxury travel, a lavish tropical sundeck and infinity-edge pool peering over the ocean, and a Club Lounge that spans an entire floor. **Pros:** prime beach location; modern seaside elegance deviates dramatically from traditional Ritz-Carlton decor; sensational Club Lounge. **Cons:** no complimentary Wi-Fi; almost too elegant for Fort Lauderdale beach. **TripAdvisor:** "lovely," "nice and fun," "wish we could have stayed longer." *Rooms from: $269* ✉ *1 N. Fort Lauderdale Beach Blvd., Along the beach* ☎ *954/465–2300* 🌐 *www.ritzcarlton.com* *138 rooms, 54 suites* *No meals.*

$$$ HOTEL **Sheraton Fort Lauderdale Beach Hotel.** As part of its global rebranding, Sheraton has reinvented (and renamed) its Fort Lauderdale landmark, the Sheraton Yankee Clipper Hotel, with updated interiors and public

spaces throughout its four towers of rooms and suites. **Pros:** Friday night retro mermaid show in swimming pool; proximity to beach; excellent gym. **Cons:** small rooms; low ceilings in lobby; faded exteriors. **TripAdvisor:** "great beach spot," "relaxing getaway," "great service." *Rooms from: $167 ✉ 1140 Seabreeze Blvd., Along the beach ☎ 954/524–5551 www.sheratonftlauderdalebeach.com 486.*

$$$ RESORT ★ **The Westin Beach Resort & Spa, Fort Lauderdale.** Smack dab in the center of Fort Lauderdale Beach and connected directly to the beach through a private overpass, the space formerly known as the Sheraton Yankee Trader has been completely transformed into a modern Westin. **Pros:** direct beach access; heavenly beds and spa. **Cons:** lenghty corridors to get to some rooms; fee for Wi-Fi. **TripAdvisor:** "nice view," "fun location combined with excellent service," "really nice beach hotel." *Rooms from: $239 ✉ 321 N Fort Lauderdale Beach Blvd., Along the beach ☎ 954/467-1111 www.westin.com/fortlauderdalebeach 433.*

$$$$ HOTEL Fodor's Choice ★ **W Fort Lauderdale.** Fort Lauderdale's trendiest hotel—equipped with a rooftop see-through swimming pool, a wide range of spectacular contemporary rooms and suites, and an easy-on-the-eyes youthful crowd—boasts a vibe highly reminiscent of South Beach. **Pros:** trendy and flashy; tony scene; amazing pool; great spa. **Cons:** party atmosphere not for everyone; impersonal service. **TripAdvisor:** "beautiful," "perfect hotel for the area," "cool place." *Rooms from: $305 ✉ 435 N. Fort Lauderdale Beach Blvd., Along the beach ☎ 954/462–1633 www.starwood.com 346 hotel rooms, 171 hotel condominiums No meals.*

$$ B&B/INN **The Worthington and the Alcazar.** Side by side and sharing common amenities—including two pools, a large hot tub, a great fitness room, and a shaded courtyard—the Worthington and the Alcazar are two of Fort Lauderdale Beach's 27 clothing-optional guesthouses for gay men. **Pros:** fresh-squeezed orange juice in the morning; nice pool area. **Cons:** not on the beach; no view. **TripAdvisor:** "exceptional staff," "clean and quiet," "laid back fun." *Rooms from: $115 ✉ 543–555 N. Birch Rd., Along the beach ☎ 954/563–6819, 954/567–2525 www.theworthington.com 17 rooms; 20 rooms and suites Breakfast.*

INTRACOASTAL AND INLAND

$$$ HOTEL **Gallery ONE by DoubleTree.** A condo hotel favored by vacationers preferring longer stays, the residential-style Gallery ONE rises over the Intracoastal, within short walking distance of both Fort Lauderdale Beach and the city's popular Galleria Mall. **Pros:** walking distance to both beach and supermarket; easy water taxi access; good for longer stays. **Cons:** pool area needs refurbishment; kitchens don't have stoves; no bathtubs. **TripAdvisor:** "excellent service," "beautiful rooms," "very helpful staff." *Rooms from: $157 ✉ 2670 E. Sunrise Blvd., Intracoastal and Inland ☎ 954/565–3800 www.doubletree.com 231 rooms No meals.*

$$$ RESORT Fodor's Choice ★ **Hilton Fort Lauderdale Marina.** With a 72 million dollar renovation, the mammoth, 589-room, 20-boat-slip Hilton Fort Lauderdale Marina infused luxury and modernity into its charming Key West style. **Pros:** sexy fire pit; outdoor bar popular with locals; easy water taxi access;

Cons: no bathtubs in tower rooms; small fitness center. **TripAdvisor:** "pools are beautiful," "great location," "good service." *Rooms from: $152 1881 SE 17th St., Intracoastal and Inland 954/463-4000 www.fortlauderdalemarinahotel.com 589.*

$$$ RESORT ★ **Hyatt Regency Pier Sixty-Six Resort & Spa.** Don't let the '70s exterior of the iconic 17-story tower fool you; this lovely 22-acre resort teems with contemporary interior-design sophistication (after a successful $40 million renovation of guest rooms and public spaces), and remains one of Florida's few hotels where a rental car isn't necessary. **Pros:** great views; plenty of activities; free shuttle to beach; easy water taxi access. **Cons:** tower rooms are far less stylish than Lanai rooms; totally retro rotating rooftop restaurant is open to non-guests only for Sunday brunch. **TripAdvisor:** "most relaxing," "nice rooms," "beautiful grounds." *Rooms from: $159 2301 S.E. 17th St. Causeway, Intracoastal and Inland 954/525–6666 www.pier66.com 384 rooms and suites No meals.*

$$ HOTEL **Il Lugano Luxury Suite Hotel.** This all-suite condo hotel on Fort Lauderdale's northern Intracoastal Waterway offers all the comforts of home (washer, dryer, kitchenette, fridge, sleeper sofa, huge terraces) with all the glamour of a hyper-modern trendsetting hotel. **Pros:** 800-square-foot rooms; easy water taxi access; good for longer stays. **Cons:** limited sunlight in pool area; need wheels to reach main beach and downtown area. **TripAdvisor:** "you'll feel like a celebrity," "great spacious room," "fantastic hotel and service." *Rooms from: $129 3333 NE 32nd Ave., Intracoastal and Inland 954/564-4400 www.illugano.com 28.*

WESTERN SUBURBS

$$$ HOTEL **Hyatt Regency Bonaventure Conference Center & Spa.** This suburban enclave targets conventioneers and business executives as well as vacationers who value golf, Everglades, and shopping over beach proximity. **Pros:** lush landscaping; pampering spa. **Cons:** difficult to find; in the suburbs; poor views from some rooms. **TripAdvisor:** "another great stay," "nice pool," "pretty surroundings." *Rooms from: $185 250 Racquet Club Rd., Western Suburbs and Beyond, Westin 954/616–1234 www.bonaventure.hyatt.com 501 rooms No meals.*

NIGHTLIFE AND THE ARTS

For the most complete weekly listing of events, check "Showtime!," the *South Florida Sun-Sentinel*'s tabloid-size entertainment section and events calendar published on Friday. "Weekend," in the Friday Broward edition of the *Herald,* also lists area happenings. The weekly *City Link* and *New Times Broward* are free alternative newspapers, detailing plenty of entertainment and nightlife options. For the latest happenings in GLBT nightlife, visit *wjumponmarkslist.com*, the online authority of all things GLBT in South Florida or pick up one of the weekly gay rags, *MARK* or *Hot Spots.*

THE ARTS

★ **Broward Center for the Performing Arts.** More than 500 events unfold annually at this 2,700-seat architectural gem, including Broadway-style musicals, plays, dance, symphony, opera, rock, film, lectures, comedy,

Lago Mar Resort & Club in Fort Lauderdale has its own private beach on the Atlantic Ocean.

and children's theater. An enclosed elevated walkway links the centerpiece of Fort Lauderdale's arts district to a parking garage across the street. ✉ *201 S.W. 5th Ave., Downtown and Las Olas* ☎ *954/462–0222* 🌐 *www.browardcenter.org.*

Chef Jean-Pierre Cooking School. Catering to locals, seasonal snowbirds, and folks winging in for even shorter stays, Jean-Pierre Brehier (former owner of the Left Bank Restaurant on Las Olas) teaches the basics, from boiling water onward. The enthusiastic Gallic transplant has appeared on NBC's *Today* and CNN's *Larry King Live*. For souvenir hunters, this fun cooking facility also sells nifty pots, pastas, oils, and other great items. ✉ *1436 N. Federal Hwy., Intrcoastal and Inland* ☎ *954/563–2700* 🌐 *www.chefjp.com* 🎫 *$65 per demonstration class, $125 hands-on class* ⏲ *Store Mon.–Sat. 10–7, class schedules vary.*

Cinema Paradiso. This art-house movie theater operates out of a former church, south of the New River near the county courthouse. The space doubles as headquarters for FLIFF, the Fort Lauderdale International Film Festival, while still playing films year-round. FLIFF's website is the easiest way to see what's playing on any given evening at the cinema. Just click on the "Cinema Events" tab on the homepage. ✉ *503 S.E. 6th St., Downtown and Las Olas* ☎ *954/525–3456* 🌐 *www.fliff.com.*

NIGHTLIFE

DOWNTOWN AND LAS OLAS

The majority of Fort Lauderdale nightlife takes place near downtown, beginning on Himmarshee Street (2nd Street) and continuing on to the Riverfront, and then to Las Olas Boulevard. The downtown Riverfront tends to draw a younger demographic somewhere between underage teens and late twenties. On Himmarshee Street, a dozen rowdy bars and clubs entice a wide range of partygoers, ranging from the seedy to the sophisticated. Approaching East Las Olas Boulevard, near the financial towers and boutique shops, bars cater to the yuppie crowd.

Maguire's Hill 16. With the requisite lineup of libations and pub-style food, this classic Irish pub is good for no-frills fun, fried eats, and daily live music. It's famous locally as the oldest award-winning Traditional Irish Pub and Restaurant in Fort Lauderdale. ✉ *535 N. Andrews Ave., Downtown and Las Olas* ☎ *954/764–4453* 🌐 *www.maguireshill16.com.*

O Lounge. This lounge and two adjacent establishments, **Yolo** and **Vibe,** on Las Olas and under the same ownership, cater to Fort Lauderdale's sexy yuppies, businessmen, desperate housewives, and hungry cougars letting loose during happy hour and on the weekends. Crowds alternate between Yolo's outdoor fire pit, O Lounge's chilled atmosphere and lounge music, and Vibe's more intense beats. Expect flashy cars in the driveway and a bit of plastic surgery. ✉ *333 E. Las Olas Blvd., Downtown and Las Olas* ☎ *954/523–1000* 🌐 *www.yolorestaurant.com.*

$$$ AMERICAN

✕ **ROK: BRG.** Downtown Fort Lauderdale warmly welcomed this personality-driven burger bar and gastro-pub in early 2011, giving the grown-ups something to enjoy in teenage-infested downtown. The long and narrow venue, adorned with exposed-brick walls and flat-screen TVs, serves up all types of burgers, from Angus beef monsters to the more en vogue sushi-grade ahi tuna burger. The hand-cut original fries and sweet-potato fries are served in their own mini fryers, accompanied by a series of sauces made from scratch every day (try the bourbon BBQ sauce). [$] *Average main: $22* ✉ *208 S.W. 2nd St., Downtown and Las Olas* ☎ *954/525–7656* 🌐 *www.rokbrgr.com.*

Fodor's Choice ★

Tap 42 Bar and Kitchen. With 42 rotating draft beers from around the USA, 50-plus bourbons, a dozen original cocktails, and 66 bottled craft beers, awesome drinks and good times headline a typical evening at classy cool Tap 42. Although the indoor/outdoor gastro-pub is a bit off the beaten path, it's well worth the detour. The 42 drafts protrude from a stylish wall constructed of pennies, surfacing more like a work of art than a beer-filling station. The venue attracts large crowds of young professionals for nights of heavy drinking and highly caloric new-age bar eats like the Florida rock shrimp mac and cheese and the "Wild" Shroom, a 9-ounce burger with wild mushrooms, swiss cheese, and Vidalia onions served on a brioche bun with a side of sweet-potato fries. ✉ *1411 S. Andrews Ave., Downtown and Las Olas* ☎ *954/463–4900.*

Tarpon Bend. This casual restaurant transforms into a jovial resto-bar in the early evening, ideal for enjoying a few beers, mojitos, and some great bar food. It's consistently busy, day, night, and late night with both young professionals and families. ✉ *200 S.W. 2nd St., Downtown and Las Olas* ☎ *954/523–3233* 🌐 *www.tarponbend.com.*

ALONG THE BEACH

Given its roots as a beachside party town, it's hard to believe that Fort Lauderdale Beach offers very few options in terms of nightlife. A few dive bars are at opposite ends of the main strip, near Sunrise Boulevard and A1A as well as Las Olas Boulevard and A1A. On the main thoroughfare between Las Olas and Sunrise, a few high-end bars at the beach's show-stopping hotels have become popular, namely those at the W Fort Lauderdale.

Elbo Room. You can't go wrong wallowing in the past, lifting a drink, and exercising your elbow at the Elbo, a noisy, suds-drenched hot spot since 1938. It seems like nothing has changed here since Fort Lauderdale's spring break heydey, though the bathrooms were redone in 2011. This watering hole phased out food (except for light nibbles) ages ago, but kept a hokey sense of humor: upstairs a sign proclaims "We don't serve women here. You have to bring your own." ✉ *241 S. Fort Lauderdale Blvd., Along the beach* ☎ *954/463–4615* 🌐 *www.elboroom.com.*

Living Room at the W. The large living-room-like space next to the lobby of the W Fort Lauderdale transforms into a major house-party-style event, mainly on weekends. There are plenty of plush couches, but it's usually standing-room-only early for this South Beach–style throwdown, with great DJs, awesome libations, and an easy-on-the-eyes crowd. A breezy and beautiful outdoor area is idyllic for the overflow, as is the downstairs lounge, Whiskey Blue. ✉ *W Fort Lauderdale, 401 N. Fort Lauderdale Beach Blvd., Along the beach* ☎ *954/414–8200* 🌐 *www.wfortlauderdalehotel.com/living-room.*

5

Parrot Lounge. An old-school Fort Lauderdale hangout, this dive bar/ sports bar is particularly popular with Philadelphia Eagles fans, those longing to recall *Where the Boys Are,* and folks reminiscing about Fort Lauderdale's big-hair, sprayed-tan, Sun-In-bright '80s heyday. This place is stuck in the past, but it's got great libations, wings, fingers, poppers, and skins. 'Nuff said. ✉ *911 Sunrise La., Along the beach* ☎ *954/563–1493* 🌐 *www.parrotlounge.com.*

INTRACOASTAL AND INLAND

Bars and pubs along Fort Lauderdale's Intracoastal cater to the city's large, transient boating community. Heading inland along Sunrise Boulevard, the bars around Galleria Mall target thirty- and forty-something singles.

Blue Martini Fort Lauderdale. A hot spot for thirty-something-plus adults gone wild, Blue Martini's menu is filled with tons of innovative martini creations and lots of cougars on the prowl, searching for a first, second, or even third husband. And the guys aren't complaining! The drinks are great and the scene is fun for everyone, even those who aren't single and looking to mingle. ✉ *Galleria Fort Lauderdale, 2432 E. Sunrise Blvd., Intracoastal and Inland* ☎ *954/653–2583* 🌐 *www.bluemartinilounge.com.*

Kim's Alley Bar. Around since 1948, Kim's Alley Bar is the ultimate no-frills South Florida dive bar, a neighborhood spot near the Intracoastal. It has two bar areas, a jukebox, and pool tables that provide endless entertainment (if the patrons aren't providing enough diversion). ✉ *1920 E. Sunrise Blvd., in the Gateway strip mall, Intracoastal and Inland* ☎ *954/763–2143.*

WILTON MANORS AND OAKLAND PARK

Fort Lauderdale's gay nightlife is most prevalent in Wilton Manors, affectionately termed Fort Lauderdale's gayborhood. Wilton Drive has dozens of bars, clubs, and lounges that cater to all types of GLBT subcultures.

Georgie's Alibi. A Fort Lauderdale GBLT institution, Georgie's Alibi is anchor for the Wilton Manors gayborhood. The gargantuan pub fills to capacity for $3, 32-ounce Long Island Iced Tea Thursdays. Any night of the week, Alibi stands out as a kind of gay Cheers of Fort Lauderdale—a neighborhood bar with darts, pool, libations, and some eye candy, offering a no-frills, laid-back attitude. ✉ *2266 Wilton Dr., Wilton Manors and Oakland Park* ☎ *954/565–2526* 🌐 *www.georgiesalibi.com.*

★ **The Manor.** Inspired by the Abbey West Hollywood, The Manor offers a one-stop gay party shop in the heart of the Wilton Manors gayborhood. The multifaceted two-story enclave mixes the likes of a massive dance club, a martini bar, a restaurant, a lounge, a small sports bar, and a beer garden with 24 beers on tap. The Manor attracts both gay men and women of all ages to indulge in the neighborhood funhouse. It's most popular on weekends. ✉ *2345 Wilton Dr., Wilton Manors and Oakland Park* ☎ *954/626–0082* 🌐 *www.themanorcomplex.com.*

★ **Matty's on the Drive.** A great meeting point for South Florida GLBT professionals, Matty's on the Drive is one of the few gayborhood bars that attracts a demographic more interested in conversation and good libations than cheap drinks and cheap times. Matty's has something fun going on every night of the week, from Wild Wednesdays to Sunday Funday. Parking can be difficult in the front lot, so look for public parking. ✉ *2426 Wilton Dr., Wilton Manors and Oakland Park* ☎ *954/564–1799* 🌐 *www.mattysonthedrive.com.*

Rosie's Bar and Grill. Rosie's is consistently lively, pumping out tons of pop tunes and volumes of joyous laughter to surrounding streets. The former Hamburger Mary's has become an institution in South Florida as the go-to gay-friendly place for cheap drinks, decent bar food, and great times. Most of the fun at Rosie's is meeting new friends and engaging in conversation with the person seated next to you. Drink specials change daily. Sunday brunch with alternating DJs is wildly popular. ✉ *2449 Wilton Dr., Wilton Manors and Oakland Park* ☎ *954/567–1320* 🌐 *www.rosiesbarandgrill.com.*

WESTERN SUBURBS AND BEYOND

South Florida's Native American tribes have long offered bingo, poker, and machines resembling slots on Indian Territory near Broward's western suburbs and in its southernmost reaches. But the laws have changed, and nowadays Broward's casinos offer Vegas-style slot machines and even blackjack. Hollywood's Seminole Hard Rock Hotel & Casino offers the most elegant of Broward's casino experiences. ⇨ *See Nightlife in Hollywood for a full listing of casinos.*

SHOPPING

MALLS

Galleria Fort Lauderdale. Fort Lauderdale's most upscale mall is just west of the Intracoastal Waterway. The split-level emporium entices with Neiman Marcus, Dillard's, Macy's, an Apple Store, plus 150 specialty shops for anything from cookware to exquisite jewelry. Upgrades in 2010 included marble floors and fine dining options. Chow down at Capital Grille, Truluck's, Blue Martini, P.F. Chang's, or Seasons 52, or head for the food court, which will defy expectations with its international food-market feel. Galleria is open 10–9 Monday through Saturday, noon–5:30 Sunday. ✉ *2414 E. Sunrise Blvd., Intracoastal and Inland* ☎ *954/564–1015* 🌐 *www.galleriamall-fl.com.*

★ **Sawgrass Mills.** This alligator-shape megamall has a collection of more than 350 outlet stores and name-brand discounters. The mall claims to be the second largest attraction in Florida, second only to Disney World. Though it's probably an exaggeration, prepare for insane crowds even during non-peak hours and seasons. ✉ *12801 W. Sunrise Blvd., at Flamingo Rd., Western Suburbs and Beyond, Sunrise.*

Swap Shop. For those who grew up in Fort Lauderdale, the Swap Shop's cheesy commercials of yesteryear will forever remain. "Where's the bargains?" "At the Swap Shop!" The South's largest flea market, with 2,000 vendors, is open daily. Thankfully, they've done away with the awful circus after years of protests by animal-rights activists. While exploring this indoor–outdoor entertainment-and-shopping complex, hop on the carousel, try some fresh sugarcane juice, or stick around for movies at the 14-screen Swap Shop drive-in. ✉ *3291 W. Sunrise Blvd., Western Suburbs and Beyond* 🌐 *www.floridaswapshop.com.*

SHOPPING DISTRICTS

Las Olas Riverfront. Largely unoccupied, Las Olas Riverfront is a shopping and entertainment complex in downtown, along the city's serene riverfront. A movie theater remains, as do a few budget eateries and nightclubs. The complex's popularity quickly waned in the late 1990s and news of its demolition has been circulating for a decade. ✉ *300 SW 1 Ave., Downtown and Las Olas.*

Las Olas Boulevard. Las Olas Boulevard is the heart and soul of Fort Lauderdale. Not only are the city's best boutiques, top restaurants, and art galleries found along this beautifully landscaped street, but Las Olas links Fort Lauderdale's growing downtown with its superlative beaches. Though you'll find a Cheesecake Factory on the boulevard, the thoroughfare tends to shun chains and welcomes one-of-a-kind clothing boutiques, chocolatiers, and ethnic eateries. Window shopping allowed. ✉ *East Las Olas Boulevard, Downtown and Las Olas* 🌐 *www.lasolasboulevard.com.*

The Gallery at Beach Place. Just north of Las Olas Boulevard on Route A1A, this shopping gallery is attached to the mammoth Marriot Beach Place time share building. Spaces are occupied by touristy shops that sell everything from sarongs to alligator heads, chain restaurants like Hooter's, bars serving frozen drinks, and a super sized CVS pharmacy, which sells everything you need for the beach. ■ **TIP→ Beach Place has covered parking, and usually has plenty of spaces, but you can pinch pennies by using a nearby municipal lot that's metered.** ✉ *17 S. Fort Lauderdale Beach Blvd., Along the beach* 🌐 *www.galleryatbeachplace.com.*

SPORTS AND THE OUTDOORS

BIKING

Among the most popular routes are Route A1A and Bayview Drive, especially in early morning before traffic builds, and a 7-mile bike path that parallels State Road 84 and New River and leads to Markham Park, which has mountain-bike trails. ■ **TIP→ Alligator alert: Do not dangle your legs from seawalls.**

Broward B–cycle. The big-city trend of "pay and ride" bicycles has now reached Broward County. With 40 station locations over 20 scenic miles, from as far south as Hallandale to as far north as Pompano Beach and Coconut Creek, bikes can be rented for as little as 30 minutes or as long as a week, and can be picked up and dropped off at any and all stations in Broward County. Most stations are found downtown and along the beach. This is an excellent green and health-conscious way to explore Fort Lauderdale. Please note, however, that helmets are not provided at the kiosks. ☎ *754/200–5672* 🌐 *www.broward.bcycle.com.*

FISHING

Bahia Mar Marina. If you're interested in a saltwater charter, check out the offerings at the marina of the Bahia Mar, a Double Tree hotel. Sportfishing and drift-fishing bookings can be arranged. A number of snorkeling outfitters also leave from here, as does the famous *Jungle Queen* steamboat. ✉ *Bahia Mar, 801 Seabreeze Blvd., Along the beach* ☎ *954/627–6357.*

SCUBA DIVING AND SNORKELING

Lauderdale Diver. A PADI 5-Star Certification Agency, this dive center facilitates daily day trips on a variety of dive boats up and down Broward's shoreline. Dive trips typically last four hours. Nonpackage reef trips are open to divers for around $50; scuba gear is extra. ✉ *1334 S.E. 17th St., Intracoastal and Inland* ☎ *954/467–2822* 🌐 *www.lauderdalediver.com.*

Pro Dive. The area's oldest diving operation offers daily trips for scuba divers to Broward's natural coral reefs or over two-dozen shipwrecks including the famous *Mercedes I.* Expect to pay $55 if using your own gear or $115 with full scuba gear for a 2-tank, half-day charter, lasting 4 hours and heading to two different diving destinations. Pro Dive also offers the full gamut of PADI dive training courses. ✉ *Bahia Mar, 801 Seabreeze Blvd., Along the beach* ☎ *954/776–3483* 🌐 *www.prodiveusa.com.*

Sea Experience Glassbottom Snorkel Tours. The *Sea Experience I* leaves daily at 10:15 am and 2:15 pm for two-hour glass-bottom-boat and snorkeling combination trips that explore Fort Lauderdale's offshore reefs. The tour costs $28; $7 more to snorkel, equipment provided. ✉ *Bahia Mar Beach Resort, 801 Seabreeze Blvd.* ☎ *954/770–3483* 🌐 *www.seaxp.com.*

SEGWAY TOURS

M.Cruz Rentals. M.Cruz Rentals offers Segway Tours of Fort Lauderdale Beach four times per day and bicycle rentals by the hour. The rental facility is at the beach entrance of Hugh Taylor Birch State Park, just north of hotel row. The Segway Tours leave from here as well. ✉ *Hugh Taylor Birch State Park, 3109 E. Sunrise Blvd., Along the beach* ☎ *954/235–5082* 🌐 *www.mcruzrentals.com.*

TENNIS

Jimmy Evert Tennis Center. With 22 courts (18 lighted clay courts, 3 hard courts, and a low-compression sand "beach" court), this is the crown jewel of Fort Lauderdale's public tennis facilities. Legendary champ Chris Evert learned her two-handed backhand here under the watchful eye of her now-retired father, Jimmy, the center's tennis pro for 37 years. ✉ *Holiday Park, 701 N.E. 12th Ave., Intracoastal and Inland* ☎ *954/828–5378* 🌐 *www.ci.ftlaud.fl.us/tennis/jetc.htm* 🎫 *$18 day pass (for Broward nonresidents)* ⏲ *Weekdays 7:45 am–9 pm, weekends 7:45 am–6 pm.*

5

NORTH ON SCENIC A1A

North of Fort Lauderdale's Birch Recreation Area, Route A1A edges away from the beach through a stretch known as Galt Ocean Mile, and a succession of ocean-side communities line up against the sea. Traffic can line up, too, as it passes through a changing pattern of beach-blocking high-rises and modest family vacation towns and back again. As far as tourism goes, these communities tend to cater to a different demographic than Fort Lauderdale. Europeans and cost-conscious families head to Lauderdale-by-the-Sea, Pompano, and Deerfield for fewer frills and longer stays.

Towns are shown on the Broward County map.

LAUDERDALE-BY-THE-SEA

Lauderdale-by-the-Sea is 5 miles north of Fort Lauderdale.

Just north of Fort Lauderdale's northern boundary, this low-rise family resort town traditionally digs in its heels at the mere mention of high-rises. The result is choice shoreline access that's rapidly disappearing in nearby communities. Without a doubt, Lauderdale-by-the-Sea takes delight in embracing its small beach-town feel and welcoming guests to a different world of years gone by.

GETTING HERE AND AROUND

Lauderdale-by-the-Sea is just north of Fort Lauderdale. If you're driving from Interstate 95, exit east onto Commercial Boulevard and head over the Intracoastal Waterway. From U.S. 1 (aka Federal Highway), turn east on Commercial Boulevard. If coming from A1A, just continue north from Fort Lauderdale Beach.

ESSENTIALS

Visitor Information **Lauderdale-by-the-Sea Chamber of Commerce** ✉ *4201 Ocean Dr.* ☎ *954/776–1000* 🌐 *www.lbts.com.*

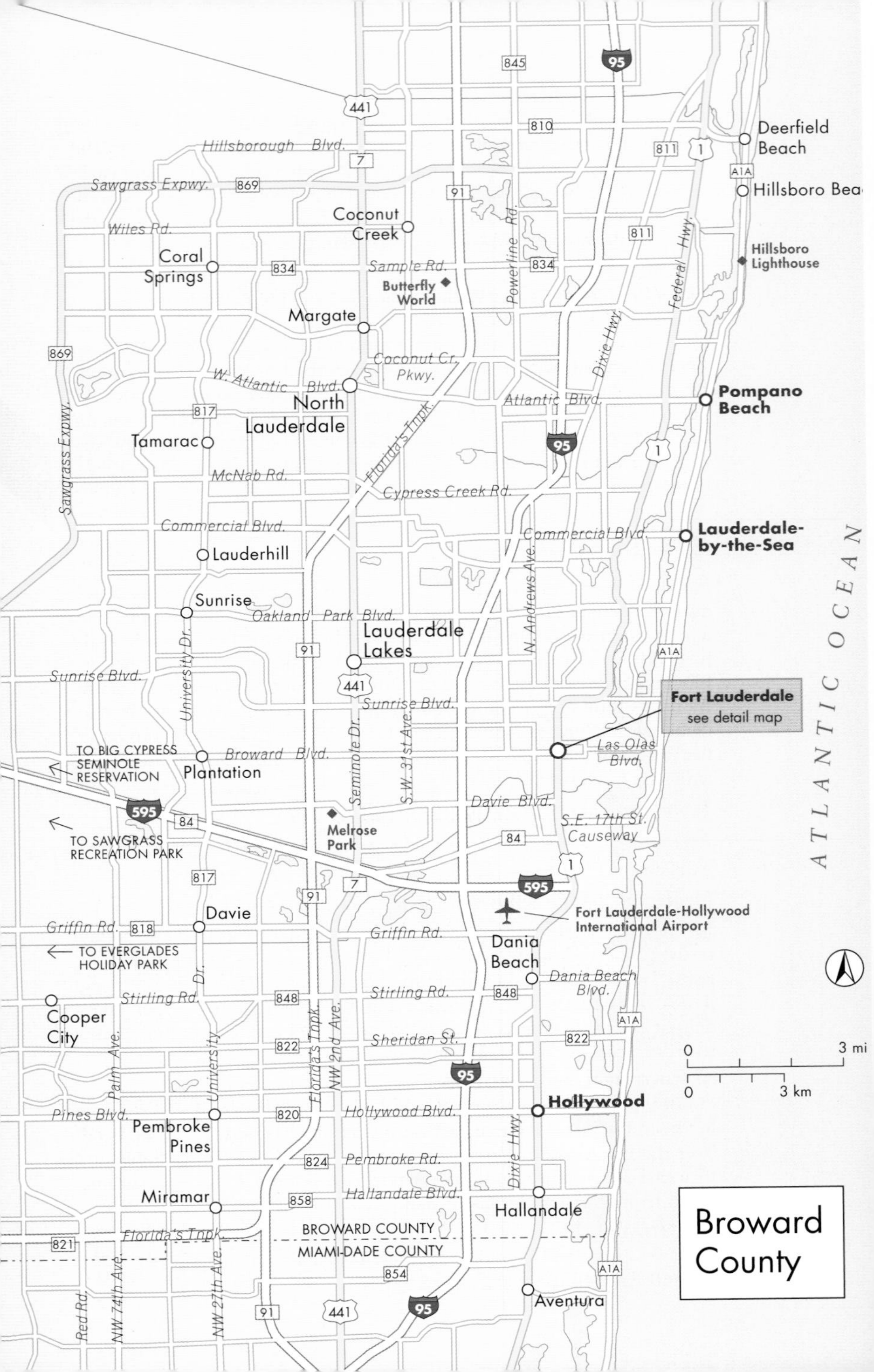
Broward County
845
95
441
810
Hillsborough Blvd.
7
811
1
Deerfield Beach
A1A
Sawgrass Expwy.
869
91
Hillsboro Beach
Coconut Creek
Wiles Rd.
Powerline Rd.
811
Federal Hwy.
Hillsboro Lighthouse
Coral Springs
834
Sample Rd.
834
Butterfly World
Margate
Dixie Hwy.
869
Coconut Cr. Pkwy.
W. Atlantic Blvd.
North Lauderdale
Atlantic Blvd.
Pompano Beach
817
Florida's Tnpk.
Sawgrass Expwy.
Tamarac
95
1
McNab Rd.
Cypress Creek Rd.
Commercial Blvd.
Commercial Blvd.
Lauderdale-by-the-Sea
Lauderhill
N. Andrews Ave.
ATLANTIC OCEAN
Sunrise
Oakland Park Blvd.
Lauderdale Lakes
91
A1A
Sunrise Blvd.
University Dr.
441
Sunrise Blvd.
Fort Lauderdale
see detail map
Seminole Dr.
S.W. 31st Ave.
TO BIG CYPRESS SEMINOLE RESERVATION
Broward Blvd.
Las Olas Blvd.
Plantation
595
84
Davie Blvd.
Melrose Park
S.E. 17th St. Causeway
TO SAWGRASS RECREATION PARK
84
817
1
91
7
595
Davie
Fort Lauderdale-Hollywood International Airport
Griffin Rd.
818
Griffin Rd.
Dania Beach
TO EVERGLADES HOLIDAY PARK
Dania Beach Blvd.
Cooper City
Stirling Rd.
848
Stirling Rd.
848
A1A
Palm Ave.
University Dr.
822
Florida's Tnpk.
NW 2nd Ave.
Sheridan St.
822
0
3 mi
0
3 km
95
Hollywood
Pines Blvd.
Pembroke Pines
820
Hollywood Blvd.
Dixie Hwy.
824
Pembroke Rd.
Miramar
858
Hallandale Blvd.
Hallandale
821
Florida's Tnpk.
BROWARD COUNTY
MIAMI-DADE COUNTY
854
A1A
Red Rd.
NW 74th Ave.
NW 27th Ave.
91
441
95
Aventura

BEACHES

Lauderdale-by-the-Sea Beach. Especially popular with divers and snorkelers, this laid-back stretch of sand provides great access to lovely coral reefs. When you're not underwater, look up and you'll likely see a pelican flying by. Gentle trade winds make this an utterly relaxing retreat from the hubbub of Fort Lauderdale's busier beaches. Families and vacationers enjoying Fort Lauderdale for longer periods of time favor this area. **Amenities:** food and drink; lifeguards; parking (fee). **Best for:** solitude; snorkeling; swimming. *Lauderdale-by-the-Sea.*

WHERE TO EAT

$$ CAFÉ **Aruba Beach Café.** This casual beachfront eatery is always crowded and always fun. One of Lauderdale-by-the-Sea's most famous restaurants, Aruba Beach serves a wide range of American and Caribbean cuisine, including Caribbean conch chowder and conch fritters. There are also fresh tropical salads, sandwiches, and seafood. The café is famous for its divine fresh-baked Bimini Bread with Aruba Glaze (think challah with donut glaze). A band performs day and night, so head for the back corner with excellent views of the beach if you want conversation while you eat and drink. Sunday breakfast buffet starts at 9 am. *Average main: $14 1 Commercial Blvd. 954/776–0001 www.arubabeachcafe.com.*

$$$ SEAFOOD ★ **Blue Moon Fish Company.** Most tables have stellar views of the Intracoastal Waterway, but Blue Moon's true magic comes from the kitchen, where the chefs create moon-and-stars-worthy seafood dishes. It's also the best deal in town with a two-for-one word-of-mouth lunch special Monday through Saturday. Start with whole roasted garlic and bread and continue on to the mussels, the langostino salad (with pecan-crusted goat cheese, spinach, and carmelized onions) or pan-seared fresh-shucked oysters. For Sunday's champagne brunch book early, even in the off-season. *Average main: $34 4405 W. Tradewinds Ave. 954/267–9888 www.bluemoonfishco.com.*

$ AMERICAN **LaSpada's Original Hoagies.** The crew at this seaside hole-in-the-wall puts on quite a show of ingredient-tossing flair while assembling take-out hoagies, subs, and deli sandwiches. Locals rave that they are the best around. LaSpada's popularity has resulted in the addition of four other South Florida locations, taking away from the joint's former one-of-a-kind appeal. Fill up on the foot-long Monster (ham, cheese, roast beef, and turkey piled high), Hot Meatballs Marinara, or an assortment of salads. *Average main: $8 4346 Seagrape Dr. 954/776–7893 www.laspadashoagies.com.*

WHERE TO STAY

For expanded reviews, facilities, and current deals, visit Fodors.com.

$$ B&B/INN **Blue Seas Courtyard.** Husband and wife team Cristie and Marc Furth run this quaint Mexican-themed motel across the street from Lauderdale-by-the-Sea's family-friendly beaches. **Pros:** south-of-the-border vibe; friendly owners; vintage stoves from 1971; memory foam mattress toppers. **Cons:** rooms lack ocean views; old bath tubs in some rooms. **TripAdvisor:** "fabulous getaway," "wonderful surprise," "charming and immaculate." *Rooms from: $121 4525 El Mar*

Dr. ☎ 954/772–3336 ⊕ www.blueseascourtyard.com ⇨ 12 rooms 🍴 *Breakfast.*

$$$ HOTEL **Sea Lord Hotel & Suites.** This attractive ocean-side hotel received major upgrades in 2010, including a new pool deck, restaurant, lobby, sundeck, entranceway, small fitness center, and room enhancements. **Pros:** terrific beach location; void of the moldy smell in nearby older hotels. **Cons:** shaky elevators; limited parking. **TripAdvisor:** "impressive customer service," "perfection on the beach," "beautiful rooms and décor." $ *Rooms from: $155 ✉ 4140 El Mar Dr. ☎ 954/776–1505, 800/344–4451 ⊕ www.sealordhotel.com ⇨ 47 rooms* 🍴 *Breakfast.*

$$$ HOTEL **Tropic Seas Resort Motel.** This two-story property has an unbeatable location—directly on the beach, flanking 150 feet of pristine sands and sparkling blues—and is a favorite of annual European vacationers looking for longer stays. **Pros:** family-owned friendliness; great lawn furniture. **Cons:** must reserve far ahead; dated bathrooms. **TripAdvisor:** "beautiful place," "Florida fun," "great place for a family." $ *Rooms from: $205 ✉ 4616 El Mar Dr. ☎ 954/772–2555, 800/952–9581 ⊕ www.tropicseasresort.com ⇨ 16 rooms* 🍴 *Breakfast.*

SPORTS AND THE OUTDOORS

★ **Anglin's Fishing Pier.** This longtime favorite for 24-hour fishing has a fresh, renovated appearance after shaking off repeated storm damage that closed the pier at intervals during the past decade. ☎ *954/491–9403.*

POMPANO BEACH

Pompano Beach is 3 miles north of Lauderdale-by-the-Sea.

As Route A1A enters this town directly north of Lauderdale-by-the-Sea, the high-rise scene resumes. Sportfishing is big in Pompano Beach, as its name implies, but there's more to beachside attractions than the popular Fisherman's Wharf. Behind a low coral-rock wall, Alsdorf Park (also called the 14th Street boat ramp) extends north and south of the wharf along the road and beach.

GETTING HERE AND AROUND

From Interstate 95, Pompano Beach exits include Sample Road, Copans Road, or Atlantic Boulevard.

ESSENTIALS

Visitor Information **Greater Pompano Beach Chamber of Commerce** ☎ *954/941–2940* ⊕ *www.pompanobeachchamber.com.*

WHERE TO EAT

$$$$ ECLECTIC ★ **Cafe Maxx.** New-wave epicurean dining had its South Florida start here circa 1984, but Cafe Maxx remains fresh. The menu changes nightly, showcasing tropical appeal with dishes such as jerk-spiced sea scallops, jumbo stone crab claws with honey-lime mustard sauce, or black-bean-and-banana-pepper chili with Florida avocado. Appetizers include caviar pie and crispy sweetbreads. Desserts such as banana spring rolls and the vanilla bean crème brulée stay the tropical course with their secondary ingredients. Select from 300 wines by the bottle, and many by the glass. $ *Average main: $42 ✉ 2601 E. Atlantic Blvd. ☎ 954/782–0606 ⊕ www.cafemaxx.com ⊙ No lunch.*

DID YOU KNOW?

Seagulls can drink both fresh and salt water, and they can make short order of your lunch, since they eat everything from crabs and fish to bread, cookies, and potato chips.

$$$$ SEAFOOD ✕ **Cap's Place.** On an island once a bootlegger's haunt, Lighthouse Point's ramshackle seafood spot reached by launch has served the famous as well as the infamous, including the likes of Winston Churchill, FDR, JFK, and Al Capone. Cap was Captain Theodore Knight, born in 1871, who, with partner-in-crime Al Hasis, floated a derelict barge to the area in the 1920s. Broward's oldest restaurant, built on the barge, is run by Hasis's descendants. Sesame-crusted mahimahi is served with soy-ginger sauce, flaky rolls are baked fresh, and tangy lime pie is a great finale. Clams and oysters are shucked to order. Cap's is no cheapie; even a plate of linguine and clams will cost you upwards of $25. *Average main: $32 ✉ Cap's Dock, 2765 N.E. 28th Ct. ☎ 954/941–0418 🌐 www.capsplace.com ⏲ No lunch. Closed Mon. May–Dec.*

WHERE TO STAY

For expanded reviews, facilities, and current deals, visit Fodors.com.

$$ RENTAL **Cottages by the Ocean.** For families wanting longer-term stays and favoring home-style comforts over resort-style bling, Cottages by the Ocean is one of five beach-area properties run by Beach Vacation Rentals offering furnished, well-equipped condo-style lodging. **Pros:** shops within walking distance, complimentary Wi-Fi; no resort fees (though there are cleaning fees). **Cons:** not directly on beach; no pool; old boob-tube TVs; sometimes 3-night minimum stay. **TripAdvisor:** "relaxing quietness," "nice spot by the ocean," "a magical cottage." *Rooms from: $210 ✉ 3309 S.E. 3rd St. ☎ 954/283–1111 🌐 www.4rentbythebeach.com 6 cottages No meals.*

SHOPPING

Sugar Chest Antique Mall. Bargain hunters and antiques junkies browse the 200 vendors' collectibles and antiques. *✉ 906 N. Federal Hwy. ☎ 954/942–8601 🌐 www.thesugarchestantiquemall.com.*

SPORTS AND THE OUTDOORS

FISHING

Pompano Pier. The 24-hour pier extends more than 1,000 feet into the Atlantic. The pier tackle shop sells beer and snacks. Admission is $4 to fish, $1 to sightsee; rod-and-reel rental is $16.50 (including admission, plus a $20 deposit) for the day. Anglers brag about catching barracuda, jack, and snapper here in the same sitting, along with bluefish, cobia, and, yes, even pompano. *☎ 954/226–6411.*

OUTFITTERS **Fish City Pride.** Morning, afternoon, and evening drift-fishing trips cost $37 and include fishing gear and bait. *✉ Fish City Marina, 2621 N. Riverside Dr. ☎ 954/781–1211.*

SCUBA DIVING

SS *Copenhagen* State Underwater Archaeological Preserve. The wreck of the SS *Copenhagen* lies in 15- to 30-foot depths just outside the second reef on the Pompano Ledge, 3.6 miles south of Hillsboro Inlet. The 325-foot-long steamer's final voyage, from Philadelphia bound for Havana, began May 20, 1900, ending six days later when the captain—attempting to avoid gulf currents—crashed onto a reef off what's now Pompano Beach. In 2000 the missing bow section was identified a half mile to the south. The wreck, a haven for colorful fish and corals and a magnet for skin and scuba divers, became Florida's fifth Underwater Archaeological Preserve in 1994, listed on the National Register of Historic Places in 2001.

EN ROUTE

Hillsboro Lighthouse. About 2 miles north of Pompano Beach you are afforded a beautiful view across Hillsboro Inlet to this lighthouse, often called the brightest lighthouse in the Southeast and used by mariners as a landmark for decades. When at sea you can see its light from almost halfway to the Bahamas. Although the octagonal-pyramid, iron-skeletal tower lighthouse is on private property inaccessible to the public, it's well worth a peek, even from afar. The Hillsboro Lighthouse Preservation Society offers tours about four times a year; call for schedule and tips on viewing vantage points. ☎ *954/942–2102* 🌐 *www.hillsborolighthouse.org.*

EN ROUTE

Hillsboro Mile. To the north, Route A1A traverses the so-called Hillsboro Mile (actually more than 2 miles), a millionaire's row of some of Broward's most beautiful and expensive homes. The road runs along a narrow strip of land between the Intracoastal Waterway and the ocean, with bougainvillea and oleander edging the way and yachts docked along both banks. Traffic often moves at a snail's pace, especially in winter, as vacationers (and sometimes even envious locals) gawk.

5

DEERFIELD BEACH

Deerfield Beach is 2 miles north of Pompano Beach.

As posh Hillsboro Mile comes to an end, Route A1A spills out onto Deerfield Beach, Broward's northernmost ocean-side community.

GETTING HERE AND AROUND

From Interstate 95, take the Hillsboro Boulevard exit east. From A1A, continue north past Pompano Beach and Hillsboro Beach.

ESSENTIALS

Visitor Information **Greater Deerfield Beach Chamber of Commerce** ☎ *954/427–1050* 🌐 *www.deerfieldchamber.com.*

EXPLORING

Quiet Waters Park. Its name belies what's in store for kids here. Splash Adventure is a high-tech water-play system with slides and tunnels, among other activities. There's also cable water-skiing and boat rental on this county park's lake, and a skate park. Note that this space functions mostly as a public park for locals rather than as a tourist attraction and is located near a highway. ✉ *401 S. Powerline Rd.* ☎ *954/360–1315* 🌐 *www.broward.org/parks* 🎟 *Park \$1 weekends, free weekdays* ⏲ *Apr.–Sept., daily 8–6; Oct.–Mar., daily 8–5:30.*

OFF THE BEATEN PATH

Deerfield Island Park. Reached only by boat (and with a new dock in the works for vessels longer than 25 feet), this officially designated Urban Wilderness Area showcases coastal hammock island and contains a mangrove swamp that provides a critical habitat for gopher tortoises, gray foxes, raccoons, and armadillos. County-operated boat shuttles run 10–3 on weekends (on the hour only). Amenities include a boardwalk, walking trails, and an observation tower. ✉ *1720 Deerfield Island*

Park ☎ *954/360–1320* ⊕ *www.broward.org/parks/DeerfieldIslandPark* *Free.*

WHERE TO EAT

$$$$ MODERN EUROPEAN ★ **Brooks.** This is one of Deerfield's more elegant dining spots, thanks to French perfectionist Bernard Perron. Brooks is now run by Perron's son-in-law Jon Howe. Updated continental fare is served in a series of rooms filled with old-master replicas, cut glass, antiques, and floral wallpaper. Fresh ingredients go into distinctly Floridian dishes, including sautéed Key Largo yellowtail snapper. Roast rack of lamb is also popular. Put your order in early for the chocolate or Grand Marnier soufflé. *Average main: $32* ✉ *500 S. Federal Hwy.* ☎ *954/427–9302* ⊕ *www.brooks-restaurant.com.*

$$ SEAFOOD **Whale's Rib.** For a casual, almost funky, nautical experience near the beach, look no farther. If you want to blend in, order a fish special with whale fries—thinly sliced potatoes that look like hot potato chips. People come from near and far for the famous whale fries. Those with smaller appetites can choose from salads and fish sandwiches, or raw-bar favorites like Ipswich clams. *Average main: $18* ✉ *2031 N.E. 2nd St.* ☎ *954/421–8880.*

WHERE TO STAY

For expanded reviews, facilities, and current deals, visit Fodors.com.

$ HOTEL **Carriage House Resort Motel.** This tidy no-frills motel, accredited as an SSL (Superior Small Lodging), is less than a block from the ocean and consists of a two-story, colonial-style building with a second-story sundeck. **Pros:** friendly staff; bargain rates. **Cons:** nothing fancy. **TripAdvisor:** "just what I was hoping to find," "nice and friendly," "outstanding service." *Rooms from: $99* ✉ *250 S. Ocean Blvd.* ☎ *954/427–7670* ⊕ *www.carriagehouseresort.com* *6 rooms, 14 efficiencies, 10 apartments* *No meals.*

SPORTS AND THE OUTDOORS

FISHING

Deerfield Pier. This picturesque pier teems with fishermen and tourists. Admission is $4 to fish, $1 to sightsee. Common catches include king mackerel, snapper, bluefish, and barracuda. ☎ *954/426–9206.*

SCUBA DIVING

Dixie Divers. Among the area's most popular dive operators, this outfit has morning and afternoon dives aboard the 48-foot *Lady-Go-Diver,* plus evening dives on weekends. Snorkelers and certified divers can explore the marine life of nearby reefs and shipwrecks. The cost is $60; ride-alongs are welcome for $40. ✉ *Cove Marina, Hillsboro Blvd. and Intracoastal Waterway* ☎ *954/420–0009* ⊕ *www.dixiedivers.com.*

HOLLYWOOD

Hollywood is 8 miles south of Fort Lauderdale.

Hollywood has had a face-lift, with more nips and tucks to come. Young Circle, once down-at-heel, has become Broward's first Arts Park. On Hollywood's western outskirts the flamboyant Seminole Hard Rock

Hotel & Casino has permanently etched the previously downtrodden section of the State Road 7/U.S. 441 corridor on the map of trendy excitement, drawing local weekenders, architecture buffs, and gamblers. But Hollywood's redevelopment effort doesn't end there: new shops, restaurants, and art galleries open at a persistent clip, and the city has spiffed up its Broadwalk (not Boardwalk)—a wide pedestrian walkway along the beach—where Rollerbladers are as commonplace as snowbirds from the north.

GETTING HERE AND AROUND

From Interstate 95, exit east on Sheridan Street or Hollywood Boulevard.

ESSENTIALS

Visitor Information **Hollywood Chamber of Commerce** ✉ *330 N. Federal Hwy.* ☎ *954/923–4000* 🌐 *www.hollywoodchamber.org.*

EXPLORING

Art and Culture Center of Hollywood. This is a visual- and performing-arts facility with an art reference library, outdoor sculpture garden, and arts school. It's southeast of Young Circle, melding urban open space with a fountain, a 2,000-plus-seat amphitheater, and an indoor theater. Nearby, on trendy Harrison Street and Hollywood Boulevard, are chic lunch places, bluesy entertainment spots, and shops. ✉ *1650 Harrison St.* ☎ *954/921–3274* 🌐 *www.artandculturecenter.org* *$7* *Tues.–Fri. 10–5, weekends noon–4. Closed Mon.*

Downtown Hollywood Art & Design District. From 21st Avenue to Young Circle on Hollywood Boulevard and Harrison Street, the streets are peppered with boutiques, bistros, sidewalk cafés, and galleries featuring original artwork (eclectic paintings, sculpture, photography, and mixed media).

★ **IGFA Fishing Hall of Fame and Museum.** This creation of the International Game Fishing Association is a shrine to the sport. It has an extensive museum and research library where seven galleries feature fantasy fishing and other interactive displays. At the Catch Gallery, you can cast off virtually to reel in a marlin, sailfish, trout, tarpon, or bass. (If you suddenly get an urge to gear up for your own adventures, a Bass Pro Shops Outdoor World is next door.) ✉ *300 Gulfstream Way* ☎ *954/927–2628* 🌐 *www.igfa.org* *$8* *Mon.–Sat. 10–6, Sun. noon–6.*

Young Circle Arts Park. This 10-acre urban park has completely transformed the run-down traffic circle linking downtown Hollywood with its beaches into a beautiful, lively public space. There's no shortage of things to do here: a huge playground beckons for the little ones, a state-of-the-art amphitheater hosts regular concerts, and educational workshop spaces host regular events, like Friday glassblowing workshops and jewelry-making classes. ✉ *1 Young Circle, Hollywood Blvd. and U.S. 1* ☎ *954/921–3500* 🌐 *www.hollywoodfl.org/index.aspx?nid=65.*

BEACHES

Fodor's Choice ★

Hollywood Beach and Broadwalk. The name might be Hollywood, but there's nothing hip or chic about **Hollywood North Beach Park,** which sits at the north end of Hollywood (Route A1A and Sheridan Street), before the pedestrian Broadwalk begins. And that's a good thing. It's just a laid-back, old-fashioned place to enjoy the sun, sand, and sea. The film *Marley & Me,* starring Jennifer Aniston and Owen Wilson and filmed in Greater Fort Lauderdale, spurred a comeback for dog beaches in South Florida, and ever since then, the year-round **Dog Beach of Hollywood** in North Beach Park has allowed dogs to enjoy fun in the sun from 3 pm to 7 pm Friday–Sunday. Farther south on Hollywood beach, the 2.5-mile **Broadwalk** is a delightful throwback to the '50s, with mom-and-pop stores, ice cream parlors, elderly couples going for long strolls, and families building sand castles on the beach. Thanks to millions in investment, this popular stretch of beach has spiffy features like a pristine pedestrian walkway, a concrete bike path, a crushed-shell jogging path, an 18-inch decorative wall separating the Broadwalk from the sand, and places to shower off after a dip. Expect to hear French spoken throughout Hollywood, since its beaches have long been a favorite getaway for Quebecois. **Amenities:** food and drink; lifeguards; parking (fee); toilets. **Best for:** sunrise; swimming; walking. ✉ *Rte. A1A from Dania Beach Blvd. to Halladale Beach Blvd.* 🎫 *Parking in public lots is $1.75 per hr.*

John U. Lloyd Beach State Recreation Area. The once pine-dotted natural area was restored to its natural state, thanks to government-driven efforts to pull out all but indigenous plants. Now native sea grape, gumbo-limbo, and other native plants offer shaded ambience. Nature trails and a marina are large draws, as is canoeing on Whiskey Creek. The beaches are also excellent, but beware of mosquitos in summer! **Amenities:** parking (fee); toilets. **Best for:** solitude; sunrise. ✉ *6503 N. Ocean Dr.* ☎ *954/923–2833* 🌐 *www.floridastateparks.org/lloydbeach* 🎫 *$6 per vehicle for 2 to 8 passengers, $4 for lone driver* ⏲ *Daily 8–sunset.*

WHERE TO EAT

$$$$ ITALIAN — **Café Martorano.** Located within Hard Rock Hollywood's massive entertainment and restaurant zone, this Italian-American institution pays homage to anything and everything that has to do with the "Godfather" and impresses with humungous family-style portions. Dishes run the full Italian-American gamut, from the classic parmigianas to the lobster and snapper française. The homemade mozzarella and fried calamari are excellent choices for starters. It's easy to gorge here, since each dish is so succulent and savory. The ever-present "Godfather" motif is taken to the extreme—dinner is interrupted hourly with clips from the movie played on the surrounding flat screens. $ *Average main: $31* ✉ *5751 Seminole Way* ☎ *954/584–4450* 🌐 *www.cafemartorano.com.*

$$ ECLECTIC — **Las Brisas.** Next to the beach, this cozy bistro offers seating inside or out, and the food is Argentine with Italian flair. A small pot, filled with *chimichurri*—a paste of oregano, parsley, olive oil, salt, garlic, and

crushed pepper—for spreading on steaks, sits on each table. Grilled fish is a favorite, as are pork chops, chicken, and pasta entrées. Desserts include a flan like *mamacita* used to make. *Average main: $18 600 N. Surf Rd. 954/923–1500 No lunch.*

$$ AMERICAN **LeTub.** Formerly a Sunoco gas station, this quirky waterside saloon has an enduring affection for claw-foot bathtubs. Hand-painted porcelain is everywhere—under ficus, sea grape, and palm trees. If a potty doesn't appeal, there's a secluded swing facing the water north of the main dining area. Despite molasses-slow service and an abundance of flies at sundown, this eatery is favored by locals, and management seemed genuinely appalled when hordes of trend-seeking city slickers started jamming bar stools and tables after Oprah declared its thick, juicy Angus burgers the best around. A plain burger and small fries will run you around $16. *Average main: $16 1100 N. Ocean Dr. 954/921–9425 www.theletub.com No credit cards.*

5

WHERE TO STAY

For expanded reviews, facilities, and current deals, visit Fodors.com.

$ B&B/INN **Manta Ray Inn.** Canadians Donna and Dwayne Boucher run this immaculate, affordable, two-story inn on the beach. **Pros:** on the beach; low-key atmosphere. **Cons:** no restaurant. **TripAdvisor:** "friendly staff," "relaxing break," "great down home service." *Rooms from: $126 1715 S. Surf Rd. 954/921–9666, 800/255–0595 www.mantarayinn.com 12 units No meals.*

$ B&B/INN **Sea Downs.** Facing the Broadwalk and ocean, this three-story lodging is a good choice for families, as one-bedroom units can be joined to create two-bedroom apartments. **Pros:** facing ocean; reasonable rates. **Cons:** minimum stay often required. **TripAdvisor:** "beautiful and clean," "slice of nostalgia," "right on the beach." *Rooms from: $109 2900 N. Surf Rd. 954/923–4968 www.seadowns.com 4 efficiencies, 8 1-bedroom apartments No credit cards No meals.*

$$$ HOTEL **Seminole Hard Rock Hotel & Casino.** On the industrial flatlands of western Hollywood, the Seminole Hard Rock Hotel & Casino serves as a magnet for pulsating Vegas-style entertainment and folks looking for 24 hours of casino, clubbing, and hedonism. **Pros:** nonstop entertainment; plenty of activities. **Cons:** in an unsavory neighborhood; no tourist sights in close proximity; endless entertainment can be exhausting. **TripAdvisor:** "a little bit for everyone," "feels like you're in Vegas," "excellent stay." *Rooms from: $179 1 Seminole Way 866/502–7529, 800/937–0010 www.seminolehardrockhollywood.com 395 rooms, 86 suites No meals.*

$$$$ RESORT ★ **The Westin Diplomat Resort & Spa.** This colossal 39-story contemporary property has been instrumental in bringing new life and new style to Hollywood Beach with its massive, 60-foot high ceilinged atrium and casual chic guest rooms. **Pros:** heavenly beds for adults and kids now, too; in-room workouts and great spa; eye-popping architecture. **Cons:** beach is eroding. **TripAdvisor:** "amazing resort," "a perfect stay," "the best bed." *Rooms from: $349 3555 South Ocean Drive*

954/602–6000, 800/327–1212 www.diplomatresort.com 900 rooms, 100 suites No meals.

NIGHTLIFE

Although Hollywood has a sleepy, small-town feel in the east, the Seminole Hard Rock Hotel & Casino brings Vegas nights to South Florida.

Seminole Hard Rock Casino. The glitzy, Vegas-style Seminole Hard Rock Casino in Hollywood has bingo, poker, blackjack, more than 2,500 gaming machines, and 89 tables over a 130,000-square-foot casino. It's open 24/7 and is connected to a hotel and an entire nightlife and entertainment complex. The Seminole Hard Rock is not to be confused with its neighbor, the smoky and seedy Seminole Casino of Hollywood. *1 Seminole Way 954/327–7625 www.seminolehardrockhollywood.com.*

SPORTS AND THE OUTDOORS

West Lake Park. Rent a canoe, kayak, or take the 40-minute boat tour at this park bordering the Intracoastal Waterway. At 1,500 acres, it is one of Florida's largest urban nature facilities. Extensive boardwalks traverse mangrove forests that shelter endangered and threatened species. A 65-foot observation tower showcases the entire park. At the free **Anne Kolb Nature Center,** named after Broward's late environmental advocate, there's a 3,500-gallon aquarium. The center's exhibit hall has 27 interactive displays. *751 Sheridan St. 954/926–2480 www.broward.org/parks/WestLakePark Weekends $1.50, weekdays free Daily 9–5.*

FISHING

Sea Leg's III. Drift-fishing trips run during the day and bottom-fishing trips at night. Trips cost $38, including rod rental. *5398 N. Ocean Dr. 954/923–2109 www.sealegs3.com.*

6

Palm Beach and the Treasure Coast

WORD OF MOUTH

"If you really want to be close to restaurants and shops in the Palm Beach area, check out the Marriott in Delray Beach or even the adjacent Residence Inn by Marriott . . . about 30 minutes south of Palm Beach."

—rattravlers

WELCOME TO PALM BEACH

TOP REASONS TO GO

★ **Exquisite Resorts:** Two grandes dames, The Breakers and the Boca Raton Resort & Club, perpetually draw the rich, the famous, and anyone else who can afford the luxury. The Ritz-Carlton and Four Seasons sparkle with service fit for royalty.

★ **Beautiful Beaches:** From Jupiter, where dogs run free, to Stuart's tubular waves, to the broad stretches of sand in Delray Beach and Boca Raton, swimmers, surfers, sunbathers—and sea turtles looking for a place to hatch their eggs—all find happiness.

★ **Top-Notch Golf:** The Bear Trap at PGA National Resort & Spa alone is worth a round; pros sharpen up at PGA Village.

★ **Horse Around:** Wellington, with its popular polo season, is often called the winter equestrian capital of the world.

★ **Excellent Fishing:** The Atlantic Ocean, teeming with kingfish, sailfish, and wahoo, and Lake Okeechobee, a great place for bass and perch, are treasure chests for anglers.

1 Greater Palm Beach. With Gatsby-era architecture, stone-and-stucco estates, and extravagant dining, Palm Beach is a must-see for travelers to the area. Plan to spend time on Worth Avenue, also known as the Mink Mile, a collection of more than 200 chic shops, and Whitehall, the palatial retreat for Palm Beach's founder, Henry Flagler. West Palm Beach and its environs—Lake Worth, Palm Beach Gardens, and Singer Island—are bustling with their own identities. Culture fans have plenty to cheer about with the Kravis Center and Norton Museum of Art, sports enthusiasts will have a ball golfing or boating, and kids love the Palm Beach Zoo and Lion Country Safari.

2 Delray Beach. Its lively downtown, with galleries, independent boutiques, and trendy restaurants right by the water, is perfect for strolling. To the west is the unique Morikami Museum and Japanese Gardens.

3 Boca Raton. An abundance of modern shopping plazas mix with historic buildings from the 1920s, masterpieces by renowned architect Addison Mizner. Parks line much of the oceanfront.

4 Treasure Coast. Northern Palm Beach County and beyond remains blissfully low-key, with fishing towns, spring-training stadiums, and ecotourism attractions until you hit the cosmopolitan—yet understated—Vero Beach.

ATLANTIC OCEAN
upiter Island
lobe Sound
Tequesta
Jupiter
Juno Beach
Singer Island
Palm Beach Gardens
Palm Beach Shores
Riviera Beach
Palm Beach
Lake Worth
South Palm Beach
Manalapan
Boynton Beach
Gulf Stream
Delray Beach
Highland Beach
Boca Raton

GETTING ORIENTED

This diverse region extends 120 miles from laid-back Sebastian to tony Boca Raton. The area's glitzy epicenter, Palm Beach, attracts socialites, the well-heeled, and interested onlookers. The northernmost cities are only about 100 miles from Orlando, making that area an ideal choice for families wanting some beach time to go with a visit to Mickey Mouse, and delightfully funky Delray Beach is only an hour north of Miami. The Intracoastal Waterway runs parallel to the ocean and transforms from a canal to a tidal lagoon separating islands from the mainland, starting with Palm Beach and moving northward to Singer Island (Palm Beach Shores and Riviera Beach), Jupiter Island, Hutchinson Island (Stuart, Jensen Beach, and Fort Pierce), and Orchid Island (Vero Beach and Sebastian).

Revised and updated by Dorothea Hunter Sönne

A golden stretch of the Atlantic shore, the Palm Beach area resists categorization, and for good reason: the territory stretching south to Boca Raton, appropriately coined the Gold Coast, defines old-world glamour and new-age sophistication.

To the north you'll uncover the comparatively undeveloped Treasure Coast—liberally sprinkled with seaside gems and wide-open spaces along the road awaiting your discovery. Speaking of discovery, its moniker came from the 1715 sinking of a Spanish fleet that dumped gold, jewels, and silver in the waters; today the *Urca de Lima*, one of the original 11 ships and now an undersea "museum," can be explored by scuba divers.

Altogether, there's a delightful disparity between Palm Beach, pulsing with old-money wealth, and under-the-radar Hutchinson Island. Seductive as the gorgeous beaches, eclectic dining, and leisurely pursuits can be, you should also take advantage of flourishing commitments to historic preservation and the arts, as town after town yields intriguing museums, galleries, theaters, and gardens.

Palm Beach, proud of its status as America's first luxe resort destination and still glimmering with its trademark Mediterranean- Revival mansions, manicured hedges, and highbrow shops, can rule supreme as the focal point for your sojourn any time of year. From there, head off in one of three directions: south toward Boca Raton along an especially scenic estate-dotted route known as A1A, back north to the beautiful barrier islands of the Treasure Coast, or west for more rustic inland activities such as bass fishing and biking on the dike around Lake Okeechobee.

PLANNING

WHEN TO GO

The weather is optimal from November through May, but the trade-off is that roadways and hotels are more crowded and prices higher. If the scene is what you're after, try the early weeks of December when "season" is not yet in full swing; however, be warned that after Easter, the crowd relocates to the Hamptons, and Palm Beach feels like another universe. For some, that's a blessing—and a great time to take advantage of lower summer lodging rates (The Breakers runs promos at a fourth its regular cost). Hurricanes can show up from June to November, but there's always plenty of notice. More important, you'll need to bring your tolerance for heat, humidity, and afternoon downpours.

GETTING HERE AND AROUND

AIR TRAVEL

If you're flying into the area, the most convenient airport is Palm Beach International Airport in West Palm, but it's possible (and sometimes cheaper) to fly to Fort Lauderdale or Orlando. Try to rent a car if you plan on exploring. Interstate 95 runs north–south, linking West Palm Beach with Fort Lauderdale and Miami to the south and with Daytona, Jacksonville, and the rest of the Atlantic Coast to the north. Florida's turnpike runs from Miami north through West Palm Beach before angling northwest to reach Orlando. U.S. 1 threads north–south along the coast, connecting most coastal communities, whereas the more scenic Route A1A, also called Ocean Boulevard or Ocean Drive, depending on where you are, ventures out onto the barrier islands. I–95 runs parallel to U.S. 1, but a few miles inland.

From the airport, call Southeastern Florida Transportation Group, a local hotline for cabs, airport shuttles, and private sedans.

Airport **Palm Beach International Airport** *(PBI).* ✉ *1000 Turnage Blvd., West Palm Beach* ☎ *561/471–7420* 🌐 *www.pbia.org.*

Airport Transfers **Southeastern Florida Transportation Group.** ☎ *561/777–7777* 🌐 *www.yellowcabflorida.com.*

BUS TRAVEL

The county's bus service, Palm Tran, runs two routes (numbers 44 and 40) that offer daily service connecting the airport, the Tri-Rail stop near it, and locations in central West Palm Beach. A network of 34 routes joins towns all across the area; regular fares are $1.50. The free Downtown Trolley connects the West Palm Beach Amtrak station and the Tri-Rail stop there. It makes continuous loops down Clematis Street, the city's main stretch of restaurants and watering holes interspersed with stores, and through CityPlace, a shopping-dining-theater district. Hop on and off at any of the seven stops. The trolleys run Sunday to Wednesday 11–9 and Thursday to Saturday 11–11.

Contacts **Palm Tran.** ☎ *561/841–4287* 🌐 *www.palmtran.org.* **Downtown Trolley** ☎ *561/833–8873* 🌐 *www.westpalmbeachdda.com/transportation.*

TRAIN TRAVEL

Amtrak has daily trains that connect West Palm Beach and Delray Beach with Miami, Orlando, Tampa, and cities in the Northeast, ending with New York. The West Palm Beach station is at the same location as the Tri-Rail stop, so the same free shuttle, the Downtown Trolley (🌐 *www.wpbgo.com*), is available.

Tri-Rail Commuter Service is a rail system with 18 stops altogether between West Palm Beach and Miami; tickets can be purchased at each stop, and a one-way trip from the first to the last point is $6.90. Three stations, West Palm Beach, Lake Worth, and Boca, have free shuttles to their downtowns, and taxis are on-call at others.

Contacts **Amtrak.** ☎ *800/872–7245* 🌐 *www.amtrak.com.* **Tri-Rail Commuter Service.** ☎ *800/874–7245* 🌐 *www.tri-rail.com.*

ABOUT THE RESTAURANTS

Numerous elegant establishments offer upscale American, Continental, and international cuisine, but the area also is chock-full of casual waterfront spots serving affordable burgers and fresh seafood feasts. Grouper, fried or blackened, is especially popular here, along with the ubiquitous shrimp. Happy hours and early-bird menus, Florida hallmarks, typically entice the budget-minded with several dinner entrées at reduced prices offered during certain hours, usually before 5 or 6.

ABOUT THE HOTELS

Palm Beach has a number of smaller hotels in addition to the famous Breakers. Lower-priced hotels and bed-and-breakfasts can be found in West Palm Beach and Lake Worth. Heading south, the oceanside town of Manalapan has the Ritz-Carlton, Palm Beach; the Seagate Hotel & Spa sparkles in Delray Beach, and the posh Boca Raton Resort & Club is by the shore in Boca Raton. In the opposite direction there's the PGA National Resort & Spa, and across from it by the water is the Marriott on Singer Island, a well-kept secret for spacious, sleek suites. Even farther north, Vero Beach has a collection of luxury boutique hotels, as well as more modest options along the Treasure Coast. To the west, towns close to Lake Okeechobee offer country-inn accommodations.

HOTEL AND RESTAURANT COSTS

Prices in the restaurant reviews are the average cost of a main course at dinner or, if dinner is not served, at lunch. Prices in the hotel reviews are the lowest cost of a standard double room in high season. Prices do not include taxes (6%, more in some counties, and 1%–5% tourist tax for hotel rooms).

VISITOR INFORMATION

Contacts **The Greater Boynton Beach Chamber of Commerce** ✉ *1880 N. Congress Ave., Suite 106, Boynton Beach* ☎ *561/732–9501* 🌐 *www.boyntonbeach.org.* **Chamber of Commerce of the Palm Beaches** ✉ *401 N. Flagler Dr., West Palm Beach* ☎ *561/833–3711* 🌐 *www.palmbeaches.org.* **Greater Lake Worth Chamber of Commerce** ✉ *501 Lake Ave., Lake Worth* ☎ *561/582–4401* 🌐 *www.lwchamber.org.* **Greater Lantana Chamber of Commerce** ✉ *212 Iris Ave., Lantana* ☎ *561/585–8664* 🌐 *www.lantanachamber.com.* **Palm Beach County Convention and Visitors Bureau** ✉ *1555 Palm Beach Lakes Blvd., Suite 800, West*

Palm Beach ☎ *561/233–3000, 800/554–7256* 🌐 *www.palmbeachfl.com.* **Palm Beach Chamber of Commerce** ✉ *400 Royal Palm Way, Suite 106, Palm Beach* ☎ *561/655–3282* 🌐 *www.palmbeachchamber.com.*

GREATER PALM BEACH

70 miles north of Miami, off I–95.

Long reigning as the place where the crème de la crème go to shake off winter's chill, Palm Beach, which is actually on a barrier island, continues to be a seasonal hotbed of platinum-grade consumption. The town celebrated its 100th birthday in 2011, and there's no competing with its historic social supremacy. It has been the winter address for heirs of the iconic Rockefeller, Vanderbilt, Colgate, Post, Kellogg, and Kennedy families. Even newer power brokers, with names like Kravis, Peltz, and Trump, are made to understand that strict laws govern everything from building to landscaping, and not so much as a pool awning gets added without a town council nod. Only three bridges allow entry, and huge tour buses are a no-no.

To learn who's who in Palm Beach, it helps to pick up a copy of the *Palm Beach Daily News*—locals call it the Shiny Sheet because its high-quality paper avoids smudging society hands or Pratesi linens—for, as it is said, to be mentioned in the Shiny Sheet is to be Palm Beach.

All this fabled ambience started with Henry Morrison Flagler, Florida's premier developer, and cofounder, along with John D. Rockefeller, of Standard Oil. No sooner did Flagler bring the railroad to Florida in the 1890s than he erected the famed Royal Poinciana and Breakers hotels. Rail access sent real-estate prices soaring, and ever since, princely sums have been forked over for personal stationery engraved with 33480, the zip code of Palm Beach (which didn't actually get its status as an independent municipality until 1911). Setting the tone in this town of unparalleled Florida opulence is the ornate architectural work of Addison Mizner, who began designing homes and public buildings here in the 1920s and whose Moorish-Gothic Mediterranean Revival style has influenced virtually all landmarks.

But the greater Palm Beach area is much larger and encompasses several communities on the mainland and to the north and south. To provide Palm Beach with servants and other workers, Flagler created an off-island community across the Intracoastal Waterway (also referred to as Lake Worth in these parts). West Palm Beach, now cosmopolitan and noteworthy in its own right, evolved into an economically vibrant business hub and a sprawling playground with some of the best nightlife and cultural attractions around, including the glittering Kravis Center for the Performing Arts, the region's principal entertainment venue. The mammoth Palm Beach County Judicial Center and Courthouse and the State Administrative Building underscore the breadth of the city's governmental and corporate activity.

The burgeoning equestrian development of Wellington, with its horse shows and polo matches, lies a little more than 10 miles west of downtown, and is the site of much of the county's growth.

Spreading southward from the Palm Beach/West Palm Beach nucleus set between the two bridges that flow from Royal Poinciana Way and Royal Palm Way into Flagler Drive on the mainland are small cities like Lake Worth, with its charming artsy center, Lantana, and Manalapan (home to a fabulous Ritz-Carlton beach resort). All three have turf that's technically on the same island as Palm Beach, and at its bottom edge across the inlet is Boynton Beach, a 20-minute drive from Worth Avenue.

Most visitors don't realize that West Palm Beach itself doesn't have any beaches, so locals and guests hop over to Palm Beach or any of the communities just mentioned—or they head 15 minutes north to the residential Singer Island towns of Palm Beach Shores and Riviera Beach, known for their marinas and laid-back vibe, to Peanut Island, which sits in the Intracoastal between Palm Beach and Singer Island, and to Juno Beach. Suburban Palm Beach Gardens, a paradise for golfers and shoppers (malls abound), is inland from Singer Island and 15 minutes northwest of downtown West Palm Beach; because of its upscale slant, it has a ton of restaurants and bars (both independents and chains).

GETTING HERE AND AROUND

Palm Beach is 70 miles north of Miami. To access Palm Beach off I–95, exit east at Southern Boulevard, Belvedere Road, or Okeechobee Boulevard. To drive from Palm Beach to Lake Worth, Lantana, Manalapan, and Boynton Beach, head south on Ocean Boulevard/A1A; Lake Worth is roughly 6 miles south, and Boynton is another 6. Similarly, to reach them from West Palm Beach, take U.S. 1 or I–95. To travel between Palm Beach and Singer Island, you must cross over to West Palm before returning to the beach. Once there, go north on U.S. 1 and then cut over on Blue Heron Boulevard/Route 708. If coming straight from the airport or somewhere farther west, take I–95 up to the same exit and proceed east. The main drag in Palm Beach Gardens is PGA Boulevard/Route 786, which is 4 miles north on U.S. 1 and I–95; A1A merges with it as it exits the top part of Singer Island. Continue on A1A to reach Juno Beach.

TOURS

DivaDuck Amphibious Tours. Running 75 minutes, these tours go in and out of the water around West Palm Beach and Palm Beach. Cruises depart two or three times most days for $25. ✉ *CityPlace, 600 S. Rosemary Ave., West Palm Beach* ☎ *561/844–4188* 🌐 *www.divaduck.com.*

Island Living Tours. Book a private mansion-viewing excursion by car, bicycle, or boat around Palm Beach, and hear the storied past of the island's upper crust. Owner Leslie Diver hosts one weekly group bike outing Saturday at 9 am ($15); call in advance for location and to reserve. ☎ *561/868–7944* 🌐 *www.islandlivingpb.com.*

EXPLORING

PALM BEACH

Most streets around major attractions and commercial zones have free parking as well as metered spaces. If you can stake out a place between a Rolls Royce and a Bentley, do so, but beware of the "Parking by Permit

Draped in European elegance, The Breakers in Palm Beach sits on 140 acres along the oceanfront.

Only" signs, as a $25 ticket might take the shine off your spot. Better yet, if you plan to spend an entire afternoon strolling Worth Avenue, valet-park at the garage next to Saks Fifth Avenue that's a block in from Ocean Boulevard (if you've reached South County Road you've gone too far); some stores validate the fare.

TOP ATTRACTIONS

Bethesda-by-the-Sea. Donald Trump and his wife, Melania, were married here in 2005, but this Gothic Episcopal church had a claim to fame upon its creation in 1926: it was built by the first Protestant congregation in southeast Florida. Guided tours after the morning services are at 12:15 on the second and fourth Sunday each month from September to May (excluding December) and at 11:15 on the fourth Sunday each month from June to August. Adjacent is the formal, ornamental **Cluett Memorial Garden.** ✉ *141 S. County Rd.* ☎ *561/655–4554* 🌐 *www.bbts.org* 🎫 *Free* ⏲ *Church and gardens daily 9–5.*

Fodor's Choice ★ **The Breakers.** Built by Henry Flagler in 1896 and rebuilt by his descendants after a 1925 fire, this magnificent Italian Renaissance–style resort helped launch Florida tourism with its Gilded Age opulence, attracting influential wealthy Northerners to the state. The hotel, still owned by Flagler's heirs, is a must-see even if you aren't staying here. Walk through the 200-foot-long lobby, which has soaring arched ceilings painted by 72 Italian artisans and hung with crystal chandeliers, and the ornate Florentine Dining Room, decorated with 15th-century Flemish tapestries. ■ TIP→ **Book a pampering spa treatment or dine on top of the Seafood Bar's whimsical aquarium, where leggy green starfish** prance below your plate, and the $20 parking is free. ✉ *1 S. County Rd.* ☎ *561/655–6611* 🌐 *www.thebreakers.com.*

Fodor's Choice ★ **Henry Morrison Flagler Museum.** The worldly sophistication of Florida's Gilded Age lives on at Whitehall, the plush 55-room "marble palace" Henry Flagler commissioned in 1901 for his third wife, Mary Lily Kenan. Architects John Carrère and Thomas Hastings were instructed to create the finest home imaginable—and they outdid themselves. Whitehall rivals the grandeur of European palaces and has an entrance hall with a baroque ceiling similar to Louis XIV's Versailles. Here you'll see original furnishings; a hidden staircase Flagler used to sneak from his bedroom to the billiards room; an art collection; a 1,200-pipe organ; and Florida East Coast Railway exhibits, along with Flagler's personal railcar, No. 91, showcased in an 8,000-square-foot beaux arts–style pavilion behind the mansion. Guided tours and audio tours are included with admission. The café, open after Thanksgiving through mid-April, offers an afternoon tea menu available for lunch. ✉ *1 Whitehall Way* ☎ *561/655–2833* 🌐 *www.flagler.org* 🎫 *$18* 🕒 *Tues.–Sat. 10–5, Sun. noon–5.*

★ **Worth Avenue.** Called the Avenue by Palm Beachers, this half-mile-long street is synonymous with exclusive shopping. Nostalgia lovers recall an era when faces or names served as charge cards, purchases were delivered home before customers returned from lunch, and bills were sent directly to private accountants. Times have changed, but a stroll amid the Spanish-accented buildings, many designed by Addison Mizner, offers a tantalizing taste of the island's ongoing commitment to elegant consumerism. It underwent a $15 million makeover in 2010: 200 mature coconut palm trees were planted, and a magnificent $600,000 clock tower was built on the beach to mark the entrance from Route A1A. Definitely explore the labyrinth of nine pedestrian "vias" off of each side that wind past boutiques, tiny plazas, bubbling fountains, and bougainvillea-festooned balconies; this is where the smaller, unique shops are. The Worth Avenue Association *(www.worth-avenue.com)* holds historic walking tours each month. ✉ *Between Cocoanut Row and S. Ocean Blvd.*

WORTH NOTING

El Solano. No Palm Beach mansion better represents the town's luminous legacy than the Spanish-style home built by Addison Mizner as his own residence in 1925. Mizner later sold El Solano to Harold Vanderbilt, and the property was long a favorite among socialites for parties and photo shoots. Vanderbilt held many a gala fundraiser here. Beatle John Lennon and his wife, Yoko Ono, bought it less than a year before Lennon's death. It's still privately owned and not open to the public. ✉ *720 S. Ocean Blvd.*

Mar-a-Lago. Breakfast-food heiress Marjorie Merriweather Post commissioned a Hollywood set designer to create Ocean Boulevard's famed Mar-a-Lago, a 114-room, 110,000-square-foot Mediterranean Revival palace. Its 75-foot Italianate tower is visible from many areas of Palm Beach and from across the Intracoastal Waterway in West Palm Beach.

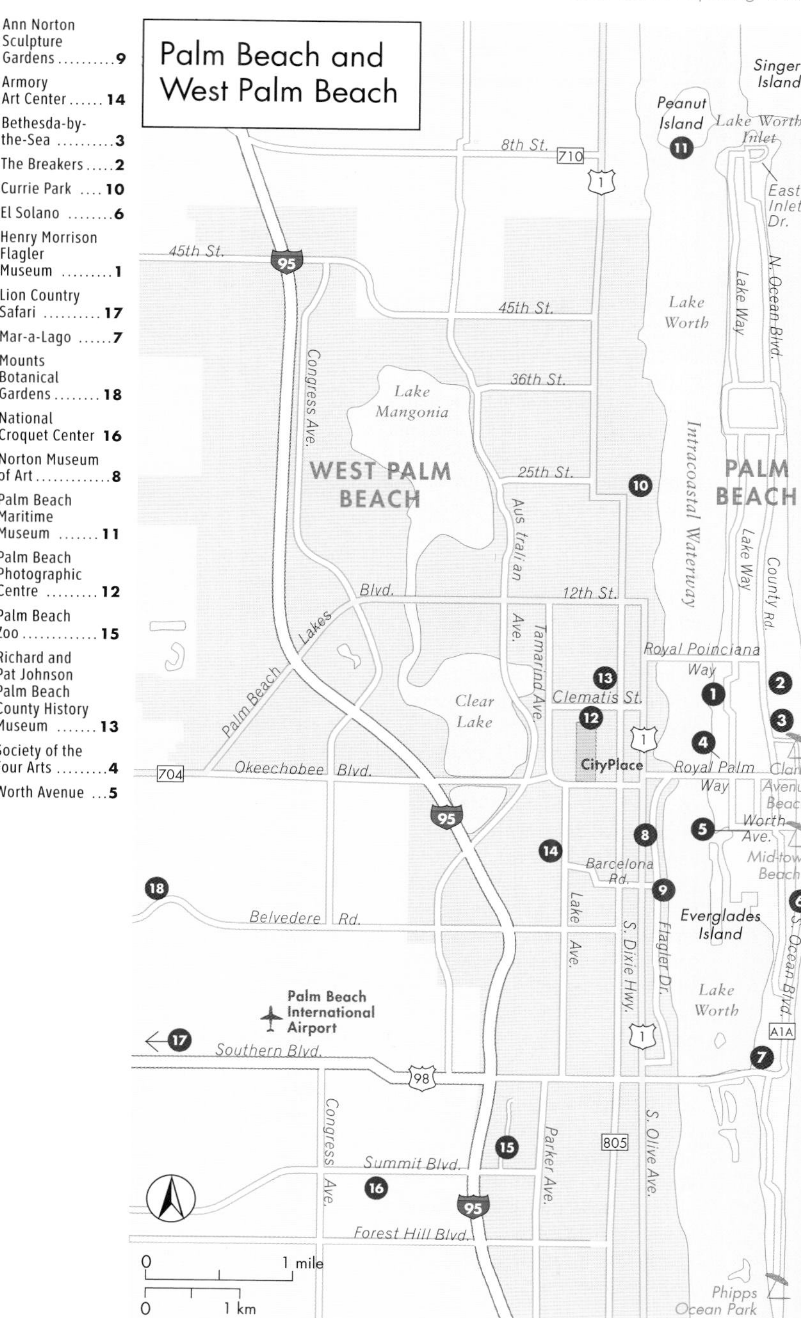
Palm Beach and West Palm Beach
Ann Norton Sculpture Gardens 9
Armory Art Center 14
Bethesda-by-the-Sea 3
The Breakers 2
Currie Park 10
El Solano 6
Henry Morrison Flagler Museum 1
Lion Country Safari 17
Mar-a-Lago 7
Mounts Botanical Gardens 18
National Croquet Center 16
Norton Museum of Art 8
Palm Beach Maritime Museum 11
Palm Beach Photographic Centre 12
Palm Beach Zoo 15
Richard and Pat Johnson Palm Beach County History Museum 13
Society of the Four Arts 4
Worth Avenue ... 5
Singer Island
Peanut Island
Lake Worth Inlet
8th St.
710
1
East Inlet Dr.
45th St.
95
45th St.
Lake Worth
Lake Way
N. Ocean Blvd.
Congress Ave.
36th St.
Lake Mangonia
Intracoastal Waterway
WEST PALM BEACH
25th St.
PALM BEACH
Australian Ave.
Lake Way
County Rd.
Palm Beach Lakes Blvd.
12th St.
Tamarind Ave.
Royal Poinciana Way
Clear Lake
Clematis St.
CityPlace
Royal Palm Way
Clark Avenue Beach
704
Okeechobee Blvd.
Worth Ave.
Barcelona Rd.
Mid-town Beach
Belvedere Rd.
Lake Ave.
S. Dixie Hwy.
Flagler Dr.
Everglades Island
S. Ocean Blvd.
Lake Worth
Palm Beach International Airport
A1A
Southern Blvd.
98
Congress Ave.
Parker Ave.
S. Olive Ave.
805
Summit Blvd.
Forest Hill Blvd.
0 1 mile
0 1 km
Phipps Ocean Park

6

CLOSE UP

The Mansions of Palm Beach

Whether or not you aspire to be a Kennedy, Donald Trump, or Rod Stewart—all onetime or current Palm Beach residents—no trip to the island is complete without gawking at the mega-mansions lining its perfectly manicured streets.

No one is more associated with how the island took shape than Addison Mizner, architect extraordinaire and society darling of the 1920s. But what people may not know is that a Fab Four was really the force behind the residential streets as they appear today: Mizner, of course, plus Maurice Fatio, Marion Sims Wyeth, and John Volk.

The four architects dabbled in different genres, some more so than others, but the unmissable style is Mediterranean Revival, a Palm Beach hallmark mix of stucco walls, Spanish red-tile roofs, Italianate towers, Moorish-Gothic carvings, and the uniquely Floridian use of coquina, a grayish porous limestone made of coral rock with fossil-like imprints of shells. As for Mizner himself, he had quite the repertoire of signature elements, including using differently sized and shaped windows on one façade, blue tilework inside and out, and tiered roof lines (instead of one straight-sloping panel across, having several sections overlap like scales on a fish).

The majority of preserved estates are clustered in three sections: along Worth Avenue; the few blocks of South County Road after crossing Worth and the streets shooting off it; and the 5-mile stretch of South Ocean Boulevard from Barton Avenue to near Phipps Ocean Park, where the condos begin cropping up.

If 10 miles of riding on a bike while cars zip around you isn't intimidating, the two-wheeled trip may be the best way to fully take in the beauty of the mansions and surrounding scenery. Many hotels have bicycles for guest use. Another option is the dependable Palm Beach Bicycle Trail Shop (☎ *561/659–4583* 🌐 *www.palmbeachbicycle.com*). Otherwise, driving is a good alternative. Just be mindful that Ocean Boulevard is a one-lane road and the only route on the island to cities like Lake Worth and Manalapan, so you can't go too slowly, especially at peak travel times.

If gossip is more your speed, in-the-know concierges rely on Leslie Diver's "Island Living Tours" (☎ *561/868–7944* 🌐 *www.islandlivingpb.com*); she's one of the town's leading experts on architecture *and* dish, both past and present.

Top 10 Self-Guided Stops: 1) Casa de Leoni, 450 Worth Avenue (Addison Mizner); 2) Villa des Cygnes, 456 Worth Avenue (Addison Mizner and Marion Sims Wyeth); 3) 17 Golfview Road (Marion Sims Wyeth); 4) 220 and 252 El Bravo Way (John Volk); 5) 126 South Ocean Boulevard (Marion Sims Wyeth); 6) El Solano, 720 South Ocean Boulevard (Addison Mizner); 7) Casa Nana, 780 South Ocean Boulevard (Addison Mizner); 8) 920 and 930 South Ocean Boulevard (Maurice Fatio); 9) Mar-a-Lago, 1100 South Ocean Boulevard (Joseph Urban); 10) Il Palmetto, 1500 South Ocean Boulevard (Maurice Fatio).

—Dorothea Hunter Sönne

Owner Donald Trump has turned it into a private membership club. ✉ *1100 S. Ocean Blvd.* ☎ *561/832–2600* 🌐 *www.maralagoclub.com.*

Society of the Four Arts. Despite widespread misconceptions of its members-only exclusivity, this privately endowed institution—founded in 1936 to encourage appreciation of art, music, drama, and literature—is funded for public enjoyment. Members do have special privileges like free admission, but anyone can enjoy the special programming that goes on here throughout the year. A gallery building artfully melds an exhibition hall that houses traveling exhibits with a 700-seat theater. A library designed by prominent Mizner-peer Maurice Fatio, a children's library, a botanical garden, and the Philip Hulitar Sculpture Garden, which underwent a major renovation in 2007, round out the facilities and are open daily. In addition to the winter art shows, the organization offers films, lectures, workshops, and concerts; a complete schedule is available on the society's website. ✉ *2 Four Arts Plaza* ☎ *561/655–7226* 🌐 *www.fourarts.org* 🎟 *$5 gallery, special program costs vary* ⏲ *Gallery, Dec.–Apr., Mon.–Sat. 10–5, Sun. 2–5; gardens, daily 10–5; children's library, weekdays 10–4:45, also Sat. 10–12:45 Nov.–Apr.*

WEST PALM BEACH

Long considered Palm Beach's less privileged stepsister, West Palm Beach has come into its own over the past 30 years, and just in this millennium the $30 million Centennial Square waterfront complex at the eastern end of Clematis Street, with piers, a pavilion, and an amphitheater, has transformed West Palm into an attractive, easy-to-walk downtown area—not to mention there's the Downtown Trolley that connects the shopping-and-entertainment mecca CityPlace with restaurant-and-lounge-lined Clematis Street. West Palm is especially well regarded for its arts scene, with unique museums and performance venues.

The city's outskirts, vast flat stretches with fast-food outlets and car dealerships, may not inspire, but are worth driving through to reach attractions scattered around the southern and western reaches. Several sites are especially rewarding for children and other animal and nature lovers.

TOP ATTRACTIONS

Ann Norton Sculpture Gardens. This landmarked complex is a testament to the creative genius of the late American sculptor Ann Weaver Norton (1905–1982), who was the second wife of Norton Museum founder, industrialist Ralph H. Norton. A set of art galleries in the studio and main house where she lived is surrounded by 2 acres of gardens with 300 species of rare palm trees, eight brick megaliths, a monumental figure in Norwegian granite, and plantings designed to attract native birds. ✉ *253 Barcelona Rd., West Palm Beach* ☎ *561/832–5328* 🌐 *www.ansg.org* 🎟 *$7* ⏲ *Wed.–Sun. 10–4. Closed Aug.*

Armory Art Center. Built by the WPA in 1939, the facility is now a nonprofit art school hosting rotating exhibitions and art classes throughout the year. ✉ *1700 Parker Ave., West Palm Beach* ☎ *561/832–1776* 🌐 *www.armoryart.org* 🎟 *Free* ⏲ *Mon.–Fri. 10–4, Sat. 10–2.*

Lion Country Safari. Drive your own vehicle along 4 miles of paved roads through a cageless zoo with free-roaming animals (chances are you'll have a giraffe nudging at your window) and then let loose in a 55-acre

The Armory Art Center in West Palm Beach helps students of all ages create works of art in various mediums.

fun-land with camel rides, bird feedings, and a pontoon-boat cruise past islands with monkeys. In total, there are just about a thousand animals in residence. A CD included with admission narrates the winding trek past white rhinos, zebras, and ostriches grouped into exhibits like Gir Forest that's modeled after a sanctuary in India and has native twisted-horned blackbuck antelope and water buffalo. (For obvious reasons, lions are fenced off, and no convertibles or pets are allowed.) Aside from dozens more up-close critter encounters after debarking, including a petting zoo, kids can go paddleboating, do a round of mini-golf, climb aboard carnival rides, or have a splash in a 4,000-square-foot aquatic playground (some extra fees apply). ⊠ *2003 Lion Country Safari Rd., at Southern Blvd. W, Loxahatchee* ☎ *561/793–1084* ⊕ *www.lioncountrysafari.com* 🎫 *$27.50, $6 parking* ⊙ *Mid-Dec.–Aug., daily 9:30–5:30 (last entry 4:30); Sept.–Dec., daily 10–5 (last entry 4).*

★ **Mounts Botanical Garden.** The oldest public green space in the county is, unbelievably, across the road from the West Palm Beach airport, but the planes are the last thing you notice while walking around and relaxing amid the nearly 14 acres of exotic trees, rain-forest flora, and butterfly and water gardens. The 2004 and 2005 hurricanes decimated the grounds, but everything is back to normal with a renewed focus on shorter, more durable plants. Feeling inspired? The main building has a lot of free brochures, and the gift shop contains a selection of rare gardening books on tropical climes. ⊠ *531 N. Military Trail, West Palm Beach* ☎ *561/233–1757* ⊕ *www.mounts.org* 🎫 *$5 (suggested donation)* ⊙ *Mon.–Sat. 8:30–4, Sun. noon–4.*

★ **National Croquet Center.** The world's largest croquet complex, the 10-acre center is also the headquarters for the U.S. Croquet Association. Vast expanses of orderly lawns are the stage for fierce competitions—in no way resembling the casual backyard games where kids play with wide wire wickets. There's also a clubhouse with a pro shop and the Croquet Grille, with verandas for dining and viewing (armchair enthusiasts can enjoy the games for no charge). You don't have to be a member to try your hand out on the lawns, and on Saturday morning there's a free group lesson with an introduction to the game, and open play; call in advance to reserve a spot. ✉ *700 Florida Mango Rd., at Summit Blvd., West Palm Beach* ☎ *561/478–2300* 🌐 *www.croquetnational.com* 🎟 *Free; full day of croquet $25* ⏲ *Tues.–Sun. 9–5.*

Fodor's Choice ★ **Norton Museum of Art.** Constructed in 1941 by steel magnate Ralph H. Norton and his wife, Elizabeth, it has grown to become one of the most impressive museums in South Florida, with an extensive collection of 19th- and 20th-century American and European paintings—including works by Picasso, Monet, Matisse, Pollock, Cassatt, and O'Keeffe—plus Chinese art, earlier European art, and photography. There is a sublime outdoor sculpture garden, a glass ceiling by Dale Chihuly, a gift shop, and a schedule of lectures, programs, and concerts for adults and children. Galleries showcase traveling exhibits, too. ■ **TIP→ One of the city's best-kept secrets is this museum's Café 1451, with its artfully presented dishes that taste as good as they look.** ✉ *1451 S. Olive Ave., West Palm Beach* ☎ *561/832–5196* 🌐 *www.norton.org* 🎟 *$12* ⏲ *Tues.–Wed. and Fri–Sat. 10–5, Thurs. 10–9, Sun. 11–5.*

WORTH NOTING

Palm Beach Photographic Centre. Local artist Fatima NeJame, who started the organization in Delray Beach in 1977, achieved her dream of a larger cultural site devoted to photography by moving into a 33,000-square-foot space in the new West Palm Beach City Hall complex in 2009. The bright, spacious museum hall showcases changing exhibits; the second floor has classrooms and a large photo studio—but with the digital age in mind, there is no darkroom. ✉ *415 Clematis St., West Palm Beach* ☎ *561/253–2600* 🌐 *www.workshop.org* 🎟 *$5 (suggested donation)* ⏲ *Mon.–Thurs. 10–6, Fri. and Sat. 10–5.*

Palm Beach Zoo. At this 23-acre wild kingdom you can admire more than 125 species of animals, from the Florida panther to the giant Aldabra tortoise—and three Malayan tigers born in 2011. A highlight is the zone that honors Central and South America with jaguars, capybaras, and tapirs, plus fantastic Mayan structures, stone sculptures, and foliage that make it seem like you're not in Florida anymore. A sizeable Australian section with koalas, emus, and wallabies is also a delight, as are the popular daily animal shows. On sweltering afternoons, kids can cool off at the large play fountain and catch a breeze on the carousel. ✉ *1301 Summit Blvd., West Palm Beach* ☎ *561/533–0887* 🌐 *www.palmbeachzoo.org* 🎟 *$18.95* ⏲ *Daily 9–5.*

Richard and Pat Johnson Palm Beach County History Museum. A beautifully restored 1916 courthouse in downtown opened its doors in 2008 as the permanent home of the Historical Society of Palm Beach County's

6

collection of artifacts and records dating back before the town's start—a highlight is furniture and decorative objects from Mizner Industries (a real treat since many of his mansions are not open to the public). ✉ *300 N. Dixie Hwy., West Palm Beach* ☎ *561/832–4164* 🌐 *www.historicalsocietypbc.org* 🎟 *Free* ⏲ *Tues.–Sat. 10–5.*

LAKE WORTH

For years, tourists looked here mainly for inexpensive lodging and easy access to Palm Beach, since a bridge leads from the mainland to a barrier island with Lake Worth's beach. Now Lake Worth has several blocks of restaurants, nightclubs, shops, and art galleries, making this a worthy destination on its own.

Museum of Polo and Hall of Fame. Start here in Lake Worth for an introduction to polo. See memorabilia, art, and a film on the history of the sport. ✉ *9011 Lake Worth Rd., Lake Worth* ☎ *561/969–3210* 🌐 *www.polomuseum.com* 🎟 *Free (donation accepted)* ⏲ *Jan.–Apr., Mon.–Fri. 10–4, Sat. 10–2; May–Dec., Mon.–Fri. 10–4.*

LANTANA

Lantana—just a bit farther south from Palm Beach than Lake Worth—has inexpensive lodging and a bridge connecting the town to its own beach on a barrier island. Tucked between Lantana and Boynton Beach is **Manalapan,** a tiny but posh residential community.

BOYNTON BEACH

In 1884, when fewer than 50 settlers lived in the area, Nathan Boynton, a Civil War veteran from Michigan, paid $25 for 500 acres with a mile-long stretch of beachfront thrown in. How things have changed, with today's population at about 118,000 and property values still on an upswing. Far enough from Palm Beach to remain low-key, Boynton Beach has two parts, the mainland and the barrier island—the town of Ocean Ridge—connected by two bridges.

Arthur R. Marshall Loxahatchee National Wildlife Refuge. The most robust part of the northern Everglades, this 221-square-mile refuge is one of two huge water-retention areas accounting for much of the River of Grass outside the national park near Miami. Start at the visitor center, which got a million-dollar face-lift in 2009 and has fantastic interactive exhibits and videos like *Night Sounds of the Everglades* and an airboat simulator. From there, you can take a marsh trail to a 20-foot-high observation tower, or stroll a ½-mile boardwalk lined with educational signage through a dense cypress swamp. There are also guided nature walks (including some specifically for bird-watching), and there's great bass fishing (bring your own poles and bait) and a 5½-mile canoe trail loop (a rental kiosk is by the fishing pier). ✉ *10216 Lee Rd., off U.S. 441 between Rte. 804 and Rte. 806, Boynton Beach* ☎ *561/734–8303* 🌐 *www.loxahatcheefriends.com* 🎟 *$5 per vehicle* ⏲ *Daily sunrise–sunset; visitor center daily 9–4.*

SINGER ISLAND

Across the inlet from the northern end of Palm Beach is Singer Island, which is actually a peninsula that's big enough to pass for a barrier island, rimmed with mom-and-pop motels and high-rises. Palm Beach Shores occupies its southern tip (where tiny Peanut Island is a stone's

The posh Palm Beach area has its share of luxury villas on the water; many are Mediterranean in style.

throw away); farther north are Riviera Beach and North Palm Beach, which also straddle the inlet and continue on the mainland.

Palm Beach Maritime Museum. You can take a guided tour of the restored "Kennedy Bunker," a bomb shelter built for President John F. Kennedy, and a historic Coast Guard station at the southern end of Peanut Island. The museum has a nice little gift shop, outdoor deck on the water, and a lawn where you can play games including horseshoes. To get there, catch a water taxi from Riviera Beach Municipal Marina (🌐 *www.peanutislandwatertaxi.com*) or Sailfish Marina (🌐 *www.sailfishmarina.com/water_taxi*). ✉ *Peanut Island, water transport only, Riviera Beach* ☎ *561/848–2960* 🌐 *www.pbmm.org* 🎟 *$12* 🕒 *Thurs.–Sun. 11–4.*

PALM BEACH GARDENS

About 15 minutes northwest of Palm Beach is this relaxed, upscale residential community known for its high-profile golf complex, the PGA National Resort & Spa. Although not on the beach, the town is less than a 15-minute drive from the ocean.

JUNO BEACH

This small town east of Palm Beach Gardens has 2 miles of shoreline that becomes home to thousands of sea turtle hatchlings each year, making it one of the world's densest nesting sites. A 990-foot-long pier lures fishermen and beachgoers seeking a spectacular sunrise.

OFF THE BEATEN PATH

Forty miles west of West Palm Beach, amid the farms and cattle pastures rimming the western edges of Palm Beach and Martin counties, is **Lake Okeechobee,** the second-largest freshwater lake completely within the United States. It is girdled by 120 miles of road yet remains shielded from sight for almost its entire circumference. Lake Okeechobee—the

Seminole's Big Water and the gateway of the great Everglades watershed—measures 730 square miles, at its longest roughly 33 miles north–south and 30 miles east–west, with an average natural depth of only 10 feet (flood control brings the figure up to 12 feet and deeper). Six major lock systems and 32 separate water-control structures manage the water. Encircling the lake is a 34-foot-high grassy levee that locals call "the wall," and the Lake Okeechobee Scenic Trail, a segment of the Florida National Scenic Trail that is an easy, flat ride for bikers. Anglers have a field day here as well, with great bass and perch catches. *See Fodors.com for more information on Lake Okeechobee.* ■ **TIP➔ There's no shade, so wear a hat, sunscreen, and bug repellent. Be sure to bring lots of bottled water, too, because restaurants and stores are few and far between.**

BEACHES

PALM BEACH

Clarke Avenue Beach. Swarms of surfers have co-opted these choppy tides almost immediately south of The Breakers' private beach club. It's somewhat amusing to witness the throng of boards in and out of the water, given the posh and polished reputation of this town, but the waves crest at a predictable spot, and 25 free two-hour parking spots are within a quarter-mile radius. The lack of basic facilities that deters most other visitors works in the riders' favor, letting them hang ten with no worries. **Amenities:** none. **Best for:** surfing. ✉ *S. Ocean Blvd. at Clarke Ave., Palm Beach* ⏲ *Daily 8–6.*

Mid-Town Beach. You know you're here if the Worth Avenue clock tower is within sight, but the gateways to the sand are actually on Chilean Avenue, Brazilian Avenue, and Gulfstream Road. It's definitely the most central and longest lifeguarded strip open to everyone and a popular choice for hotel guests from the Colony and Chesterfield. It's also BYOC (bring your own chair). You'll find no water-sport or food vendors here; however, casual eateries are a quick walk away. Free and metered street-parking spots are close by, and the town hopes to have public restrooms on the shore by 2013. **Amenities:** lifeguards; showers. **Best for:** swimming; sunsets. ✉ *S. Ocean Blvd. at Chilean Ave., Palm Beach* ⏲ *Daily 8–8.*

Phipps Ocean Park. About 2 miles south of "Billionaire's Row" on Ocean Boulevard sits the only public seaside park run by the town of Palm Beach, with two metered parking lots separated by a fire station. The north side is better for beachgoers, as there is a six-court tennis facility at the southern entrance. The beach itself is narrow and has natural rock formations dotting the shoreline. There are picnic tables and grills on-site, as well as the Little Red Schoolhouse, an 1886 landmark that hosts educational workshops for local kids. If a long walk floats your boat, venture north to see the mega-mansions, but don't go too far inland, because private property starts just a few feet from the surf. **Amenities:** parking (fee); toilets; showers; lifeguards. **Best for:** walking; solitude. ✉ *2185 S. Ocean Blvd.* ☎ *561/227–6450 (for tennis reservations)* 🎟 *$5 per hr parking* ⏲ *Daily 8–sunset.*

LAKE WORTH

Lake Worth Beach. Opening a new chapter on waterfront entertainment, Lake Worth's "casino" (not the craps and poker kind, but a retail promenade) is scheduled to debut in late 2012, with two restaurants, a surf shop, an ice cream shop, and more. This is particularly good news for Omphoy and Four Seasons guests, who are steps away; Sabal Palm House is close by too, and the Ritz is 2 miles down the coast. The beach is already buzzing, with an Olympic-size swimming pool, a fishing pier, and the always-packed luncheonette Benny's (there are plans to keep the joint jumping until midnight on weekdays and 1 am on weekends once the casino rolls out). **Amenities:** water sports; food and drink; lifeguards; parking; showers; toilets. **Best for:** partyers; sunsets; swimming. ✉ *10 Ocean Blvd., at A1A and Lake Ave., Lake Worth* *$1 to enter pier, $3 to enter and fish, $2 per hr for parking.*

LANTANA

Lantana Public Beach. Ideal for sprawling, beachcombing, or power-walking, this sandy stretch is also noteworthy for a casual restaurant, the breezy Dune Deck Café, that's perched above the waterline and offers great views. The beach's huge parking lot is directly up from the Ritz-Carlton on Ocean Boulevard, and diagonally across the street is a sizeable strip mall with all sorts of conveniences, including more eateries. **Amenities:** parking; food and drink; lifeguards; showers; toilets. **Best for:** swimming; walking. ✉ *100 N. Ocean Ave., Lantana* *$1.50 per hr for parking.*

6

SINGER ISLAND

John D. MacArthur Beach State Park. If getting far from rowdy crowds is your goal, this spot on the north end of Singer Island is a good choice. Encompassing 2 miles of beach and a lush subtropical coastal habitat, inside you'll find a great place for kayaking, snorkeling at natural reefs, bird-watching, fishing, and hiking. A 4,000-square-foot nature center renovated in 2011 has aquariums and displays on local flora and fauna, and there's a long roster of monthy activities, such as surfing clinics, art lessons, and live bluegrass music. Guided sea turtle walks are available at night in season, and daily nature walks depart at 10 am. Check the website for times and costs of activities. **Amenities:** water sports; parking (fee); toilets; showers. **Best for:** swimming; walking; solitude; surfing. ✉ *10900 Jack Nicklaus Dr., North Palm Beach* ☎ *561/624–6950* 🌐 *www.macarthurbeach.org* *Parking $5, bicyclists and pedestrians $2* ⏲ *Park daily 8–sunset; nature center and gift shop daily 9–5.*

Peanut Island Park. Partyers, families, and overnight campers all have a place to go on the 79 acres here. The island, in a wide section of the Intracoastal between Palm Beach Island and Singer Island with an open channel to the sea, is accessible only by private boat or water taxi, two of which set sail regularly from the Riviera Beach Municipal Marina (*www.peanutislandwatertaxi.com*) and the Sailfish Marina (🌐 *www.sailfishmarina.com/water_taxi*). Fun-loving seafarers looking for an afternoon of Jimmy Buffett and brewskis pull up to the day docks or the huge sandbar on the north—float around in an inner tube, and it's spring break déjà vu. Walk along the 20-foot-wide paver-lined path encircling the island, and you'll hit a 170-foot fishing pier, a campground, the lifeguarded section to the south that is particularly popular with families because of its artificial reef, and last but not least, the Palm Beach Maritime Museum's "Kennedy Bunker" (a bomb shelter prepared for President John F. Kennedy that was restored and opened to the public in 1999). There are picnic tables and grills, but no concessions. **Amenities:** lifeguards (summer only); toilets; showers. **Best for:** partyers; walking; swimming; sunrise. ✉ *6500 Peanut Island Rd. (water transport only), Riviera Beach* ☎ *561/845–4445* 🌐 *www.pbcsplash.com* 🎫 *Beach free, water taxi $10.*

JUNO BEACH

Juno Beach Park. An angler's dream, this beach has a 990-foot pier that's open daily, like the beach, from sunrise to sunset—but from November through February the gates open at 6 am and don't close until 10 pm on weeknights and midnight on weekends, making it an awesome place to catch a full sunrise and sunset (that is, if you don't mind paying the small admission fee). A concession stand on the pier sells fish food as well as such human favorites as burgers, sandwiches, and ice cream. Families plant themselves on the somewhat narrow shoreline because of the amenities and vibrant atmosphere. Just be careful not to step on any sand castles! **Amenities:** lifeguards; food and drink; parking (free); showers; toilets. **Best for:** sunrise; sunset; swimming. ✉ *14775 S. U.S. 1, Juno Beach* ☎ *561/799–0185 for pier* 🌐 *www.pbcsplash.com* 🎫 *$4 to fish, $1 to enter pier* 🕑 *Daily sunrise–sunset; Nov.–Feb., 6 am–10 pm (until midnight on weekends).*

WHERE TO EAT

PALM BEACH

$$$ ECLECTIC Fodor's Choice ★

✕ **bûccan.** Lanterns cast a soft glow as young bluebloods rocking D&G jeans slip into tightly packed copper-topped tables alongside groups of silver-haired oil scions. It's island casual in its trendiest, most boisterous, yet still refined incarnation, with a menu to match. Chef-owner Clay Conley's small plates to share (wood-fired wild mushroom pizza with black truffle vinaigrette) with unfussy presentations (house-made squid-ink orecchiette stewed with sausage and chilies in a mini–Le Creuset cocotte) and inventive, sophisticated flavor combinations and textures (hamachi sashimi with mojo and crisped lotus root) make this the place to see and be seen—and the best-tasting meal at a price more expected of the mainland. 💲 *Average main: $23* ✉ *350 S. County Rd., Palm Beach* ☎ *561/833–3450* 🌐 *www.buccanpalmbeach.com.*

$$$$ FRENCH Fodor's Choice ★

✕ **Café Boulud.** Celebrated chef Daniel Boulud opened this outpost of Café Boulud in the Brazilian Court hotel. The warm and welcoming French-American venue is casual yet elegant, with a palette of honey, gold, and citron. Plenty of natural light spills through arched glass doors opening to a lush courtyard that's just the place to be on a warm evening. Lunch and dinner entrées on Boulud's signature four-section menu include classic French, seasonal, vegetarian, and a rotating roster of international dishes. The lounge, with its illuminated amber glass bar, is the perfect perch to take in the jet-set crowd that comes for a hint of the south of France in South Florida. $ *Average main: $38* ✉ *The Brazilian Court Hotel & Beach Club, 301 Australian Ave.* ☎ *561/655–6060* 🌐 *www.cafeboulud.com* ✍ *Reservations essential.*

$$$$ ECLECTIC ★ ✕ **Café L'Europe.** Since 1980, the favorite spot of society's movers and shakers has remained a regular stop on foodie itineraries. The management pays close attention to service and consistency, a big reason for its longevity. Best sellers include Dover sole and Wiener schnitzel, along with such inspired creations as crispy sweetbreads with poached pears and mustard sauce. Depending on your mood, the champagne-caviar bar can serve up appetizers or desserts. The place has an extensive, award-winning wine list with many by-the-glass options. A pianist plays nightly from 7 till close, and the lively crowd gracefully sways to the music. $ *Average main: $43* ✉ *331 S. County Rd.* ☎ *561/655–4020* 🌐 *www.cafeleurope.com* ✍ *Reservations essential* ⏲ *No lunch Sat.–Tues. Closed Mon. June–Nov.*

$$$$ FRENCH Fodor's Choice ★ ✕ **Chez Jean-Pierre.** With walls adorned with avant garde Dalí- and Picasso-like art, this bistro is where the Palm Beach old guard likes to let down its hair, all the while partaking of sumptuous French cuisine and an impressive wine selection. Forget calorie or cholesterol concerns and indulge in scrambled eggs with caviar or homemade foie gras, along with desserts like frozen hazelnut soufflé or profiteroles au chocolat. Jackets are not required, although many men wear them. The main entrance is through a courtyard in the back. $ *Average main: $39* ✉ *132 N. County Rd.* ☎ *561/833–1171* 🌐 *www.chezjean-pierre.com* ✍ *Reservations essential* ⏲ *Closed Sun. No lunch.*

$$ PIZZA ✕ **Pizza Al Fresco.** The secret-garden setting is the secret to the success of this European-style pizzeria, where you can dine under a canopy of century-old banyans in an intimate courtyard. Specialties are 12-inch hand-tossed brick-oven pizzas with such interesting toppings as prosciutto, arugula, and caviar. There's even a breakfast pizza (part of a small morning menu) and a Nutella dessert pizza. Piping-hot calzones, salads, and baked pastas round out the choices. Next to the patio, look for the grave markers of Addison Mizner's beloved pet monkey, Johnnie Brown, and Rose Sachs's dog, Laddie (she and husband Morton bought Mizner's villa and lived there 47 years). Delivery is available. This bistro is dog-friendly. $ *Average main: $19* ✉ *14 Via Mizner, at Worth Ave.* ☎ *561/832–0032* 🌐 *www.pizzaalfresco.com.*

$$$ AMERICAN ★ ✕ **Ta-boo.** This landmark, which has been in business since 1941, with peach stucco walls, green shutters, and funky jungle accents, attracts Worth Avenue shoppers looking for a two-hour lunch and a dinner crowd ranging from tuxed-and-sequined theatergoers to polo-shirted vacationers. Entrées include super-prime Akaushi dry-aged beef with scalloped potatoes, and rotisserie duck with Asian vegetables and jasmine rice. Don't miss the signature Ta-boo Lust dessert, a coconut cream pie with a walnut cookie crust. Drop in late at night during the winter season when the music is playing, and you'll probably spot a celebrity or two. $ *Average main: $30* ✉ *221 Worth Ave.* ☎ *561/835–3500* 🌐 *www.taboorestaurant.com.*

WEST PALM BEACH

$ CUBAN ✕ **Havana.** Decorated with vintage travel posters of its namesake city, this two-level restaurant serves such authentic Cuban specialties as roast-pork sandwiches and chicken slowly cooked in Spanish sauce. Lunch and dinner dishes are enhanced by the requisite black beans and rice. Open until 1 am Friday and Saturday, this friendly place attracts a late-night crowd. The popular walk-up window serves strong Cuban coffee, sugary fried churros, and fruit juices in exotic flavors like mamey, mango, papaya, guava, and guanabana. *Average main: $10 ✉ 6801 S. Dixie Hwy., West Palm Beach ☎ 561/547–9799 ⊕ www.havanacubanfood.com.*

$ AMERICAN ✕ **Howley's.** Since 1950 this diner's eat-in counter and "cooked in sight, it must be right" motto have made it a congenial setting for meeting old friends and making new ones. Forgo the counter for the retro tables or sit out on the covered patio. The café attracts a loyal clientele during breakfast, lunch, dinner, and into the wee hours (it's open weekdays until 2 am and weekends until 5 am and has a full bar) with such dishes as turkey potpie, burgers, chicken salad, and country-fried steak. *Average main: $13 ✉ 4700 S. Dixie Hwy., West Palm Beach ☎ 561/833–5691 ⊕ www.sub-culture.org.*

$$$ ITALIAN ✕ **Il Bellagio.** In the heart of CityPlace, this European-style eatery offers Italian specialties and a wide variety of fine wines. The menu includes classics like chicken parmigiana, risotto, and fettuccine Alfredo. Pizzas from the wood-burning oven are especially tasty. Service is friendly and efficient, but the overall noise level tends to be high. Sit at the outdoor tables next to the main plaza's dancing fountains. *Average main: $21 ✉ CityPlace, 600 S. Rosemary Ave., West Palm Beach ☎ 561/659–6160 ⊕ www.ilbellagiocityplace.com.*

$ MEDITERRANEAN ✕ **Middle East Bakery.** This hole-in-the-wall Middle Eastern bakery, deli, and market is packed at lunchtime with regulars who are on a first-name basis with the gang behind the counter. From the nondescript parking lot the place doesn't look like much, but inside, delicious hot and cold Mediterranean treats await. Choose from traditional gyro sandwiches and lamb salads with sides of grape leaves, tabbouleh, and couscous. There's a big takeout business, as seating is limited, and it closes shop at 6 pm (4:30 pm on Saturdays). *Average main: $10 ✉ 327 5th St., West Palm Beach ☎ 561/659–7322 ⊙ Closed Sun.*

$$$ ✕ **Pistache.** Although "the island" is no doubt a bastion of French cuisine, this cozy bistro across Lake Worth on the Clematis Street waterfront entices a lively crowd looking for a good meal with pretention checked at the door. The outdoor terrace can't be beat, and hearty classics with slight twists, such as roasted sliced duck with lingonberry sauce rather than the ubiquitous *à l'orange,* are a delight. Save room for dessert: the house-made pudding Breton, a fluffy, raisin-accented brioche bread pudding paired with vanilla ice cream, could be straight out of a Parisian café. *Average main: $23 ✉ 101 N. Clematis St., West Palm Beach ☎ 561/833–5090 ⊕ www.pistachewpb.com.*

$$$$ AMERICAN ✕ **Top of the Point.** As you walk through a 1980s-era office tower at the foot of Royal Park Bridge, you may half expect Gordon Gekko to pop out. This trepidation belies what awaits at the penthouse: spacious

and somehow intimate, the dining room's floor-to-ceiling windows and adjacent observation deck offer gorgeous panoramic views. The menu, modern American with a focus on meats and seafood, has winners like cress salad with roasted beets, marcona almonds, and pomegranate vinaigrette; locally caught snapper with citrus-marinated lump crabmeat; and flourless chocolate cake with refreshing peppermint gelato. Service can lag, but that gives you more reason to sit back and take in the boats dotting the Intracoastal Waterway, The Breakers' iconic twin spires, and the ocean beyond. *Average main: $39 ✉ 777 S. Flagler Dr., Club Level, Palm Beach ☎ 561/832–2710 🌐 www.topofthepoint.com ⏲ Closed Sun. No lunch.*

LAKE WORTH

$ AMERICAN

Benny's on the Beach. Perched on the Lake Worth Pier, Benny's has diner-style food that's cheap and filling, but the spectacular view of the sun glistening on the water and the waves crashing directly below is what dining here is all about. Get here early—it doesn't serve dinner. *Average main: $10 ✉ 10 Ocean Ave., Lake Worth ☎ 561/582–9001 🌐 www.bennysonthebeach.com ⏲ No dinner.*

$$$$ ITALIAN

Paradiso. Arguably downtown Lake Worth's finest restaurant, with sophisticated modern northern Italian cuisine, this is a go-to place for a romantic evening. Veal chops, seafood, ravioli, and risotto are all excellent choices. Don't miss the chocolate Grand Marnier soufflé for dessert. As the name implies, the food is heavenly. *Average main: $40 ✉ 625 Lucerne Ave., Lake Worth ☎ 561/547–2500 🌐 www.paradisolakeworth.com.*

LANTANA

$$ SEAFOOD

Old Key Lime House. An informal seafood spot covered by a chickee-hut roof built by Seminole Indians, it's perched on the Intracoastal Waterway and is open and airy, with observation decks that wrap around the back. In 1889 the Lyman family, some of the earliest settlers in Lantana, built this as their house, and it has grown over the years into the popular island-style eatery it is today. Aside from being the largest viewing base for Gator football, the main appeal here for adults is the panoramic water view, and kids love feeding the fish below. Of course, order the namesake key lime pie—the house specialty has been featured in *Bon Appétit*. *Average main: $20 ✉ 300 E. Ocean Ave., Lantana ☎ 561/582–1889 🌐 www.oldkeylimehouse.com.*

SINGER ISLAND

$$$ SEAFOOD

Sailfish Marina Restaurant. This lively waterfront restaurant overlooking Peanut Island is a great place to chill out after a long day of mansion gawking, boating, or beach-bumming. Choose a table in the dining room or under an umbrella on the terrace and enjoy mainstays like conch chowder and coconut shrimp. More upscale entrées—this, after all, is still Palm Beach County—include Florida lobster tail and sautéed yellowtail snapper. Breakfast is a winner here, too. Sportfishing charters are available at the Sailfish store. *Average main: $24 ✉ 98 Lake Dr., Palm Beach Shores ☎ 561/844–1724 🌐 www.sailfishmarina.com.*

PALM BEACH GARDENS

$$$$ AMERICAN ★ **Café Chardonnay.** At the end of a strip mall, Café Chardonnay is surprisingly elegant and has some of the most refined food in the suburban town of Palm Beach Gardens. Soft lighting, warm woods, white tablecloths, and cozy banquettes set the scene for a quiet lunch or romantic dinner. The place consistently receives praise for its innovative, continually changing menu and outstanding wine list. Starters can include wild-mushroom strudel and truffle-stuffed diver sea scallops. Entrées might be Gorgonzola-crusted filet mignon or pan-seared veal scaloppine with rock shrimp. *Average main: $34 4533 PGA Blvd., Palm Beach Gardens 561/627–2662 www.cafechardonnay.com No lunch weekends.*

$$$$ STEAKHOUSE **Ironwood Steak & Seafood.** Located in the PGA National Resort & Spa, this eatery draws guests, locals, and tourists alike eager for a taste of its fired-up Vulcan steaks (Vulcan to meat-eaters is like Titelist to golfers—the best equipment around). The she-crab soup with sherry is a favorite from the sea, as are the raw bar items, like Middleneck clams and tuna tartare. Bright red banquettes, slate-tile walls, private rooms, and an impressive glass-walled wine cellar create a relaxed, contemporary setting that spills out onto the equally chic adjoining lobby bar, which becomes quite the scene on weekend nights when a DJ spins. *Average main: $38 PGA National Resort & Spa, 400 Ave. of the Champions, Palm Beach Gardens 561/627–4852 www.ironwoodgrille.com.*

$$$ SEAFOOD **Spoto's Oyster Bar.** If you love oysters and other raw bar nibbles, head here where black-and-white photographs of oyster fisherman adorn the walls. The polished tables give the eatery a clubby look. Spoto's serves up a delightful bowl of New England clam chowder and a truly impressive variety of oysters and clams. The Caesar salad with crispy croutons and anchovies never disappoints. Sit outside on the patio to take advantage of the area's perfect weather. *Average main: $26 PGA Commons, 4560 PGA Blvd., Palm Beach Gardens 561/776–9448 www.spotosoysterbar.com.*

WHERE TO STAY

For expanded reviews, facilities, and current deals, visit Fodors.com.

PALM BEACH

$$$$ HOTEL ★ **The Brazilian Court Hotel & Beach Club.** This posh boutique hotel's yellow façade, dramatic white-draped entry, red-tile roof, and lobby with cypress ceilings underscore its Roaring '20s origins, and modern touches like plush rooms and access to a shared oceanfront facility at the sleek Omphoy Resort (plus being a short stroll from Worth Avenue) present guests with the best of both worlds. **Pros:** Café Boulud is one of the best restaurants in town; attracts a hip crowd; gorgeous, charming courtyard; free beach shuttle. **Cons:** fitness center is tiny; nondescript pool; 10-minute ride to ocean with suggested 24-hour advance reservation. **TripAdvisor:** "fantastic food," "a great place to get away," "gracious rooms." *Rooms from: $499 301 Australian Ave. 561/655–7740 www.thebraziliancourt.com 80 rooms No meals.*

$$$$ RESORT Fodor's Choice ★ **The Breakers Palm Beach.** More than an opulent hotel, the Breakers is a 140-acre self-contained jewel of a resort built in an Italian Renaissance style and loaded with amenities, from a 20,000-square-foot luxury spa and grandiose beach club to 10 tennis courts and two 18-hole golf courses—not to mention Henry Flagler's heirs still run the place and invest $20 million a year to keep it at the cutting edge. **Pros:** fine attention to detail throughout with fantastic service; beautiful room views; extensive activities for families; 10 restaurants. **Cons:** big price tag; short drive to reach off-property attractions. **TripAdvisor:** "great location and amenities," "perfection even before you arrive," "worth every penny." *Rooms from: $539 1 S. County Rd. 561/655–6611, 888/273–2537 www.thebreakers.com 608 rooms No meals.*

$$$$ HOTEL **The Chesterfield Palm Beach.** A distinctly upper-crust northern European feel pervades the peach stucco walls and elegant rooms here; the hotel sits just north of the western end of Worth Avenue, and high tea, a cigar parlor, and daily turndown service recall a bygone, more refined era. **Pros:** gracious, attentive staff; nightly live entertainment in the Leopard Lounge; most room windows open, which is a treat for those who hate air-conditioning; free Wi-Fi and valet parking. **Cons:** long walk to beach; only one elevator; to some, can come off as a bit stuffy. **TripAdvisor:** "the gem of Palm Beach," "exceptional service and food," "a top notch experience." *Rooms from: $389 363 Cocoanut Row 561/659–5800, 800/243–7871 www.chesterfieldpb.com 53 rooms No meals.*

$$$$ HOTEL **The Colony.** This legendary British colonial-style hotel has sunny rooms, suites, and villas with traditional furnishings and a slight Caribbean flair in a particularly convenient location, just one block from Worth Avenue and one block from a pretty beach on the Atlantic Ocean. **Pros:** unbeatable location; classy in-house dinner cabaret; luxe touches like pillow-top mattresses abound; full English breakfast included. **Cons:** lobby is small; elevators are tight; price tag is high. **TripAdvisor:** "amazing," "a bastion of civilization," "best Easter brunch on the island." *Rooms from: $440 155 Hammon Ave. 561/655–5430, 800/521–5525 www.thecolonypalmbeach.com 90 rooms Breakfast.*

$$$$ RESORT ★ **Four Seasons Resort Palm Beach.** Couples and families seeking relaxed seaside elegance in a ritzy, yet understated, setting will love this manicured 6-acre oceanfront escape at the south end of Palm Beach, with serene, bright, airy rooms in a cream-colored palette and spacious marble-lined baths. **Pros:** accommodating service; all rooms have balconies; outstanding complimentary kids' program; pampering spa that also caters to men. **Cons:** 10-minute drive to downtown (but can walk to Lake Worth); pricey. **TripAdvisor:** "superb," "amazing experience," "wonderful service." *Rooms from: $499 2800 S. Ocean Blvd. 561/582–2800, 800/432–2335 www.fourseasons.com 210 rooms No meals.*

$$$$ RESORT **The Omphoy Ocean Resort.** From the monumental entrance and the lobby's exotic ebony pillars to a lounge with Balinese art and a pool table to the bronze-infused porcelain tile floors, this Zen-like boutique hotel has a sexy, sophisticated look and a loyal following with

6

young, hip travelers. **Pros:** most rooms have beautiful views of the private beach; ultra-contemporary vibe and luxury setting; an intimate Michelle Bernstein restaurant. **Cons:** a hike from shopping and nightlife; although itself pretty, the infinity pool is surrounded by a parking lot and you have to cross the driveway to reach it. **TripAdvisor:** "romantic getaway," "my new favorite staycation location," "a hidden gem." *Rooms from: $425 ✉ 2842 S. Ocean Blvd. ☎ 561/540–6440, 888/344–4321 www.omphoy.com 144 rooms No meals.*

WEST PALM BEACH

$$$ B&B/INN ★ **Grandview Gardens Bed & Breakfast and Vacation Homes.** The 1925 Mediterranean Revival main building with rooms that overlook a courtyard pool and its two adjacent cottages (available for weekly rental) are conveniently located next to Howard Park, across from the Armory Art Center and a short walk from the Convention Center, CityPlace, and the Kravis Center. **Pros:** multilingual owners; outside private entrances to rooms; innkeepers offer historic city tours. **Cons:** not close to the beach; steps to climb. **TripAdvisor:** "elegant," "best hospitality in WPB," "great people." *Rooms from: $199 ✉ 1608 Lake Ave., West Palm Beach ☎ 561/833–9023 www.grandview-gardens.com 5 rooms, 1 cottage Breakfast.*

$$$ HOTEL **Hampton Inn & Suites Wellington.** The four-story hotel, about 10 miles west of downtown—and the only hotel near the polo fields in the equestrian mecca of Wellington—takes cues from its surroundings and has the feeling of a tony clubhouse, with rich wood paneling, hunt prints, and elegant chandeliers. **Pros:** complimentary hot breakfast; free Wi-Fi; outdoor swimming pool; close to a large shopping center. **Cons:** no restaurant; Intracoastal Waterway is a 30-minute drive, and beach is farther. **TripAdvisor:** "very comfortable," "great beds," "nice place and location." *Rooms from: $219 ✉ 2155 Wellington Green Dr., West Palm Beach ☎ 561/472–9696 hamptoninn3.hilton.com 154 rooms Breakfast.*

$$ HOTEL **Hotel Biba.** In the El Cid historic district, this 1940s-era motel has gotten a fun stylish revamp from designer Barbara Hulanicki: each room has a vibrant mélange of colors, along with handcrafted mirrors, mosaic bathroom floors, and custom mahogany furnishings. **Pros:** great rates, especially on weekends; cool, punchy design and luxe fixtures; popular wine bar; free continental breakfast with Cuban pastries. **Cons:** water pressure is weak; bathrooms are tiny; noisy when the bar is open late. **TripAdvisor:** "too cool," "cute and charming," "old lady with character." *Rooms from: $119 ✉ 320 Belvedere Rd., West Palm Beach ☎ 561/832–0094 www.hotelbiba.com 43 rooms Breakfast.*

LAKE WORTH

$$$ B&B/INN ★ **Sabal Palm House.** Built in 1936, this romantic, two-story B&B is a short walk from Lake Worth's downtown shops, eateries, and the Intracoastal Waterway, and each room is decorated with antiques and inspired by a different artist, including Renoir, Dalí, Norman Rockwell, and Chagall. **Pros:** on quiet street; hands-on owners have a wealth of information on local sights; chairs and totes with towels provided for use at nearby beach; whirlpool tubs in some rooms. **Cons:** no pool;

peak times require a two-night minimum stay; no parking lot. **TripAdvisor:** "relaxing," "very pleasant," "off the beaten path." *Rooms from: $145* *109 N. Golfview Rd., Lake Worth* *561/582–1090, 888/722–2572* *www.sabalpalmhouse.com* *7 rooms* *Breakfast.*

LANTANA

$$$$ RESORT ★ **The Ritz-Carlton, Palm Beach.** A $130 million transformation has made this classic hotel in the coastal town of Manalapan into a sublime, glamorous destination resort by adding a 3,000-square-foot oceanfront terrace, a second pool, a huge fitness center, and a deluxe spa; the common areas also got a face-lift with richly upholstered furnishings in more contemporary, beachy patterns. **Pros:** magnificent aesthetic details throughout; indulgent pampering services; excellent on-site dining; kids love the cool cyber-lounge just for them. **Cons:** golf course is off property; 15-minute drive to Palm Beach. **TripAdvisor:** "beautiful setting," "great service," "simply breathtaking." *Rooms from: $399* *100 S. Ocean Blvd., Manalapan* *561/533–6000, 800/241–3333* *www.ritz-carlton.com* *310 rooms* *No meals.*

SINGER ISLAND

$$$$ RESORT **Palm Beach Marriott Singer Island Beach Resort & Spa.** Families with a yen for the cosmopolitan but requiring the square footage and comforts of home revel in these spacious marble-tiled, granite-topped, Kitchen Aid–outfitted condos; couples wanting a private beach without the same level of sticker shock or bustle found 10 minutes to the south also appreciate the infinity pool and quiet sundeck. **Pros:** on one of the widest stretches of sand in Palm Beach County; genuinely warm service; plenty of kids' activities, and one pool has a waterslide; sleek spa. **Cons:** no upscale dining or shopping within walking distance; unspectacular room views for an ocean-side hotel; an empty lot next door will likely be undergoing construction. **TripAdvisor:** "peaceful location to explore," "loved the accommodations," "staff was outstanding." *Rooms from: $269* *3800 N. Ocean Dr., Singer Island, Riviera Beach* *561/340–1700, 877/239–5610* *www.marriott.com* *189 suites* *No meals.*

$$ HOTEL **Sailfish Marina Resort.** A marina with deepwater slips—and prime location at the mouth to the Atlantic Ocean on the Intracoastal Waterway across from Peanut Island—lures boaters and anglers here to the perfectly nice but somewhat basic rooms, studios, and efficiencies. **Pros:** inexpensive rates; great waterfront restaurant; has a water taxi; pretty grounds. **Cons:** no real lobby; not directly on beach; area attracts a party crowd and can be noisy; dated decor. **TripAdvisor:** "very accommodating," "good concept," "loved it." *Rooms from: $115* *98 Lake Dr., Palm Beach Shores* *561/844–1724, 800/446–4577* *www.sailfishmarina.com* *30 units* *No meals.*

PALM BEACH GARDENS

$$$$ RESORT ★ **PGA National Resort & Spa.** A soup-to-nuts renovation completed in 2012 has elevated this golfer's paradise (five championship courses and the site of the yearly Honda Classic pro-tour tournament) from its Caddyshack-style beginnings to a sleek modern playground with a gorgeous zero-entry lagoon pool, seven different places to eat, and a full-service spa with unique mineral-salt therapy pools. **Pros:** dream golf

6

facilities; affordable rates for top-notch amenities; close to shopping malls. **Cons:** no beach shuttle; difficult to get around if you don't have a car; long drive to Palm Beach proper. **TripAdvisor:** "staff was phenomenal," "relaxing," "so kind and helpful." *Rooms from: $229 ✉ 400 Ave. of the Champions, Palm Beach Gardens ☎ 561/627–2000, 800/633–9150 ⊕ www.pgaresort.com ⇨ 280 rooms, 59 suites ǀ○ǀ No meals.*

NIGHTLIFE AND THE ARTS

PALM BEACH

NIGHTLIFE

Palm Beach is teeming with restaurants that turn into late-night hot spots, plus hotel lobby bars perfect for tête-à-têtes.

bûccan. A hip Hamptons-esque scene with society darlings crowds the lounge, throwing back killer cocktails like the Basil Rathbone. Don't miss the Friday-night DJ. *✉ 350 S. County Rd., Palm Beach ☎ 561/833–3450 ⊕ www.buccanpalmbeach.com.*

Cucina Dell' Arte. Though this spot is popular for lunch and dinner, the younger trendier set comes late to dance and mingle. *✉ 257 Royal Poinciana Way ☎ 561/655–0770 ⊕ www.cucinadellarte.com.*

The Leopard Lounge. The old guard gathers here for melodic live music and to dance until the wee hours; this cat's spots are even shinier now with new exotic, glam decor. *✉ Chesterfield Hotel, 363 Cocoanut Row ☎ 561/659–5800 ⊕ www.chesterfieldpb.com.*

WEST PALM BEACH

NIGHTLIFE

West Palm is known for its exuberant nightlife—Clematis Street and CityPlace are the prime party destinations. In fact, downtown rocks every Thursday from 6 pm on with Clematis by Night, a celebration of music, dance, art, and food at Centennial Square.

Blue Martini. CityPlace comes alive at this bar, where eclectic music and a mix of DJs and live bands attract a diverse crowd. *✉ 550 S. Rosemary Ave., #244, West Palm Beach ☎ 561/835–8601.*

Feelgoods. There are guitars hanging from the ceiling and a DJ booth made of a 1957 Chevy at this club, and Vince Neil, Mötley Crüe's lead singer, is a partner. *✉ 219 Clematis St., West Palm Beach ☎ 561/833–6500 ⊕ www.feelgoodswestpalm.com.*

ER Bradley's Saloon. People of all ages congregate to hang out and socialize at this open-air restaurant and bar to gaze at the Intracoastal Waterway; the mechanical bull is a hit on Saturdays. *✉ 104 Clematis St., West Palm Beach ☎ 561/833–3520 ⊕ www.erbradleys.com.*

Rocco's Tacos. Get your party started here with more than 220 choices of tequila and seriously good Mexican food. *✉ 224 Clematis St., West Palm Beach ☎ 561/650–1001 ⊕ www.roccostacos.com.*

THE ARTS

Palm Beach Dramaworks. After a stunning transformation of their home, the company reopened doors November 2011 to an intimate venue with only 218 seats; their modus operandi is "theater to think about" with plays by Pulitzer Prize winners like Arthur Miller and Eugene O'Neill on rotation. ✉ *201 Clematis St., West Palm Beach* ☎ *561/514–4042* 🌐 *www.palmbeachdramaworks.org.*

Palm Beach Opera. The organization celebrated its 50th anniversary with the 2011–2012 season. Five productions, including the Grand Finals Concert of its yearly vocal competition, are staged from December to April at the Kravis Center with English translations projected above the stage. There's an annual family opera weekend matinee performance, such as *Romeo and Juliet.* Tickets start at $20 and can be purchased at either the company's administrative offices or at the Kravis Center. ✉ *415 S. Olive Ave., administrative office, West Palm Beach* ☎ *561/833–7888* 🌐 *www.pbopera.org.*

★ **Raymond F. Kravis Center for the Performing Arts.** This is the crown jewel amid a treasury of local arts attractions, and its marquee star is the 2,195-seat Dreyfoos Hall, a glass, copper, and marble showcase just steps from the restaurants and shops of CityPlace. The center also boasts the 289-seat Rinker Playhouse, 170-seat Persson Hall, and the Gosman Amphitheatre, which holds 1,400 total in seats and on the lawn. A packed year-round schedule features a blockbuster lineup of Broadway's biggest touring productions, concerts, dance, dramas, and musicals; Miami City Ballet and the Palm Beach Pops perform here. ✉ *701 Okeechobee Blvd., West Palm Beach* ☎ *561/832–7469* 🌐 *www.kravis.org.*

6

SHOPPING

As is the case throughout Florida, many of the smaller boutiques in Palm Beach close in the summer, and most stores are closed on Sunday. Consignment stores in Palm Beach are definitely worth a look; you'll often find high-end designer clothing in impeccable condition.

PALM BEACH

SHOPPING AREAS

Royal Poinciana Way. Cute shops like resort-wear favorite Joy of Palm Beach dot the north side of Royal Poinciana Way between Bradley Place and North County Road. Wind through the courtyards past upscale consignment stores to Sunset Avenue, then stroll down Sunrise Avenue: this is the place for specialty items like out-of-town newspapers, health foods, and books. ✉ *Worth Ave., between Bradley Pl. and N. County Rd.*

South County Road. The six blocks of South Country Road north of Worth Avenue have interesting and somewhat less expensive stores. ✉ *South County Rd., between Seaspray Ave. and Worth Ave.*

★ **Worth Avenue.** One of the world's premier showcases for high-quality shopping runs half a mile from east to west across Palm Beach, from the beach to Lake Worth. The street has more than 200 shops (more than 40 of them sell jewelry), and many upscale chain stores (Gucci, Hermès, Pucci, Saks Fifth Avenue, Neiman Marcus, Louis Vuitton, Chanel, Cartier, Tiffany & Co., and Tourneau) are represented—their merchandise appealing to the discerning tastes of the Palm Beach clientele. Don't miss walking around the vias, little courtyards lined with smaller boutiques; historic tours are available each month from the Worth Avenue Association. ✉ *Worth Ave., between Cocoanut Row and S. Ocean Blvd.* 🌐 *www.worth-avenue.com.*

RECOMMENDED STORES

The Church Mouse. Many high-end resale boutique owners grab their merchandise at this thrift store. ✉ *378 S. County Rd.* ☎ *561/659–2154* 🌐 *www.bbts.org/churchmouse.*

Déjà Vu. There are so many gently used, top-quality pieces from Chanel that this could be a resale house for the brand. There's no digging through piles here; clothes are in impeccable condition and are well organized. ✉ *Via Testa, 219 Royal Poinciana Way* ☎ *561/833–6624.*

Giorgio's. Over-the-top indulgence comes in the form of 50 colors of silk and cashmere sweaters and 22 colors of ostrich and alligator adorning everything from bags to bicycles. ✉ *230 Worth Ave.* ☎ *561/655–2446* 🌐 *www.giorgiosofpalmbeach.com.*

Betteridge at Greenleaf & Crosby. Jewelry is very important in Palm Beach, and for more than 100 years the diverse selection here has included investment pieces. ✉ *236 Worth Ave.* ☎ *561/655–5850* 🌐 *www.betteridge.com.*

Spring Flowers. Specializing in European labels, beautiful children's clothing starts with newborn gown sets by Petit Bateau and grows into fashions by Léon and Fleurisse. ✉ *320 Worth Ave.* ☎ *561/832–0131* 🌐 *www.springflowerschildren.com.*

Van Cleef & Arpels. Holding court since 1940, this shop is where legendary members of Palm Beach society shop for tiaras and formal jewels. ✉ *202 Worth Ave.* ☎ *561/655–6767* 🌐 *www.vancleefarpels.com.*

WEST PALM BEACH

★ **Antique Row.** West Palm's U.S. 1, "South Dixie Highway," is the destination for those who are interested in interesting home decor. From thrift shops to the most exclusive stores, it is all here—museum-quality furniture, lighting, art, junk, fabric, frames, tile, and rugs. So if you're looking for an art deco, French-provincial, or Mizner pièce de résistance, big or small, schedule a few hours for an Antique Row stroll. You'll find bargains during the off-season (May to November). Antique Row runs north–south from Belvedere Road to Forest Hill Boulevard, although most stores are bunched between Belvedere Road and Southern Boulevard. ✉ *U.S. 1, between Belvedere Rd. and Forest Hill Blvd., West Palm Beach* 🌐 *www.westpalmbeachantiques.com.*

CityPlace. The 72-acre, four-block-by-four-block commercial and residential complex centered on Rosemary Avenue attracts people of all ages with restaurants, a 20-screen Muvico and IMAX, the Harriet Himmel Theater, and a 36,000-gallon water fountain and light show. The dining, shopping, and entertainment are all family-friendly; at night a lively crowd likes to hit the outdoor bars. Among CityPlace's stores are popular national retailers Macy's, Armani Exchange, Pottery Barn, Lucky Brand Jeans, Nine West, Sephora, BCBG MaxAzria, Gap, Banana Republic, Anthropologie, and Restoration Hardware. There are also shops unique to Florida: Behind the punchy, brightly colored clothing in the front window of **C. Orrico** (*561/832–9203*) are family fashions and accessories by Lily Pulitzer. ✉ *700 S. Rosemary Ave., West Palm Beach* ☎ *561/366–1000* 🌐 *www.cityplace.com.*

Clematis Street. If lunching is just as important as window-shopping, the renewed downtown West Palm around Clematis Street that runs west to east from South Rosemary Avenue to Flagler Drive is the spot for you. Centennial Park by the waterfront has an attractive design—and fountains where kids can cool off—which adds to the pleasure of browsing and resting at one of the many outdoor cafés. Hip national retailers such as Design Within Reach mix with local boutiques like the new Virginia Philip Wine Shop & Academy, and both blend in with restaurants and bars. ✉ *Clematis St. between S. Rosemary Ave. and Flagler Dr., West Palm Beach.*

PALM BEACH GARDENS

Downtown at The Gardens. This open-air pavilion down the street from The Gardens Mall has boutiques, chain stores, day spas, a 16-screen movie theater, and a lively restaurant and nighttime bar scene that includes the new Dirty Martini and Cabo Flats, which both feature live music. ✉ *11701 Lake Victoria Gardens Ave., Palm Beach Gardens* ☎ *561/340–1600* 🌐 *www.downtownatthegardens.com.*

6

The Gardens Mall. The premier upscale shopping center in northern Palm Beach County has a row of stores upstairs that's home to Burberry, Chanel, Gucci, and David Yurman; the mall is air-conditioned and has plenty of seating pavilions, making it a great place to spend a humid summer afternoon. ✉ *3101 PGA Blvd., Palm Beach Gardens* ☎ *561/775–7750* 🌐 *www.thegardensmall.com.*

SPORTS AND THE OUTDOORS

You can have a baseball bonanza while on vacation in the greater Palm Beach area by venturing up to the Treasure Coast's spring-training facilities, winter home to several Major League teams and Minor Leagues the rest of the year. Northern towns like Palm Beach Gardens are only minutes away.

PALM BEACH

Palm Beach Island has two good golf courses, but there are more on the mainland, as well as myriad other outdoor sports opportunities.

BIKING

Bicycling is a great way to get a closer look at Palm Beach. Only 14 miles long, ½ mile wide, flat as the top of a billiard table, and just as green, it's a perfect biking place.

Lake Trail. This palm-fringed trail, about 4 miles long, skirts the backyards of mansions and the edge of Lake Worth. The start ("south trail" section) is just up from Royal Palm Way behind the Society of the Four Arts; follow the signs and you can't miss it. As you head north, the trail gets a little choppy around the Flagler Museum, so most people just enter where the "north trail" section begins at the very west end of Sunset Avenue. The path stops just short of the tip of the island, but people follow the quiet residential streets until they hit North Ocean

Worth Avenue is the place in Palm Beach for high-end shopping, from international boutiques to independent jewelers.

Boulevard and the dock there with lovely views of Peanut Island and Singer Island, and then follow North Ocean Boulevard the 4 miles back for a change of scenery. ✉ *Parallel to Lake Way.*

Palm Beach Bicycle Trail Shop. Open daily year-round, the shop rents bikes by the hour or day, and it's about a block from the north Lake Trail entrance. ✉ *223 Sunrise Ave.* ☎ *561/659–4583* 🌐 *www.palmbeachbicycle.com.*

GOLF

The Breakers Palm Beach. The historic Ocean Course, the oldest 18 holes in all of Florida, as well as its contemporary off-site counterpart the Rees Jones Course, are open to members and hotel guests only. A $190 greens fee for each includes range balls, cart, and bag storage; the John Webster Golf Academy at The Breakers offers private and group lessons. ✉ *1 S. County Rd.* ☎ *561/655–6611.*

Palm Beach Par 3 Golf Course. The 18 holes—redesigned in 2009 by Hall-of-Famer Raymond Floyd—include six directly on the ocean, with some holes over 200 yards. Greens fees are $45; cart is an extra $9, but walking is encouraged. Nine holes are allowed (and cheaper) before 8:30 am and after 2 pm. ✉ *2345 S. Ocean Blvd.* ☎ *561/547–0598* 🌐 *www.golfontheocean.com.*

WEST PALM BEACH

POLO

International Polo Club Palm Beach. Attend matches and rub elbows with celebrities who make a pilgrimage out here during the January-through-April season. A highlight is the U.S. Open Polo Championship. ✉ *3667 120th Ave. S, Wellington* ☎ *561/204–5687* 🌐 *www.internationalpoloclub.com.*

LAKE WORTH

GOLF

Palm Beach National Golf and Country Club. This classic course has 18 holes and a Joe Lee championship layout; greens fees are $75 for 18 holes, $49 for 9 holes. The Steve Haggerty Golf Academy is based here. ✉ *7500 St. Andrews Rd., Lake Worth* ☎ *561/965–3381 pro shop* 🌐 *www.palmbeachnational.com.*

SINGER ISLAND

FISHING

Sailfish Marina. Book a full or half day of deep-sea fishing for up to six people with the seasoned captains and large fleet of 28- to 65-foot boats. ✉ *Sailfish Marina Resort, 98 Lake Dr., Palm Beach Shores* ☎ *561/844–1724* 🌐 *www.sailfishmarina.com.*

PALM BEACH GARDENS

GOLF

PGA National Resort & Spa. If you're the kind of traveler who takes along a set of clubs, this is the place for you. The five championship courses are open only to hotel guests and club members, and the Champion Course, redesigned by Jack Nicklaus and famous for its Bear Trap holes, is the site of the yearly Honda Classic pro tournament (greens fees are $301 for 18 holes and $146 for 9 holes). The four other challenging courses each carry the same greens fees ($182 and $95): the Palmer, named for its architect, the legendary Arnold Palmer; the Haig, the resort's first course, and the Squire, both from Tom and George Fazio; and the Karl Litten–designed Estates, the sole course not on the property. Lessons are available at the David Leadbetter Golf Academy. ✉ *400 Ave. of the Champions, Palm Beach Gardens* ☎ *561/627–1800.*

6

DELRAY BEACH

15 miles south of West Palm Beach.

A onetime artists' retreat with a small settlement of Japanese farmers, Delray has grown into a sophisticated beach town. Delray's current popularity is caused in large part by the fact that it has the feel of an organic city rather than a planned development or subdivision—and it's completely walkable. Atlantic Avenue, the once-dilapidated main drag, has evolved into a more-than-a-mile-long stretch of palm-dotted sidewalks, lined with stores, art galleries, and dining establishments. Running east–west and ending at the beach, it's a happening place for a stroll, day or night. Another active pedestrian area, the Pineapple Grove Arts District, begins at Atlantic and stretches northward on Northeast 2nd Avenue about a half mile, and yet another active pedestrian way begins at the eastern edge of Atlantic Avenue and runs along the big, broad swimming beach that extends north to George Bush Boulevard and south to Casuarina Road.

Morikami Museum and Japanese Gardens gives a taste of the Orient through its exhibits and tea ceremonies.

GETTING HERE AND AROUND

To reach Delray Beach from Boynton Beach, drive 2 miles south on I–95, U.S. 1, or A1A.

ESSENTIALS

VISITOR INFORMATION

Contacts **Greater Delray Beach Chamber of Commerce** ✉ *64-A S.E. 5th Ave.* ☎ *561/278–0424* 🌐 *www.delraybeach.com.*

EXPLORING

Colony Hotel. The chief landmark along Atlantic Avenue since 1926 is this sunny Mediterranean Revival–style building, which is a member of the National Trust's Historic Hotels of America. Walk through the lobby to the parking lot where original garages still stand—relics of the days when hotel guests would arrive via chauffeured cars and stay there the whole season. ✉ *525 E. Atlantic Ave.* ☎ *561/276–4123* 🌐 *www.thecolonyhotel.com.*

Fodor's Choice ★ **Morikami Museum and Japanese Gardens.** The boonies west of Delray Beach seems an odd place to encounter one of the region's most important cultural centers, but this is exactly where you can find a 200-acre cultural and recreational facility heralding the Yamato Colony of Japanese farmers that settled here in the early 20th century. A permanent exhibit details their history, and all together the museum's collection has more than 7,000 artifacts and works of art on rotating display. Traditional tea ceremonies ($) are conducted monthly from October to June, along with educational classes ($) on topics like calligraphy and sushi-making (these require advance registration). The six main gardens are inspired by famous historic periods in Japanese garden design and have South Florida accents (think tropical bonsai), and the on-site Cornell Café serves light Asian fare at affordable prices and was recognized by the Food Network as being one of the country's best museum eateries. ✉ *4000 Morikami Park Rd.* ☎ *561/495–0233* 🌐 *www.morikami.org* 🎫 *$13* ⏲ *Tues.–Sun. 10–5.*

Old School Square Cultural Arts Center. Just off Atlantic Avenue is this cluster of galleries and event spaces set in restored school buildings dating from 1913 and 1925. The **Cornell Museum of Art & American Culture** offers ever-changing exhibits on fine arts, crafts, and pop culture, plus a hands-on children's gallery. From November to April, the 323-seat **Crest Theatre** showcases national-touring Broadway musicals, cabaret concerts, dance performances, and lectures. ✉ *51 N. Swinton Ave.* ☎ *561/243–7922* 🌐 *www.oldschool.org* 🎫 *$10* ⏲ *Tues.–Sat. 10:30–4:30, Sun. 1–4:30.*

BEACHES

Fodor's Choice ★ **Delray Municipal Beach.** If you're looking for a place to see and be seen, head for this wide expanse of sand, the heart of which is where Atlantic Avenue meets A1A, close to restaurants, bars, and quick-serve eateries. Singles, families, and water sports enthusiasts alike love it here. Lounge chairs and umbrellas can be rented every day, and lifeguards man stations half a mile out in each direction. Two metered lots with restrooms are across the street at Sandoway Park and Anchor Park (bring quarters!). On the beach by Anchor Park are six volleyball nets and a kiosk that offers Hobie Wave rentals, surfing lessons, and snorkeling excursions to the 1903 SS *Inchulva* shipwreck half a mile offshore. The beach itself is open 24 hours, if you're at a nearby hotel and fancy a moonlight stroll. **Amenities:** water sports; food and drink; lifeguards; parking (fee); toilets; showers. **Best for:** windsurfing; partyers; swimming. ✉ *Rte. A1A and E. Atlantic Ave.* 🎫 *$1.50 per 1 hr parking* ⏲ *Daily 24 hrs.*

WHERE TO EAT

$$ BRITISH ✕ **Blue Anchor.** Yes, this pub was actually shipped from England, where it had stood for 150 years in London's historic Chancery Lane. There it was a watering hole for famed Englishmen, including Winston Churchill. The Delray Beach incarnation has stuck to authentic British pub fare. Chow down on a ploughman's lunch (a chunk of Stilton cheese, a piece of bread, English pork pie, and pickled onions), fish-and-chips, and bangers and mash (sausages with mashed potatoes). This is a pub's pub—nothing fancy, very hearty. Don't be surprised to find a soccer game on TV. English beers and ales are on tap and by the bottle. It's also a late-night place and has live music on weekends. [$] *Average main: $16* ✉ *804 E. Atlantic Ave.* ☎ *561/272–7272* 🌐 *www.theblueanchor.com.*

6

$$$ MODERN AMERICAN ★ **Max's Harvest.** A few blocks off Atlantic Avenue in the artsy Pineapple Grove neighborhood, a tree-shaded, fenced-in courtyard welcomes foodies eager to dig into its almost militantly farm-to-table offerings (just a few cheeses and the ketchup are not made in-house, and the ingredients are the best available). The menu encourages people to experiment with "to share," "start small," and "think big" plates. An ideal sampling: organic deviled eggs with champagne vinaigrette and truffle salt; wild-caught salmon poke, a sweet-savory Pacific Rim favorite with compressed pineapple; ricotta gnocchi, boiled then sautéed, with leek-and-fennel fondue; and a pork chop with braised red cabbage and chipotle–sweet potato puree. *Average main: $28 ✉ 169 N.E. 2nd Ave., Delray Beach ☎ 561/381–9970 www.maxsharvest.com No lunch Mon.–Sat.*

$$$ AMERICAN **The Office.** Scenesters line the massive indoor-outdoor bar from noon 'til the wee hours at this cooler-than-thou retro library restaurant, but it's worth your time to stop here for the best burger in town. There's a whole selection, but the Prime CEO steals the show: Maytag bleu cheese and Gruyère with tomato-onion confit, arugula, and bacon. It's so juicy, you'll quickly forget the mess you're making. Other upscale renditions of comforting classics like nachos (a delicate puff of whipped crab per chip served with jicama slaw), fried green tomatoes (panko-and-cornmeal crusted with crisped bits of Serrano ham), and "naughty" alcoholic shakes are worth every indulgent calorie. *Average main: $24 ✉ 201 E. Atlantic Ave., Delray Beach ☎ 561/276–3600 www.theofficedelray.com.*

$ AMERICAN ★ **Old School Bakery.** This place concentrates on sandwich making at its best, and it is known for freshly baked breads (the owner spent time in three-star Michelin restaurants before opening up shop). Particularly worthy is the cherry chicken salad sandwich with Brie on multigrain bread. Apart from sandwiches and soups served for lunch every day, you can order from a diverse menu of baked goods that includes artisan breads, pastries, several kinds of cookies, and even biscotti. The bakery is primarily takeout, but there are a few small tables in an adjacent open-air courtyard. *Average main: $8 ✉ 814 E. Atlantic Ave. ☎ 561/243–8059 www.oldschoolbakery.com.*

$$$ AMERICAN Fodor's Choice ★ **32 East.** Although restaurants come and go on a trendy street like Atlantic Avenue, 32 East remains one of the best in Delray Beach. An ever-changing daily menu focuses on refined interpretations of wood-fired pizzas, salads, soups, seafood, and meats that are all based on what is fresh and plentiful. Medium-tone wood accents and dim lighting make this brasserie seem cozy. There's a packed bar in front, an open kitchen in back, and patio seating on the sidewalk. *Average main: $29 ✉ 32 E. Atlantic Ave. ☎ 561/276–7868 www.32east.com No lunch.*

WHERE TO STAY

For expanded reviews, facilities, and current deals, visit Fodors.com.

$$$ HOTEL **Colony Hotel & Cabaña Club.** In the heart of downtown Delray, this charming building dates back to 1926 and is a member of the National

Trust's Historic Hotels of America; it maintains an air of the 1920s with its Mediterranean Revival architecture and Old Florida furnishings. **Pros:** central location; full breakfast buffet included with rooms; free use of cabanas, umbrellas, and hammocks. **Cons:** no pool at main hotel building; must walk to public beach for water-sport rentals. **TripAdvisor:** "a fun historic hotel," "comfort and charm," "fantastic quirky hotel." *Rooms from: $189 ✉ 525 E. Atlantic Ave. ☎ 561/276–4123, 800/552–2363 www.thecolonyhotel.com 69 rooms Breakfast.*

$$$$ HOTEL **Delray Beach Marriott.** By far the largest hotel in Delray Beach, the Marriott has two towers on a stellar plot of land at the east end of Atlantic Avenue—it's the only hotel that directly overlooks the water, yet it is still within walking distance of restaurants, shopping, and nightlife. **Pros:** fantastic ocean views; pampering spa; expansive manicured pool area with pretty waterfall feature and separate adults-only pool. **Cons:** chain-hotel feel; service can be impersonal; nightly charge for parking; must rent beach chairs. **TripAdvisor:** "nice property," "very attentive staff," "perfect location." *Rooms from: $279 ✉ 10 N. Ocean Blvd. ☎ 561/274–3200 www.delraybeachmarriott.com 269 rooms, 84 suites No meals.*

$$$$ RESORT ★ **The Seagate Hotel & Spa.** Those who crave 21st-century luxury in its full glory (ultraswank tilework and fixtures, marble vanities, seamless shower doors) will love this LEED-certified hotel that offers a subtle Zen coastal motif throughout. **Pros:** complimentary beach trolley and car transport within a 5-mile radius from 8 am to 11 pm; exceptionally knowledgeable and connected concierge team; two swimming pools; fabulous beach club. **Cons:** main building not directly on beach; daily resort fee and separate charge for parking; for such a grand property, service can be spotty at times. **TripAdvisor:** "excellent service," "perfect getaway," "very nice property." *Rooms from: $339 ✉ 1000 E. Atlantic Ave., Delray Beach ☎ 561/665–4800 www.theseagatehotel.com 154 rooms No meals.*

$$$ B&B/INN ★ **Sundy House.** Just about everything in this bungalow-style B&B is executed to perfection—especially its tropical, verdant grounds, which are actually a nonprofit botanical garden (something anyone can check out during free weekday tours) with an au naturel freshwater swimming pool where your feet glide along limestone rocks and mingle with fish. **Pros:** charming eclectic decor; each room is unique; renowned restaurant with popular indoor-outdoor bar and free breakfast; in quiet area off Atlantic Avenue. **Cons:** need to walk through garden to reach rooms (i.e., no covered walkways); beach shuttle requires roughly half-hour advance notice; no private beach facilities. **TripAdvisor:** "paradise," "magical," "great experience." *Rooms from: $169 ✉ 106 Swinton Ave. ☎ 561/272–5678, 877/434–9601 www.sundyhouse.com 11 rooms Breakfast.*

NIGHTLIFE

Boston's on the Beach. Groove to reggae on Monday and live music from blues to country to rock every night of the week except Wednesday at this large bar. *✉ 40 S. Ocean Blvd. ☎ 561/278–3364 www.bostonsonthebeach.com.*

6

★ **Dada.** Bands play in the living room of a historic house. It's a place where those who don't drink will also feel comfortable, and excellent gourmet nibbles are a huge bonus (a full dinner menu is available, too). ✉ *52 N. Swinton Ave.* ☎ *561/330–3232* 🌐 *www.sub-culture.org.*

Delux. A young hip crowd dances here all night long. ✉ *16 E. Atlantic Ave.* ☎ *561/279–4792* 🌐 *www.sub-culture.org.*

Jellies Bar. The Delray over-30 set floats over to this spot in the Atlantic Grille to shimmy to live music most nights; the namesake jellyfish tank never fails to entertain as well. ✉ *The Seagate Hotel & Spa, 1000 E. Atlantic Ave., Delray Beach* ☎ *561/665–4900* 🌐 *www.theatlanticgrille.com.*

SHOPPING

Atlantic Avenue and Pineapple Grove, both charming neighborhoods for shoppers, have maintained Delray Beach's small-town integrity. Atlantic Avenue is the main drag, with art galleries, boutiques, restaurants, and bars lining it from just west of Swinton Avenue all the way east to the ocean. The up-and-coming Pineapple Grove Arts District is centered around the half-mile strip of Northeast 2nd Avenue that goes northward from Atlantic.

RECOMMENDED STORES

Escentials Apothecaries. In the historic Colony Hotel, this shop is packed with all things unique and good smelling for your bath, body, and home. ✉ *Colony Hotel, 533 Atlantic Ave.* ☎ *561/276–7070.*

Furst. This studio-shop gives you the chance to watch the two designers at work—and then purchase their handcrafted bags and fine jewelry. ✉ *123 N.E. 2nd Ave., Delray Beach* ☎ *561/272–6422* 🌐 *flaviefurst.com/.*

Snappy Turtle. Jack Rogers and Trina Turk mingle with other fun resort fashions for the home and family. ✉ *1100 E. Atlantic Ave.* ☎ *561/276–8088* 🌐 *www.snappy-turtle.com.*

SPORTS AND THE OUTDOORS

BIKING

There's a bicycle path in Barwick Park, but the most popular place to ride is up and down the special oceanfront bike lane along Route A1A. The city also has an illustrated and annotated map on key downtown sights that you can pick up at the chamber of commerce.

Richwagen's Bike & Sport. Rent bikes by the hour, day, or week (they come with locks, baskets, and helmets); Richwagen's also has copies of city maps on hand. ✉ *298 N.E. 6th Ave.* ☎ *561/276–4234.*

TENNIS

Delray Beach Tennis Center. Each year this complex hosts simultaneous professional tournaments where current stars like Andy Roddick and Juan Martin del Potro along with legends like Ivan Lendl and Michael Chang duke it out (*www.yellowtennisball.com*), as well as Chris Evert's Pro-Celebrity Tennis Classic charity event (*www.chrisevert.org*). The rest of the time, you can practice or learn on 14 clay courts and 7 hard courts; private lessons and clinics are available, and it's open from 7:30 am to 9 pm weekdays and until 6 pm weekends. Since most hotels in the area do not have courts, tennis players visiting Delray Beach often come here to play. ✉ *201 W. Atlantic Ave.* ☎ *561/243–7360* 🌐 *www.delraytennis.com.*

BOCA RATON

6 miles south of Delray Beach.

Less than an hour south of Palm Beach and anchoring the county's south end, upscale Boca Raton has much in common with its fabled cousin. Both reflect the unmistakable architectural influence of Addison Mizner, their principal developer in the mid-1920s. The meaning of the name Boca Raton (pronounced boca rah-*tone*) often arouses curiosity, with many folks mistakenly assuming it means "rat's mouth." Historians say the probable origin is Boca Ratones, an ancient Spanish geographical term for an inlet filled with jagged rocks or coral. Miami's Biscayne Bay had such an inlet, and in 1823 a mapmaker copying Miami terrain confused the more northern inlet, thus mistakenly labeling this area Boca Ratones. No matter what, you'll know you've arrived in the heart of downtown when you spot the historic town hall's gold dome on the main street, Federal Highway. Much of the Boca landscape was heavily planned, and many of the bigger sights are clustered in the area around town hall and Lake Boca, a wide stretch of the Intracoastal Waterway between Palmetto Park Road and Camino Real (two main east–west streets on the southern end of town).

GETTING HERE AND AROUND

To get to Boca Raton from Delray Beach, drive south 6 miles on Interstate 95, Federal Highway (U.S. 1), or A1A.

ESSENTIALS

VISITOR INFORMATION

Contacts **Greater Boca Raton Chamber of Commerce** ✉ *1800 N. Dixie Hwy.* ☎ *561/395–4433* 🌐 *www.bocaratonchamber.com.*

EXPLORING

Boca Raton History Museum. Under the shimmering golden dome of the city's original town hall is a vital repository of archival material and special exhibits on the area's development run by the Boca Raton Historical Society. Monthly trolley tours around town and excursions to other points of interest, including an old rail depot, are also on offer; check the society's website for schedules and costs. ✉ *71 N. Federal Hwy.* ☎ *561/395–6766* 🌐 *www.bocahistory.org* 🎫 *$5* 🕒 *Weekdays 10–4.*

★ **Boca Raton Museum of Art.** Changing-exhibition galleries on the first floor showcase internationally known artists—both past and present—at this museum in a spectacular building that's part of the Mizner Park shopping center; the permanent collection upstairs includes works by Picasso, Degas, Matisse, Klee, Modigliani, and Warhol, as well as notable African and pre-Columbian art. Daily tours are included with admission. In addition to the treasure hunts and sketchbooks you can pick up from the front desk, there's a roster of special programs that cater to kids, including studio workshops and gallery walks. Another fun feature is the cell-phone audio guide—certain pieces of art have a corresponding number you dial to hear a detailed narration. ✉ *501 Plaza Real* ☎ *561/392–2500* 🌐 *www.bocamuseum.org* 🎟 *$14* 🕒 *Tues., Thurs., and Fri. 10–5; Wed. 10–9; weekends noon–5.*

Children's Science Explorium. This hands-on center in Sugar Sand Park has interactive displays designed to enhance 5- to 12-year-olds' understanding of everyday physical sciences. Outside there's a huge three-story playground with DNA-shaped climbing structures, picnic pavilions, and a classic carousel. Day camps are run during school breaks and are open to visitors. ✉ *Sugar Sand Park, 300 S. Military Trail* ☎ *561/347–3912* 🌐 *www.scienceexplorium.org* 🎟 *Free ($5 donation suggested)* 🕒 *Mon.–Fri. 9–6, Sat.–Sun. 10–5.*

Gumbo Limbo Nature Center. A big draw for kids, this stellar spot has four huge saltwater tanks brimming with sea life, from coral to stingrays to spiny lobsters, plus a sea turtle rehabilitation center added in 2010. Nocturnal walks in spring and early summer, when staffers lead a quest to find nesting female turtles coming ashore to lay eggs, are popular; so are the hatching releases in August and September. (Gumbo Limbo is one of only a handful of centers that offer the chance to observe the babies departing into the ocean.) There is also a nature trail and butterfly garden, a ¼-mile boardwalk, and a 40-foot observation tower. Free tours are conducted Wednesday at 10 am; spend a little time overlooking the tree canopy, and you're likely to see brown pelicans and osprey. ✉ *1801 N. Ocean Blvd.* ☎ *561/338–1473* 🌐 *www.gumbolimbo.org* 🎟 *Free ($5 suggested donation); turtle walks $15* 🕒 *Mon.–Sat. 9–4, Sun. noon–4.*

Old Floresta. This residential area was developed by Addison Mizner starting in 1925 and is beautifully landscaped with palms and cycads. Its houses are mainly Mediterranean in style, many with balconies supported by exposed wood columns. Explore by driving northward on Paloma Avenue from Palmetto Park Road, then weave in and out of the side streets. ✉ *Paloma Ave., north of W. Palmetto Park Rd.*

2 East El Camino Real. Built in 1926 as the headquarters of the Mizner Development Corporation, this is an example of Mizner's characteristic Spanish Revival architectural style, with its wrought-iron grilles, handmade tiles, and a towering century-old Banyan tree in the courtyard. Stop by for a peek in the daytime (at night it becomes a private-event venue). As for Mizner's grandiose vision of El Camino Real, the architect-promoter once prepared brochures promising a sweeping wide boulevard with Venetian canals and arching bridges. Camino Real is attractive, heading east to the Boca Raton Resort & Club, but don't count on feeling like you're in Venice—the canal system was never completed. ✉ *2 E. Camino Real.*

BEACHES

Boca's three city beaches are beautiful and hugely popular, but unless you're a resident or want to bike in, parking is particularly expensive. Save your receipt if you care to go in and out, or park-hop—most guards at the front gate will honor a same-day ticket from another location if you ask nicely. Another option is the county-run South Inlet Park that's walking distance from the Boca Raton Bridge Hotel at the southern end of Lake Boca; it has a metered lot for a fraction of the cost, but not quite the same charm as the others.

Red Reef Park. The ocean with its namesake reef that you can wade up to is just one draw: a fishing zone on the Intracoastal Waterway across the street, a 9-hole golf course next door, and the Gumbo Limbo Nature Center at the northern end of the park can easily make a day at the beach into so much more. But if pure old-fashioned fun in the sun is your focus, to that end there are tons of picnic tables and grills, and two separate playgrounds. Pack snorkels and explore the reef at high tide when fish are most abundant. Swimmers, be warned: once lifeguards leave at 5, anglers flock to the shores and stay well past dark. **Amenities:** lifeguards; parking (fee); showers; toilets. **Best for:** snorkeling; swimming; walking. *1400 N. Rte. A1A 561/393–7974, 561/393–7989 for beach conditions $16 parking (weekdays), $18 parking (weekends) Daily 8 am–10 pm.*

South Beach Park. Perched high up on a dune, a large open-air pavilion at the east end of Palmetto Park Road offers a panoramic view of what's in store below on the sand that stretches up the coast. Serious beachgoers need to pull into the main lot ¼ mile north on the east side of A1A, but if a spectacular sunset is what you're after, the 20 or so one-hour spots with meters in the circle driveway will do. During the day, pretty young things blanket the shore, and surfers practice tricks in the waves. Quiet quarters are farther north. **Amenities:** lifeguards; parking (fee); toilets; showers. **Best for:** sunsets; walking; swimming. *400 N. Ocean Blvd. 561/212–4530, 561/393–7989 for beach conditions $15 parking (weekdays), $17 parking (weekends) Daily 8–sunset.*

WHERE TO EAT

$$$$ AMERICAN **Racks Downtown Eatery & Tavern.** Whimsical indoor–oudoor decor and comfort food with a twist help define this popular eatery in tony Mizner Park. Instead of dinner rolls, pretzel bread and mustard get things started. Share plates like bacon-wrapped shrimp and sea bass lettuce cups to promote convivial social dining. Happy hour at the bar is 4–7 and offers half-price drinks and appetizers. *Average main: $23 402 Plaza Real, Mizner Park 561/395–1662 www.grrestaurant.com.*

$$$$ SEAFOOD **Truluck's.** This popular chain is so serious about seafood that it boasts its own fleet of 16 boats. Stone crabs are the signature dish, and you can have all you can eat on Monday night from October to May. Other recommended dishes include salmon topped with blue crabmeat and shrimp, hot-and-crunchy trout, crab cakes, and blackened Florida grouper. Portions are huge, so you might want to make a meal of appetizers. The place comes alive each night with its popular piano bar. *Average*

main: $35 ✉ *Mizner Park, 351 Plaza Real* ☎ *561/391–0755* 🌐 *www.trulucks.com.*

$$$ CHINESE ✕ **Uncle Tai's.** The draw at this upscale eatery is some of the best Hunan cuisine on Florida's east coast. Specialties include sliced duck with snow peas and water chestnuts in a tangy plum sauce, and orange beef delight—flank steak stir-fried until crispy and then sautéed with pepper sauce, garlic, and orange peel. They'll go easy on the heat on request. The service is quietly efficient. [$] *Average main: $21* ✉ *5250 Town Center Circle* ☎ *561/368–8806* 🌐 *www.uncletais.com.*

WHERE TO STAY

For expanded reviews, facilities, and current deals, visit Fodors.com.

$$$$ RESORT Fodor's Choice ★ **Boca Raton Resort & Club.** Addison Mizner built this Mediterranean-style hotel in 1926, and additions over time have created a sprawling, sparkling resort, one of the most luxurious in all of South Florida, with a particularly stunning beach club. **Pros:** super-exclusive—grounds are closed to the public; decor strikes the right balance between historic roots and modern comforts; celebrity-chef restaurants, including a Morimoto sushi bar; plenty of activities. **Cons:** all this luxury is costly; conventions often crowd common areas. **TripAdvisor:** "great getaway," "old but friendly," "holiday in the sun." [$] *Rooms from: $319* ✉ *501 E. Camino Real* ☎ *561/447–3000, 800/327–0101* 🌐 *www.bocaresort.com* *1,047 rooms* *No meals.*

$$$ HOTEL **Boca Raton Bridge Hotel.** This boutique hotel on the Intracoastal Waterway near the Boca Inlet has views of Lake Boca and the ocean that can't be beat, especially from higher-up floors and the penthouse restaurant, Carmen's at the Top of the Bridge. **Pros:** lively pool bar scene; affordable rates; great location and short walk to beach; pet-friendly. **Cons:** can be noisy if you're near the bridge; rooms are comfy and relaxed but not memorable; building is on the older side. **TripAdvisor:** "staff is nice," "amazing gem," "beautiful view." [$] *Rooms from: $179* ✉ *999 E. Camino Real* ☎ *561/368–9500, 866/909–2622* 🌐 *www.bocaratonbridgehotel.com* *142 rooms* *No meals.*

$ HOTEL **Inn at Ocean Breeze.** If golf is your game, this small resort with no-frills rooms is an excellent choice, because it is part of the Ocean Breeze Golf & Country Club, and guests can play the outstanding course that actually has 27 holes. **Pros:** rates are a steal; great value for golfers; free Wi-Fi; quiet location. **Cons:** dated decor; swimming pool not heated; old fixtures. **TripAdvisor:** "exceptional value," "we return year after year," "great deal for golfers." [$] *Rooms from: $80* ✉ *5800 N.W. 2nd Ave.* ☎ *561/994–0400* 🌐 *www.oceanbreezegolf.com* *46 rooms* *No meals.*

NIGHTLIFE

Rustic Cellar. Warm and intimate, this dark cozy nook is modeled after a Napa Valley tasting room and is perhaps the best wine bar in Palm Beach County. More than 300 hand-selected vintages, most from top domestic and rare vintners, are served—and nearly all are available by the glass. There's also an impressive collection of craft beers.

✉ *Royal Palm Place, 409 S.E. Mizner Blvd.* ☎ *561/392–5237* 🌐 *www.rusticcellar.com.*

SPIN Ultra Lounge. A newcomer on the scene, it has a large dance floor and canopied outdoor daybeds; expect Top 40 music from the DJ booth and a hip, predominantly younger crowd. ✉ *346 Plaza Real, Boca Raton* ☎ *561/361–3999* 🌐 *www.spinboca.com.*

SHOPPING

★ **Mizner Park.** This distinctive 30-acre shopping center off Federal Highway, one block north of Palmetto Park Road, intersperses apartments and town houses among its gardenlike commercial areas. Some three dozen national and local retailers line the central axis that's peppered with fountains and green space, restaurants, galleries, a movie theater, the Boca Raton Museum of Art, and an amphitheater that hosts major concerts as well as community events. ✉ *327 Plaza Real* ☎ *561/362–0606* 🌐 *www.miznerpark.com.*

Royal Palm Place. A dining and nighttime entertainment hot spot, Royal Palm is home to favorites like Lemongrass Asian Bistro and Rosarios Ristorante (which has a steal of a prix-fixe dinner menu); by day, stroll the walkable streets sprinkled with independent boutiques and have your pick of sidewalk cafés for lunch. ✉ *101 Plaza Real S, Boca Raton* ☎ *561/392–8920* 🌐 *www.royalpalmplace.com.*

Town Center at Boca Raton. This indoor megamall with 220 stores has anchor stores including Saks and Neiman Marcus and just about every major haute designer, including Bulgari, Anne Fontaine, and Ermenegildo Zegna. But it's rooted firmly down to earth with a variety of more affordable national brands, plus interesting ones such as midrange Brazilian shoe chain Santa Lolla. ✉ *6000 Glades Rd.* ☎ *561/368–6000* 🌐 *www.simon.com.*

6

SPORTS AND THE OUTDOORS

GOLF

Boca Raton Resort & Club. Legendary Sam Snead was the head pro here in the 1960s when the Resort Course (greens fee with cart $199) was the hotel's only option; nowadays there's a second one off-site, the Country Club Course (greens fee with cart $160), with a Dave Pelz Scoring Game School that is open to the public—course play is just for guests and members. ✉ *501 E. Camino Real* ☎ *561/447–3078* 🌐 *www.bocaresort.com.*

Red Reef Park Executive Golf Course. These 9 Intracoastal- and oceanfront holes, between 54 and 227 yards each, are great for a quick round. The greens fees range from $10.75 to walk in the off-season to $25.75 with a cart in season. Park in the lot across the street from the main beach entrance, and put the greens fees receipt on the dash; that covers parking. ✉ *1221 N. Rte. A1A, Boca Raton* ☎ *561/391–5014* 🌐 *www.bocacitygolf.com.*

SCUBA AND SNORKELING

Force-E. This company rents, sells, and repairs scuba and snorkeling equipment—and organizes about 80 dive trips a week throughout the region. The PADI–affiliated five-star center has instruction for all levels and offers private charters, too. ✉ *2181 N. Federal Hwy.* ☎ *561/368–0555, 866/307–3483* 🌐 *www.force-e.com.*

TREASURE COAST

In contrast to the glitzy, über-planned Gold Coast that includes Greater Palm Beach and Boca Raton, the more bucolic Treasure Coast stretches from northernmost Palm Beach County into Martin, St. Lucie, and Indian River counties. Along the east are barrier islands all the way to Sebastian and beyond, starting with Jupiter Island, then Hutchinson Island, and finally Orchid Island—and reefs, too. Those reefs are responsible for the region's nickname: ships carrying riches dating back as far as 1715 have fallen asunder and cast their treasures ashore. The Intracoastal Waterway here is called the Indian River starting at the St. Lucie Inlet in Stuart and morphs into a broad tidal lagoon with tiny uninhabited islands and wildlife galore. Inland, there's cattle ranching and tracts of pine and palmetto scrub, along with sugar and citrus production.

Despite a growing number of malls and beachfront condominiums, much of the Treasure Coast remains untouched, something not lost on ecotourists, game fishers, and people who want a break from the oversaturated digital age. Consequently, there are fewer lodging options in this region of Florida, but if 30 minutes in the car sounds like a breeze, culture vultures can live in the lap of luxury in Vero Beach and detour south to Fort Pierce's galleries and botanical gardens; likewise, families will revel in every amenity imaginable at the Hutchinson Island Marriott and be able to swing northwest to hit up the Mets spring-training stadium in Port St. Lucie or down to Jupiter for the Cardinals and the Marlins.

JUPITER AND VICINITY

12 miles north of West Palm Beach.

Jupiter is one of the few towns in the region not fronted by an island, and it's still quite close to the fantastic hotels, shopping, and dining of the Palm Beach area. The beaches here are on the mainland, and Route A1A runs for almost 4 miles along the beachfront dunes and beautiful homes.

Northeast across the Jupiter Inlet from Jupiter is the southern tip of Jupiter Island, which stretches about 15 miles to the St. Lucie Inlet. Here expansive and expensive estates often retreat from the road behind screens of vegetation, and the population dwindles the farther north you go. At the very north end, sea turtles come to nest. To the west, on the mainland, is the little community of Hobe Sound.

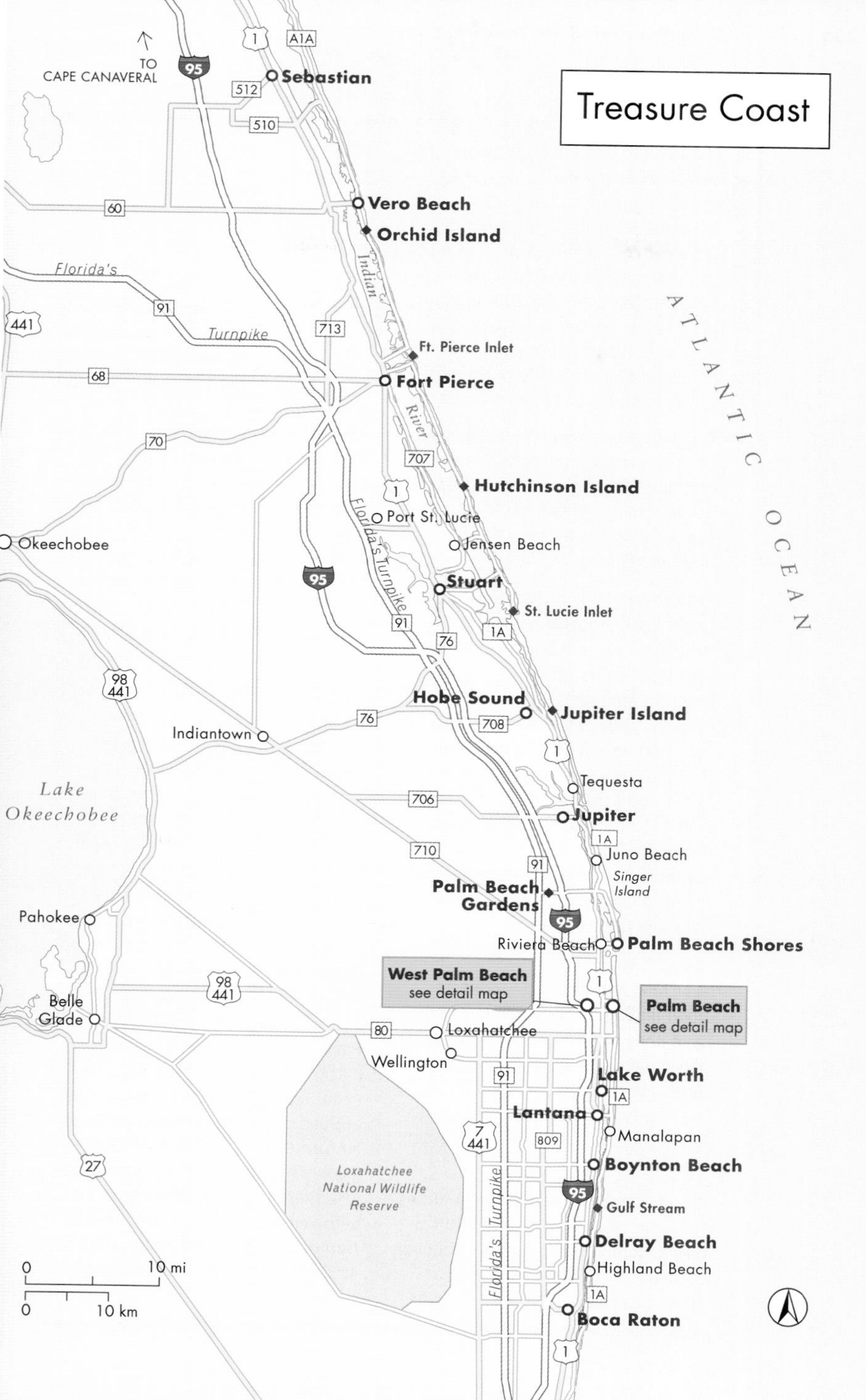
Treasure Coast
TO
CAPE CANAVERAL
Sebastian
Vero Beach
Orchid Island
Ft. Pierce Inlet
Fort Pierce
Hutchinson Island
Port St. Lucie
Jensen Beach
Okeechobee
Stuart
St. Lucie Inlet
Hobe Sound
Jupiter Island
Indiantown
Tequesta
Jupiter
Juno Beach
Singer Island
Palm Beach Gardens
Pahokee
Riviera Beach
Palm Beach Shores
West Palm Beach
see detail map
Palm Beach
see detail map
Belle Glade
Loxahatchee
Wellington
Lake Worth
Lantana
Manalapan
Boynton Beach
Gulf Stream
Delray Beach
Highland Beach
Boca Raton
Lake Okeechobee
Loxahatchee National Wildlife Reserve
Indian River
Florida's Turnpike
ATLANTIC OCEAN
0
10 mi
0
10 km

CLOSE UP

Florida's Sea Turtles: The Nesting Season

From May to October it's turtle-nesting season all along the Florida coast. Female loggerhead, Kemp's ridley, and other species living in the Atlantic Ocean or Gulf of Mexico swim as much as 2,000 miles to the Florida shore. By night they drag their 100- to 400-pound bodies onto the beach to the dune line. Then each digs a hole with her flippers, drops in 100 or so eggs, covers them up, and returns to sea.

The babies hatch about 60 days later. Once they burst out of the sand, the hatchlings must get to sea rapidly or risk becoming dehydrated from the sun or being caught by crabs, birds, or other predators.

Instinctively, baby turtles head toward bright light, probably because for millions of years starlight or moonlight reflected on the waves was the brightest light around, serving to guide hatchlings to water. But now light from beach development can lead the babies in the wrong direction, toward the street rather than the water. To help, many coastal towns enforce light restrictions during nesting months. Florida home owners are asked to dim their lights on behalf of baby sea turtles.

At night, volunteers walk the beaches, searching for signs of turtle nests. Upon finding telltale scratches in the sand, they cordon off the sites, so beachgoers will leave the spots undisturbed. Volunteers also keep watch over nests when babies are about to hatch and assist if the hatchlings get disoriented.

It's a hazardous world for baby turtles. They can die after eating tar balls or plastic debris, or they can be gobbled by sharks or circling birds. Only about one in a thousand survives to adulthood. After reaching the water, the babies make their way to warm currents. East Coast hatchlings drift into the Gulf Stream, spending years floating around the Atlantic.

Males never return to land, but when females attain maturity, in 15–20 years, they return to shore to lay eggs. Remarkably, even after migrating hundreds and even thousands of miles out at sea, most return to the very beach where they were born to deposit their eggs. Each time they nest, they come back to the same stretch of beach. In fact, the more they nest, the more accurate they get, until eventually they return time and again to within a few feet of where they last laid their eggs. These incredible navigation skills remain for the most part a mystery despite intense scientific study.

Several local organizations offer nightly turtle walks during nesting season. Most are in June and July, starting around 8 pm and sometimes lasting until midnight. Expect a $10 to $15 fee. Call in advance to confirm times and to reserve a spot—places usually take reservations as early as April. If you're in southern Palm Beach County, contact Boca Raton's **Gumbo Limbo Nature Center** (☎ 561/338–1473 🌐 www.gumbolimbo.org). The **John D. MacArthur Beach State Park** (☎ 561/624–6952 🌐 www.macarthurbeach.org) is convenient for Palm Beach–area visitors at the northern end of Singer Island. **Hobe Sound Nature Center** (☎ 772/546–2067 🌐 www.hobesoundnaturecenter.com) is farther up. Treasure Coasters in or near Vero Beach can go to **Sebastian Inlet State Park** (☎ 321/984–4852 🌐 www.floridastateparks.org/sebastianinlet).

Away from developed shorelines, Blowing Rocks Preserve on Jupiter Island lets you wander the dunes.

GETTING HERE AND AROUND

If you are coming from the airport in West Palm Beach, take I–95 to Route 706. Otherwise, Federal Highway (U.S. 1) and A1A are usually more convenient.

Northern Palm Beach County Chamber of Commerce ✉ *800 N. U.S. 1* ☎ *561/746–7111* 🌐 *www.npbchamber.com.*

EXPLORING

Blowing Rocks Preserve. An almost other-worldly-looking limestone shelf lining the shore here is the main draw, but also protected within its 73 acres on Jupiter Island are plants native to beachfront dunes, coastal strand (the landward side of the dunes), mangrove swamps, and tropical hardwood forests. The best time to come is when a storm is brewing: If high tides and strong offshore winds coincide, the sea blows spectacularly through the holes in the eroded outcropping. During a calm summer day, you can swim in crystal-clear waters on the mile-long beach and climb around the rock formations at low tide. Park in one of the two lots, because police ticket cars on the road. ✉ *574 S. Beach Rd., Rte. 707, Jupiter Island* ☎ *561/744–6668* 🌐 *www.nature.org/blowingrocks* 🎟 *$2* ⏲ *Daily 9–4:30.*

Hobe Sound Nature Center. Though located in the Hobe Sound National Wildlife Refuge, this nature center is an independent organization. The exhibit hall, renovated in 2010, houses live baby alligators, crocodiles, a scary-looking tarantula, and more—and is a child's delight. Among the center's more popular events are the annual nighttime sea turtle walks, held between May and June; reservations are accepted as early as April 1. Just off the center's entrance is a mile-long nature trail loop that snakes through three different kinds of habitats: coastal hammock, estuary beach, and sand pine scrub, which is one of Florida's most unusual and endangered plant communities and what composes much of the refuge's nearly 250 acres. ✉ *13640 S.E. U.S. 1, Hobe Sound* ☎ *772/546–2067* 🌐 *www.hobesoundnaturecenter.com* 🎫 *Free (donation requested)* ⏲ *Mon.–Sat. 9–3.*

Jonathan Dickinson State Park. From Hobe Mountain, an ancient dune topped with a tower, you are treated to a panoramic view of this park's more than 11,000 acres of varied terrain and the Intracoastal Waterway. The Loxahatchee River, which cuts through the park, is home to manatees in winter and alligators year-round; two-hour boat tours of the river depart daily (see ⇨ *Jonathan Dickinson State Park River Tours*). Kayak rentals are available, as is horseback riding (it was recently reintroduced after a 30-year absence). Among the amenities are a dozen newly redone cabins for rent, tent sites, bicycle and hiking trails, two campgrounds, and a snack bar. Don't skip the Elsa Kimbell Environmental Education and Research Center, which has interactive displays, exhibits, and a short film on the natural history of the area. The park is also a fantastic birding location, with about 150 species to spot. ✉ *16450 S.E. U.S. 1, Hobe Sound* ☎ *772/546–2771* 🌐 *www.floridastateparks.org/jonathandickinson* 🎫 *Vehicles $6, bicyclists and pedestrians $2* ⏲ *Daily 8–sunset; Elsa Kimbell Environmental Education and Research Center daily 9–5.*

★ **Jupiter Inlet Lighthouse & Museum.** Designed by Civil War hero Lieutenant George Gordon Meade, this brick lighthouse has been under the Coast Guard's purview since 1860. Tours of the 108-foot-tall landmark are held approximately every half-hour and are included with admission. (Children must be at least 4 feet tall to go to the top.) The museum tells about efforts to restore this graceful spire to the way it looked from 1860 to 1918; its galleries and outdoor structures, including a pioneer home, also showcase local history dating back five thousand years. ✉ *Lighthouse Park, 500 Capt. Armour's Way* ☎ *561/747–8380* 🌐 *www.jupiterlighthouse.org* 🎫 *$9* ⏲ *Jan.–Apr., daily 10–5; May–Dec., Tues.–Sun., 10–5. Last tour at 4.*

BEACHES

Carlin Park. About ½ mile south of the Jupiter Beach Resort and Indiantown Road, the quiet beach here is just one draw; otherwise, the manicured park, which straddles A1A, is chock-full of activities and amenities. Two bocce ball courts, six lighted tennis courts, a baseball diamond, a wood-chip-lined running path, and an amphitheater that hosts free concerts and Shakespeare productions are just some of the highlights. Locals also swear by the Lazy Loggerhead Café that's right off the seaside parking lot for a great casual breakfast and lunch. **Amenities:** lifeguards; food and drink; parking (free); toilets; showers. **Best for:** swimming; walking. ✉ *400 S. Rte. A1A* 🌐 *www.pbcsplash.com.*

Jupiter Beach. Famous throughout all of Florida for a unique pooch-loving stance, the town of Jupiter's beach welcomes Yorkies, Labs, pugs—you name it—along its 2½-mile oceanfront. Dogs can frolic unleashed or join you for a dip. Free parking spots line A1A in front of the sandy stretch, and there are multiple access points and continuously refilled dog-bag boxes (29 to be exact). Before going, read through the guidelines posted on the Friends of Jupiter Beach website; the biggest things to note are be sure to clean up after your dog and to steer clear of lifeguarded areas to the north and south. **Amenities:** toilets; showers. **Best for:** walking. ✉ *S. Rte. A1A, south of Carlin Park, Jupiter* 🌐 *www.friendsofjupiterbeach.com.*

Hobe Sound National Wildlife Refuge. Nature lovers seeking to get as far as possible from the madding crowds will feel at peace here. Even simple things like flying kites, throwing Frisbees, and eating are frowned upon on the 3½-mile-long beach, the entrance to which is on Jupiter Island. It's a haven for people who want some quiet while they walk around and photograph the gorgeous coastal sand dunes, where turtle nests and shells often wash ashore. The beach has been severely eroded by high tides and strong winds (surprisingly, surfing is allowed and many do partake). You can't actually venture within most of the 735 protected acres, so if hiking piques your interest, head to the refuge's main entrance a few miles away on Hobe Sound (*13640 S.E. U.S. 1 in Hobe Sound*) for a mile-long trek close to the nature center, or to nearby Jonathan Dickinson State Park. Amenities: parking (fee); toilets. Best for: solitude; surfing; walking. ✉ *198 N. Beach Rd., at end of N. Beach Rd., Jupiter Island* ☎ *772/546–6141* 🌐 *www.fws.gov/hobesound* 🎟 *Parking $5.*

6

WHERE TO EAT

$$ SEAFOOD

✕ **Little Moir's Food Shack.** This local favorite is not much to look at and a bit tricky to find, but worth the search. The fried-food standards you might expect at such a casual place that uses plastic utensils are not found on the menu; instead there are fried tuna rolls with basil, and panko-crusted fried oysters with spicy fruit salad. A variety of beers are fun to pair with the creatively prepared seafood dishes that include wahoo, mahimahi, and snapper. [$] *Average main: $17* ✉ *103 S. U.S. 1* ☎ *561/741–3626* 🌐 *www.littlemoirsfoodshack.com* ✍ *Reservations not accepted* ⏲ *Closed Sun.*

$$ SEAFOOD

✕ **Guanabanas.** Expect a wait for dinner, which is not necessarily a bad thing at this island paradise of a waterfront restaurant and bar. Take the wait time to explore the bridges and trails of the open-air tropical oasis and nibble on really good conch fritters at the large tiki bar until your table is ready. Try the lemon-butter hogfish for dinner and stick around for the live music (a full concert calendar is on the website). Breakfast, offered only on weekends, is great, too. [$] *Average main: $18* ✉ *960 N. Rte. A1A* ☎ *561/747–8878* 🌐 *www.guanabanas.com* ✍ *Reservations not accepted.*

$$$ SEAFOOD

✕ **Sinclairs Ocean Grill.** This popular choice for a more upscale but still laid-back setting in the Jupiter Beach Resort has sunlight streaming through the glass doors overlooking the pool. The menu has a daily selection of fresh fish, such as cashew-encrusted grouper, Cajun-spiced tuna, and mahimahi with pistachio sauce. There are also thick, juicy cuts of meat, including New York strip steak and beef tenderloin, as well as chicken and lamb dishes. The Sunday buffet is a big draw. Dine outside on the terrace to see the waves lapping and take in the beachscape. *Average main: $21 ✉ Jupiter Beach Resort, 5 N. Rte. A1A ☎ 561/746–2511 ⊕ www.jupiterbeachresort.com.*

$$ AMERICAN **Taste Casual Dining.** Located in the center of historic Hobe Sound, this cozy dining spot with a pleasant, screened-in patio offers piano dinner music on Fridays. Locals like to hang out at the old, English-style wine bar; however, the food itself is the biggest draw here. Try a lobster roll and the signature Gorgonzola salad for lunch, and any fish dish for dinner. On weekend nights, order the excellent, slow-cooked prime rib, another specialty. *Average main: $16 ✉ 11750 S.E. Dixie Hwy., Hobe Sound ☎ 772/546–1129 ⊕ www.tastehobesound.com ⊙ Closed Sun. in July and Aug.*

WHERE TO STAY

For expanded reviews, facilities, and current deals, visit Fodors.com.

$$$$ RESORT **Jupiter Beach Resort & Spa.** Families love this nine-story hotel filled with rich Caribbean-style rooms containing mahogany sleigh beds and armoires; all rooms have balconies, and many have stunning views of the ocean and local landmarks like the Jupiter Lighthouse and Juno Pier. **Pros:** fantastic beachside pool area with hammocks and a fire pit; convenient location; great restaurant; large, pampering spa. **Cons:** pricey rates and $20 nightly resort fee; beds are quite high; no covered parking. **TripAdvisor:** "perfect family getaway," "absolutely worth the money," "great resort." *Rooms from: $289 ✉ 5 N. Rte. A1A ☎ 561/746–2511, 800/228–8810 ⊕ www.jupiterbeachresort.com 168 rooms No meals.*

SPORTS AND THE OUTDOORS

BASEBALL

Roger Dean Stadium. It's a spring training doubleheader! Both the St. Louis Cardinals and the Miami Marlins call this 6,600-seat facility home base from February to April. The rest of the year two minor league teams share its turf. In the Abacoa area of Jupiter, the grounds are surrounded by a mix of restaurants and sports bars for pre- and post-game action. *✉ 4751 Main St. ☎ 561/775–1818 ⊕ www.rogerdeanstadium.com.*

BOATING AND CANOEING

Canoe Outfitters of Florida. See animals, from otters to eagles, along 8 miles of the Loxahatchee River in Riverbend County Park daily except Tuesday and Wednesday. Canoe and kayak rentals are $25 for four hours. Bike rentals are available, too. *✉ Riverbend County Park, 9060 W. Indiantown Rd. ☎ 561/746–7053 ⊕ www.canoeoutfittersofflorida.com.*

Jonathan Dickinson State Park River Tours. Boat tours of the Loxahatchee River and guided horseback rides, along with canoe, kayak, bicycle, and boat rentals are offered from 9 to 3:30 daily. *✉ Jonathan Dickinson State Park, 16450 S.E. U.S. 1, Hobe Sound ☎ 561/746–1466 ⊕ www.floridaparktours.com.*

GOLF

Abacoa Golf Club. This Joe Lee-designed 18-hole course with range is on par with nearby private courses; greens fees $99/$55 (including cart). *✉ 105 Barbados Dr. ☎ 561/622–0036 ⊕ www.abacoagolfclub.com.*

Golf Club of Jupiter. There are 18 holes of varying difficulty at this public course; greens fees with cart are $69/$29. ✉ *1800 S. Central Blvd.* ☎ *561/747–6262* 🌐 *www.golfclubofjupiter.com.*

Jupiter Dunes Golf Club. Families—or anyone who wants a quick yet challenging round—will love this 18-hole gem of a short course with views of the Jupiter River estuary. At its most expensive, it's $26 to walk and $13 per person for a cart. ✉ *401 N. Rte. A1A* ☎ *561/746–6654* 🌐 *www.jupiterdunesgolf.com.*

STUART AND JENSEN BEACH

10 miles north of Hobe Sound.

The compact town of Stuart lies on a peninsula that juts out into the St. Lucie River off the Indian River and has a remarkable amount of shoreline for its size. It scores huge points for its charming historic district and is the self-described "Sailfish Capital of the World." On the southern end, you'll find Port Salerno and its waterfront area, the Manatee Pocket, which are a skip away from the St. Lucie Inlet.

Immediately north of Stuart is down-to-earth Jensen Beach. Both Stuart and Jensen Beach straddle the Indian River and occupy Hutchinson Island, the barrier island that continues into the town of Fort Pierce. Between late April and August, more than 600 turtles come here to nest along the Atlantic beaches. Residents have taken pains to curb the runaway development that has created commercial crowding found to the north and south, although some high-rises have popped up along the shore.

6

GETTING HERE AND AROUND

To get to Stuart and Jensen Beach from Jupiter and Hobe Sound, drive north on Federal Highway (U.S. 1). Route A1A crosses through downtown Stuart and is the sole main road throughout Hutchinson Island. Route 707 runs parallel on the mainland directly across the tidal lagoon.

ESSENTIALS

Visitor Information **Martin County Convention & Visitors Bureau** ✉ *101 S.W. Flagler Ave., Stuart* ☎ *772/288–5451* 🌐 *www.discovermartin.com.* **Stuart/Martin County Chamber of Commerce** ✉ *1650 S. Kanner Hwy.* ☎ *772/287–1088* 🌐 *www.stuartmartinchamber.org.* **Jensen Beach Chamber of Commerce** ✉ *1900 N.E. Ricou Terr., Jensen Beach* ☎ *772/334–3444* 🌐 *www.hellojb.com.*

EXPLORING

Strict architectural and zoning standards guide civic-renewal projects in the heart of Stuart. Antiques stores, restaurants, and more than 50 specialty shops are rooted within the two-block area of Flagler Avenue and Osceola Street north of where A1A cuts across the peninsula (visit 🌐 *www.stuartmainstreet.org* for more information). A self-guided walking-tour pamphlet is available at assorted locations to clue you in on this once-small fishing village's early days.

Elliott Museum. Anticipating a January 2013 opening, the museum's glittering new 44,000-square-foot facility will be double its previous size and house a permanent collection along with traveling exhibits. It was founded in 1961 in honor of Sterling Elliott, an inventor of an early automated-addressing machine, the egg crate, and a four-wheel bicycle, and it celebrates history, art, and technology, much of it viewed through the lens of the automobile's effect on American society. There's an impressive array of antique cars, plus paintings, historic artifacts, and nostalgic goods like vintage baseball cards and toys. Call before visiting to check opening hours. ✉ *825 N.E. Ocean Blvd., Jensen Beach* ☎ *772/225–1961* 🌐 *www.elliottmuseumfl.org* 🎟 *$8* ⏲ *Mon.–Sat. 10–4, Sun. 1–4.*

★ **Florida Oceanographic Coastal Center.** This hydroland is the place to go for an interactive marine experience. Petting and feeding stingrays can be done at various times; in the morning, a sea turtle program introduces you to three full-time residents. Make sure to catch the "feeding frenzy" when keepers toss food into the 750,000-gallon lagoon tank and sharks, tarpon, and snook swarm the surface. Join a 1-mile guided walk through the coastal hardwood hammock and mangrove swamp habitats, or explore the trails on your own—you may see a dolphin or manatee swim by. ✉ *890 N.E. Ocean Blvd.* ☎ *772/225–0505* 🌐 *www.floridaocean.org* 🎟 *$10* ⏲ *Mon.–Sat. 10–5, Sun. noon–4. Nature trails close at 4.*

Gilbert's House of Refuge Museum. Built in 1875 on Hutchinson Island, this is the only remaining example of ten such structures that were erected by the U.S. Life-Saving Service (a predecessor of the Coast Guard) to aid stranded sailors. The displays here include antique lifesaving equipment, maps, artifacts from nearby wrecks, and boatbuilding tools. The museum is affiliated with the nearby Elliott Museum. ✉ *301 S.E. MacArthur Blvd., Jensen Beach* ☎ *772/225–1875* 🌐 *www.houseofrefugefl.org* 🎟 *$6* ⏲ *Mon.–Sat. 10–4, Sun. 1–4.*

Stuart Heritage Museum. What started off in 1901 as the tin-roofed George W. Parks General Merchandise Store and in 1946 became Stuart's feed and garden store (the name is still emblazoned on the pine facade) is now the Stuart Heritage Museum, an interesting trip down nostagia lane with Americana artifacts and goods detailing the town's history, just steps from city hall. ✉ *161 S.W. Flagler Ave.* ☎ *772/220–4600* 🌐 *www.stuartheritagemuseum.com* 🎟 *Free* ⏲ *Daily 10–3.*

BEACHES

Bathtub Reef Beach. Rough tides are often the norm in this stretch of the Atlantic Ocean, but a charming enclave at the southern end of Hutchinson Island—after the Marriott's beach and right by the Indian River Plantation luxury development—provides a perfect escape for families with young children and anyone who likes to snorkel. The waters are shallow and usually calm, and youngsters can walk up to the reef and see a dazzling assortment of fish. The parking lot is small, so get there early. Erosion is a problem, and sometimes lifeguards can't pull their hefty chairs out, leaving the beach unguarded (but it shouldn't deter you, because the sea isn't rough). **Amenities:** toilets; showers; parking (free); lifeguards. **Best for:** swimming; snorkeling. ✉ *1585 S.E. MacArthur Blvd.* ⏲ *Daily 24 hrs.*

Stuart Beach. When the waves robustly roll in, the surfers are rolling in, too. Beginning surfers are especially keen on Stuart Beach because of its ever-vigilant lifeguards, and pros to the sport like the challenges that the choppy waters here bring. Families enjoy the snack bar known for its chicken fingers, the basketball courts, the large canopy-covered playground, and the three walkways interspersed throughout the area for easy ocean access. For those who like a dose of culture with their day in the sand, the Elliott Museum is steps from the beach. **Amenities:** lifeguards; food and drink; parking (free); showers; toilets. **Best for:** surfing; swimming. ✉ *889 N.E. Ocean Blvd.* ⏲ *Daily 24 hrs.*

WHERE TO EAT

$$$ SEAFOOD **Conchy Joe's.** Like a hermit crab sliding into a new shell, Conchy Joe's moved up from West Palm Beach in 1983 to its current home, a 1920s rustic stilt house on the Indian River. It's full of antique fish mounts, gator hides, and snakeskins and is a popular tourist spot—but the waterfront location, casual vibe, and delicious seafood lure locals, too. Grouper marsala, coconut shrimp, and fried Bahamian cracked conch are menu fixtures, and live reggae gets people out of their shells Thursday through Sunday. $ *Average main: $27* ✉ *3945 N.E. Indian River Dr., Jensen Beach* ☎ *772/334–1130* 🌐 *www.conchyjoes.com.*

$$$ FRENCH **Courtine's.** A husband-and-wife team oversees this quiet and hospitable restaurant under the Roosevelt Bridge. French and American influences are clear in the Swiss chef's dishes, from rack of lamb with Dijon mustard to grilled filet mignon stuffed with Roquefort and fresh spinach. The formal dining room has subtle, elegant touches, such as votive candlelight and white tablecloths. A more casual menu is available at the bar. $ *Average main: $25* ✉ *514 N. Dixie Hwy.* ☎ *772/692–3662* 🌐 *www.courtines.com* ⏲ *Closed Sun. and Mon. No lunch.*

$$$ ECLECTIC ★ **11 Maple Street.** This cozy spot is as good as it gets on the Treasure Coast. Soft music and a friendly staff set the mood in the antiques-filled dining room, which holds only 21 tables. An extensive list of small plates can be ordered as starters or mains and includes tasty treats like black-rice calamari fritters with Thai sauce and Wagyu hanger steak with onion rings and salsa verde. The limited but superb selection of entrées includes wood-grilled venison with onion-potato hash and beef tenderloin with white-truffle-and-chive butter. All desserts are made from scratch and are also seductive, including white-chocolate custard with blackberry sauce. $ *Average main: $22* ✉ *3224 N.E. Maple Ave., Jensen Beach* ☎ *772/334–7714* 🌐 *www.11maplestreet.net* *Reservations essential* ⏲ *Closed Mon. and Tues. No lunch.*

$$ SEAFOOD **Finz Waterfront Grille.** Located on the southern end of the Manatee Pocket in Port Salerno, the popular restaurant is surrounded by boatyards and a lively gallery scene. Sit on the covered open-air deck and take in the views while eating the tastiest crab cakes south of Chesapeake Bay. The kitchen also serves up lobster bisque, peel-and-eat shrimp, maple-glazed salmon, and a variety of landlubber delights like baby back ribs and burgers. There's live music at the tiki bar Sunday afternoons from 2 to 5 and bands every weekend night. $ *Average main: $16* ✉ *Port Salerno, 4290 S.E. Salerno Rd.* ☎ *772/283–1929* 🌐 *www.finzwaterfrontgrille.com.*

WHERE TO STAY

For expanded reviews, facilities, and current deals, visit Fodors.com.

$$$$ RESORT **Hutchinson Island Marriott Beach Resort & Marina.** With a 77-slip marina, a full water-sports program, a golf course, tons of tennis courts, and children's activities, this self-contained resort is excellent for families, most of whom prefer to stay in the tower directly on the ocean. **Pros:** attentive, warm staff; rooms are comfortable and casually chic; all rooms have balconies and wet bars, and some have kitchenettes; two fitness centers and two pools on the property. **Cons:** only one sit-down indoor restaurant; common areas are a bit dated; no spa; extra charge for parking. **TripAdvisor:** "wonderful resort in an idyllic setting," "very relaxing," "super staff." *Rooms from: $249* *555 N.E. Ocean Blvd., Hutchinson Island* *772/225–3700, 800/775–5936* *www.marriott.com* *283 rooms* *No meals.*

$$$ RESORT **Pirate's Cove Resort & Marina.** This cozy enclave on the banks of the Manatee Pocket with ocean access at the southern end of Stuart is the perfect place to set forth on a day at sea or wind down after one—it's relaxing and casual, and has amenities like a swimming pool courtyard, restaurant, and fitness center. **Pros:** spacious tropical-themed rooms; great for boaters, with a 50-slip full-service marina; each room has a balcony overlooking the water; free Wi-Fi and parking. **Cons:** lounge gets noisy at night; decor and furnishings are pretty but not luxurious; pool is on the small side. **TripAdvisor:** "beautiful views," "beautiful resort," "hidden gem." *Rooms from: $160* *4307 S.E. Bayview St., Port Salerno* *772/287–2500* *www.piratescoveresort.com* *50 rooms* *Breakfast.*

SHOPPING

More than 60 restaurants and shops with antiques, art, and fashion have opened downtown along Osceola Street.

B&A Flea Market. A short drive from downtown and operating for more than two decades, the oldest and largest flea market on the Treasure Coast has a street-bazaar feel, with shoppers happily scouting the 500 vendors for the practical and unusual. *2885 S.E. U.S. 1* *772/288–4915* *www.bafleamarket.com* *Free* *Sat.–Sun. 8–3.*

SPORTS AND THE OUTDOORS

FISHING

Sailfish Marina of Stuart. Nab a deep-sea charter here, the closest public marina to the St. Lucie Inlet. *3565 S.E. St. Lucie Blvd.* *772/283–1122* *www.sailfishmarinastuart.com.*

GOLF

Ocean Club at Hutchinson Island Marriott. There are 18 holes, a warm-up aqua range, and a putting green for members and hotel guests only; greens fees $60/$30 including cart. *Hutchinson Island Marriott Bech Resort & Marina, 555 N.E. Ocean Blvd.* *772/225–6819.*

FORT PIERCE AND PORT ST. LUCIE

11 miles north of Jensen Beach.

About an hour north of Palm Beach, Fort Pierce has a distinctive rural feel—but it has a surprising number of worthwhile attractions for a town of its size, including those easily seen while following Route 707 on the mainland (A1A on Hutchinson Island). A big draw is an inlet that offers fabulous fishing and excellent surfing. Nearby Port St. Lucie is largely landlocked southwest of Fort Pierce and is almost equidistant from there and Jensen Beach; it is not a big tourist area except for two sports facilities near I–95, the Mets' Digital Domain Park and the PGA Village. If you want a hotel directly on the sand or crave more than simple, motel-like accommodations, stay elsewhere and drive up for the day.

GETTING HERE AND AROUND

You can reach Fort Pierce from Jensen Beach by driving 11 miles north on Federal Highway (U.S. 1), Route 707, or A1A. To get to Port St. Lucie, continue north on U.S. 1 and take Prima Vista Boulevard west. From Fort Pierce, Route 709 goes diagonally southwest to Port St. Lucie, and I–95 is another choice.

6

ESSENTIALS

Visitor Information **St. Lucie County Tourist Development Council** ✉ *2300 Virginia Ave.* ☎ *800/344–8443* 🌐 *www.visitstluciefla.com.*

EXPLORING

A.E. Backus Museum & Gallery. Works by one of Florida's foremost landscape artists, Albert Ernest Backus (1906–1990), are on display at this museum. It also mounts changing exhibits and offers exceptional buys on paintings, pottery, and jewelry by local artists. ✉ *500 N. Indian River Dr.* ☎ *772/465–0630* 🌐 *www.backusgallery.com* 🎟 *$2* ⏲ *Oct.–June, Wed.–Sat. 10–4, Sun. noon–4; summer hrs by appointment.*

Heathcote Botanical Gardens. Stroll through this 3½-acre green space, which includes a palm walk, a Japanese garden, and a collection of 100 bonsai trees. There is also a gift shop with whimsical and botanical knickknacks. Guided tours are available by appointment for an extra fee. ✉ *210 Savannah Rd.* ☎ *772/464–4672* 🌐 *www.heathcotebotanicalgardens.org* 🎟 *$6* ⏲ *May–Oct., Tues.–Sat. 9–5; Nov.–Apr., Tues.–Sat. 9–5, Sun. 1–5.*

★ **National Navy UDT-SEAL Museum.** Commemorating the more than 3,000 troops who trained on these shores during World War II when this elite military unit got its start, there are weapons, vehicles, and equipment on view. Exhibits honor all frogmen and underwater demolition teams and depict their history. A new addition is the lifeboat from which SEALs saved the *Maersk Alabama* captain from Somali pirates in 2009. ✉ *3300 N. Rte. A1A* ☎ *772/595–5845* 🌐 *www.navysealmuseum.com* 🎟 *$8* ⏲ *Tues.–Sat. 10–4, Sun. noon–4.*

Savannas Recreation Area. Once a reservoir, the 550 acres have been returned to their natural wetlands state. Today the wilderness area has trails and a boat ramp; camping along with canoe and kayak rentals are available October through May. ✉ *1400 E. Midway Rd.* ☎ *772/464–7855* *Free* ⏲ *Daily 6 am–7:30 pm.*

Smithsonian Marine Ecosystems Exhibit. Housed in the St. Lucie County Aquarium and run by the Smithsonian Institution, whose research facility next door is where scientists study local ecosystems (once monthly tours are organized), this facility has a 3,000-gallon coral-reef tank, originally located in the National Museum of Natural History in Washington, D.C. The parklike setting, where children love to play, makes it an ideal picnic destination. Admission is free on the first Tuesday of every month. ✉ *420 Seaway Dr.* ☎ *772/462–3474* ⊕ *www.sms.si.edu/smee* *$4* ⏲ *Tues.–Sat. 10–4.*

BEACHES

Fort Pierce Inlet State Park. Across the inlet at the northern side of Hutchinson Island, a fishing oasis lures beachgoers who can't wait to reel in snook, flounder, and bluefish, among others. The park is also known as a prime wave-riding locale, thanks to a reef that lies just outside the jetty. Summer is the busiest season by a long shot, but don't be fooled: it's a laid-back place to sun and surf. There are covered picnic tables but no concessions; however, from where anglers perch, a bunch of casual restaurants can be spotted on the other side of the inlet that are a quick drive away. **Amenities:** toilets; showers; parking (fee); lifeguards (summer only). **Best for:** surfing; walking; solitude. ✉ *905 Shorewinds Dr.* ☎ *772/468–3985* ⊕ *www.floridastateparks.org/fortpierceinlet* *Vehicle $6, bicyclists and pedestrians $2* ⏲ *Daily 8–sunset.*

WHERE TO EAT AND STAY

For expanded reviews, facilities, and current deals, visit Fodors.com.

$$ SEAFOOD ✕ **Mangrove Mattie's.** This casual spot on Fort Pierce Inlet provides dazzling waterfront views and delicious seafood. Dine on the terrace or in the dining room, and don't forget to try the coconut-fried shrimp or the shrimp scampi. Happy hour (daily 3 to 7) features roast beef or ham sandwiches, or oysters, clams, and shrimp. Many locals come by for the Champagne Sunday brunch. $ *Average main: $20* ✉ *1640 Seaway Dr.* ☎ *772/466–1044* ⊕ *www.mangrovematties.com.*

$ RESORT **Dockside Inn.** This hotel is the best of the lodgings lining the scenic Fort Pierce Inlet on Seaway Drive; it's a practical base for fishing enthusiasts, with nice touches like two pools and a waterfront restaurant. **Pros:** good value; overnight boat docking available; reasonable rates at marina; parking included. **Cons:** basic decor; some steps to climb; grounds are nothing too fancy but have great views. **TripAdvisor:** "great getaway spot," "beautiful," "amazing location." $ *Rooms from: $89* ✉ *1160 Seaway Dr.* ☎ *772/468–3555, 800/286–1745* ⊕ *www.docksideinn.com* *35 rooms* *Breakfast.*

SPORTS AND THE OUTDOORS

BASEBALL

Digital Domain Park. Out west by I–95, the New York Mets train here, and it's also the home of the St. Lucie Mets minor league team. ✉ *525 N.W. Peacock Blvd., Port St. Lucie* ☎ *772/871–2115* ⊕ *www.digitaldomainpark.com.*

BOATING AND FISHING

Dolphin Watch. This outfitter on the Dockside Inn's waterfront has for charter fishing pontoon boats and cruising boats, plus kayak rentals. Daily two-hour sightseeing, dolphin, and eco-sightseeing cruises are at 10, 1, and 3:30, but call in advance to book a spot. ✉ *1160 Seaway Dr.* ☎ *772/466–4660* 🌐 *www.floridadolphinwatch.com.*

GOLF

PGA Village. Owned and operated by the PGA of America, the national association of teaching pros, it's the winter home to many Northern instructors along with permanent staff. The facility is a little off the beaten path and the clubhouse is basic, but serious golfers will appreciate the three championship courses by Pete Dye and Tom Fazio (greens fees $119/$55 including cart), and the chance to sharpen their skills at the 35-acre PGA Center for Golf Learning and Performance that has 9 practice bunkers mimicking sands and slopes from around the globe. ✉ *1916 Perfect Dr., Port St. Lucie* ☎ *772/467–1300, 800/800–4653* 🌐 *www.pgavillage.com.*

SCUBA DIVING

The region's premier dive site is actually on the National Register of Historic Places. The *Urca de Lima* was part of the storied treasure fleet bound for Spain that was destroyed by a hurricane in 1715. It's now part of an underwater archaeological preserve about 200 yards from shore, just north of the National Navy UDT-SEAL Museum and under 10 to 15 feet of water; the remains contain a flat-bottom, round-bellied ship and cannons that can be visited on an organized dive trip.

Dive Odyssea. This shop offers tank rentals and scuba lessons; guided excursions can be arranged to dive sites like nearby reefs or the *Urca de Lima* underwater "museum." ✉ *621 N. 2nd St., Fort Pierce* ☎ *772/460–1771* 🌐 *www.diveodyssea.com.*

6

VERO BEACH AND SEBASTIAN

12 miles north of Fort Pierce.

Tranquil and picturesque, these Indian River County towns have a strong commitment to the environment and the arts, particularly the upscale yet low-key Vero Beach, which is home to the prestigious Riverside Theater, tons of galleries, and a fantastic art museum. Sebastian, a coastal fishing village that feels as remote as possible between Jacksonville and Miami Beach, has plenty of outdoor activities—including those at the Sebastian Inlet State Park, one of Florida's biggest and best recreation areas (and a paradise for surfers). It's actually within the boundaries of the federal government's massive protected Archie Carr National Wildlife Refuge, which encompasses several smaller parks within its boundaries. Downtown Vero is centered on the historic district on 14th Avenue, but much of the fun takes place across the Indian River (aka the Intracoastal Waterway) around Orchid Island's beaches.

GETTING HERE AND AROUND

To get here, you have two basic options—Route A1A along the coast (not to be confused with Ocean Drive, an offshoot on Orchid Island), or either U.S. 1 or Route 605 (also called Old Dixie Highway) on the mainland. As you approach Vero on the latter, you pass through an ungussied-up landscape of small farms and residential areas. On the beach route, part of the drive bisects an unusually undeveloped section of the Florida coast. If flying in, consider Orlando International Airport, which is larger (more flights and lower prices) and a smidge closer than Palm Beach International Airport.

ESSENTIALS

Visitor Information **Indian River County Chamber of Commerce** ✉ *1216 21st St.* ☎ *772/567–3491* 🌐 *www.indianriverchamber.com.* **Sebastian River Area Chamber of Commerce** ✉ *700 Main St., Sebastian* ☎ *772/589–5969* 🌐 *www.sebastianchamber.com.*

EXPLORING

Environmental Learning Center. Off of Wabasso Beach Road, the 64 acres here are almost compeletely surrounded by water. In addition to a 600-foot boardwalk through the mangrove shoreline and a 1-mile canoe trail, there are aquariums filled with Indian River creatures. Boat and kayak trips to see the historic Pelican Island rookery are also on offer. Call or check the center's website for times. ✉ *255 Live Oak Dr.* ☎ *772/589–5050* 🌐 *www.discoverelc.org* 🎫 *$5* ⏲ *Tues.–Fri. 10–4, Sat. 9–4, Sun. 1–4 (summer hrs can vary).*

Heritage Center and Indian River Citrus Museum. You'll learn that more grapefruit is shipped from the Indian River area than anywhere else in the world at this museum in downtown Vero Beach. The memorabilia harks back to when families washed and wrapped the luscious fruit to sell at roadside stands, and cattle hauled citrus-filled crates with distinctive Indian River labels to the rail station. ✉ *2140 14th Ave.* ☎ *772/770–2263* 🌐 *www.veroheritage.org* 🎫 *Free (donations appreciated)* ⏲ *Sept.–May, Tues.–Fri. 10–4; June–Aug., Tues.–Fri. 10–3.*

Fodor's Choice ★ **McKee Botanical Garden.** On the National Register of Historic Places, the 18-acre plot is a tropical jungle garden—one of the most lush and serene around. This is *the* place to see spectacular water lilies, and the property's original 1932 Hall of Giants, a rustic wooden structure that has stained glass and bronze bells, contains the world's largest single-plank mahogany table at 35 feet long. There's a Seminole bamboo pavilion, a gift shop, and café, which serves especially tasty snacks and sandwiches. ✉ *350 U.S. 1* ☎ *772/794–0601* 🌐 *www.mckeegarden.org* 🎫 *$9* ⏲ *Tues.–Sat. 10–5, Sun. noon–5.*

McLarty Treasure Museum. On a National Historic Landmark site, this museum underscores the credo: "Wherever gold glitters or silver beckons, man will move mountains." It has displays of coins, weapons, and tools salvaged from the fleet of Spanish treasure ships that sank here in the 1715 storm, leaving some 1,500 survivors struggling to shore between Sebastian and Fort Pierce. The museum's last video showing begins at 3:15. ✉ *Sebastian Inlet State Park, 13180 Rte. A1A, Sebastian* ☎ *772/589–2147* 🌐 *www.floridastateparks.org/sebastianinlet* 🎫 *$2* ⏲ *Daily 10–4.*

Mel Fisher's Treasure Museum. You'll really come upon hidden loot when you enter this place operated by the family of late treasure hunter Mel Fisher. See some of what he recovered in 1985 from the Spanish *Atocha* that sank in 1622 and dumped 100,000 gold coins, Colombian emeralds, and 1,000 silver bars into Florida's high seas—and what his team still salvages each year off the Treasure Coast. The museum certainly piques one's curiosity about what is still buried, and the website is all about the quest for more booty. ✉ *1322 U.S. 1, Sebastian* ☎ *772/589–9875, 772/589–0435* 🌐 *www.melfisher.com* 🎫 *$6.50* ⏲ *Oct.–Aug., Mon.–Sat. 10–5, Sun. noon–5.*

Pelican Island National Wildlife Refuge. Founded in 1903 by President Theodore Roosevelt as the country's first national wildlife refuge, the park encompasses the historic Pelican Island rookery itself—a small island in the Indian River Lagoon and important nesting place for 16 species of birds such as endangered wood storks and, of course, brown pelicans—and the land surrounding it overlooking Sebastian. The rookery is a closed wilderness area, so there's no roaming alongside animal kingdom friends; however, there is an 18-foot observation tower across from it with direct views and more than 6 miles of nature trails in the refuge. Another way to explore is via guided kayak tours from the Florida Outdoor Center. ✉ *1 mile north of Treasure Shores Park* ✣ *Take A1A and turn on Jungle Trail* ☎ *772/581–5557* 🌐 *www.fws.gov/pelicanisland* 🎫 *Free* ⏲ *Daily 7:30–sunset.*

Vero Beach Museum of Art. Part of the arts campus in the 54-acre Riverside Park on Orchid Island, the museum's five galleries and two sculpture gardens make it the largest art facility on the Treasure Coast, plus it hosts a full schedule of films, lectures, workshops, and classes. ✉ *3001 Riverside Park Dr.* ☎ *772/231–0707* 🌐 *www.verobeachmuseum.org* 🎫 *Free, temporary exhibition $10* ⏲ *Mon.–Sat. 10–4:30, Sun. 1–4:30.*

BEACHES

Most of the hotels in the Vero Beach area are clustered around South Beach Park or line Ocean Drive around Beachland Boulevard just north of Humiston Park. Both parks have lifeguards daily. South Beach, at the end of East Causeway Boulevard, is one of the widest, quietest shores on the island, and has plenty of hammock shade before the dunes to picnic in, plus volleyball nets on the beach. Humiston Park is smack-dab in the main commercial zone with restaurants galore, including the lauded Citrus Grillhouse at its southern tip.

Sebastian Inlet State Park. The 578-acre park, which spans from the tip of Orchid Island across the passage to the barrier island just north, is one of the Florida park system's biggest draws, especially because of the inlet's highly productive fishing waters. Views from either side of the tall bridge are spectacular, and a unique hallmark is that the gates never close—an amazing feature for die-hard anglers who know snook bite better at night. The park has two entrances, the entrance in Vero Beach and the main entrance in Melbourne (*9700 Rte. A1A*), and within its grounds are a brand-new two-story restaurant built in 2012 that overlooks the ocean, a fish and surfing shop (by the way, this place has some of the best waves in the state, but there are also calmer zones for relaxing swims), two museums, guided sea turtle walks in season, 51 campsites with water and electricity, and a marina with powerboat, kayak, and canoe rentals. **Amenities:** water sports; food and drink;

DID YOU KNOW?

Vero Beach is known for its arts. But like many of Florida's coastal towns, some of the top attractions here are the natural offerings, from Vero Beach's citrus trees to its beautiful sunrises.

parking (fee); showers; toilets. **Best for:** surfing; sunrise; sunset; walking. ✉ *14251 N. Rte. A1A* ☎ *321/984–4852* 🌐 *www.floridastateparks.org/sebastianinlet* 🎟 *Vehicle with up to 8 people $8, single driver $4, bicyclists and pedestrians $2* ⏲ *Daily 24 hrs (gates never close).*

Treasure Shores Park. Beautiful sand dunes and verdant grounds await at this quiet turf immediately north of the last swath of development before the drive to Sebastian Inlet. It's a perfect place to commune with nature, or it's a good spot if you want to feel like you own the beach, as sometimes there's no one except you. Children will delight in the pirate-ship-themed playground on-site, and there are plenty of picnic tables (but no grills) plus lots of shade throughout the landscaped section beside the beach. **Amenities:** parking (free); toilets; showers. **Best for:** solitude; swimming. ✉ *11300 N. Rte. A1A.*

Wabasso Beach Park. A favorite for local surfboarding teens and the families at the nearby Disney's Vero Beach Resort, the park is nestled in a residential area at the end of Wabasso Road about 8 miles up from the action on Ocean Drive and 8 miles below the Sebastian Inlet. Aside from regular amenities like picnic tables, restrooms, and a dedicated parking lot (which really is the "park" here—there's not much green space—and it's quite small, so arrive early), the Disney crowd walks there for its lifeguards (the strip directly in front of the hotel is unguarded) and the local crowd appreciates its conveniences, like a pizzeria and a store that sells sundries, snacks, and beach supplies. **Amenities:** food and drink; lifeguards; parking (free); toilets; showers. **Best for:** swimming; surfing. ✉ *1820 Wabasso Rd.* ⏲ *Daily 7–sunset.*

6

WHERE TO EAT

$$$ MODERN AMERICAN

Citrus Grillhouse. There are rooms with a view, and then there's this view: uninterrupted sea from a wraparound veranda at the southern end of Humiston Park. Even better, the food here is a straightforward, delicious celebration of what's at the market that day: only about 20 regular menu items and a few specials are presented at dinner, half as many at lunch. One such dish, the caprese salad, with different types of heirloom tomatoes, fluffy mozzarella, and a drizzling of walnut-and-arugula pesto, is an exercise in restraint that you can't help but gobble up. Speaking of gobble-gobble, the house turkey burger topped with blue cheese and avocado is the juiciest, smokiest midday indulgence on the beach. 💲 *Average main: $24* ✉ *1050 Easter Lily La.* ☎ *772/234–4114* 🌐 *www.citrusgrillhouse.com.*

$$ DINER

The Lemon Tree. If Italy had old-school luncheonettes, this is what they'd look like: a storefront of yellow walls, dark-green booths, white linoleum tables, and cascading sconces of faux ivy leaves and hand-painted Tuscan serving pieces for artwork. It's self-described by the husband-andwife owners (who are always at the front) as an "upscale diner," and locals swear by it for breakfast, lunch, and dinner (breakfast only on Sunday), so expect a short wait in season at peak hours. There's always a treat on the house, like a glass of sorbet to finish lunch, and don't miss the shrimp scampi after 11 am—the sauce is so good, you'll want to dip every bit of the fresh focaccia in it. 💲 *Average main: $19* ✉ *3125 Ocean Dr.* 🌐 *www.lemontreevero.com* ⏲ *No lunch or dinner Sun. No dinner June–Sept.*

$$$ SEAFOOD **Ocean Grill.** Opened in 1941, this restaurant combines its ocean view with Tiffany-style lamps, wrought-iron chandeliers, and paintings of pirates. Count on at least three kinds of seafood any day on the menu, along with steaks, pork chops, soups, and salads. The house drink is "Pusser's Painkiller"—a curious blend first mixed by British sailors in the Virgin Islands and rationed in a tin cup. It commemorates the 1894 wreck of the *Breconshire,* which occurred offshore and from which 34 British sailors escaped. *Average main: $25 1050 Sexton Plaza, at Beachland Blvd. and Ocean Dr. 772/231–5409 www.ocean-grill.com Closed 2 wks around Labor Day. No lunch Sunday.*

$$$ ECLECTIC Fodor's Choice ★ **The Tides.** A charming cottage restaurant west of Ocean Drive prepares some of the best food around—not just in Vero Beach, but all of South Florida. The chefs, classically trained, present a trip around the globe through food, but the setting, although effortlessly elegant (think pale blue coral-printed fabrics and a brick fireplace), is down-to-earth. Putting the crab in crab cake, an appetizer's two jumbo patties have scarcely anything but sweet, fresh flesh; the Southern-inspired corn-and-pepper sauce surrounding them is heavenly. For dinner, the inside-out chicken saltimbocca (rolled up, stuffed, and sliced) hits a high note, and the English pudding dessert is perfectly sticky and sweet. To boot, there's a notable wine list. *Average main: $27 3103 Cardinal Dr. 772/234–3966 www.tidesofvero.com Reservations essential No lunch.*

WHERE TO STAY

For expanded reviews, facilities, and current deals, visit Fodors.com.

$$ HOTEL **Aquarius Oceanfront Motel.** Right on the shore beneath the beautiful South Beach Park, this small, unpretentious resort with a relaxing seaside outdoor lounge area has loyal guests who book a year in advance for rooms that are simple but have conveniences like full kitchens. **Pros:** on a quiet, wide stretch of sand; tiki huts and loads of chairs by beach and pool; free Wi-Fi; coin laundry facilities. **Cons:** steps to climb; tight parking lot; dated decor and fixtures; no restaurant (but there are some nearby). **TripAdvisor:** "a great place to stay," "a quiet hidden gem on the beach," "attention to detail." *Rooms from: $119 1526 Ocean Dr. 772/231–5218, 877/767–1526 www.aquariusverobeach.com 28 rooms No meals.*

$$$ RESORT ★ **Costa d'Este Beach Resort.** This stylish, contemporary boutique hotel in the heart of the bustling Ocean Drive area has a gorgeous infinity pool overlooking the ocean and a distinctly South Beach vibe—just like its famous owners, singer Gloria Estefan and producer Emilio Estefan, who bought the property in 2004. **Pros:** all rooms have balconies or secluded patios, huge Italian marble showers, and other luxuries; complimentary signature mojitos on arrival indicate the fun to be had. **Cons:** spa is on the smaller side; rooms have only blackout shades, so no in-between option for natural light and privacy. **TripAdvisor:** "we'll be back soon," "enjoyable stay," "amazing beachfront hotel." *Rooms from: $179 3244 Ocean Dr. 772/562–9919 www.costadeste.com 94 rooms No meals.*

$$$$ RESORT **Disney's Vero Beach Resort.** This oceanfront, family-oriented retreat tucked away in a residential stretch of Orchid Island has a retro Old Florida design and not too much Mickey Mouse, which is a welcome

surprise for adults. **Pros:** lots for kids to do, including mini-golf, a great pool with waterslide, and campfire circle; rooms have basics like toasters and microwaves; several dining options on property. **Cons:** not the best if you're looking for a quiet couples retreat; far from shopping and dining in town; some families complain there isn't enough Disney-themed decor. **TripAdvisor:** "get away and relax," "amazing," "nice beach property." *Rooms from: $250* *9250 Island Grove Terr.* *772/234–2000, 407/939–7540* *www.disneybeachresorts.com* *181 rooms* *No meals.*

$$$ RESORT **The Driftwood Resort.** On the National Register of Historic Places, the two original buildings of this 1935 inn were built entirely from ocean-washed timbers; over time more buildings were added, and all are now decorated with such artifacts as ship's bells, Spanish tiles, and a cannon from a 16th-century Spanish galleon, which create a quirky, utterly charming landscape. **Pros:** central location and right on the beach; free Wi-Fi; laundry facilities; weekly treasure hunt is a blast. **Cons:** older property; rooms can be musty; no-frills furnishings. **TripAdvisor:** "unique and different," "comfort food," "great location." *Rooms from: $150* *3150 Ocean Dr.* *772/231–0550* *www.thedriftwood.com* *100 rooms* *No meals.*

$$$$ RESORT ★ **Vero Beach Hotel & Spa.** With a sophisticated, relaxed British West Indies feel, this luxurious five-story beachfront hotel at the north end of Ocean Drive is an inviting getaway—and its fabulous spa opened after years of waiting in 2011 as one of the best on the Treasure Coast. **Pros:** beautiful pool with restaurant on ocean; top-notch full-service medi-spa and salon with a devoted local following; complimentary daily wine hour with hors d'oeuvres. **Cons:** separate charges for valet parking and Wi-Fi; a smidge farther up from the nearby boutiques and nightlife than other resorts. **TripAdvisor:** "wonderful property," "excellent service," "beautiful luxurious paradise." *Rooms from: $239* *3500 Ocean Dr.* *772/231–5666* *www.verobeachhotelandspa.com* *102 rooms* *No meals.*

SHOPPING

The place to go when in Vero Beach is **Ocean Drive.** Crossing over to Orchid Island from the mainland, the Merrill P. Barber Bridge turns into Beachland Boulevard; its intersection with Ocean Drive is the heart of a commercial zone with a lively mix of upscale clothing stores, specialty shops, restaurants, and art galleries.

Just under three miles north of that roughly eight-block stretch on A1A is a charming outdoor plaza, **The Village Shops.** It is a delight to stroll between the brightly painted cottages that have more unique, high-end offerings. The tree-shaded, casual Coco's Village Bistro is a great spot for lunch.

Back on the mainland, take 21st Street westward and you'll come across a small, modern shopping plaza with some independent shops and national chains. Keep going west on 21st Street, and then park around 14th Avenue to explore a collection of art galleries and eateries in the historic downtown.

SHOPPING CENTERS AND MALLS

Vero Beach Outlets. Just west of I–95 off Route 60 is a discount shopping destination with 50 brand-name stores, including Ann Taylor, Polo Ralph Lauren, and Jones New York. ✉ *1824 94th Dr.* ☎ *772/770–6097* 🌐 *www.verobeachoutlets.com.*

RECOMMENDED STORES

A Pampered Life. Robes that are so fun and flirty, they can double as dresses share space with indulgent bath products. ✉ *3117 Ocean Dr.* ☎ *772/231–8864* 🌐 *www.apamperedlife.net.*

Christine. This shop is *the* place to find gorgeous gifts like Mariposa napkin holders and Michael Aram picture frames. ✉ *The Village Shops, 6220 N. Rte. A1A* ☎ *772/492–0383* 🌐 *www.christineshop.com.*

S & K Ltd. Splurge on custom jewelry and exotic home items from silver-dipped shells to whimsical pewter statues. ✉ *The Village Shops, 6290 N. Rte. A1A* ☎ *772/234–1964.*

Sassy Boutique. One of the chicest spots in town sells bright, punchy, and pretty women's designer fashions. ✉ *3375 Ocean Dr.* ☎ *772/234–3998.*

Shells & Things. Stop here for lovely handcrafted goods inspired by the sea, many by local artisans. ✉ *3119 Ocean Dr.* ☎ *772/234–4790* 🌐 *www.shellsandthings.com.*

SPORTS AND THE OUTDOORS

BOATING AND FISHING

Most of the region's fishing outfitters are based at the Capt Hiram's Resort marina in Sebastian.

Big Easy Fishing Charters. Book both guided backwater and deep-sea excursions here. ✉ *Capt Hiram's Resort, 1606 N. Indian River Dr., Sebastian* ☎ *772/664–4068, 772/538–1072* 🌐 *www.bigeasyfishingcharter.com.*

Incentive Fishing Charters. These experts on bottom-fishing do ocean trolling as well. ✉ *Capt Hiram's Resort, 1606 N. Indian River Dr., Sebastian* ☎ *321/676–1948* 🌐 *www.incentivecharters.com.*

Sebastian Watercraft Rentals. Their fleet ranges from 16-passenger pontoons to Jet Skis, and the company also organizes fishing charters. ✉ *Capt Hiram's Resort, 1606 N. Indian River Dr., Sebastian* ☎ *772/589–5560* 🌐 *www.floridawatercraftrentals.com.*

GOLF

Sandridge Golf Club. These two public 18-hole courses designed by Ron Garl allow walking and nine holes in the early morning and later afternoon. Greens fees with cart at peak times in winter season are $50; lessons and clinics are also available. ✉ *5300 73rd St.* ☎ *772/770–5000* 🌐 *www.sandridgegc.com.*

GUIDED TOURS

Florida Outdoor Center. Guided tours explore the area's natural wonders like the Pelican Island National Wildlife Refuge and begin at only $35 per person. The company is mobile and, therefore, flexible; excursions can be done by foot, bike, kayak, or paddleboard. ☎ *772/202–0220* 🌐 *www.floridaoutdoorcenter.com.*

Travel Smart South Florida

WORD OF MOUTH

"The vast majority of U.S. colleges have spring break in [early to mid March]. There are a handful of schools that might be in late February or the first week of April but not many."

—cheryllj

"The way to avoid spring breakers [isn't to avoid one area of the Florida coast or another but rather] to stay at very expensive resorts and properties."

—garyt22

www.fodors.com/community

GETTING HERE AND AROUND

AIR TRAVEL

Average flying times to Florida's international airports are 3 hours from New York, 4 hours from Chicago, 2¾ hours from Dallas, 4½–5½ hours from Los Angeles, and 8–8½ hours from London.

AIRPORTS

Most visitors to South Florida begin and end their trips at Miami International Airport (MIA). Fort Lauderdale–Hollywood International Airport (FLL) is your best bet if you are headed for the north side of Miami-Dade; it's a 30- to 45-minute drive to Miami from FLL. Of course, if you are going to Palm Beach or points to the immediate north or south, it's better to fly into Palm Beach International Airport (PBI) in West Palm Beach. If you're going to the Keys, it's more convenient but almost always more expensive to fly directly to Key West (EYW). **TIP→** Flying to secondary airports can save you money—sometimes even when there are additional ground transportation costs—so check before booking.

Airport Information **Fort Lauderdale–Hollywood International Airport (FLL)** ☎ *866/435–9355* 🌐 *www.broward.org/airport.* **Key West International Airport (EYW)** ☎ *305/809–5200* 🌐 *www.eywairport.com.* **Miami International Airport (MIA)** ☎ *305/876–7000* 🌐 *www.miami-airport.com.* **Palm Beach International Airport (PBI)** ☎ *561/471–7420* 🌐 *www.pbia.org.*

GROUND TRANSPORTATION

There's SuperShuttle service to and from Miami International Airport. The trip between the airport and South or Mid Beach takes 30 to 45 minutes and typically costs $31 per person each way. Although buying a round-trip ticket and reserving for the return trip doesn't save you money, it makes departure that much easier. Otherwise book a shuttle from your hotel to the airport at least 24 hours in advance. Expect to be picked up 2½ hours before your scheduled departure.

Although SuperShuttle doesn't pick up at either West Palm Beach or Fort Lauderdale, it does do drop-offs at both. The 90-minute trip from Miami to PBI costs $94 per person; to FLL it's $31 per person and 30 to 40 minutes.

Shuttle Service **SuperShuttle** ☎ *800/258–3826* 🌐 *www.supershuttle.com.*

FLIGHTS

AirTran. AirTran to Miami, Fort Lauderdale, Fort Myers, Jacksonville, Key West, Orlando, Pensacola, Sarasota, Tampa, and West Palm Beach. ☎ *800/247–8726* 🌐 *www.airtran.com.* **American Airlines** ☎ *800/433–7300* 🌐 *www.aa.com.* **Delta** ☎ *800/221–1212 for U.S. reservations, 800/241–4141 for international reservations* 🌐 *www.delta.com.* **Frontier.** Frontier to Fort Lauderdale, Fort Myers, Orlando, and Tampa. ☎ *800/432–1359* 🌐 *www.frontierairlines.com.* **JetBlue.** JetBlue to Tampa, Fort Lauderdale, Sarasota, Fort Myers, Jacksonville, West Palm Beach, and Orlando. ☎ *800/538–2583* 🌐 *www.jetblue.com.* **Southwest.** Southwest to Fort Lauderdale, Fort Myers, Jacksonville, Orlando, Panama City, Tampa, and West Palm Beach. ☎ *800/435–9792* 🌐 *www.southwest.com.* **Spirit Airlines.** Spirit to Fort Lauderdale, Fort Myers, Orlando, Tampa, and West Palm Beach. ☎ *800/772–7117* 🌐 *www.spirit.com.* **United** ☎ *800/864–8331 for U.S. reservations, 800/538–2929 for international reservations* 🌐 *www.united.com.* **US Airways** ☎ *800/428–4322 for U.S. and Canadian reservations, 800/622–1015 for international reservations* 🌐 *www.usairways.com.*

CAR TRAVEL

Three major interstates lead to Florida. I–95 begins in Maine, runs south through the Mid-Atlantic states, and enters Florida just north of Jacksonville. It continues south past Daytona Beach, the Space Coast, Vero Beach, Palm Beach, and Fort Lauderdale, ending in Miami.

I–75 begins in Michigan and runs south through Ohio, Kentucky, Tennessee, and Georgia, then moves south through the center of the state before veering west into Tampa. It follows the west coast south to Naples, then crosses through the northern section of the Everglades, and ends in Miami.

California and most Southern and Southwestern states are connected to Florida by I–10, which moves east from Los Angeles through Arizona, New Mexico, Texas, Louisiana, Mississippi, and Alabama; it enters Florida at Pensacola and runs straight across the northern part of the state, ending in Jacksonville.

FROM–TO	MILES	HOURS +/-
Miami–Palm Beach	70	1:15
Miami–Ft. Lauderdale	30	0:30
Miami–Naples	125	2:15
Miami–Key Largo	65	1
Fort Lauderdale–Palm Beach	45	1
Key Largo–Key West	100	2

RENTAL CARS

Unless you plan to plant yourself at a beach or theme-park resort, you really need a car to get around in most parts of Florida. Rental rates usually start at $35 a day/$160 a week, plus tax ($2 per day). In Florida you must be 21 to rent a car, and rates are higher if you're under 25.

RULES OF THE ROAD

Speed limits are generally 60 mph on state highways, 30 mph within city limits and residential areas, and 70 mph on interstates and Florida's Turnpike. Watch for signs announcing exceptions. Children younger than four years old must be strapped into a separate carrier or child seat; children four through five can be secured in a separate carrier, an integrated child seat, or by a seat belt. The driver will be held responsible for passengers under the age of 18 who are not wearing seat belts, and all front-seat passengers are required to wear seat belts.

Florida's Alcohol/Controlled Substance DUI Law is one of the toughest in the United States. A blood-alcohol level of .08 or higher can have serious repercussions even for a first-time offender.

CAR RENTAL RESOURCES		
Local Agencies		
Continental (Fort Lauderdale)	800/221–4085 or 954/332–1125	www.continentalcar.com
Sunshine Rent A Car (Fort Lauderdale)	888/786–7446 or 954/467–8100	www.sunshinerentacar.com
Major Agencies		
Alamo	877/222–9075	www.alamo.com
Avis	800/331–1212	www.avis.com
Budget	800/527–0700	www.budget.com
Hertz	800/654–3131	www.hertz.com
National Car Rental	800/227–7368	www.nationalcar.com

FERRY TRAVEL

Ferries are scarce in Florida, but if you wish to avoid traffic to the Keys and make the trip easier, Key West Express ferries people from Fort Myers Beach daily (and Marco Island in season) to the historic seaport in Key West, which is within walking distance of all major attractions as well as many hotels. The trip, just under four hours, is much cheaper than airfare and doesn't require months-in-advance booking.

Contact **Key West Express** ☎ *888/539–2628* 🌐 *www.keywestexpress.us*.

ESSENTIALS

ACCOMMODATIONS

In the busy seasons, reserve ahead for the top properties. In general, the peak seasons are during the Christmas holidays and from late January through Easter in the southern half of the state. Holiday weekends at any point during the year are packed; if you're considering home or condo rentals, minimum-stay requirements go up in these periods, too. Fall is the slowest season, with only a few exceptions (Key West is jam-packed for Fantasy Fest at Halloween). Rates are low and availability is high, but this is also the prime time for hurricanes.

Children are welcome generally everywhere in Florida; however, the buck stops at spring breakers. Hotels are fair game—and some even cater to them—but almost all rental agencies won't lease units to anyone under 25 without a guardian present.

Pets, although allowed at hotels more and more often (one upscale chain, Kimpton, celebrates its pet-friendliness with treats in the lobby and doggie beds for rooms), often carry an extra flat-rate fee for cleaning and de-allergen treatments, and are not a sure thing. Inquire ahead if Fido is coming with you.

APARTMENT AND HOUSE RENTALS

Contacts **Endless Vacation Rentals.** Unused time-share units from all major Florida cities and regions. ☎ *877/782–9387* 🌐 *www.evrentals.com.* **Florida Keys Rental Store.** Florida Keys ☎ *800/585–0584, 305/451–3879* 🌐 *www.floridakeysrentalstore.com.* **Freewheeler Vacations.** Florida Keys ☎ *866/664–2075, 305/664–2075* 🌐 *www.freewheeler-realty.com.* **Interhome.** Daytona Beach, Miami, Orlando, Sarasota, Florida Keys, Lower Gulf Coast, Tampa Bay Area ☎ *954/791–8282, 800/882–6864* 🌐 *www.interhomeusa.com.* **Villas International.** Miami, Orlando, Broward County, Florida Keys, Lower Gulf Coast, Palm Beach County, Tampa Bay Area ☎ *415/499–9490, 800/221–2260* 🌐 *www.villasintl.com.* **Wyndham Vacation Resorts.** Orlando, Daytona Beach, Broward County, Panhandle ☎ *800/251–8736* 🌐 *www.wyndhamvacationresorts.com.*

BED-AND-BREAKFASTS

Small inns and guesthouses in Florida range from modest, cozy places with home-style breakfasts and owners who treat you like family, to elegantly furnished Victorian houses with four-course breakfasts and rates to match. Since most B&Bs are small, they rely on various agencies and organizations to get the word out and to help coordinate reservations.

Reservation Services **BedandBreakfast.com** ☎ *512/322–2710, 800/462–2632* 🌐 *www.bedandbreakfast.com.* **Bed & Breakfast Inns Online** ☎ *800/215–7365* 🌐 *www.bbonline.com.* **BnBFinder.com** ☎ *888/547–8226* 🌐 *www.bnbfinder.com.* **Florida Bed & Breakfast Inns** ☎ *877/303–3224* 🌐 *www.florida-inns.com.*

HOTELS

Wherever you look in Florida, you'll find lots of plain, inexpensive motels and luxurious resorts, independents alongside national chains, and an ever-growing number of modern properties as well as quite a few classics. In fact, since Florida has been a favored travel destination for some time, vintage hotels are everywhere: there are grand edifices like The Breakers in Palm Beach, Boca Raton Resort & Club in Boca Raton, the Biltmore Hotel in Coral Gables, and Casa Marina in Key West.

All hotels listed have private bath unless otherwise noted.

EATING OUT

Smoking is banned statewide in most enclosed indoor workplaces, including restaurants. Exemptions are permitted for stand-alone bars where food takes a backseat to the libations.

One caution: raw oysters are a potential problem for people with chronic illness of the liver, stomach, or blood, or who have immune disorders. All Florida restaurants that serve raw oysters must post a notice in plain view warning of the risks associated with consuming them.

FLORIBBEAN FOOD

A true marriage of downstate's Floridian, Caribbean, and Latin cultures yields homegrown Floribbean cuisine. (Think freshly caught fish with tropical fruit salsa.) A trip to South Florida, however, is not complete without a taste of Cuban food. The cuisine is heavy, including pork dishes like *lechon asado* that are served in garlic-based sauces. The two most typical dishes are *arroz con frijoles* (the staple side dish of rice and black beans) and *arroz con pollo* (chicken in sticky yellow rice).

Key West is famous for its key lime pie (the best is found here) and conch fritters. Stone-crab claws, a South Florida delicacy, can be savored from October through May.

MEALS AND MEALTIMES

Unless otherwise noted, the restaurants listed in this guide are open daily for lunch and dinner.

RESERVATIONS AND DRESS

We discuss reservations only when they're essential (there's no other way you'll ever get a table) or when they are not accepted. It's always smart to make reservations when you can, particularly if your party is large or if it's high season. It's critical to do so at popular restaurants (book as far ahead as possible, often 30 days, and reconfirm on arrival).

We mention dress only when men are required to wear a jacket or a jacket and tie. Expect places with dress codes to truly adhere to them.

Contacts OpenTable 🌐 *www.opentable.com.*

WORD OF MOUTH

Did the food give you shivers of delight or leave you cold? Did the resort look as good in real life as it did in the photos? Did you sleep like a baby, or were the walls paper-thin? Was the service stellar or not up to snuff? Rate and review hotels and restaurants or start a discussion about your favorite (or not so favorite) places on www.fodors.com. Your comments might even appear in our books. Yes, you, too, can be a correspondent!

HEALTH

Sunburn and heat prostration are concerns, even in winter. So hit the beach or play tennis, golf, or another outdoor sport before 10 am or after 3 pm. If you must be out at midday, limit exercise, drink plenty of nonalcoholic liquids, and wear a hat. If you feel faint, get out of the sun and sip water slowly.

Even on overcast days, ultraviolet rays shine through the haze, so use a sunscreen with an SPF of at least 15, and have children wear a waterproof SPF 30 or higher.

While you're frolicking on the beach, steer clear of what look like blue bubbles on the sand. These are Portuguese men-of-war, and their tentacles can cause an allergic reaction. Also be careful of other large jellyfish, some of which can sting.

If you walk across a grassy area on the way to the beach, you'll probably encounter the tiny, light-brown, incredibly prickly sand spurs. If you get stuck with one, just pull it out.

HOURS OF OPERATION

Many museums are closed Monday but have late hours on another weekday and are usually open on weekends. Some museums have a day when admission is free. Popular attractions are usually open every day but Thanksgiving and Christmas Day. Watch out for seasonal closures at smaller venues; we list opening hours in this guide, but if you're visiting during a transitional month (for example, May in the southern part of the state), it's always best to call before showing up.

MONEY

Prices throughout this guide are given for adults. Substantially reduced fees are almost always available for children, students, and senior citizens.

CREDIT CARDS

We cite information about credit cards only if they aren't accepted at a restaurant or a hotel. Otherwise, assume that most major credit cards are acceptable.

Reporting Lost Cards **American Express** ☎ *800/528–4800* 🌐 *www.americanexpress.com.* **Diners Club** ☎ *800/234–6377* 🌐 *www.dinersclub.com.* **Discover** ☎ *800/347–2683* 🌐 *www.discovercard.com.* **MasterCard** ☎ *800/622–7747* 🌐 *www.mastercard.com.* **Visa** ☎ *800/847–2911* 🌐 *www.visa.com.*

PACKING

South Florida is warm year-round and extremely humid in summer. Be prepared for sudden storms all over in summer, and note that plastic raincoats are uncomfortable in the high humidity. Often storms are quick, usually in the afternoons, and the sun comes back in no time. (This also means that it's best to get in your beach time earlier in the day; if it's nice in the morning in August, go to the beach. Don't wait.)

Dress is casual throughout the state—sundresses, sandals, or walking shorts are appropriate. Palm Beach is more polos and pearls, Miami is designer jeans, and elsewhere the Tommy Bahama-esque look dominates. Even beach gear is OK at a lot of places, but just make sure you've got a proper outfit on (shirt, shorts, and shoes). A very small number of restaurants request that men wear jackets and ties, but most do not. Where there are dress codes, they tend to be fully adhered to. Funnily enough, the strictest places are golf and tennis clubs. Many ask that you wear whites or at least special sport shoes and attire. Be prepared for air-conditioning working in overdrive anywhere you go.

You can generally swim year-round in peninsular Florida from about New Smyrna Beach south on the Atlantic coast and from Tarpon Springs south on the Gulf Coast. Bring a sun hat and sunscreen.

SAFETY

Stepped-up policing of thieves who prey on tourists in rental cars has helped address what was a serious issue in the early 1990s. Still, visitors should be especially wary when driving in strange neighborhoods and leaving the airport, especially in the Miami area. Don't assume that valuables are safe in your hotel room; use in-room safes or the hotel's safety-deposit boxes. Try to use ATMs only during the day or in brightly lighted, well-traveled locales. Don't leave valuables unattended while you walk the beach or go for a dip.

If you are visiting Florida during the June through November hurricane season and a hurricane is imminent, be sure to follow directions from local authorities.

TAXES

Florida's sales tax is 6% or higher, depending on the county, and local sales and tourist taxes can raise what you pay considerably. Miami Beach hoteliers, for example, collect 13% for city and resort taxes. It's best to ask about additional costs up front to avoid a rude awakening.

TIME

South Florida is in the Eastern time zone.

TIPPING

FLORIDA TIPPING GUIDELINES	
Airport Valet or Hotel Bellhop	$1–$3 per bag
Maid	$1–$2 a night per guest
Hotel Room-Service Waiter	15% (unless a service charge was added)
Doorman or Parking Valet	$1–$3
Taxi Driver	15%–20%
Waiter/ Bartender	15%–20% before tax
Golf Caddies	15% of the greens fee
Spa Therapist	15%–20% of the treatment before tax

VISITOR INFORMATION

Florida has a terrific website for travelers with information about the state as a whole as well as for individual cities and regions. In addition, many cities, regions, and towns have their own visitor information offices and/or booths. What's more, some tourism offices are pumping out helpful (and smart) apps—Miami added one to instantly locate the hottest, latest dining spots, and Orlando has parkIN', which searches and compares rates at parking facilities closest to you.

Contact Visit Florida ☎ *850/488–5607, 866/972–5280* 🌐 *www.visitflorida.com.*

FLORIDA'S SCENIC TRAILS

Florida has some 8,000 miles of land-based routes (plus another 4,000 miles for paddling!). About 1,400 miles of these connect to create the Florida Trail, one of only 11 National Scenic Trails in the United States. Info on top segments is available at 🌐 *www.floridatrail.org,* and you can find a searchable list of all trails at 🌐 *www.visitflorida.com/trails.*

INDEX

A

B

C

D

E

PHOTO CREDITS

1, Visit Florida. 3, PBorowka/Shutterstock. Chapter 1: Experience South Florida: 6-7, S.Borisov/Shutterstock. 8 (top), Rick Gomez/age fotostock. 8 (bottom), borabora98, Fodors.com member. 9 (left), Visit Florida. 9 (right), Pacifi c Stock/SuperStock. 10, GlyndaK, fodors.com member. 11, funinthetub, Fodors.com member. 12 and 13, Jeff Greenberg/age fotostock. 14 (left), Visit Florida. 14 (right), Jeff Greenberg/Alamy. 15 (left), Sarah and Jason/Flickr.15 (top right), RIEGER Bertrand/age fotostock. 15 (bottom right), Danita Delimont/Alamy. 17 (left), Ken Canning/Shutterstock. 17 (right), j loveland/Shutterstock. 18 and 19, VisitFlorida. 20 (top), Ernest Hemingway Photograph Collection, John F. Kennedy Presidential Library and Museum, Boston. 20 (bottom), Visit Florida. 21 (top), Linda Brinck, Fodors.com member. 21 (bottom), George Peters/iStockphoto. 24, Andrew Woodley/Alamy. Chapter 2: Miami and Miami Beach: 25, iStockphoto. 26, Stuart Westmorland/age fotostock. 27 (top), Jeff Greenberg/age fotostock. 27 (bottom), VISUM Foto GmbH / Alamyw. 28, Roxana Gonzalez/Shutterstock. 29 (top), JUPITERIMAGES/ Brand X / Alamy. 29 (bottom), iStockphoto. 30, Ivan Cholakov/Shutterstock. 43, Joselito Briones/iStockphoto. 46, Chuck Mason/Alamy. 47 (top), Jeff Greenberg/Alamy. 47 (bottom), David R. Frazier Photolibrary, Inc./Alamy. 48 and 50, Jeff Greenberg/Alamy. 51, Jeff Greenberg/age fotostock. 52, Gregory Wrona/Alamy. 56, Robert Harding Picture Library Ltd / Alamy. 70, Jeff Greenberg / Alamy. 90 (top), Acqualina Resort & Spa on the Beach. 90 (bottom left), Nile Young. 90 (center right), Circa 39. 90 (bottom right), Morgans Hotel Group. 91 (top), Mark Wieland. 91 (center left), Kevin Syms/Four Seasons Hotels and Resorts. 91 (bottom left), Kor Hotel Group. 91 (bottom right), Mandarin Oriental Hotel Group. 93, boogie by alex de carvalhohttp://www.flickr.com/photos/adc/432547842/Attribution-NonCommercial License. 105 (left), dk/Alamy. 105 (right), Nicholas Pitt/Alamy. 107 (top), M. Timothy O'Keefe/Alamy. 107 (bottom), Miami Design Preservation League. 108 (top), Nicholas Pitt/Alamy. 108 (2nd from top), Park Central Hotel.108 (3rd from top), Ian Patrick Alamy. 108 (4th from top), Laura Paresky. 108 (bottom), ICIMAGE/Alamy. 109 (top), INTERFOTO Pressebildagentur/Alamy. 109 (bottom left), Ian Patrick/Alamy. 109 (bottom right), culliganphoto/Alamy.111, PeskyMonkey/iStockphoto. Chapter 3: The Everglades: 115, David Lyons / Alamy. 116 (top), Visit Florida. 116 (bottom), Jeff Greenberg/age fotostock. 117 (top), FloridaStock/Shutterstock. 117 (center), Pamela McCreight/flickr. 117 (bottom), Walter Bibikow/age fotostock. 118-19, tbkmedia.de/Alamy. 122 ((left), inga spence/Alamy. 122 (top center), FloridaStock/Shutterstock. 122 (bottom center), Andrewtappert/wikipedia. org. 122 (top right), wikipedia.org. 122 (bottom right), David R. Frazier Photolibrary, Inc./Alamy. 123 (top left), Larsek/Shutterstock. 123 (bottom left), Caleb Foster/Shutterstock. 123 (bottom center), mlorenz/Shutterstock. 123 (top right), umar faruq/Shutterstock. 123 (bottom right), Peter Arnold, Inc./Alamy. 124 (left), John A. Anderson/Shutterstock. 124 (top right), FloridaStock/Shutterstock. 124 (bottom center), Norman Bateman/Shutterstock.124 (bottom right), FloridaStock/Shutterstock. 125 (top left), David Drake & Deborah Jaffe. 125 (bottom left), Krzysztof Slusarczyk/Shutterstock. 125 (bottom center), Norman Bateman/Shutterstock. 125 (right), Jerry Zitterman/Shutterstock. 126, Patricia Schmidt/iStockphoto. 127 (top left), Brett Charlton/iStockphoto. 127 (bottom left, bottom center, and right), David Drake & Deborah Jaffe. 128 (left), Walter Bibikow/age fotostock. 128 (right), Stephen Frink Collection/Alamy. 129, Leatha J. Robinson/Shutterstock. 131, Larsek/Shutterstock. 138, Steven Widoff / Alamy. 143, Marc Muench / Alamy. 146, Everglades National Park by http://www.flickr.com/photos/jasonsewall/2277243977/Attribution-NonCommercial-ShareAlike License. 153, Visit Florida. Chapter 4: The Florida Keys: 157, Patricia Schmidt/iStockphoto. 158 (top), Pawel Lipiec/iStockphoto. 158 (bottom), David L Amsler/iStockphoto. 159 (top), Sheri Armstrong/Shutterstock. 159 (bottom), Visit Florida. 160, Gregory Wrona / Alamy. 161 (top), Claudio Lovo/Shutterstock. 161 (bottom), Michael Ventura / Alamy. 162, iStockphoto. 170, Stephen Frink/Florida Keys News Bureau. 177, flasporty/flickr. 184, Visit Florida. 186, PBorowka/Shutterstock. 187 and 188 (top), Douglas Rudolph. 188 (bottom), ANDY NEWMAN/Visit Florida. 189, M. Timothy O'Keefe/Alamy. 190 (top), Bob Care/Florida Keys News Bureau. 190 (bottom), Julie de Leseleuc/iStockphoto. 191 (left), Visit Florida.191 (right), Charles Stirling (Diving)/Alamy. 192 (top), Visit Florida. 192 (bottom), Gert Vrey/iStockphoto. 193, Scott Wilson, FKCC Student.197, Melissa Schalke/iStockphoto. 206, Henryk Sadura / Alamy. 215, John P Franzis. 218, CedarBendDrive/Flickr. 224, John P Franzis. 234, Starwood Hotels & Resorts. 236, Harold Smith/Alamy. 238, Laure Neish/iStockphoto. Chapter 5: Fort Lauderdale: 245, James Schwabel / age fotostock. 246, Rick Gomez. 247 (top), Dean Bergmann/iStockphoto. 247 (bottom), Jeff Greenberg / Alamy. 248, Qole Pejorian/Flickr. 251, rockindom, Fodors.com member. 257, Nicholas Pitt / Alamy. 258, Eric Gevaert/Shutterstock. 273, Lago Mar Resort & Club. 283, Pat Cahill/iStockphoto. Chapter 6: Palm Beach and the Treasure Coast: 291, RIEGER Bertrand/age fotostock. 293 (top), Perry Correll/Shutterstock. 293 (bottom), Bill Bachmann / Alamy. 294, FloridaStock/Shutterstock. 299, The Breakers Palm Beach. 304, mrk_photo/flickr. 307, FloridaStock/Shutterstock. 322, Andre Jenny / Alamy. 324, wikipedia.org. 337 and 350, Visit Florida.

NOTES

NOTES

ABOUT OUR WRITERS

After being hired sight unseen by a South Florida newspaper, Fort Lauderdale–based freelance travel writer and editor Lynne Helm arrived from the Midwest anticipating a few years of palm-fringed fun. More than a quarter century later (after covering the state for several newspapers, consumer magazines, and trade publications), she's still enamored of Florida's sun-drenched charms. Lynne updated the Everglades chapters.

Paul Rubio's insatiable quest to discover and learn has taken him to the far corners of the world—81 countries and counting. A Harvard-trained economist with a double master's degree, he took on his passion for travel writing full-time in 2008 and hasn't looked back. Paul, who updated the Fort Lauderdale and Miami chapters, currently contributes to *Ocean Home Magazine, Palm Beach Illustrated,* and *Weddings Illustrated* as well as other Fodor's guides, jetsetter.com, and various outlets of Modern Luxury Media.

Dorothea Hunter Sönne, who updated Experience South Florida, Travel Smart, and Palm Beach with the Treasure Coast, is a freelance writer who has been enchanted by Florida since her youth—so much so that after dozens of vacations there, she relocated to its sunny shores in 2010. Prior to that she was a magazine editor, spending nearly five years at *O, The Oprah Magazine*. She also co-edited the book, *Words That Matter*, and her work has appeared in publications including *The Knot* and *Chicago*.

From her home of more than 25 years on Sanibel Island, Chelle Koster Walton—author of the Florida Keys chapter—has written and contributed to a dozen guidebooks (among them *Fodor's Bahamas*), two of which have won Lowell Thomas Awards. She has penned thousands of articles about Florida and the Caribbean for *Miami Herald, USA Today,* Concierge.com, FoxNews.com, and other print and digital media.